Expositions of the Psalms

THE WORKS OF SAINT AUGUSTINE

A Translation for the 21st Century

Part III – Books

Volume 19:

Expositions of the Psalms

99-120

Contents

An alternative interpretation: verses 6-15 can be applied to the Jewish people as a whole — 250; Verses 16-17. The poor man, Christ, is persecuted in the persons of his members — 252; Verses 18-20. The curse as clothing, water, oil, and belt to wrongdoers — 254; Verses 21-22. Christ prays in his sufferings — 255; Verses 23-26. Christ prays about the weakness of his body — 256; Verses 27-29. All that has happened accords with God's saving plan — 258; Verses 30-31. The praise offered by Christ and his Church — 259

Exposition of Psalm 99

A Sermon to the People, preached in the Basilica of Celerina at Carthage[1]

Introduction: God speaks through us when we speak in God

1. You listened to this psalm when it was being sung, brothers and sisters. It is short, and there is nothing obscure about it. I say this to put you at your ease, for I do not want you to shrink from hard work. But since it is so easily approachable, let us study it all the more diligently; let us examine it very carefully to find out what it is so clearly trumpeting and, insofar as the Lord enables us, how its call is to be spiritually understood. Whatever instrument God's voice employs, God's voice it is still. Nothing but his own voice sounds sweetly in his ears. When we speak we delight him, as long as he speaks through us.

Verse 1. Universal praise

2. *A psalm of confession.* This is the psalm's heading, this is how it is entitled: *A psalm of confession.* The verses are few, but pregnant with great matters. May the seeds germinate in your hearts, so that a barn may be ready to receive the Lord's harvest.[2] In its mood of praise this psalm commands us, exhorts us, to shout with joy to God. Its exhortation is not addressed to any particular corner of the earth, or to any single dwelling or group of human beings; rather does it demand joyful shouting from every quarter, knowing that it has sown its blessing everywhere.

Verse 2. Shouting for joy

3. *Shout with joy to the Lord,[3] all the earth.* The whole earth cannot hear my voice at this moment, can it? Yet this command has indeed been heard by all the

---

1. Possibly late in 403 or early in 404.
2. *Pariant semina . . . ut paretur horreum messi dominicae.* The assonance between *pariant* and *paretur* is not easily translatable. We might have expected him to put the last clause the other way round: "that the Lord's harvest may be ready for the barn."
3. Variant: "to God" as below.

13

earth. Already the entire earth is shouting its joy to the Lord; or if any part is not shouting yet, it soon will be, for the blessing is extended to all peoples. The Church began from Jerusalem, but as it spreads it overthrows impiety in every place and builds up godliness instead. But good people are commingled with bad, for there are bad people all over the world, and good people all over the world too. In bad people the whole earth grumbles, but in the good the whole earth shouts with joy.

What is shouting with joy?[4] Even the title of the present psalm draws our attention to this word, for it says, *in confession*. What can it mean to shout for joy in confession? There is a saying in another psalm, *Blessed the people that understands how to shout with joy* (Ps 88:16(89:15)). It must be something important, if the understanding of it confers blessing on us. May the Lord our God, he who renders men and women blessed, grant me to understand what to say and grant you to understand what you hear: *Blessed the people that understands how to shout with joy*. Let us run toward this beatitude; but let us understand properly about shouting with joy, and not just make a witless noise. What would be the use of shouting for joy and obeying the injunction of the psalm, *Shout with joy to God, all the earth*, if we did not understand? What would be the point of our voice shouting on its own if our heart did not? The heart's cry of joy is its understanding.

4. What I am about to describe is something familiar to you. A person who is shouting with gladness does not bother to articulate words. The shout is a wordless sound of joy; it is the cry of a mind expanded with gladness, expressing its feelings as best it can rather than comprehending the sense. When someone is exulting and happy he passes beyond words that can be[5] spoken and understood, and bursts forth into a wordless cry of exultation. Such a person is clearly rejoicing vocally, but he is so full of intense joy that he is unable to explain what makes him happy. Notice that the same thing happens even to people who sing disreputable songs. But our joyful shouting will not be like theirs, for we must be jubilant about our justification, whereas they shout about their iniquity; and therefore we shout in confession, they in confusion. An example from common experience will make what I am saying even clearer to you. People who work in the fields are especially given to joyful shouting. Harvesters and grape-gatherers and other fruit-pickers are greatly cheered by a plentiful crop and rejoice over the fecundity and bounty of the earth. In their exultation they sing, and between the words of their songs they interject happy, wordless sounds that express the elation they feel. This is called jubilation, shouting for joy. If the example does not commend itself to any of you because you have never noticed this custom, take care to notice in the future. But I hope you will not find anyone you need to

---

4. *Iubilare.* Compare Augustine's remarks in his Exposition of Psalm 94,3.
5. Variant: "from words that cannot be. . . ."

pull up for his singing, lest God find any he must pull down.[6] However, since thorns persistently spring up, let us simply note that jubilation deserves rebuke in persons who exult in unbecoming ways, and ourselves offer to God the jubilation that wins a crown.

Contemplating God in the glories of creation

5. When should we shout for joy? When we praise what is beyond utterance. We gaze at the whole of creation: the earth, the sea, the sky, and all the creatures in them. We perceive that each has its own origin and source, its own generative power, its due time of birth, its way of maintaining itself, and its decline into death, and that each pursues its untroubled course through unfolding centuries. We watch the stars revolve from east to west and the years speed by; we see the measured months and the tension of the stretched hours.[7] And in all these there is an invisible something, called spirit or soul; in all living things there is a certain trace of unity which prompts them to seek pleasure, flee from harm, and keep themselves whole.[8] We also perceive in human beings a quality shared with the angels of God—not the faculties of life, hearing, sight, and the others we have in common with the beasts, but a quality belonging properly to the mind, one that can apprehend God and can distinguish justice from injustice as the eye tells white from black.

In all this consideration of created beings, which we have tried to name and list in some fashion, let the soul question itself: "Who made all these things? Who created them? Who created you, my soul, as one among them all? What are these things you are contemplating? And what are you, who contemplate? Who is he, who made both the things you contemplate, and you, who contemplate them? Who is he?" Speak of him, and in order to speak of him, first think of him, for you can think about something of which you may be unable to speak, but you will never be able to speak of something if you cannot think it.

---

6. *Non inveniat quos advertat, ne Deus inveniat quos evertat.* There is a play on the similarity between *advertat* and *evertat*, which the translation attempts to reflect. In the lines immediately preceding and following Augustine plays on different meanings of *adverto:* to "notice" or to "reprimand." It has been thought by some that Augustine is here alluding to a rural fertility rite.

7. *Distentiones horarum.* Compare *Confessions* 11,23,30—26,33, where Augustine grapples with the mystery of time as a dimension of created being. *Distentio* means "extension," but with the added charge of tension or strain, deriving from the unquiet mind which can grasp no element in the flux and make it stand still and call it "now."

8. Compare *Confessions* 1,20,31: "Even then [in childhood] I took good care to keep myself whole and sound and so preserve the trace in me of your profoundly mysterious unity, from which I came." He knew himself to be made in the image of God, Three in One. Similarly in the present passage Augustine evokes the enormous multiplicity and diversity of created beings yet points to the trace of unity in each and in the whole, reflecting the Creator.

Draw near to God by recovering his likeness

Think about him, then, before you speak of him; and in order to think of him, draw near to him. If you want to see something clearly, and so be equipped to speak of it, you come close to get a good view, for if you were content to look only from a distance you might make a mistake. As those bodily objects are examined with the eyes, so is he with the mind; we gaze on him and see him with the heart. But where is the heart fit to see him? *Blessed are the pure of heart, for they shall see God* (Mt 5:8), he tells us. I hear, I believe, and I understand as best I can that God is to be seen with the heart, and that only a pure heart can contemplate him. But I hear another warning from scripture: *Who will boast of having a pure heart? Or who will claim to be clean of sin?* (Prv 20:9, LXX) I have reviewed the whole of creation insofar as I could: I have considered the material creation in the sky and on earth, and the spiritual creation in myself. I speak, I animate my limbs, I direct my voice, I move my tongue, I form words and apprehend their meaning.[9] Yet when shall I ever comprehend myself in me? And if I cannot, how shall I comprehend what is above me?

To the human heart nonetheless is promised the vision of God, and we are summoned to the work of cleansing our hearts. Scripture bids us, "Before you see him, prepare in yourself the faculty for seeing him whom you love." Once we have heard of God, and heard his name, surely no one can fail to find sweetness in the sound of it, except an impious person far away, someone who has chosen to distance himself. *Lo, those who go far from you will perish,* says another psalm; and it continues, *You have destroyed everyone who leaves you to go a-whoring* (Ps 72(73):27). If the impious are far away, and therefore in darkness, if in their darkness they have such damaged eyes that they not only do not desire light but even dread it, what is said to us, who have been found in our far-off place? *Draw near to him and be enlightened* (Ps 33:6(34:5)). But if you are to draw near in order to be enlightened, your darkness must first become loathsome to you. Condemn what you are so as to deserve to become what you are not. You are unrighteous, and your duty is to become righteous, but you will never receive righteousness as long as your iniquity pleases you. Pound it to pieces in your heart and make your heart clean; drive it out from that heart of yours where he whom you long to see desires to dwell.[10] Thus the human soul draws near, the inner person recreated[11] in God's image because in that image it was created from the first. This person had been far away to the extent that he or she had lapsed into unlikeness, for it is not by spatial intervals that we approach God or distance ourselves from him. By your unlikeness to God you have gone far from

---

9. Or "distinguish sensations."
10. Variant: "Confess that it is in your heart; he wishes to dwell there."
11. Variant: "As the human soul draws near, the inner person is recreated. . . ."

him; as you become like him, you draw very near.[12] Consider how the Lord wants us to come close to him and begins by making us like himself, so that we may. *You must be like your Father in heaven, who causes his sun to rise over the good and the wicked and sends rain upon just and unjust alike* (Mt 5:45). Learn to love your enemy, if you don't want your enemy to be a threat to you. But as charity grows within you, making you more like God and recalling you to your likeness to him, it extends even to your enemies, so that you come to resemble him who causes his sun to rise not over good people only but over good and evil, and sends his rain not to the just alone but to just and unjust alike. The closer you come to his likeness, the more progress you make in charity, and the more sensitive to God you become. Of whom are you becoming aware? Of someone who has come to you, or of someone to whom you are returning? He has never left you; but God withdraws from you as you withdraw from God. Here is an analogy: all objects are present to blind persons in the same way as to those with sight. A blind man and a sighted man may stand together, and both be surrounded by the same visible forms, yet one is present to them, the other absent. Of those two men standing side by side, one is present, the other absent, not because the objects themselves are close to one and fleeing away from the other, but because of the dissimilarity in their eyes. One is called blind, because for him that light[13] has been extinguished which ordinarily is mingled with the light that clothes all things, and so it is to no purpose that he stands near objects he cannot see. Indeed, he is more properly said to be absent from them, for where there is no perception there is real absence; to be absent is not to be in a position to perceive what is there.

God, on the contrary, is present everywhere, and everywhere totally. His Wisdom reaches powerfully from end to end, disposing all things sweetly.[14] But what God the Father is, that too is his Word, his Wisdom, who is Light from Light, God from God. What are you hoping to see? What you long to see is not far from you. The apostle expressly teaches that he is not far distant from any one of us, *for in him we live and move and have our being* (Acts 17:28). How miserable a state must it then be, to be distant from him who is present everywhere?

6. Be like him, then, in tender dutifulness, and love him with your power of thought, because God's invisible reality is contemplated through things that are created.[15] Gaze at these created things, wonder at them, and seek their maker. If

---

12. Compare the "region of unlikeness" in *Confessions* 7,10,16. The formula is from Plotinus (*Enn.* 1,8,13), who derived it from Plato's "bottomless sea of unlikeness" (*Politicus* 273 D6-E1). The idea of a journey from the land of unlikeness became influential and recurs in many Christian writers and mystics.

13. The light of his eyes, which Augustine thinks of as mingling with the light all around in our act of seeing.

14. See Wis 8:1.

15. See Rom 1:20.

you are unlike him, you will be rebuffed;[16] if you are like him, you will leap for joy. As you begin to resemble him and draw near, and begin to be keenly aware of God, charity will grow in you; and since charity is also God,[17] you will be conscious of the reality you tried to talk about, though you did not truly speak of it at all. Before you became so vividly aware of him you thought yourself qualified to speak about God; but now you begin to feel what he is, and you realize that what you perceive is something that cannot be spoken.

But if you have discovered that the reality you encounter is beyond utterance, will you therefore fall silent, and not praise him? Will you be struck dumb and cease to praise God, and no longer give thanks to him who has willed to make himself known to you? While you were seeking him you praised him; will you fall silent now that you have found him? Of course not: you could not be so ungrateful. Honor is due to him, reverence is owed to him, mighty praise is his by right. Think who you are, you who are but dust and ashes. Consider who has been found worthy to see—and to see what? Think about it: who sees what? A human being has been allowed to see God! I cannot think that any human merit earned this; it comes only from the mercy of God. Praise him, then, for his mercy.

"And how shall I praise him?" you ask. The slight glimpse I can attain, a mere enigmatic reflection in a mirror,[18] even that I cannot explain, so listen to the psalm: *Shout with joy to the Lord, all the earth.* If you shout with joy to the Lord, you have understood how all the earth shouts its joy. Shout with joy to the Lord; do not dissipate your jubilation over a variety of objects. In any case, those other things can be clearly spoken about in some fashion, but he alone is inexpressible, he who spoke, and all things were made. He spoke, and we came to be, but we have no power to utter him. The Word in whom we were spoken is his Son, and to enable us weaklings to utter him in some degree, the Word became weak. We can shout in exultation over the Word, but we can find no words to articulate the Word. *Shout with joy to the Lord, all the earth.*

Freedom in the Lord's service

7. *Serve the Lord with cheerfulness.* Slavery is always very bitter; those who are bound in servile condition perform their duties, but they also grumble. Do not be afraid of slavery to this Lord of ours; there will be no complaining among his slaves, no grumbling, no resentment. No one begs to be emancipated from that service, because it is so delightful that all of us have been redeemed. It is a

---

16. Either because created things can hold us back from God, or simply because they will disappoint us if we have not the Godlike quality Augustine is talking about, which would enable us to see them in their true light.
17. See 1 Jn 4:8, but Augustine turns the text around: all true love has something of God in it.
18. See 1 Cor 13:12.

great happiness to be a slave in this magnificent household, brothers and sisters, even if you are fettered. Do not be afraid, fettered slave; confess to the Lord. You have well deserved your fetters; admit it, and confess in your fetters if you want them to be turned into adornments. Another psalm prayed with good reason, *May the groans of fettered captives come into your presence* (Ps 78(79):11), and that prayer has been heard. *Serve the Lord with cheerfulness.* Slavery to the Lord is freedom: where we serve in charity, not under coercion, there is free servitude. *You have been called to liberty, brothers and sisters,* says the apostle, *but take care not to let your freedom give the flesh its chance. Rather serve one another out of charity.* (Gal 5:13) Since the truth made you free, let charity enslave you.[19] *If you abide in my word, you will truly be my disciples,* says the Lord. *You will know the truth, and the truth will set you free.* (Jn 8:31-32) You are simultaneously a slave and a free person: a slave because you were made and a free person because you are loved by God who made you; and moreover free because you love him by whom you were made. Do not grumble as you serve him, for your complaints do not pluck you out of servitude but only leave you serving as a bad slave. You are the Lord's slave and the Lord's freedman or freedwoman. Do not look for any manumission that would be an escape from the household of the master who has manumitted you already.

Groaning amid false brethren

8. *Serve the Lord with cheerfulness.* Cheerfulness will be full and perfect only when this perishable nature has clothed itself in imperishability and our mortality has put on immortality.[20] Then will cheerfulness be perfect, and perfect too will be our jubilation; then will praise be unceasing and love free from all scandals; then will the crop be unthreatened and life unshadowed by death. But what about us here? Is there no joy for us? Joy there is indeed, for if there were no joy, we could not shout for joy, and then how could the psalm bid us, *Shout with joy to the Lord, all the earth*? Joy there certainly is, even here, joy in our hope of eternal life, as we taste here what will completely satisfy us hereafter.

Yet the crop must suffer many things here, as it grows amid the tares. The grains of wheat are among the straw, the lily blooms amid thorns. What is the Church told? *Like a lily in the midst of thorns, so is my dearest one amid the daughters* (Sg 2:2). *Amid the daughters,* it says, not "amid strangers." O Lord, how do you console us, how do you comfort us, when you terrify us so? What are you saying? *Like a lily in the midst of thorns*—but what thorns are these? *So is my dearest one amid the daughters*—but who are the daughters? Whom do you call

19. Variant: "charity enslaves you."
20. See 1 Cor 15:53.

thorns, whom daughters? He answers, "They are thorns by their behavior, though daughters because of my sacraments."[21] If only it were among strangers alone that we had to suffer! That would not be nearly so painful. But a more acute anguish is evoked in another psalm: *if an enemy had slandered me, I could have borne it; or if someone who hated me had talked arrogantly against me, I could surely have hidden from him.* These are the words of a psalm. Those who are familiar with our scriptures will know what comes next; anyone who is unfamiliar should pay attention and learn the following words. *If someone who hated me had talked arrogantly against me, I could surely have hidden from him. But it was you, a like-minded person, my guide and my familiar companion, who were wont to eat delicious food with me.* (Ps 54:13-15(55:12-14)) What is this delicious food that they eat with us, people who will not be with us for ever? What delicious food? Surely that to which scripture invites us: *Taste and see how sweet the Lord is* (Ps 33:9(34:8)). Yet among such people we must groan still.

There is no escape from tiresome neighbors

9. Is there any place to which a Christian can withdraw, to get away from the distress caused by false brethren? Where is a Christian to seek refuge? What is he to do? Should he seek lonely places? Scandals pursue him there. Is a man or woman who is making progress to seek solitude, where there will be no one at all to put up with? But what if such a person was himself impossible to put up with, before he had begun to improve? If he thinks that because he has made some progress he cannot be expected to tolerate anyone else, his very intolerance proves that he has made no progress at all. Be clear about this, beloved ones.[22] The apostle exhorts us, *Bear with each other in love, careful to maintain the unity forged by the Spirit in the bond of peace* (Eph 4:2-3). *Bear with each other,* he says; is there nothing in you that anyone else has to bear with? If there really is nothing, I am amazed. But if there is nothing, that means you must have all the more strength to put up with other people, if there is nothing in you that others have to endure. If you are no trial to others, you must be well able to bear with all the rest. "But I can't," you answer. That means there are things in you which are a trial to other people. *Bear with one another in love.* If you turn your back on human society and hide yourself away where no one can see you, whom are you going to help? Would you have reached the stage you have, if no one had helped you? Are you going to hack down the bridge, just because you congratulate yourself that your feet have been so swift in crossing it? I exhort you all, or, rather, the voice of God exhorts all of us, *Bear with one another in love.*

---

21. Schismatics therefore; he probably means the Donatists.
22. *Caritas vestra,* a customary form of address with Augustine, but perhaps with a special point in this context.

Life in a religious community is commendable but has its own difficulties

10. "Well then," someone replies, "I will withdraw from society with a few good people. Life with them will be better for me. To be of service to no one at all would be irresponsible and cruel; I recognize that." But my Lord did not so teach me, for he condemned a servant not for stealing the money in his possession but for failing to put it to good use. The punishment due to a thief can be inferred from that meted out to the lazy man. *You wicked, lazy servant* (Mt 25:26), said the Lord as he condemned him. He did not say, "I gave you money, and you did not return the full sum to me." No: "I shall punish you," he said, "because it did not increase, because you did not invest it." God is greedy for our salvation.[23] "All right, then," he persists, "I will go into seclusion with a few good people. Why should I take account of the mob?"

Fine. But what about this handful of good people: were they not strained out from the mob? However, let us grant you that these few people are all good, and that it is a good idea, a commendable plan and one attractive to our human way of thinking, to associate with others who have chosen a quiet life, far removed from the clamor of the populace, from the tumult of the mob and the towering waves of the world, as though they were safe in harbor. Does it follow that they find there the joy we await? Do they experience the jubilation we are promised? No, not yet; for they are still beset with groaning and troubled by temptations. Even their harbor must have an entrance somewhere, for if there were no way into a harbor no ship could ever enter it. So it has to be open on one side, and as often as not that means it is open to the wind. Even if there are no rocks there, the ships can be dashed against each other and wrecked. If there is no safety even in the harbor, can we be secure anywhere?

All the same, we must admit that they are to some degree better off in port than in the open sea; we must concede that much, for it is true. The ships in harbor must love each other; they need to accommodate themselves to one another with care, to avoid collisions. Fairness must be maintained all round, and constant charity. If, in spite of their circumspection, a gale blows in from the exposed quarter, careful piloting is required.[24]

11. Now there may be someone here who is a superior in one of these communities, or, as I should prefer to say, one who in that capacity serves his brethren in what is called a monastery. What answer will he give me? "I am careful not to admit any bad applicant," he says. How are you going to avoid doing so? "I will

23. It is not entirely clear which parts of this paragraph are Augustine's own words and which parts he attributes to the person arguing with him. It is possible to take the whole of "I will withdraw ... salvation" as the words of this interlocutor, who then continues, "So I will go. ..."

24. Augustine's remarks in this and the following sections are obviously applicable to religious life. It is likely that there were monks and nuns near the Basilica of Celerina, and that some were present to hear him.

refuse entry to any bad person, any brother of evil disposition. Life will be more peaceful for me with only a few, provided they are good." But how do you know whom to exclude? If an undesirable applicant is to be recognized as bad, he has to be tested within the community. How can you exclude someone who is seeking admission if he needs a period of probation but can undergo it only if he is first granted admission? Will you be able to reject all bad applicants? You tell me, "I know how to discern what they are made of." But do they all come to you with naked hearts? These people who want to enter the monastery do not even know themselves; how much less can you know them? There have been many who promised themselves that they would faithfully live a holy life, in which all things would be common to all, and no one claim anything as his own, in a community where there would be but one soul and one heart directed to God;[25] yet when such aspirants were put into the kiln, they cracked. How then do you assess someone who is still an unknown quantity even to himself? Are you really capable of excluding bad brethren from a community of good ones?

If you say that you are, prove it by shutting out all bad thoughts from your own heart. Do not admit so much as a bad suggestion. "Ah, but I don't consent to them," you reply. Perhaps not, but the thought had to get in first, didn't it, in order to make its suggestion? We all want to have such well-defended hearts that no incitement to wrongdoing can gain entry. But who knows where they find their way in? We do battle every day, each in his or her individual heart: one man or woman wrestling in a single heart with a mob of intruders. Avarice makes its suggestions; lust prompts; gluttony tempts; even that popular merrymaking insinuates its attractions. All these suggestions assail a person; he restrains himself from all of them, rejects them, turns away from them all; but if not one of them scores a hit he is very lucky. Where then is our security? Nowhere here, certainly, nowhere in this life, but only in the hope of God's promises. When we reach that fulfillment, there at last we will find perfect safety, when the doors are shut and Jerusalem's gates strongly barred;[26] there will our jubilation be perfect and our joy without limit. But for the present do not commend any form of life with complacency, nor praise anyone before his death.[27]

Take a balanced and realistic view of religious life

12. People make the mistake of either not undertaking a better form of life or of setting about it rashly. This happens because when people intend to praise it they do so in such a way as to omit all mention of the evils interspersed in it, but when they mean to belittle it they do so with so malicious and twisted a mind as

---

25. See Acts 4:32.
26. See Ps 147:13.
27. See Sir 11:30.

to close their eyes to the good things and exaggerate the bad aspects which are there or are alleged to be there. Thus it comes about that when any profession is praised in the wrong way—injudiciously praised, I mean—it attracts followers by its high reputation; but then those who enter it meet persons of a type they did not expect to find. Then, shocked by the bad characters, they recoil even from the good. Apply this principle to your own life, brothers and sisters. Listen to this teaching, that you may live.

The point may be stated in more general terms. God's Church earns praise: "Christians are fine people, and only of Christians can this be said. How great is the Catholic Church! They all love each other; they do their utmost to help one another. The Church devotes itself to prayer, fasting, and hymns the world over, and God is praised by its unity and peace." So people talk. Someone who hears this eulogy may fail to realize that the evil aspects which are mingled with the good have been passed over in silence. So the hearer comes along, attracted by such acclaim, and finds bad people mixed with the good, of a kind he was not told about before he came. He is so shocked by false Christians that he shuns good Christians.

On the other hand there are foul-mouthed slanderers, full of hatred, who rush to condemn. "What are Christians like? Christians! Misers, usurers![28] The people who fill the theatres and amphitheatres, when games or other shows are on, are the same ones who crowd into the churches on feast days, aren't they? Drunkards they are, gluttons, envious and spiteful to each other."

Yes, there are some like this, but the description does not fit all Christians. So you see, this attacker in his blindness says nothing of the good folk, while the injudicious eulogist says nothing of the bad. If you want to praise the present-day Church in the way that scripture does, remember the text I just quoted to you: *Like a lily in the midst of thorns, so is my dearest one amid the daughters* (Sg 2:2). Someone hears about the Church and weighs the matter. The lily is attractive, so he or she enters, stays close to the lily, and tolerates the thorns. Such a person will deserve the commendation and the kisses[29] of the bridegroom, who says, *Like a lily in the midst of thorns, so is my dearest one amid the daughters.*

The same holds good for the clergy. What the admirers of clerics see are devoted ministers, faithful stewards, men prepared to be patient with everyone, spending the love of their hearts on those they want to help, men who seek not their own interests but those of Jesus Christ.[30] The observers praise such conduct but forget that these good men are interspersed among bad ones. Other onlookers censure the avarice of the clergy, their improper behavior and their

---

28. See the note at Exposition 3 of Psalm 36,6.
29. Variant: "the regard."
30. See Phil 2:21; 1 Cor 13:5.

quarrels, representing them as greedy[31] for other people's money, drunkards and gluttons. You, the critic, are prejudiced in your vilification, just as you, the admirer, are injudicious in your praise. You who eulogize the clergy must admit that there are bad men among them; you who revile them must see that in their ranks there are good men too.

In the common life of brothers in a monastery the picture is the same. "Great men are to be found there, holy men whose lives are given to hymnody and prayer and the praises of God. Their business is holy reading; they work with their hands and support themselves by this means. They do not seek excessive profit; anything given to them by God-fearing neighbors is used with moderation and charity. No one claims for himself anything another does not have;[32] they all love each other and bear with one another." You praise them, yes, you praise them. But a person who does not know what goes on in the community, one who is unaware how a gale can sweep in and drive even the ships in harbor into collision—such a person enters the community in the fond hope of being secure there and finding no one who will be difficult to live with. But he finds bad brethren there, the kind who would not have been shown up as bad unless they had first been admitted. Remember that they must be tolerated for a while in the hope of their being reformed, and they cannot easily be expelled unless they have been given the chance of being tolerated first. Our newcomer, however, is impatient and in no mood for tolerance. "Who lured me into this place? I thought there would be charity here!" Exasperated by the tiresome habits of a few he abandons his holy resolve, and, since he has not persevered in what he promised, he becomes guilty of a broken vow. Moreover, having left the community he too becomes a scurrilous scandal-monger. The only things he reports are those he alleges he could not put up with; and sometimes those bad things are real enough. But the real faults of bad people must be endured if we are to have fellowship with the good. Scripture warns the one who departs, *Woe betide those who have lost the will to hold out* (Sir 2:16). What is worse, by belching out the bad smell of his resentment he frightens away others who would enter, because though he did enter himself, he lacked the strength to persevere. "What kind of people are they?" he asks. "Jealous, disputatious, intolerant, miserly! One of the community did such-and-such, and another something else just as nasty. . . ." You bad fellow, why pass over the good ones in silence? You parade the people you could not put up with, but say nothing of those who put up with your own bad ways.

---

31. Variant: ". . . quarrels and their boastfulness, seeing them as greedy."

32. Compare Augustine's *Rule* 8: "Of charity it is written that she seeks not her own, and we understand this to mean that charity makes us place what is common to all above what belongs to ourselves. Therefore in the measure that you care more for the common good than for your own, to that degree you will know that you have made more progress."

Every profession includes both worthy and unworthy practitioners

13. How true, dearest brothers and sisters, is that splendid saying in the Lord's gospel! From his own mouth we hear, *Two men will be in the field: one will be taken, the other left. Two women will be at the mill: one will be taken, the other left. Two men will be in bed: one will be taken, the other left.* (Mt 24:40-41; Lk 17:34) Who are the two men working in the field? The apostle gives us the clue: *I planted, Apollos watered, but God gave the growth. You are God's cultivated field.* (1 Cor 3:6.9) We are laboring in this field. The two men working there are clerics, but *one will be taken, the other left*; the good one will be taken, the bad left.

Then the gospel turns to the laity: *Two women at the mill.* Why *at the mill*? Because people who are under obligations to the world are bound by the cycles of temporal affairs, as though tied to a millstone. But from those obligations *one will be taken, the other left.* Who is the one taken? Someone who is exercised in good works, attentive to the needs of God's servants and of the poor, steadfast in confession of the faith, unswervingly joyful in hope, and mindful of God,[33] one who calls down curses on nobody and as far as possible loves not only friends but enemies as well. This kind of person has sexual relations with no woman except his wife, or with no man except her husband. He or she will be taken from the mill, but one whose life is not like this will be left there.

Others declare, "We want peace and quiet; we don't want to be annoyed by anyone. We will leave the crowds behind, and enjoy life in some measure of security." If you are seeking peace and quiet, you could be said to be looking for a bed on which to rest undisturbed. From there too *one will be taken, the other left.*

Make no mistake, brothers and sisters: if you do not want to be deceived, and aspire to love the brethren, be aware that there are dissemblers in every profession in the Church. I do not say that every person is a hypocrite, but that every profession has its hypocrites. There are bad Christians, but there are good Christians too.[34] You seem to see more bad ones, because they are the chaff and they block your view of the grains. But the grains are there: look more closely, feel them, shake them out, and judge by the taste. You will find undisciplined nuns; but does that mean the consecrated life itself is brought into disrepute? Plenty of them do not remain steadfastly in their houses, but make the rounds of other people's homes, indulging their curiosity and gossiping unsuitably.[35] They are

---

33. *Vigilans ad Deum.*
34. Very similar reflections are found in Augustine's Exposition 1 of Psalm 36,2; there also they are attached to the Matthean and Lukan passages quoted here.
35. See 1 Tm 5:13, though the reference there is to widows. It should be remembered that in Augustine's day many virgins consecrated to God continued to live in their own homes rather than together in communities.

proud; they are too free both with their tongues and in their drinking. Virgins they may be, but of what use is bodily integrity if the mind is debauched? Humble wedlock is better than proud virginity.[36] If such a virgin were to marry, she would not have a status to make her arrogant, but she would have a rein to guide her.[37] But the existence of unworthy virgins does not imply that we should condemn all those who are holy in both body and spirit,[38] does it? Neither, surely, are we to conclude that on account of praiseworthy virgins we must commend badly-behaved ones too. Whichever way you look, *one will be taken, the other left.*

14. Well now, brothers and sisters, let us finish the psalm; it is quite straightforward. *Serve the Lord with cheerfulness*: this invitation is addressed to you, to all of you who in charity put up with hardships and rejoice in hope. *Serve the Lord* not in bitter murmuring, but in the cheerfulness of love. *Come into his presence exulting.* It is easy enough to exult outside; you must exult in God's presence. But your exultation should be mainly in your spirit,[39] rather than with the tongue. *Come into his presence exulting.*

Verse 3. Creator and redeemer of his sheep

15. *Know that the Lord is God, and no other.* Is there anyone who does not know that the Lord is God? But the point is this: the psalm speaks of a Lord whom men did not believe to be God. *Know that the Lord is God, and no other.* Let this Lord not seem base in your eyes. You crucified him, scourged him, smeared him with spittle, crowned him with thorns, clothed him in a garment of ridicule, hung him on a tree, fixed him there with nails, pierced him with a lance, and stationed guards at his tomb. Yet he, and no other, is God.

He made us; it was not we ourselves. He made us, for all things were made through him, and without him was nothing made.[40] What cause have you for glee? What pretext for your pride? Someone else made you, and he who made you is suffering at your hands; yet you flaunt yourselves, and boast, and swagger, as though you were self-made. The best thing for you would be if he who made you were to make you perfect.[41] *He made us; it was not we ourselves.* We must not be proud, for all the good we have, we hold only from our designer. Whatever in us is solely our own work deserves condemnation, but what he has wrought in us wins us a crown. *He made us; it was not we ourselves.*

---

36. Compare his Exposition of Psalm 75,16.
37. The thought here is similar to that of *The Excellence of Marriage* 23. Some scholars have therefore assigned both works to the same period, perhaps 403-404.
38. See 1 Cor 7:34.
39. Literally "conscience."
40. See Jn 1:3.
41. Variant: "were to remake you."

We are his people, the sheep of his pasture. Many sheep and one sheep: that flock of sheep is a single sheep. And what a passionately loving shepherd we have! He left the ninety-nine and came down to search for this one; then he carried home on his shoulders[42] the sheep redeemed by his blood. The shepherd did not hesitate to die for his sheep, because risen from the dead he would make the sheep his own. *We are his people, the sheep of his pasture.*

Verses 4-5. Confession, our gateway now and our joy in heaven

16. *Enter his gates with confession.* Gates are a symbol of beginning, so you are bidden to begin by confessing. This is *a psalm of confession,*[43] which admits us to the place where we shout for joy. Confess that you did not make yourselves, and praise him by whom you were made. By departing from him you achieved your own evil work; now let your good be found in him. *Enter his gates with confession.* Let the flock come in through the gates, not linger outside exposed to the wolves. And how is it to get in? By confession. Confession must be your gateway, your beginning. This is why another psalm enjoins: *Let your first song to the Lord be one of confession* (Ps 146(147):7). What that psalm expressed by speaking of *your first song,* this one means by *gates,* when it says, *Enter his gates with confession.*

And once we are inside, shall we not continue to confess? Yes, indeed; confess always, for you always have reason to confess. It can hardly happen that any one of us is in this life so changed that nothing blameworthy remains; you need to rebuke yourself, lest he rebuke you, he who must condemn you. Once you have entered his courts, then, confess to him. When will there be no place for the confession of sins? Only in that rest which awaits us, where we shall be equal to the angels. But notice that I said, "There will be no place then for the confession of sins." I did not say, "There will be no confession"; for confession there will be, the confession of praise. You will confess for ever that he is God, and you his creature; that he is your protector and you protected. You will be in some sense hidden in him, as another psalm suggests: *You will hide them in the hidden recess of your face* (Ps 30:21(31:20)).

Come into his courts, and confess to him in hymns.[44] Confess at the gates, and when you have entered his courts, confess to him with hymns. Hymns are songs of praise. When you are making your way in, rebuke yourself; when you are in, praise him. *Open the gates of righteousness to me,* prays another psalm, *that entering I may confess to the Lord* (Ps 117(118):19). Did it say, "Once inside, I will no longer confess"? Not at all; even when I have entered there will still be

---

42. See Lk 15:4-5.
43. See verse 1, the title.
44. Variant: "in hymns of confession."

confession. What sins was our Lord Jesus Christ confessing when he exclaimed, *I confess to you, Father, Lord of heaven and earth* (Mt 11:25)? His confession was a paean of praise, not a self-accusation.

17. *Praise his name, for the Lord is sweet.* Never think that you will weary of praising him. Your songs of praise are like eating: the more you praise, the more strength you acquire, and the more delightful does he become whom you are praising. *Praise his name, for the Lord is sweet. His mercy endures for ever,* for he does not cease to be merciful when he has set you free. It is a mark of his mercy that he continues to protect you until you reach eternal life. *His mercy endures for ever, and his truth to generation after generation.* You can understand this last phrase either to mean every generation, or to indicate two generations, one earthly and the other heavenly. Here below there is a work of generation which gives birth to mortals; but there is another which gives birth to beings who are eternal. God's truth is found both here and there beyond. Do not be misled into thinking that his truth is not here. Were it not, we should not have been told in another psalm, *Truth has sprung up from the earth* (Ps 84:12(85:11)), nor would Truth himself have promised, *Lo, I am with you throughout all days, even to the end of the ages* (Mt 28:20).

Exposition of Psalm 100

A Sermon to the People

Verse 1. The era of mercy will be succeeded by that of judgment

1. This is the hundredth psalm.[1] The statement in its first verse is a key to what we must look for throughout the whole of it: *I will sing to you of your mercy and judgment, O Lord.* No one should make the assurance of God's mercy a ground for thinking he will escape punishment, for there is judgment to come as well; but neither should anyone who has reformed his life be in terror of God's judgment, for mercy is mentioned first. When human beings have to pass judgment they are sometimes overcome by merciful impulses and act contrary to what right judgment demands.[2] Thus it seems that although there is mercy in them, judgment is lacking. In other cases they try to maintain unswerving judgment but lose sight of mercy. Not so with God: the goodness that overflows in his mercy does not diminish the severity of his judgment, nor does he lose that merciful goodness in judging severely.

We may perhaps distinguish two different eras: that of mercy and that of judgment. If this is correct, it is no accident that they are mentioned in this order. The psalm does not say, "Judgment and mercy," but *mercy and judgment.* So then, if we take them to refer to two distinct periods of time, we may regard the present time as that of mercy and the future as the occasion for judgment. In what sense does the time of mercy come first? Think about it in God himself to begin with, so that in the measure he grants you, you may imitate the Father. It is no presumption on our part to say we have a duty to imitate our Father, for our Lord himself, the only Son of the Father, exhorted us to do so, saying, *You must be like your Father in heaven.* Having told us, *Love your enemies, and pray for those who persecute you*, he continued, *so that you may be like your Father in heaven, who causes his sun to rise over the good and the wicked, and sends rain upon just and unjust alike* (Mt 5:48.44-45). In this we acknowledge his mercy. When you notice that just and unjust without distinction see the same sunshine, enjoy the same light, drink from the same springs, are drenched with the same rain, are filled with the same fruits of the earth, breathe this same air, and have all the good things of this world in equal measure, do not conclude that God is acting

---

1. Augustine omits its title, which is supplied by one codex: "A psalm for David himself."
2. Variant: ". . .overcome, and exercise mercy contrary to. . . ."

unjustly in giving them to just and unjust people indiscriminately. This is the time for mercy; the time for judgment has not come yet. If God did not first spare us in his mercy, he would not find anyone to reward at his judgment. Now is the time for mercy, during which God's patience leads sinners to repentance.[3]

2. Listen to the apostle drawing a distinction between the two periods, and then draw it yourself. *You, fellow,* he demands, *you who judge people who act so, yet do the same yourself, do you suppose that you will escape the judgment of God?* Pay careful attention to this. The person he was speaking to—though to whom was he really speaking? Not just a single individual, but everyone of this kind—the person spoken to was used to seeing that although he committed many evil deeds every day, he went on living, and nothing bad befell him. He therefore believed that God was either asleep, or unconcerned about human affairs, or even pleased with human wrongdoing. The apostle banished that idea from people's hearts, or at any rate from those of sound sense. What does he say? *You, fellow, you who judge people who act so, yet do the same yourself, do you suppose that you will escape the judgment of God?* Then it seems as though the sinner retorts, "But why does nothing bad happen to me when I go on doing such bad things every day?" So Paul goes on to point out to him that this is the time for mercy: *Do you despise his generous kindness and forbearance, and his long restraint?* And indeed the sinner did despise them, but Paul warns him to be careful: *Do you not realize that God is patient only to lead you to repentance?* (Rom 2:3-4). This is the time for mercy, but Paul would not allow the sinner to imagine it would last for ever. How does he continue, how does he terrify sinners? "Watch out," he implies. "You have heard about the time for mercy. Now learn about the time for judgment. Scripture says, *I will sing to you of your mercy and judgment, O Lord.*" Now comes the threat: *But you with your hard and impenitent heart are storing up against yourself anger that will be manifest on the day of God's just judgment, for he will render to each and all as their deeds deserve* (Rom 2:5-6). This is exactly what the psalm has told us: *I will sing to you of your mercy and judgment, O Lord.*

The judgment has been spoken of in menacing terms. Does this mean that God's judgment is only to be feared? Should we not also love the prospect of his judgment? It is a fearful prospect for bad people because it will bring punishment, but lovable for the good because they will receive their crowns. In the text I have just quoted the apostle struck fear into evildoers; but listen now to another passage where he offers hope to good people concerning the judgment. He points to himself as an example, and what he says demonstrates that even in his own life he has experienced the time of mercy. If he had not found an interval of mercy, in what state would the judgment have found him? As a blasphemer and

---

3. See Rom 2:4.

persecutor, one who injured others. This is what he testifies of himself, and in so doing he makes plain to us that we too are in the era of mercy. *I was originally a persecutor and a blasphemer, and harmed people*, he says, *but I received mercy.* But perhaps he alone received it? No; listen to him as he rallies our hope too: *I received mercy so that Christ Jesus might give proof in me of his long forbearance, to instruct those who will believe in him unto eternal life* (1 Tm 1:13.16). What does he imply by saying, *That Christ Jesus might give proof in me of his long forbearance?* He wants all sinners, all who are burdened by guilt, to see that since Paul obtained pardon, they need not despair for themselves. He reported on his own case and raised up others.

Where does this apply? In this present period of mercy. But you also need to listen to what he says about the prospects for good people at the time of judgment; and notice that here again his testimony is valid both for himself and for others. At the earlier stage he obtained mercy. What for? Because he was a blasphemer and a persecutor, and he wronged people. The Lord came and conferred on Paul not his just deserts but a free pardon. If he had come to give him what he deserved, what could he have given to such a sinner? Nothing but punishment and torment. The Lord did not want to mete out retribution; he chose to bestow free grace. But now listen further: this man who was freely pardoned holds the Lord to be his debtor. In the time of mercy he found the Lord to be a donor; in the time of judgment he holds him to be a debtor. Look how he makes his point: *Already I am being poured out like a sacrificial libation, and the time for my dissolution is upon me. I have fought the good fight, I have run the whole course, I have kept the faith.* These claims refer to the time of mercy, but now he looks to the time of judgment: *All that remains for me now is the crown of righteousness which the Lord, as a just judge, will award me on that day.* He does not say, "Will freely give me," but *will award me.* When he bestowed free grace on me, he was being merciful, but when he makes his award he will be acting as a judge, for *I will sing to you of your mercy and judgment, O Lord.* By freely forgiving my offenses, he put himself in debt to me; he owes me a crown. At the first stage *I received mercy*, for then the Lord was forbearing; but now the Lord will award me the crown of righteousness. Why is he bound to award it? Because he is a *just judge.* In what respect is he judging justly? In that *I have fought the good fight, I have run the whole course, I have kept the faith.* Being a just judge, he has no option but to crown these achievements. He has found deeds that he must crown. But what did he find at that earlier stage? That *I was originally a persecutor and a blasphemer.* He freely pardoned my former deeds and he will crown my later ones; he freely pardoned the first in the era of mercy and will crown the rest in the era of judgment. And so *I will sing to you of your mercy and judgment, O Lord.*

But is Paul the only one to deserve a reward? No. I have already pointed out that just as he terrified us by another statement, so does he raise our hopes by this one, for now he says, *The Lord, as a just judge, will award me a crown of righteousness on that day, and not to me alone but to all those who love his coming* (2 Tm 4:6-8).

A warning against complacency, and hope for the members of Christ

3. Well then, brothers and sisters, we have a period of mercy; but we must not lull ourselves into complacency, we must not let ourselves down lightly, we must not say, "It's all right, God always forgives. I did that bad thing yesterday, and God forgave me; I'm doing it today, and he is forgiving me; and I will do it again tomorrow, because God forgives." You are focusing on his mercy and leaving no room for fear of his judgment. If you want to sing to him of his mercy and judgment, be clear about this: he forgives in order that you may amend, not that you may have license to continue in your villainy. Do not store up against yourself anger that will be manifest on the day of God's just judgment. Concerning this same period of mercy another psalm warns, *To the sinner the Lord says, What right have you to expound my just judgments, and take my covenant on your lips? You hate instruction, and have thrown my words behind you. Wherever you saw a thief, you would collude with him, and you threw in your lot with adulterers. You sat down to slander your brother, and put a stumbling-block in the way of your mother's son. All this you did, and I was silent.* It is speaking of the era of mercy, but what can it mean when God says, *I was silent?* It obviously cannot mean, "I did not rebuke you"; it means, "I did not judge." How could he be said to remain silent, when he cries out every day in the scriptures, in the gospel, in his preachers? "I have been silent with regard to punishment," he says, "but not from warnings." But what did the sinner say to himself in his heart when he met this silence of God, God's withholding of punishment? The same psalm tells us: *You were wrong to think that I will be like you.* It is bad enough that you were like that yourself; you went further and thought I was too. And then, after describing the time of mercy, the psalm strikes terror by signaling the time of judgment: *I will rebuke you, and bring you face to face with yourself* (Ps 49(50):16-21). You put yourself out of sight behind your back, but I will bring you round to confront yourself. Anyone who is unwilling to see his sins puts himself behind his back, and closely observes the sins of other people, though out of malice, not because he loves or cares for them. He has no desire to heal others but only to accuse them, and he forgets about himself. This is why the Lord says to people of this kind, *You see the speck of sawdust in your brother's eye, but fail to see the timber in your own* (Mt 7:3).

Since the psalm sings to us of mercy and judgment, let us too deal mercifully as in peace we await the judgment. Within Christ's body, let us sing of these things. Christ is singing about them to us. If the head were singing alone, the song would be about the Lord but would not belong to us; but if Christ is a whole, head and body, you must be among his members and cleave to him by faith and hope and charity. Then you are singing in him, and rejoicing in him, just as he labors in you, and thirsts in you, and hungers in you, and endures tribulations in you. He is still dying in you, as you have already risen in him. If it were not true that he is dying in you, he would not have pleaded in you for a respite from the persecutor, when he cried, *Saul, Saul, why are you persecuting me?* (Acts 9:4). This being so, brothers and sisters, we can say also that Christ is singing; and how we can say it, you know. We have spoken to you assiduously about Christ, and I know that these truths are familiar to you. Christ the Lord is the Word of God, through whom all things were made. In order to redeem us this Word was made flesh and dwelt among us;[4] he who is God above all things, the Son of God who is equal to the Father, became man, so that as God-man he might be the mediator between humankind and God.[5] He became man to reconcile to God those who were far off, to unite those who were divided, to recall the estranged and to bring back those sojourning away from home. He became the head of the Church, and so he has a body and limbs. Look for his limbs. At present they are groaning throughout the whole world, but at the end they will be full of joy over that crown of righteousness of which Paul says, *The Lord, as a just judge, will award it to me on that day.* Let us then sing in hope, all of us, gathered into one. Having put on Christ we, with our head, are Christ, for we are Abraham's posterity. The apostle tells us so. I have just said, "We are Christ." Let me explain that. The apostle teaches, *You are the seed of Abraham, his heirs according to the promise* (Gal 3:29). So we are Abraham's posterity. Let us go further and see whether Abraham's posterity is Christ. Paul recalls the promise, *In your seed will all nations be blessed* (Gn 12:3; Gal 3:8), and he argues, *Scripture does not say, "To his descendants," as though indicating many, but as to one only, "And to your seed," which is Christ* (Gal 3:10). And to us he says, *You are the seed of Abraham.* It is quite clear from this that we are part of Christ; and since we are his limbs and his members, we form one single person with our head. Let us make this our song, then, *I will sing to you of your mercy and judgment, O Lord.*

Verse 2. Walking in spacious innocence

4. *I will play a psalm, and I shall find understanding in a stainless path when you come to me.* Unless you walk a stainless path, you cannot either play psalms or find understanding. If you hope to understand, play psalms along a stainless way: that means working cheerfully for your God. What is a stainless path? The next line answers your question. *I was wont to walk about in the innocence of my*

---

4. See Jn 1:3.14.
5. See 1 Tm 2:5.

heart in the middle of my house.[6] So this stainless path began from innocence[7] and will reach its goal in innocence. Why seek lengthy explanations? Be innocent, and you have implemented all the demands of righteousness. But what does being innocent mean? We have it in our power to do harm in two ways: either by making someone miserable or by deserting someone who is miserable.[8] You know this from your own experience, for you do not want either to be made miserable by someone else or to be abandoned by someone when you are in distress. Who makes others wretched? Anyone who inflicts violence or entraps others, seizes other people's property, oppresses the poor, steals, seeks adulterous relationships, is a slanderer, or tries to inflict pain on other people out of deliberate malevolence. Who abandons wretched persons? Anyone who sees a destitute person in need of some help and, even though he has the means to help him, spurns the poor person, despises him, and hardens his own heart. It would be an act of pride to neglect a person in misery even if one were so secure oneself as to have no need whatever of any compassionate aid. But when we are all beset by the frailties of the flesh, and ignorant of what may befall us tomorrow, and yet we scorn the tears of the wretched, we are by no means innocent.

Who then is innocent? One who harms neither anyone else nor himself; for one is not innocent even if the harm is done to no one but oneself. An objector may say, "But look, I have not taken anyone's goods or oppressed anyone. I will make myself comfortable with my own money, for after all I earned it by honest work. I want a well-stocked table, I want to spend as much as I please, I want to drink as much as I feel like with companions of my own choice. How have I defrauded anyone? Whom have I ill-treated? Who has made any complaint about me?" The speaker seems innocent. But if he is corrupting himself, if he is wrecking God's temple within him, can you expect him to be kind to others, or compassionate toward the wretched? If he is cruel to himself, will he be kind to others? So you see, the whole of righteousness comes down to one word: innocence,[9] for *whoever loves iniquity hates his own soul* (Ps 10:6(11:5)). When he loved iniquity, the sinner thought he was harming other people. But ask that other psalm whether it really was others that he was harming. *Whoever loves iniquity hates his own soul.* Anyone who tries to hurt others hurts himself or herself first; and such a person cannot walk about in the house, because there is

---

6. The Hebrew imperfect expresses any action that is not complete and "perfect," and it is therefore used for future action. The verbs in verses 2-8 of the psalm should be understood as a declaration of intent with regard to the future: "I will walk . . . I will not set before my eyes. . . ." But the LXX, and Augustine's Latin version which derived from it, translated them into Greek and Latin imperfects, thus referring the actions to the past.

7. *Innocentia*, literally "non-harming" or "harmlessness," which Augustine contrasts in the rest of this section with tendencies that harm others or oneself.

8. Sins of commission and omission, as later writers might say.

9. Non-harming; see note above.

no room. Every kind of wrongdoing hems itself in; only innocence is broad and spacious, and leaves us room to walk about.

I was wont to walk about in the innocence of my heart in the middle of my house. By his house the psalmist may mean either the Church, in which Christ walks about, or his own heart, for our heart is like our interior house. In the latter case he would be explaining the preceding words, *in the innocence of my heart.* What is the innocence of his heart? The middle part of his house. If the center of someone's heart is bad, that person is cast out from it. It is like the situation of one who has a leaking roof in his house, or a smoky atmosphere: he leaves the house because he cannot bear to stay indoors. Similarly a person whose heart is oppressed by a bad conscience suffers from that unquiet heart and cannot easily live within it. Such persons move out from themselves by redirecting their minds and find pleasure in outward circumstances and bodily ease; they seek relief in frivolities, shows, soft living and all kinds of immorality. Why do they hope to find satisfaction outside themselves? Because conditions inside are unfavorable, and they can find no joy in their consciences.[10] This is why, after healing the paralytic, the Lord said to him, *Get up, I tell you, pick up your sleeping mat and go into your house* (Mk 2:11). A soul whose strength is dissipated as though by paralysis must do likewise: it must pull itself together by exercising its limbs in good works and pick up its sleeping mat by taking authority over its body. Then let it enter the house of its conscience, and there it will find plenty of space where it can freely walk about, and play psalms, and understand.

Verses 3-4. On treacherous associates, and on rightness of heart

5. *I did not set before my eyes anything dishonorable.* What does that mean—*I did not set before my eyes anything dishonorable*? It means, I did not set my heart on it, to love it. As you know, it is commonly said of someone who is loved by another person, "He can't take his eyes off her." Or again, someone who is being scorned complains, "He can't even spare me a glance." So what is it, to keep someone or something before one's eyes? To love. And what is it to withhold love? Not to let one's heart dwell on whatever it is. Thus the psalm declares, *I did not set before my eyes anything dishonorable*, meaning, "I did not love anything base, or set my heart on it."

Then he becomes more explicit about the dishonorable object. *I hate disloyal persons.*[11] Pay attention to this point, my brothers and sisters. If you are walking

10. Augustine speaks from experience: compare *Confessions* 10,27,38: "Lo, you were within, but I outside, seeking there for you, and upon the shapely things you have made I rushed headlong, I, misshapen."
11. *Facientes praevaricationem.* In classical Latin *praevaricatio* meant collusion between prosecution and defense to predetermine the outcome of a case, thus perverting the course of justice. It later came to carry the more general meaning of deviation from duty, or transgression.

about with Christ in the middle of his house—resting with a good conscience in your heart, I mean, or enjoying a good journey in the Church by walking a stainless path—your duty is to hate not only the disloyal outside the Church, but also any whom you find inside. Who are these disloyal transgressors? People who hate the law of God, people who hear it but do not put it into practice, are called disloyal. Hate such disloyal persons, and push them away. But it is as disloyal that you must hate them; do not hate the persons themselves. Think of a disloyal man or woman: he or she has two identities: as a human being and as a disloyal one. God made the human being; the transgressor made himself or herself disloyal. Love what God made, and zealously oppose what the transgressor made. When you hunt down the disloyalty, you put to death the human handiwork, and then God's handiwork is set free. *I hate disloyal persons.*

6. *No one of depraved heart was my companion*. What is a depraved heart? A heart that is twisted. And what is a twisted heart? One that is not straightforward, a crooked heart. But what is a heart that is not straight? First understand rectitude of heart and then you will grasp what a crooked heart is. A human heart is said to be straight if it does not refuse to accept anything that God wills.[12] Concentrate on this point. Suppose a person prays that something or other may not happen. He prays, but the calamity is not averted. Let him pray[13] with all his might, but the thing happens all the same against his will. He must then subordinate himself to the will of God, not resist that omnipotent will.

The Lord himself taught us this lesson, manifesting our weakness in his own prayer before his passion. *My soul is sorrowful to the point of death*, he said (Mt 26:38; Mk 14:34). He who had power to lay down his life, and power to take it up anew,[14] could not truly fear death. Even Paul, Christ's servant, cried out, *I have fought the good fight, I have run the whole course, I have kept the faith. All that remains for me now is the crown of righteousness which the Lord, as a just judge, will award me on that day.* (2 Tm 4:7-8) He leaps with joy because he is going to die, yet his Lord, his Commander-in-Chief, is dismayed as he faces death. Does that suggest that the servant is braver than his Master? If that were true, what would become of the Lord's teaching, *It is enough for a servant to be like his master, and a disciple like his teacher* (Mt 10:25)? Is it possible that Paul is brave when death draws near, and the Lord aghast? *I long to die and to be with Christ* (Phil 1:23), says Paul; he rejoices because his dissolution is upon him, and will bring him into Christ's company; yet is Christ himself dismayed—Christ, with whom Paul is so gladly hoping to be united? No. What was that cry uttered by Christ? It was the lament of our weakness. Many people are very daunted by

---

12. *Qui omnia quae vult Deus, non ipse non vult.* Some manuscripts amend this to the positive statement, "if it wills all that God wills."
13. Variant: "he prays."
14. See Jn 10:18.

the prospect of death, because they are still weak, but let them keep their hearts straight. Let them avoid death as long as they can, but when they cannot, let them pray the same prayer that the Lord offered on our behalf rather than on his own. What did he say? *Father, if it is possible, let this cup pass from me.* There you have the expression of his human will; now look at the rectitude of his heart: *Yet not what I will, but what you will be done, Father* (Mt 26:39).

If a straight heart follows God, a bent heart resists God. When some kind of misfortune comes the way of a person whose heart is crooked, he protests, "God, what have I done to you? What offense have I committed? How have I sinned?" He tries to make out that he is just, and God unjust. What could be more depraved? It is bad enough to be crooked oneself, but he is trying to prove that the ruler is crooked. Correct yourself and you will find that God is straight, but you have been bent out of shape by departing from him. He has acted justly, you unjustly, and therefore you are perverted in saying that a human being is just, and God unjust. And who is this human being whom you declare just? Yourself; because when you demand, "What have I done to you?" you are reckoning yourself just. But perhaps God may answer you, "You speak the truth there. You have done nothing to me; for all you did, you did to yourself. If you had done anything for me, you would have done something good. Whatever is done well is done for me, because it is done in accordance with my commandment. But whatever evil is committed strikes at you, not at me. A bad person harms himself only, because he acts as I have not ordered."[15]

When you see people like this, brothers and sisters, rebuke them, take them to task, correct them. If you cannot reprove or correct them, at least do not collude with them. Then you will be in a position to say, *No one of depraved heart was my companion.*

7. *When someone of ill-will deviated from me, I would refuse to know him.* What does *refuse to know him* imply? I would not approve or praise him, I refused to agree with him. In various texts of the scriptures we find the verb "to know" used where we would say, "find pleasing." Here is an example. Is anything concealed from God, brothers and sisters? Does he know the just only, not the unjust? Surely not. Can you entertain any thought of which he is ignorant? I am not saying, "Can you do anything?" No; can you even think anything without his knowing it? Or I should go further, and say not merely, "Can you even think it?" but, "Is there anything which you are going to think, which he has not already foreseen?" Clearly, then, God knows everything, yet at the end, at the time of judgment which will succeed the age of mercy, it will be said of certain people, *On that day many will come and say to me, Lord, Lord, did we not cast out demons in your name, and in your name work many prodigies? In your*

---

15. Or "A bad person acts for his own sake alone, since he acts as I have not ordered."

name we have eaten and drunk. But I will say to them, I never knew you. (Mt 7:22-23; Lk 13:26-27) Is there anyone whom he does not know? How then can he say, *I never knew you?* He means, I do not recognize you in relation to my rule. I know my righteous rule, but you do not conform to it. You have deviated from it, so you are distorted.

In this same sense the psalm here declares, *I would refuse to know* an unrighteous person. *When someone of ill-will deviated from me, I would refuse to know him.* But how can it say, *I would refuse to know him?* It surely cannot mean this in the same way as an ill-disposed person would, who on meeting a just man in a narrow street says to himself in the words of the Wisdom of Solomon, *The very sight of him vexes us* (Wis 2:15), and takes another road to avoid the person he does not wish to see? On the contrary, there are very many ill-disposed persons whom we see, and who see us, who not only do not turn aside from us but run toward us and even sometimes want to make us accomplices in their sins. This is our common experience.[16] How, then, can they be said to deviate from us?

To deviate from you is to be unlike you. What is "deviating" from you? Not following you. And what is "not following you"? Not imitating you. So the psalm declares, *When someone of ill-will deviated from me*—that is to say, when such an ill-disposed person was unlike me, refusing to imitate my way of life, when he or she was too ill-natured to live according to my example, as I set it forth—then *I would refuse to know* him or her. What does *refuse to know* mean? Not that I was simply ignorant but that I did not approve.

Verse 5. How are we to interpret the warning against sharing meals with the proud?

8. *Anyone who was secretly disparaging his neighbor, I would always pursue.* This is a good style of persecution, not of the sinner but of the sin. *With no one of proud eye or insatiable heart would I share meals.* What is meant by saying, "I would not share meals" with such a one? It means, "I never ate with him." But this demands your close concentration, beloved, because you are about to hear something remarkable. If the speaker refused to share meals with the person in question, he obviously did not eat with him; sharing meals with others implies that you eat with them. But then how is it that we find that the Lord himself set the example of eating with the proud? He did not eat with publicans and sinners,[17] because they were humble; they knew their sickness and sought

---

16. Variants: "Frequently they join us"; "Do they not join us? This frequently happens."

17. This is the literal meaning, and the slight manuscript variants do not soften it: *Cur ergo ipsum primo Dominum invenimus manducasse cum superbis? Non cum publicanis illis et peccatoribus, nam ipsi humiles. . . .* Perhaps we should expand the sentence slightly: "He did not eat only with publicans and sinners," or, "I am not referring to his meals with publicans and sinners, who. . . ."

their physician. No, it is with the proud Pharisees that we find him eating. A proud man invited him, that proud man who was displeased because a sinful woman, notorious in the city, approached the Lord's feet. Remember that the Pharisees were so fastidious that no sinner was allowed to touch them. If any unclean person so much as brushed against them, they would shudder, thinking that the unclean contact made them unclean too. Accordingly when the sinful woman, the one with a bad reputation in the city, approached the Lord's feet to weep there, the Pharisee observed her and said in his heart, *If this man were a prophet, he would know who this woman is, who has approached his feet.* How did he know that Christ did not know? He only suspected it from the fact that Christ did not thrust her away, for he would have done so if he had been a prophet, or so the Pharisee thought. But the Lord did know. Not only did he know this sinful woman; as a physician he also saw the incurable wounds of his proud host. Christ heard the man's thoughts, and exposed his pride. *Simon, I have something to say to you,* he began. *There was a certain creditor to whom two people were in debt. One owed him five hundred denarii, the other fifty. Since neither had the means to pay, he let them both off. Which of them will love him more?* The Pharisee gave the verdict against himself, for Truth elicited the confession from him: *I suppose, sir, the one to whom he remitted the larger debt.* Then, turning to the woman, Jesus said to Simon, *You see this woman? I entered your house, and you offered me no water for my feet; but she has washed my feet with her tears* (Lk 7:39-44), and so on; you know the rest. There is no need to dwell at length on the other elements in the story; we have cited it only to make the point that although the Pharisee was a proud man, the Lord was sharing a meal with him. What then are we to make of the psalm's testimony, *With no one of proud eye or insatiable heart would I share meals*? What does sharing meals with him imply? Eating with him, obviously. How then can the Lord recommend to us a line of conduct which he did not follow himself? He exhorts us to imitate him, and we see him accepting table fellowship with the proud; so how can he forbid us to have the same fellowship with them?

In our own case, brothers and sisters, we hold back even from our own brethren as a kind of reproof; we refuse to accept their hospitality for the sake of their correction. It is better for us to engage socially with outsiders, with pagans, than with those who belong to our number[18] if we see that they are living bad lives. In this way they may be embarrassed and correct themselves; as the apostle says, *If anyone disobeys our command conveyed in this letter, take note of such a one, and avoid his company. But do not regard him as an enemy. Correct him as a brother.* (2 Th 3:14.15) We customarily pursue this policy to

---

18. Variant: "than with those who used to be with us and still retain their connection with us."

promote their healing, although we often share meals with various outsiders and unbelievers.

9. We must examine further the meaning of the declaration, *With no one of proud eye or insatiable heart would I share meals.* A God-fearing heart has its banquets, certainly; but a proud heart has its banquets too, for it was with refer- ence to the food of the proud that the psalm spoke of an *insatiable heart.* On what does a proud heart feed? A person who is proud is also envious and cannot be otherwise. Pride is the mother of envy; it can bear no other offspring and must always be accompanied by envy. Every proud person is therefore full of spiritual envy, and if he is envious he feeds on the woes of others. This is why the apostle warns, *If you bite and try to eat each other, take care that you are not gobbled up by one another* (Gal 5:15). You are aware of such eaters, but do not share their meals, flee from that kind of feast, for they are never satisfied in their enjoyment of other people's misfortunes, having insatiable hearts. Be careful not to be caught in the devil's snare at their banquets. The Jews were eating that sort of food when they crucified the Lord. (I mean, of course, that they were feeding on the Lord's pain. We too are fed from the Lord's cross, but in a different way, when we eat his body.) When the Jews saw him hanging on the cross they mocked him, because their hearts were insatiable. *If he is the Son of God, let him come down from the cross*, they said. *He saved others, but he cannot save himself.* (Mt 27:40,42) They were feeding on the food of their cruelty, he on the food of his mercy. *Father, forgive them, for they do not know what they are doing* (Lk 23:34), he prayed. They had one kind of feast, he another. Consider also what is said elsewhere about the table of the proud: *May their table become a trap for them, let it be for them retribution and a stumbling-block* (Ps 68:23(69:22)). They were fed and captured. Just as birds go to feed at a trap, and fishes at a hook, and are snared, so too are the proud.

The impious have their feasts, then, but the God-fearing have theirs. Listen to what the devout feast on. *Blessed are those who hunger and thirst for righteous- ness, for they shall be satisfied* (Mt 5:6). If the faithful person is nourished on the food of righteousness, and the godless on the food of pride, it is no wonder that the proud person has an insatiable heart. Iniquity is his food. Do not nourish yourself on the food of iniquity and then no person of proud eye or insatiable heart will be your table companion.

Verses 6-7. The choice of good companions

10. On what were you feeding? What delicious food were you enjoying at the table where the proud did not join you? *My eyes were on the faithful in the land, that they might sit down with me.* This is the Lord speaking. He tells us, *My eyes were on the faithful in the land, that they might sit down with me.* How were they to sit down? *You will sit upon twelve thrones, judging the twelve tribes of Israel*

(Mt 19:28). They judge the faithful of the earth,[19] those to whom it is said, *Do you not realize that we shall judge angels?* (1 Cor 6:3) *My eyes were on the faithful in the land, that they might sit down with me.*

It continues, *One who walked a stainless path served me.* Served *me*, it says, not "served himself." Many who work in the service of the gospel are serving themselves, because they are furthering their own interests, not those of Jesus Christ.[20] What does it mean, to serve Christ? To pursue Christ's interests. When bad people proclaim the gospel, others are saved, but the preachers are punished, for of them it was said, *Do what they tell you, but do not imitate what they do* (Mt 23:3). Do not worry, then, if you hear the good news from a bad person. Woe betide him who serves himself by seeking his own advancement; but you, for your part, receive what is Christ's. *One who walked a stainless path served me.*

11. *No one who behaved arrogantly lived in my house.*[21] Refer this statement to the house we mentioned earlier, that is, the heart. No one who behaves arrogantly ever dwelt in my heart. Anyone of that kind would not live there but always leapt away again. No one was accustomed to live in my heart except a gentle, quiet guest; no proud person dwelt there, for the unjust do not live in the hearts of the just. However, a righteous person may be countless miles and many days' journey away from you, but if you are one in heart you are living together. *No one who behaved arrogantly lived in my house; no one who spoke wickedly continued in my presence.* This is a description of the stainless path, in which we shall find understanding when the Lord comes to us.

Verse 8. We are still in the night of temptations, but day will dawn

12. *In the morning I put to death all sinners on earth.* This is an obscure verse. Please concentrate; we are getting near the end of the psalm. *In the morning I put to death all sinners on earth.* Why? *To rid the Lord's city of all who commit iniquity.* There are people who commit iniquity in the Lord's city, then, and it seems that for the present they are spared. Why is that? Because this is the era of mercy; but the time of judgment will come, as the psalm indicated in its opening verse: *I will sing to you of your mercy and judgment, O Lord.* The psalmist has spelled out in the preceding lines the ways in which he made sure only good people would be close to him. He did not keep company with bad ones or enjoy the sinful feasts of people who ministered to themselves instead of to the Lord, by furthering their own interests. But now someone might ask him, "Why then did you put up with people like that in your city for so long?" He replies, "Because this is the time for mercy." Time for mercy? What is that? Judgment has not yet

---

19. Or "the land," as in the quoted psalm verse.
20. See Phil 2:21.
21. So the best codices. Some read "shall live."

been revealed. It is still night-time; day will dawn later, and with it, judgment. Listen to the words of the apostle: *Pass no judgment prematurely.* What does he mean by *prematurely?* Before daybreak. He was speaking of the hours before dawn; listen: *Pass no judgment prematurely, before the coming of the Lord, for he will light up the dark, hidden places, and reveal the purposes of our hearts, and then there will be commendation from God for each one* (1 Cor 4:5). As things are now, as long as you do not see my heart, nor I yours, it is still night. Suppose you make a request of some fellow-human and you do not get what you want. You think you are scorned. But perhaps you are not scorned at all. You do not see the other's heart, so you are quick with your curses. You are wrong, but pardon is granted to you as to one who has gone astray in the night. Or perhaps someone loves you, and you think he hates you; or again, he hates you, but you imagine he loves you: whichever way round it is, it is night still. Do not be afraid. Trust in Christ before the time, and be certain that you will see daylight in him. You can have no misgivings in his regard, because we are completely safe and certain that he cannot be deceived; and he loves us. We cannot yet have the same certainty with regard to one another. God knows what love we have for each other; but for our part, even though we do cherish mutual love, who knows what our motives are in doing so? Why does no one see our hearts? Because it is still night.

In the night temptations abound. Another psalm might almost have been speaking of this night when it said, *You spread the darkness and night fell. All the beasts of the forest will take advantage of it and come forth: lion cubs roaring and ready to seize their prey, seeking their food from God.* (Ps 103(104):20-21) Lion cubs hunt for food at night. Who are these lion cubs? The lackeys of the rulers and powers of the air,[22] the demons and angels who serve the devil. But how do they hunt their food? By tempting us. But they cannot approach unless God has given them the power, which is why scripture spoke of them as *seeking their food from God.* The devil asked for Job in order to tempt him. What sort of food was he begging for? Rich, succulent fare, a righteous man of God, one to whom God himself bore witness, calling him *a blameless man, honest, and a worshipper of God* (Jb 1:8, LXX). So the devil, hunting for food from God, begged for Job in order to tempt him. Job was handed over to be tempted but not crushed, to be purified but not ruined; or perhaps not even to be purified but simply to be proved. Others who are tempted are sometimes delivered into the tempter's hands through their own concealed fault, because, perhaps, they had already yielded to their own lusts. Certainly the devil harms no one, unless he has been authorized by God. But when does it happen? In the night. What does that mean—what night? In this present age. Once the night has

---

22. See Eph 2:2.

passed and day has dawned, the wicked will be cast into eternal fire along with the devil, but the just will be ushered into eternal life. There no tempter will be at work, because no lion cubs will be prowling, for the night will be over and done with. The Lord indicated all this when he said to his disciples, *This very night Satan has asked to sift all of you like wheat; but I have prayed for you, Peter, that your faith may not fail* (Lk 22:31-32). What do those words evoke—*sift you like wheat*? Just as we do not eat the wheat unless it has first been threshed to make bread, so the devil cannot eat anyone unless he has first pounded his victim with tribulation. He grinds the person down to prepare his food. But when you suffer tribulation do not be anxious; as long as you are still grain, nothing bad will happen to you. How are oxen used for threshing? Are they led into a place containing nothing but grain? No; they are taken with their sharp-studded sledge into the threshing-floor. But has the grain cause to be frightened? Not at all. Nothing is chopped up except the straw. The grain is divested of superfluous material;[23] then comes the winnowing, which will isolate a pure hoard. What the winnower finds as grain he will put into his barn, and the pile of straw he will burn with unquenchable fire.

13. Why did I say that? Because the day is ours already, in hope. In Christ it must be day for us. As long as we are beset by temptations, it is still night. God spares sinners during this night, not doing away with them but whipping them with temptations that they may be corrected; he tolerates their presence in his city. Can we think he will tolerate them for ever? If mercy is to last indefinitely there is no place for judgment; but if we are right to declare that *I will sing to you of your mercy and judgment, O Lord*, we must conclude that he spares us now but will judge us later. When will he judge? When night has passed.

This is the reason for the statement in our psalm, *In the morning I put to death all sinners on earth*. What can *in the morning* mean? When day has dawned and night is over. *In the morning I put to death all sinners on earth*. Why does he spare them until morning? Because until then it was night. What does that imply—it was night? Forbearance was appropriate then, because people's hearts were hidden. Even you tolerate someone who lives a bad life, because you do not know how he will turn out, for it is night. You cannot tell whether someone whose life is wicked today may improve tomorrow, any more than you can tell whether a person whose life is commendable today may tomorrow be wicked. It is night still, and God tolerates all of us, because he is very forbearing. He puts up with sinners so that they may be converted to him. If, however, they do not correct themselves during this interlude of mercy, they will be put to death. Why? That they may be cleared out from the Lord's city, from the

---

23. Variants: "It is not chopped up. Unless the straw is stripped away from the grain, it will be useless, and the winnowing will come. . . ."; ". . .except the straw. This is stripped from the grain, and is superfluous. Then the winnowing will come. . . ."

community of Jerusalem, from the society of the saints, from the fellowship of the Church. When will they be put to death? *In the morning.* What does that signify? When night has finally passed. And why does God spare them now? Because this is still the time for mercy. Why will he not spare them always? Because *I will sing to you of your mercy and judgment, O Lord.*

We must not deceive ourselves about this, brothers and sisters. All who commit iniquity will be slain. Christ will put them to death in the morning and exclude them from his city. But now, while the time for mercy is still with us, let them hearken to him. He shouts to them in every place, through the law, through the prophets, through the psalms, through the apostolic letters, through the gospels. Observe for yourselves that he is not silent, and that he is sparing us because he is dispensing mercy. But beware: judgment is coming.

Exposition 1 of Psalm 101

First Sermon[1]

Verse 1. Can the poor man who is praying here be the Word?

1. A poor man, one single poor man, is praying in this psalm, and he does not pray silently. We have the opportunity to listen to him and find out who he is; and perhaps we shall find that he is none other than the one of whom the apostle wrote, *Though he was rich, for your sake he became poor, so that by his poverty you might be enriched* (2 Cor 8:9). But if Christ is praying here, how can he be called poor? Surely everyone knows how rich he is. After all, what counts as wealth among us humans? Gold, I would say, and silver, and well-staffed house-holds and land; yet *everything was made through him* (Jn 1:3). How then could there be any riches greater than his, since he made all that is reckoned as wealth, even those things which are not true riches? Furthermore, through him riches of a different order were made too: intelligence, the powers of the mind,[2] our ideas of right and wrong, our bodily life and health, our senses and the coordination of our limbs. As long as these are in sound condition, even the poor are rich. Through the Word were made also greater riches still: faith and loyal fidelity,[3] justice, charity, chastity, and good character, for no one enjoys these either, except through him who justifies the ungodly.[4] Look how rich he is; for which of these two is richer: the one who has what he wants, though it is made by another, or the one who makes whatever he wants, for another to possess? In my opinion he who made what you have is the richer, for you do not have at your command the power he has. Clearly he is wealthy. How then are we to attribute to someone so rich these words: *The bread I ate was ashes, and my drink I would dilute with weeping*?[5] Has his vast wealth been reduced to this? So high was his fortune, so low his abasement. What are we to make of it? The two states are far apart.

---

1. Preached at Hippo, possibly in paschal time 395; others prefer a date between 403 and 408.
2. *Memoria*, but for Augustine this means something vaster than the faculty we call "memory," though it includes this. *Memoria* is the mind engaged in particular activities, the focus of personal identity, our link with past, present, and future. It is the storehouse of images that can be creatively combined in new ways, and the place of self-awareness. Book 10 of his *Confessions* deals at length with "the fields of *memoria*."
3. *Pietas.*
4. See Rom 4:5.
5. Verse 10 below.

45

I have not identified the poor man yet. Perhaps he is someone else; but let us go on searching. Our failure to see him as the poor man is surprising, if you conquer your terror of such riches, and put your question to the text. *In the beginning was the Word, and the Word was with God; he was God. He was with God in the beginning. Everything was made through him; no part of created being was made without him.* (Jn 1:1-3) The man who said that was rich: he must have been if he could say it; but how much richer was he of whom the evangelist was saying, *In the beginning was the Word*? He spoke not of any ordinary word, but of the Word who is God; and not in any ordinary place, but *with God*; and not idle there either, because *everything was made through him.* Could he possibly have eaten ashes for bread, or mingled weeping with his drink?

Nonetheless go on inquiring, for look what follows: *The Word was made flesh and dwelt among us* (Jn 1:14). Remember too another saying, *I am your servant and the son of your handmaid* (Ps 115(116):16). Call to mind that chaste handmaid who was both virgin and mother, for there, where he clothed himself in the form of a servant, he took on our poverty. He emptied himself[6] lest you be frightened away by his wealth and not dare to approach him with your beggarly needs. There, I tell you, there did he take the form of a servant, there he arrayed himself in the rags of our poverty, there he impoverished himself, and there he enriched us.

We are getting close to understanding how the words apply to him, but it is not time yet for confident assertions. The virginal childbearing is like the stone hewn from the mountain without hands,[7] for no human agency was at work there, nor any concupiscence involved. Faith alone burned bright, and the flesh of the Word was conceived. In due course he came forth from the womb; then the heavens proclaimed their message. Angels announced the news to the shepherds; a star drew the magi to worship the king; and Simeon, filled with the Spirit, recognized the infant God in the arms of his mother. Christ grew up not as to his divinity but in his fleshly state. Ignorant old men are shocked and amazed at the wisdom of a twelve-year-old boy. Or even if the old men are experts, what is their expertise compared with the Word of God? What is their learning in the presence of God's Wisdom? Are not those very experts bound to expire[8] without his help? He continues to make progress toward bodily maturity. He comes to the river seeking baptism, but the baptizer recognizes God and confesses himself unworthy to unbuckle Christ's sandal. Already the blind are being enlightened and the deaf recovering their hearing, the dumb are speaking and the lepers are cleansed. Limbs slack with paralysis are toned up, the weak are strengthened, and the dead arise.

---

6. See Phil 2:7.
7. See Dn 2:34.
8. Augustine has a pun here: *Nonne et periti . . . utique perituri?*

Bridegroom and bride in one voice

2. I can say with confidence that I already see a dearth of riches in him, in comparison with the wealth of the Word through whom all things were made; but even so, is he not far removed from ashes and the cup of weeping? I still hesitate to say, "It is Christ praying here"; yet that is what I want to say. Certain factors make me want to, but others make me fearful. It is he, yet it is not he. Already he bears the form of a servant, already he wears our frail, mortal flesh, already he has come for the purpose of dying; but we cannot yet see him in such penury that he could say, *The bread I ate was ashes, and my drink I would dilute with weeping.* He must add to poverty a yet deeper poverty and transfigure our lowly body into himself;[9] he must be our head and we his members; let us be two in one flesh. In order to become poor initially he left his Father and took on the form of a slave, but now, born from the virgin, let him leave his mother too, and cling to his wife, and let them be two in one flesh.[10] Thus they will be two in one voice as well,[11] and in that one voice we shall have no cause for surprise if we hear our own voice saying, *The bread I ate was ashes, and my drink I would dilute with weeping*; for he has deigned to have us as his members, and among these members there are penitents. They have not been shut out or separated from his Church; he took his bride to himself with no other invitation than *Repent, for the kingdom of heaven is near* (Mt 3:2).

Let us listen, then, to the prayer offered by the head and the body, the bridegroom and the bride. Christ and the Church together are one person, but the Word and flesh do not form one nature.[12] The Father and the Word together are one nature; but Christ and the Church together are one person, one perfect man growing toward his fullness *until we all meet in unity of faith, in knowledge of the Son of God, to form a perfect man, and attain to the mature stature of the fullness of Christ* (Eph 4:13). But until that meeting poverty is our lot here, and our business here is still hard work and groaning. Thanks be to his mercy.

How could hard work and groaning have come to be the lot of the Word, through whom all things were made? But if he has deigned to take on our death, will he not give us his life? He has lifted us up to a mighty hope, and in that mighty hope we are groaning. Groaning implies sadness, but there is a kind of groaning that also has room for joy. I think that the barren Sarah must have been

---

9. See Phil 3:21.
10. See Eph 5:31-32.
11. Augustine's central conviction with regard to the psalms, expressed repeatedly throughout the *Expositions.*
12. *Christus et ecclesia utrumque unus; sed Verbum et caro non utrumque unum.*

happy even in her groaning as she was giving birth;[13] and from our fear of you,
Lord, we, like Sarah, have conceived and brought forth the spirit of salvation.[14]
Let us then listen to the poor man, Christ, praying in us and with us and for our
sake. The title itself points to this poor person.

Give me credit for having discovered at last who this poor suppliant is. Let us
listen to his prayer and recognize the person who prays. I hope you will not be
disconcerted if you hear anywhere something unsuitable for the head. I have
prefaced my sermon with these remarks so that if you do hear anything of the
kind, you may discern in it the sound of the body's weakness and realize that the
head is speaking in the voice of his members. The title runs thus: *The entreaty of
a poor man when he was wrung with pain, and poured out his prayer in the presence of the Lord*. This same poor man says elsewhere, *From the ends of the earth
I have called to you, as my heart was wrung with pain* (Ps 60:3(61:2)). And
because this same poor man is Christ, he calls himself both bridegroom and
bride in a prophetic text: *He has adorned me like a bridegroom with his wreath,
and decked me like a bride with her jewels* (Is 61:10). He calls himself bridegroom and he calls himself bride. How can both be true, unless he means
bridegroom in his capacity as head and *bride* with respect to his body? One voice
only, then, because only one flesh. Let us listen; and, more than that, let us hear
ourselves in these words. If we perceive ourselves to be outside them, let us do
our best to be within.

Verses 2-3. The prayer of every generation, uttered by Christ

3. *Hear my prayer, O Lord, and let my cry reach you*. The first phrase, *Hear my
prayer, O Lord*, means the same thing as the second, *Let my cry reach you*;
the repetition expresses the urgency of the request. *Do not turn your face away
from me*. When did God ever turn his face away from his Son, the Father from
Christ? But because of the poverty of his members he begs, *Do not turn your face
away from me*.

On whatever day I am in trouble, incline your ear to me, for here below I am
in trouble, and you are above. Yet if I lift myself up, you become more distant,
whereas if I humble myself, you incline your ear to me. But why does he seem to
restrict it by saying, *On whatever day I am in trouble*? Is he not in trouble now?
Would he be speaking like this if he were not in trouble? Surely it would have
been enough to say, "Incline your ear to me, because I am in trouble"? No: he
prays, *On whatever day I am in trouble, incline your ear to me*, because he is
thinking of the unity of his body. If one member suffers, all the members suffer

---

13. See Gn 21:2-7.
14. See Is 26:18.

with it.[15] You are in trouble today; therefore I am in trouble. Someone else is in trouble tomorrow, so I am in trouble; after this generation others, its descendants, and their successors again, will be in trouble, and I am in trouble. Even to the end of the world, whoever in my body is troubled, I am troubled. *On whatever day I am in trouble, incline your ear to me.*

On whatever day I call upon you, hear me quickly. The same situation is evoked here. I am calling upon you now, but *on whatever day I call upon you, hear me quickly.* Peter prayed, Paul prayed, the other apostles prayed, the faithful prayed in those early days, the faithful prayed in the ages that followed, the faithful prayed in the time of the martyrs, the faithful pray in our own time, and the faithful will pray in the days of our descendants:[16] *On whatever day I call upon you, hear me quickly.* He begs, *Hear me quickly*, for I am asking for what you want to give. I do not ask, as an earthling would, for earthly things, for I am already redeemed from my former captivity,[17] and I long for the kingdom of heaven. *Hear me quickly*, for it was in response to such a longing that you promised, *While you are yet speaking, I shall say, Look, here I am* (Is 58:9). *On whatever day I call upon you, hear me quickly.* From where are you calling? Out of what trouble? What is your need? O you poor suppliant at the gate of your rich God, what are you longing for as you beg? In what penury do you seek his aid? What destitution prompts you to knock, in the hope that the door will be opened?[18] Tell us, let us hear about your need; for then we shall find ourselves in the same need, and join our plea with yours. Listen, and recognize yourself, if you can.

Verse 4. The bones in the body are roasted

4. *For my days have dwindled like smoke.* Ah, here we have a mention of *days,* and whenever we find that, we are reminded of light. But now the speaker laments, *My days have dwindled like smoke.* By *my days* he means "my life" or "my times"; but why the comparison with smoke? Surely because his days were puffed up with pride. Adam in his pride deserved days like that; but Christ derived his flesh from Adam. Christ was therefore in Adam, and Adam in Christ. He who deigned to make the voice of those smoky days his own has unquestionably freed us from smoke-filled days. *My days have dwindled like smoke.* Think how pride resembles smoke, which rises, blows into a swollen shape, vanishes and inevitably dwindles. It certainly has no permanence.

My days have dwindled like smoke, and my bones have been roasted as in a

---

15. See 1 Cor 12:26.
16. A vivid example of Augustine's understanding of the Church as a praying community united across the ages in the praying Christ.
17. He probably means "to demons," as in his Exposition of Psalm 95,5.
18. See Mt 7:7.

frying pan.[19] My very bones, my strength itself, are not free from trouble, not exempt from burning. The bones of Christ's body, the strength of Christ's body: where are these to be found? Most of all in the holy apostles. Yet look how these bones were scorched: *Is anyone tripped up, without my being afire with indignation?* (2 Cor 11:29). The apostles are strong and full of faith, men with a good understanding of the word and an ability to preach it; they live as they speak, and speak as they hear. They are indubitably strong, yet people who are tripped and stumbling are enough to scorch the apostles; for there is charity in the body, and especially in the bones. Within all its soft, fleshy parts, there are the bones, and bones carry all the flesh. But if any member is scandalized and imperiled in spirit, the bone is roasted with an intensity in proportion to its love. If love fades, no one suffers scorching. But let charity prevail, and then, if it is true that whenever one member suffers, another suffers in sympathy, how fiercely must the bones be heated—the bones that support the whole bodily frame? *My bones have been roasted as in a frying pan.*

Verse 5. Remembering the bread you had forgotten

5. *My heart is stricken and dried up like grass.* Think of Adam, from whom sprang the human race. Was not he, and he alone, the propagator of our misery? Whence comes the poverty we inherit, if not from him? Each of us can therefore say, *My heart is stricken and dried up like grass*; but though we once said it hopelessly, as from our own body, we now say it with hope, in the body of Christ. The comparison with grass is apposite, because all flesh is grass.[20]

But why did this disaster happen to you? *Because I forgot to eat my bread.* God had dispensed to us the bread of his commandment, for what else but God's word is bread for the soul? But the serpent dropped his hints and the woman transgressed; Adam touched what had been forbidden and forgot the command. Like grass he was beaten and his heart dried up: deservedly so, for he had forgotten to eat his bread. He forgot the bread and drank poison, so his heart was stricken, and withered like grass. Adam is the stricken man evoked in Isaiah: *I will not be angry with you for ever. From me, who gave life to all, a breath of life will go forth. For a little while I afflicted him on account of his sin, and struck him, and turned my face away from him.* The speaker in our psalm has good reason to pray, *Do not turn your face away from me,* for he is the one of whom God says through Isaiah, *I struck him.* But God goes on to say, *I saw where his own ways led him, and I healed him.* (Is 57:16-18, LXX) *My heart is stricken and dried up like grass, because I forgot to eat my bread.* Eat it now, the bread you had forgotten.

---

19. Or perhaps "an oven."
20. See Is 40:6.

But the true bread has come, he in whose body you can recall your forgetful condition, and cry to him now from your poverty, that you may receive his riches. Eat now, for you are within the body of him who said, *I am the living bread which has come down from heaven* (Jn 6:41). You had forgotten to eat your bread, but now that he has been crucified all the ends of the earth will be reminded and will turn to the Lord.[21] Let remembrance succeed forgetfulness, let the bread from heaven be our food that we may live, not the manna which the ancients ate, only to die.[22] Let us eat the bread of which the gospel says, *Blessed are those who hunger and thirst for righteousness* (Mt 5:6).

Verse 6. Grieving over sinners is a sign of the body's unity

6. *Through the voicing of my lament my bones have stuck to my flesh.* This is the voice I understand, the voice I know, the voice of my own lament. I am not speaking of the grief experienced by certain people for whom I feel very sorry. Plenty of people there are who do grieve, and I grieve too, but I lament because they lament for the wrong reasons. Someone who has lost a coin laments, but he or she raises no lament over the loss of faith. I weigh the coin against faith, and my grief is keener over a person who grieves for the wrong reasons or does not grieve at all. Such a one commits fraud and thinks it a laughing matter. What has he gained? And what has he lost? He has acquired some money and lost integrity. Anyone who understands what we ought to grieve about laments this loss; anyone who is close to the head and genuinely united with the body of Christ mourns over it. Carnally-minded persons do not; in fact they make themselves lamentable by their failure to lament. All the same, we cannot repudiate those who do not lament or who lament for unworthy reasons, because we want to correct them, to help them to amend,[23] and to bring them to a better state of mind. When we are unable to, we grieve, and by our grief we prove that we are not severed from them, for *through the voicing of my lament my bones have stuck to my flesh*: the strong to the weak, the firm to the infirm. What is the glue that binds them together? The lamentation of the strong, not that of the weak. What law yields such glue? Surely that which reminds us, *We who have firm footing must support the weaknesses of the infirm* (Rom 15:1). Yes, indeed *my bones have stuck to my flesh.*

---

21. See Ps 21:28(22:27).
22. See Jn 6:49.
23. Variant: "to separate from them."

Verses 7-8. Pelican, owl, and sparrow are symbols of preachers, but more particularly of Christ

7. *I have become like the pelican that lives in solitary places, like the owl*[24] *in ruined walls. I kept watch, and was like a sparrow alone on a roof.* Here we have three birds, and three habitats. May the Lord grant us to explain their significance and enable you to hear profitably what is said to further your salvation. What do these three birds with their different habitats represent? What are they? The three species are the pelican, the owl, and the sparrow; the three habitats are solitary places, ruined walls, and rooftops. The pelican is to be found in solitary places, the owl in ruined walls, and the sparrow on rooftops.

We must first discuss the pelican. Since it is an exotic bird, it is unfamiliar to us. Its birthplace is in lonely regions, especially those along the River Nile in Egypt. We should try to infer from this what kind of bird the pelican is and what the psalm wished us to understand about it. The pelican *lives in solitary places*, we are told. Why, then, inquire about its appearance, its distinctive features, its call, or its habits? All the information the psalm has given you is that it is a bird which lives in solitary places. The owl is a bird which loves the night. The ruined walls—or "ruins" as we ordinarily call them—are walls that stand roofless and uninhabited; in such places the owl lives. What the sparrow is, and the roof where it perches, you know.

Now in these birds I find a representation of someone in the body of Christ who preaches his word, is compassionate toward the weak, and seeks to increase Christ's revenue, mindful that his Lord will come and say, *You wicked, lazy servant, you should have handed my money over to the bankers* (Mt 25:26.27); for I can see in the birds a figure of three duties performed by a steward of the Lord. He must visit non-Christian peoples, and then he is like a pelican in solitary places. He must make his way among peoples who once were Christian, but have fallen away; and then he is an owl amid ruined walls, for he does not abandon these night-dwellers in their darkness but hopes to win them too. And he must be present also to people who are Christians and therefore dwell in the house; these are the ones who are not unbelievers, certainly, nor persons who have lost their faith, but they put their faith into practice only in lukewarm fashion. The sparrow cries to them, not in solitary places, for they are Christians, nor in ruined walls, because they have not tumbled down, but as to persons on a roof, or rather under a roof, because they are dominated by the flesh. The sparrow cries to them from a perch above the flesh, not hushing up God's commandments; and the sparrow does not become carnal itself by accepting a roof over its head. As the gospel warns, *One who is on the roof must not go down*

------

24. Or "night raven."

to fetch anything from the house; and again, *What you hear privately in your ear, proclaim from the rooftops.* (Mt 24:17; 10:27)

We have three birds, then, and three habitats. A single person may combine the characteristics of all three birds; alternatively, the characteristics of the birds may be distributed among three persons. But where the three habitats are in question, we must understand three different types of people; I think that solitary places, ruined walls, and the roof must represent three kinds of people. There is no other way to take it.

8. Can we say anything further about the birds? Let us look to the Lord and see whether he is himself the pelican in solitary places, and the owl in ruined walls, and the lonely sparrow on the roof, and whether he can be better known in this way. He, our head, is the poor man of the psalm; so let him tell us about it. Let him who is poor by choice speak to us who are poor by necessity. We must not ignore what some writers have said about the pelican: not that we wish to make rash assertions, but we cannot pass over in silence what certain authors have wished us to read and discuss. You must listen with discernment, so that if the report is true, you may find that it fits in with the known truth, but if false, it may not persist.

Pelicans are alleged to kill their chicks by pecking them, then for three days to mourn the dead chicks in the nest. Finally the mother is said to wound herself gravely and pour her blood over her babies, which come back to life as her blood flows over them.[25] This report may be true or false; but if it is true, observe how apt a symbol it is of him who gave us life by his own blood. It fits him very well, even though it is the mother bird who with her blood gives life to her squabs, for Christ called himself a mother hen, caring for her young: *Jerusalem, Jerusalem, how often I wanted to gather your children to myself, as a hen gathers her chicks under her wings, but you would have none of it!* (Mt 23:37) He has both a father's authority and a mother's tenderness, just as Paul too is both father and mother, not through any powers of his own, but through the gospel. He shows himself a father when he says, *However many teachers you may have in Christ, you have not many fathers, for in Christ Jesus through the gospel I have begotten you* (1 Cor 4:15), but a mother when he tells his converts, *My little children, I am in travail with you over again, until Christ be formed in you* (Gal 4:19). If the story about the pelican is true, then, this bird is a very apt image of the flesh of Christ—Christ, by whose blood we have been given life. But does her killing of her chicks fit into that picture? Yes, it does fit, for he declares, *I will kill, and I*

---

25. As a striking image of the Redeemer's love, particularly as embodied in the Eucharist, this ancient belief about the pelican influenced Christian iconography, especially in the medieval period. It is referred to in the eucharistic hymn *Adoro te devote*, attributed to Saint Thomas Aquinas: *Pie pellicane, Iesu Domine*. Dante and Shakespeare were also familiar with pelican symbolism; compare *Hamlet*, Act IV, Sc. v: "To his good friends thus wide I'll ope my arms; / And like the kind life-rendering pelican, / Repast them with my blood."

will give life; I will strike, and I will heal (Dt 32:39).Would the persecutor Saul have died, if he had not been struck from heaven? And would he have been raised to new life as a preacher, if he had not been given life by Christ's blood?

However, it is for those who have written about pelicans to settle the question; we must not base our interpretation on a doubtful report. There is another way in which we can more safely recognize in Christ the solitariness indicated by the psalm when it speaks of the *pelican in solitary places*. I think we can take it as a reference to Christ's birth from a virgin. This was true of him alone; it sets him apart from all others, and so he is in this respect solitary. He was born in solitude in the sense that he alone was born in this way.

After his birth came the time for his passion. By whom was he crucified? By upstanding people?[26] No. By people who mourned him? No.[27] He was crucified, we could say, by the Jews' benighted ignorance and in the tottering walls of their ruin. Contemplate him, the owl who was there even amid the ruins, still loving even the night. If he had not loved the night, how could he have prayed, *Father, forgive them, for they do not know what they are doing* (Lk 23:34)?

We have seen him born in solitude, because the manner of his birth sets him apart. We have watched him suffer in the darkness that enveloped the Jews, as though in the night, and through the treachery which was their ruin. What does the psalm say next? *I kept watch.* You slept amid the tumbledown walls, and in another psalm you said, *I rested.* Why did you put it that way—*I rested*? What does it mean? I fell asleep because I willed it, I fell asleep because I loved the night; but the same psalm immediately adds, *And I arose* (Ps 3:6(5)). Our present psalm also suggests the resurrection by saying, *I kept watch.* And after his dawn vigil, what did he do? He ascended into heaven, taking flight *like a sparrow alone on a roof*, which is a figure of heaven.

Christ is represented by the pelican in his birth, by the owl in his dying, and by the sparrow in his resurrection. At his birth he is solitary, because he alone was born so; in his suffering he is surrounded by ruined walls, slain by those who could not stand stable in his building. On awakening from death he flies alone to

---

26. *Numquid ab stantibus?* The contrast is with the Jews' "ruined" condition: Augustine is remembering the tumbledown walls.

27. *Numquid a lugentibus?* If this is really what Augustine said, the reference is presumably to Christ's mother, and other faithful disciples, who mourned him. But the relevance of this to the context is not very obvious, and the words seem to have puzzled copyists, generating the variants *a ludentibus* ("by those who mocked"), and *ab intellegentibus* ("by those who understood"). Neither is satisfactory. Translator's conjecture: could Augustine have said, *Numquid a lucentibus*, and a scribe misheard? The two words *lucentibus* and *lugentibus* would have sounded very similar. If *lucentibus* is the correct reading, the parallelism becomes clear. As in the preceding sentence Augustine contrasts the "upright" or "upstanding" believers with the "ruin" of the Jews, so in this sentence he asks, "Was Christ crucified by the bright, shining ones? No, but by the night-dwellers," by those in the darkness of ignorance, as he goes on to say. But the owl, the symbol of Christ, loves those ruined places and loves the night.

the roof—that is, to heaven—where he intercedes for us;[28] for our head is the sparrow, and his body the turtle-dove, as another psalm has it: *The sparrow has found himself a home.* What home is this? He is at home in heaven, there to make intercession for us. But that other psalm continues, *And the turtle-dove a nest,* for the Church of God has found a nest, made out of twigs from the wood of his cross, *where she may place her squabs* (Ps 83:4(84:3)), her little ones. *I kept watch, and became like a sparrow alone on a roof.*

Verses 9-10. Christ's readiness to forgive sinners; some objections to his policy, and refutation of them

9. *All day long my enemies insulted me, and those who pretended to praise me were cursing me.* They praised me with their lips, but in their hearts they were preparing traps. Here is an example of their praise: *Master, we know that you teach the way of God in sincerity, and are partial to no one. Is it lawful to pay tribute to Caesar?* (Lk 20:21-22) You are trying to trip up the one you pretend to praise. Why? Because the psalm foretold that *those who seemed to praise me* would be cursing me. But what was the source of their animosity toward me? Simply my mission to transform sinners into my own members, so that by repentance they may find their place in my body. This is what evokes their insults, and brings down their persecution upon me. *Why does your teacher eat with sinners and tax collectors?* Because *it is not the healthy who need the physician, but the sick.* (Mt 9:11-12) If only you could recognize your own sickness and be driven to seek your physician! Then you would not kill him, nor would you die of your pretended health, in your demented pride.

10. On what pretext did *my enemies insult me all day long?* Why did *those who pretended to praise me* utter their curses against me? Because *the bread I ate was ashes, and my drink I would dilute with weeping.* He wanted to have tax collectors and sinners among his members so that he could heal them and set them free, and this was made a ground of reproach against him. It is the same even today. What charges do the pagans bring when they want to insult us? What do you think, brothers and sisters? What do they object to? "You are undermining public decorum and corrupting human moral standards." What are you alleging? How have we done that? "By giving people the chance of repentance and promising the forgiveness of all offenses," says our accuser. "People make it an excuse to commit evil deeds, secure in the knowledge that once they have been converted, everything is forgiven."[29] This, then, is what provokes them to

---

28. See Rom 8:34.

29. Though Augustine attributes the objection to a pagan, it resembles the invective of Tertullian in *De pudicitia* (c. 217-222) against Pope Callistus, who had asserted the Church's right to forgive repentant adulterers.

insult us: that *the bread I ate was ashes, and my drink I would dilute with weeping.*

I invite you to eat this same bread, you who reproach us, for you dare not claim that you are not a sinner. Examine your conscience, take your seat in the tribunal of your own mind, do not spare yourself, interrogate yourself and allow your heart of hearts to speak to you; and then see whether you dare protest your innocence. I am quite sure that if the objector takes a good look at himself, he will find it very disturbing; if he does not flatter himself, he will confess. So what are you to do, you wretch, if there is no harbor where you can escape punishment? If we have been given only license to sin, and no forgiveness for our sins, what will become of you? Where will you go? It was certainly on your behalf that the poor man in the psalm ate ashes for bread, and mingled his drink with tears. You don't find that sort of feast attractive?

"What you say may be true," he retorts, "but it is also true that the expectation of pardon leads people to multiply their sins." On the contrary, they would multiply their sins if they had no hope of pardon. You must have noticed how licentious and brutal is the lifestyle of gladiators. Knowing themselves to be destined for the sword and ritual slaughter, they try to sate their passions before shedding their blood; how else can you account for it? Would you not do the same, would you not say to yourself, "I am a sinner already. Already I am on the wrong side of the law and under condemnation. There is no hope of forgiveness for me. Why shouldn't I indulge all my desires, as far as possible? After all, there is nothing beyond to look forward to, except torment." Would you not take this line, and deteriorate even further in your very despair? But if God promises to forgive you; if he says, *Return to your hearts, you transgressors. I do not will the death of a sinner, but that he come back, and live* (Is 46:8; Ezk 33:11), it is more likely to lead to your correction. If that harbor is pointed out to you, you will undoubtedly haul down the sail of sin, put your helm about, and set sail for righteousness. Hoping for life, you will not neglect your medicine.

But you must not find fault with God on this score either, that by promising pardon he has made sinners complacent. He has promised sinners the port of pardon lest they become worse through despair; but to make sure that they are not made worse by the hope of forgiveness he has kept the day of death uncertain. In his most wise providence he has made this dual arrangement, so that those who return to him may be sure of finding a welcome, and those who loiter may have reason to be very much afraid.

Eat ashes as your bread, then, and drop tears into your drink, for through a feast like this you will make your way to God's table. Do not despair: forgiveness has been promised to you. "Thank God for that," he replies. "Thank God it's promised. I will hold fast to that." Yes, but you must change your life for the better. "Well, I will tomorrow." Be careful. God has promised you forgiveness, but no one has promised you that you will see any tomorrow. If you have lived a bad life until now, begin to lead a better one today. *You fool: your life will be taken from you this very night*, and I do not ask you, *Who will own what you have prepared?* (Lk 12:20) but "Where will your place be, in view of the way you have lived?" Correct yourself, so that, within Christ's body, you may make these words your own: *the bread I ate was ashes, and my drink I would dilute with weeping.* Unless I am mistaken, you are ready to see the point of them.

Verse 11. The dignity and degradation of humankind

11. *As I was confronted by your anger and indignation.*[30] *You have struck me down because you lifted me up.* This means your anger against Adam, Lord. In that anger we were all born, and simply by being born we implicated ourselves in it. Your anger remains upon our iniquitous stock, upon the mass of sin[31] that is our race. The apostle confesses, *By nature we too were children of wrath, like the rest* (Eph 2:3), and the Lord warns, *The anger of God remains upon the one who has not believed in the only-begotten Son of God* (Jn 3:36). He does not say, "The anger of God will come upon" such an unbeliever; it is there already, and it *remains upon* him, because the anger into which he was born has not been lifted.

In this perspective, how are we to understand the psalm's lament, *You have struck me down because you lifted me up*? It does not say, "You lifted me up and then struck me down," but *You have struck me down because you lifted me up.* My elevation was itself the reason for my degradation. How can that be?

Human beings were created in honor, made in the image of God. Raised to such dignity, uplifted from the dust, ennobled from the earth, they received a rational soul. By reason of their vigorous rationality they were given pre-eminence over all wild beasts, cattle, birds, and fishes. Which of these is endowed with rational intelligence? None; because none of them was made in the image of God. But just as none of them enjoys that honor, so none of them is reduced to misery as humans are. Did you ever see a beast bewailing its sins? Or a bird afraid of hell fire? Because they have no share in the life of beatitude, they

---

30. This phrase connects with the preceding verse.

31. These phrases encapsulate Augustine's doctrine of original sin. Based upon Saint Paul's analogy between the work of Adam and that of Christ, and our solidarity with the one and the other, the Church's belief developed through the teaching of the Greek Fathers without arriving at any unequivocal assertion of human solidarity in the guilt of Adam, as opposed to its consequences. By the Latin Fathers Tertullian, Cyprian, and Ambrose, the assertion of our solidarity in the sin itself was made, and the mode of its transmission was held to be natural generation. Augustine inherited this theological view. He believed that concupiscence was the vehicle by which Adam's guilt was transmitted, and that humanity thereby becomes a *massa damnata* which stands in absolute need of Christ's redeeming work; see for example his *Miscellany of Questions in Response to Simplicianus*, and his Exposition of Psalm 50,10. On the controversial interpretation of Rom 5:12, see the note at Exposition of Psalm 50,10.

have no miseries to pierce them. Human beings were made in such a way that they will enjoy that blessed life if they live rightly but will be condemned to misery if their lives are evil. Thus it can be said, *You have struck me down because you lifted me up*: my punishment is the consequence of your gift of free will to me. If you had not endowed me with free will and not made me superior to the animals by my reason, I could not have been justly condemned as a sinner. By the gift of free will you raised me up, and in your just judgment you struck me down.

Verses 12-13. The transience of man, the eternity of God

12. *My days have slipped away like a shadow.* Your days need not have slipped away, if you had not slipped away yourself from daylight; but you did slip away, and you were punished with days that slipped away from you. Is there anything remarkable in this—that your days have come to resemble yourself? The slippery days that result from your deviation are the same thing as the smoky days that punish your swelling pride; earlier the psalm complained, *My days have dwindled like smoke*, and now it says, *My days have slipped away like a shadow*. But even in this shadow we must salute the day, even in the shadow we must open our eyes to daylight, lest in tardy and sterile remorse we may later be forced to ask, *What good has our pride done us? What benefit has come to us from our vaunted wealth? All these things have passed away like a shadow.* (Wis 5:8-9) You must tell yourself now, "All these will pass away like a shadow," and so avoid passing away like a shadow yourself.

My days have slipped away like a shadow, and I have withered like grass. The speaker reinforces what he said above: *My heart has been stricken and dried up like grass*; but the grass could grow green again if irrigated by the Savior's blood. *I have withered like grass*, I, a mortal, after that primal transgression. This is what I am, by your just judgment; but what are you?

13. *But you, O Lord, abide for ever.* My days have slipped away, shadow-like, but you abide for eternity. May the Eternal save his time-bound creature. My falling away does not mean that you have aged, for you who were in full vigor when you humbled me are in full vigor still to set me free. *But you, O Lord, abide for ever, and your memory[32] lasts to generation and generation.* It

---

32. *Memoriale tuum*. The word can mean "memory" or, more frequently, "that which reminds us" or "makes us remember," and so a memorial, or an abiding reputation, or some custom or institution that preserves the memory of a person or an event. In Ex 3:15 the same word is used for the revealed divine name, which will be a perpetual reminder to Israel of God's salvation. Under the New Covenant the Eucharist is the "memorial" of Christ's death and resurrection, celebrated "in memory of me." It is likely that in the present context of the psalm the meaning was that Israel would always remember the Lord, but Augustine probably takes it here as the Lord's remembering. In section 19 below he treats the word differently.

says, *Your memory*, because you, Lord, do not forget; and it adds, *To generation and generation*, because it means not this present one only, but that which is to come; for we have your promise for both the present life and the future.

Verses 14-15. The construction of the new Zion: both stones and dust from the old Zion will be built in

14. *You will arise and take pity on Zion, for the time has come for you to deal mercifully with her.* What special time is meant? *When the fullness of time had come, God sent his Son, made from a woman and made subject to the law.* And where is Zion mentioned? *That he might redeem those who were subject to the law* (Gal 4:5). The Jews were to be the first-fruits: from their race came the apostles, from them the group of more than five hundred brethren who saw the risen Lord,[33] and finally the multitude of believers in whom there was but one soul and one heart intent on God.[34] This is why the psalm predicts, *You will arise and take pity on Zion, for the time has come for you to deal mercifully with her; the time has come.* What time does it mean? The apostle tells us, *See, now is the acceptable time, lo, this is the day of salvation* (2 Cor 6:2). And who said this? God's servant and builder, who used to tell his converts, *You are God's building*, the man who claimed, *I laid the foundation like a skilled master-builder*, and warned them, *No one can lay any other foundation than that which is laid, which is Christ Jesus.* (1 Cor 3:9-11)

15. What else does the psalm say about it? *For your servants cherish her stones.* What stones? The stones of Zion. But others are to be found there who are not stones. Not Zion's stones? But let us see what follows. *And they will take pity on her dust.* Clearly, then, we must recognize stones in Zion, but dust in Zion too. It does not say, "They will take pity on her stones." What does it say? *Your servants cherish her stones, and will take pity on her dust.* They find the stones admirable, but they will pity the dust. I take the stones in Zion to be the prophets, for through them the voice of preaching first rang out. The preaching of the gospel continued their work, and through this proclamation Christ became known. Your servants, Lord, had therefore good reason to cherish those stones in Zion.

In contrast, there were the unfaithful ones who abandoned the Lord, and offended their creator by their wicked deeds. These people went back to the earth from which they were taken. They turned into dust, because they became ungodly; and of such people another psalm said, *The ungodly are like the dust which the wind sweeps away from the face of the earth* (Ps 1:4). But wait, Lord; hold your hand, Lord; be patient, Lord. Do not let the wind whistle in and sweep

---

33. See 1 Cor 15:6.
34. See Acts 4:32.

this dust from the face of the earth. Please, please, let your servants come, and acknowledge your words in the stones, but also deal mercifully with Zion's dust. May human beings be formed according to your image,[35] and let the dust pray, *Remember that we are dust* (Ps 102(103):14), that it may not perish. *They will take pity on her dust*—Zion's dust, that is. Was this not the dust that crucified Christ? It was, moreover, dust from ruined walls, which made matters worse. But in spite of all, a prayer was offered for the dust: *Father, forgive them, for they do not know what they are doing* (Lk 23:34); and it did not go unheard, for out of this dust was built a wall consisting of many thousands of believers, who laid the price of their goods at the feet of the apostles.[36] Thus there arose from this dust a new humanity, freshly formed and beautiful. Did any of the Gentiles match their generosity? We may well be amazed that so few did, in comparison with many thousands of Jews. Immediately, at the very beginning, there were three thousand; and soon afterward five thousand;[37] and all these lived in unity. They all laid the price of the property they had sold at the feet of the apostles so that provision might be made for everyone according to need, for all of them had but one soul and one heart set on God.[38] Who created all this out of dust? Who else but he who created Adam out of dust? This is what he wrought from Zion. But not only in Zion.

Verses 16-18. The construction of the new Zion: the Gentiles too are being built in

16. Let us look at the next verse. *The Gentiles too will revere your name, O Lord, and all the kings of the earth your glory*. Because you have now taken pity on Zion; because your servants have known the worth of her stones, recognizing that the apostles and prophets are the foundations; because they have taken pity on her dust, so that living men and women may be formed—or, rather, reformed—from dust, the preaching of Christ has spread among the Gentiles. Let all nations fear your name, and all earth's kings your glory; let another wall be built from the direction of the Gentiles and the cornerstone be known by all. In

---

35. There are interweaving strands of biblical imagery in this section. The "servants" are evidently Christian preachers, who acknowledge that God truly spoke through Zion's stones, that is, through the prophets of Israel, and that the apostles built on the prophets' work. The rest of Israel, who sinned and refused to believe, have gone back to dust (see Gn 3:19), and this links in Augustine's mind with the crumbling walls of section 8 above. But it was from dust that God originally formed man in his own image (see Gn 2:7), so there is hope for this dust too, since the prayer of Christ can effect re-creation. The re-created dust can then form a wall for the new Zion, the Church of Christ.

36. See Acts 4:34-35.

37. See Acts 2:41; 4:4.

38. See Acts 4:32.35.

him let the two walls be tied together: two walls that come from different quarters but no longer differ in belief.

17. *For the Lord will build up[39] Zion.* The work is going on now. Come on, then, you living stones,[40] run to take your places in an edifice that is sound and no ruin. Zion is under construction: keep clear of ruined walls. A tower is being built and an ark: watch out for the flood. The work is in progress, *for the Lord will build up Zion.* And when Zion is complete, what then? *He will be seen in his glory.*[41] To begin Zion's building, to lay the foundation in Zion, he was seen by Zion, but not in his glory, for *we saw him, and he had no beauty to attract us* (Is 53:2). It will be different when he comes to judge, escorted by his angels, when all nations will be assembled before him and the sheep on his right are separated from the kids[42] on his left.[43] Will they not see him then, him whom they pierced?[44] Then they will be ashamed, but too late, because they refused to be shamed by a timely and salutary repentance. *The Lord will build up Zion, and he will be seen in his glory,* he who once in Zion was seen in his weakness.

18. *He has had regard for the prayer of the humble,[45] and has not despised their entreaty.* This is what is happening now, while Zion is being built, for the builders of Zion are praying and groaning. One single poor person is praying, because the many poor people, the thousands among many nations, are all one person, forming the peaceful unity of the Church. This person is both one and many: one in charity but many because so widely diffused. Now, therefore, prayer is being offered, and people are running to the building. Now is the time for anyone whose character and conduct were unsuited to Zion to eat ashes for bread and drink a cup of weeping. Now is the time, while Zion is being built, now is the time when stones are being incorporated into the structure. Once the edifice is complete and the house dedicated, what will be the point of running to it? You will be seeking too late, asking fruitlessly, knocking to no purpose; you will be left outside with the five foolish maidens, won't you?[46] Run now, for the Lord *has had regard for the prayer of the humble, and has not despised their entreaty.*

Verses 19-20. In the two covenants the new creation is promised and realized

19. *Let these things be written for another generation.* At the time of writing they were not profitable to the people among whom they were written, for their purpose was to foretell the New Covenant among people who were living under

---

39. Variant: "has built up."
40. See 1 Pt 2:5.
41. Variant: "in his majesty."
42. *Haedi.*
43. See Mt 25:31-33.
44. See Zech 12:10.
45. Variant: "the poor."
46. See Mt 7:7; 25:10-12.

the Old. Yet God had given the Old Covenant too, and had settled his people in the promised land. The verse that promises, *Your memorial lasts to generation and generation*, holds good for the just, though not for the impious. For one generation it is realized in the Old Covenant, for another generation in the New.[47] The psalm indeed prophesied that it would be so, announcing the New Covenant in advance: *Let these things be written for another generation, and the people that will be created shall praise the Lord.* Not the people created already, but *the people that will be created.* What could be plainer, my brothers and sisters? What is foretold here is the new creation of which the apostle speaks: *If anyone is in Christ, there is a new creation. The old things have passed away, and lo, everything is made new! All these things are from God.* (2 Cor 5:17-18) What is meant by *all these things are from God*? Both the old and the new, for your memorial endures through one generation to another generation.

And the people that will be created shall praise the Lord, for he has looked out from his high and holy place. He looked out from his height to come to the humble; from his high dignity he became humble, in order to raise the humble to glory.

---

47. Augustine has recalled verse 13, but the crucial word *memoriale* seems now to mean the living testimony of himself which God expresses in the covenants.

Exposition 2 of Psalm 101

Second Sermon

Recapitulation of yesterday's sermon

1. Yesterday we heard a certain poor man groaning in his prayer, and we recognized him as the one who, though he was rich, became poor for us.[1] We also recognized his members, people who cling to him and speak through him who is their head. We even heard ourselves there, assuming that by his grace we too have in some degree managed to do the same. The groaning passages had come to an end yesterday, and passages about consolation succeeded them; but it was quite impossible yesterday to finish dealing with these. However, let us listen to the remaining verses today and hear in them the poor person groaning no longer but rejoicing: rejoicing because he hopes, and hoping because he places no reliance on himself. In the divine scriptures happiness was foretold for the human race, and then we read, *Let these things be written for another generation, and the people that will be created shall praise the Lord, for he has looked out from his high and holy place.* This is as far as our sermon went yesterday. See now what follows.

Verses 20-23. The Church absolves sinners and keeps its eyes on the distant prospect

2. *The Lord looked out from heaven to the earth to hear the groans of those in fetters, and free the children of the slain.* In another psalm we find the prayer, *May the groans of fettered captives come into your presence* (Ps 78(79):11), and this plea was made in a passage where we know the martyrs were speaking. But were the martyrs fettered? We know that the holy martyrs were first led before their judges and then put in chains and paraded around the provinces; but we do not hear of their being fettered.

But another use of the word "fetters" is its metaphorical application to God's discipline and our fear of him; this meaning is well known, for scripture says, *The fear of the Lord is the beginning of wisdom* (Ps 110(111):10; Sir 1:16). Inspired by such fear, God's servants did not cringe before those who kill the body but have no power to kill the soul, for they stood in awe of him who has

---

1. See 2 Cor 8:9. Some codices complete the quotation: *ut illius paupertate nos ditaremur.*

63

power to destroy both body and soul by casting them into hellfire.[2] If the martyrs had not been held fast by the fetters of this reverential fear, how could they ever have endured the harsh torments inflicted by their persecutors, when all the while they were free to cave in under pressure and so escape such suffering? God had fastened on them fetters which were certainly painful and irksome for a time, but worth bearing for the sake of what he had promised. They said to him, *Because of the words of your lips I have kept to difficult ways* (Ps 16(17):4). No one can help groaning in these fetters to implore the mercy of God, which is why the martyrs prayed in that other psalm, *May the groans of fettered captives come into your presence.* But we must not avoid such fetters in order to gain a liberty that could only harm us or the sweetness of a brief, temporal life which will be succeeded by perpetual bitterness.

To guard us against any refusal to be bound by the fetters of wisdom, scripture warns us, *Listen, my son; take my advice, and do not throw away my counsel. Thrust your feet into wisdom's fetters, and your neck into her collar. Shoulder her and carry her, and do not chafe at her bonds. Come to her with all your soul, and with your whole strength keep to her ways. Trace out her path, seek her, and she will become known to you; once you have grasped her, do not let go. In the end you will find rest in her, and she will become your joy. Then will her fetters be for you a powerful defense, and her collar a robe of glory, for in her is found a gold adornment, and her bonds are cords of purple-blue. You will clothe yourself in her as in gorgeous raiment, and place her on your head as a crown of rejoicing.* (Sir 6:24-32) Let all who wear such fetters cry out as long as they are held fast by God's discipline, in which the martyrs too were trained. Their fetters will be loosened, permitting them to fly away, and these same fetters will later be changed into an adornment. This is what happened to the martyrs; for what did the persecutors achieve by killing them except ensure that their fetters were loosed and transformed into crowns?

3. Well then, *the Lord looked down from heaven to the earth to hear the groans of those in fetters, and free the children of the slain.* The slain are obviously the martyrs, but who are meant by the children of the slain? Ourselves, surely. But in what sense are we set free? We testify that we are by saying to him, *You have burst my bonds; to you will I offer a sacrifice of praise* (Ps 115(116):16-17). Each one is freed from the bonds of evil desires or from the knotty entanglements of his own sins. The forgiveness of our sins is a liberation. What good would it have been to Lazarus to escape from his tomb if the command had not also been given, *Untie him, and let him go* (Jn 11:44)? It was the Lord's voice that awakened him in the sepulcher, and the Lord who overthrew the earthy weight that had been laid upon the dead man at his burial.

---

2. See Mt 10:28.

Lazarus emerged still bound and therefore not carried by any strength in his own feet, but only because the Lord's power brought him out. The same thing happens in the heart of a penitent. When you hear someone repenting of his or her sins, that person has already begun to live again; when you hear someone laying bare his or her conscience in confession, that person has already been led out from the tomb but has not yet been freed. When is a sinner loosed? And by whom? *Whatever you loose on earth shall be loosed in heaven* (Mt 18:18), says the Lord.[3] Absolution from sins can indeed be granted through the Church, but the dead person can be raised only by the Lord who calls within him, for this inward action is the Lord's prerogative. We speak to your ears, but how do we know what goes on in your hearts? The inner work is done not by us but by the Lord.

4. He looks forth *to free the children of the slain.* You have heard who these slain are and who are their children. What follows? *That the name of the Lord may be proclaimed in Zion.* In the early days, when fettered prisoners were being put to death, the Church was oppressed; but now that the time of persecution is over, the name of the Lord is proclaimed in Zion with all freedom—that is, in the Church, for the Church is Zion. We need not think of the original site, at first a proud city and later captured; that Zion was no more than a shadow of the true Zion, whose name means "Lookout Post." From there we look toward what lies ahead, still in the flesh though we are; we stretch our gaze not to the present scene but toward the future. That is why the Church has this name, "Lookout Post." Every watchman keeps his eyes on the distant prospect. Guards are stationed in watchtowers, and these observation posts are located on cliffs, or mountains, or in high trees, so that from their elevated position the watchers can see further. Zion is therefore a lookout post; the Church is a watchtower. Why? Because keeping watch demands the long view. Accordingly the psalmist admitted, *The problem is too hard for me until I enter God's holy place, and understand what the final outcome must be* (Ps 72(73):16-17). What kind of long-range observation is needed to understand the final outcome? We need to cross the sea not by ship but by farsightedness; we need to dwell at the sea's furthest coasts,[4] to fix our hope, I mean, on what will be when the world comes to an end. It follows, then, that if the Church is a lookout post, the name of the Lord is already being proclaimed in Zion. But in this Zion it is not only the Lord's name that is proclaimed but also *his praise in Jerusalem.*

5. How are his name and his praise proclaimed? *By the gathering of the peoples together into one, and kingdoms to serve the Lord.* How else could that

---

3. Augustine quotes the promise in the plural form addressed to all the apostles or the Church, as in the 18th chapter of Matthew, rather than the promise in the singular to Peter given in Matthew 16:19.
4. See Ps 138(139):9.

have happened if not through the blood of those who had been put to death? How could it have come about except through the groans of the fettered? The prayers of those who suffered distress and humiliation were heard so that in our day the Church might enjoy the great glory that we see, and temporal powers that used to persecute might serve the Lord.

Verse 24. The new Jerusalem responds to the Lord in his strength

6. *It responded to him in the way of his strength.*[5] To whom was the response given? To the Lord, evidently. Who responded? Let us look at the preceding lines: *his praise in Jerusalem, by the gathering of the peoples together into one, and kingdoms to serve the Lord.* Now the psalm continues, *It responded to him in the way of his strength.* What was the response, and who or what responded to him in the way of his strength?

We had better begin by finding out who or what responded, and then we shall investigate the way of his strength. The preceding words suggest that it was either *his praise* or *Jerusalem* that responded, for the psalm spoke of *his praise in Jerusalem, by the gathering of the peoples together into one, and kingdoms to serve the Lord.* Kingdoms cannot be the subject of responded, and neither can peoples, because the verb is singular. We need a singular subject for responded, and we do not find one in the foregoing verse except *his praise* and *Jerusalem.* The question is therefore open: which of these two is the subject—*his praise* or "Jerusalem"? We must consider them in turn.

When does his praise constitute a response to him? When those who have been called by him render him thanks. He calls and we respond not with our voices but with our faith, not with our tongues but by our life. If God calls you and commands you to lead a good life, and instead you lead a bad one, you are not responding to his call, nor does any praise coming from you make a response to him, because your lifestyle brings him no praise; rather is he blasphemed through your conduct. But if we so live that God is praised on our account, that praise is a response to him.

From those he has called, from his saints, Jerusalem also makes its response to him, for Jerusalem too had its vocation, though the original Jerusalem refused to listen, and so was warned, *See, your house will be left to you derelict. Jerusalem, Jerusalem* (he is calling, you see, but getting no reply), *how often I wanted to gather your children to myself, as a hen gathers her chicks under her wings, but you would have none of it!* (Mt 23: 38.37) There is no response. Rain is sent from on high, yet instead of fruit, thorns proliferate. But there is another

---

5. *In via fortitudinis suae.* The meaning should be "in the way of its strength" since *suae* refers to the subject of the verb. But in section 7 Augustine understands it of the Lord's strength after his resurrection.

Jerusalem, that which is bidden, *Rejoice, you barren one, you who are childless; leap and cry out for joy, you who have never given birth, for she who has been deserted bears many children, more than the wedded wife* (Gal 4:27; Is 54:1). This is the Jerusalem that *responded to him*. In what sense did it respond to him? By not scorning him when he called. What form did its response take? He sent the rain, and it bore fruit.

7. *It responded to him*, but where? *In the way of his strength*. Could it make any response of itself? Certainly not; for what would it have been in itself, and what voice could it have produced in itself, or from itself, except the voice of sin, articulate iniquity? Listen carefully to its own voice, and what do you find but the insistent cry, *I said it myself: Lord, have mercy on me; heal my soul, for I have sinned against you* (Ps 40:5(41:4)? If it has been justified, however, it responds to him, but not through any merits of its own; its response is his doing. Where is it given? *In the way of his strength*. This means Christ himself, for he said, *I am the way, the truth, and the life* (Jn 14:6).

Before his resurrection he was not recognized by his own people. Most especially when he was crucified in weakness[6] his true identity was hidden, but only until he manifested himself in strength at his resurrection. The Church therefore did not respond to him in the way of his weakness but *in the way of his strength*, because after rising from the dead he called the Church from every part of the round world. No longer was he weak on the cross, but powerful in heaven. The faith of Christians is not triumphant because they believe that Christ died but because they believe that Christ rose again. Even a pagan believes that he died; indeed, they mock you for having put your faith in a dead man. But in what do you really take pride? You believe that Christ is risen, and you hope that through Christ you too will rise again. This is why your faith is triumphant. *If you believe in your heart that Jesus is Lord, and confess with your lips that God raised him from the dead, you will be saved*. Notice that it does not say, "If you confess that God handed him over to be killed" but: *If you confess that God raised him from the dead, you will be saved, for the faith that issues in righteousness is in the heart, and the confession that leads to salvation is made with the lips* (Rom 10:9-10). Why do we also believe in him as having truly died? Because we cannot believe that he rose again unless we believe that he died first, for how can anyone rise again without previously dying? Who wakes up without having slept? But as another psalm asks, *Will he not go further and rise again, he who has fallen asleep?* (Ps 40:9(41:8)). This is the faith of Christians.

In this faith, the faith by which the Church is gathered together, *she who has been deserted bears many children, more than the wedded wife* (Gal 4:27; Is 54:1), and in this faith the Church responds to the Lord, giving praise to him

---

6. See 2 Cor 13:4.

according to his commandments. The Church's response is given *in the way of his strength*, not in the way of his weakness.

The unity and perpetuity of the Church: against the Donatists

8. You have already heard how it responded to him: *By the gathering of the peoples together into one, and kingdoms to serve the Lord.* This is how it responds: in unity; and so anyone who is outside that unity cannot make such a response. God is one, and the Church is a unity; only unity can respond to him who is one. But there are some people who say, "Yes, that certainly was the case. The Church spread among all nations did respond to him, bearing more children than did the wedded wife. *It responded to him in the way of his strength*, for it believed that Christ had risen. All nations believed in him. But that Church which was drawn from all nations no longer exists: it has perished."

So say people who are not within the Church. What an impudent assertion! The Church does not exist because you are not in it? Be careful lest such an attitude result in your not existing yourself, for the Church will be here even if you are not. But the Spirit of God anticipated this abominable, detestable assertion, this claim full of presumption and falsehood, a claim with nothing to support it, illumined by no spark of wisdom, seasoned by no salt. God's Spirit anticipated this empty, unfounded, foolhardy and pernicious proposition and seemingly refuted it in advance by proclaiming that the Church is united *by the gathering of the peoples together into one, and kingdoms to serve the Lord.*

Undoubtedly, then, his praise *responded to him.* Beyond question Jerusalem, our mother, *responded to him,* she who was waiting to be called back from exile, she who was found to have many children, more than those of the wedded wife. But some people would rise up to deny it, stating that the Church existed once, but exists no longer; and therefore something further was added to the psalm. *Make known to me how few are my days*, pleads the Church. "What does it mean, that some people have left me and now murmur against me? How can it happen that those reprobates maintain that I have perished? This is their contention: that I existed once, but exist no more. Tell me, then: *Make known to me how few are my days.* I am not asking you now for the days of eternity; those days will never end, and I shall be there to see them. No, I am not asking for those now. What I ask about is the days of this time-bound world. My days here are numbered, so tell me about them; make known to me the fewness of my days here, not the eternity of the days that await me. Reveal to me how long I shall last in this world, in the face of those who declare, 'It existed once, but no longer,' and those who assert, 'The scriptures were fulfilled, because all nations did believe, but the Church drawn from all nations apostatized and has been destroyed.'"

What is implied by this plea, *Make known to me how few are my days*? He made it known; the petition did not go unheard.[7] Who made it known to me, if not he, the way in person? And what was his answer? *Lo, I am with you throughout all days, even to the end of the ages* (Mt 28:20).

9. But here they stand up and object, "He said, *I am with you throughout all days, even to the end of the ages*, because he had us in view; he knew there would be the Donatist party on earth." But it was not the Donatist party, was it, that begged, *Make known to me how few are my days*? Was it not rather the same speaker who just before that had prophesied *the gathering of the peoples into one, and kingdoms to serve the Lord*? What is it that causes you grief? The very fact that emperors pass laws against heretics[8] vindicates the psalm's words, *and kingdoms to serve the Lord*. It is not you who are the children of martyrs put to death, of those fettered ones whose prayer was heard by the Lord. Far from it: your actions do not suggest that you are their descendants, nor does your pride, nor does your vanity. You have no savor left in you, and so you are thrown out of the house; you are insipid salt, fit only to be trodden underfoot.[9] Listen to what the psalm says. What Church is meant? The Church that has gathered *the peoples together into one*. What Church? The Church that has gathered *kingdoms to serve the Lord*. Troubled by your accusations and your erroneous opinions the Church begs God to make known to it the brevity of its days; but it discovers that the Lord promised, *Lo, I am with you throughout all days, even to the end of the ages*. Yet you claim, "He said that about us. We are the ones he meant; we shall last until the end of the ages." But let us ask Christ about this, for it was to him that the plea was addressed, *Make known to me how few are my days*. What did he predict? *This gospel will be preached throughout the world, as a testimony to all nations; and after that the end will come* (Mt 24:14). How then can you allege, "The Church certainly existed once, but now it has vanished"? Listen rather to what the Lord declared concerning the fewness of my days: *This gospel will be preached*, he says—where? *Throughout the world*. For whom? *As a testimony to all nations*. And what is to follow? *After that the end will come*. Do you not see that there are still nations among whom the gospel has not been preached? What the Lord said, by way of making known to the Church how few are its days, must come true. He said that the gospel must first be preached among all nations, and only after that will the end come. How then

---

7. Variant: "did not fall silent."
8. Anti-heresy decrees by the Emperor Constans in 347 and 348, and the legislation of the Emperor Theodosius in 392, would have antedated this sermon, and it may be to these that Augustine is alluding. In their dispute with the Maximianists the Donatists had attempted to invoke these laws; see Augustine's Exposition of Psalm 57,15 and the notes there. But the Act of Union promulgated by the Emperor Honorius in 405 formally assimilated the Donatists themselves to other heretical sects, so they were on shaky ground. If the present sermon is later than 405, Augustine could be playing on their discomfiture.
9. See Mt 5:13.

can you allege that the Church has perished from all nations,[10] when the gospel is being preached today for the very purpose of making it present to all nations?

The Church will undeniably be present among all nations until the end of the world; yet this period can rightly be called a few days because everything that comes to an end is a brief span of time, from which we shall cross over into eternity. May the heretics be lost, rather; let them be lost in respect of what they are, and be found to exist in a new condition, a state not theirs as yet. These few days will last until the world ends, and they are rightly called few, because the whole of time—not only from today until the end of the world but even counting from Adam to the end of the world—is but a tiny drop compared with eternity.[11]

Verse 25. Successive human generations and the eternity of God

10. The heretics have no right to crow over me because I referred to the fewness of my days, as though this meant that I shall not last until the end of the world; for what does the psalm say next? *Do not recall me when only half my days are done.* Do not deal with me in the way the heretics suppose you do. Lead me to the very end of time, not merely to the mid-point of my days. Allow me to complete these few days of mine, so that afterwards you may grant me the days of eternity.

But then why did you ask to be shown how few your days are? Why? Shall I tell you? Because, Lord, *Your years abide in the generation of generations.*[12] I inquired about my own few days because, even if these days see me through to the end of the world, they are few indeed compared with your days, for *your years abide in the generation of generations.* Why did the psalm not say, "Your years abide for ages upon ages"? That, after all, is the way scripture usually indicates eternity. But no, here it said, *Your years abide in the generation of generations.* And what are *your years*? What else can they be but years that do not come and do not pass away—years that do not come, because it is impossible for them ever not to be? In our temporal experience every day comes only to perish. Every hour, every month, every year: none of them stands still. Before each of them arrives, we say, "It will be"; but after it has come, it will be no more. Your eternal years are not like that; your years are unchanging and will abide with the *generation of generations.* There is a certain "generation of generations," and to that generation your years will be present. What is that generation? It truly exists, and if we understand properly we shall exist in it, and God's years will exist in us. How can they be in us? In the same way that God himself will be in us, so that, as

---

10. To remain in Africa alone, as the Donatists contended.
11. See Is 40:15.
12. *In generatione generationum anni tui.* The underlying idea is obviously "forever." But Augustine interprets the words literally, and his consideration of the verse requires a literal, but clumsy, English translation of it.

scripture says, *God may be all things in all of us* (1 Cor 15:28). God's years are not something different from God himself. God's years are God's eternity, and eternity is the very substance of God, in which there is no possibility of change. In him nothing is past, as though it no longer existed, and nothing is future, as though it had not yet come to be. There is nothing in God's eternity except "is." There is no "was," no "will be," because anything that "was" has ceased to be, and anything that "will be" does not yet exist. Whatever "is" in God simply *is*.

With good reason did God dispatch his servant Moses in these terms. Moses asked the name of the one who sent him; he asked and he heard it, for his initial desire was good and was not ignored. He asked God's name not out of impertinent curiosity but because he needed to know it for his ministry. *What shall I say to the sons of Israel if they challenge me, Who sent you to us?* Then the creator named himself to the creature, God to a human being, the immortal to a mortal, the eternal to an ephemeral man: *I AM WHO AM*, he said. You yourself, human creature, might use those words and say, "I am." But who would be saying it? One person says it, and it indicates Gaius. Another says it, and means Lucius. Another again, and Mark is meant. Could you say anything else to indicate the difference? Only if you were to give your name as well. This is what God was expected to give, for the question had been put to him, "What is your name? If they ask me, who shall I say sent me?" *I AM*. "I am who?" *I AM WHO AM*. Is that your name? Is that all you are called? Could that, and that alone, be your name, unless everything else that is were proved not truly to be at all, in comparison with you? This is your name, then, but I ask you to express the truth in a way I can better understand. *Go, and thus shall you say to the children of Israel, HE WHO IS has sent me to you. I AM WHO AM. HE WHO IS has sent me to you.* What a mighty "is"! What an incomparably great "is"! What is any human being beside that? A human being "is" something, but what is he or she, alongside that great "is"? Who can grasp that being? Who could share in it? Who pant for it, who aspire to it? In its presence, who dare even think he "is"?

But do not despair, frail humanity. *I am the God of Abraham, the God of Isaac and the God of Jacob* (Ex 3:13-14), he says. "You have heard what I am in myself; listen now to what I am for your sake." That eternity has called us, for the Word has burst forth from eternity. There was eternity, there was the Word, already existent, but there was as yet no time. Why was there no time? Because time is a created thing. How was time made? *Everything was made through him; no part of created being was made without him* (Jn 1:3). Ah, the wonder of it! The Word exists before time, and through him all time was made; he was born in time, though he is eternal life; he calls temporal creatures, and makes them eternal. This is what the psalm means by the *generation of generations*. A generation goes on its way, and another generation comes to replace it.[13] You observe

---

13. See Eccl 1:4.

that the generations of men and women on earth are like the leaves on a tree—but an olive tree, or a laurel, or some other that always has foliage. Similarly the earth bears the human race as its leaves: the earth is always full of people, but as some die off others are born to take their place. This tree has always been adorned with its green vesture, but notice how many dried-up leaves you are treading underfoot.

11. Thus there was a generation after Adam, and it passed away. Even at that time future participants in the eternity of God were born from it, for Abel, Seth, and Enoch were Adam's descendants. Then that generation died out, and the flood came, and only one house remained. That generation supplied a few: Noah and his three sons[14] and three daughters-in-law; for in that family of eight only one turned out to be a sinner. This number was added to those of earlier generations. Then Noah's three sons left many descendants, and the world was plentifully populated, as though filled with three measures of flour. Abraham, Isaac, and Jacob were chosen; they were holy men, patriarchs, and pleasing to God. Their generation produced yet more generations, who in their turn produced others, giving birth to prophets and preachers of God. At last came our Lord Jesus Christ himself, who put yeast into the three measures of flour, until the whole batch was leavened.[15] In the days of his earthly life there were the apostles, and other holy people; after them came other saints again; and now today all who are holy are holy in the name of Christ, as will all those be who after us will be saints, even to the world's end. From all these innumerable generations you may pick out all the holy offspring in each, and make of them one generation, and in this *generation of generations*, says the psalm, *your years abide.* Your eternity will be found in that generation which is selected from all the generations and united into one; and that one generation will participate in your eternity. All the other generations come to birth to fulfill their allotted times, but this one, elect and drawn from all of them, is brought to a new birth for eternity. It will be changed and given new life, and made able to carry you through the strength you confer on it. *Your years abide in the generation of generations.*

Verses 26-28. The whole mission of the Church is carried out in the perspective of eternity

12. *In the beginning you established the earth, O Lord.* I hear in this line an echo of your eternity, by which you precede all that you have made. *In the beginning you established the earth, O Lord, and the heavens are the work of your hands. They will perish, but you yourself abide. They will all wear out like old*

---

14. Variant: "two sons."
15. See Mt 13:33. Variant: ". . . who has put yeast . . . until the whole batch shall be leavened."

clothes, and you will discard them like a garment, and so they will be changed; but you are the selfsame. Who are you? *You are the selfsame.* You who said, *I AM WHO AM*, you are *the selfsame.* And although all those things would not exist except as deriving from you, and coming to be through you, and existing in you, nonetheless they are not what you are, for *you are the selfsame, and your years will not fail.* Those years of yours will never fail, those years of yours which will abide in the generation drawn from the generations; no, they will not fail. Knowing this, would I have inquired of you concerning the fewness of my days, unless I knew that all the days of this world, from the beginning until the end of time, are brief indeed compared with your eternity? I knew well what I was questioning you about. The heretics have therefore no ground for self-congratulation, as though the life-span of the worldwide Church were short, for even though it lasts until the end, it is still but a few days. How can they be considered few? Because they will end sooner or later. The only years that we ought to love, and long for, and pine for, are the years that will abide *in the generation of generations.* With them in view it is worth our while to maintain our unity, for them it is worth avoiding every pernicious influence from the heretics, for the sake of those years it is worth finding ways to answer the profligate, to win over the erring, and to rescue the lost; for to those years must our longing be directed. All the same, *make known to me how few are my days,* so that I may have an answer for the smooth talkers, for the gossips, the scandal-mongers, the whisperers and the detractors. *Do not recall me when only half my days are done,* lest you take me away from the earth before the entire world has been filled with the gospel, for then my Lord's command would not have been obeyed, that *this gospel must be preached throughout the world, as a testimony to all nations; and after that the end will come* (Mt 24:14).

What can we add to these words, brothers and sisters? They are abundantly clear. God established the earth: that we know; and the heavens are the work of his hands. Do not imagine that God makes one thing with his hands and something else with a word. What he makes with a word, that he also makes with his hand, for he who said, *I AM WHO AM*, is not composed of diversified bodily members. Perhaps we should even say that his word is his hand. Certainly his hand is the same thing as his power; for when he said, *Let there be a firmament,* and the firmament came to be, it seems that he created it with a word, but when he said, *Let us make humans in our own image and likeness* (Gn 1:6,26), it sounds as though he created by hand. Then consider the statement that *the heavens are the work of your hands,* which indicates that what we just now heard him creating with a word he certainly created with his hands—which is to say that he made them by his mighty power. It is advisable to concentrate on what he has made and not pry into how he made it. It is more than enough for you to understand how he did his job when he made you in such fashion that you must first be his obedient servant and afterwards, perhaps, his understanding friend.[16] *The heavens are the work of your hands.*

The destruction of the earth: in what sense will the heavens perish?

13. *They will perish, but you yourself abide.* The apostle Peter has plainly told us, *There were former heavens, established by God's word from water and with water, and this created world perished in the water of the flood. The earth and the heavens which exist now have been marked down for destruction by fire, by the same word of God.* (2 Pt 3:5-7) This text declares that the heavens did perish in the flood, and we know that they were indeed destroyed, if we understand "heavens" to mean the vast open space of the sky around us. The water gushed out, and filled the whole space where birds fly; and so it can certainly be said that the heavens closest to the earth—the heavens we mean when we speak of "the birds of heaven"—were wiped out. Higher up in the firmament are to be found the "heavens of heavens";[17] but whether they too are to perish by fire, or whether this applies only to those "heavens" which were destroyed once before by the flood, is a nice question among scholars, one which cannot easily be resolved, especially in the limited time available to us.

Let us dismiss the question, then, or at any rate postpone it; what we do know is that even if they do perish, God remains. And if certain things which were made by God remain with God, they do not remain in themselves. By refusing to be separated from God, they remain in God. What does this imply? Are we to conclude, brothers and sisters, that the angels[18] are to perish in the fire which will destroy the earth? That is unthinkable. But then, are we to say that God did not create the angels? An absurd idea. What are we to say, then? Anyway, where could they have come from, if not made by him? *He himself spoke, and they were made, he gave the order, and they were created* (Ps 32(33):9): that statement was made in connection with a review of the works of God, among which the angels were mentioned. Evidently, then, the angels will be with God even if the world is ablaze. Moreover, although fire burns the earth, it will not burn God's saints:

---

16. See Jn 15:15.

17. Taking his cue from Ps 113(115):16 according to the LXX, *Heaven's heaven is for the Lord, but he has assigned the earth to humankind,* Augustine understood the visible "heaven" or sky to be part of the earth, but above it was "heaven's heaven," or the spiritual creation. Compare *Confessions* 12,2,2: "This whole material world has been endowed with beauty of form even in its furthest parts, the lowest of which is our earth [...]; yet compared with *heaven's heaven* the heaven that overarches our earth is itself no better than earth. [...] These two vast realities—our earth and our sky—are to be regarded as mere lowly earth beside that unimaginable heaven which is for the Lord."

18. Whose proper abode was "heaven's heaven."

what the king's furnace was to the three young men,[19] the blazing world will be to the righteous on whom the Trinity has set its seal.

The prospect of bodily transformation in glory

14. It may not be far-fetched to interpret the heavens also as the just themselves, God's saints. In them God abides; he has thundered his commandments from them; he has sent forth from them the lightning of his miracles; through them he has showered the earth with wisdom and truth. These heavens have indeed proclaimed the glory of God.[20] Surely they will not perish too? Or perhaps they will, but only in one respect. What respect? As far as their clothing is concerned.[21] What do I mean by their clothing? I am referring to their bodies, for the body is the vesture of the soul. The Lord mentioned clothing when he asked, *Is not life*[22] *more than food, and the body more than clothing?* (Mt 6:25). In what sense does this garment perish? *Though our outer self is decaying, our inner self is being renewed daily* (2 Cor 4:16). The saints will perish, but only as to their bodies, whereas to God the psalm confesses, *You yourself abide.*

But if the saints are to suffer the destruction of their bodies, what becomes of the resurrection of our flesh? How is the glorification of the head a pattern for the members? How is it an example for us? Do you want to know the answer? The body will be changed; it is not destined to be the kind of body it once was. Listen to the apostle's words: *The dead will rise incorrupt, and we shall be changed.* How shall we be changed? *The body is sown an animal body; it will rise a spiritual body* (1 Cor 15:52.44). It is sown as a mortal body but will rise again immortal; it is sown as a perishable thing but will rise imperishable. We expect this transformation; and in this sense the heavens will perish, because the heavens will undergo change. Perhaps someone will think we are not correct in calling the bodies of the saints "heavens." Well, if they do not carry God, I will agree that they are not heavens. "But how can you prove that they carry God?" Has a significant text slipped your memory? *Glorify God, and carry him in your body* (1 Cor 6:20).

These heavens will be destroyed, but not for ever: they will be destroyed only to be changed. Is this not what the psalm says? Read on: *They will all wear out like old clothes, and you will discard them like a garment, and so they will be changed, but you are the selfsame, and your years will not fail.* You hear clothes mentioned, and a garment: can you interpret them otherwise than as the body?

---

19. See Dn 3.
20. See Ps 18:2(19:1).
21. Though he goes on to speak of the body as the garment of the soul, Augustine may have in his mind the clothes of the three young men, although these were not even scorched in the furnace.
22. *Anima*, which can mean either "soul" or "life."

Let us then hope that even our bodies will be transformed, but only by him who existed before we did, and abides after us, by him whose act has made us what we are, by him to whom we shall come when we have been changed. He changes us but is not changed himself; he creates but is uncreated; he moves all things but abides in stillness; he it is who, as far as flesh and blood can understand him, is the I AM WHO AM.

You are the selfsame, and your years will not fail. What are we, with our threadbare years, compared with years like his? What are they? Yet we must not despair. In his greatness, in his most excellent wisdom, he had said, *I AM WHO AM*, but for our consolation he added, *I am the God of Abraham, the God of Isaac and the God of Jacob* (Ex 3:14.15); and we are Abraham's progeny.[23] Base though we are, dust and ashes though we are, in him we hope. We are slaves, but for our sake our Lord assumed the nature of a slave;[24] for us mortals he who is immortal willed to die; and for our sake he exemplified our resurrection in himself. Let us hope, therefore, that we shall attain those steady, abiding years, wherein the days are not determined by the sun's passage, but what is remains as it is, because it alone is real.

Verse 29. The children who will enter the promised land

15. What about us? Tell us whether we can be there some day.[25] Listen to the next verse: *The children of your servants will dwell there.* Dwell where? Where else but in those unfailing years? *The children of your servants will dwell there, and their offspring will be guided unto that age.* Unto the age of ages, unto the age of eternity, unto the age that abides.

But the psalm speaks of *the children of your servants.* Should that make us worry that, since we are God's servants, our children will be there, but we shall not? Or perhaps we ourselves are the children of his servants, since we are the children of the apostles? Can we take it that way? Hardly, for what an unbecoming attitude, what impertinence, it would be on the part of the apostles' descendants, lately born and arrogant about their recent arrival, if they dared to claim, "We shall be there, but the apostles will not"! Far be such presumption from dutiful children, far be it from the faith of little ones, far be it from the intelligence of the fully grown. Of course the apostles will be there: the rams go first, and the lambs follow.[26] But then why does the psalm say, *The children of your servants,* rather than, more concisely, "your servants"? The apostles are your

---

23. See Gal 3:29.
24. See Phil 2:7.
25. These queries could be addressed by Augustine to God, or (perhaps better) by his hearers to Augustine.
26. On the apostles as rams in the flock, compare the Exposition of Psalm 64,18.

servants; and their children are your servants; and their children again, grandchildren of the first generation—what else are they but your servants? You could
have included them all in a concise phrase by saying simply, "Your servants will
dwell there." We had better try to see whether the psalm was giving us some hint.

Something happened in early times that may illuminate the phrase for us. For
forty years the people of Israel were worn down in the desert. Not one of them
entered the promised land; only their children entered it. Oh, no, we remember
that two of them did—but only two, unless I am mistaken;[27] the rest did not. Out
of so many thousands, only two entered the land. How much labor and suffering
were entailed! God does not labor, but his servants certainly did. How much
Moses had to suffer, and what burdensome tidings he heard about the people
who would not enter the land of promise! Their children did enter it, though; and
what does that signify? Those who entered it were new people; the old people
did not. Yet from the old, two did enter, two who symbolize the one and unity,
the head and the body, Christ and the Church,[28] with all that newness, the
newness of children. *The children of your servants will dwell there.*

The children of your servants can also represent the deeds of your servants,
for no one will dwell there except in virtue of his or her deeds. What is meant,
then, when the psalm says that these children will dwell there? It means that none
of us must boast that we shall dwell there if we call ourselves servants of God yet
have no deeds to show; for only the children will be dwellers in that land. What
does it mean: *The children of your servants will dwell there?* Your servants will
dwell there through their works, your servants will dwell there through their
children. Do not be sterile if you want to dwell there: send your offspring on
ahead so that you may follow them; send them ahead of you. And by that I don't
mean bury them. May your children lead you into the land of promise, the land of
the living, not the land of the dying. While you live on here, in exile, let them go
on ahead, ready to welcome you there. To secure bodily nourishment, Jacob's
son preceded[29] his family into Egypt; he said to his father and his brothers, *I
came on ahead, to ensure that you would have food* (Gn 45:7). So let your children go ahead of you, let your deeds precede you. You will follow the kind of
children you have sent on in advance.[30]

---

27. Joshua and Caleb; see Nm 14:30-32.
28. Compare section 8 above; the unity of the Church responds to the oneness of God.
29. Variant: ". . .in exile, let them go on ahead, while to secure bodily nourishment you raise
    children. Jacob's son preceded. . . ."
30. By amending *tales* to *talis* the CCL editors extract the meaning, "As are the children you have
    sent on in advance, so will you be who follow them."

Exposition of Psalm 102

A Sermon[1]

Verse 1. The voice of the soul need never fall silent as it blesses the Lord

1. Let our soul bless the Lord.[2] Let it bless the Lord our God for every gift he gives us, for every consolation he sends, for every rebuke, for the grace he has deigned to shower on us, for the forgiveness that stays the punishment that was owed to us, and for all his works. For all these let our soul bless the Lord our God. This is what we have sung; and these are the opening words of the psalm on which we are to speak. We will say whatever we are enabled to say by the grace of him whom our soul is blessing. Let each one of us arouse his or her own soul and exhort it, *Bless the Lord, O my soul.* All of us, and all who in every place are brothers and sisters in Christ, form a single person whose head is in heaven; so let this one person exhort his own soul, *Bless the Lord, O my soul.* It listens, it obeys, it acts accordingly and is persuaded, not in response to anything with which we endow it but because of the bounty of him whom our soul blesses.

This psalm sets out to demonstrate to us the reasons why our soul should bless him, as though our soul's reaction had been, "Why are you telling me to bless the Lord?" Let us listen to it, then; let our soul listen, and ponder carefully all those instances of the Lord's kindness that should rouse it to respond. Let it see the justice of the invitation addressed to it, *Bless the Lord, O my soul.* Let it consider too whether anything other than the Lord deserves such blessing. *Bless the Lord, O my soul,* says the psalm.

2. It then repeats the invitation already issued, but urges more expressly, *Bless the Lord, O my soul, and let all that is within me bless his holy name.* I do not think this is addressed to the internal organs of the body: I hardly think it means that our lungs and liver, or any other internal physical organs, should burst out into blessings offered to the Lord. It is true that inside the chest there are our lungs, which are like a pair of bellows breathing in and out alternately. The air breathed in is pushed out and expressed in the voice and other sounds when we articulate[3] words. No vocal sound can proceed from our mouths except

---

1. Preached at Carthage, on a martyrs' festival, probably in or shortly before 411; see the note at Exposition of Psalm 66,1.
2. One codex inserts the title, "For David himself," omitted by Augustine.
3. Variant: "direct."

78

through the compression of the lungs. But this process is not in question here, because it is entirely concerned with sounds audible to human ears.

God also has ears, and the heart has a voice. In the psalm a human speaker is exhorting his inner faculties to bless the Lord; he says to them, "All you inward powers of mine, bless the Lord's holy name." What are your inward powers? Your soul, nothing else. Thus after the psalm has said, *Bless the Lord, O my soul*, it says the same thing again, urging, *Let all that is within me bless his holy name.* Use your voice to shout, if there is a human hearer; but let your voice be silent[4] when no man or woman is at hand to listen. The one who can hear the cry of your inner being is never absent. Those words of blessing rang out from our lips for some considerable time as we continued to sing, *Bless the Lord, O my soul, and let all that is within me bless his holy name.* We sang it for as long a time as was required, and then we fell silent; but does that mean that our inward faculties should cease to bless the Lord? The sound of our voices comes and goes, but the voice of our inner being must be perpetual. When you come to church to join others in singing a hymn, your voice must chant the praises of God. When you have sung as long as your strength allows, you go home; but then let your soul go on caroling the praises of God. Perhaps you are engaged in business: let your soul praise God. You are eating: observe the apostle's injunction, *Whether you eat, whether you drink, do everything for the glory of God* (1 Cor 10:31). I even dare to say, when you are asleep, let your soul bless the Lord. Let no memory of a shameful deed keep you awake, no planning of theft disturb you, no commitment to bribery trouble your rest. Your innocence is the voice of your soul even as you sleep. *Bless the Lord, O my soul, and let all that is within me bless his holy name.*

Verse 2. How do we repay the Lord?

3. *Bless the Lord, O my soul, and do not forget all the ways in which he has repaid you.*[5] It says, *Bless the Lord, O my soul.* What is your soul? The same thing as "all that is within you." *Bless the Lord, O my soul*: the repetition conveys an urgent appeal. But to ensure that you always bless the Lord, *do not forget all the ways in which he has repaid you.* If you do forget them, you will fall silent. But you will be able to keep in sight all the ways in which the Lord has repaid you only if your sins are also before your eyes. This does not mean keeping in sight

---

4. Variant: "He uses his voice . . . he lets his voice be silent."

5. *Omnes retributiones eius.* The noun *retributio*, like its cognate verb, is often translated by "favor, benefit," which meaning is included here. But Augustine's emphasis in this and the following section falls on two contrasts: 1) that between *tributio* and *retributio*, the former being a gift of what belongs to the donor and the latter being a repayment of what rightly belongs to the recipient; 2) that between the just recompense for our sins (punishment) and the merciful forgiveness with which God has chosen to repay us.

the pleasure you derived from your past sins; it means that you must keep an eye on the condemnation they deserve. For the condemnation you are responsible, but the forgiveness is from God. The Lord's manner of repaying you forces you to ask, *What return shall I make to the Lord for all the repayment he has made to me?* (Ps 115(116):12)

This was the question that preoccupied the martyrs whose memorial we celebrate today, and indeed all the saints who scorned the present life, and laid down their lives for their brethren. As you heard in the Letter of John,[6] such an act is the perfection of charity, for, as the Lord affirmed, *no one can have greater charity than this, to lay down his life for his friends* (Jn 15:13). Pondering this matter, the martyrs set little store by their life here, because they hoped to find it hereafter, according to the Lord's promise, *Anyone who loves his life will lose it, but anyone who loses it for my sake will preserve it for eternal life* (Mt 10:39; 16:25; Jn 12:25). They wanted to make some repayment to him—but who wanted to? With what? And to whom? Men and women repaid God with their service even unto death. But had they anything to offer in repayment that he had not first given? What did they give that they had not received in the first place? He who is truly the source of gifts, he alone has repaid us; but he has not repaid us for our sins, because one kind of recompense was owed to us, and quite another was made. *Do not forget all the ways in which he has repaid you*, the psalm warns us—not simply the things he has given you, but the ways in which he has repaid you.[7] Something was indeed owed to us, but what was given to us was something not owed. That is why a psalmist asks, *What return shall I make to the Lord for all the repayment he has made to me?* He does not say, "for all he has given[8] me" but *for all the repayment he has made to me.* You have repaid the Lord with evil for good, but he has repaid you with good for evil.

How did you repay God with evil for good, mortal creature? You were originally a persecutor and a blasphemer and acted unjustly,[9] so you were repaying him with blasphemies. For what good gifts were you making that repayment? In the first place, for your existence; but a stone exists too. Then, for your life; but an animal also has life. What recompense will you offer to the Lord for giving you a higher dignity than all the animals and all the birds, for making you in his own image and likeness? Do not cast about for some repayment; simply return his own image to him. He seeks no more than that; what he wants is his own coin.[10] But instead of giving him thanks, instead of the humility, the obedience,

---

6. See 1 Jn 3:16.
7. *Non tributiones, sed retributiones.*
8. *Tribuere* in classical Latin meant the giving of something according to justice. The common definition of justice was *ius suum cuique tribuere.*
9. See 1 Tm 1:13.
10. See Mk 12:13-17 and parallels. As Caesar has a right to the coin because his own image is stamped upon it, God has a right to the human beings created in his image and likeness.

the religious worship you owed to God, instead of all the good recompense you owed him for the good things you received, you repaid him with blasphemies. And what was his response? "Confess, and I will forgive you. I too make repayment, but not as you have repaid me. You have repaid good with evil, but I repay evil with good."

4. Think then, my soul, about all the ways in which God has repaid you, but think about them in the context of all your evil deeds. Manifold as are your wicked acts, manifold too are his repayments of good. Will you offer him some special presents,[11] perhaps? Some gifts? Some sacrifices? What, then? There is one sacrifice that delights him: if you, remembering all the ways in which he has repaid you, cry out, *Bless the Lord, O my soul.* He has told us, *By a sacrifice of praise I shall be honored; offer to God a sacrifice of praise, and address your prayers to the Most High* (Ps 49(50):14,23). God desires to be praised, but for your profit, not his aggrandizement. There is nothing at all that you can give him by way of repayment. What he demands, he demands not for his own benefit, but for yours; it is to your advantage and will be kept for you. The gift he enjoys from you is not anything that can add to his happiness but one that will lead you to him.

With this in mind the martyrs looked for a gift they could offer him, and almost despaired when they found none. They wondered, *What return shall I make to the Lord for all the repayment he has made to me?* They found no means of repayment, save one: *I will take in my hands the cup of salvation, and call on the name of the Lord* (Ps 115(116):13). With what will you repay the Lord? You were wondering but found no suitable gift. *I will take in my hands the cup of salvation.* What do you mean? Was this cup of salvation not the Lord's own gift to us? Make your repayment from your own resources if you can. But no, I would advise you not to attempt that; do not render to God anything that has its origin in yourself, for God does not want to be repaid with what is yours. If you look to yourself to find the means of repayment, all you will give him is sin. The repayment he wants is not from your resources, but from his. If you harvest a crop for the farmer from the land he has sown, you are paying the farmer back with the fruit that belongs to him; if you give him only thorns, you give what is your own. Make truth your repayment, and praise the Lord in truth. If you try to speak from yourself, you will be lying. *One who tells lies speaks from what is his own* (Jn 8:44). Anyone who lies is speaking from himself, but anyone who speaks the truth is speaking from what belongs to God.

But what does it mean, to take the cup of salvation? Nothing less than to imitate the sufferings of the Lord. This is what the martyrs did, and this was the advice the Lord gave to the proud, to those who were prematurely ambitious for exalted thrones, who hoped to avoid the narrow valley of weeping and wanted to

---

11. *Exenia* were properly gifts offered to a guest, then gifts in general.

sit, one at his right hand, the other at his left. What did he reply? *Are you able to drink the cup I am to drink?* (Mt 20:22). A martyr preparing to be immolated as a holy sacrifice declares, "I will take into my own hands the cup of salvation: I will take up Christ's cup, I will drink the Lord's passion." Be careful that you do not weaken. "No fear of that, because *I will call on the name of the Lord.*" If any did weaken, it was because they did not call on the name of the Lord, but presumed on their own strength.

Render your homage in full awareness that you received everything that you offer. Let your soul bless the Lord in such wise that you do not forget all the ways in which he has repaid you.

Verses 3-5. Christ, the omnipotent healer

5. Now listen to all the ways in which he has repaid you. *He is ready to forgive all your iniquities, and he heals all your diseases. He will redeem*[12] *your life from corruption, he crowns you in his pity and mercy. He satisfies your longing with good things, your youth will be renewed like an eagle's.* These are the forms his repayment takes. What was due to a sinner except torment? What was owed to a blasphemer except the fires of hell? Yet these were not the repayment he made to you; do not be afraid, do not shrink back appalled, do not give way to loveless terror. Do not forget all those good ways in which he has repaid you; allow yourself to be changed now, and so avoid experiencing his—what shall I say? His bad ways of repaying you? But they cannot be bad if they are just. They seem bad to you, but to God[13] not even the bad things you suffer are bad; for if they are just, they are good, and only to you who endure them do they seem bad. Would you prefer not to experience your fate as bad, just though it is in God's sight? Then make sure there is no sinful badness on your part in his presence. He has never ceased to call you, nor has he neglected to instruct the one he has called; he has never ceased to perfect the one he has instructed, nor will he neglect to crown you when he has made you perfect. What have you to say? That you are a sinner? Be converted, then, and be open to receive the repayments he offers, for *he is ready to forgive all your iniquities.*

Even after your sins are forgiven you still carry with you a weak body. Inevitably there will be carnal desires that titillate you and tempt you to forbidden pleasures; these result from your sickness, for you still carry weak flesh. Death has not yet been swallowed up in victory, nor has this corruptible nature yet been clothed in incorruptibility.[14] The soul itself is still shaken by manifold disturbances, even after the forgiveness of its sins. It is still battered by dangerous temptations, and all

---

12. Variant: "he redeems."
13. Variant: "The bad things are from you, the good things are from God."
14. See 1 Cor 15:54,53.

sorts of suggestions assail it. Some of these it finds pleasurable, others it does not; but from time to time it consents to some of those in which it takes pleasure, and then it is trapped. This is a disease, but the Lord *heals all your diseases*. All your maladies will be healed, never fear. "They are great," you say; but the physician is greater. An omnipotent doctor is never confronted with an incurable disease. All you need to do is to allow yourself to be cured. Do not thrust his hands away, for he knows what he is doing. You must not simply enjoy it when he pampers you; you must also bear it when he plies the knife. Hold out under the painful treatment by fixing your mind on the health it will bring you.

Just think, my brothers and sisters, how much people put up with in their bodily illnesses, and only to gain a few extra days of life before they die and uncertain days at that. Plenty of people have endured excruciating pain under surgery, and then died in the hands of the doctors, or else recovered only to succumb to some other illness that carried them off. If they had looked for such a speedy death, would they have consented to undergo that agonizing pain? But you are not suffering for the sake of a doubtful outcome; he who has promised you health cannot make a mistake. A doctor is sometimes mistaken in promising health where a human body is concerned. Why can he be mistaken? Because what he is trying to heal is not something he made himself. But God made your body, and God made your soul. He knows how to re-create what he created; he knows how to form anew what he once formed. Your job is simply to stay under the doctor's hands; anyone who pushes his hands away offends him. People do not behave so to human doctors. On the contrary, they let themselves be tied down and cut. For the sake of uncertain recovery they are willing to pay the high price of certain pain. God who made you cures you with absolute certainty, and he charges no fee. Yield to his hands, then, O soul, you who bless him, mindful of all the ways in which he repays you, for *he heals all your diseases*.

6. *He will redeem your life from corruption*. This is the root of the healing he brings to your ailments: that he redeems your very life from corruption. You know well how the corruptible body weighs down the soul;[15] for the soul lives its life in a body subject to corruption. What kind of life is that? One that bears burdens and carries heavy weights. Even when we try to think about God, as it is proper for human beings to do, how many things get in the way, interrupting us on the pretext of some need of our corruptible nature? How many things call us away? How many divert us from our noble purpose? How many cares distract us? What a crowd of fantasies! What a rabble of suggestions! All this goes on in the human heart, as though it were swarming with the maggots of our corruption. We have described the gravity of the disease, so let us praise our physician. Will he not heal you, he who made you the kind of creature who would not have fallen ill if you had consented to observe the rule of health he gave you? Did he not

---

15. See Wis 9:15.

draw it up for your benefit, indicating to you what you might touch, and what you must not touch,[16] if you were to keep your salutary condition?[17] You refused to listen in order to keep it, so listen now to regain it. Your illness has taught you how right his orders were. Men and women would not hear when they were warned, but let them hear now, at last, in the light of experience. It is a stubborn mind indeed that even experience cannot teach. Will God not heal you, God who made you such that you would never have been ill, if only you had chosen to keep his commandments? Will he not heal you, he who made the angels and will make you their equal once you have been re-created? Will he who made heaven and earth not heal the creature made in his own image and likeness? Heal you he will; but you need to will your healing. He heals people with every possible kind of disease, but he heals no one who is unwilling.

What could be a more blessed state than yours, when your healing is there within your grasp, conditional only on your consent?[18] Suppose you coveted some elevated rank on this earth, aspiring to military leadership, or the proconsulate, or a prefecture: could you get it immediately, the moment you began to want it? Would fulfillment come on the heels of desire? Many people wish to attain such positions and fail; but even if they did attain them, what use would high rank be to sick persons? And who in this life is not sick? Is there anyone who does not have to drag his way through a long illness? Even to be born here, in a mortal body, is the onset of our maladies. Our needy condition is supported by daily doses of medicine, for the means we use to relieve our wants are like remedies applied every day. Would hunger not kill you if you did not treat it with the appropriate medicine? Would thirst not destroy you if you neglected to drink? Yet your drinking only keeps thirst at bay; it does not quench it entirely, for after that temporary relief thirst will return. With remedies like these we alleviate the distress of our sickness. You were wearied with standing; you are rested by sitting down. Sitting is a remedy for your fatigue, but the remedy itself tires you, for you cannot continue to sit for very long. Wherever our fatigue is relieved, another form of fatigue makes its entrance.

Why then hanker for temporal things when you are unwell? Concentrate first on getting better. Sometimes a person is ill in bed in his own house. His sickly state is quite obvious, though there is another sickness, just as unmistakable, which people are unwilling to recognize.[19] However, in the case of the physical complaint, human doctors are called in. The patient is ill in his own home, gasping with fever in his bed. Perhaps he tries to think about his financial affairs,

---

16. See Gn 2:16-17.
17. *Salutem.* In the preceding sentence Augustine used *sanitas*, health; now he changes it to *salus*, which connotes both health and salvation.
18. Variant: ". . . than yours, than to have your healing dependent on your consent, as though you had your life in your hand?"
19. That is, a spiritual malady, as he will explain in a minute.

or to give orders about his staff, or his farm, or to make some other arrangements. But he is immediately recalled from these anxieties by the solicitude of his relatives who fuss and murmur all round him. He is advised, "Forget about all that; just concentrate on getting better."[20] The same advice is apposite for you. Whoever you are, think about other things if you are well; but if some malady proves to you how sick you really are, concentrate on your salvation. Christ is your salvation, so fix your mind on Christ. Accept his cup of salvation, for *he heals all your diseases.* If you truly want this salvation,[21] you will get it. If you seek honors and riches you will not have them as soon as the desire arises, but what Christ gives you is more precious and is yours as soon as you desire it. *He heals all your diseases; he will redeem your life from corruption.* Every desire that plagues you will be healed when this corruptible nature is clothed in incorruptiblity. Your life has been redeemed from corruption; there is no need to be afraid anymore. A contract has been signed in good faith; no one can deceive your redeemer, no one outwit him, no one bully him. He has struck this business deal, and he has paid the price already by shedding his blood. That is what I am saying, no less: that God's only Son has poured out his blood for us. Walk tall, human soul, for you are worth so high a price.

He will redeem your life from corruption. What he has promised us as a reward he has shown us in himself by way of example. He died for our offenses, and rose for our justification.[22] Let the members hope for what has been demonstrated in their head. Will he not care for the members if he has raised their head to heaven? Surely; *he will redeem your life from corruption.*

You conquer in God's strength; he crowns you for the victory he wins in you

7. *He crowns you in his pity and mercy.* You began to be arrogant, did you, when you heard those first words, *he crowns you?* "Aha, how important I am: it shows that I acquitted myself well in the fight!" But in whose strength did you contend? Your own, yes, but supplied by him. It is evident that you are wrestling, and because you will overcome, you will be crowned; but consider who overcame in the first place, making you a victor after him. *Be glad,* he said, *for I have overcome the world* (Jn 16:33). Why should his victory over the world make us glad, as though it had been our victory? Because we did indeed win that victory, and therefore we must most certainly rejoice. We were vanquished in ourselves but victors in him.[23] He therefore puts the wreath on you, because he crowns his

---

20. *De salute tua,* which could also mean "on your salvation."
21. Or healing.
22. See Rom 4:25.
23. Insofar as we are allied with the world as sinful, we are defeated along with it; but as members of Christ we share his victory over it, including over its manifestations in ourselves.

own gifts,[24] not your merits. *I have worked harder than any of them*, claims the apostle; but notice what he adds: *only not I, but the grace of God with me* (1 Cor 15:10). After all those labors he confidently looks forward to his crown: *I have fought the good fight, I have run the whole course, I have kept the faith; all that remains for me now is the crown of righteousness which the Lord, as a just judge, will award me on that day* (2 Tm 4:7-8). Why should you be crowned, Paul? Because *I have fought the good fight*. Why? Because *I have run the whole course*. Why? Because *I have kept the faith*. But what empowered you to fight? How did you keep the faith? *Not I, but the grace of God with me*.

If you too are crowned, you are crowned by his mercy. There is no room at all for you to be proud. Praise the Lord always and never forget the manifold ways in which he repays you. He repaid you by calling you when you were a sinner and an unbeliever, that you might be justified. He repaid you by holding you upright and guiding you lest you fall. He repays you by giving you strength to persevere even to the end. He repays you by assuring you that even your flesh, the flesh that weighs so heavily upon you, shall rise again, without even a hair on your head perishing.[25] After rising again you will be crowned, and that too is his repayment. You will praise God for ever without wearying, because that is his repayment to you. Never forget all his ways of repaying you, if you want your soul to bless the Lord who *crowns you in his pity and compassion*.

8. "What shall I find to do, after receiving my crown? I was helped while I wrestled, certainly; and when the contest is over I shall be crowned. But after that there will be no lingering trace of the enemy's suggestions or corrupt temptations for me to fight." In this life we have to struggle all the time against those corrupt influences, but what does scripture say? *Death, the last enemy, will be destroyed*. Once death is destroyed, you will have no enemy to fear; from that moment *the saying will come true: Death is swallowed up into victory* (1 Cor 15:26.54). That will be the day of triumph; then you will receive your crown.

"Very well, then: I will be crowned after the contest, but what shall I be doing after that?" God will *satisfy your longing with good things*. Even now you hear about what is good, and you are fired with longing; you hear about goodness and you sigh for it. Even when perhaps you fall into sin, you are deceived by your eagerness to choose what is good. You are trapped and guilty, because you did not listen to God's good advice about what to shun and what to choose. If you went wrong in your judgment of what the good was that you ought to choose, it must have been because you were too careless to learn. In whatever matter you sin, you are seeking some apparent good and desiring some kind of relief. The things you reach out for are good things, but they are bad for you if you have forsaken him who made them good. Seek your proper good, human soul. Another good thing

---

24. For this classical phrase, compare Expositions of Psalms 70,5, and 98,8 and Letter 194,19.
25. See Lk 21:18.

may be proper to some other creature, for all creatures have their own good ends, which promote their integrity and the perfection of their nature. Each imperfect being needs something different to make it perfect; and you must seek the good proper to yourself. *No one is good except one, God alone* (Mk 10:18). Your proper good is the highest good of all. If the supreme good is our good, can we lack anything? There are lower goods, to be sure, and various good things are right for various creatures. What is good for an animal, brothers and sisters, beyond filling its belly, having all its needs met, sleeping, playing happily, staying alive and well, and perpetuating its kind? These things are good for it. A measure of goodness is supplied and conceded to it within appropriate limits by God, the creator of all that exists. Is that the kind of good you are seeking? God gives that too, but do not seek that only. You are a fellow-heir with Christ;[26] can you regard fellowship with a beast as a cause for joy? Lift your hope higher to the Good of all goods. He made you good in your own kind, as he made all things good in their own kind, for God made all things exceedingly good, and he himself will be your good.

How, then, can we speak of that good which is God as "exceedingly good," when it has already been said of creation that *God made all things exceedingly good* (Gn 1:31)? What are we to say of that good, of whom scripture also says, *No one is good except one, God alone*? Is it enough to say that he is "exceedingly good" when we are immediately reminded of the paean uttered over creation, that *God made all things exceedingly good*? But what else can we say? Words fail us, but love does not. Our consideration of another psalm occurs to us: when we cannot articulate our thoughts, we must shout for joy.[27] God is good, but what kind of good he is, who can tell? We cannot put it into words, but we are not allowed to remain silent. This is our problem: we cannot find words, but our sheer joy does not permit us to be silent; so let us neither speak nor hold our tongues. But what are we to do, if we can neither speak nor keep silence? Let us shout for joy. *Let us shout for joy to God, our salvation; shout with joy to God, all the earth* (Pss 94(95):1; 99(100):1). What does that mean: *Shout for joy?* Give vent to the inarticulate expression of your joys, belch out[28] all your happiness to him. What kind of belching will there be after the final feasting, if even now after a modest meal our souls are so deeply affected? When we have been redeemed from every form of corruption, when the psalm's prediction has come true, that *he satisfies your longing with good things*, what will our joy be then?

---

26. See Rom 8:17.
27. *Iubilemus.* See Augustine's remarks in his Exposition of Psalms 94,3, and 99,3-4.
28. *Eructate*, as in Ps 44:2(45:1). Augustine maintains the gastronomic metaphor in the following lines.

The myth of the eagle

9. The psalmist seems to hear you asking, "When will he satisfy me? I am not satisfied now. Whichever way I turn it is the same: something kindles my desire, but when I get it, it seems to me contemptible. As long as I don't possess certain things I crave them, but as soon as I have them they seem not worth having. Is there any good thing that can satisfy me?" Yes, there is: praising God. "But even with that my soul is not filled or brought to perfection,[29] for *the corruptible body weighs down the soul, and this earthly dwelling oppresses a mind that considers many things* (Wis 9:15). Other pleasures[30] concerning the demands of my perishable nature wrench me away from the praise of God. When will my longing be satisfied with good things?"

When, you ask? *Your youth will be renewed like an eagle's.* Are you wondering when your soul will be sated with good things? When your youth has been restored. But the psalm adds, *like an eagle's.* Undoubtedly there is some hidden meaning here. All the same, we cannot pass over without comment what is often reported about the eagle, since to understand it is germane to our purpose. This conviction only must be lodged in our hearts: that the comparison, *your youth will be renewed like an eagle's,* was not made by the Holy Spirit without good reason. He used it to signify to us some kind of resurrection, for indeed an eagle's youth is restored, though not for immortal life. A simile was drawn from a mortal object to signify as best it could an immortal reality, though it could never reveal that clearly.[31] When an eagle is oppressed by its aging body, popular belief holds that it is prevented from eating by the excessive growth of its beak. The upper section of the beak, which hooks over the lower section, has grown so excessively long with advancing age that it hinders the opening of the mouth by blocking the aperture between the upper and the lower parts of the beak. If there is no space between them, the bird cannot use its beak like pincers, to tear off the food before swallowing it. Thus as the upper part of the beak grows to excess and hooks over too far, the eagle cannot open its mouth to seize anything. This is what old age does to it. Weighed down by the weariness of age and malnutrition it becomes extremely weak, for both misfortunes afflict it at the same time—age and starvation. Accordingly, so it is said, the eagle responds to a certain natural instinct that enables it in some sense to restore its youth. It dashes and hits against a rock what we might call its upper lip, that overgrown piece that blocks the food passage. The bird chips it away by beating it on the rock and thus rids itself of the onerous beak that has prevented it from eating. Then it finds

---

29. So the CCL editors. Variant, supported by all codices: "Even that is not carried out properly or brought to perfection in my soul."
30. Variant: "other thoughts."
31. On the myth of the eagle, which Augustine proceeds to expound, see the note at Exposition of Psalm 66,10.

food, and everything about it is restored; after that period of old age it becomes like a young eagle again. Strength returns to the limbs, the plumage regains its sheen, the wings recover full power and skill, and the bird soars to the heights as it used to. A kind of resurrection has taken place.

This is the meaning that the simile was used to convey, like the other simile of the moon, which, after waning and being apparently spirited away, is reborn and grows full again. The moon too is a sign of resurrection for us, but it does not remain at the full; it wanes once more, that the sign may be repeatedly present. The same is true of the myth about the eagle, for the eagle is not restored to immortal life as we are. Nonetheless the eagle is valuable for us as a sign that what gets in our way can be removed from us by the rock.[32]

Do not be over-confident in your own powers. The firmness of the rock smashes your old degeneracy away from you, and the rock is Christ.[33] In Christ our youth, like the eagle's, will be restored. It is true that old age has come upon us as we live among our enemies; the lament of another psalm is well known: *I have grown old in all my enemies* (Ps 6:8(7)). What caused this aging process? Our mortal flesh, this flesh that is but grass,[34] and so a psalmist confesses, *My heart is stricken and dried up like grass, because I forgot to eat my bread* (Ps 101:5(102:4)). He points to the trouble: *I forgot to eat my bread.* Old age has brought excess and closed his mouth; let it be battered against the rock.

The Holy Trinity alone will satisfy our longing

10. The assurance in our present psalm, that *he satisfies your longing with good things*, might prompt the soul to reply, "I shall never be satisfied with mortal things. No temporal goods will ever satisfy me. Let him grant me something eternal, let what is eternal be his gift to me. Let him give me his Wisdom, let him give me his Word who is God with God. Let him give me himself, God the Father, the Son, and the Holy Spirit. I am standing like a beggar at his door. I am calling out to him, and he is not asleep; so let him give me those three loaves."

You remember the gospel: look how useful it is to be familiar with God's letter.[35] Those who have read it were stirred when I said this. You will recall how a certain man who was in need went to his friend's house and begged for three loaves. The friend had been asleep and answered him, *I have already gone to bed, and my children here with me are asleep* (Lk 11:7). But the caller persisted

---

32. The immediate verbal allusion is to Ps 136(137):9, but Augustine goes on to point out the Christological sense.
33. See 1 Cor 10:4.
34. See Is 40:6.
35. Evidently the congregation's reaction indicated that they had picked up the allusion. On the designation of the scriptures as a letter from God, see Exposition of Psalm 73,5 and the note there.

with his request and, by making a nuisance of himself, wheedled out of the other what he could not get as a friendly favor. God, by contrast, wants to give, but he will give only to one who asks, for he is careful not to give to anyone who lacks the capacity to receive. He does not want to be awakened by your wearisome demands,[36] for when you pray you are not being a nuisance to a sleeper: *He will not sleep or be drowsy, the guardian of Israel* (Ps 120(121):4). Once only did Christ fall asleep, that his bride might be drawn from his side: he fell asleep on the cross, that is plain to see. He died, that he might say, *I rested and fell asleep.* But will he not go further and rise again, he who has fallen asleep?[37] Indeed he will, and therefore in that earlier psalm he goes on, *And I arose, because the Lord will uphold me* (Ps 3:6(5)). What does the apostle say? *Rising from the dead, Christ will never die again, nor will death ever again have the mastery over him* (Rom 6:9).

He does not sleep, but make sure that your faith does not sleep. Let the soul, already filled with longing, voice its desire to be satisfied with that sublime, inexpressible good, that good to which and about which we can shout for joy, but which we can scarcely explain at all. Already the soul wants it, and has some inkling of it, but knows itself to be hampered by the crushing weight of the body and therefore unable to attain total satisfaction in this life. And so the soul protests, "How can you promise me, 'Your longing will be assuaged with good things'? I well know what good it is that I desire, I know what will content me, for I find Philip expressing the same desire: *Show us the Father, and that is enough for us.* He seemed to imply that the Father alone was the object of his desire; but the Lord showed him the three desirable loaves. The Lord himself, true bread, was one loaf and directed Philip's attention to the gifts already given: *Have I been all this time with you, and yet you have not known the Father? Whoever sees me, Philip, also sees the Father.* He also promised the Spirit, *whom the Father will send in my name*, he said; but of this Spirit he also promised, *I will send him to you from the Father* (Jn 14:8,9,26; 15:26). The Spirit is a gift equal to himself. Yes, I know very well what I am longing for. But when shall I be fully satisfied? Even now I think about the Trinity, and I have some notion of the Trinity. But it is like looking at a confused reflection in a mirror;[38] I dare to claim some notion of it, but when shall I be satisfied?"

Your youth will be renewed like an eagle's. You are not fully satisfied now because your soul is not adapted to that great food, that solid food. It lacks the capacity for that food while its beak is closed. Old age has blocked your mouth, but the rock has been provided for you, on which you may chip away the

---

36. *Non taedio tuo vult excitari*, so most codices. A variant substitutes *nam* for *non*, reversing the sense: "For he wants to be awakened. . . ."
37. See Ps 40:9(41:8). Commenting on that verse in his Expositions of Psalm 40, Augustine alludes to the creation of the Church, the new Eve, from the side of the new Adam, as here.
38. See 1 Cor 13:12.

encrustation of age. Then will your youth be restored like that of the eagle, and
you will be able to eat your bread, which is he who said, *I am the living bread
which has come down from heaven* (Jn 6:41). *Your youth will be renewed like an
eagle's*, and then you will be satisfied with good things.

*Verse 6. Demand justice only if there is nothing in you that deserves
punishment*

11. *The Lord it is who exercises mercy, and gives judgment for those who are
injured.* This is what he is doing now, brothers and sisters, even before we attain
that eagle-like renewal, even before we are satisfied with good things; for how is
it with us here, on this journey we are making? How is it with us in this life?[39] Are
we forsaken? No. *The Lord it is who exercises mercy.* But notice how he shows
himself merciful, not abandoning us in the desert, never leaving us alone in the
wilderness, until we reach our homeland. He is certainly the one who exercises
mercy, but to whom? *Blessed are the merciful, for they shall obtain mercy* (Mt
5:7). You heard him say that, brothers and sisters, when the gospel was being
read. No one whose own attitudes are unmerciful should expect to find God
merciful toward himself.

But now learn what the scope of your mercy must be; make sure that you do
not think of it as due to your friend but not to your enemy. The gospel commands,
Love your enemies (Mt 5:44). You hope to be fully satisfied with the good things
of God; make sure then that mercy gets its fill in you. A mercy fully satisfied is
mercy made perfect, mercy that loves, that deliberately loves,[40] even someone
who hates the lover. I stress this because of your objection, "What am I to do? If I
undertake to love my enemy, does it mean that I shall have to accept injuries, and
suffer under them, and not avenge myself, even though the laws are available to
award me my rights?" That you should demand redress is no more than justice;
you are granted this concession because it is just. First make sure there is nothing
in yourself calling for punishment, and then go ahead and claim your rights.
When you object, "Can't I avenge myself then? Surely I can?" you make it sound
as though God were suppressing the justice of the plaintiff's cause, whereas he is
in fact stamping out the pride of the one who seeks to punish a wrongdoer.

What about the adulterous woman in the gospel? Did she not deserve to be
stoned? If she had been stoned, would any injustice have been done? If such a
punishment was inequitable, so was the law that enjoined it. The law did enjoin
it, God enjoined it; but you, you zealots for its enforcement, are you not sinners
yourselves? The adulterous woman was led to judgment, to be stoned under the

---

39. Variant: ". . . on this road?"
40. *Quae amat, quae diligit. . . .* The choice of words brings out the willed element. *Amor* can be
instinctual; *dilectio* is the love of choice.

law, but he to whom she was brought was the lawgiver. You are ferocious, you who dragged her there, but consider who you are, who breathe fury, and against whom your ferocity is directed. If you are a sinner ferociously pursuing a sinner, lay your ferocity aside and confess first; if you, a sinner, are loosing your savagery against a sinner, let it go. He knows what he ought to think about this woman, how he should judge her case, how to spare her and how to heal her. Your ferocity is authorized by the law, is it? But the legislator knows how to act according to the law on which you take your stand; he knows even better than you.

At the time when the woman was presented to him, the Lord had already bent down and was writing on the ground. He wrote on the earth when he bent down to the earth; before bending down to the earth he had written not on earth but on stone. The earth began to be fruitful, for it was to bring forth its abundance when sown with the letters of the Lord. Of old he had written the law on stone to signify the hard-heartedness of the Jews; now he wrote on earth, to signify the fertility of Christians.

The Jews came, leading the adulterous woman to him. They were like raging waves, dashing themselves against the rock; but his response broke their force. *Anyone of you who knows himself to be without sin shall be the first to throw a stone at her* (Jn 8:7), he said. And bending down again, he continued to write on the ground. Each one of them examined his own conscience, and they melted away. It was not the weak, adulterous woman who drove them off, but their own befouled consciences. They wanted to punish her, they decided to judge; they came to the rock, but on the rock the judges foundered.[41]

Almsgiving is mercy shown to the just

12. *The Lord it is who exercises mercy*, but to whom? *Blessed are the merciful, for they shall obtain mercy*. Show mercy to everyone. But what mercy can you show to a just person? Mercy in this case means attending to his or her bodily needs. Resources may be scanty on your part, but God will not be short of anything, and therefore you will be the chief beneficiary from what you do. Give to the passing beggar who asks you. You are on the lookout for a just person to whom you can give alms, through whose intercession you may hope to be welcomed into the tents of eternity,[42] for *anyone who welcomes a just person inasmuch as he is a just person will receive the reward due to a just person* (Mt 10:41). This means that even as the beggar is on the watch for you, you are on the watch for a just person. Of the one it is said, *Give to everyone who asks you* (Lk 6:30), while of the other it is said: "Your alms should be sweating in your hands

---

41. See Ps 140(141):6.7.
42. See Lk 16:9.

until you find a just person to whom you may give it."[43] It may take you some time to find such a recipient, but go on looking and you will find one.

What will you give? Are you not rather the one who receives?[44] *If we have sown spiritual seeds for your benefit*, asks the scripture, *is it too much to ask that we reap a carnal harvest from you?* (1 Cor 9:11). Not long since, at the Lord's prompting, we expounded to you the scriptural teaching on this subject. The earth produces grass for grazing animals,[45] that is to say, carnal food for creatures that do the threshing, which is hard work, and we are warned, *You shall not muzzle an ox while it is threshing* (Dt 25:4; 1 Cor 9:9; 1 Tm 5:18). We exhorted you to be diligent in this matter, though with due caution and moderation. You should regard your charitable works as your assets. You surely do not suppose, brothers and sisters, that we are saying this to ensure that we ourselves benefit from your generosity? I think you can take this appeal as made in the name of the Lord. Weak though the voice may be that relays it to you, it is the apostle who speaks, reminding you that you yourselves will gain: *Not that I seek your gift: all I seek is the fruit accruing to you* (Phil 4:17).

What alms are you going to give, then, to a just person?[46] Elijah was fed not by the widow but by a raven,[47] because he who created the raven supplied Elijah's food. God is never without the means to provide for his own. For your part, consider what you are buying, when you must buy it, and what you must pay. You are purchasing the kingdom of heaven and the only chance you have to make the deal is now, in this life. But look how cheaply you can buy it! Whatever you are able to give, that is what it will cost you.

Distinctions to be observed with regard to gifts made to persons of immoral life

13. Exercise mercy toward a scoundrel, but not in his character as a scoundrel. You may not welcome an unrighteous person for the sake of his unrighteousness, as though your kindness were a mark of approval of his wicked conduct. We are forbidden to give to a sinner or to welcome sinners. But in that case, what becomes of the Lord's injunction, *Give to everyone who asks you?* And what about the command, *If your enemy is hungry, feed him* (Rom 12:20)?

---

43. These words, which are cited again in Exposition 3 of Psalm 103, 12, are treated by Augustine as if they were scriptural. They appear for the first time in *Didache* 1,6, where they are likewise quoted together with Lk 6:30.
44. Augustine goes on to apply the same principle to contributions made to Christian preachers and pastors.
45. See Ps 103(104):14.
46. A resumption of the question posed at the beginning of section 12, "What mercy can you show to a just person?"
47. See 1 Kgs 17:4-6.12.

There seems to be a contradiction here, but to those who knock in Christ's name the door will be opened, and these contradictory statements will become plain to all who seek. *Do not give to a sinner*, says scripture, and *Do not welcome a sinner* (Sir 12:6,4); yet the Lord commands, *Give to everyone who asks you.* "What if the person who asks me is a sinner?" you object. Then give, but not as to a sinner. In what circumstances would you be giving to someone precisely as to a sinner? When his or her sinful conduct so appeals to you that you want to give.

You must concentrate for a little while, beloved, until this question is sorted out with the help of examples, for it will be very useful for us to understand it. Scripture has told us, "If anyone, anyone at all, is hungry, and you have anything to give, give it. If you see that something must be given to relieve a person's needs, give it." Do not let your merciful, compassionate instincts remain dormant because it is a sinner who accosts you, for the one who accosts you is both a sinner and a human being. When I say, "A human being who is a sinner confronts you," I am giving that person two names, and neither name is redundant. This person bears the name, "human being," and the other name, "sinner." Their significance is different: as the work of God, he or she is a human being; as the work of a mortal creature, he or she is a sinner. Give, then, to God's work, but withhold your gift from the handiwork of a mortal.

"But how can you forbid me to give to what a mortal has made?" you ask. Well, think what it would mean to give to what someone has made of himself. It would mean to give to a sinner inasmuch as he is a sinner, bestowing your gift on him because you like him for his sin. "But who would ever do that?" you reply. Who would do it? I only wish that no one ever did, or at least not many, and at any rate not openly! But they do: what about those who make donations to gladiators?[48] Let them tell me why they give to such persons. Why does anyone offer presents to a gladiator? Because what he loves in such a person is his very depravity; what he feeds and clothes in a gladiator is the wickedness that is publicly displayed before all the spectators. If someone offers gifts to actors, to circus charioteers,[49] or to harlots, why does he offer them? You could say, "But those who make such gifts are giving to human beings, are they not?" All the same, what they have in view is not the nature that is God's work but the wickedness that is human work. Do you wish to see clearly what it is you are honoring in a gladiator when you adorn him? Only let someone say to you, "Be like him yourself!" After all, you are enamored of him, you applaud his triumphs, you are even willing to strip yourself to deck him out; so do not feel insulted if someone

---

48. *Venatoribus.* The word *venator* properly meant a hunter but was often used by Christian writers for one who fought with wild beasts in the arena.

49. On Augustine's severe attitude to all kinds of "shows" see his Expositions of Psalms 39,8 and 93,20 and the notes.

says to you, "I hope your children will turn out like him!" "But that is an insult," you reply. Why an insult, if not because of the wickedness involved? Why an insult, if not because it is a disgraceful occupation? When you make your donation you are giving not to courage but to depravity.

You can see now why anyone who gives payment to a gladiator is contributing not to a man but to a very wicked profession, for if the recipient were simply a man and not a gladiator you would not hold him in honor. What you laud in him is his vice, not his nature. Now look at the opposite case. Suppose you make a gift to a just person, or you give to a prophet, or you give to one of Christ's disciples something he needs, but you do not think of the one you help as a disciple of Christ, or as a servant of God, or as a dispenser of God's mysteries; all you think about is some temporal advantage to be gained. For instance, you may have tried to bribe him by slipping him some money, so that he will support your cause when you need him. If you make your gift in that spirit, you have no more given it to a just person than the contributor at the arena gave to a human being when he rewarded the gladiator.

So you see, dearest friends, that the distinction is perfectly plain, and although the matter was obscure to begin with, I think it is clear enough now. The Lord laid an obligation on you when he said, *Anyone who welcomes a just person. . ,* and that should have been sufficient. But it was possible that a just person might be welcomed with the wrong intention because he or she is thought useful in some temporal ploy, perhaps to pander to the donor's greed, or to help him entrap or oppress someone else. You might welcome a just person into your home because you hope for some such service from him. In this case the Lord debarred you from the reward due to a just person, but he did so only by the phrase he added. He said, *Anyone who welcomes a just person inasmuch as he is a just person,* which means, "welcomes him for that reason, in his capacity as a just person." He also said, *Anyone who welcomes a prophet,* but he did not leave it at that; he added, *inasmuch as he is a prophet,* which implies that you are honoring your guest because he is a prophet. Finally the Lord said, *Anyone who gives a cup of cold water to one of my little ones simply because he is a disciple*—that is, precisely because he is a disciple of Christ, precisely because he is a steward of Christ's mystery—*I tell you, he will not miss his reward* (Mt 10:41-42). It follows then that, as you understand the promise, *Anyone who welcomes a just person inasmuch as he is a just person will receive the reward due to a just person,* you must also understand that anyone who welcomes a sinner inasmuch as he or she is a sinner will lose all reward.

Be merciful to all; discipline your subordinates with charity; trust God to see justice done

14. To sum up, brothers and sisters, exercise mercy. This alone is the bond of charity, this alone is the vehicle which carries us from the present life into our homeland. Let your love extend even to your enemies, and be free of anxiety. Christ came to exclude revenge; that is why before he came a psalm said to him, *Out of the mouths of infants and nurslings you have perfected praise, in order to destroy the enemy and the avenger* (Ps 8:3(2)). Some codices read *defender* here, but *avenger* is the better reading.[50] The Lord willed to destroy the avenger—anyone, that is, who tries to avenge himself—by warning us that if we seek revenge our own sins will not be forgiven. "But does that mean all discipline must be relaxed?" you ask. "Will there be no place for correction?" Yes, there will be a place for it. What will you do with your son if he is living in a dissolute way? Will you not chastise him with a beating? And if you see that even your slave is living immorally, will you not check him with some penalty, perhaps with blows? This is perfectly proper; it has to be done. Not only does God allow it; he condemns us if we neglect it. But you must impose discipline with a loving intention, not in a spirit of vengeance.

In some circumstances, however, you will suffer from harm inflicted by people more powerful than yourself, where you are in no position to apply corrective discipline or even to admonish or give orders. Put up with it. Endure it with an untroubled mind. Listen to the gospel that was read just now: *Blessed will you be when people persecute you, and speak all kinds of evil against you untruthfully, because of my name* (Mt 5:11). Notice the concluding words: the Lord added *because of my name* to show that he did not mean evil spoken of you because you deserve it but only that which you incur because of God's righteousness. A person is not just simply because others curse him; but if he is just, and is unjustly cursed, he earns a reward.

In all situations, then, be merciful and do not worry. Extend your love even to your enemies. If offenders are under your authority, castigate and control them, but with love, with charity. Keep their eternal salvation in view, lest by sparing their bodies you allow their souls to perish. Make this your practice. You will have to endure injustice from many people[51] upon whom you have no right to impose discipline, since they are not under your authority; in these cases tolerate the wrongs done and keep your peace of mind, for *the Lord it is who exercises mercy, and gives judgment for those who are injured.* He will exercise mercy toward you if you have been merciful yourself; but you will deal mercifully,

---

50. When commenting on Psalm 8 Augustine preferred "defender"; see the note at Exposition of Psalm 8,6.

51. Variant: ". . . your practice and you will not have suffered sinners without being avenged."

secure in the knowledge that the injuries you suffer will not go unpunished. *Revenge is for me; I will see justice done, says the Lord* (Rom 12:19; Dt 32:35).

Verse 7. God's mysterious purpose in giving the law

15. *He made his ways known to Moses.* What were these ways of his that he made known to Moses? Why is Moses singled out? You must understand that Moses represents all just and holy people; the psalm mentioned one, but all are included.

However, it was through Moses that the law was given, and there is something mysterious about the promulgation of the law. The law was given that the patient's sickness might be diagnosed, and that he might beg for the doctor's aid. This is God's secret way. In an earlier verse you heard that *he heals all your diseases.* There was a time when those diseases in sick people were concealed; but then the five books were given to Moses. The pool was ringed by five porches; the law brought out the sick so that they could lie there, but only to be exposed, not healed. The five porches displayed the sick, without curing them. The pool did cure, but only when a single person went down and the pool was disturbed.[52] This disturbance of the pool occurred at the time of the Lord's passion, for he came as someone unknown, and some said, "He is the Messiah"; others, "No, he isn't." "He is a good man." "He is a sinner." "He is a fine teacher." "He is a charlatan." He stirred up the water, which means that he disturbed the people; and in all that stirring of the water only one was healed, because unity is preserved by the Lord's passion. No one who is outside this unity can be healed, even though he may lie in the porches, because even if he holds to the law, he does not reach salvation.

All this conceals a mystery, for scripture teaches that the law was given in order to show up sinners and drive them to appeal to the doctor for grace. Paul portrayed himself in the character of one thus diagnosed: *Who will deliver me from this death-ridden body, wretch that I am?* The conflict within himself had been revealed to him by means of the commandment, as he explained: *I am aware of a different law in my members that opposes the law of my mind, and imprisons me under the law of sin inherent in my members.* He recognized his miserable condition as he groaned and struggled in the conflict; he was at war with himself, out of tune with himself and pulled apart. He longed for peace, true peace, heavenly peace; and what did he say? *Who will deliver me from this death-ridden body, wretch that I am? Only the grace of God, through Jesus Christ our Lord* (Rom 7:23-25). But *where sin abounded, grace abounded all the more.* How did sin abound? *The law entered stealthily that sin might abound*

---

52. See Jn 5:2-4.

(Rom 5:20). How did the intrusion of the law cause sin to increase? Because men and women had refused to confess that they were sinners, when the law was introduced they became law-breakers as well. No one is a law-breaker unless he or she has transgressed against a law; the apostle himself points out that *where there is no law, there is no violation of it* (Rom 4:15). Sin abounded, therefore, only that grace might be superabundant.

This is why, as I was saying, there is a deep mystery about the law. It was given so that, as sin multiplied, proud people might be humbled, and being humbled might confess, and having confessed might be healed. These are the hidden ways that God made known to Moses, through whom he gave a law which would serve to increase sin, in order that grace might increase even more. This was no cruel dealing on God's part but medical strategy. Sometimes a person who is genuinely ill thinks himself well, and because he is unaware of his sickness he does not seek a doctor. But if the disease worsens and becomes more threatening the doctor is called in, and there is complete healing.

He made his ways known to Moses, and his will to the children of Israel. To all the children of Israel? No, only to the true children of Israel—but in fact that means all of them, because the guileful, the treacherous and the hypocritical are not children of Israel. Who are the children of Israel? *Look, there is a true Israelite, in whom there is no guile* (Jn 1:47). *He made his will known to the children of Israel.*

Verse 8. God's long patience calls sinners to repent

16. *The Lord is compassionate and merciful, long-suffering and richly merciful.* Could there ever be any greater instance of long-suffering? People sin, yet go on living; sins are piled on sins, yet life only increases; God is blasphemed every day, yet he makes his sun rise over good and bad alike.[53] On every side he calls us to amend, from every quarter he summons us to repent. He calls through the blessings of creation, he calls by granting us a prolongation of our lives, he calls through the reader, he calls through the preacher, he calls through our inmost thoughts, he calls through the corrective scourge, he calls through his comforting mercy: he is *long-suffering and richly merciful.*

But be careful not to abuse the long-drawn mercy of God and store up anger for yourself against the day of his wrath, as the apostle warns: *Do you despise his generous kindness and forbearance, and his long restraint, not realizing that God is patient only to lead you to repentance?* (Rom 2:4) Do you imagine that you are pleasing to him, just because he spares you? Not at all. *All this you did, and I was silent; you were wrong to think that I will be like you* (Ps 49(50):21), he says. "Your sins are not acceptable to me; but in my endless patience I look for good actions on your part. If I were to punish sins, I would never find any people

_____

53. See Mt 5:45.

confessing their sins." By sparing you, God in his long-suffering kindness leads you to repentance, yet you keep on saying with every day that passes, "Today is nearly over, and I can carry on in the same way tomorrow, for tomorrow will not be my last day. And then there will be another. . . ." And suddenly his anger falls on you. My brother, my sister, *do not delay in turning back to the Lord* (Sir 5:8). There are people who mean to be converted, but keep putting it off; they are for ever crying, "Cras, cras!" like a raven.[54] A raven was sent out of the ark, and did not return. What God wants is not the procrastination of the raven's cry but the moaning confession of the dove. When the dove was sent forth, she did return.[55] How long will you go on crying, "Cras, cras"? Watch out for that last "tomorrow." You do not know when the last one will be; all that matters is that you have lived as a sinner until today. You have heard the warning, you are accustomed to hearing it frequently and you have heard it again today; but though you hear it daily, you daily neglect to correct yourself. *With your hard and impenitent heart you are storing up against yourself anger that will be manifest on the day of God's just judgment, for he will render to each and all as their deeds deserve* (Rom 2:5-6). Do not so misrepresent God's mercy to yourself as to lose sight of his justice. "*The Lord is compassionate and merciful*: I am glad to hear that," you say. Fine: hear it and rejoice. The psalm went further and added, *Long-suffering and richly merciful*; but the final words tell you that he is also constant.[56] You find joy in the earlier statements; tremble at the closing phrase. God is merciful and long-suffering in such a way that he is also constant. If you have stored up anger for yourself against the day of wrath, will you not then experience as just the God with whose kindness you have trifled?

Verses 9-13. God's merciful dealings: chastisement, forgiveness, and grace

17. *He will not be angry to the end, nor will his indignation last for ever.* The very fact that we live amid the scourges and corruption[57] inseparable from our mortality is a mark of his indignation, for our lot is the result of the first sin. We should not concentrate on avoiding only his threats about the future, brothers and sisters; we must also shun his anger in the present. The apostle teaches that both we and he himself inherit a nature marked by God's anger, for he confesses, *By nature we too were children of wrath, like the rest* (Eph 2:3). The lot of men and women is to be pilgrims here, and to labor, and this is the effect of God's anger. Can we doubt that his anger was expressed, brothers and sisters, in the

54. Literally "Tomorrow, tomorrow!" but the harsh sound of *cras, cras* in Latin reminds Augustine of a raven's cry.
55. See Gn 8:6-12.
56. Some witnesses omit these last words.
57. Variant: "correction."

sentence passed upon our primal ancestor:[58] *In the sweat of your face you shall eat your bread, for the earth will bring forth thorns and thistles for you* (Gn 3:19.18)? If you think this is not a fair picture of our life, see if you can find any pleasure in which there are no thorns. Choose what you want to be—a miser, a libertine, to mention only two. Or add a third possibility—an ambitious place-seeker. What a crop of thorns springs up in the quest for honors! How many thorns there are in the indulgence of lust, how many thorns in burning avarice! How much harassment do base loves bring with them? How much vexation do they create in this life? I am not even speaking of hell. Be careful not to become a hell for yourself.

All this is the effect of God's anger, brothers and sisters. Even if you have turned back to God and are living righteously, you cannot be exempt from hard labor on earth; and the labor does not end until our wayfaring itself is finished. We have to labor on the way, that we may rejoice when we reach home. The psalm therefore comforts you in your toil, your sweat and all your vexations; it comforts you with the promise, *He will not be angry to the end, nor will his indignation last for ever.*

18. *He has not dealt with us according to our sins.* Thanks be to God, that he did not will to do so. We have not received what we deserved. *He has not dealt with us according to our sins, nor requited us in accordance with our iniquities; for in proportion to the height of heaven above earth has the Lord consolidated his mercy over those who fear him.* Consider that statement. *The Lord has consolidated his mercy over those who fear him*: in what measure? *In proportion to the height of heaven above earth.* What has the psalm said? If heaven can ever desert its duty of protecting the earth, God will be able to cease protecting those who fear him. Look up at the sky. Everywhere, on every side, it serves as a protective covering for the earth; there is no place on earth not shielded by the sky. People sin under the sky, they commit all sorts of evils under the sky, yet still the sky protects them. From there comes light for the eyes, from there comes the air we breathe, from there the winds, from there the rain needed by the earth to nourish its crops. All this merciful provision comes from the sky. Take away from the earth the sky's bounty, and the earth will promptly wither. As the sky's protection abides over the earth, so does the Lord's protection abide over those who fear him. If you hold God in awe, his protection is over you. Perhaps you are buffeted by misfortune and think God has forsaken you. Only if the sky's protection has withdrawn from the earth could that be true, for *in proportion to the height of heaven above earth has the Lord consolidated his mercy over those who fear him.*

---

58. Variant: "spoken by our creator."

19. What has he done? We have heard that he has not requited us according to our sins. *As far as the east is from the west has he distanced our sins from us.* In proportion to the sky's height above earth has the Lord consolidated his mercy over us. I have told you why: for protection. How does he protect us? *As far as the east is from the west has he distanced our sins from us.* Those who are initiated into the sacraments know what this means; but I will speak of what everyone may hear. When sin is pardoned your sins set and your grace rises: it is sunset for your sins and sunrise for the grace that liberates you. *Truth has sprung up from the earth* (Ps 84:12(85:11)). What does that mean—*truth has sprung up from the earth*? Your grace is newly-born, your sins die, and you are somehow made new. You should be looking toward the east and away from the west.[59] Turn away from your sins and turn toward the grace of God. As your sins sink down you arise and stride forward.

Admittedly the region of the sky that sees the sunrise will be overcome by darkness again later. Similes can never be perfectly adequate, but the thing used for purposes of comparison can be helpfully aligned with the realities to which they correspond. We saw this in connection with the eagle and with the moon, and the same is true here. One quarter of the sky sinks into darkness, while sunrise irradiates another, but the region that is bright now will lose its light twelve hours later. Very different is the sunrise of grace for us: our sins sink down for ever, and grace abides everlastingly.

20. Why *has he distanced our sins from us, as far as the east is from the west,* so that they set as grace arises? Why do you think he has done so? Because *as a father feels compassion for his children, so has the Lord been compassionate toward those who fear him.* Let him be as angry with us as he likes: he is still our father. "But he has whipped us and afflicted us and beaten us!" Yes, because he is our father. If you must weep, child, weep in submission to your father; do not weep in anger or out of wounded pride. What you endure, what makes you cry, is a medicine, not a punishment; it is chastisement, but not condemnation. If you do not want to be thrust out of your inheritance, do not thrust away the whip. Focus your mind not on how much the whipping hurts but on keeping your place in his will.[60] *As a father feels compassion for his children, so has the Lord been compassionate toward those who fear him.*

---

59. This was done literally during the richly symbolic rites of baptism. Cyril of Jerusalem gives in his *Catecheses* a full description of the practice at Jerusalem in the fourth century. The candidate for baptism solemnly renounced Satan facing west, "since the west is the region of darkness, and Satan, being darkness himself, has darkness as his dominion." Then the candidate turned to the east, because "there is opened for you God's paradise, which he planted in the east . . . which is why you turn from west to east, to the place of lights." A profession of faith in the Holy Trinity followed. See Cyril, *Cat.* 19,4.9.

60. *In testamento*. "Will" here, rather than "covenant," since the context deals with inheritance; but the word is always laden with meanings in Christian Greek or Latin. Compare Heb 8:6-13; 9:15-17.

Verses 14-16. The transience of frail humanity; the eternity of the Word

21. *For he knows how we are framed*, and therefore knows our frailty. He knows what he made, how it fell, how it is to be repaired, how enriched. We were created from mud: *the first man was from the earth, earthly, but the second man is from heaven, heavenly* (1 Cor 15:47). God even sent his own Son; he who is God, pre-existent before all things, was created as a man. He was the "second man" as to the time of his coming, but the first to return, for many had died before he died, but he rose again before them all. *He knows how we are framed*. What is this frame we bear? Ourselves. Why do you speak of his knowing it, psalmist? Because he looked on it with pity.

Remember that we are dust: the psalmist turns to God himself to make this plea, as though God could forget. No; so well does he know us, so compassionately does he understand us, that he does not forget. Why, then, the plea, *Remember*? May your mercy continue unfailingly in our regard. You do know how we are fashioned, certainly, but do not forget how weak is this frame of ours, lest we forget your grace. *Remember that we are dust*.

22. *As for human beings, their days are like grass*. Let human beings keep in mind what human nature is, and not be proud, for *their days are like grass*. What pretext has grass for pride, grass which is in flower for the moment but withers so soon? What is the point of pride in grass which is green only for a little while, until the sun grows hot? We are fortunate that God's mercy rests upon us, to make gold out of grass. *As for human beings, their days are like grass; they shall bloom like a flower of the field*. The whole panoply of human glory—honors, sovereignty, wealth, men's bluster and conceit—all this is no more than a transitory wild flower. A great house flourishes, a family flourishes, many great people flourish, but how many years do they last? It seems like many years to you, but it is a brief span to God. God does not reckon as you do. Compared with the duration of long-drawn ages, any great house flourishes as fleetingly as a flower in the field. The whole beauty of our year is scarcely of a year's duration. The vigorous growth, the brilliant blossom, the fair display will not last out the year; none of these can be persuaded to put on their show all the year round. In how short a season do the flowers fade away, those flowers which are the plants' beauty! What is most lovely falls soonest. *All flesh is but grass, and human glory like the flower of grass. The grass is dried up and its flower wilted, but the word of the Lord abides for ever.* (Is 40:6,8)

The Father recognized our fragile frame and knew that we were but grass, flowering only for a brief spell; and therefore he sent his Word to us. He made his eternally abiding Word a brother to that grass. He caused the Word, who is his only-begotten Son by nature, his only Son born from his own substance, to become the brother of a multitude of adopted brothers and sisters. Do not be amazed to hear that you will share in his eternity, for he first willed to share in your ephemeral humanity. Will he deny you a destiny far above you, he who first took to himself your lowliness? Men and women, considered in themselves, are *like grass; they shall bloom like a flower in the field.*

23. *The wind will blow*[61] *over them and they will not tarry, nor will they know their place any more.* This looks like ruin and destruction. Consider people who are puffed up and conceited, exalting themselves: *The wind will blow over them and they will not tarry, nor will they know their place anymore.* Look at such people dying every day; that will be all there is, that will be the end of them. But the psalmist is not addressing grass as grass; he speaks to you, on whose account even the Word became grass. You are human, and for your sake the Word himself became human. You are flesh, and for your sake the Word was made flesh. *All flesh is but grass*, yet *the Word was made flesh* (Jn 1:14). How greatly, then, should grass hope, since the Word became flesh! That which abides eternally did not disdain to take to himself our grass, that grass might not despair of itself.

Verses 17-19. God's ultimate justice; charity fulfills the law

24. When you consider yourself, think about your lowly nature, and remember that you are dust. Do not give yourself airs. If you are anything better than this, you are so by his grace; only his mercy has endowed you with anything more. Listen to the next verse: *But the mercy of the Lord is from eternity and unto eternity upon those who fear him.* If you do not fear him you will be no more than grass, mixed with other grasses and in torment with all the rest; for though your flesh will rise again, it will only be for anguish. But let all who fear him rejoice, because his mercy rests upon them.

25. *And his saving justice is for their children's children.* The psalm speaks of rewards in store for our *children's children*, but how many servants of God have no children, much less grandchildren? By our *children* the psalm means our actions; and our *children's children* are the rewards of our actions. *His saving justice is for the children's children of those who keep his covenant.* This is a warning that all and sundry must not presume that the rewards are meant for them; they must choose while it is still open to them to choose: *Those who keep his covenant*, says the psalm, *and hold his commandments in their memory, to observe them.* You were getting ready to show off, weren't you, when you heard the word *memory*, and were about to reel off the psalter to me, which I do not

---

61. Variant: "has blown."

know by heart, or perhaps to recite the whole law from memory?[62] You are undoubtedly better than I in the matter of memory, and better than any righteous person who cannot reproduce the law word for word; but make sure you keep an equally firm hold on the commandments.[63] How are you to keep hold of them? Not with your memory, but with your life. Keep his commandments in mind, but not in order merely to recite them, but rather *to observe them.*

Someone may be troubled in spirit on hearing that. "Who can keep all God's commandments in mind? Who can remember the whole of scripture? Truly I want to keep the commandments in my actions, not just to keep hold of them in my memory, but who can ever remember them all?" Don't worry; the task will not be too burdensome. *On two commandments depend all the law and the prophets* (Mt 22:40). "But I want to remember the whole law." Remember it if you can, wherever you can, however you can. Whatever page of it you consult, it will tell you, "Hold onto what you hold already, but above all hold onto charity, for *the end of the commandment is charity*" (1 Tm 1:5). Do not worry about the multitude of branches; grasp the root, and you have the whole tree in you. Such people *hold his commandments in their memory, to observe them.*

26. *The Lord has established*[64] *his throne in heaven.* Of whom can this be said, that he has established his throne in heaven—of whom but Christ? He who descended and later ascended, who died and rose again, who raised up to heaven the humanity he had assumed, he has established his throne in heaven. A throne is where a judge sits; take care, then, you who hear this, for he *has established his throne in heaven.* Let each do as he or she has determined on earth; but sin will not go unpunished, nor will righteous living be without fruit, for the Lord who was mocked when he stood before a mortal judge has established his own judicial throne in heaven. *The Lord has established his throne in heaven, and his kingdom will be sovereign over all.* As another psalm says, *the kingship is the Lord's, and he will hold sway over the nations* (Ps 21:29(22:28)). *His kingdom will be sovereign over all.*

Verses 20-22. Angelic homage

27. *Bless the Lord, all you his angels, mighty in strength and obedient to his word.* Apply this verse to yourself, mortal. You are not yet just or faithful when you hear the word; you must also carry it out. The angels are *mighty in strength and obedient to his word, ready to hearken to every word he speaks.*

---

62. From various remarks in the course of his *Expositions* it is evident that many of Augustine's hearers were illiterate. The teasing in the text here casts an interesting light on the power of memory in societies less dependent than ours on the written word.

63. Augustine plays on different senses of *tenere* in the rest of this section: to "keep something in one's memory" and to "keep the commandments."

64. Variant: "will establish."

28. *Bless the Lord, all you who are his powers, his servants who do his bidding.* All you angels, all you who are mighty in strength, all you who obey his word, all you his servants who do his bidding, all of you, bless the Lord. Among us humans, all who live sinfully curse the Lord by their lives, even if their tongues are silent. What is the use of singing a hymn with your tongue, if your life breathes sacrilege? By your wicked conduct you have set many tongues wagging in blasphemy. Your tongue is occupied with hymn-singing, but the tongues of those who see you are busy with blasphemies.

If you want to bless the Lord, do his will. Build on rock, not on sand. To hear and not carry out what you hear is to build on sand. Anyone who neither hears the word nor acts according to it does not build at all. If you build on sand, you are building something ready to topple; if you build nothing, you will be exposed to rain, floods and wind, and you will be swept away before you can secure a footing.[65] Our job is not to take things easy but to build, and not to put up a shaky structure that will crumble into ruins but to build on rock so that temptation does not overthrow our work. If this is what you are engaged on, bless the Lord. If it is not, do not congratulate your tongue, but interrogate your life, and let that give you an account of itself. When you find what is evil there, groan and confess. Your confession itself can be a way of blessing the Lord, but let a change of conduct in you be a continuous blessing.

29. *Bless the Lord, all his works, in every place where he rules.* That means everywhere. If there is any place where his lordship is not supreme, let him not be blessed there; but there is none. Let him be blessed *in every place where he rules.* No one can plead, "I cannot bless the Lord in the east, because he has departed for the west," or "I cannot bless him in the west, because he is in the east." *Neither from the east, nor from the west, nor from the deserted mountains,* for the judge is God (Ps 74:7-8(75:6-7)). Universal is his presence, that universal may be the blessing offered him; universally is he blessed, that from every place we may shout with joy to him; universal is the blessing sung to him, that in every quarter he may be praised by holy lives. *Bless the Lord, all his works.* When you begin to bless the Lord by living a good life, it is his own works and not your merits that are blessing him. He performs good actions through you and in you, as the apostle teaches: *Work out your own salvation in fear and trembling; for it is God who is at work in you* (Phil 2:12-13). You might have prided yourself on obeying his word and carrying out his will, but he made sure you would not; he wanted you to be humbled about it by acknowledging his grace, which enabled you to act *in every place where he rules.*

---

65. See Mt 7:24-27.

Bless the Lord, O my soul. This last verse is the same as the first. The psalm began with blessing and ends with blessing. We set out from blessing; let us return to blessing, that in blessing we may reign at last.

Exposition 1 of Psalm 103

First Sermon[1]

The spiritual and the literal senses of this psalm

1. We trust that you remember, holy friends,[2] how lavishly you were fed the day before yesterday; yet even after that lengthy sermon you were still very hungry when you let us go. For this reason we did not think you should be denied what we owe you today. The present sermon stands on the debit side, though the preceding one stands as credit.

The psalm which has been read to us is almost entirely composed of figurative statements and mysterious expressions, which demand close attention not on our part only but also on yours. However, all that the psalm says is rich in religious significance even when taken literally; for many of God's creative works are enumerated here, though not all. To us who contemplate them these works are pointers to God, provided that we have learned to discern his invisible reality through the created things we can see.[3] We behold a vast fabric consisting of sky and earth and all things within them, and from the greatness and beauty of all that is crafted we have some inkling of the greatness and beauty of the craftsman himself. We do not yet see him, but we already love him. We do not yet possess the purity of heart that would make us fit to contemplate him, but he has never ceased to display his works before our eyes, so that through seeing what we can see we may love him whom we cannot see and be enabled to see him eventually in virtue of our love.

Nonetheless we must also search for the spiritual sense in everything the psalm has said. Your desires will help us in Christ's name as we seek it out, for with those desires you knock with invisible hands at an invisible door, that it may be invisibly opened to you and you may invisibly enter to be invisibly healed.

---

1. Probably preached at Carthage. Tentatively assigned to the summer of 411; on this dating see the Exposition of Psalm 66,1 and the note there. Other commentators prefer 404 or 409.
2. *Sanctitatem vestram.*
3. See Rom 1:20.

Verse 1. If God is always great, how can he be magnified?

2. Let us all say, then, *Bless the Lord, O my soul.*[4] Let us all address our one soul, because on account of our common faith all of us have but one soul. All of us who believe in Christ, whoever we are, form one single person in virtue of the unity of his body. Let our soul bless the Lord for his great favors and for all his gifts of grace, so many and so splendid. We shall find these gifts of God in our psalm if we approach it with keen attention, shaking off the murk of carnal thoughts. We must listen with our minds alert insofar as we can, with the eye of our heart pure, to the extent that this is possible for us. In the measure that our present life does not get in the way, nor the desire for temporal things distract us, nor worldly greed blind us, we shall be alert to hear of the glorious gifts of God, gifts joyous and beautiful, desirable and full of gladness.[5] The writer who conceived this psalm was contemplating such gifts in his spirit, and in the delight of his vision he burst out, *Bless the Lord, O my soul.*

3. *O Lord my God, you are exceedingly magnified.* Consider the magnificent things of which the psalmist is about to tell us. God alone, the author of all that is magnificent, is to be praised for these magnificent works. *You have clothed yourself in confession and seemliness.*

O Lord my God, you are said to be *exceedingly magnified*, but how can this be so? Are you not always great? Are you not always magnificent? Is it possible for you to be less than perfect, and so have room to grow? Do you ever weaken, are you ever diminished? No, because you are what you are; and because you exist in all fullness, you revealed your name to your servant Moses: *I AM WHO AM* (Ex 3:14). You are therefore unquestionably great, and your greatness is everlasting, without beginning or end. It does not begin with the beginning of time, nor does it run out when time ends, nor does it undergo change anywhere in between; for your greatness is immutable. How then can it be said that *you are exceedingly magnified*?

Another psalm gives us a hint when it says, *Your knowledge has become wonderful in my eyes* (Ps 138(139):6). If it is correct to say, *Your knowledge has become wonderful in my eyes*, it is also correct to say, *O Lord my God, you are exceedingly magnified* in my regard. But this too leaves us with a question. Is my God magnified in consequence of anything I do? That would imply that he becomes great through my agency.

A prayer we say every day, a salvific prayer, has something to teach us on the subject. Daily we pray: *Hallowed be thy name* (Mt 6:9). Day after day we go on asking that this may happen. Now suppose someone questions us, "What is your request, when you pray that God's name be hallowed? Is there ever a time when it

---

4. One witness inserts the title, "For David himself," omitted by Augustine.
5. Variant: "magnificent and beautiful desires."

is not holy, a time when God's name could be hallowed?" A fair question; and yet if we did not want this hallowing of God's name to occur, we should not pray for it. Thanksgiving and petition are two different modes of prayer: we give thanks for what is the case, but we make a petition for something which is not yet the case to happen. What does it mean, then, when it says, *Hallowed be thy name*? If we understand that, we shall understand also what is meant in the psalm by the words, *O Lord my God, you are exceedingly magnified*. The prayer, *Hallowed be thy name*, means: "May your name be held holy among mortals." Your name is always holy, but it is not yet reckoned holy by some unclean persons. The apostle teaches that *to the pure all things are pure, but to the impure and unbelievers nothing is pure* (Ti 1:15). If nothing is pure to the impure and unbelievers, I ask why, and the apostle explains: *Their minds and consciences are polluted*. If nothing is pure to them, even God cannot be, unless you suppose that people who daily blaspheme God think him to be pure. If he seems pure in your eyes, let him delight you, and if he delights you, let him be praised; but if he is blasphemed, it must be because you take no delight in him, and if you do not find him delightful, how can he appear pure to you?

What, then, are we asking when we say, *Hallowed be thy name*? We beg that God's name be held holy among people who until now have not regarded him as holy by reason of their unbelief, though of himself and in himself, and in his saints, he is always holy. We make the petition for the whole human race, we make it for all the world, for all those people who daily sit down and argue that God is not right-minded and does not judge in an upright way. We make the petition that they may sooner or later correct themselves, and make their heart right by bringing it close to God's rectitude, so that by clinging to him and straightening themselves against him who is upright they may cease to insult him. In him may they find their joy, as straightforward men and women in their straightforward Lord; for *how good God is to Israel!* But only *to those of straightforward hearts* (Ps 72(73):1).

When the singer in our present psalm—though in truth this singer is ourselves, the body of Christ, the members of Christ—when this singer saw what splendid gifts God had given to the human race, even though people had disbelieved in his existence, or worshipped false gods, or at least not believed him to be so good; when, as I say, the psalmist saw God in his works, he exclaimed, *O Lord my God, you are exceedingly magnified*. I did not understand you before, he implies, but now I understand you to be great. You are great always, even when you are hidden, but you became great for me when you revealed yourself. In this sense you have been magnified through me, in the same way as *your knowledge has become wonderful in my eyes*, since it has become wonderful because of me. When I turn toward it I wonder at it, but your knowledge remains whole and unimpaired whether I turn to it or not, and even if having turned toward it I turn away again. But I have become great myself because of it, and having left behind my impaired state and become whole, I wonder at what I did not know earlier. I am not marveling at something that has become great from the time I learned about it; I marvel because I have become great myself since I learned.

Listen now, and the psalm will tell us where God, always great in himself, is seen as magnified by us. He has become magnified exceedingly in the works he performs in our regard.

To redeem us who were ugly, the beautiful one became ugly

4. *You have clothed yourself in confession and seemliness.* Notice that the psalm indicates beauty by the term *seemliness* and that confession comes before beauty. If you seek beauty, you are seeking something good. But why, O soul, do you seek beauty? Surely so that your bridegroom may love you, for when you are ugly you do not please him. What about the bridegroom himself, what is he like? *Fair,* he is, *beyond all the children of men.* You who are ugly want this beautiful bridegroom to kiss you; you forget that you are full of iniquities. But *grace bedews* his *lips,* for of him scripture said, *Fair are you, beyond all the children of men, and grace bedews your lips; therefore have maidens loved you* (Ps 44:3(45:2); Sg 1:2). Someone is described here as fair to see, lovely *beyond all the children of men*; for though he is himself the Son of Man, he is more beautiful than any of humankind. Do you hope to please him, human soul, you one soul, made from many? We must understand that the Church is in view here, for in the Church there was from the beginning but one soul and one heart intent on God,[6] and to the Church our psalm speaks. Do you want to please him? You cannot please him as long as you are ugly, but what will you do to become beautiful? First of all you must find your deformity displeasing, and then you will receive beauty from him whom you hope to please by being beautiful. He who formed you in the beginning will reform you.

Your first duty is therefore to see clearly what you are; that will deter you from going in your ugliness to receive the kisses of the beautiful bridegroom. "But where shall I look, to see myself?" you ask. He has provided his scriptures as a mirror for you, and there you are told, *Blessed are the pure of heart, for they shall see God* (Mt 5:8). In that text a mirror is held out to you. See whether you are one of the pure-hearted it mentions, and grieve if you are not yet like that; grieve in order to become so. The mirror will reflect your face to you. You will not find the mirror flattering you, and neither must you beguile yourself. The reality that is yourself, that is what the mirror shows forth. Look at what you are,

---

6. See Acts 4:32.

and if what you see disgusts you, seek to become otherwise. If in your ugly condition you find yourself repulsive, you are already pleasing to your beautiful bridegroom.

What are you to do? Since your ugliness is offensive even to yourself, your first step must be to approach him by confession; as another text recommends, *let your first song to the Lord be one of confession* (Ps 146(147):7). Begin by admitting your ugliness, the deformity of soul that results from sins and iniquity. Initiate your confession by accusing yourself of this ugliness, for as you confess you become more seemly. And who grants this to you? Who else but he who is fairer of form than any of humankind?

5. Now I am going to make a bold statement: to render her beautiful he loved her even when she was ugly. How can that be said, that he loved her even in her ugly state? *Christ died for the godless* (Rom 5:6). Think what sort of life he must be keeping for you now that you are justified, if he gave you his death when you were godless! He who is beautiful, he who is *fair of form beyond all the children of men* because more just than any of the children of men, he came to the ugly one to make her beautiful. And that is not all; I will say something more daring still, since I find it in scripture: to make her beautiful he became ugly himself. Do not listen to me saying such a thing; after all, I could have made a rash mistake. I have told you already that he loved her even in her ugliness, and that would not have been a fitting statement to make in the presence of people who love him, but for the fact that scripture bore witness to it before I did. I was quoting the apostle. Do you want proof that he can be said to have loved her in her ugly condition? *Christ died for the godless.* Now I am going further, and telling you this: in order to come to her while she was ugly, he became ugly, he was himself deformed. How am I to demonstrate that, when the word of God has already told us that he is *fair of form beyond all the children of men*?[7] But in the same word of God I also find the following: *We saw him, and there was no fair form or seemliness in him* (Is 53:2). He is *fair of form beyond all the children of men*, yet *we saw him, and there was no fair form or seemliness in him*. Scripture does not say, "We have not seen him, and therefore we did not know whether he had any fair form or seemliness." What it says is, *We saw him, and there was no fair form or seemliness in him.*

Let us put a question to the speaker who proclaimed him as *fair of form beyond all the children of men*. Where did you see him? And then let us ask the

---

7. Running through Augustine's remarks to the end of section 5 is the idea of "form," the principle of differentiation which gives to each thing its distinctive identity, but also (usually) connotes beauty. Thus the bridegroom is "fair of form" (*speciosus forma*); the eternal Son was "in the form of God" (*in forma Dei*), but took the form or nature of a slave (*formam servi*). Compare Augustine's *Confessions* I,7,12: "From you derives all manner of being, O God most beautiful, who endow all things with their beautiful form." *Forma* is often close in meaning to *species;* the suffering Servant had neither *speciem neque decorem.*

same of him who testified: *We saw him, and there was no fair form or seemliness in him.* What about you? Where did you see him? Listen to the answer from the former: *"Being in the form of God he deemed it no robbery to be God's equal* (Phil 2:6). Of course he is superior to all humankind, because he is equal to God." I accept that; and now I know where this witness saw him, the one who spoke of him as *fair of form beyond all the children of men.* He has given us a convincing answer. "You ask where I saw him? *In the form of God."* But how could you have seen him in the form of God? How was that possible? "Because *the invisible reality of God is plainly to be understood through created things that are seen"* (Rom 1:20). Yes, that satisfies me perfectly. Now I know whom you saw, what he whom you saw was like, when you saw him, and how you were able to see him. Whom did you see? Our bridegroom. What was he like? He was *fair of form beyond all the children of men.* When did you see him? When he was *in the form of God.* How were you able to see him? Because his *invisible reality is plainly to be understood through created things that are seen.*

Now let us examine what is said of him by a different prophet, though in no different spirit,[8] for there is no disagreement between them. The first speaker has displayed Christ to us as *fair of form beyond all the children of men*; now let this one tell us his perception of Christ, this prophet who said, *We saw him, and there was no fair form or seemliness in him.* The one apostle Paul unites these two prophets; one single chapter in Paul endorses both views. In Paul I find the Christ who was fairer than any human being, because *being in the form of God he deemed it no robbery to be God's equal.* But in the same text Paul supports what the other prophet said of him, that he was devoid of beauty and majesty, because *he emptied himself and took on the form of a slave; and bearing the human likeness, sharing the human lot, he humbled himself and was made obedient to the point of death, even death on a cross* (Phil 2:7-8). Most assuredly did people see him stripped of beauty and majesty. Understandably they shook their heads before his cross, taunting, "Is this all that the Son of God amounts to? *If he is the Son of God, let him come down from the cross"* (Mt 27:40). But he had neither beauty nor seemliness. This is how you saw him, you who despised him because he was empty of beauty and seemliness. You shook your heads before the cross, failing to find steadiness for your heads[9] in that head who was hanging on the cross. The heads of the mockers necessarily go on wobbling until he whom they mocked becomes their head. Watch him: he is resuming his majesty, and great majesty it is. What you propose as a challenge to him is less than what he did. You suggest, *If he is the Son of God, let him come down from the cross.* He did not come down from the cross, but he rose from the tomb.

8. Or possibly "Spirit."
9. Variant: "for the cross."

6. You see then, O soul, that you cannot be decorous and beautiful unless you first confess your ugliness to him who is always beautiful, but for your sake renounced his beauty for a time. He was stripped of his beauty for a season, taking the form of a slave, though he lost no whit of that beauty which is his in his nature as God. This is why you, the Church, have beauty too, for in the Song of Songs you are acclaimed, *Most beautiful among women* (Sg 5:9). Of you the question is asked, *Who is this who comes up from the wilderness, made white?* (Sg 8:5, LXX). What does *made white* signify? It means that she has been illuminated,[10] not that she is made up in the manner of women who paint themselves in order to seem what they are not. Neither does it mean whitewashed like a wall; the apostle used the phrase "whitewashed wall"[11] as a metaphor for hypocrisy and deceit, due for destruction. A whitewashed wall is mere mud within, for its shiny coat is only superficial.

Very different is the illuminated Church, gleaming white and said to be *made white* because her whiteness does not derive from herself. *I was originally a blasphemer*, says Paul, and again, *By nature we too were children of wrath, like the rest* (1 Tm 1:13; Eph 2:3). Grace comes to you, the grace that illumines you and makes you white. You were black formerly, but you have been made white by God's grace. *You were darkness once, but now you are light in the Lord* (Eph 5:8). Therefore the question is now asked concerning you, even you, *Who is this who comes up from the wilderness, made white?* So marvelous are you already that we would almost make you the object of our contemplation, for it is the voice of wonder that asks, "*Who is this who comes up from the wilderness, made white*, so lovely, so radiant, free from stain or wrinkle? Is this not she who used to lie in the filth of her iniquities? Is she not the one who wallowed in the harlotry of idol-worship? Is this not she who was unclean through every kind of lust and carnal desire? Who, then, is this, *who comes up from the wilderness, made white?*"

Remember who he is, he who for her sake was divested of beauty and seemliness, and you will appreciate how honored she is by the luminosity that now is hers. If the lowliness he accepted for her sake astounds you, you will be less amazed by the eminence she enjoys because of him. How great must be the happiness of the whitened bride as she remembers how, even when she was black, she drew down to herself the beautiful one, that he might die for the godless! This is why our psalm says that the Lord our God clothed himself in confession and seemliness: he clothed himself in the Church, for the Church is confession and seemliness. Confession first, then seemly beauty: confession of sins, then decorous good deeds. *You have clothed yourself in confession and seemliness.*

---

10. A term often used of baptism.
11. See Acts 23:3.

*Verse 2. God stretched out the sky: literally this suggests effortless work,
figuratively the scriptures*

7. *Arrayed in light as in a garment.* The Church is his garment, the Church
which, as I have already reminded you, is *free from stain and wrinkle* (Eph 5:27).
The Church is called "light," and of this too I have reminded you by quoting the
text, *You were darkness once, but now you are light in the Lord.* In the Lord,
notice; you were darkness in yourself, but in the Lord you are light. *Arrayed in
light as in a garment, he stretched out the sky like a skin.*[12] The psalmist now
wishes to clarify how Christ was able to clothe himself in light, that light being
the Church; and he explains it by symbolic expressions that point beyond themselves. Let us listen as he relates how the Church became light, how she was
rendered free from every stain and wrinkle, and how she became shining and
white, radiant as the clothing of her bridegroom, in whom she dwells.

He stretched out the sky like a skin. This at any rate is clear to me; for who
stretched out the sky at which we gaze with our bodily eyes, if not God? The
comparison, *like a skin,* is added to illustrate the ease with which it was done, if
you take it at face value. You have looked at this vast construction, and you
reflect on how hard it is for a human being to put up even a small vault or arch,
how much effort and trouble he has to put in, and how long the job takes. The
limitations of our minds might therefore have suggested to us that similar stren-
uous labor was entailed in the works of God; and to rule out such a misunderstanding the psalmist used a symbol of effortless operation which you can grasp.
With the help of this comparison you may begin to believe that God works with
ease, and not suppose that he stretched out the sky in the way that you put a roof
on your house. It was as easy for him to spread out this vast sky as it is for you to
spread out a hide. That is a wonderful facility indeed, and yet the Spirit is still
speaking to you as to a slow learner. Yes, that is what I said, the Spirit is still
speaking to you as to a slow learner;[13] for it was not even in the way that you
spread out a skin that God spread the sky. Imagine that a hide is laid down in
front of you, crinkled or folded. Order it to stretch out flat. Stretch it out simply
by your command. "I can't," you say. Even in your action of spreading out a skin
you are a long way from God's easy act, then, for *he spoke, and all things were
made* (Ps 148:5). God said, *Let there be a vault between upper and lower waters,
and so it was* (Gn 1:6). Nevertheless you can take the comparison literally for the
present to aid your understanding, since it signifies the ease of God's action.

8. Turn now to a figurative interpretation of the same words. If we try to make
accessible what is obscure and knock hopefully at a closed text, we find that the

---

12. *Pellis* is primarily the hide, skin or pelt of an animal, then by extension what is made from it:
clothing, tents and parchment. Augustine will focus primarily on the last.
13. Variant: "the Spirit is still speaking slowly to you," in both occurrences.

psalm speaks of God stretching out the sky like a skin because it means us to understand this as a reference to holy scripture. God established the authority of scripture in his Church first of all, and from it other things flowed, as also he established the sky, stretching it out like a skin. Now this comparison, *like a skin*, was not chosen without good reason. The first thing God did in his Church was to spread the name and fame of his preachers, a fame that was like a skin because skin symbolizes mortality. The symbolism is unmistakable, because after our first parents, Adam and Eve, the progenitors of the human race, had spurned God's command in paradise, and at the serpent's persuasion and proposal had transgressed the law God had given them, they became mortal and were driven out of paradise. As a sign of their mortality they put on skin tunics, for they had been provided by God with tunics made out of animal hides; and hides are not usually removed from animals until after they are dead. Thus in our psalm skin symbolizes mortality. What are we to understand, then, when the psalm speaks of God making the sky out of skin, and spreading it out like a skin, if divine scripture is represented by this comparison? It means that those who promulgated the scriptures to us were mortal men.

The Word of God himself is always the same, ever unchanging and indefectible. Remember how *in the beginning was the Word, and the Word was with God; he was God* (Jn 1:1). Are we to infer from this that he *was* but no longer is? Of course not; he is, and he always will be. So if the Word of God is God-with-God, go ahead and read him, if you can! What do you say? That he is too high up, and that is why you are unable to read him? But the Word of God is everywhere; he stretches mightily from end to end and touches everything by his purity.[14] *He was here in the world, a world made by him* (Jn 1:10); when he came, he was already here, for he came in the flesh to a world from which he had never been absent in his divinity. Why, then, were you unable to read him? *Because by the wisdom of God the world failed to recognize God by its wisdom* (1 Cor 1:21), although the world was created in God's wisdom; for in that wisdom all things are contained and, were it removed, they would not be anything at all. But the world, even so created, was unable to recognize God through its wisdom, and the necessary consequence was that *it pleased God to save believers through the foolishness of our preaching* (1 Cor 1:21).

Those who believed were to be saved through the foolishness of preaching, and so God chose mortal creatures, human beings subject to death and destined to die. He employed a mortal tongue and uttered mortal sounds, he employed the ministry of mortal men and made use of mortal instruments, and by this means a sky was made for you, so that in this mortal artifact you might come to know the immortal Word, and by participating in this Word you too might become

---

14. See Wis 8:1; 7:24.

immortal. Moses lived[15] and died, for God ordered him, *Go up onto the mountain, and die* (Dt 32:49). Jeremiah died, and all the multitude of prophets died, but the oracles of these dead men remain for their posterity, even for us, because those words, spoken through them, were truly the words of him who *stretched out the sky like a skin.* Think about it: the apostle who declared that to die and to be with Christ would be far the best for him[16] has been released from this life and now lives with Christ, just as all the prophets are living with Christ now; but what did God use to make available to us these scriptures that we read? He used what was destined to die, their mouths, tongues, teeth and hands. The apostle produced what we read through the instrumentality of these bodily organs; but his soul commanded them, and God was commanding his soul. Thus was the sky spread out like a skin. We read now under this sky, under this skin of the divine scriptures spread out for us.

Moreover we are told that *the sky will be rolled up like a scroll* (Is 34:4; Rv 6:14). There is a good reason for this double comparison, brothers and sisters: here the sky is a skin, there a scroll, because something important concerning the divine scriptures is being shown to us under these images. The speech of dead persons is extended and is therefore described as stretched out like a skin; what is more, it is given much wider extension by the fact that the speakers are dead. The prophets and apostles became much better known after their deaths than they had been in their lifetime, for only Judea had access to living prophets, but all nations know them now that they are dead. While they lived the skin had not yet been stretched, nor was the sky spread out to cover the whole earth. But later God *stretched out the sky like a skin.*

Verse 3. The water above the sky is charity

9. *He covers its higher regions with waters.* When we read this the literal sense is easily grasped. When God issued his command, a vault came into being between one set of waters and another,[17] so that there are lower waters to pour themselves over the earth, and upper waters too far away from us to be seen, but commended to our faith. Another psalm mentions them: *Let the waters that are above the heavens praise the name of the Lord, for he spoke, and they were made; he gave the command, and they were created* (Ps 148:4-5). The literal meaning is evident: God covers the sky's *higher regions with waters.*

Now what about the figurative sense? We took the skin to be a symbol of holy scripture and of the authority of the divine word as mediated to us through

---

15. A well-supported variant is "Moses spoke."
16. See Phil 1:23.
17. See Gn 1:6-7.

mortals, because it is since their deaths that knowledge of the word so dispensed has become widespread. In line with this interpretation, how are we to understand the words: *He covers its higher regions with waters*? The higher regions of what? Of the sky. And what is the sky? Holy scripture. What are the higher regions of holy scripture? Do we find anything described as higher in the holy scriptures? Ask Paul. *Now I will point out to you a higher way*, he says. *If I speak in the tongues of mortals or angels, but have no love, I have become like a booming gong or a clashing cymbal* (1 Cor 12:31-13:1). If nothing more eminent than charity can be found in holy scripture, and thus the higher regions of the scriptures are the precepts of charity, how can we say that the upper regions of the sky are covered with waters? Listen, for Paul tells you how: *The charity of God has been poured out into our hearts through the Holy Spirit who has been given us* (Rom 5:5). The words, *has been poured out*, give you the clue: waters are to be understood as the charity of the Holy Spirit. These are the waters of which another scriptural text warns, *Let your waters run widely in your streets, but let no stranger communicate with you* (Prv 5:16-17);[18] for though all who are strangers to the way of truth, whether pagans, Jews, heretics, or bad Christians, may have many gifts, they cannot have charity. And what kind of gift is that? We are not speaking of the external gifts which everyone enjoys, since God makes his sun rise over good and bad alike;[19] these are certainly gifts of God, but they are common not only to good and bad people but even to wild beasts and cattle. Existence itself, life, sight, feeling, hearing and the functions of all our senses: these are gifts of God; but consider with how many and what kind of creatures you share them, some of whom you have no wish to imitate. Even the most depraved characters may have acute intelligence, even thoroughly disreputable actors have highly developed skill in the arts, even robbers have wealth, and many bad men have wives and children. All these are delightful gifts from God; no one would deny it. But look who shares them with you.

Think now of the gifts conferred on the Church. There is the gift of the sacraments: baptism, the Eucharist, the other holy sacraments. What a gift that is! Yet even Simon Magus acquired it.[20] Then consider what kind of gift prophecy is. Yet the evil king Saul prophesied, and he prophesied at the very time when he was persecuting holy David. Note this point carefully: I did not say, "After he had persecuted David." If that had been the case, he could perhaps have repented after persecuting David, and become worthy to receive the gift of prophecy. No. Not after he had persecuted, not before he began to persecute, but precisely when

18. The context in Proverbs is marital fidelity and the metaphors warn against adultery. The omission of a negative clause at the beginning of this verse by some witnesses to the Septuagint text has reversed the meaning.
19. See Mt 5:45.
20. See Acts 8:13.

he was bent on persecution, he prophesied. He sent his servants to arrest David, who at that time was staying with some prophets, among whom was holy Samuel. Saul's envoys were filled with the spirit of prophecy, and they prophesied too. Well, yes; but we might guess that they had come with good intentions, either because their office left them no alternative, or because they did not mean to carry out the order. Saul sent others, and the same thing happened. Very well, let us interpret their intentions in the same benign way. Furious at the servants' dalliance, Saul came himself, breathing slaughter and thirsting for the blood of an innocent and holy man, to whom he should rather have been grateful. Yet even he was filled with the spirit of prophecy, and he too prophesied.[21]

These events should be a warning against pride to any who have received from God a holy gift such as baptism, and yet lack charity. They would do better to think about the reckoning with God to be faced by all who make use of holy things in an unholy manner. They will find themselves among people protesting, *But we prophesied in your name!* The answer they will receive is not "You are lying;" but *I never knew you; depart from me, all you who act unjustly* (Mt 7:22.23). This is because *if I have the gift of prophecy, yet have no love, it avails me nothing* (1 Cor 13:2). Saul too prophesied, but he acted unjustly. And who acts unjustly if not one who has never had charity? Charity is the fulfillment of the law.[22]

Well then, what does the psalm mean by saying, *He covers its higher regions with waters*? Throughout the scriptures charity chooses the highest way and claims the highest place. Only good people aspire to charity; the wicked do not communicate with us in charity. They may communicate with us in baptism, they may communicate with us in the other sacraments, they may communicate with us in prayer. They may share these very walls with us and be part of this congregation, but they do not communicate with us in charity. The true wellspring of good things, the proper fount of all that is holy, is that charity of which scripture warns, *Let no stranger communicate with you.* Who are the strangers? All those who hear the dismissal, *I never knew you; depart from me*; for if the Lord never knew them, they must be strangers. The higher way of charity lays hold on those who properly belong to the kingdom of heaven.

The commandment of charity is higher than the skies and higher than all books; for the books are subordinate to it and the tongues of all the saints fight in its service, as does every movement, spiritual or physical, on the part of God's stewards. Charity is the supereminent way, and we can rightly say that God covers the higher regions of the sky with waters because you will find nothing loftier than charity in the sacred books.

---

21. See 1 Sm 19:18-24.
22. See Rom 13:10.

The water above the sky is the Holy Spirit

10. Listen now to an even plainer demonstration of what water symbolizes in the psalm. We have mentioned that God's charity has been poured abroad in our hearts through the Holy Spirit who has been given to us; we also quoted the text, *Let your waters run widely in your streets*. But someone may say to me, "It is not expressly stated there that this is to be understood as meaning charity. What if someone else takes it in a different sense?" Simply keep in mind the apostle's words, *The charity of God has been poured out into our hearts*. By whose agency? *Through the Holy Spirit who has been given us* (Rom 5:5). Now hearken to the Lord, the teacher of the apostles: *Let anyone who is thirsty come and drink*. Go on listening as he promises, *If anyone believes in me, as scripture says, rivers of living water shall flow from within that person*. What does he mean? Let the evangelist explain: *He said this of the Spirit which those who believed in him were to receive; for the Spirit had not yet been given, because Jesus was not yet glorified.* (Jn 7:37-39) You see, brothers and sisters, that the reason why the Spirit had not yet been given was that Jesus at that time had not yet been glorified; but once he had been glorified and had ascended to heaven, the Holy Spirit was sent, and the apostles were filled with the charity that was poured abroad in their hearts by the Holy Spirit who was given to them. And this happened because the upper regions of the sky are covered by the waters. This is quite evident, for the Lord ascended into heaven in order to be above the heavens[23] and to send charity down from there. We must not think that, since God is said to cover the sky, he is supported by the element that he covers. He uplifts what he covers; he does not impose a weight on it. He covers the sky with waters in such a way that the sky is uplifted by the divine Spirit. Now what uplifts something else is above that other thing; what is uplifted is below. The one suspends, the other is suspended. Well now, if one suspends the other, and the lower hangs from the higher, we might expect that the sky, by which I mean the scriptures, would hang from and depend on charity. And this is indeed the case, for there are two commands of love which are the most notable of all, and *on these two commandments depend all the law and the prophets* (Mt 22:40). *He covers the sky's higher regions with waters.*

His clouds are preachers who lift us up to an understanding of the scriptures

11. *He makes the clouds his chariot*. This too can very well be taken literally. The Lord ascended into heaven as the apostles watched. In what sense were clouds used as the chariot that bore him there? *After he had said these things, a*

---

23. Augustine uses the same word *caelum* for both "heaven" and what we would call "sky."

cloud received him (Acts 1:9), says scripture. The same thing is foretold concerning our own resurrection: *Those who have died in Christ will be the first to rise. Then we who are still alive will be snatched up together with them in the clouds to meet Christ in the air; and thus we shall always be with the Lord.* (1 Th 4:16-17) There you have the clouds described as the vehicle of ascent to heaven, but now I am going to show you how clouds are also your means of ascent to that sky which is the divine scriptures. What do I mean by that, brothers and sisters? Would that the Lord my God may graciously number me among all his manifold clouds! Let him see, though, what a dense cloud I am.[24] Nonetheless you must understand clouds represent all preachers of the truth. People who because of their weakness are unable to ascend to the sky—to an understanding of the scriptures, I mean—should mount by means of these clouds. Perhaps this is happening even now in your own case. If we are achieving anything, if our hard work and sweat are not altogether unfruitful, you are traveling upwards to the sky of the divine scriptures—to an understanding of them, that is—by means of our preaching.

Here are two examples of the process. How high and far away the sky seemed in our psalm! None of you had been able to see what the simile meant when the psalm said, *He stretched out the sky like a skin, and covers its higher regions with waters.* And the same thing is happening in this verse, for now you understand what it means by saying, *He makes the clouds his chariot,* and you have understood through our preaching, but only in the measure that the Lord granted it, for the clouds do not send down rain from their own resources. Mount up then, by understanding, and bear fruit through the insight you have gained, for you must not be like that vineyard of which the Lord says through a prophet, *I will forbid my clouds to send rain upon it* (Is 5:6). A certain vineyard was being rebuked because instead of grapes it had yielded thorns; it had not been suitably grateful for the gentle rain. Anyone who hears good preaching but acts sinfully is soaked by wholesome rain yet brings forth thorns. The Lord did not issue this threat against some earthly, visible vineyard, as we might have surmised, brothers and sisters. He did not want any obscurity in the oracle to provide the hearers with an excuse for their sin, and he therefore stated clearly whom he was addressing and what vineyard he had denounced: *The vineyard of the Lord of Hosts is the house of Israel.* "What are you doing, you sinners, roving mentally through the mountains and hills where vines are grown?" he asks. "I know what vineyard I am talking about, I know where I came looking for grapes, to find only thorns. All your divergent ideas and interpretations are beside the point. You are unwilling to understand, because if you did you would have to reform your behavior." Another psalm makes the same accusation: *He has refused to under-*

---

24. *Quam nebulosa nubes sim.*

stand, so as to act well (Ps 35:4(36:3)). Away with all your theories! *The vineyard of the Lord of Hosts is the house of Israel, and his cherished young shoot is everyone in Judah* (Is 5:7). Cherished, because God planted it, but condemned when it sprouted thorns.

Can we suppose, brothers and sisters, that the house of Israel was the Lord's vineyard, but we are not? Hardly. We must see that it was said to the Jews, but we too must listen with fear. Observe how the apostle terrifies the engrafted branches by pointing to the fate of the branches broken off. True, he commends to the broken branches God's fearful severity, and to the inserted branches God's lovable goodness;[25] but you who have experienced his goodness must not prove sterile, lest in your unfruitfulness you feel his severity.

"But I am not a vine," you object. Really? What about the Lord's saying, *I am the vine, you are the branches, and my Father is the vinedresser* (Jn 15:5.1)? And what about the apostle's question, *Who plants a vineyard, and receives no fruit from it?* (1 Cor 9:7) A vineyard you are, holy Church, and God is the keeper of your vines. No human farmer can send rain on his vineyard.

Listen then, most beloved brethren, you who are the dearest, the most intimate parts of the Church's being, the pledges of the Church's love, the children of this heavenly mother: listen while there is still time. Of old God uttered an appalling threat against that vineyard: *I will forbid my clouds to send rain upon it.* It was carried out. The apostles went to the Jews, but the Jews scorned them; and the apostles announced, "We were sent to you, but since you have rejected the word of God, we are going to the Gentiles."[26] In that instance the same Spirit of God, who was dwelling in their hearts, gave inward orders to those clouds to withhold rain from the vineyard that had been expected to yield grapes, but produced thorns.

It is clear, then, that the Lord made the clouds into a chariot and stretched out the sky like a scroll. You have no cause for complaint. The authority of the scriptures has been extended over the whole earth, and clouds are plentiful: the word of truth is preached, and all obscure matters are explained, so that your hearts may use the clouds to ascend. Take care how you believe, and take care how you accept what you hear, for the judge will come on the heels of the preacher, and after the steward will come the master who demands an account. *He makes the clouds his chariot.*

---

25. See Rom 11:22.
26. See Acts 13:46.

The winds are souls, their wings are charity toward God; but God's love for us is higher

12. *He walks on the wings of the winds.* Now it is rather risky to take this in its literal sense. What are the wings of the winds? Are we supposed to imagine it in the way an artist might, and picture to ourselves winds flying with outstretched wings? Surely not, brothers and sisters; the wind is nothing but a movement and rush of air that we feel, blowing away whatever its strength permits. What are the wings of the winds? But then, what are the wings of God? Another psalm has said, *They will hope under the shelter of your wings* (Ps 35:8(36:7)).

But let us make some attempt to find a literal meaning in this verse also, one that corresponds to the particular characteristic of this created element, the wind. Perhaps scripture wishes to remind us of the wind's swiftness. We spoke about that swiftness a long time ago, when commenting on the psalm that says, *Very swiftly runs his word* (Ps 147:15). Human beings know of nothing swifter than wind. Just as we saw that God's effortless activity was suggested by the simile of the skin, because nothing is easier for us than to spread out a hide, so here the psalmist wants to convey that God, or his Word, is present everywhere, so rapid in motion that he never deserts anything. The psalm uses this metaphor because you cannot conceive of anything swifter than wind. *He walks on the wings of the winds*, it says, meaning that he outstrips the wind in speed. You are invited to understand that the wings of the wind are a symbol of its velocity and that God's word travels faster than any wind.

This is the most obvious meaning. Now let us knock and seek something more hidden; may these words reveal some figurative sense to us.

13. We can quite reasonably take winds to be a symbol of souls—not that the soul is wind, but because the wind is invisible. It is a physical thing, and exerts its force on bodies, yet it escapes the perception of the human eye. The soul too is invisible, and therefore the wind is a good symbol of it. This is why God is said to have blown the breath of life into the human he had formed, whereupon *the man became a living creature* (Gn 2:7). Thus we are justified in taking the winds to be an allegorical representation of souls.

Be careful not to seize on the mention of allegory and think I am talking about music and dancing on the stage.[27] There are some words that are in common use both among us and in frivolous theatrical circles, including disreputable ones; they are only words, after all, sounds made with the tongue. They have their place in the Church, and they have their use on the stage as well. I have not said anything that the apostle did not say when, referring to Abraham's two sons, he told us, *These are two covenants, allegorically prefigured* (Gal 4:24). Some-

---

27. *Pantomimi aliquid.* See Exposition 4 of Psalm 30,11 and the note there.

thing is said to be an allegory when one meaning seems to be conveyed by the words, and a different meaning is symbolized for our minds. How can Christ be called a lamb? He is not a domestic animal, is he? Christ is also called a lion, but is he a wild beast? He is a rock, but does that mean he is hard? Christ is a mountain, but we should not think of him, should we, as a raised area of earth? Many expressions seem to say one thing by their words, but something else is signified; then the expression is allegorical. When I mention allegory I am no more talking about the stage than the Lord was talking about the amphitheatre when he used the word "parable."[28] You have before your eyes the bustle of a city[29] where shows are numerous. I would have been more comfortable talking about allegory in the country, where people might never have heard of allegory except in God's scriptures. We must explain, then, that as an allegory is a figurative mode of speech, so the figurative representation of a sacred mystery is an allegory.

What are we to understand by the expression, *He has mounted*[30] *on the wings of the winds*? We have already remarked that the winds can very well be taken as a symbol of souls. What are the wings of souls, then? What else but the means by which they are raised aloft? The wings of souls are therefore virtues, good works, deeds rightly done. Souls have all the pinions they need in the form of paired wings, for all the commandments are summed up in two precepts. Anyone who loves God and neighbor has a winged, free soul that flies to the Lord in holy love; but anyone who is entangled in carnal love has wings sticky with bird-lime. If this interpretation is not well founded, if the soul does not have wings and feathers, what are we to make of the groans of someone in trouble who asked, *Who will give me wings, as to a dove?*[31] And the distressed soul continues, *Then I will fly away and find rest* (Ps 54:7(55:6)). Similarly another voice in the psalms cries out, *Whither shall I go from your spirit, and whither flee from your face? If I mount to heaven, you are there; if I sink down to hell, even there you are present. If I take wings like a dove, and fly to the uttermost parts of the sea. . . . It is as though he were saying, "I can escape from your anger if I take wings like a dove and fly to the sea's furthest limits." To fly to those extreme regions means to stretch one's hope even now to the end of the world, as did he who said, *It is too hard for me, until I enter God's holy place, and understand what the final outcome must be* (Ps 72(73):16-17). But how is he to reach those distant parts of the sea, even if he takes wing? *Even there your hand will lead me, your right*

---

28. Augustine is conscious of the Greek root of the Latin *parabola*. The παραβολή was something "thrown alongside" something else to illustrate a truth; and the related noun παράβολος, a fighter in the arena, evokes the amphitheatre.
29. Carthage.
30. *Sic.*
31. For the translation "to a dove" rather than "of a dove" see Augustine's Exposition of Psalm 54,8 and the notes there.

hand bring me through (Ps 138(139):7-10), he says, for even with my wings I shall fall unless you guide me.

Souls who sincerely obey God's commandments, fostering charity from a clear conscience and unfeigned faith,[32] have good strong wings, unhampered by sticky substances. Yet however richly endowed they may be with virtues animated by charity, what is that compared with the elective love of God that embraces them and that embraced them even when they were stuck in their gluey impediments? God's elective love for us is greater than our love for him. Our love is our wings, but he *walks* even above *the wings of the winds.*

14. The apostle spoke about this to some of his correspondents: *I bend my knees to the Father* on your behalf, that your inmost being may be strengthened and Christ may dwell in your hearts through faith, so that rooted in love and built up on love—God is already giving them charity, you see, already giving them wings and pinions—*you may come to grasp what is the height and breadth and length and depth.* Perhaps he means us to think of the Lord's cross. In the cross there was the breadth, where his hands were stretched out; we see length in the upright that rose from the earth, the part to which the body was attached; there was height in the limb which thrust upward from the cross-piece; and depth in the earth where the cross was made firm. In the cross is all our hope of life. Breadth signifies reaching out in good works, length our perseverance even to the end, and height our aspiration to "Lift up our hearts."[33] So we are reminded to exercise ourselves in good works, persevering in them even to the end, having wide space in which to act as we should and long perseverance to see our works through, but all this only in the hope of heavenly rewards. The height of charity, the height of the cross, is to seek no recompense here but only on high, lest we hear the Lord say of us, *I tell you truly, they have had their reward* (Mt 6:2). But I mentioned depth as well, the place into which the cross was made fast, the part which was unseen, from which the visible parts arose. Now what is hidden in the Church and not open to public view? The sacrament of baptism and the sacrament of the Eucharist. Even the pagans see our good actions, but our sacraments are concealed from them. Yet the actions that are seen arise from what is unseen, just as from the deepest part of the cross which is fixed in the earth rises the whole cross, visible to our gaze.

How did the apostle continue? After speaking of breadth, length, height and depth, he added, *May you know the charity of Christ that is beyond knowing*, although he had also urged them to be *rooted in love and built up on love* (Eph 3:14-19). You love Christ, and therefore all you do is done in the power of his cross. But do you love him as much as he loves you? By no means. Yet by loving him to the utmost of your capacity you fly toward him, so that there you may

---

32. See 1 Tm 1:5.
33. See the note at Exposition of Psalm 10,3.

come to know how he has loved you—come to know, in other words, that charity of his that is beyond knowing. You love him as much as you possibly can, and you fly to him as fast as your strength permits, but he walks even above your soul's flight. *He walks on the wings of the winds.*

Verse 4. Angels and fire, God's ministers

15. *He makes spirits into his angels, and blazing fires into his servants.* We do not see the angels as present; this is something hidden from our eyes, something that belongs to the mighty commonwealth of God, our supreme ruler. But we know from our faith that angels exist, and we read of their having appeared to many people. We hold this firmly, and it would be wrong for us to doubt it. The angels are spirits. When they are simply spirits, they are not angels, but when they are sent, they become angels; for "angel" is the name of a function, not of a nature.[34] If you inquire about the nature of such beings, you find that they are spirits; if you ask what their office is, the answer is that they are angels. In respect of what they are, such creatures are spirits; in respect of what they do, they are angels. Make a comparison with human affairs. The name of someone's nature is "human being," the name of his job is "soldier." The name of someone's nature is "man," the name of his office is "herald." A human being becomes a herald; in other words, one who was already a man becomes a herald. We cannot say the opposite, that one who was a herald becomes a man.

Similarly some beings existed who were created by God as spirits, but he makes them angels by sending them to announce what he has ordered them. He also makes blazing fires his servants, for we read of fire appearing in a bush,[35] and we also read of fire that was sent down from heaven to carry out God's commands.[36] It was God's servant when it acted as he bade it. In respect of its existence it was what its nature made it, namely fire; when it did what it was told to do, it fulfilled a ministry. So much for the literal sense of this verse, referring to God's creatures.

16. Can we find a figurative sense verified in the Church? How are we to take this: *He makes spirits into his angels, and blazing fires into his servants*? "Spirits" here means spiritual persons. God makes spiritual persons into his messengers, to announce his word, for *the spiritual person judges everything, but is not himself judged by anyone* (1 Cor 2:15). Consider an example of a spiritual man who was made God's angel: *Not as spiritual persons could I speak to you, but only as carnal*, he lamented (1 Cor 3:1). His affection for them was spir-

---

34. The original meaning of ἄγγελος in Greek is "messenger" or "envoy."
35. See Ex 3:2.
36. See 1 Kgs 18:38; 2 Kgs 2:11.

itual in quality, but he was sent to carnally-minded people, like an angel sent from heaven to earth.

What does the psalm mean by saying, *And blazing fires into his servants*? The same thing, surely, as another passage of scripture means by *ardent in spirit* (Rom 12:11). Every servant of God who is ardent in spirit is a blazing fire. Was not Stephen a man on fire? What was the fire that burned in him? What kind of fire was it that drove him to intercede for his murderers even while they were stoning him?[37] When you hear it said, "Fire is God's servant," do you think it is going to burn you? Well yes, it will, but all it will burn up is the chaff in you. God's servant burns up all your carnal desires by preaching his word. Listen to Paul: *Everyone should regard us as servants of Christ, and dispensers of the mysteries of God* (1 Cor 4:1). How fiercely he was burning when he declared, *Our mouth is open to you, Corinthians, and our heart is thrown wide open* (2 Cor 6:11)! He burned and blazed with charity, and he went to them that he might set them alight. The Lord promised to send this fire when he said, *I have come to set fire to the earth* (Lk 12:49). As the sword does its work, so does the fire: the sword divided by shearing away carnal affection,[38] and the fire consumes it. You must understand all this as the effect of God's word and recognize here the work of God's Spirit. Begin to burn with charity through the word you hear, and then see what the fire that is God's servant has wrought in you. *He makes spirits into his angels, and blazing fires into his servants.*

Verse 5. The firmly founded Church

17. *He has founded the earth on its firmness; it will not be dislodged for ever.* Take this first as applying to the earth. I do not know whether the earth will come to an end, or whether we can rightly say, *It will never be dislodged*; for scripture also says, *Heaven and earth will pass away* (Mt 24:35). This is a difficult question, if you seek to interpret the verse literally. It may be that in saying, *He has founded the earth on its firmness*, the psalm is referring to some firm structure hidden from us but holding the earth together, and that was why it said, *He founded* it. Founded it on what? On the firmness of the earth itself, a firmness the Lord has put underneath it to hold it up, though your eyes cannot see it. The truth of these matters may be hidden from us with regard to the creation, but the Creator is not hidden by obscurities in his creatures. Let us see as much as we can, and from what we see, let us praise and love him.

Now let us turn to the figurative meaning and see what we can find there. When the psalm says, *He has founded the earth*, I understand this to mean the

37. See Acts 7:59.
38. See Lk 12:51-53; Mt 10:34.

Church, just as when another psalm declares that *the earth is the Lord's, and all that fills it* (Ps 23(24):1), I take *earth* to mean "Church." The Church is the thirsty earth crying out in the psalms (for the one voice speaks in all of them), *My soul is like waterless earth before you* (Ps 142(143):6). What does *waterless* evoke? Thirst. My soul thirsts for you like parched land, for if it is not thirsty it will not be irrigated to its profit. To a soul already soaked, rain seems like a flood. It ought to be thirsty. *Blessed are those who hunger and thirst for righteousness* (Mt 5:6); let the Church cry out, *My soul is like waterless earth before you*, as it cries elsewhere, *My soul has been athirst for the living God* (Ps 41:3(42:2)). These passages demonstrate why I understand the earth to be a figure of the Church.

Now what is the firmness on which it is established? Its proper foundation must be meant. Surely we are on the right lines if we understand the firmness on which the earth rests to be a figure of the foundation on which the Church is built? And what is this foundation? *No one can lay any other foundation than that which is laid, which is Christ Jesus*, says scripture (1 Cor 3:11). On that we have been securely established. Being founded so, we can justifiably say that we shall never be dislodged, for nothing could be more stable than that foundation. Infirm you were in yourself, but a firm foundation bears you. You had no possibility of standing firm in yourself, but you will stand firm for ever if you do not depart from that firm foundation. The Church *will never be dislodged*; it is the predestined pillar and bulwark of the truth.[39]

Verses 6-17. Why God leaves some things beyond our understanding

18. *The deep enwrapped it like a garment, and the waters will overtop the mountains. They shall flee before your rebuke, fearing the voice of your thunder. The mountains soar and the plains slope down to the place you have assigned to them. You have set the waters a limit which they may not overrun, nor shall they return to overwhelm the earth. You unseal springs in the valleys, and streams shall flow midway between the mountains. All the woodland beasts will drink there, and the onagers will quench their thirst. On the mountains birds of the sky will dwell, singing their song from among the rocks. From his high dwelling he pours rain on the mountains, and the earth will be enriched with the fruit you have created.*[40] *It brings forth grass for cattle, and plants for the service of human beings, that we may produce*[41] *bread from the ground, and the wine that cheers the human heart, that our faces may shine cheerfully with oil, and bread*

---

39. See 1 Tm 3:15.
40. Variant: ". . .created, O Lord."
41. Variant: "that you may produce."

strengthen our hearts. The trees of the plain shall drink their fill, and the cedars he planted[42] on Lebanon. There will the sparrows nest; but their leader is the home[43] of the coots. You gaze at the expanse of the sky, and you long to soar there with your intelligence. I see it too; but I think you ought to reflect with me, dearly beloved, how high it is. I recited a long string of verses on purpose, to show you how lofty God has made his holy mysteries, to ensure that we shall neither scorn what is easily available to us nor consider what we are offered unworthy of our attention, but rather go on searching, however difficult this may be, so that our delight may be all the greater when we find what we have sought.

However, among the statements that may perhaps be taken literally, brothers and sisters, we find the following: *There will the sparrows nest, but their leader is the home of the coots.* Surely the home of coots, or of waterfowl, cannot be the leader of the sparrows? Or does it mean that the home of waterfowl is the leader of the cedars? Cedars have been mentioned just before this: *Cedars he planted on Lebanon. There will the sparrows nest, but their leader is the home of the coots.* No, the cedars cannot be meant, since "cedars" is a feminine noun in Latin and the pronoun is masculine. *The home of the coots* must be the leader of the sparrows, then; but how can that be the case? If we confine our attention to the creatures before our eyes, the statement is unintelligible, for we know that coots or waterfowl are sea-birds or pond-dwellers. The *home* of the coot, or waterfowl, could mean its nest, but how could the home of the waterfowl be leader of the sparrows? Why would the Holy Spirit include apparently absurd statements about visible things, unless because our very inability to make sense of it literally may drive us to seek a spiritual meaning?

Conclusion: ponder what has been said, act on it, and pray as Christ taught you

19. So, as I say, you want to fly up to the sky with your understanding, up to that scroll stretched out above us; and the clouds are the means of ascent God has provided. But this particular cloud who is talking to you has no more energy left today to expound all these matters. Spare my weakness, even if you do not spare your own. I can see that you are so intensely eager that you are always ready to listen, but there are two considerations to which you should give due weight. One is our bodily weakness, and the other is your need to remember all the explanations you have been given. In the interval, think over what you have heard. What did I say? Chew the cud with what you have eaten; thus you will be clean animals, fit for God's banquets.[44]

---

42. Variants: "the Lord planted"; "will plant"; "you have planted."
43. Literally "house."
44. See Lv 11:1-8. The clean animals were ruminants with cloven hooves, typically sheep and cattle.

But you must take care to demonstrate in your actions the wholesome effects of what you hear. Anyone who hears accurately but does not act well has an extremely bad digestion, because the Lord our God never tires of feeding us. Everyone knows that we shall have to render an account both of the bread we have received and of the bread we have handed out. You know this very well, dearly beloved, for the sacred page does not leave us in ignorance, nor does God mislead us. You can observe for yourselves how frankly we have spoken to you from this place where we stand; and if perhaps I have been less than frank—or if any of us who speak to you from this place have been less than frank—at any rate God's word is no respecter of persons. For our own part, whether we are timid or whether we speak boldly, we are obliged to proclaim him who is afraid of no one. It is not human preachers, but God, who has given you what you have heard, so you can hear him who speaks frankly to you even through cowardly spokesmen. At God's judgment you will have nothing to plead in your defense unless you have employed yourselves in good works and have yielded fruit commensurate with what you have heard, as if it were nourishing rain. The proper fruit is good works; the proper fruit is sincere, willed love, not only for your nearest and dearest, but also for your enemy. You must turn no suppliant away; even if you cannot give him what he asks, do not treat him scornfully. If you can give, give; if you cannot, be kind to him. God crowns your inner intention, even if you lack material means. Let no one protest, "I have nothing." Charity is not something you dole out from your wallet. Whatever we say, whatever we have said in the past, whatever we may manage to say in the future, whether we personally, or our successors, or our predecessors—all of it has one purpose only, and that is charity, because charity is the goal of the commandment: charity from a pure heart, from a clear conscience and from sincere faith.[45]

When you pray, question your hearts and watch how you get past this verse: *Forgive us our debts as we forgive our debtors* (Mt 6:12). You will not be praying unless you say that. If you make a different prayer God will not hear you, because it will not be the one drawn up for you by the expert advocate he sent.[46] If we use our own words in prayer it is essential that they accord with the Lord's Prayer; and when we say the Lord's Prayer itself, we must clearly understand what we are saying, because God has willed it to be quite plain to us.

To sum up: if you do not pray, there is no hope for you. If you pray otherwise than as your Master taught you, you will not be heard. If you are untruthful in your prayer, you will not get what you pray for. We must pray, then; we must speak the truth in prayer; and we must pray as he taught us. Whether you like it or not, you will have to say every day, *Forgive us our debts as we forgive our debtors*. Do you want to say it safely? Then act in accordance with what you say.

_____

45. See 1 Tm 1:5.
46. The counsel for the defense, who helped the accused to prepare his case.

Exposition 2 of Psalm 103

Second Sermon

Introduction: Augustine is discharging a debt; please help by being quiet and patient

1. I am well aware that you hold us to be in your debt, not by necessity but by the more pressing obligation of charity. However, our debt is in the first place to the Lord our God who, as he dwells within you, demands this sermon of us in your name. Secondly we owe this sermon to our revered father,[1] who is present and orders me to speak, and who is praying for me. Finally we owe it to you, whose violent demands drag it from us, however lacking in strength we may be. Nonetheless it is the Lord himself who supplies the strength we need in response to your prayers; and insofar as he empowers us we must undertake to deal with the next verses of the psalm we began to study yesterday. We have looked at its opening sections, and with the help of him in whose name we began to study it we must try to finish it now.

We have already pointed out to those of you who were here yesterday, beloved friends, that this whole psalm is composed of figurative expressions, signifying mysteries beyond the words; but as the search for meaning is more difficult, so is the discovery, as always, more rewarding. You must not think that the obscurity of the text will debar you from these mysteries; rather they are stored safely for you by the difficulty itself, to the very end that, as we have often remarked, those who ask may receive, those who seek may find, and to those who knock admission to the hidden truths may be granted.[2]

We particularly need you to be quieter and more patient than usual, so that the few things we have to say may not take longer than is necessary on account of competing noise. Shortage of time obliges us to speak briefly, and you also know, beloved friends, that we owe our solemn service to the funeral of a faithful Christian.[3] Do not compel us to repeat what has been said or explain it over again. Perhaps there were some here who were absent yesterday and did not hear what was said; well, they should not have been absent. But perhaps it may be a

---

1. Probably Aurelius, Bishop of Carthage, Augustine's friend and mentor.
2. See Mt 7:7-8.
3. This is the most obvious interpretation of *debere nos exsequiis fidelis corporis sollemne obsequium*, though some think it is another and more elaborate reference to Augustine's own indifferent health.

salutary lesson for them, because if they do not hear today what yesterday's congregation heard, they may learn to come along themselves in the future. Let us run through the opening verses briefly.

Verses 1-4. Recapitulation of yesterday's interpretation of the opening verses

2. *Bless the Lord, O my soul.* The one soul of all of us must say this, for it has become one single soul in Christ.[4] *O Lord my God, you are exceedingly magnified.* How are you magnified? *You have clothed yourself in confession and seemliness.* Confess then, O Church, that you may gain decorum and he may clothe himself in you. *Arrayed in light as in a garment.* Christ is arrayed in his Church, because she who once was darkness in herself has become light in him; this is the teaching of the apostle, who said, *You were darkness once, but now you are light in the Lord* (Eph 5:8). *He stretched out the sky like a skin*: if you take this literally it means that he did it as easily as you would spread out a hide. Alternatively we should interpret the skin as the authority of the scriptures extended over the whole world; this is called a skin because skin represents mortality, and the authoritative scriptures were made available to us through mortal human beings, whose fame was spread wider after their deaths.

3. *He covers its higher regions with waters.* The higher regions of what? Of the sky. What is the sky? Confining ourselves to the figurative sense, we said that the sky is the divine scriptures. What is the highest reach of God's scripture? The precept of charity, for nothing is more lofty than that. But why should charity be compared with water? Because *the charity of God has been poured out into our hearts through the Holy Spirit who has been given to us* (Rom 5:5). But then why is the Spirit himself represented by water? Remember the gospel passage: *Jesus stood up and shouted, Let anyone who is thirsty, come to me and drink. If anyone believes in me, as scripture says, rivers of living water shall flow from within that person.* And how can we prove that this promise referred to the Spirit? The evangelist himself tells us: *He said this of the Spirit which those who believed in him were to receive* (Jn 7:37-39).

He walks on the wings of the winds, that is, on the powers of the soul. And what is the power of the soul? Charity, nothing else. But then how does God walk on charity? He does so because God's charity toward us is greater than ours toward him.

4. *He makes spirits into his angels, and blazing fires into his servants.* Those who are already spirits, being spiritually-minded and not carnal, he makes into his angels by sending them to preach his gospel. *And blazing fires into his*

---

4. See Exposition 1 of this psalm, sections 2 and 4.

servants: for unless the minister who preaches is himself on fire, he cannot set his hearers alight.

Verses 5-7. The waters of persecution once submerged the eminent leaders of the Church

5. *He has founded the earth on its firmness.* This seems to say that he made the Church firm on the Church's own firmness. But what is the firmness of the Church? Nothing else but the Church's foundation. And what is its foundation? That of which the apostle says, *No one can lay any other foundation than that which is laid, which is Christ Jesus* (1 Cor 3:11). If the Church is supported on a foundation like that, small wonder that it received the assurance, *It will not be dislodged for ever.* The psalm declares that God *founded the earth on its firmness*, and this means that he made the Church firm on the foundation that is Christ. If that foundation ever totters, the Church will totter; but how can Christ totter? Before he came to us, before he assumed flesh, *everything was made through him; nothing came to be without him* (Jn 1:3). He holds all things together by his majesty, and holds us by his goodness; how can he ever be shaken? And if Christ is unshakable, the Church will never be dislodged. What becomes of the allegation that the Church has vanished from the world if it cannot even totter?

6. But when did the Lord begin to plant his Church? When did he begin to make it known, to launch it, manifest it, spread it? When did he begin this process? What happened before it could begin? *He founded the earth on its firmness, and it will never be dislodged. It was enwrapped with the vast deep as with a garment.* Obviously this is not God's garment that is in question: the psalm has already stated that he is *arrayed in light as in a garment*, so I know that light is God's clothing, and we ourselves are that light, if we consent to be. What do I mean by that—if we consent? If we are darkness no longer. Well then, if God is arrayed in light, who or what has the great deep as a garment? The immense volume of waters is called the vast deep; this one term, *deep*, applies to all water, all the dampness in nature, all that is spread around us in seas, rivers, and hidden caves. When we read that *the vast deep enwrapped it like a garment*, we should take it, I think, to refer to the earth, of which the psalm has declared, *He founded the earth on its firmness, and it will never be dislodged.* The sea is like raiment for the earth, surrounding it and covering it. But there was a time when this garment around the earth increased to such a point that it covered everything in the flood, and submerged the highest mountains to a depth of about fifteen cubits, as scripture testifies.[5] Possibly the psalm was alluding to that time when it said, *Enwrapped with the vast deep as with a garment.*

---

5. See Gn 7:20.

7. *The waters will overtop the mountains.* The earth's clothing, the vast deep, rose so high that the waters stood even above the mountains. We read this in the psalm and, as I have pointed out, it was what actually happened during the great flood. Was that what the prophet meant? Was he relating past events or fore-telling the future? If he were recalling the past, he would not have said to us, *The waters will overtop the mountains,* but rather, "The waters overtopped the mountains." Scripture quite frequently uses the past to indicate future events, for the Spirit foresees future events as though they had occurred already, and we are used to reading it so. We all recognize the same convention of speech when in another psalm it seems as though the gospel is being read: *They dug holes in my hands and my feet, and numbered all my bones. They cast lots for my tunic* (Ps 21:17-19(22:16-18)). All this is recounted as though it had happened already, though in fact that psalm refers to future events, foreseen long before. But why need we labor this point? What does all our diligent research achieve? What does our careful inquiry reveal? When are we so confident in the result of our study that we can say with certainty, "This is how it is"? We observe that the prophets often use verbs in the past tense to predict the future; but it is not easy to find an example of the future tense being used to indicate past happenings. I do not presume to say that there is no such example; I would merely suggest to students of those writings a suitable object for their research. If they find an instance of it and report it to us, we busy older people will applaud the studies of younger scholars who have more time, and we too will learn something from their industry. We shall not think this beneath our dignity, for Christ uses all means to teach us.[6]

Well then, the psalm declares, *The waters will overtop the mountains.* The prophet was concerned to foretell the future, not to rehearse past events; and he said this because he wanted people to understand that the Church would be flooded by persecutions in the future. There was indeed a time, not so long ago, when God's earth—God's Church, I mean—was covered by the waters of the persecutors. So deeply was it submerged that not even the greatest Christians were visible, the leaders represented by mountains; for since they were every-where put to flight, they naturally disappeared from view. Perhaps the cry in another psalm envisaged these same waters: *Save me, O God, for the waters have flooded in even to my soul* (Ps 68:2(69:1)); it perhaps meant especially the waters that make up the sea, stormy and sterile waters, for if any region of the earth is covered by sea water it is not made fruitful thereby, but left barren. The mountains were submerged because the waters rose and stood higher; obstinate

---

6. The argument is an *a fortiori*: it is well known that prophetic writings sometimes use past tenses to recount future events, as in Psalm 21(22). It is hard to find an example of the opposite case. Therefore if we find a psalm using future tenses, as here with regard to flood-waters, we are all the more justified in concluding that it was talking about the future.

nations had overpowered the authority of all those preachers of God's word who had been promulgating the good news so strongly on all sides. The waters had covered them and stood over them, saying, "Oppress these folk, oppress them!" And oppress them they did. "Snuff them out, get rid of all trace of them!" said the persecutors. They prevailed against the martyrs, and Christians everywhere were put to flight. Even the apostles fled into hiding. Why were the apostles hidden in flight? Because the waters were standing over the mountain-tops. Great was the force of those waters, but how long did it last? Listen to the next verse.

8. *They shall flee before your rebuke.* Yes, brothers and sisters, this was what happened: at God's rebuke the waters fled, they fell back and stopped afflicting the mountains. Nowadays Peter and Paul, those lofty mountains, are plainly visible, and how they soar! These men who once were oppressed by persecutors are now revered by emperors. The waters were put to flight by God's rebuke, for the hearts of kings are in the hand of God, and he changes their course in whatever way he wills.[7] He commanded that through them peace should be granted to Christians, and then the towering authority of the apostles was plainly seen. Was their eminence in any way diminished while they were hidden beneath the waters? Certainly not; but all the same, brothers and sisters, those waters were banished by God's rebuke so that everyone might see the height of the mountains through whom salvation was to be made available to the human race; as a psalm says, *I have lifted my eyes to the mountains, from where comes help for me* (Ps 120(121):1).

They will fear the voice of your thunder. Is there anyone today who is not afraid of the voice of God sounding through the apostles, the voice of God thundering through his scriptures and his clouds? The sea grew calm, the waters became fearful, the mountains were exposed, the emperor issued his orders. But would any emperor have given such orders if God had not thundered? Only because God willed it did they command, and so it was done. No human being can claim the credit; the waters were afraid, but only at *the voice of your thunder.* The facts are plain: when God decreed it the waters fled away and threatened the mountains no more; but before this happened the mountains stood firm, even beneath the waters.

Verses 8-10. The waters of life flow between the mountains, and are common to all

9. *The mountains soar and the plains slope down to the deep place you have assigned to them.* The psalm is still talking about waters. We should not take this verse to refer to mountains of rock and earth, or to earth's plains; but to waves so

---

7. See Prv 21:1. The part of the verse not directly quoted is about waters.

high that they seemed mountainous. Time was when the sea was raging and its billows were like mountains, so high that they covered even the mountains that were the apostles. But how long could it be said that *the mountains soar and the plains slope down*? They raged, and then they were calmed. While they raged, they were like mountains; when calmed they became plains, for God assigned a deep place to them. There is a fear[8] that resembles a deep place, and it became a kind of lodging for all the savage hearts of mortals. How many are there today who are salty and bitter, yet quiet? How many refuse to become sweet and wholesome? Who are these? People who still refuse to believe in Christ. And yet, though there are many who have not yet come to faith, what do they do to the Church? They were mountains once; now they are no more than plains. All the same, brothers and sisters, a dead calm sea is still the sea. Why are they not raging now? Why do they not unleash their mad fury? Why are they not striving at least to submerge our earth, if they are powerless to destroy it? Why not? Listen to the psalm: *You have set the waters a limit which they may not overrun, nor shall they return to overwhelm the earth.*

10. Now that these fierce waves have been checked, so that we are free to preach like this; now that they have been assigned their due limit, and are unable to overrun the boundary appointed for them or to return and overwhelm the earth; now that we are in this state of peace, what is happening in our land? The sea has withdrawn from this earth of ours, so what goes on here, what kind of activity? Some feeble waves fling themselves on the beach, and pagans still growl, but all I hear is echoes from the shore; I do not fear a flood. So then, what is happening in our land? *You unseal springs in the valleys*, says the psalm. To God it says, *You unseal springs in the valleys.* You know what valleys are: the low regions of the earth. Valleys and ravines are the opposite of hills and mountains. Hills and mountains are like swollen ground; valleys and ravines are humble, lowly areas. But do not underrate these lowly places, for *you unseal springs in the valleys.* Listen to a mountain speaking: *I have worked harder than any of them.* Something great is being described; but immediately the mountain abases itself into a valley, so that the waters may gush out: *Only not I, but the grace of God with me* (1 Cor 15:10). There is no contradiction in mountains being also valleys, for as they are called mountains on account of their spiritual greatness, so too are they deep valleys in their humility of spirit. *Not I*, says one of them, *but the grace of God with me.* When he avows, *not I*, he is a deep valley; when he adds, *but the grace of God with me*, he is a spring of water. The verse that says, *You unseal springs in the valleys*, was speaking of the Spirit whom I mentioned earlier, for the Lord promised, *Let anyone who is thirsty come to me and drink. If anyone believes in me, as scripture says, rivers of living water shall flow from within that person. He said this of the Spirit, which those who believed*

---

8. *Metus.* Variant: *meatus*, a channel.

in him were to receive. (Jn 7:37-39) Let us see whether there are any valleys in our land, so that the promise of springs opening in the valleys may come true. Yes, for so a prophet testifies in God's name: *Upon whom shall my Spirit rest, but upon the humble, peaceable person, the one who trembles at my words?* (Is 66:2) What does that imply: *Upon whom shall my Spirit rest, but upon the humble, peaceable person*? It means, "In whom shall my fountain be unsealed? In a deep valley."

11. *Streams shall flow midway between the mountains.* This is the point reached by the lector when reciting the psalm, and commentary to this point will be enough for you, I hope, beloved. We will speak about this verse, and then conclude the sermon in God's name.

What does it mean that *streams shall flow midway between the mountains*? We have heard who the mountains are: great preachers of the word, men who are sublime angels of God even though they are still mortal as to their flesh. They are exalted not by their own strength but by his grace; but for their own part and in their own estimation they are valleys that humbly gush with springs. The psalm declares that *streams shall flow midway between the mountains,* and we may take this to mean, "midway between the apostles the preachers of the word of truth will make their way." But why "midway between the apostles"?

What is in the middle belongs to all. It is common property, on which everyone depends equally for life. It is centrally placed; it does not belong to me, but not to you either; it is not the private possession of any of us. This is why we say of certain people, "They have peace among themselves," or, "They keep faith between themselves," or, "They foster charity in their midst." We certainly use such expressions. What do we mean by "among themselves"? Midway, centrally placed among them. And what does "midway" suggest? That it is common to all of them.

Now think about the streams flowing midway between the mountains. They are so described because faith was shared among them as something common to all; no one claimed those waters as private or as an exclusive possession. If the waters were not flowing in the middle they would look like private streams, not flowing for public use: I would have my own, and he would have his, and she hers; there would be nothing central and common which could be mine and his and hers equally. But the preaching that creates peace is not like that. Listen to the words of a mountain who wanted to make sure that the streams would flow midway between the mountains: *May the God of peace grant you to have a common understanding among yourselves* (Rom 15:5). And again: *I beg you to be united in what you say, and not to allow schisms to form among you* (1 Cor 1:10). What I think is what you think; the stream flows down the middle. None of it is my private property, none of it yours. *Streams shall flow midway between the mountains.*

Now listen to a particular mountain putting this principle into practice, a mountain I have already mentioned. *Whether it is I, or whether they, this is what we preach, and this is what you have believed* (1 Cor 15:11). With complete confidence he said this, *Whether it is I, or whether they, this is what we preach, and this is what you have believed,* because the streams were flowing midway between the mountains. There was no dissension between one mountain and another, but peaceful agreement and fellowship in charity. If anyone tried to preach something different, such a person would be preaching his own ideas, not drawing from the central stream. Listen to what was said of such a one by the Lord who unsealed the springs in the valleys: *One who tells lies speaks from what is his own* (Jn 8:44). The apostle wished to make sure that no mountain would be accepted if it supplied water from itself rather than from the stream in the middle, so he warned, *If anyone preaches to you a gospel different from the one you have received, let him be accursed.* He wanted them to place no trust whatever in a mountain that might shift away from the centrally-flowing stream and try to introduce some water of its own. *Even if we ourselves*—wait a minute! Think what a magnificent mountain is speaking! Think how plenteous were the waters gushing from his valley! Yet all he wanted was to run midway between the mountains so that the faith of his people might be safe and assured, because it would be the faith that the apostles held centrally among themselves. So, warned Paul, *Even if we ourselves* —even you, Paul? Could you ever preach anything different? But even Paul must face the test, so he admonishes them, *Even if we ourselves or an angel from heaven should preach to you anything other than what you have received, let such a messenger be anathema!* (Gal 1:9.8) If some mountain appears preaching a different gospel, let that mountain be accursed; if an angel comes preaching a different gospel, let the angel be accursed. Why? Because he wants to be a private stream, not the one in the middle.

A human being, hampered by the obscurity of the flesh and straying away from the common spring to his own false belief, might perhaps do this. But is it possible that an angel could? An *angel*? Surely not? But remember: if an angel who flowed in his own private stream in paradise had not been hearkened to, we should not have been flung down into death. A central stream had been provided for human beings: God's commandment. It was centrally-placed water, water in the middle, public water, we might say. It was there to be used honestly, as I have reminded you, beloved; it was water free from pollution, flowing clear and unmuddied. If we had drunk that water always, we should not have died. But an angel appeared, one fallen from heaven. He had become a snake, because he sought to disseminate his poison by crafty means; he spat out poison because he spoke from his own store, from what was private to himself; and the Lord told us that *one who tells lies speaks from what is his own.* The wretched humans who listened to him forsook the common provision which was the source of their blessedness. They were led away from it to what was their own, perversely trying to be like God, for this was what the tempter had told them: *Taste, and you will be like gods* (Gn 3:5). Craving to be what they were not, they lost what they had received.

To sum up, brothers and sisters: we have spoken to you about springs in the valleys. Let what we have said to you, beloved, help you to be valleys yourselves, so that springs may well up in you. Make sure that what you receive from God is shared with all the others. Let the streams flow in the middle. Do not be jealous of anyone else but drink your fill, and when you are satisfied, flow for others. May this water, common everywhere to all, reflect the glory of God, not the private lies of human beings.

Exposition 3 of Psalm 103

Third Sermon

Preliminary remarks: the eager audience

1. You remember, beloved friends, that we are still in your debt with regard to the exposition of the remaining verses of this psalm. There is therefore no need for any introduction designed to fix your minds on it. Indeed, I see that you are all agog, eager to understand the mysteries of this prophecy. Anything I might say to focus your attention would be superfluous, since the Spirit of God has done that already. All we have to do is to act as he urges us. Explanations have been given of the springs unsealed in deep valleys, and of the streams that flow midway between the mountains. We treated of the psalm thus far, so let us take it up again from this point.

Verse 11. Forest animals signify the nations; on their journey they drink from God's word and apostolic teaching, but in heaven they will contemplate the Word

2. The psalm continues, *All the woodland beasts will drink there.* What will they drink? The streams that flow midway between the mountains. What will they drink? The springs unsealed in the deep valleys. Who will drink? The woodland beasts. In our created world we see animals doing this, to be sure; we watch them drinking from streams and from the brooks that run between mountains. Yet God has willed to hide his wisdom under figurative interpretations of such common sights, not in order to conceal it from earnest seekers but to put off the careless and to open the door to those who knock. It has also pleased the Lord our God to exhort you through us to seek diligently. We must look for the latent spiritual meaning in statements made concerning the material, visible creation, and when we find it, rejoice.

Thus we understand the woodland beasts to be the nations. There are plenty of places in scripture where this meaning is attested, but two clear examples spring to mind. Noah's ark is generally recognized as a prefiguration of the Church, and the only reason why all species of animals were taken aboard was that through their close-knit assembly all nations might be figuratively suggested. This must be the reason, for we can hardly think that God lacked power to command the earth to produce them over again, if all of them had been

139

wiped out by the flood, just as he had ordered it to produce them in the first place by his mere word. No; it was not without purpose, nor randomly, nor on account of any want of power on God's part that all living creatures were ordered into the ark, but as a preparation for what was to happen much later, when the time was right. And this brings us to the second example. When the time came for the symbolism of the ark to be revealed and fulfilled in the Church, the apostle Peter was hesitating over whether he should pass on the mystery of the gospel to uncircumcised Gentiles. Or, rather, I should say that he was not even hesitant, but convinced that he should not. Now on a certain day he was hungry and looking forward to his dinner, and he went upstairs to pray. The story in the Acts of the Apostles is familiar to all who read or listen attentively.[1] While Peter was praying he experienced the kind of spiritual rapture that the Greeks call ecstasy; that is to say, the natural function of his mind was suspended, and he was abstracted from present objects to contemplate something offered to his spiritual sight. Then he beheld what seemed like a sheet being lowered by four linen ropes from heaven, containing all living creatures, every species of animal. A voice called to him, *Now, Peter, slaughter and eat.* But he had been trained under the law and had grown up imbued with Jewish customs. All his life he had held onto the command delivered through God's servant, Moses, and kept it faithfully. He therefore replied, *Far be that from me, Lord; nothing common has ever entered my mouth.* Anyone well versed in ecclesiastical usage is aware that unclean food is called "common" by the Jews and by their law. The voice insisted, *What God has cleansed, do not call unclean* (Acts 10:13-15). This happened three times, and then the round dish,[2] which had three times been shown lowered from heaven, was taken away. This round dish, supported on four linen ropes, was the round earth with its four quarters. Scripture often mentions these four quarters: east and west, north and south. Since the whole of this round world was summoned through the gospel, four gospels were written. The three descents of the container point to the command laid on the apostles, *Go, baptize all nations in the name of the Father, and of the Son, and of the Holy Spirit* (Mt 28:19), and, as you already know, implied in this commission is the number twelve, since this was the number of the disciples. Not without clear purpose did the Lord choose to have twelve, and so sacred was this number that when one fell, an extra one had to be ordained in his place. Why were there twelve apostles? The earth consisted of four quarters, and this whole round world was called to believe the gospel, which was why four gospels were written. But this whole round world was called in the name of the Trinity to be gathered as the Church; and four times three makes twelve.

---

1. See Acts 10:9-16.
2. *Discus.*

Small wonder, then, that all the woodland beasts drink from the streams flowing midway between the mountains, from the teaching of the apostles which flows centrally because of the peaceful communion between them. All these animals were in the ark, all were in the round dish, and Peter slaughters and eats all of them, because Peter is the rock, and the rock is the Church.[3] What does it mean to slaughter and eat them? To kill what they were, and take them into his own vitals. When you have dissuaded a pagan from his sacrilegious practices you have slain what he was; when you have conferred Christ's sacrament on him and incorporated him into the Church, you have eaten him.

3. These, then, are the animals that drink from the waters, but the waters are running streams, coursing by and never standing still. All the teaching dispensed in this present age is transient. The apostle says of it, *Knowledge will be destroyed, and prophecy annulled.* Why will these things cease to count? Because *we know only in part, and utter partial prophecies, but when perfection comes, what is partial will be superseded* (1 Cor 13:8-10). In the city which is bidden, *Sing united praise to the Lord, O Jerusalem, praise your God, O Zion, for he has strengthened the bars of your gates* (Ps 147:12-13); in that place where the bars are strengthened and the city closed; there, whence no friend departs and where no enemy gains entrance, as we have told you before,[4] dearly beloved; in that city we shall need to have no book read to us, no sermon preached as it is preached to you now. It is preached now that it may abide in your memory in that heavenly city; the word is broken down into syllables now, that there you may contemplate it whole and entire. The word of God will be there indeed, but not mediated through letters, or sounds, or books, or reader, or homilist. How, then? As *the Word was in the beginning, the Word who was with God, the Word who was God.* He did not come to us in such a way as to forsake his heaven, for though *he was here in the world, the world was made by him* (Jn 1:1.10). Such is the Word we shall contemplate, for *the God of gods will be seen in Zion* (Ps 83:8(84:7)).

When will this be? After our pilgrimage, when our journey is finished, provided that when the journey is over we are not handed over to the judge and flung into prison.[5] But if when our wayfaring is done we arrive at our homeland—as we hope, and long, and strive to do—there we shall contemplate the reality that we are to praise for ever. It will be freely available to us, and neither it nor we who enjoy it will ever fail. The one who eats will never weary of that food, nor will the food run short. That will be contemplation indeed, glorious and wonderful.

---

3. *Petrus petra, petra ecclesia.*
4. See Exposition of Psalm 147,9.13.
5. See Mt 5:25.

Who can speak of it worthily in this present age, when the streams are flowing between the mountains? But let them flow on, let them course by, for as they flow past us we drink on our pilgrimage, lest we faint from thirst on the way. *All the woodland beasts will drink there.* That is where you come from; you were collected from the woods. What kind of woods were they? No human passed through them, for no prophet had been sent there. Yet trees from those forests were felled to build the ark. From the woods came trees and animals; from the woods you came too. Drink, then. *All the woodland beasts will drink there.*

There is water for all animals, large and small; the wild asses represent celibates

4. *The onagers will quench their thirst.* The psalm calls large animals *onagers*, and everyone knows that this is a common name for wild asses. It is therefore talking about certain powerful, untamed people. The Gentiles bore no yoke of the law; many of them were living according to their own ideas of right and wrong, roaming in their boastful pride as though in the desert. The same was true of all animals, but the psalm singled out onagers as a symbol of great size. They too will drink to slake their thirst, for the waters flow for them as well. The coney[6] drinks, and the onager drinks; the coney is small, the onager large; the coney is timid, the onager fierce. Both drink, but each to quench its own thirst. The water does not drive the onager away, saying, "I have only enough to satisfy the coney"; nor does it say, "Let the onager approach, but if the coney comes too near, he will be swept away." The stream flows so steadily and evenly that it will satisfy the onager as surely as it does not frighten the coney.

Imagine a voice resounding—Tully's, perhaps. Some book of Cicero is read, or a dialogue, one of his or one of Plato's, or of some other great writer. Uneducated folk hear it, people of limited understanding. Which of them is bold enough to aspire to such works? These books are like crashing, turbulent waters, or at least like water flowing so dangerously that a timid animal dare not approach to drink. But when we hear, *In the beginning God made heaven and earth* (Gn 1:1), is there anyone who is too shy to drink? Is there anyone who hears a psalm ring out, and says, "That is above my head"? Take the strains of our present psalm, for instance: they conceal mysteries, to be sure, but so sweet are they that even children delight to listen to them. The unskilled approach to drink, and being satisfied they burst out into psalmody.

Little animals drink, and larger animals drink too, because *the onagers will quench their thirst.* Let the little ones drink that scripture which urges, *Husbands, love your wives, as Christ loved the Church. Let wives be subject to their husbands.* (Eph 5:25.24) Let the smaller animals drink that.

---

6. See the note at section 18 below on the identification of this animal.

But a question was put to the Lord: *Is it lawful for a man to divorce his wife on any grounds?* The Lord forbade it, denying that it was lawful. *Have you never read*, he asked, *that God created them male and female from the beginning? What God has joined together, no one may divide.* (Mt 19:3,4,6) Then he added, *Anyone who divorces his wife, apart from the case of unfaithfulness, causes her to commit adultery; and if he marries someone else, he commits adultery* (Mt 5:32). Christ affirmed the bond that exists between husband and wife, and that is a comfort to those who are married. Anyone who objects should have taken care not to be bound in the first place. *Are you bound to a wife? Then do not seek to be unbound. Are you free of a wife? Do not seek one.* (1 Cor 7:27) If you are not yet an onager, and are unmarried, you have the chance to drink as a coney, for if you do marry you have committed no sin.[7] But when the disciples heard the Lord say that marriages could not be dissolved for any reason (leaving aside a case of unfaithfulness), they protested, *If things stand thus between husband and wife, it is better not to marry!* And the Lord answered, *Not everyone can accept that.* (Mt 19:10,11) You are right to say that if this is the situation between husband and wife, it is better not to marry. But is it the onagers alone who will be able to drink? Not everyone can accept that doctrine; many cannot. Who are the ones who do accept it? *The onagers will quench their thirst.* What does that mean—*the onagers will quench their thirst*? The same as: *Let anyone accept this who can.*

Verse 12. Mountain-dwelling birds represent spiritual persons, who are to be listened to if they sing from amid the rocks

5. The text of the psalm proceeds thus: *On them birds of the sky will dwell.* On what? On the onagers, or on the mountains? Probably the latter, because the sense follows on better that way: *Streams shall flow midway between the mountains. All the woodland beasts will drink there, and the onagers will quench their thirst. On them birds of the sky will dwell.* It is more intelligible if we take it as "on the mountains" because they are a habitat suited to this particular creature. Flying creatures can dwell on mountains but not on wild asses; we would only understand it in the latter sense if we had no alternative. Well, then, creatures that fly beneath heaven will dwell on the mountains. We certainly do observe birds dwelling there; but many other birds live in fields, many in valleys, others in woods, others in gardens. Not all birds are mountain-dwellers, though some species will live nowhere but on mountains.

Now birds represent spiritual souls. Winged creatures symbolize the hearts of spiritual persons which enjoy the freedom of the air. These birds exult in calm

---

7. See 1 Cor 7:28.

skies, yet their food is on the mountains, and that is where they make their home. You know what mountains are: that has been explained already. The prophets are mountains, the apostles are mountains, all preachers of truth are mountains. Whoever aspires to a spiritual life should live among them and beware of getting lost by following his own heart. Let him live there and grow strong by flying.[8] We can be sure, then, that birds represent something spiritual; it was no idle promise that *your youth will be renewed like an eagle's* (Ps 102(103):5).

Nor is it without significance that we are told concerning Abraham, *He did not divide the birds* (Gn 15:10). You remember that very mysterious sacrifice? Abraham took three animals: a three-year-old ram, a three-year-old heifer, and a three-year-old she-goat; he also took a turtledove and a pigeon.[9] The ram was cut in half, and its two halves arranged opposite each other; the she-goat was halved, and the pieces placed opposite each other; the heifer was cut in half and its carcass arranged similarly. Scripture then states, *He did not divide the birds.* What is more, it tells us that the ram, the heifer and the she-goat were all three years old but says nothing of the age of the birds. Why is that? I am asking you. Could it be because the birds represent spiritual persons? Their temporal age is not mentioned because they meditate on eternal realities, and by their desire and understanding they transcend all the things of time.

Then as to the undivided state of the birds: these are a symbol of spiritual men[10] who are judges of all but judged themselves by no one;[11] they alone, therefore, do not splinter into heresies and schisms. The ram is a figure of prelates who lead the flock; the heifer stands for the Jewish people because they wore the yoke of the law and labored under it; the she-goat represents the Church gathered from the Gentiles, because it used to leap about unrestrainedly and feed on wild olives.[12] These three animals are named because it was in the third age that grace was revealed. The first age was that which preceded the law; the second opened when the law was promulgated; the third, in which we live, is the time when the kingdom of heaven is preached.

Can we truly say that the ram, taken in the figurative sense, is not divided? Were not schisms and heresies initiated by bishops? Yes, but if the peoples themselves had not been divided—if neither heifer nor she-goat had been divided, we might say—the leaders would perhaps have been ashamed of their divisions and would have returned to union with the rest. When leaders are

---

8. *Habitet, perferat volando.* The phrase is difficult, and some copyists seem to have found it so. Some codices omit the first two words and extract the meaning, "Let him not live in his own heart, whence he might go astray in his flight."
9. See Gn 15:9-17.
10. *Viri.*
11. See 1 Cor 2:15.
12. See Rom 11:17.

disunited, the peoples are disunited too, and then the blind lead the blind, and they fall into the pit together.[13] All these are placed in opposition to each other. *But he did not divide the birds.* Spiritual persons are not so divided. They harbor no thoughts of schism but live tranquilly. They encourage peace in others insofar as they can, and when it fails in other people they preserve it in themselves. *If a son of peace is there,* the gospel tells us, *your peace will rest upon him; but if not, it will revert to you* (Lk 10:6). If that other person is no son of peace, he has been wanting division, and in that case your peace will come back to you. This is what is suggested by the fact that Abraham did not divide the birds.

Sooner or later, the brazier will appear. The story relates that Abraham remained sitting there until nightfall, and then he was overcome by a mighty terror of judgment day. That nightfall signifies the end of the world, and the brazier the future day of judgment. The parts of the animals were separated already, but the brazier came to reinforce the separation, for if it passed down the middle, it must have made a sharp distinction between those to the right of it and those to the left. There are people of carnal disposition still within the embrace of the Church; they live in their own fashion, and we should be apprehensive lest they be seduced by heresies, because being carnal they are prone to division. *He did not divide the birds,* but the carnal are divided. *Not as spiritual persons could I speak to you, but only as carnal,* Paul complains. How do we prove that carnally-minded persons are divided? By Paul's reproof: *When everyone of you is saying, I belong to Paul; I belong to Apollos; I belong to Cephas, are you not carnal still, conducting yourselves in a merely human way?* (1 Cor 3:1; 1:12; 3:3) Listen to this warning, brothers and sisters, I beg you, and take it to heart. Tear yourselves away from the carnal position and take your place with the turtledove and the pigeon, for *he did not divide the birds.* If anyone neglects to change, and persists in a lifestyle characteristic of carnal persons yet does not leave the bosom of the Church and is not seduced by heretics, the brazier will come to separate him or her from the opposing party, for in the end it will not be possible to be on the right side[14] without the intervention of the brazier. Anyone who dreads being burnt by it should join the turtledove and the pigeon now. Let those who can accept this accept it. What if such a person does not, but *builds in wood, hay and straw* (1 Cor 3:12); that is to say, superimposes the love of worldly things upon the foundation of his faith? Even so, provided that Christ is there as the foundation and holds first place in such a person's heart, worldly loves can be borne and tolerated, for the brazier will come and burn up the wood, hay and straw, *but he himself will be saved, though it be through fire* (1 Cor

---

13. See Mt 15:14.
14. Implicitly, Christ's right hand as in Mt 25:33, though the scene is still that of Abraham's vision.

3:15).[15] It will be the work of the burning brazier to separate people. Some will be to the left, others sifted out for the right.

He did not divide the birds. But the birds must watch out, if they are the kind of birds adapted to life on the mountains. They must not be led astray into any self-exaltation like the people of whom it is said, *Their boastful talk is directed to the sky* (Ps 72(73):9). Let them roost on the mountains lest they be snatched away by the winds. The authority of the saints is there for them, so let them roost on the mountains, on the apostles and the prophets. Let birds of such plumage dwell there, for on the mountains they find rocks, the stable firmness of the commandments. As there is one single rock, Christ, the Word of God, there are also many words of God like so many rocks, and these rocks are to be found on the mountains. Watch the birds that dwell there, for *on the mountains birds of the sky will dwell.*

6. Do not imagine, though, that these creatures flying under heaven claim any authority for themselves, for the psalm continues, *They will sing their song from among the rocks.* Suppose I were to say to you today, "You have to believe this, because Cicero said it, Plato said it, Pythagoras said it," wouldn't you all laugh at me? I would be like a bird chirping, but not from the rock. What ought every one of you to say to me? How should a person respond who has heard Paul's warning, *If anyone preaches to you a gospel different from the one you have received, let him be accursed* (Gal 1:9)? You should reply, "Why talk to me about Plato, or Cicero, or Virgil? You have the mountains and the rocks right in front of you; speak from a place amid the rocks." *They will sing their song from among the rocks.* Only those who listen to the rock deserve to be heard.[16] Let them be heard, because even in these many rocks the voice of one rock is speaking, and *the rock is Christ* (1 Cor 10:4). Yes, let us hear them eagerly, those who utter their cries from the heart of the rocks. Nothing is sweeter than this kind of birdsong. They chirp, spiritual persons discuss, the rocks ring with it, and the teaching of scriptures answers. Listen to the winged creatures giving voice from amid the rocks, for they dwell on the mountains.

Verse 13. We receive nourishing water from the rocks and mountains; they receive it from God

7. But where do the mountains and rocks learn their song? If we need to be watered by the scriptures, we rush to the apostle Paul. But where did Paul get it? We have recourse to Isaiah. But who taught Isaiah? Listen, the psalm tells us:

---

15. Augustine seems to envisage the possibility of some purification after death from attachment to things other than God. His remarks give some insight into an early stage in the development of the doctrine of purgatory, taken further in *The City of God* 21,13.

16. Variant: "Let those who listen to the rock listen to such people."

From his high dwelling he pours rain on the mountains. Suppose an uncircumcised Gentile comes to us, prepared to believe in Christ. We baptize him, and we do not direct him to the works of the law. If a Jew challenges us on this policy, we sing our song from the rock: we say, "Peter acted so, Paul acted so." We send forth our song from amid the rocks. But that great mountain, that mighty rock, Peter himself, was watered from on high when he saw his vision; and the apostle Paul told the Gentiles, *If you have yourselves circumcised, Christ will be useless to you* (Gal 5:2). When Paul says this he speaks as a mountain, and we say it too, singing our song from the rock; but the Lord had to irrigate that very mountain from his own heights. He did, for when that particular rock was still a rugged unbeliever, and the Lord intended to water him from on high so that the water might flow in the valley, he shouted, *Saul, Saul, why are you persecuting me?* (Acts 9:4). He did not read him some passage from a prophet, nor anything from another apostle; a mighty mountain might have scorned these. He watered Paul from his own heights, and no sooner was Paul irrigated than he wanted to gush with water himself. *What do you want me to do, Lord?* he asked (Acts 9:6).

Take this mountain, this rock, as your stronghold, so that from there you too may sing your song. Take him as your own. Watch him being watered from above and flowing down to places below.[17] There is one place where you hear him speaking about this: *If we are beside ourselves, it is for God; if in our right mind, it is for you* (2 Cor 5:13). By *beside ourselves* he means, "You cannot comprehend these things, for we have left all carnal considerations behind, whereas you are still carnal. When we are beside ourselves we commune with God, and what we see in those states we cannot put into words"; for there *he heard things beyond utterance, of which no human tongue may speak* (2 Cor 12:4). "But what about us?" protest those carnal people, the coneys. "Are we not to be watered? Will no drop of it filter down to us? How does God unseal springs in the valleys? How will streams run midway between the mountains?" The answer has already been given: *If we are in our right mind, it is for you.* What drives us? Whom are we imitating? *The charity of Christ constrains us* (2 Cor 5:14). You participate in the Word, Paul. Today you are a spiritual man, but only yesterday you were carnal. Humble yourself, then, and come down to the level of flesh and blood, since the Word himself was made flesh and blood in order to live among us.[18]

8. Let us bless the Lord and praise him who waters the mountains from his high places. From the mountains the earth will receive its irrigation, so that even the lowest regions will be satisfied. The psalm therefore continues, *The earth*

---

17. These last sentences could be understood as transferring Paul's example to the Christian: "Take this mountain, this rock, as your example. . . . Take him, and see yourself being watered."
18. See Jn 1:14.

will be enriched with the fruit you have created. What does that phrase indicate, *the fruit you have created*? That no one may boast of his own works; anyone with a mind to boast must boast in the Lord.[19] If the earth is drenched it is drenched with God's grace, and it cannot say that grace was given in response to its deserving. If it is grace, it is given gratis; if it is given in view of work done, it is paid as wages. Receive it, then, as sheer grace, because you, impious though you were, are justified.[20] *The earth will be enriched with the fruit you have created.*

Verse 14. The laity should give material support to their pastors, symbolized by oxen, which are their servants

9. *It brings forth grass for cattle, and plants for the service of human beings.* This evokes something I know about and have observed in creation. The ground produces grass for cattle, and crops to meet the needs of humans. But I see in this verse other cattle, which are referred to in the injunction, *You shall not muzzle an ox while it is threshing* (Dt 25:4; 1 Cor 9:9; 1 Tm 5:18). And on this prohibition an ox itself demands, *Does God care about oxen? Scripture is talking about us, clearly.* (1 Cor 9:9-10) In what sense does the earth bring forth grass for cattle? *The Lord ordained that those who preach the gospel should earn their living by the gospel* (1 Cor 9:14). He sent out his preachers and instructed them, *Eat what they set before you, for the laborer deserves his pay* (Lk 10:8.7). He had said to them, *Eat what they set before you,* and the disciples might have objected, "We shall have no right to eat at people's tables when we have no means to pay. Do you intend us to be so shameless?" "No," he might have replied. "It is not a donation from them, but the wages you deserve." Wages for what? What are they giving, what receiving? They give spiritual goods and receive carnal payment; they give gold and receive grass, for *all flesh is but grass, and human glory like the flower of grass* (Is 40:6). All the temporal goods you have over, things you do not need, are grass for cattle. Why? Because they are carnal.

Now I will tell you what the oxen are, the ones you supply with grass. *If we have sown spiritual seeds for your benefit, is it too much to ask that we reap a carnal harvest from you?* (1 Cor 9:11) This is what the apostle asked, and what a hard worker he was, how indefatigable, how strenuously determined to give the very grass back to the earth! *I made no use of any of these rights* (1 Cor 9:15), he says. He pointed out that though recompense was owed to him, he did not accept it, though he did not condemn others for accepting what was due to them. Only those who demanded what was not due deserved condemnation, not those who took their just wages; yet Paul gave away even the wages he had earned. But it does not follow that because one preacher has been so generous to you, you owe

---

19. See 1 Cor 1:31.
20. See Rom 4:4-5.

nothing to another: if you take that line you will not be the well-watered earth that produces grass for the cattle. *The earth will be enriched with the fruit you have created*, says the psalm; *it brings forth grass for cattle*. Do not be barren; bring forth grass for those cattle. Even if they do not want your grass, do not on that account let them find you barren earth. You receive spiritual riches, so give back carnal ones. They are due to a soldier, and it is to the soldier's upkeep that you, as Christ's civilian,[21] are contributing. *Does anyone ever serve in the army at his own expense? Who plants a vineyard, and receives no fruit from it? Does a person ever tend a flock, without drinking its milk?* (1 Cor 9:7) I am not saying this because I want you to give your money to me. There certainly was a soldier who handed back even his allowance[22] to civilians, but that does not excuse the civilians from making the contribution.

I would like to speak further on this subject. Your preachers are beasts of burden: the law enjoins, *You shall not muzzle an ox while it is threshing.* Our psalm first says that the earth *brings forth grass for cattle* and then goes on to explain this by adding, *and plants for the service of human beings.* In case you might not understand the words, *it brings forth grass for cattle*, the psalm clarified the phrase by repeating it in different terms. Thus *grass* in the first half becomes *plants* in the second, and *for cattle* in the first is repeated in the second as *for the service of human beings.* It therefore looks as though the grass is provided for creatures bound to servitude, not for free creatures. What then becomes of the statement, *You have been called to liberty*? But listen to what Paul claims elsewhere: *Though I am a free man and beholden to no one, I have made myself the slave of all, to win over more people* (1 Cor 9:19). Further, though he had said to some of his converts, *You have been called to liberty*, he immediately added, *But take care not to let your freedom give the flesh its chance. Rather serve one another out of charity* (Gal 5:13). Having declared them free he then made slaves of them, not as to their condition but because of Christ's redemption not as a matter of compulsion but out of charity, for he said, *Serve one another out of charity.*

Someone objects, "But it is to Christ that we render our service, not to people generally or carnal folk or the weak." Yes, and it is Christ whom you truly serve, if you serve those whom Christ served. Was it not said of him, *He gave good service to many* (Is 53:11, LXX)? That is a text from prophecy, and it is usually referred to Christ alone, but let us listen to his command in the gospel: *Whoever wishes to be greater among you will be your servant* (Mt 20:27). You must say to us, "He who made you a free man by his own blood has made you my slave"; and you are right to say that. Quite correct. And listen to another admonition by Paul:

---

21. *Provincialis.* On the contribution of the *annona* by civilians to the support of the military, see the note at Exposition of Psalm 90,10.
22. *Annonam*: see the preceding note.

We are your slaves, through Jesus (2 Cor 4:5). Take care to love your slaves, but in your Lord; and may he grant us to serve you well. Whether we like it or not, we are servants, but if we consent to be servants, we serve not under compulsion but out of charity.

What prompted the Lord to say, *Whoever wishes to be greater among you will be your servant,* seems to have been a proud, peevish outburst on the part of his servants, for the sons of Zebedee were already looking for the most honorable seats. One wanted to sit at his right, the other at his left, and they expressed their ambition through their mother. The Lord did not begrudge them their thrones, but he first pointed to the vale of tears, as though asking them, "You want to reach the place where I am? Then travel by the road I take." What does it mean to travel by his road? "Travel by humility. I came down from sublime heights, and I ascend only after being humbled. I found you on earth; and yet you aspire to fly before you have even been fed. Take your nourishment first, allow yourselves to be trained, bear the restraints of the nest." This must be what he meant, for what did he say to them? How did he recall these seekers of high places to sage humility? *Are you able to drink the cup I am to drink?* And they, proud even in such a matter as this, replied, *We are.* They were like Peter, who boasted, *I will go with you even to death* (Lk 22:33). He was a strong man, until a woman said, *This man was with them too* (Mk 14:69). James and John were just the same: *We are able,* they declared. *Are you able? We are.* And Jesus predicted, *You shall indeed drink my cup,* even though you cannot do so now. *You shall drink it,* he said, as he also promised Peter, *You will follow me later* (Jn 13:36). He warned James and John, *You shall indeed drink my cup, but to sit at my right or my left is not mine to grant you.* (Mt 20:22-23) Why did he say that—*not mine to grant you*? "It is not in my power to grant this to proud persons," he implied. "As I speak to you today, you are proud. That is why I have to tell you that it is *not mine to grant you.*" Perhaps they countered, "But we will be humble!" "Then you will not be yourselves. What I said was addressed to you, to you as you are. I did not say, 'I will not grant this to the humble,' but 'I cannot grant it to the proud.'" When a proud person becomes humble, he will not be what he once was.

Try to anticipate the needs of God's servants

10. As I was saying, the preachers of the word are laboring oxen and your servants. If the earth has been watered, it must bring forth *grass for cattle, and plants for the service of human beings.* Production of such crops makes possible the happy outcome mentioned in the gospel: *They will welcome you into the tents of eternity* (Lk 16:9). Look what you can do with your grass! Consider what you can buy at so cheap a price! *They will welcome you into the tents of eternity,* says scripture. They will be there; let them welcome you there too. How does that happen? *Anyone who welcomes a just person inasmuch as he is a just person will*

receive the reward due to a just person. Anyone who welcomes a prophet inasmuch as he is a prophet will receive the reward due to a prophet. And anyone who gives a cup of cold water to one of my little ones simply because he is a disciple, I tell you, he will not miss his reward. (Mt 10:41-42) What is the reward that he or she will not miss? A welcome into the tents of eternity.

Who would not be in a hurry to get there? Who would not run as fast as possible? If you are the earth, allow yourself to be irrigated by God's husbandry, and do not make excuses: "There is no one to whom we can render these services. Our preachers, the threshing oxen, those who serve us—they do not need us." All the same, make inquiries; there may be one who is in need. In any case, even if he does not need your contribution, let him find you ready to give what he declines to accept. He does accept your good will, and you for your part receive his peace,[23] and even if he is not seeking your gift, he does seek the fruit accruing to you.[24] Go looking, then, in case there is one of them in need, and do not say, "I will give if someone asks." Are you going to wait for him to ask? Are you going to treat God's ox like a passing beggar? You give to the beggar because scripture bids you, *Give to everyone who asks you* (Lk 6:30). But what else does scripture tell you? *Blessed is everyone who understands about the needy and poor man* (Ps 40:2(41:1)). Look for someone to whom you can give help, for *blessed is everyone who understands about the needy and poor man*, blessed is the one who forestalls the request. If Christ's soldiers are among you, yet are so badly off that they even have to ask you for assistance, do not be surprised if they judge you sooner than begging from you. "But how am I to look for them?" you ask. Be inquisitive, try to foresee the need. Look around, find out how each one makes his living, how he does for transport, how he manages. This will not be frowned on as curiosity on your part, for you are simply the earth which *brings forth grass for cattle, and plants for the service of human beings*. Be inquisitive, and try to understand about the needy and the poor. One poor person seeks you out to beg from you; but you must forestall the other so that he has no need to beg. Concerning the one who seeks you out, you are bidden, *Give to everyone who asks you*; and something similar has been said to you about the one you must seek out: "Your alms should be sweating in your hand until you find a just person to whom you may give it."[25]

Alms should certainly be given to those who openly ask you. God has put no curb on such donations. On the contrary, Christ commanded, *When you give a feast, invite the blind, the lame, and the frail. They have no means of repaying you, but you will be rewarded at the resurrection of the just* (Lk 14:13-14). Yes, invite these by all means, and feed them. Feast while they feast, enjoy it when

---

23. See Lk 10:6.
24. See Phil 4:17.
25. Quoted already by Augustine in his Exposition of Psalm 102,12. See the note there.

they eat their fill, for as they are nourished on your food, you are nourished on God's righteousness. Let no one tell you, "Christ commanded us to give to a servant of God, not to a beggar." That is completely wrong, and only a godless person would say it. By all means give to the beggar, but far more to God's servant. The one asks, and by his request you know that this is someone to whom you ought to give; the other does not ask, but that means you must be all the more vigilant to give before he asks—or rather to give to someone who is not going to ask now, but may condemn you later. Be alert and inquisitive about such cases, brothers and sisters. You will discover poverty in many servants of God, as long as you really want to discover it. But you don't, of course. You eagerly seize on the excuse, "We didn't know." And that is why you fail to discover it.

The Lord himself accepted contributions from believers and gave alms to the poor; he left us an example in both respects

11. The Lord himself owned purses, and necessary funds were kept in them.[26] He had money to defray his own expenses and those of his companions. The evangelist was not writing fiction when he told us that Jesus was hungry:[27] Jesus willed to be hungry for your sake, to free you from hunger in him who, though rich, became poor for us, so that through his poverty we might become rich.[28] However, he did own purses, and it is related that certain faithful women followed in his footsteps[29] wherever he went to preach the good news and ministered to him from their own resources.[30] These women are named in the gospel; among them was the wife of a certain Chuza, who was Herod's steward.

Try to understand the reason for these arrangements. Later on there would be Paul, who asked for nothing like this and handed everything back to the civilians. But later still there would be plenty of weak ministers of the gospel who would seek payment, and so Christ preferred to take on the role of the weak. Was Paul acting more nobly—more nobly even than Christ? Far from it: Christ's policy was nobler, because more merciful. He foresaw that Paul would not demand fees, and to ensure that anyone who did demand them would not be condemned for doing so, he set an example for his weak servants. His attitude was similar when he saw that many would hasten to suffer martyrdom, joyful and eager, exulting in their passion, brave men and women who would represent the Lord's hundredfold, a mature crop ready for the barn.[31] Christ saw that there would also be weaker people who would be dismayed by the prospect of

26. See Jn 13:29.
27. See Mk 11:12.
28. See 2 Cor 8:9.
29. Literally "his feet," recalling the "beautiful feet" of Is 52:7; Rom 10:15.
30. See Lk 8:2-3.
31. See Mt 13:23.

suffering, and in his own passion he willed to identify with them, that they might be empowered to unite their human wills with the will of their creator. Accordingly he admitted, *My soul is sorrowful to the point of death,* and again he prayed, *Father, if it is possible, let this cup pass from me.* By this prayer he exemplified what a weak person would say; but he went on to show us what a weak person must do: *Yet not what I will, but what you will be done, Father.* (Mt 26:38,39)

In his passion he identified himself with his weak followers by prefiguring them in his own body, for they too are his members, and it was not for nothing that a psalm prayed, *Your eyes beheld my imperfection, and in your book all shall be written* (Ps 138(139):16). In parallel fashion he made the poverty of his followers his own by possessing funds and in a certain sense inviting a contribution, not by demanding it but by laying on the faithful an obligation to give.[32] Zacchaeus offered hospitality to Christ and rejoiced.[33] Who benefited? Christ or Zacchaeus? Suppose Zacchaeus had not invited him in, would he who fashioned the world have been without a place to lodge? Or if Zacchaeus had not fed him, would he have gone hungry, he who satisfied so many thousands of people with five loaves? When anyone gives hospitality to a holy person, it is the host, not the guest, who gains. Was Elijah not fed in a famine? Did not a raven, a creature serving God's servant, bring him bread and meat? Yet he was sent to a widow's house to be fed there,[34] in order that the civilian might receive a gift, not the soldier.

12. We spoke about the duty of caring also for the poor, brothers and sisters, when commenting on the fact that the Lord had money in his purse. Now when he said to Judas, who was plotting to betray him, *What you are going to do, do quickly* (Jn 13:27), the other disciples did not understand what he meant and thought he had told Judas to get something ready to give to the poor. Judas had charge of the purse, as we know from scripture. They could hardly have entertained that idea, could they, if it had not been the Lord's custom to act like this? So we can infer that it was usual for donations to be given to him and put into the purses and for alms to be given from them to the poor people whom God has taught us not to despise. But if you must not despise a beggar, how much less the ox who tramples the threshing floor? How much less your own servant? He does not need food? Very well, perhaps he needs clothing. He does not need clothing either? But perhaps he needs a roof over his head, perhaps he is building a church, or struggling with some useful work in God's house and is waiting for you to notice, waiting for you to understand about the poor and needy person.

---

32. Variant supported by many codices: ". . .not by demanding it but as a favor he was granting to them."
33. See Lk 19:6.
34. See 1 Kgs 17:4-16.

But no, you are hard, stony earth, not watered, or watered to no purpose. You cling to your excuse: "I did not know, I never found out, nobody told me." Nobody told you! Christ never stops telling you, the prophet never stops telling you, *Blessed is everyone who understands about the needy and poor man.* Perhaps you cannot see that your pastor's[35] coffers are empty, but you can certainly see the fabric rising, the building which you will later enter to pray. Does it not stare you in the face? You surely do not think, brothers and sisters, that your bishops[36] are hoarding money? We have known many of them who, so far from hoarding, are in want of everyday necessities, though no one believes it. You could find some in this condition if you wanted to, if you looked around, if you were on the watch to yield proper fruit.

I have said what I could, as forcefully as I could; but I think you know us too well, as the apostle would say, to suppose that we are reminding you of all this to induce you to increase your contributions to us. May God grant that I have not said it all in vain; may he grant you to become well-watered earth, earth that after being irrigated yields its crop to the farmer. Even the stony hearts of the Jews, symbolized by the stone tablets, used to give tithes.

Do I hear you groaning? Nothing is coming out, though! If you are groaning, go into labor, and if you are in labor, give birth to something! Why groan to no purpose? Why groan if you are sterile? Your bowels are in anguish: is there nothing within that can come to birth? *From his high dwelling he pours rain on the mountains, and the earth will be enriched with the fruit you have created.* Blessed are those who act on this, blessed are those who listen fruitfully to these things, blessed are they whose groaning is no empty noise.

The earth will be enriched with the fruit you have created. It brings forth grass for cattle, and plants for the service of human beings. And why? *That we may produce bread from the ground.* What bread is this? Christ. And what is the earth that brings him forth? Peter, Paul, and the other dispensers of truth. I will tell you why he is said to be brought forth from the earth: *We carry this treasure in earthen vessels,* says Paul, *so that the sublime power may plainly belong to God* (2 Cor 4:7). Christ is the bread that came down from heaven,[37] to be drawn from the earth when he is proclaimed through the flesh of his servants. The earth yields grass, so that God may bring forth bread from the earth. Which is the earth that yields grass? Devout peoples, holy peoples. And from which earth is bread drawn forth? From the apostles; for God's word is drawn from apostles and from ministers of God's mysteries who are still walking about on the earth, still carrying their earthly bodies.

---

35. *Praepositi tui*: "of the one set over you."
36. *Praepositi.*
37. See Jn 6:33.41.

Verse 15. True wine of joy, true bread: Christ the anointed one

13. *And wine that cheers the human heart.* Let no one expect to get drunk—or, rather, let everyone get drunk! *How excellent is your intoxicating chalice!* (Ps 22(23):5) We do not mean to say, "Nobody must be inebriated," but rather, "Go ahead and get inebriated, but from the right source." If the Lord's excellent chalice intoxicates you, your inebriation will be evident in your actions. It will show itself in your holy love for justice, and finally it will be obvious from the way you lose your senses, but lose them only in the estrangement of your mind from earthly things to fly to heaven. *That our faces may shine cheerfully with oil.* I see now what impressive fruit is derived from this earth, if it produces grass for cattle. These servants do not sell what they give you; they are not merchants of the gospel, for they freely give what they freely receive.[38] They are delighted at your good works because such works enrich you; your pastors are not looking for the gift itself but for the profit that accrues to you.[39] Now, what is a face glistening with oil? It is the grace of God, or a radiance that manifests the presence of grace, according to the apostle's statement: *To each is granted the Spirit for manifestation* (1 Cor 12:7). A special grace in human beings, which is evident to other people and so makes holy love attractive to them, is called oil because of its Godlike radiance. It appeared in fullest splendor in Christ himself, and that is why the whole world loves him. Here below he was despised, but now he is adored by every nation, *for the kingship is the Lord's, and he will hold sway over the nations* (Ps 21:29(22:28)). So powerful is his grace that many who do not put their faith in him nonetheless praise him: they maintain that their reason for not believing in him is that no one can possibly measure up to his commands. The same people who once insulted him in their rage are now constrained to praise him in their embarrassment.

Yet he is loved by all, and preached by all, because he is the supremely anointed one. This is why he is called Christ. The anointed Christ derives his name from "chrism." His name is *Messiah* in Hebrew, *Christos* in Greek, *Unctus* in Latin. But he anoints his entire body. All comers receive grace, that their faces may shine with oil.

14. *And the bread that strengthens our hearts.* What does this refer to, brothers and sisters? The phrase almost forces us to understand what bread is meant; for ordinary, visible bread strengthens the stomach and the digestion, but there is another bread that strengthens the heart, because it is the bread proper to the heart. The psalm spoke of bread before this when it said, *That we may produce bread from the ground*; but it did not make unambiguously clear what kind of bread that is. Now it adds, *And wine that cheers the human heart.* This

---

38. See Mt 10:8.
39. See Phil 4:17.

wine that gladdens the human heart certainly seems to be spiritual wine. But it still could be understood as ordinary wine, because drunken persons appear to be happy. (I wish they would just be happy, and not brawl.) You say to me, "Who is happier than a drunken man?" I would rather say, Who is crazier than a drunk? And who more quarrelsome, often enough? No, there is a wine that truly gladdens the heart and nothing but the heart. Even so, you still might have thought that while a spiritual interpretation was appropriate for the wine, it did not hold for the bread. The psalm therefore makes it clear that the bread too is to be understood as spiritual, by saying, *And the bread that strengthens our hearts.* Take both bread and wine in the same sense. Hunger inwardly, and be thirsty inwardly: *Blessed are those who hunger and thirst for righteousness, for they shall be satisfied* (Mt 5:6). This bread is righteousness, and this wine is righteousness; they are real, they are the truth, and Christ is the truth. *I am the living bread which has come down from heaven*, he claimed, and *I am the vine, you are the branches* (Jn 6:41; 15:5). *The bread strengthens our hearts.*

Verse 16. The cedars of Lebanon, some planted by the Lord, others doomed to be uprooted

15. *The trees of the plain shall drink their fill* from the grace drawn out of the earth.[40] The *trees of the plain* are the peoples, all nations. *And the cedars he planted on Lebanon.* The cedars of Lebanon are the powerful in this world: they too will be satisfied, for the bread, the wine, and the oil of Christ have reached senators, and nobles, and kings. The trees of the plain have been satisfied; humble folk were satisfied first, and then the cedars of Lebanon. But only those whom the Lord had planted: the God-fearing cedars, the devout believers, for these are the trees planted by the Lord. We must keep the distinction, because there are also godless cedars on Lebanon, of whom another psalm says, *The Lord will shatter the cedars of Lebanon* (Ps 28(29):5). In the literal sense Lebanon is a mountain on which grow very ancient, magnificent trees. But interpreted figuratively Lebanon means "whitening," according to works we have read on the subject. If Lebanon means "whitening" it must be the whitening of this world, with all its false glitter and ostentation. But even in this world there are to be found cedars of Lebanon which the Lord has planted, and they will be satisfied. Still, the Lord warns, *Any tree that my Father has not planted will be uprooted* (Mt 15:13). *The cedars he planted on Lebanon.*

---

40. The earth in the sense of apostles and preachers, as at the end of section 12.

Verse 17. Sparrows nest in cedars which provide for them, but their ultimate refuge is the rock

16. *There will the sparrows nest; but their leader is the home of the coots.* Where will the sparrows build their nests? In the cedars of Lebanon. We have heard already whom the cedars of Lebanon represent: the nobles of this world, people illustrious by their birth, their wealth, their rank. These cedars will be satisfied, but only if they are the ones the Lord has planted. In these cedars the sparrows nest; so who are the sparrows? Sparrows are birds, winged creatures of the sky, to be sure; but it is usually the smallest of these winged creatures that we call sparrows. It seems, then, that there are certain spiritual persons who nest in Lebanon's cedars: those servants of God who hear the gospel's invitation, "Leave everything you possess," or *Sell all you have and give the money to the poor, and you will have treasure in heaven; then come, follow me* (Mk 10:21). It is not important people only who have heard this; little people have heard it too, little people have heard the invitation and longed for a spiritual way of life. They have chosen not to marry, not to be burdened with responsibility for children, not to be tied to homes of their own, but to enter some form of common life. But what have these sparrows left behind? Sparrows seem to represent the very least in this world. What have they renounced? Have they given up anything significant? One such person is converted, and leaves his father's poor hovel, abandoning scarcely one bed, one chest. All the same, he is converted and becomes a sparrow: he has opted for a spiritual way of life. Splendid: let us not insult him by saying, "You haven't left much!" Another, who had much to leave, has no right to be proud on that score. We know that Peter was a fisherman; what could he have left behind in order to follow the Lord? And what about his brother Andrew? Or John and James, the sons of Zebedee, who were fishermen? Yet what did they claim? *Look, we have given up everything, and followed you* (Mk 10:28). The Lord did not reply, "You forget how poor you were. What did you give up, in order to gain the whole world?" Brothers and sisters, anyone who has renounced not merely whatever he had but also what he desired to have has given up very much; yes, he or she has given up a great deal. Is there any poor person who does not passionately hope for more in this world? Is there anyone in that state who does not long every day to augment his possessions? But in the apostle this covetousness was sheared away; it aspired to great wealth, but it was restrained. Was nothing renounced, then? On the contrary, Peter forsook the whole world, and Peter was given the whole world in exchange. The apostles were men who seemed to have nothing yet possessed everything.[41]

There are many others who do the same. Many who have few possessions do it; they come, and they make useful sparrows. They seem so insignificant,

---

41. See 2 Cor 6:10.

lacking any high position or worldly dignity, but they nest in the cedars of Lebanon. Moreover these Lebanon cedars, the nobles, the rich, persons of rank in this world, tremble when they hear, *Blessed is everyone who understands about the needy and poor*; they take stock of their goods, their houses, and all their superfluous riches—of the very things which give them their prestige—and donate them to the servants of God. They give fields and gardens, they build churches and monasteries, they assemble the sparrows so that in these cedars of Lebanon the sparrows may build their nests. Thus it comes about that the cedars of Lebanon which the Lord has planted are satisfied, and *there will the sparrows nest*. Cast your eyes round the whole world, and see if it is not so. I am not telling you this on hearsay. I have seen it for myself; my own experience has taught me. Investigate even the most distant regions known to you, and see in how many cedars of Lebanon there are the nesting sparrows of which I have spoken to you.

17. All the same, brothers and sisters, if these sparrows are truly spiritual, they must not overestimate the cedars of Lebanon, even though they nest there. The cedars that supply their needs are not on that account to be reckoned superior. Spiritual persons are sparrows, the others are cedars of Lebanon. The psalm states that *the sparrows' leader is the home of the coots*. The sparrows nest in the cedars of Lebanon, yet the cedars are not their leaders. Certainly the trees of the plain—that is, all nations—will be satisfied; and the cedars of Lebanon too, all those the Lord has planted, all the noble and high-ranking persons among the faithful, they shall be satisfied. Among these cedars the sparrows will build their nests, for the mighty trees provide the branches of their wealth to accommodate the tiny winged creatures. These cedars of the Lord's planting provide the habitat; they do it and do it willingly; they know what they are doing and how they will be rewarded. Nonetheless, the leader of those sparrows who will nest in the cedars *is the home of the coots*.

What is the home of the coots? As we all know, coots are water birds. They live either on ponds or near the sea. Rarely if ever do they nest on shore; they prefer a place surrounded by water, especially on a rock with sea all around. We can well understand why a rock provides a good habitat for coots, for there could be none stronger or steadier. What kind of rock? A rock out to sea. It may be battered by waves, but it breaks their force; it is not broken itself. This is what a great rock is like, as it towers from the sea.

How great are the billows that have poured over our rock, the Lord Christ! The Jews dashed themselves against him; they were broken, but he remained whole. Anyone who imitates Christ must so live in this world, in this sea where we cannot but feel storms and hurricanes, as to yield to no wind and no wave, but accept them all and stay whole. Thus the dwelling of the coots is both strong and humble. A waterfowl does not build a nest in lofty places. Nothing is stronger than its dwelling, and nothing humbler. Sparrows nest in cedars on account of present needs; but they look to that rock as their leader, the rock that is battered by waves but not broken. They imitate the sufferings of Christ. If it happens that the cedars of Lebanon grow angry and stir up trouble or scandal against God's servants who lodge in their branches, the sparrows will fly away. But woe to the cedar that is left bare of sparrows' nests. The sparrows will neither be ship-wrecked nor die, for *their leader is the home of the coots.*

Verse 18. The rock is needed by all kinds of creatures

18. What comes next? *The highest mountains are for the harts.* The harts are the spiritually great, who in their swift course leap over all the thorny patches in brambles and woods. Another psalm says of God, *He made my feet perfect like a hart's, he will set me on the high places* (Ps 17:34(18:33)). Let them claim for their own the high mountains, the lofty precepts of God, let them reflect on sublime mysteries and take possession of the most elevated passages in the scriptures, let them be justified on the heights, for the towering mountains are for the harts.

What about the lowly animals? What of the coney?[42] The hedgehog? The coney is a tiny, weak animal, and the hedgehog is also spiny: the one is a timid animal, the other is covered with spines. What do the spines suggest? Sinners, surely. Those who sin daily, even if their sins are not grave, find themselves covered with tiny prickles. In respect of their timidity, they are coneys, and in their prickly condition they are hedgehogs; they are therefore incapable of frequenting the heights of the precepts that lead to perfection. The lofty mountains are the abode of the harts.

Does this mean that the small, fearful, spiny creatures must perish? No. The psalm has told us that *the highest mountains are for the harts,* but it goes on to explain what provision is made for the others: *The rock is a refuge for hedgehogs and coneys*; the Lord has made himself a refuge for the poor.[43] If you think of a rock on land, it is a refuge for hedgehogs and coneys; if you think of a rock in the sea, it is the habitat of coots. The rock is useful everywhere. Even in the mountains it serves a necessary purpose, for without that rocky substrate the mountains would collapse into the deep. Has the psalm not already said of the

---

42. In the original Hebrew only one small animal is mentioned in the second part of verse 18; the word is the same as in Lv 11:5 and Prv 30:26, and is best translated "hyrax" or "rock-rabbit" or "coney," a small, shy animal living among rocks. In the Septuagint, which underlies Augustine's Latin translation, again there is only one small animal in this half-verse, and the meaning is the same as that of the Hebrew. However, the word in Greek, χοιρογρυλλίοις, is similar to words related to pigs, which perhaps gave rise to the extra animal, the hedgehog. A variant reading of the Septuagint gives a word meaning "hares." Augustine's version may have been influenced by this variant, since he read *leporibus,* "hares." However, he emphasizes the smallness of the animal, so it seems better to retain "coney" in the English translation.

43. See Ps 9:10(9).

mountains, *Birds of the sky will dwell there, singing their song from among the rocks*? Wherever we are, we need to take refuge on the rock, whether it be the lofty crag in the mountains, or the reef at sea that is battered by waves but not broken, or the land rock that gives stability. To the rock flee the harts, the water-fowl, the coneys and the hedgehogs. Let the coneys beat their breasts and the hedgehogs confess their sins. Even though small daily sins cover them all over like prickles, the rock is still there for them, the rock that taught them to pray, *Forgive us our debts, as we forgive those who are in debt to us* (Mt 6:12). So *the rock is a refuge for hedgehogs and coneys.*

Verse 19. The moon is the Church within time; the sunset is Christ's passion

19. *He made the moon as a sign of the passage of time.* We take this in a spiritual sense to mean the Church which grows from its small beginning, and grows old with the passing of this mortal life, though it ages only in order to approach the sun. I am not talking about the moon we can observe with our eyes but about the Church which this represents. When the Church was in its obscure phase, when it was not plainly visible, not yet widely famous, people were deceived by false opinions. "This is the Church, this is Christ," some would tell them, in order to *shoot those of honest heart when the moon was darkened* (Ps 10:3(11:2)). But today things are very different: how blind people must be if they lose their way at full moon! *He made the moon as a sign of the passage of time*, for the Church is making its way through a time-bound world. Mortality will not last for ever, the phases of waxing and waning will pass away eventually. It is appointed for determinate seasons.

The sun knew its setting. Who is this sun? Surely the sun of righteousness[44] whom the godless will bewail on the day of judgment, because it never rose for them. On that day they will lament, *No doubt of it, we strayed from the path of truth. On us the light of righteousness did not shine, nor did the sun rise for us.* (Wis 5:6) But for the Church that sun does rise, for we understand the sun to be Christ. Yet if anyone becomes so angry with a brother or sister as to cherish hatred, Christ has withdrawn from that person's mind. Heed the warning, *Be angry, and do not sin* (Ps 4:5(4)). Charity may grow angry at times because it needs to rebuke something; in that case anger is not blameworthy because it has not hardened into hatred. But if anger has become hatred, the sun has set over your anger. Make sure, then, that *the sun does not set over your wrath* (Eph 4:26).

20. You must not think, brothers and sisters, that because the sun sometimes represents Christ in scripture, people are right to worship the sun. Some folks are so mad that when they hear, "The sun represents Christ," they think it a proper

---

44. See Mal 4:2.

object for adoration. All right, worship a rock too, since that represents Christ! And scripture also says of him, *He was led like a sheep to the slaughter* (Is 53:7), so worship a sheep, since it is a figure of Christ! Then again, *the lion from the tribe of Judah has conquered* (Rv 5:5), so worship a lion as well! See how many things are symbols of Christ, but all of them are Christ only figuratively, not in the real sense. Are you looking for what Christ truly is? *In the beginning was the Word, and the Word was with God* (Jn 1:1). That is the reality of Christ, the reality through whom you were made. And now would you like to consider the reality through whom you were made anew? *The Word was made flesh, and dwelt among us* (Jn 1:14). All the rest are metaphors. Have some sense, stretch your mind to take in scripture's meaning. Try to understand that one thing is put before your eyes, but something else is intimated to your heart.

21. We can say with certainty that this sun, the sun of righteousness, does not rise for the godless, and with good reason. Yet they seem to wish it would, for Wisdom declares, *The wicked will seek me, but not find me.* Why not? *They will seek me, but not find me*, because they hate wisdom. Wisdom herself testifies to this: *They will seek me, but not find me, because they hate wisdom.* (Prv 1:28-29, LXX) If they hate it, why do they seek it? They seek wisdom not to enjoy it but to enhance their own reputation; they profess to seek it but deny it by their conduct. But *the holy spirit of discipline rejects falsehood, and withdraws from stupid thinking* (Wis 1:5). This sun rises for no godless people, for none who are wicked. And yet what does scripture say about the visible sun? God *causes his sun to rise over the good and the wicked, and sends rain upon just and unjust alike* (Mt 5:45). This passage makes it clear that when our psalm says, *The sun knew its setting*, it must be using the word *sun* in a mystical sense, for we see what happens in the visible creation.

What then does the psalm mean by *the sun knew its setting*? Christ "knew" his passion, and Christ's "setting" is a symbol of his passion. But did that sun so set as never to rise again? Far from it: *Will he not go further and rise again, he who has fallen asleep?* (Ps 40:9(41:8)). Did he not say himself, *I slept, but never completely at rest*? And to him that same psalm cried out, *Be lifted up above the heavens, O God.* (Ps 56:5,6(57:4,5)) This is what is meant by *the sun knew its setting*. But what about that word, "knew"? It means he approved it, it was something he desired. How can we prove that this is the meaning? Well, is there anything God does not know? Or anything Christ does not know? Yet he will say to certain people at the end, *I never knew you* (Mt 7:23). Just as in that gospel text the words, *I never knew you*, do not mean, "You are unknown to me," but, "You do not please me," so too when the psalm says, *The sun knew its setting*, it means that Christ's passion was something he desired. If it had not been pleasing in his sight, how could he have suffered? Any ordinary person, one who is not the sun of righteousness, may not will to suffer, but he or she has to suffer what is not willed. Christ would not have suffered unless the path of suffering found favor in his sight, which is to say, if he had not *known his setting*, he would not have set at all. He stated this himself: *I have the power to lay down my life, and I have the power to take it up again. No one takes it away from me; but I lay it down of my own accord.* (Jn 10:18) This is why we can say, *The sun knew its setting.*

Verses 20-21. The lion cubs that hunt in darkness

22. What happened when the sun set, when the Lord suffered? Darkness fell in the minds of the apostles, and their hope sagged, because they had believed him to be the mighty redeemer of us all. Why did this happen? *You spread the darkness and night fell. All the beasts of the forest will take advantage of it and come forth: lion cubs roaring and ready to seize their prey, seeking their food from God.* What spiritual interpretation can I find for these lion cubs, if not wicked spirits?[45] How else can I understand them than as evil demons, the demons who feed on human wrongdoing? There are some demons in powerful positions, and others that are mere underlings. These latter try to seduce human souls but only where the sun has not risen, for then it is dark. And in this darkness the lion cubs look for souls to devour. Remember what is said about the prince of all these lions: *Do you not know that your enemy the devil prowls about like a roaring lion, seeking whom he may devour?* (1 Pt 5:8) The lion cubs are said to *seek their food from God* because no one can be tempted by the devil unless God allows it. Holy Job found himself face to face with the devil, and yet the real distance between them was great; the devil had Job in front of him yet was far removed as far as his power was concerned. How could he have dared to attack even Job's body, even his possessions, unless he had been authorized to do so? But why is authorization given? Either to condemn the godless or to test the God-fearing. God determines the whole matter justly. The devil has no power over anyone or over anyone's property, unless God, who is supreme and all-holy in his power, grants the devil permission. As for the devil, so for every human aggressor: no one has power over anyone else unless it is granted from above. The judge of the living and the dead once stood before a human judge. The human judge, looking at Christ before him, puffed himself up and asked, *Are you unaware that I have the power either to release you or to put you to death?* But Christ had come to teach even this man by whom he was being judged, and he replied, *You would have no power over me, had it not been given you from above* (Jn 19:10.11). Human aggressor, the devil, subordinate demons—none of them do any harm except insofar as they have been empowered, and to those who are making progress they do no harm at all. For bad people they are like fire to straw, for good people like fire to gold. Judas was eaten like straw; Job was proved like gold.

---

45. The following lines closely resemble Augustine's Exposition of Psalm 100,12. Pauline teaching in Eph 2:2 and 6:12 colors the passage.

You spread the darkness and night fell. All the beasts of the forest will take advantage of it and come forth. Here we find a different significance for these beasts of the forest.[46] These images can often support different interpretations, just as the Lord can be called a lamb and a lion. What could be more different than lamb from lion? But what kind of lamb was he, who could defeat the wolf and even the lion? He is a rock, a shepherd, a door. The shepherd enters by the door and says, *I am the good shepherd*; but he also says, *I am the door* (Jn 10:11.7). Indeed, the one name, *lion*, stands for the Lord, since scripture says, *The lion from the tribe of Judah has conquered* (Rv 5:5), and for the devil, because it also says, *On both lion and snake he has trampled* (Ps 90(91):13). You must learn to understand these figures of speech properly, because otherwise you might read that a rock represents Christ and then go on to think that wherever a rock is mentioned it is always Christ. Symbols can mean different things, just as you discern the force of a letter of the alphabet from the place where it occurs. If you read the name of the Deity and observe that its first letter is D,[47] you might think that it belongs there only and should be deleted from the beginning of "devil." The name of God, *Deus*, and the name "devil" both have the same initial letter, yet no one thing could be more different from another than God is from the devil. Suppose someone said of the letter D, "It ought not to be used as the initial of the devil's name," and you asked, "Why not?" and he replied, "Because I have read that letter in God's name." Such a person would be judged quite uncouth, ignorant of both human and divine custom. He or she would simply be laughed at; you would not even bother to argue with a person like that. You must not think in childish ways yourselves about these divine truths; for example, none of you must think I am contradicting what I said earlier, if then I said that the woodland beasts were the nations, and now I say the beasts of the forest represent demons and traitorous angels. These are metaphors, and wherever they occur they must be interpreted in the light of the particular context.

All the beasts of the forest will come forth. Where? In the darkness which the Lord has cast, because *the sun knew its setting. Lion cubs roar and are ready to seize their prey, seeking their food from God.* As the Lord approached his sunset, he, the sun of righteousness who knew his setting, warned his disciples of what was to come. He foresaw that darkness would fall[48] and that the lion would be on the prowl, in search of someone to devour. But that lion would savage no one unless he obtained his victim from God, so the Lord said, *This very night Satan has asked to sift all of you like wheat; but I have prayed for you, Peter, that your faith may not fail* (Lk 22:31-32). Was Peter not in the lion's jaws when he denied

---

46. A long digression follows: Augustine interpreted the woodland beasts in verse 11 as the nations (see sections 2-3 above). He defends the apparent inconsistency by the polyvalence of many images used in scripture, and the need to understand each in the light of its context.
47. The following argument depends on *Deus* and *diabolus* beginning with the same letter.
48. Variant: " that the disciples would be in darkness."

the Lord three times? *Lion cubs roar and are ready to seize their prey, seeking their food from God.*

Verses 22-23. The Church's daylight; the lion cubs slink away

23. *The sun has risen.* Christ said, *I have the power to lay down my life, and I have the power to take it up again* (Jn 10:18). He knew his setting, and he laid down his life; but *the sun has risen*: he has taken it up again. *The sun has risen,* because though it set, it was never extinguished. Those who have no understanding of Christ are still in the night; for them the sun has not yet risen. Let them draw near that they may come to know him and not be seized by the roaring lion. You can see for yourselves how the lion cubs dare not attack those for whom the sun has risen, for the psalm continues, *The sun has risen, and they have gathered together; they will go and lie down in their dens.* As this sun rises, as Christ becomes known throughout the world and his name is glorified, the lion cubs gather together more and more hungrily; for the demons are withdrawing from their persecution of the Church, from that open hostility they instigated against the house of God, in order to concentrate on unbelievers. So does scripture characterize them: *The prince of the power of the air, who is now at work in the children of unbelief* (Eph 2:2). None of them dares to persecute the Church now, for *the sun has risen* and so they have gathered for a concerted attack. And where are they? *They will go and lie down in their dens.* Their dens are the hearts of unbelievers. How many people carry sleeping lions in their hearts? The lions do not spring out, they do not attack Jerusalem on her journey. Why not? Because now *the sun has risen*, and sheds its radiance throughout the whole world.

24. Now see the effects of the sunrise. *The sun has risen, and they have gathered together; they will go and lie down in their dens.* And what about you, man of God, woman of God? What of you, Church of God? What of you, the body of Christ whose head is in heaven? What will you do, you whom he forms into one man? *The man will go out to his work*, says the psalm. Let this one person work at his good task in the security of the Church's peace; let him work at it until the end. One day darkness will fall again, and once more there will be an onslaught, but these things will come in the evening, at the end of the world. For the present, let the Church do its work in peace and tranquillity. *The man will go out to his work, to labor until evening.*

Verse 24. The glories of creation and of the new creation, wrought in the Wisdom of God

25. *How magnificent are your works, O Lord!* Great indeed they are, glorious indeed. Where were these mighty works wrought? Where was God's workplace,

where did he sit, to create it all? Where was his workshop? Whence did these
beautiful things first emerge? If you take the verse literally, you can ask these
questions about the whole of this creation, so elegantly ordered: ordered in its
swift movement, ordered in its beauty, ordered in its rising, ordered in its
decline, pursuing its ordered course through time. Where does it come from? But
what of the Church itself? How does it grow, and develop, and reach perfection?
How is it oriented to an immortal destiny? What kind of proclamation makes it
known? For what high mysteries do we venerate it? Under what sacred signs is it
hidden? How does preaching reveal it?

Where did God bring all this into being? I contemplate his mighty operations
and cry, *How magnificent are your works, O Lord!* But I ask where he did it, and
I find no place. But then my eye lights on the next phrase: *In wisdom you have
created all things.* You created them in Christ. He was despised, he was slapped,
he was spat on, he was crowned with thorns, he was crucified; yet in him you
created all that exists. I hear what you announce to us about him through a soldier
of yours;[49] I hear what you preach about him to the Gentiles through your holy
herald; yes, that indeed I hear: that Christ is the power of God and the wisdom of
God. Let the Jews scoff at Christ crucified because he is an offense to them; let
the pagans scoff at Christ crucified because to them he is an absurdity. But, says
Paul, *We preach Christ crucified, to Jews a stumbling-block and to Gentiles
folly; but to those who are called, both Jews and Greeks, a Christ who is the
power of God and the wisdom of God* (1 Cor 1:23-24). *In wisdom you have
created all things.*

26. *The earth is filled with your creative work.* The earth is filled with Christ's
creation. We see this to be true, for does anything exist that was not created by
the Father through his Son? Everything that walks and everything that crawls on
earth, everything that swims in the waters, everything that flies in the air, everything that circles in the heavens, and still more the earth itself, the entire
world—all is God's creation. Yet it is a sign of something more, of that new
creation of which the apostle says, *If anyone is in Christ, there is a new creation.
The old things have passed away, and lo, everything is made new! All these
things are from God.* (2 Cor 5:17-18) This new creation by God comprises all
who believe in Christ, who are stripping themselves of the old self and putting on
the new.[50] *The earth is filled with your creative work.* Christ was crucified in one
small place on earth; in that one small spot the grain fell into the ground and died;
but it yielded a great harvest.[51] Before your passing you were all alone, Lord
Jesus; I recognize your voice in another psalm, crying, *I am all alone, until my*

---

49. Possibly the centurion who acknowledged, *Truly this was a/the Son of God* after Jesus' death
   (Mt 27:54); but it seems more likely that Augustine means Paul, as in the following lines.
50. See Eph 4:22.24.
51. See Jn 12:24-25.

passover (Ps 140(141):10). You were alone until you had achieved your pass-over, you were all alone when you knew your sunset; but you passed from sunset to sunrise. You rose, a new sun in splendor, you were glorified as you climbed the sky, and now *the earth is filled with your creative work*.

We have not yet finished the psalm, brothers and sisters. Let us in Christ's name postpone the remainder until Sunday.

Exposition 4 of Psalm 103

Fourth Sermon

Introduction: today we will discharge the debt

1. There is but one single utterance of God amplified throughout all the scriptures, dearly beloved. Through the mouths of many holy persons a single Word makes itself heard, that Word who, being God-with-God in the beginning, has no syllables, because he is not confined by time. Yet we should not find it surprising that to meet our weakness he descended to the discrete sounds we use, for he also descended to take to himself the weakness of our human body. The psalm which we are studying has already given rise to many words on our part. Mysteries were concealed in it to be opened to those who knock, and these mysterious verses occupied us for no little time over several days, as they were read out and your attention was directed to them, as they were shown to hold more than met the eye, and as their meaning was drawn out and interpreted. As you will recall, beloved, this long treatment did not leave us time to finish the psalm on the previous occasion and compelled us to defer what was left until today. Now the Lord has provided us with the opportunity to pay the outstanding debt and make you, our creditors, happy. May he himself give us good things to pay the debt with, though whatever we have done ill so far is our doing, not his.

Verse 24. *The glorious creativity of Wisdom*

2. We cried out from the innermost depths of our hearts, *How magnificent are your works, O Lord! In wisdom you have created all things. The earth is filled with your creative work.* You remember how our hearts shouted this in harmony with the psalm, and the memory brings you devotion and joy. Everything that has been made by God was made in wisdom and by wisdom. Everything that is aware of wisdom, and everything that is unaware of it, yet is still part of God's creation, was made in wisdom and by wisdom. People who acknowledge wisdom enjoy wisdom as their light; those who do not recognize it still have wisdom as their designer, even though they are themselves trapped in folly.[1] All who have wisdom as their light also have wisdom as their designer, but the converse is not true, for not all of those who have wisdom as their designer have

---

1. Many codices omit "even though . . . folly." Others read, "are trapped by wisdom."

wisdom as their light. Among human beings there are many who participate in wisdom, and they are called wise; many others know nothing of it, and are reckoned fools. They deserve this insulting name, because if they will only apply themselves to the pursuit of wisdom, and beg for it, and seek it, and knock at wisdom's door, they will attain some share in wisdom, for it is denied not to anyone's nature but to carelessness.

There are other creatures, such as all wild beasts, domestic animals, and trees, which lack intelligence and are unable to participate in wisdom. But does this inability mean that they were not made in wisdom and by wisdom? Far from it. God does not demand understanding from a horse or a mule; but to human beings he says, *Do not be like a horse or a mule, devoid of understanding* (Ps 31(32):9). What is natural in a horse is a matter for reproach in a man or woman. God says to us, "I do not expect creatures that I have not made in my own image to participate in my wisdom. But from you, who are made in my image, I do demand it. I require you to use the gift I have given you."

As human beings render to Caesar what belongs to Caesar when they hand back to Caesar the coin that bears his image, so do they render to God what belongs to God[2] when they give themselves back to him whose image they bear and lift their minds above themselves to their designer, to the light from which they came and to the spiritual fire which warms them. If they withdraw from it they grow cold, if they move away they sink into darkness. But if they return to that light, that fire, they are illumined. Faithful and loving, they pray, *You, Lord, will light my lamp; my God, you will enlighten my darkness* (Ps 17:29(18:28)), and in response to that prayer the darkness of their earthly folly is dispelled. They open their mouths and draw breath, and then, as I said, they trustingly raise the eyes of their hearts. Mentally they contemplate the entire world that lies around them: earth, sea and sky; they see how beautifully all things are disposed, how they pursue their ordered courses, distinguished by their species, preserved by their generative powers, changing, evolving, and surviving through swiftly-running time. When wise people observe creation they delight in its creator and so give their creator delight in them, who also are his creation. Then they exclaim for sheer joy, *How magnificent are your works, O Lord! In wisdom you have created all things.*

Where is the wisdom in which you made all these? What mind can reach it, what eye behold it, what study seek it? How can it be gained? How else, but by God's grace? By his gift we exist, and by his gift also we become good. This gift he bestows on those who have come back to him. But did he not seek them before their return, when they were estranged from him and intent on their own ways? Did he not come down to look for them? Did not the Word become flesh to live

----

2. See Mk 12:17.

among us? Did he not light the lamp of his flesh when he hung upon the cross, searching for his lost coin? He searched and he found it, and his neighbors rejoiced with him, for every spiritual creature who keeps close to God is his neighbor. To the neighbors' glee the coin is found; to the angels' joy is found a human soul.[3] It is found; let it rejoice, and exclaim, *How magnificent are your works, O Lord! In wisdom you have created all things.*

3. *The earth is filled with your creative work.* What creative work fills the earth? All trees and bushes, all animals, both wild and tame, and the whole human race itself: with all these creatures of God the earth teems. We observe them all, we know them, read about them, recognize them, praise them, and proclaim their creator as we gaze on them. Yet our praise falls short, for we cannot praise him in the measure that our heart overflows when in wonder we contemplate his creative work. Nonetheless we should attend even more closely to that particular creative work of which the apostle says, *If anyone is in Christ, there is a new creation. The old things have passed away, and lo, everything is made new!* (2 Cor 5:17) What are the old things that have passed away? All the idolatry that was practiced among the Gentiles, all the slavery to the law that prevailed among the Jews, and all the sacrifices that were harbingers of our present sacrifice. The human race was old and worn out, but Christ came to renew his work, he came to melt his silver and re-mint his coinage; and now we see the earth filled with Christian peoples believing in God, forsaking their former foul practices and their idolatry, and turning away from their old hopes to hope of a new world. This new world is not yet fully realized in fact but is ours already in hope; and in the strength of that hope we sing, *The earth is filled with your creative work.* Not yet in our homeland do we sing it, not yet in the rest promised to us, not yet within the barred gates of Jerusalem.[4] But even now on our pilgrimage, as we behold this entire world we know, where men and women are running from every side to embrace the faith—men and women who fear hell, defy death, love the life that lasts for ever and make light of the present life—we are filled with exultant joy, as we say, *The earth is filled with your creative work.*

Verse 25. The perilous sea

4. This world is still shaken by the waves of temptation, still battered by storms, still in commotion with the billows of distress;[5] yet this is the voyage we must make. Even though the sea threatens and the waves rise higher and storms break over us, this is the voyage appointed for us, and a boat[6] has been given us in

---

3. See Lk 15:8-10.
4. See Ps 147:13.
5. Variant: "fears."
6. *Lignum,* "wood." The thought of the cross runs through this section.

which we may set our course aright. *The earth is filled with your creative work.* We are not yet at home in the land of the living. But, still in the land of the dying, we cry out in prayer, *You are my hope, my portion in the land of the living* (Ps 141:6(142:5)). You are my hope in the land of the dying and my portion in the land of the living; and yet even this earth I know is full of your creative work. What way are we to take, we who are still in this land of the dying and have not yet reached the land of the living? Listen to the next verse: *This is a wide, vast sea, and in it are crawling creatures beyond counting, living things both small and great.* The psalm evokes a terrible sea, full of *crawling creatures beyond counting.* Crafty temptations crawl about in this world and seize the unwary without warning. Can anyone count these creeping temptations? They move stealthily: take care they do not steal.[7] We must be watchful in our boat, but we are safe even on the high seas, even amid the waves. Do not let Christ fall asleep—your faith, I mean; do not let it doze off. If it has gone to sleep, wake it up. It will command the waves, and the sea will grow calm;[8] the voyage will soon be over and you will rejoice in your homeland.

In the sea are crawling creatures beyond counting, living things both small and great. Yes, for I can still see some unbelievers in this frightening ocean. They swim about in salty, sterile waters. Among them are small creatures and larger ones. We know how true this is. Many who are small fry in this world have not yet come to faith, but many important people have not either: there are *living things both small and great* in this sea. They hate the Church and feel oppressed by Christ's name. They do not rage openly because that is unlawful; savagery lurks in their hearts but dares not express itself in their hands. All those who regret the closure of temples, the destruction of altars, the smashing of idols, and the legislation that makes idolatrous sacrifices a capital crime—all these people, whether obscure or prominent, *living things small and great*, are still in the sea. But what about us? Are we not there too? What other route can take us home? We have to cross the sea, but we must cross in our wooden boat. Do not fear the world, for the ship that carries you holds the world together. Listen to the psalm: *This is a wide, vast sea, and in it are crawling creatures beyond counting, living things both small and great.* Do not be afraid, do not let it daunt you. Long for your homeland, and understand the conditions of the voyage.

Verse 26. The great sea-serpent, the devil

5. *There the ships ply.* Reassure yourself: in that element which seemed so alarming ships make their way and do not sink. We understand these ships to be the churches. Let them sail among storms, through the gales of temptation,

---

7. Word-play: *repunt, sed cave ne subripiant.*
8. See Mk 4:37-39.

through the breakers of the world, through the living creatures both small and great. Christ is the pilot, Christ on his wooden cross. *There the ships ply*. The ships must not be afraid nor be too preoccupied about their course but rely on their pilot. *There the ships ply*. How can they regard any voyage as unlucky, when they know Christ is at the helm? Let them hold calmly to their course, for if they sail on steadily they will reach their appointed haven; they will be guided to the land of peace.

6. There is something else in this sea, something that dwarfs all the other living creatures, small and great. What is it? Let us listen again to the psalm: *The dragon you made to play with*.[9] Countless crawling creatures are there; living things both small and great are there. The ships will sail through them without fearing the countless crawling things, or the small creatures, or the great; but they will not fear the dragon either, the dragon which God *made to play with*.

What I am going to tell you is a great secret, and yet you already know it. You know that the Church's arch-enemy is a certain dragon whom you have not seen with your bodily eyes but see with the eyes of faith. He is called a lion as well, and of him scripture says, *On both lion and dragon you will trample* (Ps 90(91):13). He is already subjected to your head; let him be subjected to the body as well. All that the members need do is cling tightly to their head in order to be his members. Something very significant was said about the first woman, whom the dragon deceived. I mean Eve, of course, Eve, to whom the tempter offered lethal counsel, into whose feminine heart he sidled snake-like. What happened, we know. We bewail the fact that we too did it, for in these two original humans our whole race was comprised. From them was death propagated, and from them sins, even the debt of sin inherited by babies; for *no one is pure in your sight, not even an infant whose life on earth has been but one day* (Jb 14:4-5, LXX). The transmission of sin means the transmission of death resulting from the first sin.[10] Now, you know what was said to the woman, or rather about the woman to the snake, when God heard about the sin of the first human: *She will watch for your head, and you for her heel* (Gn 3:15). This highly mysterious promise was made to the Church of the future, prefigured by Eve; but it was directly spoken about Eve, who had been formed from the side of her husband as he slept. Adam prefigured one who would come after him; the apostle says this: *Adam was a type of the one who was to come* (Rom 5:14).What was to happen in the future

9. This dragon of the psalm is identified by Augustine in section 9, below, with the Leviathan of Jb 40:15–41:34. Leviathan was a mythical beast, a representation of the primeval chaos defeated by the creative power of God but sometimes thought to be still dwelling deep in the sea. Its description in Job includes features of the crocodile. In Augustine's comments on this verse the figure of the dragon merges with that of the snake in Gn 3.

10. *Tradux peccati, tradux mortis*. The word *tradux* literally means a vine-layer, trained across a space between vines. In Augustine's thinking the concupiscence involved in carnal generation provided a link: see the note at Exposition 1 of Psalm 101,11, on his doctrine of original sin.

was foreshadowed by the type, for the Church was formed from the Lord's side
as he slept on the cross. When the side of the crucified Christ was struck with a
lance, the sacraments of the Church gushed forth.[11] Very well, then, what was
promised to the Church? Listen carefully, make sure you understand, and take
warning: *She will watch for your head, and you for her heel.* Watch closely, O
Church, for the snake's head. What is the snake's head? The first suggestion of
sin. Some unlawful thought enters your mind. Do not dwell on it, do not consent
to it. What came into your mind was the snake's head: trample on it, and you will
be safe from any more of his movements. What does this mean, to trample on his
head? Repudiate the suggestion. But suppose what he has suggested is a way of
enriching yourself? "There is a tidy profit in this, plenty of money to be made.
Just a little cheating, and you will be rich." That is the snake's head: tread on it.
"Tread? How?" Denounce the fraud he suggests. "But it would win me lots of
money!" And what profit is it to anyone to gain the whole world, if he loses his
soul thereby?[12] Say to the snake, "Let all this world's wealth perish sooner than
my soul." If you can say that, you have watched for the snake's head and trampled on it.

But the devil watches for your heel. What does that mean? He watches for
you to slip off God's path. You are watchful for his initial suggestion; but he is
alert for you to slip, for if you slip, you will fall, and if you fall, you will be in his
power. To avoid falling, do not leave the way. God has laid down a narrow path
for you, and all the ground off the path is slippery. Christ is our light, and Christ
is our way. *He was the true light, which illumines every human person who
comes into this world*, says scripture; and again: *I am the Way, the Truth and the
Life* (Jn 1:9; 14:6). You travel by me, and you travel to me. If he is light and he is
the way, and you leave him, you will be neither in the light nor on the way. And
what will follow you? The fate that another psalm envisages for the godless:
May their path be dark and slippery (Ps 34(35):6).

7. This dragon, our ancient enemy, boiling with anger, astute and crafty, is at
large in the vast sea. But he is the dragon God *made to play with.* Now it is your
turn to make fun of the dragon; that is what he was created for. By his sin he fell
from his sublime status in heaven; from being an angel he was turned into a
devil, and he found a place in this wide, vast sea. What you think is his kingdom
is really his prison. Many people do not understand this: they ask, "Why has the
devil acquired so much power, enough to dominate in this world and act with
such terrible strength and effect?" But what strength has he, how much can he
effect? He can do nothing unless he is given permission. For your part, conduct
yourself in such a way that no permission is given him with regard to you, or, at

11. See Jn 19:34; compare Expositions of Psalms 40,10 and 102,10.
12. See Mt 16:26.

any rate, in such a way that if he is permitted to tempt you, he will slink off
defeated and not take you over.

A digression on Job illustrates the limitations placed on the devil's power

He has sometimes been permitted to tempt certain holy men[13] who were
servants of God, but they overcame him because they did not leave the way, and
though he kept a close watch on their heels, they did not slip. Holy Job was
seated on a dunghill, yet all the while running along in the way; notice how he
was on the watch for the snake's head, while the snake concentrated on Job's
heel. Job rebuffed the snake's suggestion, but the snake went on hoping Job
would slip. The devil captured Job's little wife.[14] He robbed him of all his
possessions, but left him his consort, not to be a comforter for her husband but
rather a temptress.[15] The devil had captured her because she did not watch for his
head. She was still Eve, though Job was no Adam. Stripped of everything, Job
was left with his wife, who was tempting him, and with God, who was ruling
him. If you consider his house, could anything be poorer than this man, so
suddenly ruined? But could anything be richer, if you look to his heart? His
house was utterly destitute: everything had been taken away. But look at how
rich his heart was: *The Lord gave, and the Lord has taken away. This has
happened as the Lord willed: may the Lord's name be blessed.* (Jb 1:21) *The
Lord gave, and the Lord has taken away*: he knew who ruled him and who
tempted him, and he knew who had given his tempter permission. "Let the devil
make no claims on his own account," said Job. "He has the will to hurt me, but he
would have no power to hurt unless he had received it. I suffer only insofar as he
has been given permission, and therefore I am suffering not at his hands but at
the hands of the one who gave him power. Let the pride of my tempter be routed,
and the scourges of my Father be borne." The tempter was beaten back, for his
head had been detected and he failed to penetrate Job's heart. He attacked a
walled city from the outside but could not overthrow it.

Then came another temptation. The devil was allowed some power over
Job's body. He struck him with a serious ulcer from head to foot. Job oozed pus
and crawled with maggots; he left his house and sat down on the dunghill. There
Eve approached him, herself already captured and supplied by the devil not as an
ally for her husband but as a means to his fall.[16] She suggests that he blaspheme
God. The devil first suggested in paradise that God be ignored; now he suggests
that God be blasphemed. Of old he prevailed against a man in perfect health;

13. *Viros.*
14. *Mulierculam*, a contemptuous diminutive.
15. Several codices omit "but rather a temptress."
16. Some codices read, "Eve, already captured, was an ally for the devil, left with her husband as a
    means to his fall."

now he is beaten by one in a state of rottenness. In paradise he overthrew the man, on a dunghill he is himself overcome.

But the dragon was watching carefully for Job to slip with his tongue. Whenever a person acts it is as though he had feet, for when he moves in any way, it is as though he were walking. Now Job said a great many things. Anyone who has read the book knows what a lot Job said, and throughout all those long discourses the snake was watching his heel for any slip. But Job was equally attentive to the snake's head and repulsed every suggestion. He replied to the woman in the way she deserved: *You have spoken like the silly woman you are. If we have received good things from the Lord's hands, should we not endure the bad too? And throughout all he said, Job never slipped.* (Jb 2:10) Unfortunately many people who read the discourses do not understand this and interpret things according to their own way of thinking, supposing that he did speak harshly against God.

Job's words foreshadow the Mediator

8. There is one place in particular where people judge him to have spoken in anger against God because they do not fully understand, whereas in fact Job was speaking as a great prophet, uttering profound truth. In the course of his eloquent speeches he flung this at God: *I wish there could be some arbiter between us!* (Jb 9:33, LXX) "I wish someone would come between us, to give judgment between me and you!" A man says this to God; a man says it from a dunghill. Or, come to that, an angel in heaven says it to God: "I wish someone would arbitrate between us!"

But what did Job foresee? What was he hoping for? The Lord told us that *many righteous people and prophets longed to see what you see, but never saw it* (Mt 13:17). Job wanted an arbiter; but what is an arbiter? Someone who stands between opposing parties to settle a dispute. But were we not once God's enemies, with a bad case against God? Who else could have brought that bad case to a good end but he who stood as arbiter between us, he without whose intervention the way of mercy would have been closed to us? Of him the apostle says, *God is one, but there is a mediator between God and humankind, the man Christ Jesus* (1 Tm 2:5). He could not have been a mediator had he not been human, because as God he is equal to the Father. As the apostle says elsewhere, *No intermediary is required where only one party is involved, and God is one* (Gal 3:20). An intermediary stands between two, and so Christ is the mediator between humanity and God, not because he is God but because he is man; for as God he is equal to the Father, and as the Father's equal he cannot be a mediator.[17] If he is to be a mediator he must come down from the greatness of God, down

---

17. Variant: "not because he is God, equal to the Father, but because as man he is less than the Father. If [as man] he had been equal to the Father, he would not have been a mediator."

from his equality with the Father to one who is lower. He must do as the apostle says he did: *He emptied himself and took on the form of a slave, bearing the human likeness, sharing the human lot* (Phil 2:7). He must shed his blood to blot out the handwriting on the decree that stood against us;[18] he must settle the case between us and God by correcting our wills to conform with justice and bending God's sentence to mercy.

Insofar as God has enabled us we have clarified this one instance where Job seems to have spoken harshly against God. Other passages which appear rough or blasphemous can be similarly explained. We might have thought otherwise if God had not himself borne witness both before Job began to speak and after he had concluded all his discourses. Near the beginning of the story God gave his testimony, describing Job as *a blameless man, honest, and a worshiper of God* (Jb 1:8, LXX). These are God's own words, spoken before Job's temptation. Possibly, though, someone might misunderstand and be scandalized, suspecting that, while Job was indeed a just man before he was tempted, he weakened under severe temptation and fell into sacrilegious blasphemy. To exclude this mistake God gave his verdict after all the discussion was over, both on Job himself and on the friends who had offered him comfort. They had not spoken the truth, as God's servant Job had done. *You did not say anything true before me, as my servant Job did* (Jb 42:7), said God. Then he ordered that Job should offer sacrifices for them, to expiate their sins.[19]

Even the most exalted angels act only as God wills; how much more a degraded angel

9. Well, as we were saying, brothers and sisters, we have to accept the fact that since the devil who fell from heaven was consigned to the sea as his own place, that old snake still lives here in it.[20] Anyone who means to watch for the snake's head must beware of both fear of the world and greed for the world, for the snake will be making suggestions about what you should fear from it, and what you should crave in it. He tempts you either in your love or in your fear, but if you are afraid of hell and in love with God's kingdom, you will be on the watch for the snake's head. If you avoid his head you will be safe, and he will neither catch you out as you slip nor rejoice over your downfall. As I have pointed out already, no one should say, "He has enormous power." People see what they think is great power, but they do not see what he has lost. Holy Job himself, in those mysterious and deeply significant sayings of his, referred to the power

---

18. See Col 2:14.
19. See Jb 42:8.
20. Augustine is picking up the thread from the beginning of section 7, after his long digression on Job.

which the devil is alleged to have. He described the devil in a variety of symbolic images, exposing his nature and the limits of his capacity. One of the things said of him is this: *There is nothing like him on earth, made for my angels to deride.* This is God speaking in the Book of Job, *There is nothing like him on earth, made for my angels to deride. He surveys all that is lofty, and he is king of all the creatures in the waters.* (Jb 41:24-25, LXX) This corresponds to what is said in our psalm. While the psalm was considering the wide, vast sea, with its living things both small and great and its crawling creatures beyond counting, that sea where ships sail safely with their wooden hulls, it spoke of *the dragon you made to play with.* But if he is made for mockery, how does God mock him? Perhaps God has handed him over to others, to be mocked by them. We might have thought that God himself mocked the dragon, were it not that the Book of Job settled the question, for there it is written that he is *made for my angels to deride.* Do you want to deride the dragon? Then be an angel of God. But you are not yet one of God's angels. In the meantime, provided that you are on the way to becoming one, there are angels who can deride the dragon and prevent him from hurting you. The angels of heaven have been given authority over the powers of the air,[21] and from heaven issues the word which is effective on earth. They contemplate the fixed, eternal law of God, the law which gives orders without writing, without syllables, without noise, the law which abides unchanged for ever. The angels contemplate it in purity of heart, in obedience to it they do whatever is to be done here below, and in accordance with it all powers are regulated, from the highest to the lowest. Now, if the powers of the highest heavens are controlled by the word of God, how much more the lower powers and those on earth?

We can be certain, then, that nothing more than the wish to do harm remains in the wicked. A human being may harbor this desire to hurt, this will to cause another's ruin. But if he has succeeded in hurting someone, he has no reason to brag, for of himself he did no harm at all. The power was given to him. It has been stated once for all that *there is no power except from God* (Rom 13:1).

Why, then, are you afraid? Yes, the dragon is in the waters, the dragon is in the sea, and by that route you have to cross. He was made to be mocked, he was designed for that place; the sea was assigned to him as his domain. You think his throne there is mighty, but only because you have no idea of the angelic thrones from which he fell. What looks to you like his promotion is truly his damnation.

10. Consider the following analogy, which I will sketch for you briefly, for it is truly important to grasp this point and understand it clearly. Think of the whole ordering of creation as some great estate. In this great household there is the master, and he has servants. Among these are some whom he keeps close to

21. See Eph 2:2.

himself, and to them he entrusts the care of more important matters, such as his clothing, valuables, storehouses and major possessions. He also has servants engaged in more menial tasks; so completely are all ranks subject to him that some are even assigned to cleaning the drains. How many grades there are, from the highest officials down to these lowly, servile functionaries! Now suppose one of the important officials commits some fault, and his master decides to punish him by degrading him to the post of doorkeeper in some remote part of the building. While exercising the power given him, this servant then harasses people who want to enter or depart. It is real power that he wields, in the measure conferred on him by his master, but the people whom he vexes have no idea that he was formerly a senior official. They regard him as very powerful, because they do not know what he has lost.

All the same, brothers and sisters, the doorkeeper whom I have described to you in this parable of a great earthly household can do things without his master's knowledge or trouble someone without his master's authorization. But the devil is not stationed at the doorway through which we enter into God. Christ is that door,[22] and through Christ we enter eternal life.

However, there is a door that admits us to this world, the door of mortality, and amid all the ups and downs to which our feeble flesh is subject there is a keeper at that door. He has power in the sea where our ships ply, but not enough power to do anything without the Lord's knowledge or contrary to the Lord's will. No one must say, "But he was degraded from a high and mighty position, where he had great responsibilities, while I am of very low rank. He has me in his power here, so I had better serve him." Do not be deceived. Your Lord knows all about you. So well does he know you that he even keeps count of the hairs on your head.[23] What are you afraid of? Perhaps he will attack your body. If that happens it will be a whipping from your Lord, not something due to the power of the tempter. The tempter wants to undermine the salvation promised to you, but he is not given permission. To make sure that he never is given permission, have Christ as your head. Kick away the dragon's head; do not consent to his suggestions; do not slip off your path. He is only the dragon God *made to play with.*

Verses 27-29. God feeds all his creatures; the serpent's food is earth, which means earthly-minded people

11. Would you like further proof that the devil can do you no harm unless he gets permission? *All creatures look to you, O Lord, for you to give them their food at the proper time.* The dragon is hungry too, but he does not get everyone he wants to eat. *All creatures look to you, O Lord, for you to give them their food*

---

22. See Jn 10:9.
23. See Mt 10:30.

at the proper time, says the psalm. *All creatures*, the crawling ones that cannot be counted, all living things small and great, even the dragon himself, all this vast creation of yours with which you have filled the earth: *All creatures look to you, for you to give them their food at the proper time*, and to each its own food. You have your food, and the dragon has his. If you live as you should, you have Christ as your food; if you forsake Christ, you will be food for the dragon.

All creatures look to you, for you to give them their food at the proper time. What was the dragon told? *You shall eat earth all the days of your life* (Gn 3:14). Now you know what the dragon's food is. If you do not want God to hand you over to the dragon to be eaten, do not be dragon's food, do not turn your back on the word of God. In the same passage where God said to the dragon, *You shall eat earth*, he said to the disobedient man, *Earth you are, and back to earth you shall go* (Gn 3:19). So you do not fancy being snake's food? Then don't be earth. "But how can I not be earth?" you ask. By not having a taste for the things of earth. Listen to the apostle's advice on not being earthbound. Your body is earth, but you yourself must not be earth. What does that mean? *If you have risen with Christ*, says the apostle, *seek what is above, where Christ is seated at the right hand of God. Have a taste for the things that are above, not the things on earth.* (Col 3:1-2) If you do not have a taste for earthly things, you will not be earth, and if you are not earth, you will not be eaten by the snake, which was given earth as its food. God gives the snake its proper food when he wills, and he gives it to whomsoever he wills; but he judges justly. He cannot be deceived, and he never gives the snake gold instead of earth.

All creatures look to you, O Lord, for you to give them their food at the proper time. When you give it to them, they will gather it up. Their prey is there before them, but they will not pick it up unless you give it to them. Job was there in front of the devil, but so far from devouring Job, the devil did not even dare to tempt him except after God had given him permission. *They look to you; when you give them their food, they will gather it up*; but if you have not given it, they will not gather it.

12. What about ourselves, brothers and sisters? What food shall we get? The psalm goes on to tell us about our food. *When you open your hand, all shall be filled with goodness.* What does it mean, Lord, that you open your hand? Your hand is Christ. *To whom has the arm of the Lord been revealed?* (Is 53:1) The one to whom it is revealed is the one to whom it is opened, for revelation implies opening. *When you open your hand, all shall be filled with goodness.* When you reveal your Christ, *all shall be filled with goodness.* Their goodness does not derive from themselves and sometimes you make this clear to them, for *if you turn your face away, they will be troubled.* Many people who were full of goodness have attributed what they had to themselves, and tried to boast about it as though their justification was the result of their own actions. They said to themselves, "I'm all right; what a fine fellow I am!" And they were complacent. The

apostle thundered a challenge to such people: *What have you that you did not receive?* (1 Cor 4:7) God wills to prove to men and women that whatever they have they hold as a gift from him, so that they may have humility along with their goodness. He therefore troubles them from time to time; he turns his face away from them and they fall into temptation. He thus demonstrates to them that their previous righteousness and honorable way of life were possible only because he was ruling them. *If you turn your face away, they will be troubled.* Compare this with what was said in another psalm: *I said in the midst of my plenty, I shall be unmoved for ever.* That speaker had relied on himself; he was full of goodness and imagined that he was the source of it all. So he said in his heart, *I shall be unmoved for ever.* But by the time he sang his psalm he had realized that he had received God's grace, and he gave thanks for what he had experienced: *Lord, in your kindly will you have added strength to my beauty, but you turned your face away from me, and I became distraught* (Ps 29:7-8(30:6-7)). The same insight is expressed here: *When you open your hand, all shall be filled with goodness.* Not the speaker's own goodness, but God's open hand, brings it about. But *if you turn your face away, they will be troubled.*

13. Why do you do this? Why do you turn your face away and throw them into confusion? *When you withdraw their breath, they faint.* Their breath was their pride. They boast, they claim their goodness as their own, they think to make themselves righteous. Turn your face away, then, and let them be troubled; take their breath away and let them faint. Let them cry to you, *Make haste to hear me, O Lord, for my spirit has fainted away* (Ps 142(143):7).[24] *When you withdraw their breath, they faint, and return to the dust whence they came.* When we repent of our sins we find ourselves and discover that we had no strength of our own. We confess to God that we are earth and ashes. You have been reduced to your native dust, proud sinner, and your breath, your spirit, has been taken away from you. You are not swaggering now, or exalting yourself, or claiming to be the author of your justification; you see now that you were made from dust, and that when the Lord turns his face away you fall back into your native dust again. Pray to him, then. Confess your dustiness and your infirmity.

Verse 30. The Spirit of the new creation

14. Now look at what follows: *You will breathe forth your Spirit and they will be created.* You will take away their spirit and send forth your own. *You withdraw their breath,* so that they will have no breath, no spirit, that they can call their own. Are they destitute, then? No, blessed rather, for *blessed are the poor in spirit: the kingdom of heaven is theirs* (Mt 5:3). Having renounced their own

---

24. The same word, *spiritus*, is used for "breath," "spirit," and "Spirit" in Augustine's Latin, as also in Hebrew and Greek.

spirit, they will have God's Spirit. This is what the Lord promised to his future martyrs: *When they arrest you and deliver you up, do not wonder how to speak, or what you are to say. It is not you who are speaking, but the Spirit of your Father who speaks in you* (Mt 10:19.20). Do not attribute any strength to yourselves, the Lord tells them. If it is yours, it is not mine, and in that case it is not courage but insensitivity.

When you withdraw their breath, they faint and return to the dust whence they came. But you will breathe forth your Spirit and they will be created. The apostle reminds us, *We are his own handiwork, created for good works* (Eph 2:10). From God's Spirit we have received the grace to live for righteousness, for it is he who justifies the godless.[25] *When you withdraw their breath, they faint and return to the dust whence they came. But you will breathe forth your Spirit and they will be created, and you will make the face of the earth new*; make it new, that is, for new men and women, who confess that their righteousness is nothing of their own but rather that they have been justified by God, so that his grace may be in them.[26] See what they are like, these people for whom the whole aspect of their earth has been made new: *I have worked harder than any others*, Paul claims. What are you saying, Paul? Was it you, was it the work of your own spirit? *Not I*, he confesses, *but the grace of God with me* (1 Cor 15:10).

Verses 31-32. God's dealings with the proud

15. What are the consequences? When God has taken our own spirit away from us, we shall be reduced to our dust. Then we shall see to our profit how weak we are, so that we may receive his Spirit and be re-created. Now observe what follows: *May the glory of the Lord last for ever.* Not your glory, not mine, not his, not hers, but the Lord's glory; and may it last not for a time but for ever. *The Lord will rejoice in his works.* Not in your works, as though they really belonged to you. If your works are bad, they are the fruit of your sinfulness; if good, they are wrought through God's grace. *The Lord will rejoice in his works.*

16. *He looks on the earth and makes it shudder, he touches the mountains and they pour forth smoke.* You were exulting in your goodness, O earth, you were attributing your mighty wealth to yourself; but now the Lord looks down on you and sets you shuddering. Yes, let him look down on you, let him send shudders through you, for trembling humility is better than confident pride.

---

25. See Rom 4:5.
26. The idea of *spiritus* has developed through sections 13 and 14. At first it was the vital breath of the Creator, giving life to all creatures, and in a special sense giving life to man's dust (see Gn 2:7). Then it became the earthbound spirit of pride, from which God turns his face away. Then it is the penitent spirit, the attitude of the "poor in spirit," and then the inspiration of God who gives eloquence to martyrs. Finally it is revealed as the Spirit of the new creation in justified human beings.

Notice how God gazes on the earth to make it shudder. The apostle admonishes an earth that seems overconfident and boastful, *Work out your own salvation with fear and trembling. With fear and trembling*, he says, and then he adds, *for it is God who is at work in you* (Phil 2:12-13). You tell us to work at it, Paul, but why *with fear and trembling*? Because, he answers, *it is God who is at work in you*. That is the reason why we must work with trembling: because it is God who is at work. Because what you have is his gift, not something originating in yourself, you are to work *with fear and trembling*, for if you do not tremble before him, he will take away what he gave you. Work with trembling, then. Compare the injunction in another psalm: *Serve the Lord in reverence, and rejoice before him with awe* (Ps 2:11). If we are to rejoice with awe it is because God is beholding us. And this means an earthquake: when God looks upon us, let our hearts quake, and then God will find his rest in our hearts. Remember what God says elsewhere: *Upon whom shall my spirit rest, but upon the humble, peaceable person, the one who trembles at my words?* (Is 66:2) God *looks on the earth and makes it shudder, he touches the mountains and they pour forth smoke*. The mountains stand for proud and ostentatious people, whom God had not yet touched. Now he touches them, and they send up smoke. What does this represent, this smoke issuing from the mountains? It is a symbol of prayer offered to the Lord. Think what some lofty mountains used to be like: they were proud, towering folk, who never asked God for anything. They wanted other people to beg favors from them; they acknowledged no higher power to whom they would need to offer petitions. What proud, conceited, domineering person in this world ever lowered himself to petition God in humility? Of course, I am talking about unbelievers, not about the cedars of Lebanon that the Lord planted. Every impious person is a wretched soul who has no idea how to ask God for anything, though he or she likes being approached by others who seek favors. Such a person is a mountain, and God needs to touch that mountain and make it smoke. When it begins to send up smoke it will offer prayer to God, the sacrifice of its heart. It sends its smoke up to God, and it beats its breast. Then it begins to weep as well, for smoke draws forth tears. *He touches the mountains and they pour forth smoke*.

Verses 33-34. Praise, joy, conversation with God

17. *I will sing to the Lord all my life*. What will sing? Everything that exists will sing. Let our lives sing to the Lord. Hope is our life now, eternity will be our life later. Our present life is mortal, our hope is for life immortal. *I will sing to the Lord all my life; I will play psalms to my God as long as I exist*. Since I shall exist in God without end, I will play psalms to him unendingly. We must not think that, having begun to play psalms to God in that city, we shall then pass on to doing something else; no, our whole life will consist of playing psalms to God.

We shall only become bored with praising if we can ever become bored with him whom we praise. If he is always loved, he will be always praised. *I will play psalms to my God as long as I exist.*

18. *May my conversation be pleasing to him; but for my part, I will find joy in the Lord.* The psalmist prays, *May my conversation be pleasing to him.* What kind of conversation can a human being hold with God, except a confession of sins? Confess to God what you are, and you have held a conversation with him. Hold a conversation with him, then go and do good works, and then converse again with him. *Wash yourselves, make yourselves clean,* the Lord bids us through Isaiah. *Get rid of the wickedness of your hearts and take it out of my sight; have done with your evil ways, learn to do good, deal justly with the orphan and the widow. Then come, and let us argue it out, says the Lord.* (Is 1:16-18) What does it mean to hold a conversation with God? Show yourself to him who knows you, that he may show himself to you who do not know him. *May my conversation be pleasing to him.* This is what the Lord finds pleasant about your conversation: that it is a sacrifice offered by your humility, the contrition of your heart, the holocaust of your life; this is sweet and pleasing to God. But what is pleasing to you? *I will find my joy in the Lord.* This is the two-way conversation I have suggested to you: that you show yourself to him who knows you, so that he may show himself to you who do not know him. Your confession is sweet to him, his grace is sweet to you. He has told you about himself. How did he himself speak to you? Through his Word. What Word? Christ. He uttered himself, and to you. By sending Christ, he spoke himself. This is quite certain; let us listen to the Word himself telling us so: *Whoever sees me sees the Father* (Jn 14:9). *For my part, I will find joy in the Lord.*

Verse 35. The ultimate conversion of sinners. A thankful conclusion

19. *May sinners disappear from the earth.* This sounds like a savage request, yet it is a holy soul that is singing and sighing here. If only our soul were close to his! If only ours were united with his, attuned to his, closely allied with his! Then it would understand the merciful intention beneath the harsh plea. Can anyone understand this? Yes, but only a person full of charity. *May sinners disappear from the earth.* You are horrified to hear the psalmist cursing! And who is cursing? A holy man. Moreover, there is no doubt that his request is granted. Yet the saints have been told, *Bless, and do not curse* (Rom 12:14). What, then, does he mean by praying, *May sinners disappear from the earth*?

Let them vanish, let their spirit[27] be taken away from them and let them faint away, so that God may send forth his Spirit, and they may be recreated. *May sinners disappear from the earth, and the wicked vanish, to be no more.* What is

---

27. Or breath.

not to be anymore? The wicked. Let them be justified, so as not to be wicked. The psalmist saw that this would come about, and he was filled with joy. He repeated the first verse of the psalm: *Bless the Lord, O my soul.*

May our soul too bless the Lord, brothers and sisters, for he has graciously bestowed on us ability and eloquence and on you concentration and eagerness to learn. Each one of you must try to recall what he or she has heard. Chew over the choicest parts and share them with one another;[28] ruminate on what you have received, and do not let it slip away into the bowels of oblivion. Let it rather be a desirable treasure, reposing in your mouth.[29] It cost us much labor to research and discover all this, and great labor again to proclaim it and discuss it with you. May our labor bring forth fruit for you, and may our soul bless the Lord.

---

28. Literally "belch the richness/fat to each other." All the metaphors used here for the reception and assimilation of the word are gastronomic.
29. See Prv 21:20, LXX.

Exposition of Psalm 104

Verses 1-3. Praise precedes petition

1. This psalm, the one hundred and fourth, is the first of those to which "Alleluia" is prefixed.[1] The meaning of this word—or rather of this fusion of two words—is "Praise God." The psalm therefore begins, *Confess to the Lord, and call upon his name*, because this kind of confession is a form of praise. We find it in the passage, *I confess to you, Father, Lord of heaven and earth* (Mt 11:25). When praise has been offered first, it is usual for invocation to follow, and to this invocation the one who is praying attaches his desires.[2] The Lord's Prayer itself conforms to this pattern. After a very brief expression of praise, *Our Father, who art in heaven*, requests follow. Similarly in another psalm we find, *We will confess to you, O God; we will confess to you and call upon your name* (Ps 74:2(75:1)), and elsewhere, more plainly still, *I will call upon the Lord in praise, and I shall be saved from my enemies* (Ps 17:4(18:3)). So in the present psalm the speaker urges, *Confess to the Lord, and call upon his name*, which is the same thing as saying, "Praise the Lord, and call upon his name." The Lord listens to one who calls upon him when he sees that the praying person is praising him; and he sees that we are praising him when he verifies our love as genuine. There was a certain good servant whose love for him was genuine, and how did the Lord will to demonstrate that? By commanding, *Feed my sheep* (Jn 21:17). A comparable command follows here: *Proclaim[3] his deeds among the nations*; or, if we translate the Greek exactly, as other Latin codices do, *Proclaim the good news[4] of his deeds among the nations*. To whom is this command addressed? Surely to the evangelists, by prophetic anticipation.

2. *Sing to him and play psalms to him.* Praise him by word and work, for songs are sung with the lips, but psalms are played on the psaltery, which requires the hands. *Tell of all his wonders, be praised in his holy name.* These two injunctions can reasonably be seen as expressed already in the two that preceded them. In saying, *Tell of all his wonders*, the psalm re-emphasizes what it has just said in *Sing to him*; by continuing, *Be praised in his holy name*, it echoes what it has said in *Play psalms to him*. The good word is suggested first, by the reference to

---

1. This Exposition, different in tone from the preceding consideration of Psalm 103, was evidently written rather than preached.
2. Variant: ". . . in this, desires bind the sinner."
3. *Annuntiate.*
4. The CCL editors amend the verb to *evangelizate*, which seems necessary to the sense, though all codices read *annuntiate*, as before. The translation assumes that the emendation is right.

singing and telling of the Lord's wonders. Then good actions are enjoined on us by the command to play psalms to him; but then the danger arises that a person who performs good works may seek to be praised on that account, as though he had acted in his own strength. Accordingly the psalm first says, *Be praised*, for those who act well deserve commendation; but it immediately adds, *in his holy name*. It reminds us that anyone minded to boast must boast only in the Lord.[5] Those who intend to play psalms to him, rather than to themselves, must beware of performing their righteous actions in such a way as to be observed by other people, or they will have no reward from their Father in heaven.[6] However, those same works should shine out where others can see them, not to attract attention to those who so act, but that people may see the good works themselves and glorify the heavenly Father of those who perform them.[7] This is what is meant by being praised in his holy name. Another psalm expresses the same idea: *In the Lord shall my soul be praised; let the gentle hear it and be glad* (Ps 33:3(34:2)). Something similar follows here: *Let the heart of those who seek the Lord rejoice.* The gentle are gladdened when they emulate those who act well, but not in any bitter spirit of jealousy.[8]

Verse 4. *The unending search for God, powered by love*

3. *Seek the Lord and be strengthened.*[9] This is a close translation of the Greek, though the expression is not usual in Latin; other codices therefore have either *confirmamini* or *corroboramini*.[10] Scripture addresses God elsewhere as *My strength* (Ps 17:2(18:1)), and promises him, *I will guard my strength as yours* (Ps 58:10(59:9)). We are bidden to seek him and draw near to him that we may be enlightened and strengthened, so that blindness may not conceal from us what needs to be done, nor weakness prevent us from doing even what we see to be right. With regard to seeing, we are invited, *Draw near to him and receive his light* (Ps 33:6(34:5)); and as for doing, the present psalm tells us, *Seek the Lord and be strengthened.*

Seek his face always, it continues. What is the Lord's face? Nothing else but the presence of God. Scripture speaks of the face of the wind and the face of fire: *like straw in the face of the wind*, and *as wax flows liquid in the face of fire* (Pss 82:14(83:13); 67:3(68:2)). There are plenty of other scriptural examples of the use of the word "face" to signify the presence of something. But what is meant

---

5. See 1 Cor 1:31.
6. See Mt 6:1.
7. See Mt 5:16.
8. *Non amaro zelo*. This "bitter zeal" is a harsh, self-righteous pharisaism alien to the true spirit of the gospel. The phrase recurs in a key chapter of the Rule of Saint Benedict (Chapter 72).
9. *Confortamini.*
10. The three words are almost synonymous.

by *seek his face always*? I certainly know that it is good for me to cleave to God,[11] but if he is always being sought, when is he ever found?

Perhaps the psalm said *always* with reference to our life here on earth from the moment when we first came to know that we must seek God, this life in which we must still seek him even after we have found him. Faith does indeed find him, but hope seeks him still. Charity both finds him through faith and seeks to possess him in vision, where he will be found so completely that he will wholly satisfy us and need be sought no longer.[12] If faith were not capable of finding him in this life, the prophet would not have bidden us, *Seek the Lord*, and, when you have found him, *let the godless abandon his way, and the wicked man his thoughts* (Is 55:6.7). Yet if after we have found him in faith there were no need to go on searching for him, scripture would not say, *If we hope for what we do not see, we wait for it in patience* (Rom 8:25), nor, as John has it, *We know that when he appears, we shall be like him, because we shall see him as he is* (1 Jn 3:2). May we think, perhaps, that even when we do see him face to face, as he is, we shall still need to search for him, and search unendingly, because he is unendingly lovable? Even now we can say to someone who is present, "I'm not looking for you," meaning, "I do not love you." Conversely, if someone is loved with the love of choice he is sought even when present, as long as our love is everlasting love, lest he become absent. When we love another, even when we can see that person, we never tire of the presence of the beloved, but want him or her to be present always. This is what the psalm conveys by the words, *Seek his face always*: let not the finding of the beloved put an end to the love-inspired search; but as love grows, so let the search for one already found become more intense.[13]

Verses 5-7. *God reveals his name and his nature to his people*

4. But now this ardent praise-singer restrains himself and descends to words whose content we can more easily grasp; he nourishes our weak love by nursing us on the temporal wonders wrought by God. *Remember the wonders he has wrought, his mighty exploits and the judgments he has uttered*. This sequence of thought recalls the one we find on that occasion when God replied to Moses, who had asked him who he was, *I AM WHO I AM. Thus shall you say to the children of Israel, HE WHO IS has sent me to you.* (Ex 3:14) It is a rare mind that can understand this even in the smallest degree; and so it was that God mercifully accommodated his grace to human beings by going on to reveal his name in

---

11. See Ps 72(73):28.
12. Augustine modifies this statement on further reflection, below.
13. The voice of experience is plainly audible in these remarks. The tension between seeking and finding, finding and more ardent seeking, recurs in the testimony of the mystics down the ages.

these terms, *I am the God of Abraham, the God of Isaac and the God of Jacob. This is my name for ever* (Ex 3:15). The further revelation implied two things. First, he willed to show that those whom he named, saying that he was their God, are alive with him for ever.[14] Second, he expressed himself in a form that even little ones could understand, so that those who knew how to make use of the powerful forces of charity in seeking his face might always, in their measure, grasp his earlier statement, *I AM WHO I AM.* The same is true in our own case: if you find it too difficult to see, or even inquire, what God is, *remember the wonders he has wrought, his mighty exploits and the judgments he has uttered.*

5. And to whom is this said? *O seed of Abraham, his servant, O children of Jacob, his chosen one.* You, who are Abraham's progeny, Jacob's children, *remember the wonders he has wrought, his mighty exploits and the judgments he has uttered.* However, someone might mistakenly suppose that only the single race is intended here, Israel according to the flesh, failing to understand that the children of the promise are more truly Abraham's progeny than are the children of his flesh. To Gentiles the apostle says, *You are the descendants of Abraham, his heirs according to the promise* (Gal 3:29). The psalm makes the same point by continuing, *The Lord and no other is our God; his judgments are in force through all the earth.* Similarly Isaiah assures the free Jerusalem, the Jerusalem that is our mother, *Your God, who delivers you, will be called the God of all the earth* (Is 54:5). Is he the God of Jews only?[15] Far from it. *The Lord and no other is our God; his judgments are in force through all the earth,* because his Church, in which his judgments are promulgated, extends worldwide.

Why, then, does another psalm say of him, *He announces his word to Jacob, his just decrees and judgments to Israel. He has not dealt so with any other nation; he has not revealed his judgments to them* (Ps 147:19-20)? It says this because God wanted us to understand that Abraham's progeny comprises one single nation called from all nations. All peoples are said to belong to it, but in such a way that the nation called into adoption is but one. Outside this one people God has manifested his judgments to no other nation, because where people have refused to believe in God's revelation, even when it has been announced to them, it has not truly been manifested. Unless they believe, they will not understand.[16]

---

14. See Mk 12:25-27.
15. See Rom 3:29.
16. Faith is required for true understanding of what is revealed. Augustine's remarks anticipate Anselm's dictum, *Credo ut intellegam.*

*Verses 8-11. The eternal covenant referred to in the psalm is the covenant of
faith, not the Old Covenant as such*

6. *He has been mindful throughout the ages of his covenant.* Some codices
have *for eternity,*[17] instead of *throughout the ages;*[18] the difference arises from
an ambiguity in the Greek. If we take *throughout the ages* to mean "as long as
this age lasts, but not for ever," why does the psalm go on to say, as a way of
specifying what covenant God has remembered, *the word he enjoined on a thousand generations*? Well, I suppose even that could be considered as a process
that will end eventually; but the psalm then adds, *The word he entrusted to
Abraham, and his oath to Isaac; he established it as a command for Jacob, to
Israel as an eternal covenant.* There is no room for ambiguity here: the Greek
has αἰώνιον, which our translators have never rendered as anything but *eternity,*
or, in a few instances, *eternal.* (Possibly it could be argued that since αἰῶνα is
more usually translated "this world" or "this age," αἰώνιον must mean not
"eternal" but "pertaining to this world"; but I do not remember anyone being so
presumptuous as to say so.)

There is a difficulty, though. The psalm goes on to mention the land of Canaan:
*he established it as a command for Jacob, for Israel as an eternal covenant, saying,
To you will I give the land of Canaan, as your allotted inheritance.* This might
seem to suggest that the covenant means the Old Covenant. But then how could it
be eternal, when that earthly inheritance cannot possibly last for ever? The Old
Covenant is called old precisely because it has been superseded by the New. Moreover the phrase *a thousand generations* does not appear to signify anything eternal,
because they would come to an end. But in any case, a thousand generations are too
many for a temporal span, for although a generation, which the Greeks call γενεά, is
restricted to a very few years—fifteen years, according to some, reckoning from
the time when a person can procreate—what is the sum of these thousand generations, counting not merely from the time of Abraham, who received the promise, to
the era of the New Covenant, but even from Adam to the end of the world? Who
dare assert that this world will last for fifteen thousand years?

7. In view of this I do not think that we should understand *"covenant"* to
mean the Old Covenant, which according to a prophet was superseded by the
New: *Lo, the days are coming, says the Lord, when I will conclude with the
house of Israel and the house of Judah a new covenant, not like the covenant that
I established with their ancestors when I led them out of the land of Egypt* (Jer
31:31-32). Rather is it to be understood as the covenant of faith which the apostle
commends, proposing Abraham to us for our imitation and refuting those who
make the works of the law their boast. The apostle proves that Abraham put his

17. *in aeternum.*
18. *in saeculum.*

faith in God even before his circumcision and that this was reckoned to him as righteousness.[19] What is more, after saying that God *has been mindful throughout the ages of his covenant*, which we must take to mean that he is mindful to eternity of his covenant of justification and of the eternal inheritance he has promised to believers, the psalm goes on to call it *the word he enjoined on a thousand generations*. What does *enjoined* suggest? The words, *to you will I give the land of Canaan*, are not something enjoined, not a command, but a promise. What is enjoined on us as a command is something we must do; a promise is something we receive. Thus faith is a command; the righteous person must live by faith,[20] and to this faith an eternal inheritance is promised.

The psalm speaks of a thousand generations because this perfect number stands for all generations. As long as one generation continues to succeed another, so long does the command to live by faith hold good. God's people sees this happening; we watch new children of the promise coming to birth and others departing by death, until the time for begetting and bearing is over. This is symbolized by the number one thousand because the number ten squared makes a hundred, and when this is multiplied by ten again we get a thousand.

This word God *entrusted to Abraham, and his oath to Isaac. And he established it for Jacob*; gave it, that is to say, as *a command to Jacob*. These are the three patriarchs of whom he particularly said that he was their God. The Lord also names them in the New Testament, predicting that *many will come from east and west and will sit down with Abraham and Isaac and Jacob in the kingdom of heaven* (Mt 8:11). This is the eternal inheritance. Here too when the psalm says, *He established it as a command to Jacob*, it stresses that faith is a command laid upon us; for it would not call a promise a command. A command entails work; promise implies a reward. *This is the work God wants*, said the Lord, *that you believe in the one he has sent* (Jn 6:29). The Lord is *mindful throughout the ages of his covenant*, and he established his word—the word of faith which we preach[21]—*as a command for Jacob, for Israel as an eternal covenant*. This means that on the basis of his word and of the fulfillment of his command, he will give us something eternal. But he says, *To you will I give the land of Canaan as your allotted inheritance*. How can that be eternal? Only inasmuch as it symbolizes something eternal. Indeed, it was called the land of promise, a land flowing with milk and honey, and this is a figure of grace, whereby we taste and see how sweet the Lord is.[22] But not everyone reaches it, because not all have faith. The psalm added *as your allotted inheritance*, as also

---

19. See Rom 4:3.10-11.
20. See Hb 2:4; Rom 1:17. The original sense was probably "one who by faith is righteous has life"; but the meaning offered in the present translation seems to be what Augustine had in mind.
21. See Rom 10:8.
22. See Ps 33:9(34:8).

in another psalm we hear the progeny of Abraham, that progeny which is Christ, exclaiming, *The measuring-lines have fallen for me in bright, glorious places; indeed, my inheritance is glorious to me* (Ps 15(16):6).

If we wonder why the land was called Canaan, an interpretation of the name itself provides the answer, for Canaan means "humble." If this is compared with Noah's judgment, whereby he condemned Canaan to be the slave of his brothers in the future,[23] the additional idea of servile fear is included. But *a slave does not stay in the house permanently, whereas a son stays for ever* (Jn 8:35). Canaan is thus excluded, and the land of promise is given to the progeny of Abraham, for when charity is made perfect it casts out fear,[24] allowing the son to stay in the house for ever. This is why the psalm says that God's word came *to Israel as an eternal covenant.*

Verses 12-15. The patriarchs in Canaan: few and foreign, but protected, and Christian by anticipation

8. The psalm then resumes a story very well known to us from the reliable account in the holy books. *While they were few in number, very sparse, and foreign sojourners in it* . . . that is, in the land of Canaan. When the patriarchs Abraham, Isaac, and Jacob lived there, before they had received the land as their inheritance, they had very few descendants and were no better than resident aliens in the land.[25]

9. *While they were few in number, very sparse, and foreign sojourners in it, they traveled from tribe to tribe, and from the kingdom to another people.* This last phrase, *from the kingdom to another people,* is a repetition of the preceding one, *from tribe to tribe.* The psalm then relates that God *allowed no one to hurt them,*[26] and rebuked kings on their account. *Do not touch my anointed,*[27] he said, *or malign my prophets.* These are the words God spoke to rebuke or admonish

---

23. See Gn 9:22-25.
24. See 1 Jn 4:18.
25. Augustine here argues about phrases which are intolerable in Latin, being an over-literal translation of the Greek. The argument makes no sense in English; hence a few sentences are omitted in the translation above. The omitted passage runs as follows: "But some codices have not *paucissimi et incolae,* but *paucissimos et incolas.* It is clear that those who so translated these words followed a Greek idiom which cannot be carried over into Latin without an absurd effect which is quite intolerable. If we were to transfer this usage into Latin for the whole phrase we would have to say, *In eo esse illos numero brevi, paucissimos et incolas in ea.* But when the Greek says, *In eo esse illos,* it means what Latin means by saying, *Cum essent,* which cannot be followed by a noun in the accusative, but only by a nominative. Who would ever say, *Cum essent paucissimos?* We would say, *Cum essent paucissimi.*"
26. Augustine's brief observations on different ways of expressing this are omitted from the English translation. The omitted phrase runs: "The Greek expression is *nocere illos,* but the Latin is *nocere illis.*"
27. *Christos meos.*

kings, forbidding them to harm[28] the holy patriarchs who were few in number, very sparse, and only sojourners in the land of Canaan. The words are not recorded in the historical books that deal with the period but are to be understood either as spoken secretly, as God sometimes does speak in human hearts by hidden means and through reliable manifestations, or perhaps as having been transmitted by an angel. Both the king of Gerar and the king of Egypt were divinely warned not to hurt Abraham,[29] and another king not to hurt Isaac,[30] and sundry others not to hurt Jacob; for they were very few and only sojourners before Jacob migrated with his descendants to dwell in Egypt. It is this period in Canaan that is recalled by the psalm's statement, *They traveled from tribe to tribe, from the kingdom to another people.*

We might wonder how the patriarchs, so few in number before they went to Egypt and increased there, so sparse, and only sojourners, could have survived at all in a foreign land. The psalm therefore explains that God *allowed no one to hurt them, and rebuked kings on their account. Do not touch my anointed or malign my prophets.*

10. Another point may possibly perplex us: how could they be called God's anointed ones[31] before any rite of anointing had been introduced, before the time when this title was applied to the kings? It was ascribed first to Saul, and then to David who succeeded him in the kingship, and then to the other kings of Judah and the kings of Israel who were anointed as the sacred custom was perpetuated. In them was prefigured Christ, the one, true, anointed king; and to him scripture testifies, *God, your God has anointed you with the oil of joy, more abundantly than your companions* (Ps 44:8(45:7)). How, then, could the patriarchs, already in their day, have been called "anointed ones"? We certainly do read that they were prophets, or at least that Abraham was; and we can reasonably infer that what is openly stated of him may be understood of the others. Can we think, then, that they were "anointed ones"[32] because they were already Christians,[33] though in a hidden sense? Though Christ's flesh derived from them, he truly existed before them, as he asserted to the Jews: *Before Abraham came to be, I AM* (Jn 8:58). But in that case, how could the patriarchs have failed to know him or to believe in him, when they deserved the name of prophets because they proclaimed the Lord in advance, even though in a hidden way? The Lord himself declared plainly, *Abraham desired to see my day; he saw it, and rejoiced* (Jn 8:56). They must have believed in him, because no one is reconciled with God, whether before the incarnation or after it, except through the faith that is in Christ

---

28. Variant: "neglect."
29. See Gn 20:1-18; 12:10-20.
30. See Gn 26:7-11.
31. *Christi.*
32. *Christi.*
33. *Christiani.*

Jesus; the apostle declared with absolute certainty that *God is one, and there is one mediator between God and humankind, the man Christ Jesus* (1 Tm 2:5).

Verses 16-17. The great hunger

11. The psalm now begins to tell the story of how they came to travel from tribe to tribe, and from the kingdom to another people. *He summoned hunger into the land, and shattered their entire support, the bread on which they relied. But he sent a man ahead of them, Joseph, sold into slavery.* This is what caused them to travel from tribe to tribe, to migrate from the kingdom to a different people. But the expressions used in the holy scriptures should not be passed over carelessly. It says, *He summoned hunger into the land*, as though hunger were a person, or some live material creature, or some spirit that could obey the one who summoned it, whereas hunger is a ruinous condition consequent on not eating, and so is like a disease in those who suffer it. As a disease is often banished by medicine, so we might say that hunger is cured by food. Why, then, does the psalm say that God summoned hunger? Should we suppose that the evils visited upon human beings are all in the charge of various bad angels? Another psalm says that God afflicted men and women by launching evil angels against them,[34] and that interpretation cannot be wrong. Does it hold good here as well, so that the words *he summoned hunger* mean that God summoned a bad angel, the angel of hunger, and that this angel was named after the calamity in his charge? The ancient Romans had the same idea, and dedicated such phenomena to particular gods, like the goddess Febris[35] and the god Pallor.[36]

Perhaps it is preferable to take *he summoned hunger* to mean, "He said that there should be hunger." "Summon" means "call"; "call" means "decree"; "decree" means "command." He who summoned hunger is he who also *calls into being things that do not exist as though they already were* (Rom 4:17). The apostle did not say that God *calls into being things that do not exist* in order that they may come to be, but *as though they already were*. Whatever is to come about in the future by God's decision is already accomplished in him; elsewhere it is said of him that *he has done future things* (Is 45:11, LXX). So in our psalm: when famine occurred it is said to have been summoned; for what was in existence already, inasmuch as it was organized in God's secret providence, was commanded to arrive. The psalm then immediately states how God summoned the famine: *He shattered their entire support, the bread on which they relied.* To say that *he shattered it* is an unexpected turn of phrase, meaning, "he caused it to fail."

---

34. See Ps 77(78):49.
35. Fever.
36. Paleness, the god of fear.

12. *He sent a man ahead of them.* Who was this man? Joseph. How did he send him ahead? *Joseph was sold into slavery.* That happened through the sin of his brothers, and yet it was God who sent Joseph into Egypt. We should look deeply into this and see something great, something we very much need to see: God's way of making good use of the bad actions of human beings. They, on the contrary, make bad use of the good works of God.

Verses 18-22. Joseph's oppression and advancement. He educates the Egyptian elders

13. The psalmist goes on weaving his story, recalling what Joseph endured in his lowly condition, and how he was raised out of it. *They forced his feet into fetters; and a sword entered his soul until his word came true.* We do not in fact read that Joseph was fettered, but we have no reason to doubt that this did happen to him. Some details may have been omitted from the history which were none-theless well known to the Holy Spirit who speaks in these psalms. We should interpret the sword which is said to have pierced his soul as the harsh treatment he was forced to endure, for it is said to have transfixed his soul, not his body. A similar metaphor is used in the gospel when Simeon says to Mary, *This child is set for the fall and the rising of many in Israel, and for a sign that will be gain-said—and a sword will pierce your own soul—that the thoughts of many hearts may be laid bare* (Lk 2:34-35). The Lord's passion did indeed spell ruin for many and exposed the secrets of many hearts, for it forced into the open what they thought about the Lord. Unquestionably it also brought great sadness to his mother, who was grievously struck by the sword of bereavement.[37]

Joseph remained in that distressed condition *until his word came true,* the word in which he had accurately interpreted certain dreams. His reputation brought him to the notice of the king, to whom also Joseph foretold future events from his dreams. However, we should not take the word "his," in the phrase *until his word came true* to mean that so awesome a power was to be attributed to a human being. To exclude such a misunderstanding the psalm promptly added, *The Lord's utterance enkindled him*; or, as other codices have it, keeping more closely to the Greek, *The Lord's utterance set him on fire.* This puts Joseph among those to whom the psalm earlier said, *Be praised in his holy name.*

The Lord's utterance set him on fire. When the Holy Spirit was sent by the Lord, separate tongues, seemingly of fire, were seen by the disciples, and there was a profound reason for this. The apostle tells us to be *ardent in the Spirit*

---

37. A good example of the connection Augustine can establish between apparently disparate scriptural passages. The superficial similarity of the words (a sword piercing someone's soul) enables him to point out the analogy between the spiritual suffering of Joseph in prison and the much greater spiritual suffering of the mother of Jesus.

(Rom 12:11). Those who distance themselves from the fire are those of whom it is said: *The love of many will grow cold.*

14. The narrative continues, *The king sent and released him, the prince of the peoples, and set him free.* The same person is meant by *the king* and *the prince of the peoples.* He released Joseph from the fetters, and set him free from prison. *He appointed him ruler of his house, and administrator of all his possessions, that he might instruct his leading men like himself, and teach his old men*[38] *prudence.* The Greek has for this last phrase, *teach his elders wisdom.* Translating the Greek exactly, we get, *that he might instruct his leading men like himself, and make his elders wise*; for the Greek has πρεσβυτέρους, which we usually render "elders," not γέροντας, "old men." It also has σοφίσαι, which we cannot translate by a single word; it is derived from "wisdom," in Greek σοφία, not from "prudence," which would be φρόνησις. Here we have something reported about Joseph in his exalted station that we do not read elsewhere, just as we read nothing about fetters in his lowly condition. But how could it have been possible for so great a man, a worshipper of the one true God, to be solely intent on nourishing bodies in Egypt, and on the administration of material goods, and take no care of the people's minds, if he had the opportunity to improve them? In the history only such things were recorded as were judged sufficient to foreshadow future events—judged, that is, by the mind of the writer, in whom dwelt the Holy Spirit.

Verses 23-25. Israel in Egypt; the ill-will of the Egyptians is not caused, but is used, by God

15. *So Israel went to Egypt, and Jacob was a sojourner*[39] *in the land of Ham.* Israel is the same as Jacob; Egypt is the same as the land of Ham. This is a plain demonstration that the Egyptian race sprang from the stock of Ham, one of the sons of Noah. The eldest son of Ham was Canaan. Hence where some codices read, *the land of Canaan,* they should be corrected. The translation, *was a sojourner,* is better than that of some codices which have *dwelt.*[40] Our reading, *was a sojourner,*[41] comes to the same as saying, "was an *incola*"; there is no difference in meaning between the two words. In fact the Greek uses the same word here as it used earlier when it said that the patriarchs were *very sparse, and foreign sojourners* in the land. A sojourner (whether we use *incola* or *accola*) is someone who is not indigenous but a stranger.

---

38. Variant: "elders."
39. *Accola.*
40. *Inhabitavit.*
41. *Accola.*

This is how the family of Israel came to *travel from tribe to tribe, and from the kingdom to another people*. The fact was briefly stated earlier and has now been briefly explained in the narrative. But we may well ask from what kingdom they migrated to lodge with another people, for they were not kings in the land of Canaan. The monarchy had not yet been established among the people of Israel. How can the verse be understood? Only, perhaps, proleptically: it refers to the kingdom that would later be founded there, ruled by their descendants.

16. There follows an account of what happened in Egypt. *He multiplied his people exceedingly, and made them strong against their enemies*. This too is a brief anticipatory statement, to be filled out by the subsequent narrative, for God's people had not been strengthened against the hostile Egyptians at the time when their male children were being slaughtered, or when they were being crushed by the labor of making bricks. They became strong later when by the mighty hand of the Lord their God, and through his signs and portents, they were rendered terrifying and awesome, until the resistance of an obstinate king was overcome and the Red Sea overwhelmed the pursuing enemy with his army.

17. As though we were inquiring how the changed situation came about—the situation so briefly described by the statement, *He made his people strong against their enemies*—the psalm now begins to tell the story which will make this development clear. *He turned their heart to hate his people, and to deal dishonestly with his servants*. We surely must not take this to mean that God turns the human heart toward sin? Or are we to think that it is no sin, or only a slight sin, to hate God's people and deal dishonestly with his servants? That cannot be right; who would defend such an opinion? Are we to maintain, then, that God was the author of such grave sins, he who cannot be thought responsible for any sin at all, even the least?

Who is wise enough to understand this?[42] It is characteristic of the amazing goodness of God that he makes good use even of bad agents, whether angelic or human. People are bad because of their own depravity, yet he makes good use of their badness. The Egyptians had not been good before they began to hate God's people; they were malevolent, wicked people, prone to envy the fortunate immigrants in their midst. God was conferring a benefit on his people by causing them to multiply, and by this very kindness he steered those bad people to envy, for envy is hatred of another's good fortune. In that sense he turned their heart to hatred of his people arising out of envy, and to deceitful dealing with his servants. Not by making their heart bad, but by doing good to his own people, did he direct their heart toward a hatred that was their own choice. God did not pervert a straightforward heart; he acted on a heart already perverse of its own accord, turning it toward hatred of his people so that he might bring good out of their evil attitude. Not by making the Egyptians bad did he do so, but by

_____

42. See Ps 106(107):43.

bestowing on the Israelites good things which could very easily arouse envy in bad people. How God made use of their hatred for the training of his people and the glory of his name, so profitably also for us, the following verses demonstrate. When "Alleluia" is sung, these events are recalled and he is praised.

Verses 26-36. The plagues

18. *He sent Moses, his servant, and Aaron whom he had chosen [him].*[43] It would have sufficed to say, *whom he had chosen*; nothing is added to the meaning by the addition of *him.* But this is a scriptural idiom, found also in the phrase, the land in which they dwell in it.[44] The divinely inspired pages are full of examples.

19. *He sent the words of his signs and prodigies among them in the land of Ham.* Although the psalm calls them *the words of his signs and prodigies* we must not take *words* literally, as though spoken words set off the signs and prodigies, as commands that such things should happen. Many of the plagues were initiated without words, through the instrumentality of a rod, or an outstretched hand, or ash tossed into the air. But the events were not empty of meaning, any more than are the words we speak, and therefore the plagues are called "words," words formed not by voices and sounds but by signs and prodigies. *He sent* these words *among them*; that is to say, God caused the plagues to happen among them.

20. *He sent darkness, and all was obscured.* This too was mentioned among the plagues with which the Egyptians were afflicted. But in the next phrase there are divergent readings among the codices. Some have, *And they provoked him to angry words*, others, *And they did not provoke him to angry words*. The former we have found in many witnesses, but the latter reading, with the negative inserted, in two codices at most. It may be that the text has been corrupted to produce a smoother reading, for what could be easier to understand than the assertion that *they provoked him to angry words* by their obstinate resistance?[45] We have attempted, therefore, to make good sense of the alternative reading. *They did not provoke him to angry words*, and this is the explanation that occurs to us at present: *they did not provoke* Moses and Aaron *to angry words*, because these men tolerated even the most stubborn Egyptians with the utmost patience, until all that God intended to do among them should be duly completed.

21. *He turned their waters into blood, and killed their fish. He gave their land over to frogs, even in the private chambers of their kings.* This seems to say, "He

---

43. This grammatically redundant word engages Augustine's attention.
44. See Num 13:20, LXX; compare Lv 18:3, LXX.
45. Augustine was familiar with the principle beloved of textual critics, *lectio difficilior est praeferenda.* Many corruptions in the copying of ancient manuscripts crept in through scribes' attempts to smooth difficult readings.

turned their very land into frogs." So great were the swarms of frogs that this hyperbole could be justified.

22. *He spoke, and flies and stinging insects swarmed throughout their terri-tory.* If we ask when he spoke, the answer must be that the event was present in his word before it came to pass, and in this same non-temporal word the decision on its timing was also present. Yet when the time came for it to be implemented, God did in a sense command it to happen through his angels and through his servants, Moses and Aaron.

23. *He turned their rain into hail.* This is the same expression as that used above, *He gave their land over to frogs,* except that it cannot have been the entire land that was turned into frogs, whereas the whole of the rain could have been turned into hail. *A devouring fire in their land:* the words "he sent" are under-stood.

24. *He struck their vines and their fig-trees, and smashed every tree in their country.* This happened under the impact of hail and lightning, which explains the reference to *the devouring fire.*

25. *He spoke, and there came locust and hopper, an uncountable swarm.* This is a single plague, for the locust is the parent, the hopper its young.

26. *They ate up all the grass in their land, and devoured all the fruit their soil produced.* Even grass is a kind of fruit, and scripture customarily calls fruit crops "grass"; but here the psalmist probably wanted two words to correspond to the two insects just mentioned, locust and hopper. The choice of words is simply a device for varying the expressions to relieve monotony, not an indication of difference in meaning.

27. *He smote every firstborn in their land, and the firstfruits of all their toil.* This plague is the last one, except for the slaughter at the Red Sea. I think that *the firstfruits of their toil* must mean the firstlings of their cattle. Although there were ten plagues, not all are mentioned, nor are they mentioned by the psalm in the order in which they occurred; the composer of a praise-song is free from the rules that bind one who narrates and weaves a history. The speaker and author of this praise-song is the Holy Spirit, acting through the prophet. The authority of the Spirit worked through the man who wrote the history, and that same authority was at work here in the psalm, recording some events not mentioned in the history and passing over others that are found there.

Verses 37-38. The exodus

28. The psalm adds another point in praise of God, that he led the Israelites out of Egypt enriched with silver and gold. They were not yet the kind of people who could disregard the due and just recompense for their labors, even though the payment was only a temporal one. They tricked the Egyptians into lending them gold and silver ornaments; but it must not be thought that God commands

people whose hearts are uplifted to practice fraud of this kind, or, if they have already committed it, that he approves. They were permitted, rather than ordered, to behave so by the instructions of God, who certainly saw their hearts and scrutinized their greedy desires. Yet in furthering their own material interests they were taking advantage of people who deserved to be treated so and removing from unjust employers what they had earned, even though they did so by cunning. As God made use of the Egyptians' iniquity, so did he in his divine wisdom make use of the Israelites' weakness, to symbolize and prefigure what needed to be revealed through these events.

And he led them out in silver and gold. This again is a scriptural turn of phrase, meaning "with silver and gold." *And there was no sick person in their tribes*, physically, that is; it would not have been true spiritually. This too was a great kindness on God's part, that when the need to migrate was upon them, no one was ill.

29. *Egypt rejoiced at their departure, for fear of them lay heavy upon it*—fear of the Hebrews lay on the Egyptians, that is. Fear of the Hebrews means not that the Hebrews were afraid, but that they were feared.[46] Someone may ask, "In that case, why had the Egyptians been so reluctant to let them go? Why did they give them leave only on the supposition that they would return? Why did they lend their gold and silver to the Hebrews in the expectation that they would return and give it back, if *Egypt rejoiced at their departure*?" We must take this to mean that after the last deadly plague among the Egyptians, and after the huge slaughter at the Red Sea of so great a pursuing army, the surviving Egyptians feared that the Hebrews would come back and very easily crush the Egyptian stragglers. In this way a declaration made earlier in the psalm was verified. *He multiplied his people exceedingly*, it said, and immediately added, *He made them strong against their enemies.* In order to explain how what he announced in that verse came about, the psalmist has told us this story of catastrophe[47] down to the point where he could say, *Egypt rejoiced at their departure, for fear of them lay heavy upon it.* The psalm has set a seal on what it said earlier, that God made his people strong against their enemies.

Verses 39-44. God's kindness to his people in the desert and the promised land

30. The psalm now proceeds to relate the divine favors conferred on the travelers through the desert. *He spread a cloud to protect them, and fire to give them light through the night.* These statements are as clear as their content is familiar.

---

46. Objective genitive.
47. Some codices omit "of catastrophe."

31. *They entreated him, and quails came.* What they craved was not quails, but meat. However, since quails are meat, and since this psalm is not concerned with the bitter obstinacy of those with whom God was not well pleased[48] but with the faith of the elect who are Abraham's true descendants, we must assume that these faithful ones begged God to send something to silence the angry murmuring of the discontented. In the next verse, *and he satisfied them with bread from heaven*, the manna is not expressly named; but no one who has read those stories will find anything obscure in this.

32. *He split the rock and waters flowed; rivers ran down onto the dry land.* This is immediately intelligible as we read it.

33. By all these kindly provisions God reminds them of Abraham's meritorious faith; for the psalm continues, *Because he was mindful of his holy word, which he swore to his servant Abraham. And he led his people out with gladness, his elect with joy.* The expression, *his people*, is repeated as *his elect*; and *with gladness* has its counterpart in *with joy.* It continues, *He gave them the territories of the Gentiles; they took possession of the labors of the nations.* Here again we have repetition: *the territories of the Gentiles* corresponds to *the labors of the nations*, and *he gave them* is echoed in *they took possession.*

Verse 45. The purpose of it all; Augustine indicates the Christian application of the whole psalm

34. We might perhaps inquire about God's purpose in conferring all these gifts. To exclude the danger that God's people should regard this good fortune in temporal matters as its supreme good, the psalm immediately pointed to where the supreme good must be sought: *That they might keep his righteous ordinances, and zealously follow his law.* The lesson in this for us is that God's servants, the elect children of the promise, the true and authentic posterity of Abraham who imitate his faith, receive such earthly gifts from God not in order to abandon themselves to self-indulgence or grow lazy in decadent complacency but in order to be free for that essential work whereby they may attain their supreme good: the work, namely, of keeping his righteous ordinances and zealously following his law. They are provided with all they need, prepared for them by God's mercy, because otherwise they might be so preoccupied by the demanding labors of acquiring these things that they would have no time for the essential task.

Another point that emerges from this verse is that the psalmist wanted to present Abraham's descendants as the sort of people who could claim to be true children of Abraham. There certainly were some of these in the Israelite people, as Paul clearly shows, for he declares that *God was not pleased with all of them*

48. See 1 Cor 10:5.

(1 Cor 10:5). If God was not pleased with all of them, there evidently were some among them with whom he was pleased. The present psalm is concerned to commend such people, so it says nothing of the sins and provocation and bitter resentment of which others were guilty, those others with whom God was not pleased. But not only was divine justice manifested toward the wicked; the mercy of our omnipotent and kindly God was also displayed, and therefore the psalm which follows this one praises God even while speaking of the delinquents. Both sorts of people co-existed in the one nation, but the wicked did not pollute the good with the contagion of their sins. *The Lord knows his own*, and if in this world a just person cannot hold aloof from the unjust, at least let *everyone who calls on the name of the Lord keeps clear of iniquity* (2 Tm 2:19).

35. Let us try now to discern the soul of this psalm hiding in its body, so to say; let us try to find the interior meaning concealed by the exterior words. It seems to me that Abraham's progeny, by which I understand all the children of the promise with a right to the eternal inheritance, the heirs to the eternal covenant, are being warned in this psalm that they must choose as their inheritance nothing else but God. They must worship him disinterestedly, that is to say, for his own sake, not in order to gain some reward other than himself. In doing this they must praise him, invoke him, and proclaim him, performing through faith good actions to his glory, not their own, rejoicing in their hope and fervent in charity.[49] This whole way of life is set forth in the psalm's opening verses: *Confess to the Lord, and call upon his name; proclaim his deeds among the nations. Sing to him and play psalms to him. Tell of all his wonders, be praised in his holy name. Let the heart of those who seek the Lord rejoice. Seek the Lord and be strengthened, seek his face always.*

36. The psalm then addresses the hearts of the little ones in need of nourishment. To them it proposes the example of the patriarchs, stressing both their faith and the promise of God. By imitating their faith, and by hope, we may become their true posterity, which consists not only of the Hebrew nation but of all throughout the world who accept the same grace. All of this is contained in these verses: *Remember the wonders he has wrought, his mighty exploits and the judgments he has uttered. O seed of Abraham, his servant, O children of Jacob, his chosen one, the Lord and no other is our God; his judgments are in force through all the earth. He has been mindful throughout the ages of his covenant, the word he enjoined on a thousand generations, the word he entrusted to Abraham, and his oath to Isaac; he established it as a command for Jacob, to Israel as an eternal covenant, saying, To you will I give the land of Canaan, as your allotted inheritance.* According to my small ability I have explained how all this should be understood.

----

49. See Rom 12:11.12.

37. A mind not well endowed with faith raised a question here. If God is to be worshiped disinterestedly, if the inheritance promised by the eternal covenant is God himself and he is to be sought for his own sake alone, does this not mean that, in spite of the multiplication of his mercies, he neglects the mortal life of those who seek him and their temporal needs?[50] The psalm replies: Listen carefully to what he granted to our fathers, both those ancestors whom God set up as examples of faith and those who, sprung from them by carnal descent, also imitated their faith. *While they were few in number, very sparse, and foreign sojourners in it*—that is, in the land of Canaan—*they traveled from tribe to tribe, and from the kingdom to another people. He allowed no one to hurt them, and rebuked kings on their account. Do not touch my anointed or malign my prophets.*

38. If you now inquire how it happened that they *traveled from tribe to tribe, and from the kingdom to another people*, listen to what comes next. *He summoned hunger into the land, and shattered their entire support, the bread on which they relied. But he sent a man ahead of them, Joseph, sold into slavery. They forced his feet into fetters; and a sword entered his soul until his word came true. The Lord's utterance set him on fire. The king sent and released him, the prince of the peoples, and set him free. He appointed him ruler of his house, and administrator of all his possessions, that he might instruct his leading men like himself, and teach his elders prudence. So Israel went to Egypt, and Jacob was a sojourner in the land of Ham.* This was how they came to *travel from tribe to tribe, and from the kingdom to another people.*

39. *He multiplied his people exceedingly, and made them strong against their enemies.* But perhaps you may wonder how he did this? Listen: *He turned the heart* [of the Egyptians] *to hate his people, and to deal dishonestly with his servants. He sent Moses, his servant, and Aaron whom he had chosen. He sent the words of his signs and prodigies among them in the land of Ham. He sent darkness, and all was obscured, and they provoked him to angry words. He turned their waters into blood, and killed their fish. He gave their land over to frogs, even in the private chambers of their kings. He spoke, and flies and stinging insects swarmed throughout their territory. He turned their rain into hail, and sent devouring fire in their land. He struck their vines and their fig-trees, and smashed every tree in their country. He spoke, and there came locusts and grasshoppers, an uncountable swarm. They ate up all the grass in their land, and devoured all the fruit their soil produced. He smote every firstborn in their land, and the firstfruits of all their toil. Then he led* [Israel] *out in silver and gold, and there was no sick person in their tribes. Egypt rejoiced at*

50. So the older codices. Others have ". . . sought for his own sake alone, why does he grant mortal life to those who seek him? Does he not neglect their temporal needs, in spite of the multiplication of his mercies?"

their departure, for fear of them lay heavy upon it. This was how he made his own people strong against their enemies.

40. You have heard how God's justice inflicted all these calamities on the enemies of his people. Hearken now to how his mercy showered benefits upon his own, even temporal benefits. *He spread a cloud to protect them, and fire to give them light through the night. They entreated him, and quails came, and he satisfied them with bread from heaven. He split the rock and waters flowed; rivers ran down onto the dry land, because he was mindful of his holy word, which he swore to his servant Abraham. And he led his people out with gladness, his elect with joy. He gave them the territories of the Gentiles; they took possession of the labors of the nations,* not that they might worship him for the sake of these good things but that they might refer even these things to their eternal good and use them for that end, which is to say, *that they might keep his righteous ordinances, and zealously follow his law.* Whatever good things God gives us are to be subordinated to the disinterested, pure worship we must give him, for then our service will truly be offered free. The ancient enemy himself challenged us, when he dared to say to God, *Job hardly worships the Lord for nothing, does he?* (Jb 1:9)

But there is more. If Joseph was sold into slavery and humiliated, but then exalted, if he prepared a place where temporal goods would be provided for God's people, that it might be strengthened against its enemies, how much more has Jesus, sold and humiliated by his brethren according to the flesh, but then exalted in heaven, prepared a place where eternal goods may be provided for God's people, as it triumphs over the devil and his angels? Listen, then, O progeny of Abraham, you who do not boast of carnal descent but imitate his faith; listen, you servants of God, you chosen ones of God who hold the promise of life both now and in the future.[51] If trials are hard for you to bear in this world, think of Joseph in prison and Jesus on the cross.[52] If temporal prosperity is within your reach, do not use God to secure it, but use it for God's sake. Do not imagine that his worshipers serve him with an eye to gaining what they need in the present life; after all, he bestows the same good things on those who blaspheme him. No; seek first God's kingdom and his righteousness, and all these things will come your way as well.[53]

---

51. See 1 Tm 4:8.

52. Augustine's parallel between the Hebrew Joseph and Jesus Christ is powerful and has deep scriptural roots. The motif of humiliation followed by exaltation in the life of one who plays a key role in God's saving plans is present already in the Old Testament, notably in the Servant prophecies of Second Isaiah. In the present instance Joseph's suffering and subsequent exaltation are the means whereby temporal salvation is secured for God's chosen Hebrew people, who will later triumph over the Egyptians; but this is a type of the suffering and exaltation of Christ, who wins eternal salvation for all the true descendants of Abraham, destined to triumph over their angelic enemies.

53. See Mt 6:33.

Exposition of Psalm 105

Verse 1. Should Alleluia be prefixed here?

1. Like its predecessor, the one hundred and fifth psalm is headed Alleluia, and this time there are two Alleluias. Some people maintain that one of these belongs to the conclusion of the previous psalm, and the other to the opening of this one. They base their assertion on the fact that all the Alleluia psalms have Alleluia at the end, but not all have it at the beginning; therefore if a psalm lacks an Alleluia at the end, it cannot have it at the beginning either, and if it seems to have one at the beginning, this Alleluia must really belong to the end of the psalm that precedes it. For our part, we prefer to follow the custom of most interpreters who, whenever they read Alleluia at the beginning of a psalm, ascribe it to that same psalm; and we shall continue to take this view until the proponents of the opposite opinion persuade us by irrefutable arguments that their view is correct. Another point is this: there are very few codices which have Alleluia at the end of the one hundred and fiftieth psalm, after which no other psalm follows in our canon, and none of the Greek codices which I have been able to inspect contain it there. Yet even if all codices did have it there, this would not be enough to establish such a rule as they propose, because it could have happened that the requirements of God's praise dictated that the entire Book of Psalms should close with a final Alleluia after all the songs are over. (The Book of Psalms is generally considered to consist of five books, and scholars believe that the words, *So be it, so be it,*[1] mark the end of each book.) Even if Alleluia were always found at the end of the one hundred and fiftieth psalm, therefore, I do not see that this would necessarily mean that all psalms using the Alleluia must have Alleluia at the end.

With regard to the duplication of Alleluia, the Lord in the gospel sometimes says Amen once and sometimes repeats it, so I do not know why Alleluia should not similarly be said once in some places, and repeated in others. This is especially evident where both Alleluias occur after the number which is inscribed over the psalm as its heading, such as 105. If one of these Alleluias really belonged to the end of the preceding psalm we would expect one Alleluia to be put before the numeral and the other one after it, attached to the psalm that follows, to which the numeral applies.

It is possible that the prevailing custom was initiated by ignorance, and that some arguments, of which we are still unaware, may be adduced whereby the

---

1. *Fiat, fiat.* These are found at the end of Psalms 40(41), 71(72), 88(89), 105(106).

conviction of truth rather than the prejudice of habit may persuade us otherwise. For the present, however, and until we are better informed, we shall attribute the Alleluia, whether single or repeated, to the same psalm to which it is prefixed, in all instances where the Alleluia comes after the number of the psalm. In this we are conforming to the very well-known custom of the Church. We confess, however, that all the titles of the psalms, and the order in which the psalms occur, are in our belief matters laden with mystery, which we have not yet been able to fathom as we would wish.

The present psalm has connections with its predecessor; confession of sin and belief in God's mercy

2. I do see, however, that these two psalms, the one hundred and fourth and the one hundred and fifth, are connected.[2] In the former God's people is presented in a favorable light in the persons of his chosen ones, with whom no fault is found. These, I think, are among the Israelites with whom God was well pleased.[3] But in this psalm which follows, the rebellious troublemakers among God's people are to the fore, although even for them the divine mercy was not lacking. The story is told from the viewpoint of people who have been converted and are praying for pardon; hence the psalm recalls the example of those to whom God's rich mercy was revealed, sinners as they were. This psalm accordingly opens with the same exhortation as did the preceding one, *Confess to the Lord*, but whereas Psalm 104 continued, *and call upon his name*, this one continues, *because he is good, because his mercy endures to the end of the age*. This verse can certainly be understood as an invitation to a confession of sins, for a few verses further on the psalm acknowledges, *We sinned with our fathers; we have acted unjustly and committed iniquity* (verse 6); but since it says, *because he is good, because his mercy endures to the end of the age*, it is clearly also an invitation to praise God, and to combine confession of sin with praising him. When a person confesses even his or her own sins, it must be accompanied by praise offered to God; no confession of sins can be loving and filial unless it is made in an attitude far removed from despair, begging the mercy of God. It therefore includes praise of him, whether expressed in words, by acclaiming him as good and merciful, or in the intention only, when the sinner believes him to be so. The only words recorded as having been spoken by the tax collector in the gospel are, *Lord, be merciful to me, a sinner* (Lk 18:13); he did not say, "because you are good and merciful," or anything to that effect, but he must have believed it or he would not have spoken as he did. He prayed in hope, and hope could not

---

2. This Exposition was evidently written very soon after that of Psalm 104, to which it alludes.
3. See 1 Cor 10:5, and Augustine's explanation in his Exposition of Psalm 104,34 that there must have been some who found favor with God.

have existed without such faith. Praise of God can be genuine and reverent where there is no confession of sins, and praise of this kind is frequently called "confession" in the scriptures; but there can be no filial, profitable confession of sins where God is not praised, whether in the heart alone or with lips and words also.

Where some codices have *because he is good*, others have *because he is kind*;[4] these are alternative translations of the same Greek word, χρηστός. Similarly where the Greek has εἰς τὸν αἰῶνα, our translation has *because his mercy endures to the end of the age*,[5] but it could equally well be taken to mean "for ever."[6] If we take mercy to mean that no one can ever be happy and blessed apart from God, it is better to translate, "for ever"; but if we take it to refer to the mercy shown to miserable people, either to console them in their misery or even to rescue them from it, we do better to translate to the end of the age or to the end of the world, in which there will always be wretched people who need mercy.[7]

It is possible that someone may boldly speculate that some kind of divine mercy will not be denied even to those who will be damned with the devil and his angels, not in the sense that they will be freed from damnation but in that their punishment may be to some degree mitigated; in this perspective God's mercy could be understood as eternal because operative in their eternal misery. Yet since we read that some will be condemned to a more tolerable damnation than others, who would be so rash as to assert that a punishment assigned to someone can be further mitigated, or interrupted by some kind of respite, when the rich man in hell did not qualify even for a drop of water?[8] But this question demands more careful discussion, when time allows. As far as the present psalm is concerned, let what has already been said on it suffice.

Verses 2-3. To obey the commandments is to proclaim the Lord's praise

3. *Who can tell of the mighty works of the Lord?* The one who is pleading for mercy is rapt in wonder as he considers the works of God, and he cries, *Who can tell of the mighty works of the Lord, or make all his praises heard?* We need to supply a word or two to bring out the meaning of the second clause: "Who is to make all his praises heard?" Who has the power to make all those praises audible? Who can speak of the Lord's mighty deeds and declare his praises in such a way that they are effectively preached to those within earshot? All his praises? How can anyone do that?

4. *Suavis.*
5. *In saeculum.*
6. *In aeternum.*
7. Augustine discussed these alternative interpretations in his Exposition of Psalm 104,6.
8. See Lk 16:24-26.

There is a hint of the answer in the verse that follows: *Blessed are those who observe right judgment, and do justice at all times.* This perhaps indicates that God's praises are those works of his which are recognized when his commandments are kept, for, as the apostle says, *It is God who is at work in you* (Phil 2:13). Moreover the preceding psalm bade Abraham's descendants, *Sing to him and play psalms to him*, and we understood that to suggest, "You must both say good things about him and perform good deeds, and both to his praise." We saw that these two verbs—singing and playing psalms—corresponded to the exhortations in the next two phrases: *tell of all his wonders* means the same as *sing to him*, and *be praised in his holy name* resumes *play psalms to him*. To this same family of Abraham the Lord himself says, *Let your deeds shine before men and women in such a way that they see the good you do, and glorify your Father who is in heaven* (Mt 5:16). The psalmist therefore meditates on God's commandments, reflecting that when they are observed, God is praised, for he himself is at work in his faithful servants. With this in mind the psalmist asks, *Who can tell of the mighty works of the Lord?* Who indeed, since God works in a way inexpressible for us? *Who shall do all the praises heard?*[9] This means, "Who hears and then acts on what has been heard so as to praise him? Who implements his commands?" None of us can carry out everything we have heard, but insofar as we do, God is praised, God *who is at work in us, inspiring both will and work, for his own good purpose* (Phil 2:13). The psalm could have said "all his commandments" or "all that is done in conformity with his commandments," but it preferred to say, *all the praises* of God, because, as we have explained, insofar as the commandments are kept, God is acknowledged as worthy of praise. Yet who, having heard these praises, has the strength to act on them all? Who is equal to doing all that has been heard?

4. *Blessed are those who form right judgment, and do justice at all times.* Obviously this means from the point where they begin to live in time. The person who perseveres to the end will be saved.[10] It might seem that we have in this verse a simple repetition, doing justice being the same thing as forming right judgment. In that case each clause leaves out something we must supply from the other; reading them in full we would get this: *Blessed are those who form right judgment* at all times, and blessed are those who *do justice at all times.* So it might seem, but if there were no difference between judgment and justice, scripture would hardly have said in another psalm, *Until justice is changed into judgment* (Ps 93(94):15), or, in yet another psalm, *Justice and judgment guide his throne* (Ps 96(97):2). Again, another psalm promises, *He will bring forth your justice like light, and your judgment like high noon* (Ps 36(37):6). Admittedly,

9. Augustine's Latin in this verse had *quis auditas faciet laudes eius?* which he takes in the double sense of "making them heard" and "doing what has been heard."
10. See Mt 10:22.

though, it does look like a repetition of the same idea there also. The two words are so close in meaning that they may perhaps be used interchangeably—judgment for justice, or justice for judgment—but properly speaking I do not doubt that there is this difference, that someone who judges fairly is said to form right judgment, whereas someone who acts rightly is said to do justice. I think we can even go so far as to say that the text just quoted, *until justice is changed into judgment*, is a kind of beatitude pronounced even here over people who form right judgment by their faith and do justice in their conduct; for the time will come when the judgment they form in their faith will be vindicated in fact. This will be when *justice is changed into judgment*, which is to say when the just have been given power to judge justly those by whom they themselves are at present unjustly judged. In another passage the body of Christ can be heard to promise, *When my time comes, I will pronounce just judgments* (Ps 74:3(75:2)), which implies, "I will judge equitably." It does not say, "When my time comes, I will act in accordance with justice," for that is to be done at all times, as our present psalm also enjoins by saying that they are blessed who *do justice at all times*.

Verses 4-5. A prayer for God's salvation; Augustine thinks his Latin version confuses the sense of the Greek verbs

5. It is God who justifies, God who makes people righteous by healing them of their iniquities, and therefore the psalm proceeds, *Remember us, O Lord, among the people with whom you are pleased*. This means, "Let us be numbered among those on whom your favor rests," because God was not well pleased with all of them.[11] *Visit us in your salvation*: this means the Savior himself, in whom sins are forgiven and souls healed so that they are able to form right judgment and do justice. The speakers in the psalm understood how blessed such people are and therefore beg the same blessing for themselves. Elsewhere we find another prayer concerning this salvation: *Let us know your way upon earth*. In answer to a question we might have posed about what earth is meant, it continues, *among all nations*; and then again, in case we might wonder about God's *way*, it clarifies, *your salvation* (Ps 66:3(67:2)). The old man, Simeon, spoke similarly of Christ: *My eyes have seen your salvation* (Lk 2:30); and Christ also said of himself, *I am the way* (Jn 14:6). The prayer, *Visit us in your salvation*, therefore means, "Visit us in your Christ."

That we may see in the felicity of your chosen ones, and rejoice in the gladness of your people. These are the consequences of your visiting us in your salvation, the consequences for which we pray: the power to see in the felicity of your elect and to share in your people's gladness. Where our reading is *felicity*, other

11. See 1 Cor 10:5.

codices have *sweetness,* just as earlier we saw a similar variant: *because he is good,* or *because he is kind.* The word is the same in the Greek. We find it differently translated in another psalm too, where some codices have *the Lord will give sweetness* (Ps 84:13(85:12)), while others interpret it as *goodness,* and others again as *kindness.* What favor is the present psalm asking for, when it prays, *Visit us in your salvation, that we may see in the felicity of your chosen ones, and rejoice in the gladness of your people?* Surely the grace not to remain blind, like those who were warned, *Because you say, We see, your sin remains in you* (Jn 9:41); for *the Lord gives sight to the blind* (Ps 145(146):8) not in consideration of their own merits but *in the felicity of his chosen ones,* in the grace he grants to his elect. The same is true of the invocation, *O salvation of my countenance,* for there the addition of the words, *my God* (Ps 42(43):5), immediately emphasizes that the salvation does not derive from the speaker. Again, we pray for *our daily bread*—ours, yes, but we preface this with the plea, *Give us.* So too in our present psalm: *Visit us in your salvation.*

That we may see in the felicity of your chosen ones, and rejoice in the gladness of your people. We should understand this one nation of God to be the whole posterity of Abraham: the children of the promise, that is, not his carnal progeny. The people whose voice we hear in the psalm are hoping to share the joy of that nation. And what is its joy if not God himself? In him other psalms rejoice: *You who make me dance with happiness, save me* (Ps 31(32):7), and elsewhere, *The light of your countenance is stamped upon us, O Lord; you have given joy to my heart* (Ps 4:7(6-7). To God are these prayers addressed as to the highest, most true, unchangeable, and beatific good, the good that is God himself.

That you may be praised, with your inheritance. It puzzles me that this verse is so translated in many codices, although one and the same Greek expression is used in three successive lines. If this translation is correct, *that you may be praised, with your inheritance,* we should have to translate the preceding lines as follows, in order to be consistent: "That *you* may see in the felicity of your chosen ones, and that *you* may rejoice in the gladness of your people." So the whole passage would run like this: *Visit us in your salvation, that you may see in the felicity of your chosen ones, and that you may rejoice in the gladness of your people, and that you may be praised, with your inheritance.* Alternatively, if we take as correct the translation adopted, namely, *Visit us . . . that we may see in the felicity of your chosen ones, and rejoice in the gladness of your people,* we should logically continue, "And that we may be praised, with your inheritance." That inheritance has, after all, been bidden, *Be praised in his holy name* (Ps 104(105):3). The expressions in the present psalm seem to be ambiguous, but if the translators are right in rendering the third line, *That you may be praised, with your inheritance,* the two previous lines should be adjusted accordingly, as I have explained, since the same Greek expression is used in all three. We should therefore interpret the whole verse as follows. *Visit us in your salvation, that you may see in the felicity of your chosen ones*: visit us to this purpose, that you may cause us to be there, in your salvation, and you may see us there; *that you may rejoice in the gladness of your people*: you are said to rejoice yourself when your nation rejoices over you; *that you may be praised, with your inheritance*: praised along with it, for it is praised on your account, not otherwise.

Whichever way we translate the three verbs—whether the subject of them is God or those who pray—at any rate they are pleading to be visited by God's salvation, that is to say, by his Christ, that they may not be estranged from his people or from those with whom God is well pleased.

Verses 6-7. Israel's sins of forgetfulness

6. Let us listen now to what they set themselves to confess. *We sinned with our fathers; we have acted unjustly and committed iniquity*. What does it mean by saying *with our fathers*? Is it thinking in the way that the Letter to the Hebrews thinks? There we are told that tithes were exacted even from Levi, because he was present in the loins of Abraham when he gave tithes to the priest Melchizedek.[12] Should we think of the later generation as having sinned with their fathers because they were in the loins of the generation that was in Egypt? The people who were living at the time when the psalm was composed, and especially their descendants (because the psalmist could be speaking either in the name of his own contemporaries, or prophetically in the name of their posterity), were far removed in time from those who sinned in Egypt by not understanding God's wonderful works. The psalm continues, explaining how the speakers sinned with their ancestors: *Our fathers, when they were in Egypt, did not understand your wonderful works*; and it goes on to record many facts about the sins of that earlier generation.

Or should we rather take the admission, *We sinned with our fathers*, to mean, "We have sinned, just as our fathers did, by imitating their sins"? But if this is the right interpretation we ought to support it by producing some other example of this turn of phrase. When I hunted for such an example I found none to be available—no instance, I mean, of anyone saying that he had sinned with somebody else, or done anything with somebody else, when he meant he had behaved in a similar fashion by imitating that other after a long lapse of time.

7. What, then, is meant by the words: *Our fathers did not understand your wonderful works*? Surely, that they did not comprehend what God wanted to give them through those wonders. And what else was that but eternal life and the gift not of fleeting but of unchangeable good, the good we must await in patience? But no, they grumbled impatiently and were bitterly contumacious and sought happiness in the deceptive and transient goods of the present.

---

12. See Heb 7:4-10.

They did not remember your abundant mercy. The psalm shows them to have
been at fault with regard to both their comprehension and their memory.
Comprehension was needed if they were to understand to what eternal good
things God was calling them through temporal benefits; memory was required
so that at least they might not forget the temporal wonders wrought on their
behalf and might confidently believe that God would exert the same power to
free them from future persecution by their enemies that he had already demonstrated for them in the past. Yet they forgot what he had done for them in Egypt
by his impressive signs and how he had crushed their foes.

They provoked him as they went up toward the sea, the Red Sea. The codex I
consulted had the text as given here, but the last words, *the Red Sea,* were
preceded by an asterisk, which signifies that they are found in the Hebrew but
not in the interpretation by the Septuagint. However, several codices of both
Greek and Latin which I have been able to inspect read. *They provoked him* (or
they embittered him, which renders the Greek more exactly) *as they went up over
the Red Sea.* Anyone who reads the history of how they left Egypt and crossed
the Red Sea will bemoan their infidelity, for it relates how terrified and desperate
they were in spite of the many spectacular miracles they had so recently
witnessed in Egypt, and how the multifarious mercies of God had slipped from
their memory. They are described as having "gone up" toward the Red Sea
because the relationship of the two countries was such that people spoke of
"going down" into Egypt from Canaan and returning thence as "going up."

We should observe that scripture plainly regards it as culpable not to understand what should be understood and not to remember what should be retained in
the memory. Men and women are reluctant to look on this kind of failure as their
own fault, but only because they want an excuse to pray less and to avoid
humbling themselves before God. If only they will confess in his presence what
they are, they will obtain help to become what they are not. Even sins of ignorance or negligence are better confessed in order that they may be destroyed,
than excused that they may remain. They are more profitably purged by our
invocation of God than entrenched by our offending him.

Verses 8-11. God reveals his power at the crossing of the sea

8. The psalm goes on to say that God did not act in a way that matched their
unfaithfulness. *He saved them for the sake of his own name,* it says, *to make his
power known.* His action was not prompted by any merits on their part.

9. *He rebuked the Red Sea, and it dried up.* We do not read that any voice was
heard from heaven, rebuking the sea; more probably the psalm meant by
"rebuke" the divine power by which the miracle was effected, though some may
prefer to think there was some kind of secret admonition that the water could

hear but human ears could not. The power with which God acts is exceedingly mysterious and secret, so much so that even creatures devoid of understanding immediately obey his will. *And he led them out through the deep as though through a desert.* The psalm calls the mighty waters *the deep.* Some interpreters have wished to explain this verse by reading, "He led them out through the mighty waters." but what else does it mean by saying *through the deep as though through a desert* if not that the terrain became as dry as a desert, where there had been deep waters?

10. *He saved them from their haters' hand.* Some have preferred to alter the translation of this verse to avoid an awkward expression. They read, *He saved them from the hand of those who hated them.*[13]

And he redeemed them from the hand of the enemy. What price was paid in this act of redemption? Or is it a prophecy? Was this done to prefigure baptism, in which we are redeemed from the hand of the devil at an enormous price, no less than Christ's blood? If so, it was especially significant that the event occurred at the Red Sea, evoking the redness of blood.

11. *He submerged those who harassed them beneath the water; not one of them was left.* Not all the Egyptians were drowned but only those who pursued the Hebrews, bent on capturing or killing them.

Verses 12-18. Immediate backslidings: impatience, greed, schism

12. *Then they believed in his words,*[14] *and praised his praise.* This last is the same idiom we employ when we say that someone fought a fight or lived a life of whatever it was. But it also recalls a very special hymn of praise sung to God, one very well known to us, beginning, *Let us sing to the Lord, for he is glorious in his might: horse and rider he has hurled into the sea* (Ex 15:1).

13. *Yet they lost no time,*[15] *but forgot his deeds.* Other codices express it more intelligibly: *They hastened to forget*[16] *his deeds.* It continues, *They did not wait upon his plan.* Their business was to reflect that such mighty works of God on their behalf were not pointless but were calling them to a bliss without end, which they ought to have awaited in patience. But they were in a hurry to find blessedness in temporal things which yield nobody true happiness because they

---

13. The change is from *de manu odientium* to *de manu eorum qui oderant eos.*
14. Augustine here remarks that the expression *in verbis eius* (ablative) is rather ill-suited to Latin, which would have preferred dative or accusative. He says, "This seems a rather un-Latin expression, because it does not say *verbis eius* or *in verba eius*, but *in verbis eius*; however, such usage is very common in the scriptures." These points on case usage cannot be conveyed in English, so the sentence is omitted in the English translation.
15. *Cito fecerunt.*
16. *Festinaverunt.*

do not quench the insatiable longing that is in us. As the Lord said, *A person who drinks this water will be thirsty again* (Jn 4:13).

14. *They hankered after their hankerings*[17] *in the desert, and put God to the test in that waterless land.* The idea conveyed by *the desert* is repeated in *that waterless land*; and the content of *they hankered after their hankerings* is resumed in *they put God to the test.* The special turn of phrase, *they hankered after their hankerings*, is the same as the one we saw in *they praised his praise.*

15. *He granted them what they asked, and filled their soul to satiety.* But he did not thereby render them blessed, for their satiety was not like that of which it is said, *Blessed are those who hunger and thirst for righteousness, for they shall be satisfied* (Mt 5:6). We should not take the word, *soul,* in this context as the rational soul but only as the animating principle of the body, which makes it a living thing. Food and drink sustain this soul, which is why the Lord asks in the gospel, *Is not the soul*[18] *more than food, and the body more than clothing?* (Mt 6:25). This question implies that the soul needs to be fed, as the body needs to be clothed. Isaiah uses the word in the same way: *Why have we fasted, and you did not notice, stinted our souls, and you ignored it?* (Is 58:3).

16. *In their camp they provoked Moses, and Aaron, the Lord's holy one.* The following verses clearly reveal what was implied in the provocation mentioned here, or the embittering, as other interpreters more vividly express it.

17. *The earth opened and swallowed up Dathan, and engulfed the clan of Abiram.* The same idea is expressed by both *swallowed up* and *engulfed.* Dathan and Abiram together were the sole cause of the proud, sacrilegious schism.[19]

18. *Fire broke out in their gathering, and flame burnt up the sinners.* The term "sinners" is not customarily applied by scripture to people who generally live in a just and commendable fashion, though not altogether free from sin. Rather there is a distinction between those who sin and sinners, as between those who sometimes mock and mockers, those who occasionally murmur and murmurers, those who happen to write something and writers, and so forth. So scripture uses the term "sinners" to denote very wicked persons who are weighed down by heavy loads of sin.[20]

---

17. Or "they lusted after their lusts," *concupierunt concupiscentiam,* another cognate object as in verse 12 above, as Augustine goes on to remark.
18. *Anima,* which can mean "soul" or "life."
19. See Nb 16.
20. Professional sinners, as it were.

Verses 19-23. The golden calf; Moses' intercession

19. *They fashioned a calf at Horeb, and worshiped a graven image; they changed their glory into the image of a bull-calf that eats grass.*[21] The psalmist chooses his words carefully in saying not, "They changed the glory of God," as he might have done, and as the apostle does when he recalls, *They exchanged the glory of the immortal God for the image of a mortal man* (Rom 1:23), but, "They exchanged their own glory." God would have been their glory if they had waited on his plans and not been over-hasty: God, whom another psalm calls *my glory, you who lift up my head* (Ps 3:4(3)). It was their own glory, their God, whom they exchanged for *the image of a bull-calf that eats grass*, making themselves into fodder for the calf, like all who judge according to the wisdom of the flesh; for *all flesh is but grass* (Is 40:6).

20. *They forgot God, who had saved them.* How had he saved them? He *had wrought great signs in Egypt, wonders in the land of Ham, and terrible deeds at the Red Sea.* The *wonders* and the *terrible deeds* are the same, for all wonderment includes some tinge of fear, even though in this case God's exploits could be called terrible for the enemy but admonitory for the Hebrews in showing them what they needed to fear.

21. *And he said he would destroy them.* They had deserved to perish, because they had not only forgotten the God who saved them; they had also committed the heinous crime, the incredible impiety, of fashioning and worshiping a graven idol. God therefore *said he would destroy them, but Moses, his chosen one, stood in the breach in his presence.* This does not mean that Moses *stood in the breach* in the sense of making a breach in God's anger.[22] He stood amid the breaking, shattering plague that would have struck the people; that is to say, he stood there to draw it on himself and shield them with his own person, beseeching God, *If you are willing to forgive them this sin, forgive them; but if not, blot me out of your book* (Ex 32:31-32). This episode proves how powerful with God is the intercession of the saints. Moses was so certain of divine justice that he knew God could not blot him out, and thus he obtained mercy for others, that God might not blot out the people, as he could most justly have done. This was how Moses *stood in the breach in his presence to avert God's anger, that he might not destroy them.*

---

21. Augustine here comments on an un-Latin usage similar to the one he noted in verse 12. His comments are omitted in the English translation. The omitted passage runs as follows: "The psalmist says not *in similitudinem*, but *in similitudine*. This is the same idiom we found just now when he said, *Et crediderunt in verbis eius.*"

22. To "stand in the breach" (*in confractione*) averting God's anger from a sinful people was the particular duty of the prophet-intercessor; compare Ez 22:30. But Augustine seems to take it here as a "breaking" or "shattering"; that is, a shattering calamity such as plague. In section 26 below he regards it as synonymous with *quassatio*, affliction.

*Verses 24-31. Sins in the desert: unbelief, grumbling, idolatry; Phineas'
intervention*

22. *They scorned the desirable land.* But they had not seen it, had they, so
how could they despise what they had not yet seen? The psalm immediately
explains: *Nor did they believe in his words.* The promised land was said to be
flowing with milk and honey, and in this respect it was like a visible sacrament,
designed to lead people who had understood God's wonderful deeds to invisible
grace and the kingdom of heaven. If the land had not been a sign of something
much greater the Israelites could not have been held guilty for despising it; after
all, we too are bound to set little store by that temporal kingdom and to love the
free Jerusalem in heaven, our mother,[23] holding her alone to be truly desirable.
But the main reason why the Israelites are here denounced for scorning the land
they should have longed for is their lack of faith: they did not believe in the assur-
ances of God, who was leading them through small gifts to much greater things.
In so much of a hurry were they to find happiness in temporal goods, which they
evaluated in a carnal way, that *they did not wait upon his plan*, as an earlier verse
recorded.

23. *And they grumbled in their tents; they did not listen to the voice of the
Lord*, who strictly forbade them to murmur.

24. *He raised his hand over them to strike them down in the desert, to scatter
their descendants among the nations, and to disperse them far and wide.*

25. Before relating how someone interceded in this time of God's fierce
anger, to some extent appeasing him, the psalm adds more detail: *They were
initiated into the cult of the Baal of Peor*,[24] which means that they dedicated
themselves to a pagan idol; *and they ate sacrifices offered to lifeless gods. They
provoked him to anger with their evil practices, and devastation spread widely
among them.* It seems as though God deferred his punishment, that sentence he
had passed when he raised his hand over them to strike them down in the desert,
to scatter their descendants among the nations and disperse them in foreign
countries. He waited until they were so far gone in their depraved way of
thinking that they perpetrated even this monstrous crime, in order that their
punishment should be more manifestly just. The apostle testifies, *Because they
did not see fit to acknowledge God, he gave them over to their own depraved way
of thinking, to do things that should not be done* (Rom 1:28).

---

23. See Gal 4:26.
24. The sanctuary at Peor was on the boundary between later Israel and Moabite territory and, like
     other shrines of the Baalim, was dedicated to the powers of agricultural and animal fertility.
     Such cults constantly tempted the Israelites to both idolatry and sexual immorality and were the
     target of prophetic denunciation. The ancient story in Nb 25:1-5 presents this seduction as
     powerful even before Israel's occupation of the promised land.

26. They had dedicated themselves to an idol, and feasted on sacrifices offered to lifeless beings (to dead men, that is, whom the pagans worshiped as deities with their sacrifices), and in the end their wickedness was so great that God refused to be propitiated in any way at all, except by the action of the priest Phineas. Catching a man and a woman locked in adulterous embrace, Phineas slew both of them together. If he had been motivated by hatred of them, rather than love, being devoured as he was by zeal for God's house,[25] his action would not have been accounted righteous. But it was, for there would have been a far more terrible slaughter among the people[26] had he not, in striking one man, struck the whole people to save their souls from death. Admittedly Christ our Lord has willed that discipline should be gentler, now that the New Covenant has been revealed. Yet the threat of hell is much more horrifying, and we do not read that God included hell in his menaces under the dispensation in force at that time. Thus *devastation spread widely among them,* for they were devastated by the grave punishment for their grave sins. *But Phineas arose, and appeased God, and the distress abated.* The psalm summarizes the event briefly because it is not instructing ignorant people, but reminding those who know. The afflic-tion[27] is the same as the breaking, the shattering, mentioned earlier;[28] the same word is used in both places in the Greek.

27. *And this was accounted to him as righteousness, from generation to generation and for ever.* God accounted the action to his priest as righteousness, not only as long as the generations last, but for ever. God scrutinizes hearts, and he knew how to assess the intense charity for his people that prompted Phineas' action.

Verses 32-33. Moses lacks faith and is punished

28. *They provoked the Lord at the water of contradiction, and Moses was vexed with them, for they grieved him in spirit. And he made a distinction with his lips.* What was this distinction? It seems he doubted that God, who had already performed such mighty wonders, had power to cause water to flow from the rock; for Moses struck the rock with his staff in a hesitant manner,[29] thereby distinguishing this from the other miracles, over which he had not doubted. In this he offended, and for this he deserved to die without entering the promised land.[30] He was upset by the murmuring of an unbelieving people and did not stand fast in confidence as he should have done. Nonetheless God bore witness

---

25. See Nb 25:7-13.
26. By reason of the plague.
27. *Quassatio,* a shaking, disturbance, affliction.
28. Verse 23.
29. See Nb 20:1-13. The exact nature of Moses' fault is unclear.
30. See Dt 32:48-52.

to his chosen servant even after his death, in order to make clear to us that Moses' staggering in faith was punished only by God's refusal to allow him to enter the land to which he was leading the people. It would be quite wrong to think he was excluded from the kingdom of God's grace, which was symbolized by the land of promise, flowing with milk and honey. This kingdom of grace was guaranteed by the covenant God established with Abraham, our father not according to the flesh but in faith.

Verses 34-39. The Israelites imitate Canaanite sins

29. The psalm now proceeds to tell of the sins of the people after they had entered the temporal land of promise. *They did not destroy the nations, as the Lord had ordered them. They mingled with the nations, and learned their customs, and served their idols; and this became a stumbling-block for them.* It was a stumbling-block because, having failed to destroy the pagans, they mingled with them instead.

30. *They immolated their sons and daughters to demons, and they spilt inno-cent blood, the blood of their sons and daughters whom they sacrificed to the idols of Canaan.* The history does not relate that they immolated their sons and daughters to demons and idols; but the psalm cannot be lying, and neither can the prophets, who frequently include this among their reproaches. Moreover we know from the writings of pagans themselves that this custom prevailed among them.

31. But what do the next lines say? *The land was slain by bloodshed.* We might have thought this the mistake of a scribe, who wrote *slain*[31] in place of the true reading, *infected*;[32] so we might have supposed, were it not for the goodness of God, who willed us to have his scriptures in many languages. Thus we have been able to ascertain from Greek codices that *the land was slain by bloodshed* is indeed the correct reading. How, then, should we interpret the statement that *the land was slain*? We must, I think, take it as a metaphor for the people who dwelt in the land, the content being signified by what contained it. Just so we speak of "a bad house" if bad people live in it or "a good house" where the inhabitants are good. This makes excellent sense here, for the people who dwelt in the land were habitually slaying their own souls by sacrificing their children and shedding the blood of little ones who in no way consented to the crime; indeed, the psalm explicitly says, *They spilt innocent blood.* The result was that *the land was slain by bloodshed and defiled by their conduct*, in the sense that they themselves were slain in their souls and personally defiled by what they did.

---

31. *Interfecta.*
32. *Infecta.*

They went a-whoring in their evil practices.[33] The psalm calls *adinventiones* what the Greeks call ἐπιτηδεύματα. This word occurs in the Greek codices both here and in verse 29 above, where we found *They provoked him to anger with their evil practices.* In both instances it means the evil practices they picked up from other people. We should not understand these *adinventiones* to be anything they invented for themselves, without any example to follow in the conduct of others. To emphasize this point, some of our translators have preferred the word, *pursuits;*[34] others again have translated it as "*inclinations,*"[35] or "*inordinate desires,*"[36] or *pleasures.*[37] Even some of those who put *adinventiones* here have *studia* in the other place. I wanted to be exact on this point in case the word *adinventiones* might be thought inappropriate for a practice they did not devise for themselves but learned by imitating others.

Verses 40-43. The wrath of God

32. *And the Lord was stirred to anger against his people.* Some of our translators shrank from writing *anger*, even though the Greek has θυμός. Some rendered it as "strong feeling,"[38] others as "indignation," others again as "vehemence."[39] But whichever term we prefer, there can be no perturbation in God. We translate according to our accustomed mode of speech, which may refer to the power to punish as "anger." (33) *He came to hate his inheritance. He delivered them into the hands of the nations, and peoples who hated them ruled over them. Their enemies harassed them, and they were humiliated at their hands.* By calling the people God's inheritance the psalmist plainly indicates that it was not to destroy them that God hated them and handed them over to their enemies, but for purposes of discipline. Indeed, it continues, *He very often freed them.*

34. *But they provoked him with their own plan.* This is to be compared with verse 13 above, where we read, *They did not wait upon his plan.* The plans of men and women are extremely harmful to themselves when they seek their own ends rather than God's. Our inheritance is God, for he deigns to give himself to us that we may enjoy him. In fellowship with the saints we shall suffer none of the restrictions that result from seeking our own private advantage. In that most glorious commonwealth which is in possession of the promised inheritance, where no one will die, no one be born, there will be no citizens who delight in

---

33. *In adinventionibus suis.* The word generally has a pejorative sense in Christian writings.
34. *Studia.*
35. *Affectiones.*
36. *Affectationes.*
37. *Voluptates.*
38. *Mentem.*
39. *Animum.*

their own exclusive property, for God will be all things to all of them.[40] If while still wayfarers we faithfully and ardently long for that society, we become used to preferring the common good to our private concerns and seek not our own ends but those of Jesus Christ.[41] We shall be wary of self-seeking cleverness and the pursuit of our own advantage, lest we provoke God by our plans. Rather must we hope for what we do not see yet and be in no hurry to seek happiness in the things that are seen; we shall await unseen happiness with patience[42] and conform to the plan of God enshrined in his promises, as we pray for his help in our trials. Those who so bear themselves will also be humble in their confession and in no danger of resembling the people of whom it is said, *They were humiliated by their iniquities.*

Verses 44-45. God pre-ordains all that happens, including our prayer and his response

35. Nonetheless, God is full of mercy, and he did not abandon them. *He had regard for them when they were distressed, when he heard their prayer. He remembered his covenant, and he changed his mind, in accordance with his abundant mercy.* The psalm says that God *changed his mind* because he altered his apparent intention to put an end to them. With God all things are, of course, disposed and settled; he does not alter his decision as though on a sudden impulse or do anything he did not foreknow from eternity he would do. Amid the temporal changes that take place in the creation which he so wonderfully governs, he is not subject to any temporal changes himself, as though he could be said to act on a sudden whim. He has ordained events to occur in response to their appropriate causes by his immutable and most mysterious purpose. In the light of this purpose all events are so known as to be realized at their due times; he makes some of them occur as present, just as he has already created those which will be realized in the future. Is any of us able to grasp this? No; so let us hearken to scripture, which conveys sublime truths in humble guise, for it proffers easily assimilable food to nourish babies but proposes to those of mature age truths that will stretch their minds.

He had regard for them when they were distressed, when he heard their prayer. He remembered his covenant. This evidently means the eternal covenant *he entrusted to Abraham* (Ps 104(105):9), not the Old Covenant, which is abolished, but the New, which is hidden even in the Old. *He changed his mind, in accordance with his abundant mercy.* In doing this he did what he had already decided, but he had known in advance that he would make this concession to

---

40. See 1 Cor 15:28.
41. See Phil 2:21.
42. See Rom 8:25.

distressed people who prayed to him; for their very prayer was undoubtedly known to God before it existed, while it was still to be offered in the future.

Verse 46. Deliverance from diabolical captivity

36. *He assigned them to mercies*, that they might be vessels of mercy, not vessels of wrath.[43] I think the psalm spoke of mercies in the plural because each one of us has his or her proper gift from God, one in one way, another person in another.[44] He therefore *assigned them to mercies in the sight of all who had captured them.*

Consider this carefully, whoever you are who read this. You recognize the grace of God by reading of it in the apostolic letters but also by searching the prophetic oracles, where you encounter that same grace whereby we are redeemed unto eternal life through our Lord Jesus Christ. You perceive the New Covenant veiled in the Old, and the Old Covenant revealed in the New. Remember, then, as you read this, who it was that the apostle Paul called the ruler of the powers of the air *who is now at work in the children of unbelief* (Eph 2:2). Remember too what he urges upon certain persons: *that they come to a better mind concerning the snares of the devil, by whom they were entrapped according to his will* (2 Tm 2:26). Recall the words spoken by our Lord Jesus Christ when he drove the devil from the hearts of the faithful: *Now has the ruler of this world been cast out* (Jn 12:31). Remember the testimony of his apostle that *he has plucked us away from the power of darkness and brought us across into the kingdom of his beloved Son* (Col 1:13).

With all this in mind, turn your attention back again to the Old Testament, and consider what is sung in the psalm entitled, *When the house was being built after the captivity.*[45] It opens with the invitation, *Sing a new song to the Lord.* And to make sure that you do not take this as addressed to the Jewish people exclusively, it continues, *Sing to the Lord, all the earth. Sing to the Lord, bless his name, worthily declare his salvation as day from day*—or, rather, *proclaim the good news of his salvation as day from day.* The altered translation I give here more exactly represents the Greek and points us toward evangelization, toward the gospel in which Christ the Lord is proclaimed as day from day, light from light, the Son from the Father. This is indeed *his salvation*, for Christ is God's salvation, as we demonstrated earlier.[46] *Proclaim his glory among the nations, and his marvels among all peoples. For great is the Lord and exceedingly worthy of praise; he is more to be feared than all the gods, for all the gods of the*

---

43. See Rom 9:22-23.
44. See 1 Cor 7:7.
45. Psalm 95(96).
46. See section 5 above.

heathen are demons. (Ps 95(96):1-5) These are the enemies who, under their commander the devil, held God's people captive. When we are ransomed from captivity and the prince of this world is cast out, the house is built after the captivity. Its cornerstone is Christ, who bonded the two peoples in himself and built them into one new person, making peace. Coming to us as day from day, he proclaimed the gospel of peace to those who were near and to those who were far off, forming them into one.[47] He brought in other sheep who did not belong to this sheepfold, that there might be but one flock and one shepherd.[48]

This was how God *assigned to mercies* those whom he had predestined, for salvation depends *not on the one who wills it, nor on the one who runs, but on God who shows mercy* (Rom 9:16). He *assigned them to mercies in the sight of all who had captured them.* These enemies, the devil and his angels, had captured those predestined by God for his kingdom and glory. They were accustomed to dominate unbelievers from within and to attack believers from without, though they could only attack and not defeat people who take their stand in the impregnable tower against the enemy.[49] These assailants have been cast out by our redeemer. But even their attacks on us are possible only because they sense in us the residual traces of our weakness, those traces concerning which we pray, *Forgive us our trespasses,* and beg, *Lead us not into temptation, but deliver us from evil.*

Having cast out all his enemies, Christ the Lord has brought healing and wholeness to his body, that body of which he is the head and Savior, so that on the third day he may reach perfection in his body. This he foretold: *I cast out demons and bring healing and wholeness today and tomorrow, and on the third day I am consummated* (Lk 13:32). I am made perfect, he declares, when all meet in me to form one perfect man,[50] who attains to the full stature of the maturity of Christ.[51]

Verses 47-48. Consummation in Christ

37. Once he has cast out the demons who held us as their prisoners, Christ completes the process of healing. Accordingly, after confessing that *he assigned them to mercies in the sight of all who had captured them* and proclaiming the expulsion of the demons, the psalm goes on to pray that God may bring his healing work to perfection. *Save us, O Lord our God, and gather us from all nations into one flock, that we may confess to your holy name and glory in*

---

47. See Eph 2:13-17.
48. See Jn 10:16.
49. See Ps 60:4(61:3).
50. *Virum.*
51. See Eph 4:13.

praising you. Then it briefly summarizes the content of the praise we shall offer him: *Blessed be the Lord, the God of Israel, from age to age*, which we understand to mean "from eternity to eternity," because he will be praised without end by his elect, of whom another psalm says, *Blessed are they who dwell in your house; they will praise you for ever and ever* (Ps 83:5(84:4)). For the body of Christ this will be the consummation of the third day, when the demons have been expelled and the body's health brought to such perfection that it attains immortality and becomes the eternal realm of those who praise God perfectly because they love him perfectly and love him perfectly because they contemplate him face to face. The prayer formulated early in this psalm will then be fully answered: *Remember us, O Lord, among the people of your good pleasure. Visit us in your salvation, that we may see[52] in the felicity of your chosen ones, and rejoice in the gladness of your people, that you may be praised, with your inheritance*. He gathers not only the lost sheep of the house of Israel,[53] scattered among the nations, but also other sheep who did not belong to that sheepfold, that there may be, as he said, but one flock and one shepherd.

If the Jews imagine that this prophecy refers to their visible kingdom, their mistake arises from their inability to rejoice in the hope of good things as yet unseen and they will blunder into the traps set by the one of whom the Lord spoke: *I came in the name of my Father, and you have not accepted me; another will come in his own name, and him you will accept* (Jn 5:43). Of this same impostor the apostle Paul says, *The man of sin, the son of perdition, must be exposed. He is the one who opposes and exalts himself against anything claiming to be God, everything that people worship, even to the point of seating himself in God's temple, and showing himself off as though he were God*. And a little further on: *Then will the wicked man be revealed, whom the Lord Jesus will slay with the breath of his mouth, and annihilate by the radiant light of his presence. The coming of the wicked one will be Satan's work; he will display all kinds of powers and signs and lying prodigies to seduce into sin those who are doomed to perish because they would not open themselves to love of the truth, and so be saved. Therefore God will visit upon them the active power of error, to induce them to give credence to a lie, so that all who have refused to believe in the truth, and have consented to iniquity, may be judged*. (2 Th 2:3-4,8-12)

It seems to me likely that the carnally-minded among the Israelites will view this rebel, who exalts himself against anything claiming to be God, everything that people worship, as the fulfillment of the psalm's prophetic prayer, *Save us, O Lord our God, and gather us from all nations into one flock*, for they will think that under God's guidance they will win visible glory in the presence of those visible enemies who in a visible sense took them captive. They will believe this

---

52. For the meaning Augustine attaches to this petition, see section 5 above.
53. See Mt 15:24.

lie because they have not opened their minds to love of the truth, which would have taught them to desire not carnal but spiritual liberation. So completely were they deceived by the devil that they slew Christ. *If we leave him alone like this,* they said to each other, *everyone will believe in him, and then the Romans will come, and sweep away our land and our nationhood. But one of them, Caiaphas, being high priest in that year, said to them, You know nothing. You do not consider that it is expedient for us*[54] *that one should die for all, rather than the whole nation perish. He did not say this as of himself,* comments the evangelist, *but in virtue of his office as high priest he prophesied that it was necessary for Jesus to die for the nation, and not for the nation alone*—that is, not only for the lost sheep of the house of Israel—*but to gather into one all the children of God who were scattered.* (Jn 11:48-52) Other sheep he had, not belonging to that sheepfold, and all these sheep, both from the Israelites and from the Gentiles, the devil and his angels had captured.

Now that the devil's hold over them has been broken in full view of the malicious spirits who imprisoned them, the voice of prophecy is raised in a prayer that the elect may be saved and made perfect for ever: *Save us, O Lord our God, and gather us from all nations into one flock.* The victory will not be won through the Antichrist, as the Jews suppose, but through Christ our Lord, who comes in the name of his Father as *his salvation, day from day* (Ps 95(96):2), to whom the psalm referred when it prayed earlier, *Visit us in your salvation.*

And, finally, *Let all the people*—this whole people predestined for salvation, gathered from the circumcised and the uncircumcised, this holy nation, the people of God's adoption—*let all the people say. So be it, so be it.*

---

54. The CCL editors amend "us" to "you."

Exposition of Psalm 106

A Sermon to the People

Verse 1. Tasting God's sweetness

1. This psalm reminds us of the mercies of God that we have known in our own lives, and its accord with our experience makes it all the more delightful. It would be strange if anyone who had not personally learned the truth of what the psalm proclaims were able to perceive its sweetness. However, it was not written for one or two hearers only but for all God's people, and proposed to them as a means of self-knowledge, like a mirror.

We need not examine the title, for it consists simply of Alleluia, or rather of two Alleluias. It is our custom to sing this acclamation solemnly on certain days, in conformity with the ancient tradition of the Church, and this practice of singing it on special days is itself fraught with holy mystery. On particular days we sing Alleluia, but we have it in our minds every day, for if the word signifies praise of God, it is always in the mouth of our hearts, even when absent from our bodily mouths. As another psalm declares, *His praise shall be in my mouth always* (Ps 33:2(34:1)). The doubling of Alleluia in the title of this psalm is not something proper to this one alone, for the preceding psalm is also headed by a double Alleluia. Moreover, although the psalm was sung about the people of Israel, as is evident from its content, it is also sung about the whole Church of God spread throughout the world, and in this perspective it is hardly surprising that we sing the Alleluia twice, since we also cry out, *Abba! Father!* The word *Abba* means the same as *Father*, yet the apostle had good reason to say that in the Spirit *we cry, Abba! Father!* (Rom 8:15); for one wall that comes to join the corner cries *Abba!* while the wall coming from another quarter cries *Father!* but both cry out in that cornerstone who is our peace and builds the two into one.[1]

Let us consider, then, the lessons this psalm offers us about what should give us joy and what evoke our groans, from whom we should expect help, why we are abandoned and how we are to be rescued. Let us see if it can teach us anything about what we are of ourselves and what through the mercy of God, about how our pride is to be shattered and his grace glorified. What I am about to say should commend itself inwardly to the mind of each person who listens, as far as

---

1. See Eph 2:14,20.

possible. I am speaking to people who are walking in the way of God[2] and have already made some spiritual progress. If therefore there are any here present who do not fully understand me, let them take their bearings and hasten forward toward comprehension. All the same, I do not think that God is likely to abandon us in our efforts; so we may expect that what we have to say will be accessible to all, whether experienced or not. Thus the experienced may confirm it and the inexperienced find something to long for, and my exposition may be sweet to all. It will be sweet in the first place if it is truthful, and it will be truthful if it proceeds not from me but from God.

The psalm begins:

2. *Confess to the Lord, because he is sweet, for his mercy endures for ever.* Confess this, that he is sweet,[3] confess it, if you have tasted.

No one who refuses to taste can make this confession, for how can anyone say that a thing is sweet without personal experience of it? But you, for your part, if you have tasted how sweet the Lord is,[4] *confess to the Lord, because he is sweet.* If you have tasted eagerly, belch forth in confession; for *his mercy endures for ever*, which is to say, to eternity. We find the expression, *in saeculum*, here, because in various scriptural passages the phrase (which in the Greek is εἰς αἰῶνα) means "for all eternity."[5] Clearly God's mercy cannot last through time only and not for eternity, since the whole purpose of the outpouring of his mercy on men and women is to enable them to live with the angels for eternity.

Appeal to experience: in each believer is enacted what the psalm speaks of in collective terms

3. *Let them speak, those who have been redeemed by the Lord.* It may look as though the redeemed people referred to are the people of Israel redeemed from the land of Egypt, from their servile condition, from their sterile labor, and from their drudgery with bricks. However, let us investigate whether it really is the people freed from Egypt by the Lord who speak here. In fact it is not. Who are they, then? *Those whom he redeemed from the hands of their enemies.* It is still possible for someone to argue that it does mean the Israelites redeemed from the hands of their Egyptian foes. But now let them be unmistakably identified, the

---

2. A theme to be resumed later; see sections 9 and 14.

3. *Suavis.* On the interchangeability between *suavis* and *bonus* see Augustine's remarks in his Exposition of Psalm 105,2.5. But the occurrence of *suavis* here gives him the opportunity to speak of "tasting" the Lord, a personal experience, and so relevant to his point in the preceding section. He will return to the idea later in a negative sense when considering the trial that many people undergo, boredom and distaste. See section 11.

4. See Ps 33:9(34:8); 1 Pt 2:3.

5. Literally it could mean "to the end of the world" or "to the end of the age"; but these meanings are inappropriate here, as he goes on to say. Compare his discussion of the same point in Expositions of Psalms 104,6, and 105,2.

people on whose account the psalm wishes the following verses to be sung. *From different regions he gathered them into a single flock.* Well, I suppose this could just mean different regions in Egypt, for even in a single province there can be many regions. Let the psalm make its point plainly, then: *From east and west, from the north and from the sea.* This makes it clear to us that the redeemed people are to be found all over the world. The people of God have been freed from a vast, widespread Egypt. They are led through a kind of Red Sea for the destruction of their enemies, for in the sacrament symbolized by the Red Sea—in baptism, consecrated by the blood of Christ—their sins, the pursuing Egyptians, are slain. You escape, and not one of the enemies who formerly oppressed you is left alive.

It is the baptized who are invited by the psalm to speak. Let us listen, brothers and sisters, to what happens in this flock gathered from all nations and redeemed by Christ, for it is God's people that is led through these things.[6] I do not mean that the experiences recorded here in song happen to the whole people all at once. They happen to the faithful individually, and in this respect God's people today differs from that other people. The whole race of Israel, the whole nation descended from Abraham according to the flesh, the entire house of Israel, was led out of Egypt once only, was led once through the Red Sea, and once brought through to the promised land. They experienced these things collectively and at the same time; but, says scripture, *All these things happened to them, but with symbolic import, for they are written down as a rebuke to us, upon whom the climax of the ages has come* (1 Cor 10:11). In our case it happens differently: we are not all gathered at once into a single city, the one people of God, but little by little and one by one as we come to believe. But as these things that are written take place in each one of us individually they take place also in God's people, for the people is made up of individual persons, not the other way round. Does a single human come into being from the people? No; but the people comes into being from the individual persons. If, then, you recognize anything in yourself as I am speaking, if anything I say corresponds to your own experience, do not let your reflections remain confined to yourself, as though you were the only person to whom these things happen, but realize that they happen to all, or nearly all, who join this people and are redeemed from their enemies' clutches by Christ's precious blood.

---

6. Variants: "for it is called God's people"; "and whither it is led, this people of God."

Four acknowledgements of the Lord's merciful deliverance evoke the idea of four typical temptations

4. The verse we have just sung will be repeated frequently: *Let them confess to the Lord his merciful works, and the wonders he has wrought for mortals.*[7] As far as I could discover, these lines recur four times, but you can check that for yourselves. With the Lord's help we have partially succeeded in discerning the mystery of this number four: it signifies four temptations or trials, from which we are delivered by the Lord, to whom his merciful works confess.

First scene: wandering and hunger

First of all picture to yourselves a person who is not seeking anything much, someone living in the deceptive security of the old life, not expecting anything to follow this present life when sooner or later it runs out, someone negligent and brutish, with a heart weighed down by the allurements of the world and stupefied by its lethal pleasures. It takes the hand of God to arouse such a person, doesn't it? God's action is needed to awaken him or her, to arouse the sleeper and prod him into seeking God's grace and living with greater care. He still does not know who aroused him, but he will begin to belong to God[8] when he has recognized the true faith; at present, though, before he recognizes it, he bewails his error. He finds himself to be on the wrong path; he wants to know the truth, he knocks on any door he can find, he tries everything, he wanders about, and he hungers for the truth.[9]

Thus the first temptation is that of error and hunger. Once the wanderer has wearied of this temptation and has cried out to God, he is led into the way of faith and begins his journey to the city of peace. He is led to Christ, who said, *I am the way* (Jn 14:6).

Second scene: concupiscence

5. Once he is on the way and knows what his duties are, he begins to want to do battle with his sins. But it may happen that pride is his downfall, because he

---

7. These lines recur as a refrain at verses 8, 15, 21, 31. Augustine's congregation had evidently sung them as a response. The Latin, *confiteantur Domino miserationes eius, et mirabilia eius filiis hominum,* is ambiguous, since *miserationes* and *mirabilia* could be either the subject of the verb *confiteantur* or the object. Augustine takes it sometimes one way, sometimes the other, in this sermon.
8. Variants: "to taste the sweetness of God"; "to belong to God and taste his sweetness."
9. Hunger for truth characterized Augustine's own life, both before and (differently) after his acceptance of Christ. There are echoes of his own experience in the four temptations he describes, corresponding to the fourfold demonstration of the Lord's mercy evoked by the refrain in the psalm.

expects too much of himself and relies on his own strength. He is therefore left to discover how hampered he is by the difficulties that result from his disordered desires and finds himself unable to walk along the way because of his fetters. He feels himself shut in by the obstacles his vices have set up. They are like an unscalable wall, with all doors closed, and he can find no way by which to escape into a good life. He already knows how he ought to live. Formerly he was lost in error and suffered hunger for the truth, but now he has been given the food of truth and set on the right path. He hears the admonitions, "Live a good life as you have been taught. Once you did not know how to conduct your life, but now you have been given instruction, and you do know." He tries, but he cannot. He feels himself bound, and he cries out to the Lord.

This second temptation is that of difficulty in right action, as the first was the temptation of error and hunger. In the second temptation he again cries out to the Lord, and the Lord frees him from his plight, breaking the chains of difficulty and setting him firmly into habits of just conduct. What was arduous for him before now begins to come easily: to steer clear of wrongdoing, not to commit adultery, not to steal, not to kill, not to profane what is holy, not to covet what belongs to another. Where there was difficulty before, now there is the possibility of right action.

The Lord could have granted this possibility without the antecedent difficulty, but if we had the power without experiencing the struggle we should not acknowledge the donor of such a blessing. If the power had been available to this convert in the first place, whenever he wanted it, if he had never felt the strength of his concupiscence warring against him, and if his burdened soul had never chafed against its bonds, he would have attributed to himself the possibility of right action he knew he had. And then the Lord's merciful works would not have confessed to him.

Third scene: boredom and disgust

6. After these two temptations—the first of error and being starved of the truth, the second of difficulty in acting rightly—a third temptation overtakes a person. I am speaking now to those who have passed through the first two, which, I admit, are familiar to many people. Are there any who do not know themselves to have come from ignorance to truth, from error to the way, from hungering for wisdom to the word of faith? Then again, many people wrestle with difficulties consequent upon their vices, shackled by their bad habits and groaning as though fettered in prison. Many are familiar with this temptation. But let them say, if say it they must: *Who will deliver me from this death-ridden body, wretch that I am?* (Rom 7:24) For the chains are very tight indeed: *The flesh lusts against the spirit, and the spirit against the flesh, so that you do not act*

as you want to (Gal 5:17). But then there is the man or woman who has been strengthened in spirit, who has willed not to be an adulterer and is so no longer, who has willed to steal no more and is no longer a thief, and so on. All these things people try to overcome, but often they are beaten down and worsted, so they cry out to God to free them from their predicament. On being relieved let them confess to the Lord his merciful works. Well then, let us picture a person of this kind, who has overcome these difficulties and now lives honorably among other men and women, accused of no wrongdoing. Such a one is then entrapped by the third temptation, the trial of boredom with the tedium of this life, so that he or she may sometimes find no pleasure at all in either reading or prayer.[10] This third temptation is the opposite of the first: the person was then in danger from hunger, but now from distaste. How can this happen? It can only be the effect of a sickness in the soul. Adultery no longer attracts you, yet God's word gives you no pleasure. You are glad to have escaped the dangers of ignorance and concupiscence; but watch out, for weariness and boredom may kill you.

This too is no light temptation. Recognize yourself in it, and cry out to the Lord to deliver you from your plight in this matter as well. And when you have been freed from this temptation, let the Lord's merciful works confess to him.

Fourth scene: storms rock the boat

7. You have been freed from error, freed from things that hamper you when you want to act as you should, and freed from weariness and distaste for the word of God. Perhaps you are now ready to be responsible for other people, perhaps you are worthy to steer the ship, to rule a church. And there you meet the fourth temptation. The storms at sea batter the church and trouble the pilot. The first three temptations may be experienced by any loyal believer among God's people, but the fourth is ours.[11] The more highly we are honored, the greater the risk we run. Certainly we must fear lest dangerous error turn any one of you away from the truth; certainly we must fear lest anyone's inordinate desire overcome him or her, and that person choose to follow it rather than crying out to the Lord amid the struggle; certainly we must fear lest any one of you lose all relish for God's word and die of disgust; but the temptation in piloting the ship, the perilous temptation encountered in ruling a church, touches us most of all.

Yet how can you be indifferent to it, if the whole ship is at risk? I have spoken about it in case you might be less concerned about this fourth temptation, considering it to be our problem alone. If that were so, you would pray less for us,

10. *Acedia*, the classic temptation well known to the desert fathers and frequently mentioned in subsequent ascetical literature: a weariness of soul and disgust with all things spiritual.
11. The trial of pastors.

precisely in this matter where it is most necessary that you not slacken in your prayers, for you will be the first to suffer shipwreck. Think of that, brothers and sisters! You may not be sitting at the helm, but are you not sailing in the same ship?

A summary of the four temptations, and a sketch of the whole psalm

8. After these four temptations, after the four pleas addressed to God, after the four confessions of the Lord's mercy, it is the Church itself that is brought to mind in the rest of this psalm, so that you may clearly perceive what the psalm had in view from the outset. The Church is presented in such a way that in all that happens the grace of God may be proclaimed to us, the grace of him who *thwarts the proud, but gives grace to the humble* (Jas 4:6; 1 Pt 5:5), because he came *so that they who do not see may see, and those who see may become blind* (Jn 9:39); for *every valley shall be filled in, and every mountain and hill brought down* (Is 40:4). After the Church has been presented to us, something further is said which may be understood of the heretics, by whose activity the Church is shaken as if by civil war. And thus the psalm draws to an end.

I have expounded it more briefly than you expected, haven't I? Yes, in fact I think I have so comprehensively explained this whole psalm, fairly long though it is, that if you retain what I have said you cannot expect me to serve you any further as a teacher but only as a reader—scarcely anything more. The main points have been put before you for your examination, I think; but to make them even more memorable, we will now briefly recapitulate.

The first temptation is error and starvation of the word; the second is the difficulty of conquering one's lusts; the third is boredom and distaste; the fourth is the danger of storms in the government of churches. In all these trials we must cry out; from them all the Lord delivers us, and we confess the merciful works of God. Finally we are shown the Church itself, which has been saved by the grace of our God, not by its own merits. We are also shown how its enemies are afflicted for their pride. After their defeat the Church stands upright, and the divine blessings conferred on it are acknowledged, for it will have been saved from the damage it has suffered through the treachery of heretics and from the harm inflicted on it by its own members. And thus the psalm concludes. Let us now stop discussing, and read it.

Verses 2-9. Wanderers are directed and the hungry fed

9. *Let them speak, those who have been redeemed by the Lord, those whom he redeemed from the hands of their enemies. From different regions he gathered them into a single flock, from east and west, from the north and from the sea.* Christians should be the ones to speak, for they have been called together from all parts of the world. *They wandered in the desert, in a waterless land, unable to*

find the way to a city where they could live. We have heard now about their wretched wandering; what about their sheer poverty? *They were hungry and thirsty, and their soul fainted within them.* Why did it faint? What was God's purpose in this? He is not cruel. But he reminds us of himself, which is for our good, so that when we are at the end of our resources we will pray to him, and then he can come to our help and win our love. In this extremity, after their wandering and their hunger and thirst, *they cried to the Lord in their distress, and he snatched them out of their plight.*[12] They had been wandering: what did he do for them? *He led them into the right way, guided them to a city where they could dwell.* The psalm does not yet tell us what he did about their hunger and thirst, but wait: it will. *Let them confess to the Lord his merciful works, and the wonders he has wrought for mortals.* You who are now set on the way, you who are now directed toward the city you must find, you who have experienced these mercies, tell those who have not. You, finally, who have now been freed from your hunger and thirst, speak about it, *for he has satisfied the empty soul, and filled the hungry soul with good things.*

Verses 10-17. God's help in the struggle against our concupiscence

10. Now you are established on the right path and have been told what you must hope for. Live a good life, then. But you are wrestling and being defeated: what else is catching up with you? *Some sat in darkness and the shadow of death, in helpless need and in irons.* How did that befall you? Only because you failed to acknowledge the grace of God and rejected the Lord's plan for you. This is what the psalm indicates: *They bitterly resented the Lord's words* through pride, being ignorant of the Lord's righteousness and desirous of setting up their own.[13] *They rebelled against the plan of the Most High. And their heart was humbled as they toiled.* So now, fight against your concupiscence. If God withdraws his help you may toil strenuously, but you cannot overcome. When you find yourself hard pressed by your depraved habits your heart will be humbled in your toil, in order that you may learn to cry out from your humbled heart, *Who will deliver me from this death-ridden body, wretch that I am?* (Rom 7:24). The heart of the Hebrew people was thus *humbled as they toiled; they became weak, and there was no one to help them.* What remains to us but to ask why this happened? *If a law capable of giving life had been granted to us, then of course righteousness would have been obtainable through the law; but scripture has included all things under sin, so that through faith in Jesus Christ the promise may be given to believers. The law entered stealthily that sin might abound.* (Gal 3:21-22; Rom 5:20) You have received God's word and accepted his commandment, yet

---

12. This verse recurs several times as a refrain, but the second verb varies: *eripuit, salvos fecit, liberavit, eduxit.* The English translation varies accordingly.

13. See Rom 10:3.

you do not cease your former wrongdoing. Moreover, since you have been given the commandment, you are compounding your sins by disobedience. Proud sinner, if you did not know yourself in your old life, learn what you are now that you have been humbled. You will cry out, and you will be rescued from your predicament, and being delivered you will confess the Lord's merciful works. *They cried to the Lord in their distress, and he saved them in their need.*

Thus they were freed from the second temptation; there remains the temptation to weariness and disgust. But first notice what the Lord did for them after their liberation. *He brought them out from darkness and the shadow of death, and broke their chains apart. Let them confess to the Lord his merciful works, and the wonders he has wrought for mortals.* Why? What difficulties did he surmount? *He smashed bronze doors, and shattered iron bars. He steered them away from the path of their iniquity, for it was on account of their wrongdoing that they had been humbled.* Because they had thought to succeed by their own efforts, because they tried to set up a righteousness of their own, disregarding God's righteousness, they were humbled. They had presumed on their own unaided powers, but they discovered that they could do nothing without God's help.

Verses 18-22. The danger of boredom and distaste for God's word

11. What else is left in the matter of temptation? *Their soul shrank from all food with disgust.* Now they are suffering disgust, they are ill with their disgust, they are imperiled by their disgust. You surely do not imagine, do you, that although they could have died from hunger, they could not be killed by disgust? They certainly could; observe what the psalm goes on to say. *Their soul shrank from all food with disgust,* it says; but then, to make sure you do not think them safe because fully fed, but rather see how likely they were to die from their aversion, it continues, *And they came close to the gates of death.* What lesson is there in this for you? That you should not claim the credit for any delight you experience in God's word, lest you become puffed up with pride and caper arrogantly in your eagerness for that food, scorning others who are endangered by their disgust. Be clear in your mind that this too is a gift conferred on you, not something attributable to yourself, for *what have you that you did not receive?* (1 Cor 4:7) If you understand this, and if you find yourself imperiled by this vice, this sickness, act as the psalm suggests: *They cried to the Lord in their distress, and he freed them.* It emphasizes that inability to find pleasure in that food is indeed a sickness, by adding, *He sent his word and healed them.* Look how dangerous that disgust is, and look at the peril from which he freed you when, overcome by disgust, you cried to him. *He sent his word and healed them*—from what? Not from error and hunger this time, nor even from the difficulty of defeating their sins, but *from their disease.* It is a disease, a corruption of the mind, to find distasteful what is delicious. For this divine gift, as for the others received

earlier, *let them confess to the Lord his merciful works, and the wonders he has wrought for mortals, and let them offer him a sacrifice of praise.* The Lord is sweet,[14] and his sweetness deserves our praise. *Let them proclaim his deeds as they leap for joy*—not with weariness, not with sadness, not with anxiety, not with distaste, but leaping for joy.

Verses 23-31. Pilot and passengers are at risk from stormy seas

12. The fourth one is still to come, the trial that puts us all in jeopardy, for we are all aboard the ship. Some are crew, others are passengers, but all are in peril from a storm, and all alike are safe when she reaches harbor. After all the earlier vicissitudes comes this one: *Those who go down to the sea in ships, pursuing their business in vast waters,* that is, among many peoples. The Revelation of John proves to us that "waters" often stand for "peoples" in scripture, for when John asked what the waters were, the answer he received was, *They are the peoples* (Rv 17:15). The people who work among vast waters *have seen the works of the Lord, and his wonders in the deep;* for what is deeper than human hearts? Winds often rise in force from them; storms of sedition and discord rock the ship. Then what happens? It is God's will that both those who steer the ship and her passengers cry out to him. *He spoke, and stormy weather set in.* What does *set in* suggest? That it came to stay, it lasted a long time. In fact it is still causing disturbance, it goes on tossing the ship, it rages and does not abate. Why? Because the Lord himself *spoke, and stormy weather set in.* And what effect did this stormy weather have? *The waves were whipped up. They mount as high as the sky* in their daring;[15] *they sink right down to the abyss* in their fear. It matches our experience: *they mount as high as the sky, they sink right down to the abyss,* for there are fights without and fears within.[16] *Their soul was flinching amid the calamities, they were shaken and tottering like a drunkard.* Those who sit at the helm and those who loyally love the ship will understand what I am saying: *They were shaken and tottering like a drunkard.* When they speak, or read, or interpret,[17] they look wise and competent enough, but woe betide them in a storm! *All their skill was swallowed up,* says the psalm. It sometimes happens that all human plans are insufficient: whichever way one turns the waves are crashing and the storm raging, and every arm has lost its strength. The navigators are completely powerless to see where the prow may be struck, or when the ship may come broadside onto some wave, or whither she may be driven, or from what rocks she must be held off lest she be wrecked. What recourse have they? One only: *They cried out to the Lord in their distress, and he led them safely*

---

14. See Ps 33:9(34:8).
15. *Audendo.* Variant: *audiendo,* "at what they hear."
16. See 2 Cor 7:5.
17. Or "handle their business."

out of their perils. He commanded the storm, and a gentle breeze set in. It was no stormy weather that set in now but *a gentle breeze. And the waves grew quiet.*

Listen to what a certain ship's captain had to say about this experience, a captain who had faced danger, and been humiliated, but then delivered: *I would not have you ignorant, brethren, about the afflictions that beset us in Asia, for we were crushed under such an excessive weight of troubles that we felt too weary even to live* (2 Cor 1:8). All his skill and wisdom were gone, it seems. But did God abandon them in their exhaustion? Did he not rather allow them to reach that low point in order to win glory in them? Surely that was so, for the apostle continues, *In ourselves we found nothing but the token of death, to ensure that we should put our trust not in ourselves, but in God, who raises the dead* (2 Cor 1:9). God *commanded the storm, and a gentle breeze set in.* They had already found the token of death in themselves, as far as their own power was concerned, for all their skill was gone; but *the waves grew quiet. They rejoiced at the calm, and he led them into the harbor they were making for. Let the Lord's merciful works confess to him.* Everywhere, absolutely everywhere, *let the Lord's merciful works confess to him*—not our merits, or our strength, or our wisdom, but *his merciful works.* May he be loved in every deliverance he grants us, he who has been invoked in our every trouble. *Let the Lord's merciful works confess to him, and the wonders he has wrought for mortals.*

Verses 32-38. God thwarts the proud and gives grace to the humble: how this relates to Jews and Gentiles

13. Now consider the background to everything that the psalm says, the standpoint from which it has told its story, the place whence it has enumerated all these mercies, the setting in which they occur. *Let them exalt him in the church of the people, and praise him in the seat of the elders.* The words *let them exalt him* mean the same as *let them praise him.* Let them all exalt him, let them all praise him, both people and elders, those engaged in business and those who steer the ship, for what has he done in this Church? What has he established? From what has he delivered it? What gifts has he bestowed on it? Just as he has thwarted the proud, so has he given grace to the humble. The proud are primarily the original people of God, the Jews, who became arrogant and boastful because they were of Abraham's race and to them God's words had been entrusted.[18] But those words brought them not healing but self-importance in their hearts, not true greatness but morbid swelling. What did God do, he who thwarts the proud and gives his grace to the humble, he who excised the natural branches for their pride

18. See Rom 3:2.

and engrafted the wild olive in its humility?[19] What did God do? Hear now two things that he did, as the psalm relates them. First, how God thwarts the proud, and then how he confers grace on the humble.

He turned rivers into desert. Among the Jews waters used to flow: prophecies ran freely. Look for a prophet among them now! You will not find one, for *he turned rivers into desert, springs of water into parched ground.* The psalm states that *he turned rivers into desert*, but not only this psalm: let the Jews admit it themselves: *There is no prophet now, and he recognizes us no longer* (Ps 73(74):9). *He turned rivers into desert, springs of water into parched ground, and fruitful land into salty waste.* Look for the faith of Christ there, and you will not find it; look for a prophet, and you find none; look for a priest, and you find not a single one; look for a sacrifice, and there are no sacrifices; look for the temple, and look in vain. How can this be? Because God *turned rivers into desert, springs of water into parched ground, and fruitful land into salty waste.* But why? How did they deserve it? *Because of the malice of those who lived there.*

You know now how God thwarts the proud. Listen to how he gives grace to the humble. *He turned the desert into lakes, and a waterless country into springs. There he made a home for the hungry.* Why? Because to him it was said, *You are a priest for ever after the order of Melchizedek* (Ps 109(110):4). If you look among the Jews for a sacrifice you find none offered according to the order of Aaron, because God has turned their rivers into a desert; but neither will you find any sacrifice there according to the order of Melchizedek. Not there will you find it, not among the Jews, but it is celebrated in the Church throughout the world. *From the rising of the sun to its setting, the name of the Lord is praised* (Ps 112(113):3). To those people whose rivers he turned into desert scripture says, *I take no pleasure in you, the Lord declares, nor will I receive any sacrifice at your hands; because from the rising of the sun to its setting, in every place a clean oblation is offered to my name* (Mal 1:10-11). In Gentile regions plenty of unclean sacrifices used to be offered in the days when they were desert lands, when they were drought-stricken and filthy,[20] when all nations were salty wastelands. But now there are fountains gushing there; now there are rivers and lakes and springs. See how God thwarts the proud but gives his grace to the humble.

There he made a home for the hungry, for *the poor shall eat, and be satisfied* (Ps 21:27(22:26)). *They founded a city to dwell in,* a dwelling in hope, at present, because, as scripture says, *Anyone who listens to me will dwell in hope* (Prv 1:33, LXX). *They founded a city to dwell in, they sowed their fields and planted vineyards, and reaped plentiful grain.* Such plenty delighted a certain laborer who

---

19. See Rom 11:17-24.
20. *Quando squalebant*: a nice choice of verb in this context, because *squaleo* means, first, to be stiff and rough, as through drought, and, second, to be filthy or squalid.

said, *I do not seek your gift: all I seek is the fruit accruing to you* (Phil 4:17). *God blessed them, their numbers greatly increased, and in their livestock there was no diminution.* All this well-being is assured, for *God's foundation stands firm, and the Lord knows his own* (2 Tm 2:19). The cattle and livestock represent those who walk with simplicity in the Church, without pretensions, but useful; not highly educated, but full of faith. *God blessed them,* the spiritual and the carnal[21] alike; *their numbers greatly increased, and in their livestock there was no diminution.*

Verses 39-42. The fate of those who leave the unity of the Church

14. *They became few, and were harassed.* What are we to make of this? It seems to cut across what we have just heard. No, it arises from within, for the people who became few were those who *went out from us, but they had never belonged to us* (1 Jn 2:19). The reason why the psalm seems to make the statement, *They became few, and were harassed,* about the people so recently mentioned is this: we are meant to understand that these few seemed to belong to the main group, because they shared the sacraments. They are the kind who belong to God's people by an appearance of devotion, though not by genuine virtue. We have heard the apostle predict concerning them, *In the last days lawless times will threaten, for people will be lovers of themselves* (2 Tm 3:1-2). There is the root cause of the trouble: people will be lovers of themselves and will find themselves pleasing. They would do better to find themselves displeasing and so become pleasing to God;[22] they would be better off crying out to him in their need, that they might be freed from their distress. But no, they expected great things of themselves, and so they became few.

It is quite obvious, brothers and sisters, that all who cut themselves off from unity become few. They are many to begin with, but many within a unity, and remain so as long as they are not separated from it. If the multitude-in-unity ceases to be their home, they are in heresy and schism, and then they are few. *They became few, and were harassed by tiresome misfortunes and grief. Scorn was poured out upon those leaders,* for they were repudiated by God's Church, and scorned all the more because they tried to set themselves up as leaders. They became like insipid salt, thrown out of doors and fit only for people to trample on.[23] *Scorn was poured out upon those leaders.*

And he led them astray, off the path, and not in the way. The people we heard of earlier[24] were on the way, led along in the right way toward their city, led

---

21. Evidently the word carries no pejorative overtones here.
22. Variant: "love God."
23. See Mt 5:13.
24. See section 9.

straight forward and not astray. But now these few are off the track, missing their way. What can it mean, to say that God *led them astray?*[25] *God delivered them to their own lusts* (Rom 1:24). This is what it means by saying, *He led them astray*: he handed them over to themselves. Strictly speaking it is they who lead themselves astray, for *anyone who thinks he is something, whereas he is nothing, deceives himself* (Gal 6:3) and leads himself astray. What, then, was the effect here, when, as the psalm says, God *led them astray?* He left them to their own devices, *off the path, and not in the way*; for how could people who cling to a part, abandoning the whole, be on the way? How could they be in the way? What is this way, and how can it be known? *May God have mercy on us and bless us*, another psalm prays. *May he make his face shine upon us, that we may know your way on earth.* What earth? *Your salvation among all nations.* (Ps 66:2-3(67:1-2))

Clearly then, they go out from among us to be diminished and reduced; they have all left the multitude-in-unity. The text already quoted applies to them: *they went out from us, but they had never belonged to us; for if they had truly belonged, they would have stayed with us* (1 Jn 2:19). Perhaps, though, in the secret foreknowledge of God, they are really ours, in which case they must return. How many are there who seem to be within but are not truly ours, and how many others are ours, though still outside? *The Lord knows his own* (2 Tm 2:19). People who are still inside, but not really ours, leave when the opportunity presents itself; and those who are ours, though still outside, return when they find their opportunity. Accept the fact that God knows all, and in the light of this understand how *he led them astray, off the path and not in the way.*

What use has he made of them? I began to explain this point, and you must listen carefully. God could perfectly well have allowed them to stay inside all their lives, but then we would have derived no profit from them. As it is, they have been separated from us, and by their malicious carping they disturb us, thereby forcing us to study the points they raise, and at the same time providing us with a salutary warning. Every one of us trembles on seeing another leave the Church, as though that person's departure were saying to us, *Anyone who thinks he stands must take care not to fall* (1 Cor 10:12). Those who leave do us a service, therefore, whereas if they were still within, bad as they are, they would not profit us at all. What was said about them in another psalm? *A batch of bulls* (that is, of stiff-necked, proud persons) *is among the cows of the peoples.* By *cows* that other psalm suggests souls that are easily seduced, and liable to consent readily to the seductive bulls. But why is this allowed to happen? *So that*

---

25. *Seduxit eos.* The verb *seducere*, used with emphasis and intensity in the following lines, means "to lead astray" in its etymological sense, but carries the moral overtone of "seduction" and, in the quotation from Rom 1:24, "self-seduction."

those who have been proved sound by silver may be pressed out (Ps 67:31(68:30)). What does that phrase mean: *may be pressed out*?[26] It means that those who have been proved sound by God's word may be clearly seen or may stand out plainly. To reply to the heretics is necessary, but to build up Catholics in the process is very useful. Paul made the same point unambiguously: *Heresies there must be, so that those who have been proved sound may be clearly identified among you* (1 Cor 11:19). For the same reason there must be bulls bent on seduction *so that those who have been proved sound by silver may be pressed out*, that is, clearly identified. But what does *proved sound by silver* mean? We need to think of yet another psalm: *The words of the Lord are pure words, silver tried by fire for the earth, purified seven times* (Ps 11:7(12:6)). Those who have been proved by this silver, this word of the Lord, cannot fully shake out their rich silver for display except when the questions of the heretics agitate them.

One particular point has been mentioned here, that *scorn was poured out upon the leaders*, upon those bulls. Why were they scorned? Because they proclaimed a different message. In what sense were they scorned? They were regarded as anathema, for the apostle ordered, *Even if we ourselves, or an angel from heaven, preaches to you a gospel different from the one you have received, let him be anathema!* They are leaders, they are learned, important people, they are precious stones.[27] Yes, and what more can you say of them—that they are angels? Nonetheless, *even if an angel from heaven preaches to you anything other than what you have received, let him be anathema!* (Gal 1:8-9) For the devil himself is an angel who fell from heaven. Rightly, then, is *scorn poured out upon the leaders*.

But he helped the poor beggar. What is this, brothers and sisters? The princes scorned, but the poor helped? Yes, the proud have been rejected and the humble instructed; for God cast out the proud and in so doing *helped the poor beggar*. This poor person is a beggar who attributes nothing to himself and expects everything from the mercy of God. He stands outside the Lord's door every day, shouting, knocking, and waiting for the door to be opened, naked and shivering in the hope of being clothed, with eyes lowered to the earth, beating his breast. God constantly helps this beggar, this poor person, this humble suppliant, and helps him even by the separation of heretics from the Church, because they have become so few, and have been harassed, and led astray off the path, so that they are no longer on the way.

But after they have been reduced in number, and seduced, diminished, and harassed, what happens for the poor person who has been helped? God *made the families like flocks of sheep.* When the psalm said just now that God *helped the*

---

26. *Ut excludantur.* Augustine uses this word in his Expositions of Psalms 54,22 and 67,39; and in *The Spirit and the Letter* 17. The root idea is that pressure is applied to bring about the emergence of significant form or meaning, to make something "stand out."

27. This sentence could be understood as spoken by the "separated," perhaps the Donatists.

poor beggar, you understood it of a single poor person, a solitary beggar; but now this poor person has become many families, and numerous peoples. There are many churches but only one Church: one people, one family, one sheep. *He made the families like flocks of sheep.*

These are great mysteries. Sacred signs[28] are here, wonderful, profound, fraught with mystery. How delightful it is to discover them: all the more so in that they lay hidden for so long. Accordingly *the upright will see and be joyful, and all sin will shut its mouth.* Sin has been convicted, that sin which prated against our unity, but only succeeded in forcing the truth into the open, and now *it must shut its mouth.*

Verse 43. Conclusion: the poor contemplate all these instances of God's mercy and praise him

15. *Who is wise? The wise will treasure these things, and understand the merciful deeds of the Lord.* Notice how the psalm concludes: *Who is wise? The wise will treasure these things.* And what are the wise to treasure? These wise persons must be poor if they are to keep it all; they must not be proud or puffed up, or they will never treasure these things. Why do they treasure them? Because they will *understand the merciful deeds of the Lord.* He guided them aright when they were wandering and fed them in their hunger; he freed them when they were fighting against the difficulties in which their sins had left them, and he broke the chains of their bad habits; he sent the medicine of his word to heal and renew them when they felt distaste for God's word and were almost dying from their disgust and weariness; he calmed the sea and guided them into port when they were at risk of shipwreck amid the stormy waves. Finally he gave them a place within that people where he gives grace to the humble, not among those where he thwarts the proud; he made them his own, that they might remain within and multiply and never depart to be diminished.

This is what the upright see, what makes them joyful. Therefore *all sin will shut its mouth*, and *the wise will treasure these things.* How will they treasure them? By humility, and by understanding the merciful works of the Lord, for throughout the psalm the refrain is heard, *let them confess to the Lord his merciful works, and the wonders he has wrought for mortals.*

---

28. *Sacramenta.*

On Psalm 107

Why no exposition is provided here

The composite character of Psalm 107

1. I deemed it unnecessary to expound Psalm 107, because it consists of the later verses of Psalm 56 plus the later verses of Psalm 59; and I have commented on these already in their proper places. The last part of Psalm 56 forms the opening part of this Psalm 107, down to the verse, *May your glory pervade the whole earth.*[1] The rest of Psalm 107 is the same as the last part of Psalm 59. Similar repetitions are found elsewhere in the psalter: for instance, the last part of Psalm 134, beginning from the verse, *The idols of the Gentiles are fashioned of silver and gold*, is the same as a passage beginning with that verse in Psalm 113.[2] Again, Psalm 13 and Psalm 52 are the same throughout, apart from a few slight variations in the middle.

With regard to Psalm 107, we notice that it presents no difficulty at the few points where it differs from the other two psalms of which it is made up. Where Psalm 56 has: *I will sing and play the psaltery: arise, O my glory* (Ps 56:8-9(57:7-8)), Psalm 107 has: *I will sing and play the psaltery in my glory* (Ps 107:2(108:1)). The exhortation *Arise!* was added to make it clear that it is in glory that the singing and playing of psalms are carried on. Similarly we find in Psalm 56: *Your mercy is magnified* (or *raised*, as some translate) *even to the heavens* (Ps 56:11(57:10)); but in Psalm 107 this appears as: *Your mercy is great above the heavens* (Ps 107:5(108:4)). The purpose of God's mercy being magnified even to the heavens is that it may be great in heaven, for this is what *above the heavens* means.

When we turn to Psalm 59 we read: *I will rejoice and divide Shechem* (Ps 59:8(60:6)), but here: *I will be exalted, and will divide Shechem* (Ps 107:8(108:7)). This variant shows us what was signified by the division of Shechem, something prophesied as due to happen after the Lord's exaltation. The rejoicing belongs to the exaltation, for joy is the consequence of his being exalted. The same thought occurs in another psalm: *You have turned my lamentation into joy; you have torn up my sackcloth and girded me with happiness* (Ps 29:12(30:11).

---

1. Pss 56:6 and 107:6 (57:5 and 108:5).
2. Pss 134:15 and 113B:4 (135:15 and 115:4).

Again, in Psalm 59 we read: *The strength of my head is Ephraim* (Ps 59:9(60:7)), but in Psalm 107: *My head's receiving*[3] *is Ephraim* (Ps 107:9(108:8)); for our strength comes from God's reception of us. He takes us up and makes us strong by renewing us and bringing forth fruit in us, for the name Ephraim means "bearing fruit." But the act of receiving can also be understood either as our receiving Christ or as his reception of us, since he is the head of the Church. Finally, where Psalm 59 has *those who harass us* (Ps 59:14(60:12)), Psalm 107 has *our enemies* (Ps 107:14(108:13)); obviously the same people are referred to.

Seemingly divergent psalms point to one end, Christ

2. However, this psalm has an important lesson to teach us. Some of the titles attached to the psalms apparently refer to events recorded in history, but we are undoubtedly right to interpret them as prophecy whenever we see that this is the perspective in which the psalms were composed. If we took them in a purely historical sense, what could be more divergent than the title of Psalm 56: *To the end, as an inscribed title for David himself that is not to be tampered with, when he fled into a cave from Saul's pursuit*, and the title of Psalm 59: *To the end, for those who will be changed, into an inscribed title, into teaching, for David himself, when he burnt Mesopotamia of Syria, and the Syrians of Zobah, and Joab turned round and smote Edom, twelve thousand men, in the Valley of the Salt-pits?* The only elements common to both titles are the words, *an inscribed title, for David himself*, and *to the end*. Apart from these, the two titles are so different that the former evokes David's lowly state, the latter his time of strength; the former speaks of his flight, the latter of his victories. And yet our Psalm 107 is composed of the last verses of those other two psalms which bear such divergent titles.

We could have no clearer indication that both the earlier psalms are oriented to a single end not in their superficial historical sense but in the depth of the prophecy they express.[4] The closing verses of both are united in our present psalm, which bears the title, *A song for David himself*. This title resembles neither of the earlier ones, except for the words, *for David himself*. By many fragmentary sayings and in many ways God spoke of old to our fathers through the prophets, as the Letter to the Hebrews reminds us;[5] but what he spoke was the One whom he sent later to fulfill the oracles of the prophets, for *however many were the promises of God, all find their "yes" in him* (2 Cor 1:20).

---

3. *Susceptio.* On the overtones of this word see the notes at Expositions of Psalms 3,3; 45,11; and 83,9.
4. A summary statement of Augustine's constant Christological interpretation of the psalms.
5. See Heb 1:1.

Exposition of Psalm 108

Introduction: this psalm speaks of Judas, but as a representative figure

1. Anyone who attentively reads the Acts of the Apostles will be aware that this psalm contains a prophecy relating to Christ. The petition in the psalm, *May his days be few, and let another take over his sacred office*[1] (verse 8), is clearly asserted in the Book of Acts to be a prophecy about Judas, who betrayed Christ.[2] It was recalled on the occasion when Matthias was added as the twelfth to the college of the apostles. If, however, we attempt to interpret everything the psalm says about a bad man as referring to the single individual, Judas, we can scarcely, if at all, produce a convincing exposition. On the other hand, if we understand all that is said here about this type of person more generally—of Christ's enemies, that is, and of the ungrateful Jews—it all seems to me to lend itself to much clearer explanation. Just as certain things in the gospel are apparently said to Peter in person, but cannot be fully luminous unless they are referred to the Church, which he represented by reason of the primacy he held among the disciples—I am thinking of such promises as *I will give to you the keys of the kingdom of heaven* (Mt 16:19)—so too Judas in a sense personifies the Jews who were Christ's enemies, both those who hated him in his own days and their successors in the unbelieving yet enduring race.[3]

It is reasonable to refer to these people and to that race not only the things plainly said about them in this psalm but also those which are specifically said about Judas himself, such as the verse I have already quoted: *May his days be few, and let another take over his sacred office*. With the Lord's help we hope to make this clear when in the course of our exposition we reach those lines.

Verses 2-3. Guileful speech erupts into spiteful action

2. The psalm accordingly begins, *Do not pass over my praise in silence, O God, because the mouth of the sinful and cunning person has been opened against me*. From this it is evident that the insults from which a crafty sinner never falls silent are lies, but the praise about which God is not silent is truthful.

---

1. *Episcopatum eius*. Literally his "oversight," the office of a superintendent. In later Christian usage it came to mean the office of a bishop.
2. See Acts 1:20.
3. Both Peter and Judas are seen as representative figures (*gestasse personam . . . personam sustinet*), the former of the Church, the latter of Christ's enemies. Toward the end of the Exposition Augustine adopts a different contrasting parallel; see note at section 25.

God alone is true; every human being is a liar (Rom 3:4), for the only person who speaks truthfully is one in whom God is speaking. But the most sublime praise of all is that of God's only-begotten Son, the praise that proclaims him for what he truly is, the only Son of God. When the mouths of sinful, deceitful people were opened against him the reality of his person was concealed, and all that appeared was his weakness. Only because his strength was hidden could those guileful mouths speak against him. The psalm declares that the mouth of a cunning person has been opened because the hatred that had been craftily suppressed now burst forth into speech. The point is more plainly made in the following verses.

3. *With deceitful tongues they spoke against me.* This was certainly the case when they praised Christ as a good teacher, but with insincere flattery.[4] Another psalm makes a similar charge: *Those who pretended to praise me were cursing me* (Ps 101:9(102:8)). But they soon burst into shouts of *Crucify him! Crucify him!* (Jn 19:6), so the psalm immediately continues, *And they surrounded me with words of hatred.* At first they had spoken with deceitful tongues, proffering words that appeared to be expressions of esteem, not hatred; but because their attitude was full of trickery they went on later to speak not in feigned friendliness but *with words of* open *hatred, and attacked me for no reason.* Christ's dedicated followers love him gratis, for no reason, just as unbelievers hate him gratis, for no reason. Truth is pursued by the most honorable people for its own sake, not for any advantage it may bring them, and wickedness is similarly sought by the worst characters. Even among secular writers the judgment was passed on a very depraved person that he "was evil and cruel from choice, without provocation."[5]

Verse 4. Returning good for evil; the example of Christ

4. *Instead of loving me they disparaged me.* In this matter there are six possible responses; if they are listed here they can be easily recognized. They are: to return good for evil; not to return evil for evil; to return good for good; to return evil for evil; not to return good for good; and to return evil for good. The first two attitudes are characteristic of good people, and of these two the former is better. The last two denote the responses of bad people, and of these two the latter is worse. The two middle attitudes are those of mediocre persons, but of these two the former is closer to the stance of the good, the latter close to that of the wicked.

We should notice how all these are mentioned in the holy scriptures. The Lord himself renders good for evil. He *justifies the impious* (Rom 4:5), and, hanging on the cross, he prayed, *Father, forgive them, for they do not know what*

---

4. See Mk 12:14.
5. Sallust, *The Cataline War* 16.

they are doing (Lk 23:34). Saint Stephen followed in his footsteps, for he knelt and prayed for those who were stoning him, *Lord, do not hold this sin against them* (Acts 7:60). The Lord's command urges this: *Love your enemies, do good to people who hate you, and pray for those who persecute you* (Mt 5:44). The apostle Paul teaches us not to retaliate by matching the evil we have suffered: *Repay no one with evil for evil* (Rom 12:17); and the apostle Peter likewise commands, *Do not return evil for evil, or curse for curse* (1 Pt 3:9). In the psalms too we find, *if I have repaid those who have paid me back with evil* (Ps 7:5(4)).

Of the last two attitudes of the six we enumerated, the less reprehensible was exemplified in nine lepers who after being cleansed by the Lord neglected to thank him.[6] But the last one, the worst attitude of all, is that of the people who figure in our present psalm, of whom we read, *Instead of loving me, they disparaged me*. Love was what they certainly owed the Lord for his great acts of kindness; yet not only did they fail to render him love for love but they even repaid his goodness with evil.

We spoke of two other responses which are found in the middle of the six enumerated. These two are characteristic of mediocre people, but the former—returning good for good—is the instinct of good people too. It is found in the good, in the fairly good, and in the fairly bad. The Lord does not, therefore, denounce it; but he does not want his disciples to remain stuck there. He wishes them to advance to better things, telling them that *if you love only those who love you* (which means repaying kindness with kindness) *what reward can you expect? Are you doing anything extraordinary? Do not even the tax collectors do that?* (Mt 5:46). He wants them to reach that standard but to go much further by loving not only their friends but their enemies as well.

The second of the two middle attitudes, that which repays evil with evil, is characteristic of bad people and also of the fairly bad and the fairly good. In this spirit the law set bounds to revenge: *An eye for an eye, a tooth for a tooth* (Dt 19:21);[7] it established the justice of the unjust, so to speak. I do not mean that there is anything inequitable about each person incurring the penalty for his or her own deeds, for if that were the case the law would give no such permission. It is the thirst for revenge that is vicious. The business of a judge is to see fair play between opposing parties, and this is the justice a good person must seek.

But if people have fallen away from the summit of kindness, where good is rendered for evil, to what a depth of malevolence must they have fallen if they render evil for good? They have fallen headlong, passing through all those other grades of behavior on their way down. We should not try to excuse their attitude by pointing out that the psalm does not, after all, complain, "Instead of loving

---

6. See Lk 17:17.
7. The "law of the talion" was not intended to encourage revenge but to limit its effects and prevent escalation.

me, they sought to kill me," but only, *Instead of loving me, they disparaged me.* They were in fact murderers through their disparagement, denying the Son of God and alleging, *It is by the power of the prince of demons that he casts demons out* (Lk 11:15), and, *He has a demon, he is possessed. Why do you listen to him?* (Jn 10:20), and the like. By such disparagement they turned away from him people whose conversion he hoped for. The psalm made this complaint to show that enemies who disparage Christ and thereby murder souls do more damage than those who in their savagery put him to death in his mortal flesh, which was very soon to rise again.

5. After complaining that *instead of loving me, they disparaged me*, how does he continue? *But I went on praying.* He does not indicate what he prayed for, yet surely our best way of understanding this is to assume that he prayed for them. Their worst insults were hurled at him when they mocked him on the cross as a mere human being whom they had defeated; but from that cross he prayed, *Father, forgive them, for they do not know what they are doing* (Lk 23:34). As they, from the depths of malice, were repaying his good deeds with evil, so he from the highest point of his kindness wanted to repay their evil with good. To be sure, we also know that he prayed for his disciples, because before his passion he told them that he had prayed that their faith should not fail.[8] But while hanging on the cross he did not display his strength in the face of those detractors whom he could have annihilated by his divine power, and this restraint was meant to give us an example of patience. It was more profitable for us that he should give an example of patient suffering than that he should slay his enemies forthwith, as we might be in a hurry to avenge ourselves on bad people who are cruel to us. He wanted to build us up to an attitude like his own, for, as scripture says, *Better than a mighty warrior is one who overcomes anger* (Prv 16:32).

Thus sacred scripture makes use of our Lord's own example to instruct us. When we hear in the psalm, *Instead of loving me, they disparaged me; but I went on praying*, we understand that we too must pray when we encounter ingratitude in others who not only fail to repay our kindness but even render us evil for the good we have done to them. Christ himself prayed for others, both for his savage attackers and for the disciples who would be grieved and in danger of losing faith. But we need to pray in the first instance for ourselves, that by God's mercy and aid we may conquer the anger which sweeps us toward a lust for revenge, when we are belittled either to our face or when absent. And, finally, when we remember Christ's patience we are, so to say, awakening him, as the apostles did on that occasion when he was asleep in the boat.[9] He calms the storm and turbulence in our hearts. Then with a mind tranquil and at peace we can pray even for those who slander us, and so say with confidence, *Forgive us, as we forgive.*

---

8. See Lk 22:32.
9. See Mk 4:38-39.

Remember, though, that he who forgave had no sin at all for which he needed to seek forgiveness.

Verse 5. The psalm does not pray for disasters but predicts them

6. The psalm proceeds, *They committed evil against me in response to my good deeds.* Then, as though we might have asked, "What evil? And what good deeds?" it answers, *And they repaid my love with hatred.* This is the sum of their guilt and its most heinous aspect; for what harm could the persecutors have done materially to one who died not of necessity but of his own free will? The greatest wickedness on the part of a persecutor is hatred, even though the victim suffers voluntarily. He said just previously, *Instead of loving me,* and now he adds, *they repaid my love with hatred,* to explain that the debt they owed him was not a general debt: they were indebted to his love. He speaks of his love in the gospel: *Jerusalem, Jerusalem, how often I wanted to gather your children to myself, as a hen gathers her chicks under her wings, but you would have none of it!* (Mt 23:37)

7. The psalm now begins to prophesy how these people will be requited for their impiety. It does so in such a way that the speaker seems to be prompted by a desire for vengeance. But the reason for this mode of speech is that future retribution is foretold as absolutely certain and destined to fall on those sinners in accordance with the justice of God.[10] Some people fail to understand this way of foretelling future events under the guise of hoping for disaster; they think that hatred is being met with hatred and evil intent with evil intent. Few are able to see the distinction between the pleasure taken by an accuser of wicked persons who longs to sate his enmity and the very different pleasure felt by a judge who with honorable intention punishes sins. The former is rendering evil for evil; the latter, even when he metes out punishment, is not rendering evil for evil but handing down a just sentence on an unjust offender; and inasmuch as it is just, it must be good. He imposes punishment not because he enjoys someone else's misery, which would be to render evil for evil, but out of delight in justice, which is to render good for evil. Blind interpreters have therefore no ground for finding fault with the light shed by the scriptures, alleging that God cannot punish sins; but neither can unjust persons seek to justify themselves by claiming that even God renders evil for evil.

Let us listen, then, to how the divine word weaves its account, and hear the predictions of a prophet in what sounds like someone praying for calamities. Let us discern in this account the God who metes out just retribution, as we raise our minds to his eternal law.

---

10. A principle Augustine states elsewhere, but with particular relevance in treating this imprecatory psalm.

Verses 6-8. Judas appears; his sin, futile prayer, death, and replacement

8. *Set a sinner over him, and let the devil stand at his right hand.* Until this point the psalm has spoken of several adversaries, but now it envisages only one. It had complained, *With deceitful tongues they spoke against me; they surrounded me with words of hatred, and attacked me for no reason. Instead of loving me, they disparaged me, but I went on praying. They committed evil against me in response to my good deeds, and they repaid my love with hatred.* Many foes are envisaged. But now there is a change. When the psalm considers what those enemies deserve for their iniquities and foretells what will happen to them by God's judgment, it prays, *Set a sinner over him.* It seems that the speaker has in view the individual who handed him over to the sort of enemies of whom he has been speaking. He is referring here to the traitor Judas, who is to be punished by a condign fate, as the Acts of the Apostles record.[11] What then can be meant by *Set a sinner over him*? Nothing else but what is indicated in the next line: *Let the devil stand at his right hand.* He deserved to have the devil over him, which meant being subject to the devil, for he had refused to be subject to Christ. The expression, *Let the devil stand at his right hand,* is used because Judas gave the works of the devil precedence over the works of God; for a person's right hand signifies something to which he gives priority, as the right hand is superior to the left.[12] Another psalm speaks of those who rate this world's prosperity higher than God and so reckon a race blessed if it enjoys such prosperity; and of them it most aptly says, *Their right hand is a hand that deals unjustly* (Ps 143(144):11), for in judging that race blessed which enjoys such temporal benefits, their mouths speak empty words, as the same psalm-verse declares. On the contrary, one whose mouth speaks truthfully is obliged to assert, against those who reckon such a people fortunate, that *blessed is the people whose God is the Lord* (Ps 143(144):15). It is the Lord, not the devil, who stands to the right of this people, as another psalm testifies: *I kept the Lord always before my eyes; he is at my right hand, and so I shall not be thrown off course* (Ps 15(16):8).

We conclude, then, that the devil stood at Judas' right hand when he gave greed precedence over wisdom, and money over his salvation, to such a point that he betrayed Christ. He ought to have been possessed by Christ, and if he had been he would not have been possessed by the devil. But by refusing to be Christ's possession he came to be possessed by the one whose works Christ came to destroy.[13]

9. *When he is judged, may he go out condemned,* for he was unwilling to be the kind of person who will be invited, *Enter into the joy of your Lord,* but preferred to be the one concerning whom the order will be given, *Cast him into outer darkness* (Mt 25:21.30).

---

11. See Acts 1:16-20.
12. See the Exposition of Psalm 16,8 and the note there.
13. See 1 Jn 3:8.

And may his very prayer be accounted sinful. This comes about because no prayer can be righteous unless offered through Christ, whom Judas sold by his monstrous sin. A prayer made otherwise than through Christ is not merely powerless to efface sin; it even becomes a sin. We may wonder when Judas could have prayed in such a fashion that his prayer was itself a sin. I think it must have been before he betrayed the Lord but when he was planning to do so, for at that stage he must have been already incapable of praying through Christ. After he had betrayed him he suffered remorse; and if he had prayed through Christ then, he would have begged forgiveness. If he had begged forgiveness, he would have had hope; if he had had hope, he would have hoped for mercy; if he had hoped for mercy, he would not have hanged himself in despair.

After saying, *When he is judged, may he go out condemned*, the psalm immediately adds, *And may his very prayer be accounted sinful*, because it wishes to explain why Judas could not have escaped his imminent condemnation by offering the prayer he had learned with his fellow disciples: *Forgive us our trespasses, as we forgive those who trespass against us.* But no prayer that Judas offered would be offered through Christ, whom he had chosen not to follow but to persecute;[14] hence the psalm adds, *May his very prayer be accounted sinful.*

10. *May his days be few.* By *his days* it means the days of his apostolate; they were few indeed, because even before the Lord's passion they were ended by Judas' crime and his death. But this raises the question, "What was to become of the sacred number twelve?" The Lord had good reason to choose twelve as his first apostles. In answer to the question the psalm promptly adds, *Let another man take over his sacred office.* It implies, "Let him be punished, and let that special number be made good." Anyone who wishes to know how this was achieved must read the Acts of the Apostles.[15]

Verses 9-15. The fate of Judas' family and property; he carries the guilt of his ancestors

11. *May his children become orphans, and his wife a widow.* This was the inevitable consequence of his death, that his children were orphaned and his wife widowed.

12. *May his children be driven out, may they wander and beg.* They are described as wandering because they will not know where to go, being stripped of protection. *Let them be cast out from their homes*: this expands the idea already suggested in *may they be driven out.* The following verses indicate how all this befell his wife and children.

---

14. *Quem noluit sequi, sed persequi.*
15. See Acts 1:15-26. This chapter seems to have furnished Augustine with his theme for the entire Exposition.

13. *May the creditor search out all his property, and strangers seize all his work.* Then to exclude the idea of any care being taken of his descendants, the psalm goes on, *Let there be no one to help him, no one to show mercy to his orphaned children.*

14. There might still be a chance, however, that even without helper or defender, even amid hardship and poverty, his children could grow up and keep the family going by producing children themselves. But no; the psalm continues, *May those born to him perish, and his name be blotted out in one generation.* Let no one generated by him generate in turn, but quickly vanish.

15. What does the next petition mean? *Let the iniquity of his fathers be remembered before the Lord, and his mother's sin not be effaced*: are we to understand that he will be held responsible for the sins of his forebears? Such sins are not laid at the door of anyone who has been transformed in Christ, because by not imitating the conduct of previous generations such a person has ceased to be their child. Yet it is written with absolute truth both that *I will visit the sins of the fathers upon the children* (Ex 20:5) and that *the father's soul is mine, and the child's soul is mine; the soul that sins is the one that will die* (Ezk 18:4). The latter saying refers to those who have been converted to God and do not imitate the wicked deeds of their parents; the prophet makes this fact perfectly clear by declaring that their ancestors' iniquities will constitute no obstacle to people who by their righteous living have proved themselves unlike their parents. But the other text, *I will visit the sins of the fathers upon the children*, is completed by the qualification, *the children who hate me*; that is, it applies to children who hate the Lord as their parents did. Imitation of good people earns us the deletion of our own sins, but those who imitate bad people make themselves liable not only to retribution for their own offenses but also to that incurred by the people they copy.

If Judas, therefore, had held fast to his vocation, neither his own past sins nor those of his parents would have been in any sense chargeable to him. But because he did not hold to his adoption into God's family but instead chose the iniquity of a past generation, the sins of his forebears returned to the Lord's sight, so that those sins too were punished in the person of Judas, and his mother's offenses were not effaced in him.

16. *Let them be over against the Lord always.* This means, "Let his ancestors and his mother *be over against the Lord always*," not in the sense of being opposed to the Lord but in the sense that the Lord should not forget their very wicked deeds when he punishes Judas for those sins too. The phrase, *over against the Lord*,[16] simply means *in the Lord's sight*,[17] which is how other trans-

---

16. *Contra Dominum.*
17. *In conspectu Domini.*

lators have rendered it, while others again translate *in the Lord's presence.*[18] The idea is the same as that expressed in another psalm: *You have placed our iniquities where you can see them* (Ps 89(90):8). The word *always* indicates that so great a crime should find no forgiveness either here or in the world to come.

Let their memory disappear from the earth, the memory of his ancestors and his mother. The psalm calls *their memory* that trace of themselves which is preserved in succeeding generations; it predicts that this will perish from the earth because Judas himself, along with his children who are like a memorial of his ancestors and his mother, died without leaving survivors, as has been said already. In one swift generation they were extinguished.

But are the dead conscious of, or affected by, what happens to their relatives?

17. Someone objects, "But can we really believe these consequences to have been part of Judas' punishment, that after his death his wife and children were reduced to poverty, and displaced, and thrown out of their homes; that a creditor sought out all his property, and strangers seized all his work; that no one supported or pitied his children, and that they all died off swiftly without issue? Can we really suppose that the dead experience any grief over things that happen to their nearest and dearest after their own demise? Do they even know about it, when their perception is engaged elsewhere in accordance with their deserts, whether good or bad?"

In reply I must say that it is an enormous question, and one that cannot be dealt with now because it needs extensive treatment, whether, or in what measure, or in what way, the spirits of the dead are aware of things that happen to us. But it can be said briefly that if the dead were entirely unconcerned with us, the Lord would not have represented the rich man who was suffering the torments of hell as saying, *I have five brothers; let them not come to this place of torment too* (Lk 16:28). Others may try to understand this differently; and certainly we must admit that even though the dead may know that their relatives are still alive (since they see them neither in the places of torment where the rich man was, nor in the place of rest where he recognized Lazarus and Abraham, albeit from afar), it does not follow that they must know what is happening to their dear ones and whether their fate is happy or sad. However, this I will assert: there are very few people disposed to take no care about what weal or woe may befall their relatives after their death—very few who will make no provision for it in their lifetime or think it a matter of no importance. On the other hand, there are many who do their best to ensure that when they are dead, things will go well with their relatives. A proof of this is the great store people set by making their

---

18. *Coram Domino.*

dying wishes known and leaving some kind of last will and testament. The only ones who make light of the continuance of their posterity through successive generations—the only ones, I mean, who do so in a way that can be admired—are those who make eunuchs of themselves in view of the kingdom of heaven,[19] or hope that their children will, and long for their offspring to be crowned with martyrdom so that none of their posterity may remain on earth. But all the rest, or nearly all, hope that after their deaths their descendants will survive, and their family not die out.

It was thus a terrible fate for Judas that after his tragic death his wife should remain so defenseless as a widow and his children as orphans that a creditor could search out all his property and strangers seize his work, that his family should be expelled from their homes and his children find no one to take pity on them, and that they should perish in one generation leaving no posterity. If the dead are conscious of all this, it is the culmination of their woes; if not, it is a fearful warning to the living.

Some may wonder how Judas could have had any property for a creditor to lay hands on or strangers to seize, when he was following the Lord like the other eleven disciples. We must suppose that he had left all he formerly possessed to his children and his wife, in such a way that he did not sincerely and steadfastly break the chain of desire for it. He must have pretended to sell all and distribute to the poor, while in fact he was behaving as Ananias did after the Lord's ascension.[20] He would not have been afraid that the Lord with divine insight might detect this, for he supposed the Lord to have been deceived when he abstracted from the common purse the offerings placed in it.[21]

An alternative interpretation: verses 6-15 can be applied to the Jewish people as a whole

18. Insofar as we are able, and the Lord helps us, let us now see how the preceding verses may apply equally well to the Jewish people, whose hostility to the Lord has persisted with unrelenting hatred. As we said earlier, Judas personifies that people, as Peter personifies the Church.

Set a sinner over him, and let the devil stand at his right hand. This is to be understood of the whole people in the same way as it was of Judas: having rejected Christ it became subject to the devil and refused the offer of salvation in favor of the devil's seductive offers of all sorts of earthly and debased advantages. *When it is judged, may it go out condemned,* for by persisting in its wickedness and unbelief it is storing up anger against itself, anger that will be

19. See Mt 19:5.
20. See Acts 5:1-5.
21. See Jn 12:6.

manifest on the day of God's just judgment, for he will render to each and all as their deeds deserve.[22] *And may its very prayer become sinful*, as it must do because it is not offered through the mediator between God and human beings, the man Jesus Christ, who is priest for ever according to the order of Melchizedek.[23] *May its days be few*: this must be understood of the Jewish kingdom, which did not last long after Christ's passion. *And let another take over its sacred office.* I think we are justified in regarding the Lord Christ himself as the Jewish people's sacred office, for he was born from the tribe of Judah according to the flesh, and the apostle says, *I maintain that Christ Jesus was a servant of the circumcised, to save the faithfulness of God and confirm the promises made to our fathers* (Rom 15:8). And the Lord himself declared, *I was not sent except for the lost sheep of the house of Israel* (Mt 15:24), since it was to them that he was bodily present. The wise men who came from the East acknowledged him in like terms: *Where is he who is born King of the Jews?* (Mt 2:2). The same truth was proclaimed by the title affixed to the cross; and not without good reason did Pilate rebuff those who wanted him to change it, retorting, *What I have written, I have written* (Jn 19:22). But *another* people, namely the Gentiles, took over the sacred office that had belonged to the Jews, the sacred office that was the Lord Christ himself. *May its children become orphans*: of those children it was prophesied, *The children of the kingdom will be thrown into the outer darkness* (Mt 8:12). They were orphaned by the loss of their kingdom, which was like the loss of a father; but we may well understand the verse to mean that they also lost God as their Father, because the Truth itself testifies that *anyone who does not have the Son does not have the Father either* (1 Jn 2:23). *May its wife become a widow.* The ordinary populace might be called the wife of the kingdom, since it was subject to the kings who dominated it; but when the kingdom was lost this populace was widowed. *May its children be driven out, may they wander and beg.* They were indeed driven out by the enemies that pressed upon them, and they wandered amid perils. The children of the Jewish realm were vanquished. What does begging imply if not to live in dependence on the pity of others? And this is how they live now, under the rulers of the Gentile nations to which they were deported. *Let them be cast out from their homes*: this has happened to them. *May the creditor search out all its property*, all the wealth which that people possesses. We can find no better application for this verse than to interpret it as a request that their sins, their debts, be not remitted, for they can be remitted only in Christ, whom the Jews have rejected. He it was who taught us to pray, *Forgive us our debts, as we forgive those who are in debt to us.* But the reference to *all its property* indicates that its whole way

---

22. See Rom 2:5-6.
23. See 1 Tm 2:5; Heb 5:6.

of life is in question, and so none of its debts, none of its sins, are to be remitted. *Let strangers seize all its work*: these strangers are the devil and his angels. None can lay up profits in heaven if they refuse to have Christ. *Let there be no one to help it*, for what helper can anyone expect, if Christ does not help? *Nor let there be anyone to show mercy to its orphaned children*, for once they had lost the kingdom, which symbolized their father, they were left bereaved. Alternatively, it could mean that they lost God by persecuting and hating his Son, and therefore they had no one to supply them with compassionate aid: they were bereft not in the matter of embarking on temporal life and sustaining it but in respect of their true life, life eternal. *May those born to them perish*, perish eternally. *May their name be blotted out in one generation*: because they were generated but never regenerated[24] they were blotted out in a single generation; if they had been willing to recognize the possibility of regeneration and seize their chance, they would not have been blotted out and denied that new birth. *Let the iniquity of its fathers be remembered before the Lord*; let the Lord visit upon that people as it obstinately continues in its malice even the punishment due to its ancestors' sins. He warned them of this: *You bear witness against yourselves, proving yourselves children of those who slew the prophets*. And shortly afterward he continued, *So that upon you may be all the innocent blood shed on earth, from the blood of Abel to the blood of Zechariah*. (Mt 23:31,35) *May their mother's sin not be effaced*: this means the sin of Jerusalem, which is in slavery along with her children,[25] which kills the prophets and stones those who are sent to her.[26] *Let them be over against the Lord always*. Let their iniquity and their sin be over against the Lord, let them never be swept out of the Lord's sight, but rather may God punish them for eternity. *Let their memory disappear from the earth*. God's earth is the place God cultivates, and God's cultivated field is the Church. From this earth their memory has disappeared, for though they were the natural branches of the olive, they were broken off in consequence of their unbelief.[27]

Verses 16-17. The poor man, Christ, is persecuted in the persons of his members

19. *Because he did not remember to show mercy*. We must say "he" if it means Judas; but it could also mean the Jewish people, in which case we should

---

24. In Christ.
25. See Gal 4:25.
26. See Mt 23:37.
27. See Rom 11:20-21.

translate, *Because it did not remember to show mercy*.[28] The latter is preferable, for even after killing Christ the Jewish people might at least have remembered in a spirit of repentance what it had done and shown mercy to his members instead of relentlessly persecuting them. But persecute it did, as the psalm goes on to say: *It persecuted an indigent beggar.* However, the reference could, even so, be to Judas' persecution of Jesus, because the Lord, though rich himself, did not disdain to become a poor man, that by his poverty we might become rich.[29] But did he ever beg? Yes, for he besought the Samaritan woman, *Give me a drink* (Jn 4:7); and on the cross he cried, *I am thirsty* (Jn 19:28).

I see no way, however, in which the following lines can be understood of our head, the Savior of his body, whom Judas persecuted; for after the accusation, *it persecuted an indigent beggar*, the psalm adds, *and sought to kill one who was pierced to the heart*.[30] Now a person is said to be pierced to the heart only when goaded by his sins and suffering the pain of repentance. This is why the expression is used of those who listened to the apostles after the Lord's ascension: *They were pierced to the heart* (Acts 2:37) because they had killed the Lord. But the most blessed Peter addressed them, and among other things urged them, *Repent, and let every one of you be baptized in the name of the Lord Jesus Christ, that your sins may be forgiven* (Acts 2:38). These hearers became members of him whose limbs they had nailed to a tree, but the Jewish people as a whole did not remember to show mercy. Instead, it persecuted the indigent beggar, but now in the persons of his members. This is the same thing as persecuting himself, for one day he will say, *What you did not do for one of the least of those who are mine, you did not do for me either* (Mt 25:45). When the psalm says that the Jews *sought to kill one who was pierced to the heart*, we must understand it, certainly, of Christ, but in his members.

Among the persecutors who sought to kill the one pierced to the heart was Saul, who consented to the killing of Stephen; for Stephen surely was pierced to the heart: he had been one of the many pierced with compunction at the apostles' preaching. But Saul did remember to show mercy; he who had been like a ravening wolf in the morning came back at evening to divide the prey.[31] He was pierced to the heart himself, so that in Saul's passion too the persecutors might harass a needy man, and seek to kill one who was pierced to the heart. Saul was on his way to do that himself—to persecute the indigent beggar, Christ, and to kill one pierced to the heart, though in Christ's members—when he heard the voice from heaven, *Saul, Saul, why are you persecuting me?* (Acts 9:4). Saul

---

28. The Latin is the same either way, *Judas* and *populus* both being masculine singular. After the long digression in section 18, where Augustine applied verses 6-15 to the Jews, he now returns to the double perspective, Judas and the Jewish race in parallel.
29. See 2 Cor 8:9.
30. *Compunctum corde.*
31. See Gn 49:27. Saul was of the tribe of Benjamin (see Phil 3:5), of whom this prophecy was uttered in the "Blessings of Jacob."

was pierced to the heart, and thereafter suffered in his own person the injuries he had been wont to inflict on those who were pierced to the heart.

Verses 18-20. The curse as clothing, water, oil, and belt to wrongdoers

20. The psalm goes on, *He made a curse his own, and on him it will fall*. Judas, to be sure, made a curse his own, both by stealing from the purse and by selling and betraying the Lord; but the Jewish people more explicitly made a curse its own when it shouted, *His blood be upon us, and upon our children!* (Mt 27:25) *He spurned blessing, and it will be far removed from him*. This can be referred to Judas, who rejected Christ, in whom is eternal blessing; but here again it is better to take it as the rejection of blessing by the Jewish people. The blind man whose eyes had been illumined by the Lord challenged them, *You don't want to be his disciples too, surely?* But his people spurned that blessing and treated it as a curse. They retorted, *You be his disciple yourself* (Jn 9:27.28), and the blessing was far removed from them, for it migrated to the Gentiles.

He put a curse on like a garment; this could apply either to Judas or to the people. *It poured into him like water*: a curse both outside and inside, then; outside like clothing, inside like water, for the sinner falls under the judgment of one who has power to destroy both body and soul in hell.[32] He can destroy the body outwardly and the soul inwardly.[33] *And it soaked into his bones like oil*. This suggests that the sinner enjoyed acting wickedly and claiming a curse as his own. Since the blessing is eternal life, the curse means eternal punishment. Sinful deeds give pleasure in the short term, like water gulped down, or oil for the bones, but the curse falls on the sinner in God's forecast of the torments that will follow. The curse is compared to oil in the bones because people consider themselves strong when they are allowed to do bad things with apparent impunity.

21. *Let it be like a garment that covers him*. The psalm has used the comparison with a garment already; why is it repeated? Can it be that a difference is implied between the earlier statement, *He put a curse on like a garment*, and this one, where, not content with merely putting it on, he covers himself completely with it? A person puts on a tunic, but is covered by a cloak. And what does a cloak signify, if not pretentiousness in the sight of other people? *And like a belt with which he is girded all the time*. People generally put belts around themselves when they want to be ready for work and not hampered by their clothes. A person who girds himself with a curse is therefore not one who does wrong on

---

32. See Mt 10:28.
33. Variant: "The body is outside, the soul within."

the spur of the moment but one who tackles a premeditated evil deed and is so thoroughly schooled in wrongdoing that he is always prepared for it. This is why the psalm says that the curse is *like a belt with which he is girded all the time.*

22. *This is the work of those who slander me in the Lord's presence.*[34] The psalm does not say their "recompense" but their *work*; for it is plain that under the figures of a garment, a covering, water, oil, and a belt it was alluding to the works that earn an eternal curse. There is not one Judas only, but many, and of all of them the psalm says, *This is the work of those who slander me in the Lord's presence.* Admittedly a plural is sometimes used in place of a singular, as when, after Herod's death, the gospel says, *They who sought the child's life are dead* (Mt 2:20). But who were more guilty of slandering Christ in the Lord's presence than they who scorned the very words of the Lord, denying that he was the one whom the law of the Lord and the prophets foretold? *And speak wickedly against my life,* he continues. They spoke against his life by denying that he had the power to rise again when he chose, though he claimed, *I have the power to lay down my life, and I have the power to take it up again* (Jn 10:18).

Verses 21-22. Christ prays in his sufferings

23. *And you, Lord, Lord, work with me.* Some interpreters think we should understand this to mean "act with mercy in my regard," and some translators have inserted these words. But the more carefully corrected codices read, *And you, Lord, Lord, work with me, as befits your name.* This gives a hint of a deeper meaning, one we should not omit to mention: the Son would be saying to his Father, *Work with me,* because the works of Father and Son are inseparable. Even if we do take *"work"* to mean "deal mercifully with me" (and there are some grounds for doing so, since the psalm continues, *For your mercy is sweet*), we can still very well take it to mean that the Father and Son together exercise mercy toward the vessels of mercy;[35] for the psalm did not say, "Act toward me," or "deal in my regard," or anything like that, but *work with me.*

We may also understand *work with me* to mean simply "help me." In everyday speech when something is turning out favorably for us we say, "It's working out for us." The Father did indeed help the Son, in the sense of God helping a man, inasmuch as the Son had taken the form of a servant. To this man God is Father, and to this servant the Lord too stands as father. But inasmuch as he is in the form of God, the Son needs no help, for he is equal to the Father and

---

34. *Qui detrahunt mihi apud Dominum.* The obvious meaning of the words is "slander me before the Lord," but toward the end of this section Augustine seems to read more into *mihi apud Dominum*: in slandering Christ they were speaking against the Lord in Christ, Christ in the Lord.

35. See Rom 9:23.

omnipotent, which is why he too is helper to human beings, *for as the Father raises the dead and gives them life, so too does the Son give life to whom he wills* (Jn 5:21). This does not mean that the Father raises some people, and the Son others, nor that Father and Son act differently; their action is identical in object and manner. The consequence is that inasmuch as the Son of God is a man, God—that is, the Father—raised him from the dead. He prays to God for this in another psalm: *Raise me up; then I will requite them* (Ps 40:11(41:10). But inasmuch as he is God, he raised himself, to which fact he bore witness by claiming, *Dismantle this temple, and in three days I will raise it up again* (Jn 2:19). The same truth is suggested here in our psalm for anyone who studies it carefully; the Lord commanded us to search the scriptures which bear witness to him,[36] not to skim them. Notice, then, that the psalm does not simply say, *You, Lord, Lord, work with me*; it says, *And you*. What does *and you* indicate? Surely "I and you."

The repetition, *Lord, Lord,* conveys the intense ardor of the one who prays, as elsewhere in the invocation, *O God, my God* (Pss 21:2(22:1); 62:2(63:1)). After the plea, *Work with me*, he adds, *as befits your name*, to emphasize the reality of grace, for human nature had no antecedent merits that could have entitled it to the sublime honor of being united with the Word in such a way that Word and flesh together, God and man, should be called the only-begotten Son of God. But this was effected so that what had perished might be sought by him who had created it, by the power of what had not perished. Accordingly the psalm confesses that *your mercy is sweet*.

24. *Set me free, for I am needy and poor.* Need and poverty spell weakness, and in weakness he was crucified.[37] *And my heart is in turmoil within me*: this refers to his agony as his passion drew near; he confessed, *My soul is sorrowful to the point of death* (Mk 14:34).

Verses 23-26. Christ prays about the weakness of his body

25. *Like a lengthening shadow I was swept away.* This directly signifies his death, for as the lengthening of a shadow presages nightfall, so does the mortality of the flesh lead to death. *I was shaken off like locusts.* I think it is preferable to refer this to what happened in his members, his faithful disciples.[38] To make the reference a little clearer, the psalm says not "like a locust," but *like locusts*, even though a crowd can be signified by a singular number, as when another psalm says, *He spoke, and there came the locust (Ps 104(105):34). But*

---

36. See Jn 5:39.
37. See 2 Cor 13:4.
38. As in the imprecatory verses of the psalm there were frequent transitions from the individual, Judas, to the Jewish people whom he personified, so in the later, more prayerful, verses there are transitions between the individual person of Christ and the faithful who are his members, though in this latter case the identification is far closer.

if the singular had been used, the allusion to his members would have been less clear. The faithful were shaken off when they were put to flight by persecutors, and the comparison with locusts was made either to suggest their great numbers or because they jumped from place to place.

26. *My knees were weakened from fasting.* We read that Christ our Lord kept a fast for forty days, but did hunger gain such a hold over him that his knees were weakened? Is it not better to refer this statement to his members, his saints? *And my flesh was changed, because of oil*: that means, because of spiritual grace. Christ's name derives from chrism, and chrism signifies anointing. His flesh was changed because of oil, but for the better, not the worse; it was changed from the ignominy of death into the glory of immortality as it rose.

The psalm said just now, *My knees were weakened from fasting*, and I think this signifies that those of his members who had seemed to be strong, because sustained by the presence of their bread, became weak when in Christ's passion that presence was withdrawn, weakened even to the point of denying him. This occurred in the case of Peter. But the Lord strengthened them and saved them from final defeat, and so he goes on, "*And my flesh was changed, because of oil*, that by my resurrection I might strengthen those who had failed at the time of my death, and by sending the Holy Spirit I might anoint them. If I had not departed, he could not have come to them." The Lord told us this explicitly: *He cannot come unless I go away* (Jn 16:7). And the evangelist recorded, *The Spirit had not yet been given, because Jesus was not yet glorified* (Jn 7:39): his flesh was not yet changed. The Spirit may be symbolized by water, which evokes cleansing or irrigation, or by oil, which suggests joy and the fire of charity, but the diversity of the signs does not mean that he is divided within himself or from himself. A lion is very different from a lamb, yet Christ is signified by both. The lion suggests one aspect, the lamb another, but Christ is one and the same. A lamb is not strong, a lion is not harmless;[39] but Christ is innocent like a lamb and strong like a lion. Finally we notice that in Isaiah Jesus Christ testifies, *The Spirit of the Lord is upon me, for the Lord has anointed me* (Is 61:1).

27. *I became a disgrace to them* by dying on the cross, for *Christ redeemed us from the curse of the law, becoming a curse for us* (Gal 3:13). *They saw me, and shook their heads.* This was because they saw him on the cross but did not see him risen; they saw him when his knees were weakened but not when his flesh had been changed.

28. *Help me, Lord my God, save me according to your mercy.* This prayer can be understood as offered by the whole Christ, head and body: by the head, who had taken the form of a servant, and by the body, that is, by the servants themselves. In them Christ could say to God, *Help me* and *Save me*, as he also said in them to Saul, *Why are you persecuting me?* (Acts 9:4) But the addition of the

---

39. *Innocens.*

words, *according to your mercy*, emphasizes that grace is purely gratuitous, not a payment due for works performed.

Verses 27-29. All that has happened accords with God's saving plan

29. *Let them know that this is your hand, and that you, Lord, have made it.*[40] The plea, *Let them know,* was for those who raged against him but for whom he prayed, for among those who looked on him as a disgrace, those who shook their heads at him in mockery, there were some who later believed in him. But people who suppose that God has a bodily form like that of human beings[41] should learn from this passage in what sense it is true that God has a hand. If what he makes, he makes with his hand, can he make that hand itself by hand? No? How then can the psalm say, *Let them know that this is your hand, and that you, Lord, have made it*? We must understand here that God's hand is Christ, as elsewhere scripture says, *To whom has the arm of the Lord been revealed?* (Is 53:1) This hand already existed, and yet we can also say that it was made by God, for *in the beginning was the Word, and the Word was made flesh* (Jn 1:1.14). He existed outside time in his godhead; and he was made for God from David's stock according to his flesh.[42]

30. *They will curse, and you will bless.* This shows how futile is the cursing of human beings who love emptiness and chase falsehood;[43] but when God blesses anyone, his blessing effectively does what it says. *May those who rise up against me be confounded.* If they attack me it can only be because they think they can overcome me in some way, but when I have been exalted above the heavens, and my glory pervades the whole earth,[44] they will be confounded. *But your servant will be glad*: either at the Father's right hand, if we refer it to Christ personally, or else in his rejoicing members, who are happy in hope amid their trials but will be happy for eternity when the trials are over.

31. *Let those who disparage me be clothed with shame*, embarrassed at having spoken scornfully about me. This could also be taken in a positive sense, because shame may lead to their correction. *And may they be covered with their confusion as with a double cloak.* The word used here, *diplois*, means a mantle of double thickness, and some translators have made this explicit. But clearly it

---

40. *Sciant quoniam manus tua haec, et tu, Domine, fecisti eam.* The more obvious meaning would be: "Let them know that your hand is at work here, and that you have done this, Lord," but Augustine takes the verb *facere* in its other sense of "make" and reads a different meaning in the verse.

41. Augustine had been confused about this himself in youth, imagining that the scriptural teaching that man is made in the image of God must imply that God has some kind of vast corporeal shape. See *Confessions* 6,3,4; 7,1,1.

42. See Rom 1:3.

43. See Ps 4:3(2).

44. See Pss 56:12(57:11); 107:6(108:5).

means that they should be discomfited both inwardly and outwardly, before God and before other people.

Verses 30-31. The praise offered by Christ and his Church

32. *I will vehemently*[45] *confess to the Lord with my mouth.* In Latin *nimis* generally implies excess, something more than ought to be present, just as *parum* means something less than is appropriate. But *nimis* is represented in Greek by εἰς, and the Greek text in this passage has not ἄγαν but σφόδρα. Some of our translators reflect this by putting *valde*[46] instead of *nimis*. Now if *nimis* is to be considered as equivalent to *valde*, it can quite suitably be used with reference to praising God, for the confession mentioned is praise. So the psalm continues, *And I will praise him in the midst of the great crowd.* Similarly in another psalm it is said, *In the midst of the Church I will sing your praise* (Ps 21:23(22:22). But if it is the Church that is singing, the body of Christ, how can the Church sing in the midst of the Church? And what about our present text? The great crowd of which it speaks is composed of Christ's members, so if they praise him, he himself is praising, since they are his limbs. But then how can he sing praise in the middle of the great crowd when the very fact that they are praising already means that he is praising? Perhaps we should understand it in this sense, that because he is with his Church until the end of the world,[47] the words, *in the midst of the great crowd*, mean that he is honored by this same multitude. We say that someone is central when special honor is paid to that person.

But the central part of a human being, we might say, is the heart. Our text could therefore mean, "I will praise him in the hearts of many people." Christ dwells in our hearts through faith,[48] and he therefore speaks of praising with his mouth, because he means that he praises with the mouth of his body, the Church. *The faith that issues in righteousness is in the heart, and the confession that leads to salvation is made with the mouth* (Rom 10:10).

33. *For he has taken his stand at the poor person's right hand.* It was said of Judas earlier in the psalm, *Let the devil stand at his right hand*, because Judas tried to enrich himself by selling Christ. But here it is the Lord who *has taken his stand at the poor person's right hand*, so that the Lord himself may be riches to this pauper. *He has taken his stand at the poor person's right hand* not to lengthen the present life for him, for that must end sooner or later; not to increase his wealth; not to fortify his bodily condition; not even to keep him safe for the time being; but *to save my soul from the persecutors.* A person's soul is saved

---

45. *Nimis.*
46. Vigorously, very much.
47. See Mt 28:20.
48. See Eph 3:17.

from persecutors if it does not consent to their wicked persuasions; and it does not consent to them if the Lord stands at the poor person's right hand to prevent him or her from succumbing under the very pressure of that poverty, which is a source of weakness. This assistance has been granted to the body of Christ in the experience of all the holy martyrs.

Exposition of Psalm 109

A Sermon to the People

A solemn introduction to this messianic psalm: the era of promises and the age of fulfillment

1. The Lord has appointed us ministers of his word and his sacrament, to serve you in the riches of his mercy. Relying on his bounty, we have undertaken to speak to you about the psalm that we have just sung, a psalm short indeed as to the number of its words but vast and weighty as to its content. May the Lord who has focused your attention also send us his help, to make us fit to study and expound it as well as we possibly can. Let your minds be alert and vigilant toward God.[1]

God established an era of promises and another era for the fulfillment of his promises. The time for promises was the age of the prophets down to that of John the Baptist. From his day, and thenceforth until the end, is the era of fulfillment. God is faithful and has put himself in our debt not because we have given him anything but because he has promised us so much. Yet even promising was not enough for him. He wanted to be bound in writing as well, so he gave us a signed copy of his promises, as it were, so that once he had begun to fulfill them we could study the scriptures and learn the sequence of their realization. Thus the era of prophecy was that in which things were promised for the future. We have often explained this. God promised us eternal salvation, a life of happiness with the angels that would never end, an unfading inheritance, everlasting glory, the delight of seeing his face, his holy home in heaven, and resurrection from the dead, after which we need never fear death again. This last is like his ultimate promise, to which all our hope aspires, so that when we reach it we shall look for nothing further nor ask anything more. Yet in his promises and predictions God has not kept silent even about the stages through which we shall reach that final destiny, for he has promised divinization to human beings, immortality to mortals, justification to sinners, glorification to the outcast. Whatever he has promised, he has promised to the undeserving, so that it should not be like wages pledged for work done but grace given gratis, as its name implies. Even the fact that a person lives righteously (in the measure that any man or woman can) is not

---

1. This psalm has been recognized as formally messianic in both Jewish and Christian tradition. Augustine's solemn tone in the introduction prepares his hearers to consider its central importance.

attributable to human merit but to divine generosity. Nobody lives a just life except as a consequence of being justified—that is, rendered just—and a human being is made just only by him who can never be unjust. As a lamp is not kindled from itself, so no human soul grants light to itself. It can only cry to God, *You, Lord, will light my lamp* (Ps 17:29(18:28)).

2. The kingdom of heaven has been promised to sinners: not to those who persist in sin but to those who have been freed from sin and live for righteousness.[2] Yet they can do this only, as we have said, when they are aided by grace and justified by him who is always just. That God should lavish so much care on human beings seemed incredible, and there are those today who despair of divine grace. They are unwilling to give up their foul way of life and turn to God, that they may be justified by him, receive his forgiveness, see all their sins destroyed, and begin to live justly in him who has never lived unjustly. They have a most baneful idea about themselves, maintaining that God takes no notice of human affairs, and that the designer and ruler of this world cannot be concerned with how any mortal lives on earth. Thus a human being, made by God, thinks that God takes no account of human beings![3]

If we could speak directly to someone of this persuasion, if he were prepared to give us access initially to his ears and then to his heart, if he were willing to offer no resistance and not to rebuff one who sought him when he was lost but would let himself be found, we could say to him, "Ask yourself this question, mortal creature: if God took the trouble to bring you into being, how can he take no account of you now that you exist? Why do you think you are not counted in the array of created beings? Do not believe[4] any deceiver; in your creator's sight all the hairs on your head are numbered.[5] In the gospel the Lord gave this assurance to his disciples, to dispel their fear of death and convince them that when they died no part of them would perish. They were terrified about the fate of their souls after death, but he gave them security even about their hair. If a person's hair is to survive, can you suppose that his soul will perish?"

However, brothers and sisters, what God had promised did seem incredible to men and women:[6] that out of the mortality, the squalor, the vileness, the weakness, and the dust and ashes of the human condition we should one day be equal to the angels of God. He was therefore not content to provide us with a written guarantee of his promises to help us believe in him. He even appointed a mediator to establish his good faith: not some nobleman, nor an angel, nor an archangel, but his only Son. Through his Son God could show us the way whereby he

---

2. See Rom 6:18.

3. The opinion was widespread among ancient philosophers, notably the Epicureans.

4. Variant: "Do not yield to. . . ."

5. See Mt 10:30. The Latin has an assonance not reproducible in English: *Noli credere/cedere seductori; capilli tui numerati sunt conditori.*

6. He is returning to the charge of incredibility mentioned near the beginning of section 2.

meant to lead us to the destiny he had promised us. But he wanted to do more than simply show us the way. It would not have been enough for God only to appoint his Son as a signpost to the way; he made him the Way, that you might walk in him who guides you.[7]

3. He promised that we would come to him, to that immortal life no tongue can describe, to equal status with his angels. But how far off were we? How high above was he, how low were we? He was in highest heaven; we lay in the depths, hopeless. We were ill, with no prospect of health. God sent the physician, but the patient did not recognize him, for if *they had known him, they would never have crucified the Lord of glory* (1 Cor 2:8). Yet the sick man's very action in killing the doctor was his means of healing, for the doctor who came to see the patient was killed to cure him. To those who would believe he intimated the reality of his being as God and man: the God by whom we were made, and the man by whom we were made anew. Something was visible in him, something else hidden. What was hidden was far more excellent than what appeared, but that more excellent substance could not be seen. Through Christ's visible nature the patient began to be cured, that he might later become capable of a vision that was withheld only for a time, not refused and put for ever beyond our reach.

The only Son of God therefore decided to come to human beings, to become a man himself by taking our humanity, to die, to rise again, to ascend into heaven, to take his seat at the Father's right hand, and to fulfill among the Gentiles the promises he had made. After fulfilling them there he means to implement his final promise: that he will come again and demand the interest on the gifts he gave,[8] separate the vessels of wrath from the vessels of mercy,[9] and render to the wicked what he threatened and to the just what he pledged. It was necessary that all this should be prophesied, announced in advance. We needed to be told so that our minds might be prepared. He did not will to come so suddenly that we would shrink from him in fear; rather are we meant to expect him as the one in whom we have believed.

Our psalm deals with these promises. It speaks prophetically of our Lord and Savior Jesus Christ with such certainty and clarity that we cannot doubt that it is he who is proclaimed here. Still less can we doubt it if we are Christians, who already believe the gospel. When our Lord and Savior Jesus Christ challenged the Jews to tell him whose son the Messiah would be, and they replied, *David's*, he immediately turned the argument against them: *Then how is it that David in spirit calls him Lord, saying, The Lord said to my Lord, Sit at my right hand, until I put your enemies under your feet? If David in spirit calls him Lord, how can he be David's son?* (Mt 22:43-45) From this verse our psalm begins.

---

7. A beautiful Augustinian epigram: *ut per illum ires regentem te, ambulantem per se.*
8. See Mt 25:14-28.
9. See Rom 9:22-23.

Verse 1. Christ is David's son and David's Lord

4. *The Lord said to my Lord, Sit at my right hand, until I make your enemies into your footstool.* As we approach the psalm we must begin by considering that question put to the Jews by the Lord. If the same question were put to us, if we were asked whether we confess or deny the truth, it is unthinkable that we would deny it. If we are asked, "Is Christ the son of David or not?" we cannot say, "No," for that would be to contradict the gospel. Matthew's gospel begins, *A book of the descent of Jesus Christ, the son of David* (Mt 1:1). The evangelist states his intention of tracing the genealogy of Jesus Christ, son of David. Hence when Christ asked the Jews whose son they believed the Messiah would be, they answered correctly, *David's.* The gospel accords with their reply; this is not just a notion entertained by the Jews but the faith of Christians. I can find other supporting evidence. The apostle speaks of Jesus as the one who *was made for God from David's line, according to the flesh* (Rom 1:3), and to Timothy he writes, *Remember Jesus Christ, risen from the dead, born of David's lineage, whom my gospel proclaims.* Of this gospel he goes on to say, *In its service I am laboring even to the point of being fettered like a criminal, but God's word is not bound.* (2 Tm 2:8,9) The apostle was laboring in the service of his gospel to the point of being fettered for it, so earnest was he to spread the good news which he was preaching to the nations and on which he was expending all his energies for their sake. He who had been like a ravening wolf in the morning was distributing the prey when evening fell.[10] For his witness to the gospel he labored even to enduring chains; but what was this gospel? *Jesus Christ, risen from the dead, born of David's lineage.*

That was the gospel for which Paul worked so hard, and yet Christ questioned it; moreover, when the Jews gave him an answer conformable to the apostle's preaching he seemed almost to contradict them: *Then how is it that David in spirit calls him Lord?* And he cited the testimony of our psalm: *The Lord said to my Lord. . . . If David in spirit calls him Lord, how can he be David's son?* At this challenge the Jews fell silent, unable to find any further retort. They did not seek after him as the Lord, for they did not recognize him as David's descendant either.

For our part, brothers and sisters, let us both believe and speak the truth in the matter, for *the faith that issues in righteousness is in the heart, and the confession that leads to salvation is made with the lips* (Rom 10:10). Let us believe and proclaim that he is both David's son and David's Lord. Let us not be ashamed of David's descendant, lest we have to face the wrath of David's Lord.

---

10. See Gn 49:27; compare Exposition of Psalm 108,19 and the note there.

The Eternal made himself transient in Christ's mysteries

5. When a couple of blind men had the good sense to hail Jesus by this title as he passed by, they deserved to receive their sight. He was walking past, and the blind men heard the sound of the passing crowd. Recognizing with their ears what they could not yet see with their eyes, they shouted loudly, *Take pity on us, son of David!* (Mt 20:30) The crowds rebuked them and told them to be quiet, but in their longing to see the light the blind men shouted down the crowds' protests. They brought Jesus up short in his walking and deserved to receive the light from him when he touched them; for they kept saying to him while he passed by, *Have pity, son of David*, but when he stood still, and heard that they had silenced the clamor of the objectors, he asked them, *What do you want me to do for you?* They answered, *Lord, let us see.* (Mt 20:32-33) He touched them and opened their eyes, and they saw him face to face, this man of whom they had been aware as he passed by. From this episode we learn that the Lord did something transitory[11] but that there is something else that is stable. I repeat, there are transient acts performed by the Lord, and there is the stable reality of the Lord. The Lord's transit was accomplished through the Virgin's childbearing and the incarnation of the Word, through his growth to maturity, his display of miracles, and his endurance of sufferings, through his death, his resurrection, and his ascension into heaven. All these acts were transient; for Christ is not being born now, nor is he still dying, or still rising, or still ascending into heaven. You can see, can't you, that these deeds unfolded in a temporal sequence, and that as the ages pass they have represented something transient to us wayfarers, encouraging us not to stop on the way but to press on toward our homeland? The two blind men were sitting by the road; they heard the Lord passing by; they stopped him by shouting. On this world's journey the Lord made himself transient, and this transient character was his as son of David. That is why the blind petitioners cried out to their passing Lord, *Take pity on us, son of David!* They implied, "We recognize the son of David in this passer-by; we understand that in his passing he has become the son of David." Let us learn the same lesson and confess him to be the son of David so that we too may deserve to be illuminated. We hear of him as the transient son of David, and are illuminated by David's Lord.[12]

---

11. *Transitorium*, echoing the participle *transiens* which has been repeatedly used in the preceding lines. The idea of "passage" and "wayfaring" runs through the section. Compare Augustine's meditation on Christ's plunging into the ever-passing stream of human life in the last section of this sermon.

12. The theme of "passing" or "transitoriness" has been elaborated at different levels. 1) Jesus is passing by when hailed by the blind men as son of David; when he stops, he gives them sight and light. 2) Jesus lived through a temporal sequence of events in his birth, life, ministry, death, and glorification; these events are transient in the sense of unrepeatable. 3) To pilgrims, wayfarers through this world, Christ's mysteries are dynamic, leading us toward our homeland. 4) Underlying the temporal, transient character of Christ's acts is the "stable" reality of the Lord who illuminates believers in faith and baptism.

The Christian response to the question that silenced the Jews

6. Now recall how our master questioned the Jews and how they refused to answer because they did not want to be his disciples. What about ourselves: if he questioned us, how would we answer him? The Jews failed under this interrogation, but Christians ought to profit from it; they should be not disconcerted but instructed. The Lord did not put his questions because he was seeking information; he was asking as a teacher asks. But the wretched Jews would want to say, "You tell us." They preferred to blow themselves up in proud silence until they burst rather than be taught through humble confession.

So let our master speak to us, and let us see what reply we shall make to his question. *What do you think of Christ? Whose son is he?* (Mt 22:42) Let us answer exactly as the Jews did but not stick where the Jews stuck. Let us call to mind the gospel that we believe, the *book of the descent of Jesus Christ, the son of David.* We must not forget under the stress of interrogation that Christ is the son of David, as the apostle reminds us: "Now, Christian, *remember Jesus Christ, risen from the dead, born of David's lineage.*" Let us face the interrogation and give our answer. *What do you think of Christ? Whose son is he?* Let Christian tongues reply unanimously, *David's.* Then let our teacher take the argument further by reminding us of another passage: *Then how is it that David in spirit calls him Lord? The Lord said to my Lord, Sit at my right hand, until I put your enemies under your feet.* How can we answer, unless we learn from you? But now that we have learned, we give him our response: in the beginning you were the Word, and as the Word you were with God, and you, the Word, were God. All things were made through you, and in this we know you to be David's Lord. But because of our weakness, because we lay prostrate, hopeless flesh, you, the Word, were made flesh in order to dwell among us;[13] and in this we know you to be David's son. Being in the form of God you certainly deemed it no robbery to be God's equal: lo, you are David's Lord. But you emptied yourself and took on the form of a slave:[14] lo, you are David's son. When you put to us the question, *Whose son is he?* you were not denying this but seeking to draw from us a confession of how it came about. *David calls him Lord,* you say. *How can he be David's son?* I am not repudiating that title, says Christ, but tell me how it came to be mine.

The Jews should have found the answer in the scriptures which they read but did not understand. If under Christ's questioning they had remembered it, would they not have said to him, "How can you ask that? *Lo, a virgin shall conceive and bear a son, and they shall give him the name, Emmanuel, which means "God with us"* (Is 7:14; Mt 1:23). A virgin will be with child, a virgin from David's

---

13. See Jn 1:1-3.14.
14. See Phil 2:6-7.

line will bear a son so that the child will be David's son; for Joseph and Mary were of the house and kindred of David.[15] This virgin gave birth to him, that he might be David's son. Yet to him whom she bore they *shall give the name, Emmanuel, God with us*, and there you have David's Lord.

The glorification of the son of David

7. The psalm itself will perhaps give us some hint about this puzzling matter: how Christ can be both David's son and David's Lord. Let us listen to it and study it; let us knock with devotion at its door and wrest the answer from it by our love. David himself states the fact, and not even the Lord himself can gainsay it: *David in spirit calls him Lord*, says Christ. What then does David say about Christ? This, after all, is *A Psalm for David himself*; that is the title it bears, a simple, unambiguous title that contains no knotty points or difficulty. What does David say, then? *The Lord said to my Lord, Sit at my right hand, until I make your enemies into your footstool*. The last phrase is also rendered as *under your feet*, for that is where a footstool is placed. *The Lord said to my Lord*, says David. David heard this said, he heard it in spirit, in a place where we have not heard what he heard, though we have believed what he who did hear it has said and written. Hear it he undoubtedly did in some secret place of truth, in some sanctuary of mysteries, where the prophets heard in a hidden manner what they preached publicly. There David heard what he proclaimed with great confidence: *The Lord said to my Lord, Sit at my right hand, until I make your enemies into your footstool*. Now we know that since his resurrection from the dead and his ascension into heaven Christ has been seated at the Father's right hand. This is already the case: we have not seen him there, but we have believed it; we read it in the scriptures, we have heard it preached, and we hold firm to it with our faith. This means that in virtue of the very fact that Christ was David's son, he became David's Lord. You find this surprising? But the same thing happens in human affairs. Suppose a man's son becomes king while the father remains an ordinary citizen, will the son not be lord over his father? And something even more remarkable may happen: not only is a commoner's son who has become king thereafter sovereign over his father, but when a layman's son becomes a bishop, he becomes a father to his father. From the fact that Christ took flesh, that he died in the flesh, rose in the same flesh, and in that same flesh ascended into heaven and sits at the Father's right hand, it follows that in the same flesh that was so honored, so glorified, and so wonderfully transfigured into heavenly apparel, he is both David's son and David's Lord. The apostle testifies, concerning this dispensation whereby Christ made his passover, that God *raised*

---

15. See Lk 1:27.32; 2:4.

him from the dead, and gave him a name above every other name, so that at the name of Jesus every knee should bow, in heaven, on earth or under the earth (Phil 2:9-10). This passage states that God *gave him a name above every other name*: gave it to Christ in his manhood, to Christ who in the flesh died, rose, and ascended, *gave him a name above every other name, so that at the name of Jesus every knee should bow, in heaven, on earth or under the earth*. Where then could David be, outside Christ's lordship? Whether David be in heaven, on earth, or under the earth, Christ will be his Lord, for he is Lord of all things, heavenly, earthly, and infernal.[16]

Let David then rejoice with us, David who is honored by his son's birth and set free by his son's lordship. Let him declare with joy, as we hear him with joy, *The Lord said to my Lord, Sit at my right hand, until I make your enemies your footstool.*

Believing in what we do not yet see

8. Be seated, be enthroned, says the psalm, but not only on high: be enthroned in a hidden way as well; shine out gloriously to reign, but hide yourself to be believed in. How could our faith deserve a reward if its object were not hidden? The reward of faith is to see what we believed in before we saw. Scripture trumpets, *The one who lives by faith is just* (Hb 2:4; Rom 1:17). We can therefore never be justified through faith unless we believe in something hidden but preached to us and by believing attain to vision. *How great, how immense, is your sweetness, Lord, which you have hidden from*[17] *those who fear you!* You have hidden it, then; does that mean your believers are left so? By no means, for *you have brought it to perfection for those who hope in you* (Ps 30:20(31:19)). This is the wonderful thing about the mystery of Christ's enthronement at God's right hand: his presence is hidden that he may be believed in and withdrawn that he may be hoped for, because *in hope we have been saved. But if hope is seen, it is hope no longer, for when someone sees what he hopes for, why should he hope for it?* These are the words of the apostle. You are quite familiar with them, of course, but I am recalling them for the sake of those less well instructed. What does the apostle say? *In hope we have been saved. But if hope is seen, it is hope no longer, for when someone sees what he hopes for, why should he hope for it? But if we hope for what we do not see, we wait for it in patience.* (Rom 8:24-25) Because *we hope for what we do not see, and wait for it in patience,* you *have brought it to perfection for those who hope in you.*

This is important, dearly beloved, so concentrate on what I am about to say. Because our righteousness comes through faith, and our hearts are cleansed by

---

16. In other words, Christ is David's Lord not only in his godhead but also in his glorified humanity.
17. See Exposition 4 of Psalm 30,6 and the note there.

faith so that we may be fit to see what we have believed in (for both these state-ments are made in scripture: *Blessed are the pure of heart, for they shall see God* (Mt 5:8), and *God cleansed their hearts by faith* (Acts 15:9))—because, as I say, the righteousness that comes from faith means believing in what you do not see and by the merit of your faith attaining to vision in due time, the Lord stated in the gospel, when promising the Holy Spirit, *He will convict the world concerning sin, and righteousness, and judgment* (Jn 16:8). Concerning what sin? And what righ-teousness? And what judgment? The Lord did not leave the answers to human conjecture; he himself went on to explain what he meant: *Of sin, inasmuch as they have not believed in me* (Jn 16:9). What a lot of other sins the Jews committed! Yet the Lord singled this one out as though it had been the only one: *Of sin, inasmuch as they have not believed in me.* This is the sin of which he says elsewhere, *If I had not come, they would not be in sin* (Jn 15:22). What can he have meant by that: *If I had not come, they would not be in sin*? Did you come to righteous people, Lord, and turn them into sinners? No, but he passed over all the other sins, which might have been forgiven through faith, and mentioned this one sin, because if they had not committed that one, they could have found pardon for all the rest. *Of sin, inas-much as they have not believed in me*, he said, and *if I had not come, they would not be in sin.* They fell into sin precisely in this: that he came and they did not believe in him, whereas if they had not fallen into that sin all their other sins could have been met by the grace of forgiveness, obtained through faith. This is why he said, *Of sin, inasmuch as they have not believed in me.*

He continued, *Of righteousness, because I am going to the Father, and you will see me no longer* (Jn 16:10). Righteousness for us depends on your going to the Father and your disciples seeing you no more, because this kind of righteous-ness is the outcome of faith. *The one who lives by faith is just*, and we live by faith only when we do not see that in which we believe. Living by faith is essential to righteousness, and none of us can live by faith unless we are unable to see the object of our faith. The Lord wanted to establish this righteousness among us by making it possible for us to believe without seeing, and so he said, *Of righteous-ness, because I am going to the Father, and you will see me no longer.* Your righ-teousness will consist in this, he tells us, that you believe in him whom you do not see, that being cleansed by faith you may later, on the day of resurrection,[18] see him in whom you have believed.

Psalm 2 and Psalm 109: both messianic prophecies

9. Christ is seated at the right hand of God; the Son is seated at the Father's right hand but hidden from us, so let us believe. But notice, God says two things

---

18. Many codices omit "on the day of resurrection."

in the psalm. He says, *Sit at my right hand*, but adds, *until I make your enemies your footstool*, that is to say, "Until I put them under your feet." You do not see Christ sitting at the Father's right hand, but this at least you can see: how his enemies are being made into his footstool. Since the latter prophecy is being visibly fulfilled, believe that the hidden one is too. Which enemies are being made into his footstool? Surely those who devise futile schemes, who are challenged in another psalm, *Why have the nations raged, and the peoples devised futile schemes? The kings of the earth have arisen, and the rulers conspired together, against the Lord and against his Christ. Let us burst their chains asunder*, they said, *and throw their yoke away from us*; let them have no dominion over us, nor subject us to themselves. But *he who lives in heaven will laugh them to scorn.* (Ps 2:1-4)[19] You,[20] whoever you are, were once his enemy; you will find yourself under his feet, either adopted or subjugated. Which place will you have under the feet of the Lord your God? The choice is yours, for you must have either grace or punishment.

Christ sits, then, at God's right hand until his enemies are thrust beneath his feet. This is happening; the process is going forward; it may be slow but it never ceases. Though the nations have raged and the peoples have devised futile schemes, though the kings of the earth have arisen and the rulers conspired together against the Lord and against his Christ, what will their raging, their scheming, or their conspiracies against Christ achieve? Will they ever frustrate the fulfillment of that promise, *I will give you the nations as your heritage, and the ends of the earth for your possession* (Ps 2:8)? Of course not. It will certainly be fulfilled, in spite of their raging and their futile schemes: *I will give you the nations as your heritage, and the ends of the earth for your possession.* The schemes they devise are futile; but it was no one mouthing futile and empty plans who promised, *I will give you the nations as your heritage, and the ends of the earth for your possession*; no, for *the Lord said* it *to me* (Ps 2:7). Equally in our present psalm we can proclaim that the Lord said it, not any unauthorized speaker, not those who rage or devise futile schemes, but the Lord, who *said to my Lord, Sit at my right hand, until I make your enemies into your footstool.* Let them rage, let them devise their futile schemes: will not this promise too be fulfilled? Most certainly it will. *Their memory has perished with an uproar*: it is a different psalm speaking here, but not a different spirit:[21] *Their memory has perished with an uproar, and the Lord abides for ever* (Ps 9:7-8(6-7)). He who abides for ever, while their memory vanishes noisily, he himself *said to my Lord,*

---

19. Augustine's linking of Psalm 2 with Psalm 109(110) is in full accord with Christian interpretation down to the present day.
20. Singular.
21. Or perhaps "Spirit."

Sit at my right hand. Christ sits at the Father's right hand until God makes all his enemies into his footstool.

Verse 2. "Beginning from Jerusalem": Christ's paschal victory inaugurates his temporal reign

10. *From Zion will the Lord send forth your scepter of power.* It is very obvious, brothers and sisters, that the prophet is not speaking about Christ's eternal sovereignty in the bosom of the Father, who is Lord of all the things he created through his Word. No, clearly that sovereignty is not meant here, for when does the Word ever not reign as God with God? Scripture proclaims, *To the King of ages, invisible, immortal, to God alone be honor and glory for ever and ever* (1 Tm 1:17). To whom is this ascribed? *To the King of ages, to God alone be honor and glory for ever and ever.* Who is this King of ages? He who is *invisible, immortal.* Inasmuch as Christ is invisible and immortal with the Father, being his Word, his Strength, his Wisdom, God with God, he through whom all things were made, he is the King of ages. But with regard to the transient economy of salvation,[22] whereby he called us to eternity through the medium of his flesh, his reign begins with us Christians, though it will have no end.

His enemies are therefore being put under his feet while he sits enthroned at the Father's right hand, as we have explained. This is a process, and it will go on inexorably until the end of time. Let no one say that what has been begun cannot be completed. You surely do not fear that the end of it will not be reached? The Almighty has begun it, and the Almighty has promised to bring to completion what he has begun. But at what point did it begin? *From Zion will the Lord send forth your scepter of power.* Zion is Jerusalem. Now listen to the Lord's words: *It was necessary for Christ to suffer, and to rise from the dead on the third day* (Lk 24:46). From that moment of his resurrection he is seated in his own place, at the Father's right hand. And once he is enthroned there, what process begins? What has to happen, for his enemies to be subjected beneath his feet? Listen to his own words as he teaches and explains it: *And for repentance and forgiveness of sins to be preached in his name throughout all nations, beginning from Jerusalem* (Lk 24:47), because *from Zion will the Lord send forth your scepter of power.* The kingdom where he reigns mightily is called *your scepter of power*; as the other psalm predicts, *You will rule them with an iron rod* (Ps 2:9). *From Zion will the Lord send forth your scepter of power* because the preaching of his lordship will begin from Jerusalem.

22. See Augustine's meditation on transience in section 5 above.

11. When the scepter of his power has been sent forth from Zion, what will its effects be? *Have dominion in the midst of your foes.* This must come first, your *dominion in the midst of your foes,* amid the raging Gentiles. This must refer to the first stage, because he will scarcely be exercising his sway amid his enemies later, will he, when his saints have received their glorious reward and the impious their condemnation? In any case, is there any need to marvel that he will indeed be Lord of all then, when the just are reigning with him for ever, and the wicked are burning in eternal punishment? Would that need to be remarked upon? But now it is a different matter. Now you reign amid your enemies, Lord: now in this transient age while the centuries roll on, while mortal humanity propagates itself and the generations succeed each other, while the torrent of time slips by, now is the scepter of your power sent forth from Zion that you may hold sway in the midst of your enemies. Be Lord of them: be Lord amid pagans, Jews, heretics, and false brethren. Be Lord of them; be Lord, you son of David who are also David's Lord, be Lord amid pagans, Jews, heretics, and false brethren. *Have dominion in the midst of your foes.* We do not understand this verse aright unless we see it being realized already. Sit at the right hand of God, but stay hidden that we may have faith in you, until the times of the Gentiles have run their course.[23] Scripture attests the fact, for you are he *whom heaven must receive until the age of the Gentiles is complete* (Acts 3:21; Lk 21:24). If you were to rise again, you had to die; in order to ascend, you rose from the dead; and therefore you died in order to take your seat at the Father's right hand: all this originated in your death.[24] The splendor of your glory springs from your humility. Now that you are enthroned at the right hand of the Father, the era of the Gentiles is running its course, and all your enemies are being turned into your footstool. To bring about your final victory you will first establish your authority in the midst of your foes, for to this end will the Lord *send forth your scepter of power* from Zion.

But if you were to be put to death and through your death blot out the written record of sins,[25] and if repentance and remission of offenses were to be preached throughout all nations, beginning from Jerusalem, it was necessary that blindness should fall upon the Jews. The blindness of some served for the illumination of others, for *blindness fell upon part of Israel that the full tally of the Gentiles might come in, and so all Israel be saved* (Rom 11:25-26). The blindness that afflicted part of Israel killed you; but after being killed you rose again and with your blood washed away the sins of the nations. Seated at the Father's right hand you have gathered from every quarter of the world those who suffer and fly to you for refuge.

---

23. See Lk 21:24. In the following sentence Augustine attaches this text to his quotation from Acts, as though they belonged together. Both passages are expressions of eschatological hope.
24. The unity of the paschal mystery is stressed.
25. See Col 2:14.

Blindness fell upon part of Israel, and that blindness was allowed so that *the full tally of the Gentiles might come in, and so all Israel might be saved*, and all your enemies become your footstool. This is being verified now. What of the future?

Verse 3. The economy of salvation: God's acts in Christ in the past and present, and promised for the future

12. *With you is the beginning, on the day of your strength*. What is this day of his strength? When was the beginning with him? What beginning is meant, and how could the beginning be with him, when he is himself the beginning? May the Lord help us with these questions, so that I may not become confused as I explain it, nor you as you listen.

I see what has been effected already, and along with you I see it with the eyes of faith. I also see with my bodily eyes what is even now taking place. Again with the eyes of faith I, like you, am looking forward to what will come to pass in the future. Now, what has been done already, what is taking place now, and what will happen later? Christ suffered, he died, he rose on the third day, and, as we know, he ascended on the fortieth day to heaven, where he sits at the right hand of the Father. All this is done; we did not see it, but we believe it.

What is taking place now? His scepter of power has been sent forth from Zion, and he holds sway in the midst of his enemies. This is happening now, the process is under way. In the form of a servant his servants once beheld him, present with them; in the form of a servant his servants now believe in him, in his absence. We believe as much about him in his servant-form as we are capable of taking in, given our own condition as servants. What we believe is babies' milk, adapted to our age; for it is bread processed through his flesh.[26] That *in the beginning was the Word* is the bread of angels; but to make it possible for humans to eat the bread of angels[27] the creator of angels was made man. Thus the incarnate Word became assimilable to us. We would not have had the strength to feed on him if the Son who is the Father's equal had not emptied himself, taking on the form of a slave, and been born bearing the human likeness, sharing the human lot.[28] To make it possible for us to receive him who is beyond the power of mortals to receive, the immortal one became mortal, that through his death he might make us immortal. He gave us something to be verified by the senses, something to be believed in, and something to be seen hereafter. To his own contemporaries he offered his form as servant, and he offered it not only for their

---

26. A favorite image of Augustine's inspired by the "spiritual milk" of 1 Pt 2:2, and the infants' milk dispensed by Paul in 1 Cor 3:1-2. As a mother's body processes adult food to produce milk for her baby, so Christ's humanity made truth that would otherwise have been beyond our grasp assimilable to human minds.
27. See Ps 77(78):25.
28. See Phil 2:6-7.

eyes to see but even for their hands to grasp.[29] In that same form he ascended to heaven, commanding us to believe in what he granted them to see. Yet we too have something we can see, for while they beheld the sending forth of his scepter of power from Zion, we behold him exercising dominion in the midst of his enemies. All this, brothers and sisters, belongs to the economy of his self-revelation in the form of a servant, a revelation which we can bear now as his servants, but can love as his children-to-be. The unchangeable Truth who is the Word of God, God-with-God, the Word through whom all things were made, abides in himself yet imparts newness to all.[30] If we are to contemplate unchangeable Truth we need great purity, perfect purity of heart, and this can be gained only through faith.

The Truth revealed himself in the form of a servant, but delayed his self-revelation in the form of God. Speaking still in the form of a servant he made this promise to his servants, *Whoever loves me will be loved by my Father, and I will love him, and will show myself to him* (Jn 14:21). To those who could already see him, he promised to show himself. What were they looking at? What was he promising? They were looking at the form of a servant, but he was promising them the form of God. *I will show myself to you*, he said. To this glory he is leading his kingdom, the kingdom that is being gathered to him now, as this world goes on its way. It is being led to a vision unutterable, of which unbelievers will not be found worthy. Remember too that the servant-form in which he was present during his life on earth was seen also by unbelievers: those who believed saw it, but those who killed him saw it too. You need not rate too high the privilege of seeing that servile form: his friends saw it and his foes saw it; some who saw it slew him, others who did not see it have believed.[31] Here in his humble lifetime his servant-form was seen by the good and the wicked, and on judgment-day too both good and wicked will see it. This we know, for as the Lord was borne up to heaven before the gaze of his disciples, a prophecy was trumpeted by angelic voices: *Why stand here gazing up to heaven, men of Galilee? This Jesus will come again, even as you have seen him go.* (Acts 1:11) *Even as you have seen him*, notice: even as you have seen him, in the same form. Elsewhere it was prophesied of the wicked, *They will gaze on him whom they pierced* (Zech 12:10; Jn 19:37). They will see him coming as judge whom they mocked when he was judged. On judgment day his servile form will be plainly seen by just and unjust, by the good and the wicked, by believers and unbelievers alike. What is it, then, that the wicked will not see? Something there must be. While of them it was said, *They will gaze on him whom they pierced*, of these

---

29. See 1 Jn 1:1.
30. See Wis 7:27.
31. See Jn 20:29.

same people it was also said, *Away with the impious, he shall not see the glory of the Lord* (Is 26:10, LXX). What can it mean, brothers and sisters? Let us puzzle it out, let us try to learn.[32] A wicked person will be awakened to see something, yet this wicked person will be driven away, prevented from seeing something else. We have explained already what he or she will see: that form of which the angels prophesied that he will come again *even as you have seen him.* Then what will the wicked be forbidden to see? That of which the Lord promised, *I will show myself.* What does that word, *myself*, point to? Not the form of a servant. What is *myself*, then? The form of God, in which he deemed it no robbery to be God's equal. What does this *myself* pledge to us? *Dearly beloved, we are children of God already, but what we shall be has not yet appeared.* We know that when he appears, we shall be like him, because we shall see him as he is (1 Jn 3:2). The glory of God is light beyond all telling, a fountain of light never dimmed, truth that never fails, Wisdom that while abiding in herself renews all things.[33] This is the very substance of God. The wicked must therefore be banished, forbidden to see this holy magnificence of God; it is written, *Blessed are the pure of heart, for they shall see God* (Mt 5:8).

The psalm also hints at the eternal power and dominion of the Son

13. It seems to me, brothers and sisters,[34] insofar as the Lord communicates the meaning to our capacity, that the phrase, *With you is the beginning, on the day of your strength*, refers to that time—if indeed we can speak of time then, since we shall proceed from time to non-time—well, it seems to me that this was stated in the psalm (but I am keeping an open mind in what I am about to say, in case anyone can understand it better or more conveniently or more convincingly)—it seems to me, as I was saying, that this verse is satisfactorily explained by its context. The psalmist has spoken of Christ's power, whereby he has subjected the nations to his yoke and subdued the peoples not by the sword but by the wood of his cross. Even in his fleshly condition, even in his humility, his great power is perceptible to the extent that his servile form allows it to show, for the weakness of God is stronger than human might.[35] Well, then, since Christ's power has been indicated here too, as the psalm mentioned in the words, *from Zion will the Lord send forth your scepter of power; have dominion in the midst*

---

32. Variant: "Let us discuss it."
33. See Wis 7:27.
34. This section 13 shows Augustine at his stylistic worst. The point he wants to make is that the psalm indicates not only the dominion over his enemies won by Christ through his redemptive work but also the essential power of the Son, who is the Wisdom and the Power of God. But it takes Augustine a long time, many parentheses, and many subordinate clauses to make it. The translation reflects the involved style of the passage.
35. See 1 Cor 1:25.

of your foes—for how great is his power indeed as he rules in the midst of his noisy enemies who are powerless to withstand him, but every day ask themselves, *When will he die, and his name disappear?* (Ps 40:6(41:5)) while all the time his glory increases among the peoples, while nations are brought into allegiance to his name, while the sinner is enraged at the sight, gnashes his teeth and pines away[36]—as I was saying, since this power of Christ has been demonstrated, the prophet wants to draw our attention to his power in another sense: in that Christ is the Power of God and the Wisdom of God[37] in the perpetual light of immutable truth. For this vision we are being kept safe, from this vision we are held back for a time, for this vision we are being cleansed by faith, from this vision the impious is banished, being forbidden to see the glory of the Lord—since, then, the prophet wants to make this clear, he says, *With you is the beginning, on the day of your strength.*

What does *With you is the beginning* mean? If Christ himself were meant, the psalm would have said, "You are the beginning," rather than *With you is the beginning,* for when questioned, *Who are you?* he replied, *The Beginning, and now I am speaking to you* (Jn 8:25). The Father also is the Beginning, from whom is born the only Son; and the Word was in that Beginning, for the Word was with God. Does that mean there are two beginnings, since the Father is the Beginning, and the Son is the Beginning? Absolutely not. As the Father is God and the Son is God, yet Father and Son are not two gods but one God, so too the Father is the Beginning and the Son is the Beginning, but Father and Son are not two but one Beginning.

With you is the beginning. At the end of time you will be seen, and then we shall see how the Beginning is with you, though not even here is the Beginning distant from you. Did you not say yourself, *Lo, you are departing, each to his own way, and leaving me alone; yet I am not alone, for the Father is with me* (Jn 16:32)? Even here the Beginning was with you. Elsewhere you said, *The Father, who abides in me, himself performs his works* (Jn 14:10). *With you is the beginning,* for the Father is never absent from you. But when at last we see that the Beginning is with you, then the truth will be manifest to all who have become like you, because they will see you as you are.[38] Here below Philip asked to see the Father, even though he was looking at you;[39] but then, at the end, we shall see what we now believe. Then the Beginning will be seen to be with you by the eyes of the saints, by the eyes of the just, while the impious are banished, forbidden to see the glory of the Lord.

---

36. See Ps 111(112):10.
37. See 1 Cor 1:24.
38. See 1 Jn 3:2.
39. See Jn 14:8.

Seeing Christ: in the form of a servant, but later in his glory

14. Let us believe in him now, brothers and sisters, that we may see him hereafter. Philip was chided because, not recognizing the Father's presence in the Son, he asked to see the Father. Jesus asked him, *Have I been all this time with you, and yet you have not truly seen me? Whoever has seen me, Philip, has seen the Father.* (Jn 14:9) But *whoever has seen me* does not mean the one who merely regards the form of a servant in me. Only the one who has seen me in the form I have hidden from those who fear me, but am perfecting for those who trust me,[40] only such a person *has seen the Father.* But if this vision is withheld until later, what is there for us in the meantime? Let us see what Christ had to say to Philip, after telling him that *whoever has seen me has seen the Father.* We might think Philip had silently replied, "But how else can I see you, if you are to be seen otherwise than in the form of a servant? How can I ever see the Father—I, a weak mortal, only dust and ashes?" Christ turned to him, delaying that vision but demanding faith. He who had just declared, *Whoever has seen me has seen the Father*, knowing that this was too much for Philip, who was far from seeing, asked him, *Do you not believe that I am in the Father, and that the Father is in me?* (Jn 14:10) Believe now in what you lack the strength to see, that you may deserve to see it.

When at last we come to see that vision, the truth of the psalm's assertion will be plain to us: *With you is the beginning, on the day of your strength.* When it says, *your strength*, it does not mean the strength of your weakness; it is your strength[41] that is spoken of here. Human beings exercise their virtues now, in faith, in hope, in charity, in all good actions, but they will progress from many virtues to the one virtue, the one Power.[42] *With you is the beginning*: you will be seen at last with the Father, in the Father; you will be so seen that we know that the Father is *with you on the day of your strength*, on the day when your strength is so manifested that the wicked shall not see it. Even your weakness is stronger than human strength, but *on the day of your strength* we shall see that the Beginning is with you.

15. Now tell us, psalmist, what strength you have in mind. His power has been alluded to already, when we heard that the scepter of his strength is sent forth from Zion, that he may wield power in the midst of his enemies. Of what strength are you speaking here? Of that which is manifest *in the splendor of the saints*,

---

40. See Ps 30:20(31:19).
41. The power of his godhead.
42. The Latin *virtus* usually means strength, but the root idea is that of any kind of "virile" excellence, and hence also moral perfection or "virtue." In his commentary on verse 8(7) of Psalm 83(84), to which he alludes here, Augustine speaks of the believer's progress from many virtues to the one "virtue" which is Christ, the Power of God. See his Exposition of Psalm 83,11 and the notes there. In the present passage he is playing on the ambiguity: strength or virtue.

says the psalm. *In the splendor of the saints*: it is telling us, then, of a power to be revealed when the saints are in glory, a power not yet manifest while they carry mortal flesh, while they still groan in a mortal, perishable body that weighs down the soul, while this earthly dwelling depresses the mind that ponders many things,[43] while people's thoughts are not transparent to others. This is not the splendor of the saints. What does the psalm mean by *in the splendor of the saints*? The apostle speaks of this present age *until the Lord comes; for he will light up the dark, hidden places, and reveal the purposes of our hearts, and then there will be praise for everyone from God* (1 Cor 4:5). That will be the era of the splendor of the saints, because then *the righteous will shine like the sun in their Father's kingdom*. Listen to what the gospel says about the spendor of the saints: *The harvest will come at the end of the world. The householder will send his angels to gather up from his kingdom all that makes people stumble, and throw it into a blazing furnace. Then the righteous will shine like the sun in their Father's kingdom.* (Mt 13:41-43) What kingdom? See if the gospel has anything to tell of a vision in store for us, the vision hinted at by the psalm's words, *With you is the beginning.* In what kingdom shall we enjoy it? *Come, you who are blessed by my Father, take possession of the kingdom prepared for you since the creation of the world* (Mt 25:34). But when he has singled out the righteous, and praised them, and invited them, *Take possession of the kingdom*, what follows for the wicked whom he has condemned? *The wicked will go into eternal burning, but the righteous into eternal life* (Mt 25:46). What he first called a *kingdom* he subsequently called *eternal life,* into which the impious will not be admitted. But eternal life is a state of vision, for the Lord also said, *This is eternal life, to know you, the one true God, and Jesus Christ, whom you sent* (Jn 17:3). Then we shall see that *with you is the beginning on the day of your strength*, and this is why the psalm tells us that we shall see it *in the splendor of the saints.*

Christ is the twice-born

16. But this vision is withheld until later. What about now? *From the womb before the morning star I begot you.* What can that mean? God has a Son, yes, but surely not a womb? If we think of the human, fleshly body, then no, he does not, any more than he has a bosom; and yet scripture says, *The only-begotten Son, who is in the bosom of the Father, has made him known* (Jn 1:18) *Bosom* and *womb* mean the same thing here; both are figurative expressions for what is hidden. What, then, is implied by *from the womb*? From a hidden, secret place, from my very self, from my intimate substance; for, as another passage asks, *Who shall recount his generation?* (Is 53:8) We must take the psalm's words to

---

43. See Wis 9:15.

be those of the Father addressing his Son: *From the womb before the morning star I begot you.*

But what is the meaning of *before the morning star?* The morning star[44] stands for all the stars, for scripture names a part for the whole, and indicates all the other stars by one of extraordinary brightness. But how were these other stars created? *To be signs of seasons, and days, and years* (Gn 1:14). If, therefore, the heavenly bodies stand for the passage of time, and the morning star represents all the heavenly bodies, the expression, *before the morning star,* means "before all the stars"; and whatever is before the stars is before time began. What is before time is from eternity; do not ask when that was, because "when" has no meaning in eternity. "When" and "sometimes" are notions that belong to time. He through whom time was created was not born from the Father within time. The psalm spoke in a figurative, prophetic mode proper to the subject matter when it called God's hidden substance a womb and used the morning star to represent time.

Would you like to consider the application of this birth to David also, since he called the Lord his son?[45] David could speak thus only because he had listened to his Lord and heard the truth from one who could not deceive him. Already, therefore, he could call Christ his Lord: *The Lord said to my Lord, Sit at my right hand.* It is David who speaks here; the whole passage is presented as his utterance. And so we can perhaps understand David too as saying, *From the womb before the morning star I begot you.* It would then mean, "From a virginal womb, before the morning star, I begot you." A virgin descended from David's flesh gave birth to Christ from her womb, and so it could be said that he was born from the womb of David. *From the womb* untouched by any male: the phrase, *from the womb,* carries its full and proper meaning, because only he was born from a womb alone. David, who had acknowledged Christ as his Lord, could thus rightly say, *From the womb I begot you.* The words, *before the morning star,* are used deliberately and with clear significance, for that was how the prophecy was fulfilled. The Lord was born from the womb of the virgin Mary in the night; we know this from the shepherds who were keeping the night watches over their flocks.[46] *From the womb before the morning star I begot you.* You, my Lord, you who sit at the right hand of my Lord, how can you be my son, unless *from the womb before the morning star I begot you?*

---

44. *Lucifer,* the light-bringer, a name often applied by Greeks and Romans to the planet Venus.
45. The preceding paragraphs contemplated the eternal birth of the Word. Augustine now turns to his temporal birth.
46. See Lk 2:8.

Verse 4. The Aaronic priesthood is superseded by the priesthood of Melchizedek

17. To what purpose were you born? *The Lord has sworn, and will not revoke it: you are a priest for ever according to the order of Melchizedek.* This is why you were born from the womb before the morning star: to be a priest for ever according to the order of Melchizedek. If we take the words about his being born from the womb to refer to his birth from the virgin, and the mention of the morning star to mean that he was born at night, as the gospels record, there is no doubt that the purpose of his birth from the womb before the morning star was that he should be a priest according to the order of Melchizedek. By his birth from the Father, as God-with-God, co-eternal with his Begetter, he is not a priest. He is a priest only because of the flesh he assumed, the body he received from us to offer as a sacrificial victim for us.

The Lord has sworn: what does this mean? Is it possible that God swears, when he has forbidden human beings to swear?[47] Or should we not think, rather, that he forbids humans to swear because of the danger of their slipping into perjury but that God can swear because there is no possibility of his swearing falsely? If a man or woman gets into the habit of swearing there is the risk of a slip into perjury, and so the warning against oaths is necessary: the more oaths are avoided, the less likely are people to be forsworn. A human being who swears may swear either to what is false or to what is true, but one who avoids oaths altogether cannot swear to falsehood. Why, then, should the Lord not swear? His oath is the confirmation of his promise. He has every right to swear. Think now: when you take an oath, what are you doing? You are calling God to witness; that is what an oath is: an appeal to God to witness to what you say. This is why it is dangerous, for you may invoke God as witness to some falsehood. But if you when taking an oath call God to witness, why should God not invoke himself as witness by giving his oath? God's manner of swearing is to say, *As I live.* That is how he uttered his oath concerning the posterity of Abraham: *As I live, says the Lord: because you have hearkened to my voice, and for my sake have not withheld your beloved son, I will bless you exceedingly, and multiply your seed more and more, like the stars in the sky and the sand on the seashore; and in your seed shall all the nations of the earth be blessed* (Gn 22:16-18). Now Christ is the seed of Abraham. He who took flesh from Abraham's stock will be a priest for ever according to the order of Melchizedek. It is about Christ's priesthood according to the order of Melchizedek that *the Lord has sworn, and will not revoke it.*

But what about the priesthood of the order of Aaron? Is it conceivable that God should repent, as humans do, or slip into doing something against his will,

47. See Mt 5:34.

or fall into some action imprudently, and afterwards be sorry for his fall? No, of course not. He knows what he is doing and knows where any process is leading; it is within the power of him who rules it to redirect it and change it into something else. But a change in things can seem like a revocation of a prior decision. When you repent of something, you are sorry about what you did. In an analogous way, if God changes something in a manner humans did not want or expect, God is said to repent or revoke his decision; he even says he repents of the punishment inflicted on us, if we repent of our evil ways. When the psalm says, therefore, that *the Lord has sworn* (meaning that he confirmed his promises with an oath) *and will not revoke it*, it means that he will not change. Will not change what? His promise that *you are a priest for ever*. It must be *for ever* if he is never going to revoke it.

But what kind of priesthood is envisaged? Will it require those victims and sacrifices offered by the patriarchs, altars running with blood, and the sacred tent, and all the other emblems of the first covenant, the old one? By no means. All those things have been swept away with the destruction of the temple, the abolition of the old priesthood, and the disappearance of the victims and sacrifices that belonged to them. Not even the Jews have these now. They see that their priesthood according to the order of Aaron has ceased to exist, and they fail to recognize the priesthood according to the order of Melchizedek. *You are a priest for ever, according to the order of Melchizedek.* I am speaking to believers. If some of this is obscure to the catechumens, let them throw off their sluggishness and hasten toward knowledge. There is no need for us to parade our mysteries openly; the scriptures inform us as to what is meant by priesthood according to the order of Melchizedek.

Verse 5. The stone that trips and crushes

18. *The Lord is at your right hand.* The Lord had said, *Sit at my right*, yet now we find the Lord God at his right hand, as though they had exchanged thrones! A better way to read it is this: the words, *the Lord has sworn, and he will not revoke it*, refer to the Lord's promise to Christ: *You are a priest for ever*; the Lord has sworn this to you. The Lord? Which Lord? The Lord who issued the invitation *to my Lord: Sit at my right hand*, the Lord who gave his oath, *You are a priest for ever, according to the order of Melchizedek.* Thus it is to this same Lord who swore the oath that our present verse is addressed: *The Lord is at your right hand.* O Lord, you swore your oath; you said, *You are a priest for ever, according to the order of Melchizedek*; and he to whom you made that promise, he the eternal priest, he is the "Lord" at your right hand, he is the everlasting priest who is "my Lord." To him you have said, *Sit at my right hand, until I make your enemies into your footstool.*

This Lord who is at your right hand, about whom and to whom you swore your oath, *You are a priest for ever, according to the order of Melchizedek*, has *shattered*[48] *kings on the day of his anger*. Christ who is the Lord at your right hand, to whom you gave your irrevocable oath—what is he doing,[49] this eternal priest? What is he doing as he sits at God's right hand and intercedes for us?[50] He is like the priest entering the innermost place, the holy of holies, the secret recess of heaven, and cleansing us easily from sins because he has no sin himself.[51] Sitting at your right hand, *he has shattered kings on the day of his anger*.

What kings, you ask? Have you forgotten that other passage, *The kings of the earth have arisen, and the rulers conspired together against the Lord and against his Christ* (Ps 2:2)? He shattered those kings with his glory and left them helpless under the weight of his name, so that they could not do what they planned. They tried hard to blot out the Christian name from the earth, but they could not do it, because *anyone who trips over this stone will be shattered against it*. They tripped over the stumbling block, and so those kings have been shattered. They say, "Christ? Who is Christ? Some Jew, some Galilean fellow. He was put to death, he died thus and thus. . . ." The stone is in front of your feet, lying there lowly and contemptible. You scorn it and so you trip over it; in tripping you fall; in falling you are shattered against it. If the anger of one still hidden is so devastating, what will his judgment be when he is revealed? You have heard about the anger of the hidden one, for another psalm bears the title, *Concerning the hidden things of the Son*; it is the ninth psalm, if I remember rightly. It is inscribed, *Concerning the hidden things of the Son*, and it sets forth the concealed judgment imposed by concealed anger. Those who stumble against the stone are the people whose lives provoke God's anger, and they are dashed to pieces. And what does this present shattering portend? Listen to the gospel words about future judgment: *Anyone who trips over this stone will be shattered against it, and anyone on whom it falls will be crushed* (Lk 20:18). When people trip over him and are shattered it is because he seems to be lying there humbly; but when he crushes them it will be because he comes from above. Notice how the different phases of Christ's victory are suggested by these two verbs: shattering and crushing, tripping over him and being beneath him as he comes from on high. The two periods are those of Christ's lowliness and glory, of hidden punishment and future judgment. Anyone who is not shattered by him as he lies humbly will not be crushed when he comes. "Lies humbly," I said, because he appears contemptible. He is at the right hand of God, yet he shouts loudly from on high, *Saul, Saul, why are you persecuting me?* (Acts 9:4) In

---

48. Variant: "will shatter."
49. Variant: "what will he do."
50. See Rom 8:34.
51. See Heb 9:12-14.24.

heaven as he is, untouched by anyone, he could not call out, *Why are you perse-cuting me?* unless his enthronement at the Father's right hand still allowed him to be present to us as lying visibly on earth. *The Lord at your right hand has shattered kings on the day of his anger.*

Verse 6. Rebuilding humble ruins

19. *He will execute judgment among the nations.* Now, today, is the time of the *hidden things*; but there will come a time for his judgment to be manifested. *He will execute judgment among the nations* one day; but at present another prophecy is being fulfilled: that *their memory has perished with an uproar.* This is found in the psalm headed, *For the hidden things.* It runs, *Their memory has perished with an uproar, and the Lord abides for ever. He has prepared his seat in judgment, and he himself will judge the earth with equity.* There too it was said, *You have rebuked the heathen, and the ungodly has perished; their name you have blotted out for ever.* (Ps 9:7-9.6(6-8,5)) All this is going on in secret. Thus *he has shattered kings on the day of his anger*, and *he will execute judgment among the nations.* How does he judge them? Listen to the words that follow: *He will rebuild the ruins.* His judgment of the nations at the present time is of a kind to rebuild their ruins; but when he judges at the end he will condemn the ruins. For now, *he will rebuild the ruins.* What ruins are these? Anyone who comes to fear the name of the Lord falls down, and in the falling what he or she used to be is destroyed, making way for the person to be built up into something that was not there before. *He will execute judgment among the nations and rebuild the ruins.* If you are stubbornly opposed to Christ, you have built a high tower destined to fall.[52] It would be better for you to demolish yourself, come back humbly and prostrate yourself at the feet of him who sits at the Father's right hand, that the ruin in you may be fit for reconstruction. If you persist in your high and mighty sinfulness you will be torn down, and then there will be no prospect of rebuilding for you. Of such people scripture says elsewhere, *You will overthrow them, and not build them up* (Ps 27(28):5). Now it would not have said of certain people, *You will overthrow them, and not build them up*, unless there were others whom he meant to overthrow in such a way that he could rebuild them. This is taking place in our day, when Christ is exercising judgment among the nations in order to restore their ruins. *He will shatter many heads on earth.* Here, on earth, in this life, *he will shatter many heads.* He transforms the proud into humble people. I venture to say, my brothers and sisters, that to walk humbly here, even with a wounded head, is better than falling under the sentence of eternal death with head held high. He will shatter plenty of heads as he reduces them to ruin, but he will restore and rebuild many.

---

52. An ancient symbol of hubris; compare the tower of Babel, Gn 11:1-9.

Verse 7. The Messiah who drank from the river of mortality is exalted in glory

20. *He will drink from the torrent beside the way, and therefore he will raise*[53] *his head.* Let us also contemplate him drinking from the torrent on his journey. But first, what torrent is this? The cascade of human mortality. A stream is formed from rainwater; it swells, roars, rolls swiftly, and as it surges forward it is running downward to the end of its course. The course of mortal life is like this. Human beings are born, they live, they die; as some die, others are born, and as they die in their turn others again rise up. There is succession, arrival, departure; none of them abide. Can we hold onto anything? Is there anything that does not run through our fingers? Or anything that does not disappear into the ocean, like the rain that gathered to form the stream? The river surfaced suddenly[54] as rain-water accumulated, swelled by many drops from many showers, but it vanishes into the sea and we cannot distinguish it, any more than we could see it before it was formed by the rain. So too the human race is formed from hidden sources and flows out into the open but then disappears into death. In the middle part of its course it raises its hubbub, but then it passes on.

Christ drank from this river; he did not disdain to drink from the torrent by being born and dying. The torrent is the stream of birth and death, and Christ accepted it. He was born and he died; thus he *drank from the torrent beside the way,* for *he leapt up like a giant to run his course with joy* (Ps 18:6(19:5)). Because he refused to stand still and linger *in the way of sinners* (Ps 1:1) he *drank from the torrent beside the way,* and therefore *he will raise his head.* Because he *humbled himself and was made obedient to the point of death, even death on a cross, God raised him high and gave him a name above every other name, that at the name of Jesus every knee should bow, in heaven, on earth or in the underworld, and every tongue confess that Jesus Christ is Lord, in the glory of God the Father.* (Phil 2:8-11)

---

53. Variant: "has raised."
54. He is perhaps thinking of rivers that flow only in winter.

Exposition of Psalm 110

A Sermon

The symbolism of the forty days of Lent and the fifty of Easter

1. The time for singing Alleluia has arrived.[1] Be mentally alert, brothers and sisters, to whatever instruction the Lord may give us to nourish our charity, for our good is to hold fast in charity to God.[2] Be mentally alert, you skillful singers, dedicated as you are to the praise and everlasting glory of the true, immortal God.[3] Listen intently, all of you who know how to sing and play psalms to the Lord in your hearts, giving thanks to him for everything;[4] and praise God, for this is what Alleluia means.

These Easter days arrive only to pass away again, and they pass only to come round once more; but they signify a day that neither comes nor passes, because it is not preceded by any yesterday that moves out of the way to make room for it, nor is there any tomorrow pressing on its heels to displace it. When we reach that day we shall be fully at home in it, and we shall no longer be ephemeral ourselves. Scripture somewhere says to God, *Blessed are they who dwell in your house; they will praise you for ever and ever* (Ps 83:5(84:4)); this will be the employment of the leisured, the work of the unencumbered, the activity of those at rest, the care of those free from care.[5] How do these Easter days signify that eternal day? As our paschal days, with their solemn and most welcome gladness, succeed the days of Lent, which before the Lord's bodily resurrection symbolized the sorrows of our present life, so will that eternal day after our resurrection be granted in all its everlasting happiness to Christ's fully perfect body,[6] his holy Church, when all the pains and sorrows of our present life are over and done with.

But this life on earth requires us to practice self-control. Even as we groan under the weight of our labors and struggles, even as we long to be clothed with our heavenly habitation over this earthly one,[7] we must restrain ourselves from worldly pleasures. The symbol of our earthly life is that period of forty days

---

1. Plainly a sermon preached in paschaltide, but commentators differ as to the year.
2. See Ps 72(73):28.
3. Literally, "you sons of the praise and . . . immortal God," a Hebraism.
4. See Eph 5:19-20.
5. These thoughts recur at the end of the sermon, together with the evocation of Psalm 83(84).
6. *Plenario corpori Domini.*
7. See 2 Cor 5:2.

during which Moses and Elijah fasted,[8] as ultimately our Lord did himself. We are commanded to curb our greed by a temperance that is like fasting, and hold back from all the worldly enticements that captivate people to the forgetting of God. Both the law and the prophets lay this command upon us, and so too does the gospel, to which the law and the prophets lend their witness; this is why the transfigured Savior appeared on the mountain between two persons who represented them.[9] The perfect observance of the ten commandments is like a melody played on a ten-stringed psaltery, and this observance must be preached to the four corners of the world. Since ten multiplied by four makes forty, the duty of temperance is incumbent on us throughout the time of preaching, as though we were living a forty-day Lent.

However, what is signified by the fifty days after the Lord's resurrection, the days in which we sing, Alleluia, is no passage of time, no time that will ever run out. These fifty days stand for our blessed eternity, because the just reward for those who toil faithfully in this life is a denarius, that equal reward which the householder has prepared for the early workers and the late-comers alike.[10] Now a denarius is a coin of ten units, and when we add ten to forty we get the fifty days of our Eastertide.

Let us, then, attune ourselves to the heart of God's people, a heart filled with his praise.[11] Listen to how he fills this psalm with the song of someone who exults in joy and jubilation and prefigures God's people, Christ's body, as it will be when it is freed at last from all evil and overflows with heartfelt love of God

Verses 1-2. God's will is accomplished, whatever humans may do

2. *I will confess to you, O Lord, with all my heart.* "Confession" does not always mean confession of sins; the praise of God can also be declared in devout confession.[12] The former is made in sorrow, the latter in joy; by the one we show our wound to the physician, by the latter we give thanks for health. The confession uttered in this psalm bespeaks a person who has not only been set free from every evil but is also separated from everyone of malicious intent. Let us notice, then, where he is as he confesses to the Lord with all his heart: *in the assembly of the upright, in their congregation.* These, I think, must be the people who are to sit upon twelve thrones, judging the twelve tribes of Israel.[13] No wicked person finds a place among them, no Judas-like thefts are tolerated there, no Simon

8. See Ex 34:28; 1 Kgs 19:8.
9. See Mk 9:3 and parallels.
10. See Mt 20:1-16.
11. Variant: "Let us listen to a psalm that refreshes the heart of God's people with praise."
12. Compare the Expositions of Psalms 104,1 and 105,2 on these two senses of the word.
13. See Mt 19:28.

Magus is baptized in the expectation of buying the Spirit in order to sell,[14] no coppersmith like Alexander does his manifold harm,[15] no one clothed in sheepskin sneaks in with a show of feigned brotherliness.[16] The Church has no option but to groan among such people now, but they must be excluded in the future when all the just are gathered into one flock.

Great are the works of the Lord to be seen on that day. *They are finely wrought to fulfill all his purposes.* What he wills is that no one who confesses shall be bereft of mercy and no one's iniquity go unpunished, for he whips even his children, every one whom he acknowledges as his.[17] But if the just are barely saved, where will there be room for the sinner and the unbeliever?[18] Let men and women choose as they wish; the works of the Lord are not so wrought that a creature endowed with freedom of choice can override the will of the creator, even by acting contrary to his will. God does not want you to sin, and he forbids you to do so; but if you have sinned, do not delude yourself that a human being has done what he wanted, while God has had to suffer what he did not want. No: just as he wills human beings not to sin, he also wills to pardon the sinner so that he or she may turn back again and live,[19] but so too does he will in the end to punish one who perseveres in sin, that no defiant sinner may evade the power of his justice. It follows that whatever you choose, the Almighty will not lack the means to carry out completely his will in your regard, for *great are the works of the Lord; they are finely wrought to fulfill all his purposes.*

Verses 3-5. The magnificence of God's works: justification, miracles, compassion

3. *Confession and magnificence are his work.* What work is more magnificent than to justify a sinner? But it might be said that there is a work on our part that precedes this magnificent work of God, and that when he has confessed his sins a person earns justification. The gospel tells us, *The tax-collector went down to his house at rights with God, rather than the Pharisee,* because the tax collector *had dared not even raise his eyes to heaven, but beat his breast, saying, Lord, be merciful to me, a sinner* (Lk 18:14,13). This is the Lord's magnificence, that he justifies a sinner, for *anyone who exalts himself will be humbled, but the one who humbles himself will be exalted* (Lk 18:14). This is the Lord's magnificence, that one who has had most forgiven, loves most.[20] This is the Lord's

---

14. See Acts 8:18-24.
15. See 2 Tm 4:14.
16. See Mt 7:15.
17. See Heb 12:6.
18. See 1 Pt 4:18.
19. See Ezk 18:23; 33:11.
20. See Lk 7:41-48.

magnificence, that *where sin abounded, grace abounded all the more* (Rom 5:20).[21] But perhaps our justification comes about through our own efforts. No, says the apostle, *it does not come from works, lest anyone boast. We are his own handiwork, created in Christ Jesus for good works.* (Eph 2:9-10) No human being can act justly unless first justified; but by *believing in him who justifies the impious* (Rom 4:5) he begins with faith. Thus his good works do not precede his justification as an entitlement but follow it to demonstrate what he has received.

How does confession come about, then? It is not yet a righteous work, but it is a detestation of the offence committed. In any case, whatever its nature, no human being may take any pride in it. Rather *let anyone who boasts, boast in the Lord. What have you that you did not receive?* (1 Cor 1:31; 4:7). The Lord's work is not only the magnificence he displays in justifying the sinner; both *confession and magnificence are his work. What are we to say, then?* God *has mercy on whom he chooses, and hardens whom he chooses. Is there iniquity in God? Absolutely not.* (Rom 9:14.18) For *his justice abides for ever and ever.* But you, a child of this world, *who are you, a mere mortal, to answer back to God?* (Rom 9:20)

4. *He has made us remember his wonderful deeds*, humbling one person, exalting another. *He has made us remember his wonderful deeds*, reserving the right to perform prodigies when occasion demands, unusual feats that weak human beings, whose attention is caught by novelty, will easily remember, even though his everyday miracles are greater. He creates innumerable trees all over the world, and no one remarks on it; he caused one to wither away by his word,[22] and the minds of mortals were stupefied. He wanted them to *remember his wonderful deeds.* That miracle would stick in the memory of those who had witnessed it, because familiarity had not devalued it for them.

5. But what good would miracles have done, if they had not led people to fear him? And what purpose would fear have served, unless *the merciful and compassionate Lord* had given *food to those who fear him*? It was an incorruptible food, the bread that came down from heaven,[23] given to the wholly undeserving; for Christ died for the wicked.[24] No one therefore could give such food except *the merciful and compassionate Lord.* But if he has given us so much in this life, if a sinner in need of justification has received the Word made flesh, what will the believer, once glorified, receive in the world to come? The Lord *will be mindful of his covenant for eternity.* He has given us his pledge, but he has not yet given all.

---

21. Speaking of magnificence as a human virtue, Cicero said, "Magnificence is the discussing and administering of great and lofty undertakings, with a certain broad and noble purpose of mind" (*De invent. rhet.* 2). Human magnificence is a reflection of divine power and generosity.
22. See Mt 21;19-20.
23. See Jn 6:32.33.50.51.
24. See Rom 5:6.

Verses 6-9. The trustworthy promises attached to the New Covenant

6. *He will proclaim*[25] *to his people the power of his works.* Those holy Israel-ites who left their all and followed Christ had no reason to enquire sadly, *Who can be saved?* on hearing that *it is easier for a camel to squeeze through the eye of a needle than for a rich person to enter the kingdom of heaven,* for Christ proclaimed to them the power of his works. He assured them that *what is too difficult for human beings is easy for God.* (Mt 19:24-26) *So that he may give them the heritage of the nations*: the gospel was extended to the Gentiles as well, and the rich of this world were enjoined not to be arrogant in their attitude nor to trust in unreliable riches but only in the living God,[26] for whom it is easy to bring about what human beings find difficult. Many accordingly were called, and the apostles took over Gentile lands as their inheritance. The result was that even among people who did not renounce all their possessions in this life to follow Christ, a great multitude spurned even life itself for the confession of his name. Like camels kneeling to take on their backs a load of suffering, they squeezed through the needle's eye, through the lacerating straits of pain. The Lord achieved this, he to whom all things are possible.

7. *The works of his hands are truth and judgment.* Let those who are subjected to judgment here below hold fast to the truth of the Lord's promise. The martyrs are judged here, but they are conducted to another tribunal where they will judge not only the officials who judged them but even the angels[27] against whom they had to struggle while they were apparently facing their human judges. Let not affliction, hardship, hunger, nakedness, or the sword separate us from Christ,[28] for *all his commands are trustworthy*; he does not deceive us, and he will deliver what he has promised. We must not expect his promises to be fulfilled here: no, we should not hope for that; but *they are guaranteed in perpetuity, being estab-lished in truth and justice.* This is what truth and justice dictate: that we labor here and rest hereafter, because *he has sent redemption to his people.* But from what do they need redemption? Surely from the captivity they endure on their pilgrimage.[29] We must seek rest in our heavenly homeland, nowhere else.

8. It is true, of course, that God gave to the carnal Israelites the earthly Jeru-salem, which *is in slavery, together with her children* (Gal 4:25); but that was part of the Old Covenant, appropriate to the old humanity. Those who under-stood that the earthly Jerusalem was no more than a symbol were accounted heirs to the New Covenant, for *the Jerusalem on high is free, and she is our mother* (Gal 4:26), eternal in heaven. Hence it is self-evident that under the Old

---

25. Variant: "has proclaimed."
26. See 1 Tm 6:17.
27. See 1 Cor 6:3.
28. See Rom 8:35.
29. Redemption in the strict sense of buying back captives.

Covenant God promised only transient blessings, whereas the psalm declares, *He decreed that his covenant should last for ever.* What covenant? The New Covenant, clearly. I warn you, whoever you are who want to be an heir to this New Covenant, do not deceive yourself. Do not dream of a land flowing with milk and honey in a material sense, nor of pleasant estates, nor of shady, fruitful gardens; do not fantasize about gaining possession of any such things that the greedy eye always covets. *Covetousness is the root of all evils* (1 Tm 6:10). Avarice must be extinguished and made to perish here, not protracted to be sated hereafter. Make it your first job to flee from punishment and avoid hell; before you desire the God who promises, fear the God who threatens, for *holy and terrible is his name.*

Verse 10. Wisdom, approached through fear of the Lord

9. Instead of all the pleasures of this world, whether those you have experienced already or those you can increase and multiply for yourself in your imagination, set your desire on wisdom, the mother of delights that never die;[30] but the beginning of wisdom is the fear of the Lord. Wisdom will be your joy; she will infallibly lead you to the chaste, eternal embrace of truth, in a delight beyond description. But you need to have your debts forgiven before you demand rewards. *The fear of the Lord,* therefore, *is the beginning of wisdom.*

Understanding is good. Who would deny that? But to understand without acting in conformity with what you have understood is perilous, and the psalm warns us of this by its next words: *Understanding is good for those who so act.* Do not let your understanding make you conceited. The beginning of wisdom is fear of God, whose *praise lasts for ever and ever.* This will be your reward, your final destiny, your everlasting stability and place of rest. There will be found God's trustworthy commands, guaranteed in perpetuity; this is the inheritance of the New Covenant, decreed for all eternity. *One thing have I begged of the Lord, and that will I seek after,* says another psalm, *to live in the Lord's house all the days of my life* (Ps 26(27):4), for they are blessed who live in the Lord's house, blessed because they will praise him for ever.[31] *His praise lasts for ever and ever.*

---

30. Wisdom, the intermediary between holy fear and eternal blessedness, is presented by Augustine as the opposite of the cupidity discussed in the preceding section.

31. See Ps 83:5(84:4).

Exposition of Psalm 111

A Sermon to the People

Verse 1. The prophets of the new temple

1. I think you will have noticed the title of this psalm, brothers and sisters, and will have committed it to memory. It runs, *The turning back of Haggai and Zechariah.*[1] When the psalm was first sung, these two prophets did not yet exist. Between the time of David and the exile of the Israelite people to Babylon fourteen generations intervened, as divine scripture attests, and the evangelist Matthew in particular.[2] But according to the prophet Jeremiah the reconstruction of the ruined temple was expected after seventy years had passed from the beginning of the exile;[3] and after this period had elapsed, the two prophets Haggai and Zechariah were filled with the Holy Spirit in the reign of Darius, King of Babylon.[4] They began to prophesy one after the other within the same year[5] about the restoration of the temple, which had been foretold so long before.[6]

However, any readers who confine their hearts' vision to these material happenings and do not move on to the grace of spiritual understanding are living mentally among the stones with which the visible fabric was raised up by human hands but are failing to become living stones themselves. Living stones are shaped and fitted for that temple which the Lord first embodied in himself, of which he said, *Dismantle this temple, and in three days I will raise it up again* (Jn 2:19). In a fuller sense the body of the Lord is holy Church itself,[7] whose head has ascended into heaven. He is the living stone *par excellence*, the cornerstone concerning which the blessed Peter exhorted us, *You have come close to him, the*

---

1. This title is absent from the original Hebrew, which heads the psalm only with Alleluia. It may have been added to suggest that after the people's return from exile the two prophets encouraged them to sing the psalm, as a reminder of the way of life enjoined by the law.
2. See Mt 1:17.
3. See Jer 25:12; 20:10.
4. See Hag 1:1; Zech 1:1. Darius I (522-486 B.C.) was of course King of Persia, Babylon having been conquered by Cyrus in 538 B.C. and absorbed into the Persian Empire; but since Babylonia was now a Persian satrapy Darius could be loosely styled King of Babylon. The building of the Second Temple in Jerusalem took place during the years 520-515; see Ezra 6:15; Hag 2:15.
5. 520 B.C.
6. That is, by the title of the present psalm, which Augustine takes to belong to David's time.
7. *Plenius ipsa sancta ecclesia.* Compare *plenario corpori Domini* in the Exposition of Psalm 110,1. These two psalms have several points of doctrine in common, as do Augustine's Expositions of them.

living stone rejected by men, but chosen by God. You too must allow yourselves to be built, like living stones, into a spiritual house, a holy priesthood, offering spiritual sacrifices acceptable to God through Jesus Christ. For scripture says, Lo, I am laying in Zion a cornerstone, chosen and precious. No one who believes in him will be condemned. (1 Pt 2:4-6) If anyone wants to become a living stone, fit for such an edifice, he or she must understand the restoration of the temple in a spiritual sense. It symbolizes the re-creation of the new people after the ruin caused by Adam. This new people is remodelled on the pattern of the new man, the heavenly man, so that, as once we bore the image of the earthly man, we may henceforth bear that of the man from heaven.[8] The ages of this world roll on like the prophesied seventy years, a number that mystically stood for perfection; but when they are past, when our captivity and our long trudge are over, we shall not be built into an edifice liable to crumble again. Through Christ we shall be consolidated for ever in immortality.

You should not regard the spiritual Jerusalem as more the Jews' property than your own. The apostle declares, *You are pilgrims and lodgers[9] no more; rather are you fellow-citizens with the saints and members of God's household, built up on the foundation of the apostles and prophets, Christ Jesus himself being the chief cornerstone. In him the whole edifice is bound together and grows into a holy temple for the Lord. In him you too are being built with all the others into a spiritual dwelling for the Lord.* (Eph 2:19-22) This is God's temple, to which the prophetic ministry of Haggai and Zechariah, like a sacred sign, was pointing. The same apostle speaks directly to it in another passage: *God's temple is holy, and that temple is yourselves* (1 Cor 3:17). Anyone who turns away from the crumbling ruins of this world is like a living stone dedicated to the communal work of building and hoping for a place in this holy, firm structure. Such a one will understand the title of the psalm, and understand too the "turning back" of Haggai and Zechariah. Let any such person sing the verses that follow, not so much with the tongue as by the honesty of a life; for the perfection of the building will be the indescribable peace of wisdom, of which the initial stage is fear of the Lord.[10] Anyone whose "turning back" is building him or her into the common structure should therefore begin from fear of the Lord.[11]

2. *Blessed is the man[12] who fears the Lord; he will be full of good will about his commands.* Let God, who alone judges both truly and mercifully, assess what progress each person has made in the commandments, for *human life on earth is all temptation* (Jb 7:1), as holy Job confirmed. And again scripture says, *The*

---

8. See 1 Cor 15:49.

9. *Inquilini.* See the note at Exposition of Psalm 38, 21 for the overtones of this word.

10. An echo of the last section of the preceding sermon.

11. The following sections 2 and 3 are quoted verbatim by Augustine in his *Eight Questions of Dulcitius* 4.

12. *Vir.*

corruptible body weighs down the soul, and this earthly dwelling oppresses a mind that considers many things (Wis 9:15). It is the Lord who judges us with discernment. We have no right to pass judgment prematurely, before the coming of the Lord, for he will light up the dark, hidden places and reveal the purposes of our hearts, and then there will be commendation from God for each one.[13] Let him then determine how much progress each has made in his commandments. Nonetheless anyone who deeply loves the peace of that shared building work will undoubtedly be very much in earnest. Let such a one not despair, for *he will be full of good will about* God's commandments, and there is *peace on earth for people of good will* (Lk 2:14).

Verses 2-3. The true wealth of honest hearts

3. The psalm continues, *His seed will be mighty on earth.* The apostle testifies that works of mercy are the seeds of a future harvest: *Let us not weary of doing good, for in his time we shall reap without weariness* (Gal 6:9), and again: *This I want to emphasize: whoever sows sparingly will also reap sparingly* (2 Cor 9:6). What can be mightier, brothers and sisters, than to be so placed that you can buy the kingdom of heaven? Not only did Zachaeus purchase it with half his property,[14] but a widow even bought it with two mites,[15] yet both of them gained it equally! What can be mightier than this, that the same kingdom costs a rich man his fortune and a poor person only a cup of cold water?[16]

There are some who do these good deeds to gain earthly advantages, either hoping to receive a reward from the Lord here and now or seeking to enhance their reputation in the eyes of other people. But the psalm warns us that *the generation of straightforward people will be blessed.* This is obviously a blessing on the deeds of those to whom the God of Israel is good, those of straightforward hearts. Straightforwardness, rectitude of heart, is characteristic of those who do not resent their Father's chastisement and who believe in his promises. It is quite different from the attitude of those whose feet slip, those whose steps slide out of control as they envy sinners, seeing the peace that wrongdoers enjoy.[17] Another psalm sings about these misguided folk, who imagine that their good deeds perish because no perishable reward comes their way. But the man[18] in our present psalm, the one who fears the Lord and through his conversion to rectitude of heart is being shaped for God's holy temple, neither seeks the approval of other people nor covets earthly riches. Yet in spite

---

13. See 1 Cor 4:5.
14. See Lk 19:8.
15. See Mk 12:42-44.
16. See Mk 9:40.
17. See Ps 72(73):1-3.
18. *Vir.*

of this, *glory and wealth are in his house.* His house is his heart where, secure in God's commendation, he dwells in richer style than others who depend on human flattery and live in marble-adorned mansions, beneath panelled ceilings, with the fear of eternal death to keep them company. Such a person's *righteousness abides for ever,* and that righteousness is his glory and his wealth. Purple, fine linen and sumptuous banquets pass away even as they are within a rich person's grasp, and when they are finished, his burning tongue will be begging for a drop of water from someone's finger.[19]

Verses 4-9. The honorable conduct of the just person

4. *A light has arisen in the darkness for those of straightforward hearts.* They have strong motives for directing their hearts toward God and strong motives for walking honestly with their God, preferring his will to their own and putting no reliance on anything they can do themselves; for they remember that they were once darkness but now light in the Lord.[20] *The Lord God is merciful and compassionate and just.* We love to think of how merciful and compassionate he is, but perhaps we are terrified when we remember that *the Lord God is just.* Do not fear, do not despair, you blessed one, you who fear the Lord and are full of good will about his commands; simply be kind, be merciful and lend. The Lord God proves his justice by judging without mercy anyone who has not shown mercy.[21] But *the pleasant man shows mercy and lends;* God does not spit him out of his mouth like something unpleasant.[22] He bids us, *Forgive, and you will be forgiven; give, and gifts will be given to you* (Lk 6:37-38). When you forgive, that you may be in turn forgiven, you are showing mercy; when you give, that gifts may be given you, you are lending. In a general sense any action designed to relieve another's misery can be called mercy, but there is a difference when you are not spending money or putting bodily effort into your action, but pardoning someone who has sinned against you, and thereby winning pardon for your own sins. These two kindly acts—pardoning offences and almsdeeds—are enjoined by the gospel passage just quoted, *Forgive, and you will be forgiven; give, and gifts will be given to you;* and I think they are also distinguished in this verse of the psalm: *The pleasant man shows mercy and lends.*

Let us not be dilatory about this, brothers and sisters. A person who craves revenge is looking for a glorious triumph, but remember what scripture says, *Better is the one who overcomes anger than the one who captures a city* (Prv 16:32, LXX). Another who is unwilling to give to the poor is looking for wealth,

---

19. See Lk 16:19-31.
20. See Eph 5:8.
21. See Jas 2:13.
22. See Rv 3:16.

but remember what scripture says, *You will have treasure in heaven* (Mt 19:21). You will not lack glory when you grant pardon, because it is a noble triumph to overcome anger; nor will you be impoverished by generous giving, because a heavenly treasure is more safely acquired thereby. This verse was born from the preceding one: *Glory and wealth are in his house.*

5. A person who behaves like this *will regulate his words judiciously.* His very deeds will be like words that plead in his defence on judgment day. And the judgment passed on him will not be without mercy, because he has treated others mercifully. *He will never be dislodged* because, being assigned to the Lord's right hand, he will hear the invitation, *Come, you who are blessed by my Father, take possession of the kingdom prepared for you since the creation of the world* (Mt 25:34). The only deeds mentioned there are their works of mercy. The just will hear the summons, *Come, you who are blessed by my Father,* because *the generation of straightforward people will be blessed.* Thus it will come about that *the just one will be held in eternal remembrance; woeful tidings hold no terrors for him.* The sentence he will hear being passed on those at the Lord's left will strike no fear into him: *Depart from me, you accursed, into the eternal fire which was prepared for the devil and his angels* (Mt 25:41).

6. Every believer who here below seeks not his own interests but those of Jesus Christ[23] bears all hardships with the utmost patience and confidently looks forward to what we have been promised. *His heart is ready to hope in the Lord.* No adversities break him down, for *his heart has been strengthened, and he will not be moved until he has seen what is above his enemies.* His enemies craved to see good things in this world, and when invisible blessings were promised, they merely carped, *Who has anything good to show us?* (Ps 4:6). May our hearts be strengthened and may we not be moved until we have seen what is above our enemies. They aspire to see the good things humans value here in the land of the dying, but we believe we shall see the good things of the Lord in the land of the living.[24]

7. But it is a hard thing to keep one's heart strong and not be moved, when other people who value only what they can see are making merry and jeering at anyone who hopes in what is unseen. One who can do this *will not be moved* until he sees not what his enemies see, here below, but what is on high, *above his enemies.* That is something no eye has seen, no ear heard, no human heart conceived, something God has prepared for those who love him.[25] How much is it worth, this reality that cannot be seen and costs everything that each of us can pay? For the sake of that treasure the just person has *dispersed freely, and given to the poor.* He did not see it, yet he was buying it all the while. The Lord, who

---

23. See Phil 2:21.
24. See Ps 26(27):13.
25. See 1 Cor 2:9.

graciously willed to hunger and thirst in the persons of the poor on earth, was keeping the treasure safe for him in heaven. No wonder, then, that *his righteousness abides, world without end*, for he who created the world is guarding it. *His horn will be raised up in glory*, though his humility was despised on earth by the proud.

Verse 10. The ultimate triumph of the just

8. *The sinner will be enraged at the sight*, but his remorse will come too late and remain sterile. With whom shall a sinner be more enraged than with himself, when he asks in chagrin, *What good has our pride done us, what benefit has come to us from our vaunted wealth?* (Wis 5:8) He will see the one who freely dispersed his goods to the poor, and see him with his horn raised up in glory. The sinner *will gnash his teeth and pine away*, for in the place where he is there will be weeping and grinding of teeth. He will not put forth leaves and grow green and lustrous, as he could have done if he had repented at the proper time; he will feel remorse only when *the desire of sinners is doomed to perish*, with no consolation to follow. The desire of sinners will fade away when all things pass like a shadow, when the grass withers and the flower falls. But the word of the Lord abides for ever,[26] and as that word was derided by the empty glee of the falsely happy, so will it laugh last, and better, over the perdition of the truly miserable.

---

26. See Is 40:8.

Exposition of Psalm 112

A Sermon to the People

Verses 1-3. The praise offered by the childlike

1. There is something that you know well, brothers and sisters, for you have very often heard the Lord saying in the gospel, *Allow the children to come to me, for the kingdom of God belongs to such as these*; and again, *Anyone who fails to receive the kingdom of God like a child shall not enter it* (Mk 10:14-15). In many other passages our Lord uses this striking example of humility to rebuke the pride of our old selves and encourage us humbly to renew our lives, holding before us the image of childhood. This is why, when you hear the words, *Praise the Lord, you children*, sung in the psalms, you must not conclude that such an exhortation does not concern you, dearly beloved, because you have attained a bodily stature beyond that of childhood, or because you are in your full flush of youthful strength, or because you are beginning to display the venerable white hair of old age. This is not so, for the apostle is speaking to all of you when he says, *Do not be childish in your outlook; but be babes in your innocence of evil, so as to be mature in mind* (1 Cor 14:20). But what kind of evil, particularly? Surely pride above all. Pride, with its puffed-up delusions of greatness, does not leave room for a person to walk in the narrow way or through the narrow gate;[1] but a child gets through a narrow opening easily, and that is why no one who lacks childlike qualities gets into the kingdom of heaven. What is worse than the evil pride which can acknowledge no one's authority, not even God's? As scripture says, *the starting-point of human pride is rebellion against God* (Sir 10:14). Such pride, with its swollen, conceited obstinacy, rears up against the commandments of God and refuses the sweet yoke of the Lord. Break it, smash it to pieces, and get rid of it altogether, and then, *praise the Lord, you children, praise the name of the Lord*. When pride has been thrown down and stamped out, then is praise perfected out of the mouths of infants and nurslings.[2] Once pride has been crushed and destroyed, anyone with a mind to boast must boast only in the Lord.[3] People who think themselves important do not sing these words, nor did those who, though knowing God, did not glorify him as God or give him thanks;[4] they

---

1. See Mt 7:13-14.
2. See Ps 8:3(2).
3. See 1 Cor 1:31.
4. See Rom 1:21.

praise themselves, not God, for they are not children. They do not praise the name of the Lord because they would much prefer their own names to be proclaimed. *Their thoughts have wandered into futility and their stupid hearts have been darkened; believing themselves to be wise, they have sunk into folly* (Rom 1:21-22). Though they wanted their name to be lauded long and widely, they will quickly stumble into straitened ways. For God alone is it fitting, for the Lord alone is it proper, to be proclaimed always and everywhere. Let the proclamation resound always: *May the name of the Lord be blessed, from now on and for ever.* Let the proclamation be made everywhere: *From the rising of the sun to its setting, praise the name of the Lord.*

2. Perhaps one of these holy children who praise the Lord may put a question to me: "I understand *for ever*: that means 'to eternity.' But why *from now on*? Why not before now, indeed, before all ages? Was it not right that *the name of the Lord be blessed* before our time?" I will give this little child an answer, for the question was not posed in any argumentative spirit. To you, both masters and children, to you is the exhortation addressed, *Praise the name of the Lord.* By you *may the name of the Lord be blessed, from now on*, from the time this is said to you. You are beginning to praise him now, but go on praising him without end. *From now on and for ever* means "Never stop praising him." Do not say, "Yes, we are beginning to praise the Lord now, because we are only children, but when we have grown up and become adults, we shall praise ourselves." No, children, no; that is not the way. Through Isaiah the Lord says, *I am; and even to your old age, I am* (Is 46:4). HE WHO IS must be praised always.

Praise the Lord, you children, from now on; and praise him, you elderly folk, *for ever*, for though wisdom announces itself in your declining years by your white hair, it will not fade as the flesh grows old.[5] Childhood seems to signify humility in this context, a childlikeness that is the antithesis of empty, false pride; and therefore only children praise the Lord, because proud people have no idea how to praise him. Your old age must therefore have a childlike quality about it, and your childlikeness the wisdom of age. Your wisdom must be free from pride, and your humility must be no stranger to wisdom; then you may praise the Lord *from now on and for ever.* Wherever the Church of Christ is spread abroad through its childlike saints, let it *praise the name of the Lord.* Thus will the psalmist's injunction be obeyed: *From the rising of the sun to its setting, praise the name of the Lord.*

---

5. A pun: *canis sapientiae, sed non carnis vetustate.*

Verses 4-6. The Most High looks down on the humble, both heavenly and earthly

3. *The Lord is most high above all nations.* The nations are part of the human race, so what wonder that the Lord is most high above human beings? There are some among them who, seeing with their bodily eyes the sun and moon and stars in the sky, and observing that these shining objects are above them, worship them as gods, serving creatures and deserting the creator. But not only is the Lord *most high above all nations*; the psalm confesses that *his glory is higher than the heavens.* The heavens themselves look up at him[6] who is above them, yet the humble have him dwelling with them, because they do not worship the sky instead of God, even though they are bound by flesh to a lower plane than the heavens.

4. For *who is like the Lord our God, who dwells in high places and looks down on what is lowly?* Anybody could have guessed that he would dwell in highest heaven and from there look down on lowly things on earth; but there is more: *He looks down on what is lowly in heaven and on earth.* What high places can be his dwelling, if he can look down from there on lowly things both in heaven and on earth? Or should we understand it to mean that even the high places in which he dwells are regarded by him as themselves humble? This could be right, for he exalts the humble, but in such a way that he does not make them proud. Thus he dwells in high places in the sense that he dwells in people whom he exalts and makes into his heaven, his throne. But he regards them always not as proud persons but as subject to himself, and so even in heaven he looks down on lowly creatures, whom he yet dwells in as in lofty places. Through Isaiah the Spirit speaks: *Thus says the Most High who dwells in lofty places, he whose name is eternal, the most high Lord who has rest in his holy ones.* The prophet explains what was meant by *who dwells in lofty places*: he spells it out more fully by adding, *who has rest in his holy ones.* But who are the holy ones, if not the humble, the childlike ones who praise the Lord? Accordingly the prophet continues, *Granting nobility of soul to the pusillanimous, and giving life to those who live in humility of heart* (Is 57:15, LXX). The holy ones in whom he finds rest are the pusillanimous to whom he grants nobility of soul. By endowing them with such magnanimity he obviously raises them to the heights, and when he takes his rest in them he is dwelling in high places. But since it is on the pusillanimous that he confers this nobility, he is looking down on what is lowly even as he looks down on those high places. As the psalm testifies, *He looks down on what is lowly in heaven and on earth.*

5. By these words the psalm has provoked us into asking whether it means that the Lord our God looks down on the same lowly things both in heaven and on earth or on one sort of holy beings in heaven and different lowly beings on

---

6. Variant: "receive him."

earth. If it means that they are the same, I see a clue to understanding how this can be in the apostle's words, *Though we live in the flesh, our fighting does not rely on the flesh, for the weapons of our warfare are not carnal, but divinely potent* (2 Cor 10:3-4). How could they be potent, unless spiritual? If the apostle, then, although living in the flesh, nonetheless wages war spiritually, it is no wonder that God looks down on his humility both in heaven on account of his free spirit and on earth because of his body's servitude. Moreover in another passage the apostle says, *We have citizens' rights in heaven* (Phil 3:20), while also admitting that the best thing for him would be *to die and to be with Christ* but that *it is necessary for you that I remain in the flesh* (Phil 1:23-24). From these texts it follows that anyone who understands both the apostle's citizenship in heaven and his remaining in the flesh on earth ought also to understand how the Lord our God looks down on the lowly things both in heaven and on earth. On the heights he dwells in his holy ones; he knows these saints as humble before him, and knows them to be even now in heaven because they relish the things that are above, and have risen with Christ in hope;[7] at the same time he looks on them as still on earth, for they are not yet freed from the restrictions of the flesh to be in Christ's company with all their being.

If, however, we are to understand that the Lord our God looks on some lowly beings in heaven and different ones on earth, I think that the ones he already sees to be in heaven must be those whom he has called and in whom he now dwells; but those he regards on earth are the ones he is calling, that he may dwell in them. The former are his possession as they meditate on the things of heaven; the latter he awakens as they dream of things on earth.

6. It may be difficult for us to accept, though, that people who have not yet bowed willing necks to the Lord's sweet yoke can be called humble. This is especially difficult when the divine scripture instructs us throughout the whole text of this psalm to understand the humble things it refers to as holy things. There is therefore another possible interpretation which I would like you to consider with me, dearest friends.[8] In this new perspective I think that the heavens symbolize those who will sit upon twelve thrones and judge with the Lord,[9] while by the word "earth" the psalm indicates the multitude of other blessed people who will be placed at the Lord's right hand whence, commended for their works of mercy, they may be welcomed into the tents of eternity by the friends they made for themselves through unrighteous mammon in this mortal life.[10] This interpretation seems plausible to me because the apostle demands of such people, *If we have sown spiritual seeds for your benefit, is it too much to ask*

---

7. See Col 3:1.
8. *Caritas vestra.*
9. See Mt 19:28.
10. See Lk 16:9.

that we reap a carnal harvest from you? (1 Cor 9:11) We could paraphrase that as follows: "If we have sown heavenly seeds for your benefit, is it too much to ask that we reap an earthly harvest from you?" God looks down on those who sow heavenly seed and looks on them in heaven; and he looks down on earth to see those who yield an earthly harvest. Yet both the one group and the other he sees as humble. *He looks down on what is lowly in heaven and on earth* because both groups remember what they were through their own bad will, and what they have become through God's grace. It was not to his hearers only that Paul, God's chosen instrument,[11] was speaking when he recalled, *You were darkness once, but now you are light in the Lord* (Eph 5:8); and again, *By grace you have been saved, through faith, and this is not your own doing but the grace of God. It does not come from works, lest anyone boast.* But then he includes himself by continuing, *We are his own handiwork, created in Christ Jesus for good works.* (Eph 2:8-10) Furthermore he makes separate explicit statements concerning himself and others who are regarded as "in heaven." *By nature we too were children of wrath, like the rest* (Eph 2:3), he says; and again, *We too were once foolish and unbelieving, going astray, enslaved to all sorts of desires and pleasures, acting out of malice and envy, hateful ourselves and hating one another. But when the kindness and humanity of God our Savior appeared he saved us, not in view of any righteous deeds we might have done, but because of his own mercy, through the laver of rebirth.* (Ti 3:3-5)

Such are the humble creatures upon whom God looks down in heaven. They are spiritual persons and judge all things,[12] yet they remain humble lest they be cast down and judged. And has Paul anything to say of himself in particular? Yes, for does he not associate himself with what he said earlier? *I am not worthy to be called an apostle, because I persecuted God's Church; but I received mercy, because I acted in ignorance* (1 Cor 15:9; 1 Tm 1:13).

Verses 7-9. The exaltation of the humble; the fruitfulness of the Church

7. The Spirit, speaking through the preceding verses of the psalm, has asked us to consider the words: *who is like the Lord our God, who dwells in high places and looks down on what is lowly in heaven and on earth?* Now he wants to teach us why people can be called lowly in heaven, even when they are already persons of great spiritual stature, worthy to take their places on judges' seats. He therefore immediately adds that the Lord *raises up the needy from the earth, and exalts the pauper from the dungheap, to give him a place among princes, with the princes of God's people.* Let not the heads of those exalted ones disdain to bow down under the Lord's hand. Even though a faithful steward of his Lord's

---

11. See Acts 9:15.
12. See 1 Cor 2:15.

wealth be given a place with the princes of God's people, even though such a person be found worthy to sit among the twelve thrones and even to judge angels,[13] nonetheless he or she is a needy person when raised from the earth, a pauper when exalted from the dungheap. Can you deny that they were lifted up from a dungheap, those who used to be enslaved to all sorts of desires and pleasures? Well, yes, you say; but when those things were said of them they were not needy, not poor any longer. Are you sure? Then why do they still groan under the weight of the body, longing to have their heavenly dwelling put on over it?[14] Why are they still buffeted to save them from becoming arrogant, and subjected to a messenger from Satan, a sting in the flesh?[15] They are on the heights, certainly, for the Lord dwells in them; they possess the Spirit who searches all things, even the heights of God,[16] and thus they are truly in heaven; yet even in heaven the Lord looks down on what is humble.

8. Well then, brothers and sisters, we have heard about the lowly in heaven, and about their being raised from the dungheap to be given places with the princes of God's people. What about the lowly upon whom the Lord looks down on earth? Are there any prophecies here about them? Surely there must be, because only a few people will qualify as the friends of the Lord who will judge with him, but far more numerous are they who will be welcomed into the tents of eternity. When you think of the whole harvest, the grain seems paltry compared with the quantity of straw attached, but considered in itself the grain is nevertheless very plentiful. *Many are the children of the forsaken one, more than of her who has a husband* (Is 54:1); the children of her who conceived in her old age through grace are more numerous than those of her who from her early youth was wedded under the bond of the law. When I say, "in her old age" I am thinking of Sarah who is our mother, for through her one child Isaac she is the mother of all believers throughout the nations.[17]

9. But the woman alluded to in another passage in Isaiah seems to be mother of no one at all, a woman who has borne no children. Look at what he says, *The children whom you had lost will be saying in your hearing, This place is too cramped for us; make us a place now where we can live. But you will say in your heart, Who has begotten these children for me, when I knew myself to be child-*

---

13. See 1 Cor 6:3.
14. See 2 Cor 5:2.
15. See 2 Cor 12:7.
16. See 1 Cor 2:10. *Altus, altitudo* can mean either "high, height" or "deep, depths," and the phrase in 1 Cor 2:10 is usually translated "the depths of God." But since Augustine has used *altus* to mean "high" at the beginning of the sentence, the sense seems to demand "the heights of God" here.
17. The contrast is between the regime of grace already exemplified in Abraham, Sarah, and Isaac, the child of promise, and the regime of law inaugurated at the time of Israel's "early youth" (see Jer 2:2-3) under Moses. Compare the argument in Gal 3:6-22; 4:22-31. Sarah thus prefigures the Church. But the antithesis between law and grace is strengthened in the following lines.

less and widowed? Who has raised these up for me? I was abandoned and alone; where have these come from? How are they mine? (Is 49:20-21, LXX) The Church makes these words her own when she considers what seems to be her barrenness among all the crowds of people who did not leave all things to follow the Lord, and thereby win a place on the twelve thrones. Yet how many among that crowd make friends for themselves by means of unrighteous mammon, and through their works of mercy will stand at the Lord's right hand? Not only does the Lord raise up from the dungheap a person to whom he will assign a place with the princes of his people; he goes further: *He makes the barren woman dwell at home, a joyful mother of children.* He who dwells in the heights does both these things. He multiplies Abraham's seed like the stars of heaven, for he establishes sublime holiness on heavenly thrones.[18] But he also multiplies Abraham's seed like the sand on the seashore by separating that merciful, uncountable multitude from the waves on the left[19] and from the bitter, salty sea of unbelief.

---

18. Variant: "establishes it on heavenly thrones in recognition of its sublime holiness."
19. *A sinistris fluctibus*: a play on the double meaning of *sinister*, which signifies primarily "pertaining to the left hand" and hence alludes to the Lord's left in the parable of Mt 25:31-46, and by extension "unfavorable, unlucky, bad." Compare Exposition of Psalm 16,8 and the note there.

Exposition 1 of Psalm 113[1]

First Sermon[2]

Verses 1-6. Both the experiences of God's ancient people and the psalmist's reinterpretation of them are the work of the Spirit and types of our salvation

1. We have read in the Book of Exodus, beloved brothers and sisters, how the people of Israel were set free from the unjust oppression they had endured under the Egyptians and how the waters of the sea were divided to allow them to cross on dry land.[3] Having read about this we have it firmly fixed in our minds. We remember too what happened when the people were about to enter the promised land: as soon as the River Jordan came into contact with the feet of the priests who carried the ark of the Lord, the water above that place was held in check, while the lower part flowed down and away into the sea, until the priests could stand on dry ground and the whole people could cross.[4] We know about all these events; but when we consider this psalm, to which we respond by saying and singing, *Alleluia*, we should not assume that the Holy Spirit intends us simply to recall what was done in the past, giving no thought to similar happenings in the future. As the apostle says, *All these things happened to them, but with symbolic import, for they are written down as a rebuke to us, upon whom the climax of the ages has come* (1 Cor 10:11). The psalm opens with the words, *When Israel went forth from Egypt, the house of Jacob from a barbarous people, Judah became his sanctification, Israel his display of power. The sea saw it and fled, the Jordan was turned back.* When we hear these words, we should not suppose that past events only are being related to us but rather understand that the future is being foretold. The wonderful things that took place among the people of Israel were present to them at the time, certainly, but they were not without import for the future.

Now the one same Spirit was at work in both the happenings of old and the words of the psalm later. In foretelling the future by singing these words in the psalm he wished to show us that the same mystery was being revealed by both the actions[5] and the words, so that though the full truth was held back to be mani-

---

1. Verses 1-8 of Psalm 113A in the LXX and Latin = Psalm 114 in Hebrew.
2. Probably preached in paschal time, though the year is not certain.
3. See Ex 14:22.
4. See Jos 3:15-17.
5. Variant: "the figurative events."

fested at the end of time, it might be figuratively announced through both events and words long beforehand.[6] To make this amply clear the Spirit did not in the psalm describe events exactly as we learn of their happening historically. He introduced some differences, lest we should imagine that the psalm was simply recounting deeds over and done with rather than foretelling[7] the future. To begin with, we do not read in the history that the Jordan was turned back in its course, only that it was restrained in its upper reaches while the people crossed. Secondly, we read nothing of mountains and hills skipping joyfully. But the psalm added these touches in order to take them all up again in the repetition; for after saying, *The sea saw it and fled, the Jordan was turned back*, it continued, *The mountains skipped like rams, and the hills like new-born lambs*, and then turned the same expressions into questions: *What ailed you, sea, that you fled away, or you, Jordan, that you turned back? What ailed you, mountains, that you skipped like rams, and you, O hills, like new-born lambs?*

2. Let us pay close attention, then, and try to understand the instruction we are given, for the events were types with significance for us, and the words encourage us to recognize ourselves. If we hold on with steady hearts to the grace God has given us, we are Israel, we are Abraham's posterity. The apostle assures us: *You are the descendants of Abraham* (Gal 3:29). In another passage he says, *Abraham's faith was reckoned to him as justification, not when he was circumcised but in his uncircumcised condition. He accepted circumcision as a seal on the justification he had received through faith, a faith that is present in the uncircumcised, to be reckoned as justifying them also. Thus Abraham is indeed the father of the circumcised, but of those who do not rely on their circumcision but tread in the footprints of his faith, the faith that was in our father Abraham when he was still uncircumcised.* (Rom 4:9-12) It was not only to a race circumcised in the carnal sense that he became father; to him was the assurance given, *I have made you the father of many nations* (Gn 17:4). "Many" in this context means not certain people only, but all. This was made clear when God promised Abraham, *In you shall all the nations of the earth be blessed* (Gn 22:18).

No Christian should therefore consider himself or herself alien to the name Israel. In Christ, the cornerstone, we are bound to those from the Jewish race who have come to believe, foremost among whom are the apostles.[8] The Lord says in another passage, *Other sheep I have, not counted in this fold; them too I must lead in, that there may be but one flock and one shepherd* (Jn 10:16). The Christian people has therefore a better right to the name Israel; it is more truly the house of Jacob. (Israel is, of course, the same as Jacob.) But the great majority of

---

6. Compare Vatican II: *Dei Verbum* 2.
7. Variant: "foreseeing."
8. See Eph 2:20.

the Jews, rejected on account of their faithlessness, were seduced by carnal indulgence to sell their prerogative as the firstborn and so belong more to Esau than to Jacob.[9] You know the mystical significance of the prophecy, *The elder shall serve the younger* (Gn 25:23).

3. The name Egypt is interpreted "affliction" or "one who afflicts" or "oppressor." Egypt is therefore often used as a symbol of this world, which we must spiritually leave in order not to be yoked in fellowship with unbelievers.[10] Just as the chosen people would not be led into the promised land until it had left Egypt behind, so no one becomes a fit citizen of the heavenly Jerusalem except by first renouncing this world. But Israel was able to leave Egypt only because set free by God's help, and so too no one's heart turns away from this world unless fortified by the gift of divine mercy. That escape from Egypt happened once and served as a prophetic sign; but it is fulfilled daily as the Church becomes fruitful in every new believer in this final age of the world, this *last hour* (1 Jn 2:18), as blessed John calls it. Listen to the apostle, the teacher of the Gentiles, spelling this out for our instruction: *I would not have you ignorant, brothers and sisters, that all our ancestors walked under the cloud, and all crossed the sea, and all were through Moses baptized in cloud and sea; all of them ate the same spiritual food and all drank the same spiritual drink, for they drank from the spiritual rock that followed them, and that rock was Christ. Yet God was not pleased with all of them: they fell in the desert. These events are types for us.* (1 Cor 10:1-6) What clearer instruction can you ask for, beloved brothers and sisters? The truth is plain to see, demonstrated not by human conjecture but by apostolic teaching, which means divine teaching, the lesson given us by the Lord; for God spoke through the apostles. The Lord was the thunderer, even though his roar came through the clouds of human flesh. On the strength of such irrefutable testimony it is clear that all these things which happened with symbolic meaning are now being fulfilled in our salvation. Long ago they were foretold as future; now they are read about as past, but recognized as present.

Within the Old Testament itself past events were recognized as having been prophetic; an example from Micah

4. Now listen to something even more wonderful. Obscure, veiled mysteries in the books of the Old Testament are sometimes unveiled by those ancient books themselves. The prophet Micah says this: *As in the days when they came out of Egypt, I will show them marvels. The Gentiles will see, and they will be confounded and lose their strength; they will cover their mouths with their*

---

9. See Gn 25:29-34.
10. See 2 Cor 6:14.

hands, and their ears will be deafened. They will lick the earth, dragging them-selves along the ground like snakes; they will come trembling out of their strong-holds, they will be distraught and terrified by you, our Lord God. Who is like you, O God, who take away iniquity and overlook guilt for the remnant of your inheritance? He has not harbored his anger against his covenant people, for he is propitious and merciful; he will turn to us and have pity on us, he will drown our sins, plunging all our offenses into the depths of the sea. (Mic 7:15-19) You can see here, brothers and sisters, that sacred mysteries are being opened in a quite unambiguous way.[11]

Our psalm, likewise, is ostensibly recounting events in the past, yet the wonderful Spirit of prophecy is looking to the future. *Judah became his sanctifi-cation . . . the sea saw it and fled,* says the psalm. The words *became, saw,* and *fled* are all verbs in the past tense; similarly the phrases, *the Jordan was turned back, the mountains skipped,* and *the earth trembled,* all sound like statements about the past, yet this still allows the possibility of referring them to the future. Were it not so, we should be obliged to fly in the face of gospel testimony and take the text, *They shared out my garments among them, and cast lots for my tunic* (Ps 21:19(22:18)), as a record of past events, rather than as a prophecy of what was to come. The verbs in that passage are in the past tense, to be sure, but the prophecy was fulfilled long afterward in the Lord's passion.

The prophet whom we quoted just now was acting similarly, beloved friends. He refined the rough hearts of his hearers, and did not hesitate to stretch them toward an understanding of the future derived from the events of the past. This means that when we believe those events to hold symbolic meaning for us, we believe it not on apostolic authority alone; we find that the prophets themselves did not neglect to teach the same lesson. When their words open this truth for us, we can therefore see and rejoice, and bring forth from God's treasures both new things and old,[12] secure in the conviction that old and new are in harmony and mutually coherent. When the prophet already quoted sang these lines, so long after the exodus of his people from Egypt, and so long before the era of the Church, he was unquestionably claiming to foretell the future. *As in the days when they came out of Egypt, I will show them marvels,* he said. *The Gentiles will see, and they will be confounded.* This casts light on our psalm, which says, *The sea saw it and fled.* Since those verbs in the psalm are in the past tense, the fact that they announce future events might not seem obvious; but there is no doubt that the prophet's words, *The Gentiles will see, and they will be confounded,* are a statement about the future. These verbs are in the future tense; who would be so

---

11. The principle that the Old Testament is in some passages the interpreter of itself is one recognized by modern scholars. Some of the later parts of Isaiah, for example, are evidence of a re-reading of the exodus traditions, as are certain psalms.
12. See Mt 13:52.

perverse as to refer them to events in the past? Just after this the same prophet makes it clear, clearer than daylight, that those enemies of ours who pursued us with murderous intent as we fled from them—our sins, I mean—were drowned and annihilated in baptism, like the Egyptians overwhelmed by the sea; for he says that the Lord *is propitious and merciful; he will turn to us and have pity on us, he will drown our sins, plunging all our offenses into the depths of the sea.*

Christians are Israelites, and in them the types are fulfilled

5. What conclusion shall we draw, dearly beloved? Already you know yourselves to be Israelites, being Abraham's descendants; you recognize yourselves to be the house of Jacob and heirs according to God's promise;[13] realize also that once you have renounced this world you have left Egypt. By distancing yourselves from pagan blasphemies and devoutly confessing your faith you have accomplished your exodus from a barbarous people. It is not your language but a barbarian tongue that is unable to praise God, but you sing Alleluia to him. *Judah has become his sanctification* in you, for *a Jew is not one who is so outwardly, nor is circumcision an external mark in the flesh. A Jew is one who is such inwardly, by circumcision of the heart.* (Rom 2:28-29) Question your own hearts, then: if faith has circumcised them, if confession has purified them, *Judah has become his sanctification* in you, and in you *Israel is his display of power*, for he has given you power to become children of God.[14]

6. Now let each one of you cast his or her mind back. Your heart had been laboring in the carnal servitude of this world, laboring fruitlessly, as though condemned to make bricks in Egypt under the harsh domination of the devil. But the day came when you heard the Lord's voice calling, *Come to me, all you who labor and are heavily burdened, and I will give you relief* (Mt 11:28). Your heart longed to draw closer to God; it withdrew from the desires that belonged to its ignorance, and sincerely subjected itself to Christ's sweet yoke. It abandoned its servile labors, casting them aside and running to take up Christ's light burden instead. Now, I am asking each of you to remember how all the worldly things that had been hampering you fell away, and how the voices of those who tried to dissuade you either dared not blurt out their arguments or were terrified into silence when they observed how Christ's name has been exalted and honored in every land. In your own experience, then, *the sea saw it and fled*, so that a way to freedom lay open before you, with no one to block your path.

7. As for the words, *the Jordan was turned back*, I would not wish you to seek a meaning outside yourselves for these either, or to take them in a bad sense. The Lord rebukes certain people who turned their backs, not their faces, toward

---

13. See Gal 3:29.
14. See Jn 1:12.

him.[15] People who desert the author of their being and turn away from their creator hurtle down into the salty wickedness[16] of this world like rivers into the sea. The best thing for such people is to turn back from their course, so that God, whom they had thrust behind them, is before their faces as they return. The sea of this world, which they had been facing as they were sliding into it, will now be behind them. Henceforth they must forget what is behind and stretch out to what lies ahead;[17] this is right for those who have turned round. The situation is different before their conversion, for if they then forget what is behind them, they are forgetting God, whom they have put behind their backs, and if they stretch out to what lies ahead they are stretching out toward the world to which they have turned their faces, eager to plunge into it.

The Jordan therefore represents those who have received the grace of baptism. For them the Jordan is turned back when they are converted to God, so that they no longer have him behind them but with unveiled faces behold the glory of the Lord and can be transformed into his likeness from glory to glory.[18]

8. *The mountains skipped like rams*: these rams are the holy apostles, faithful dispensers of the word of truth and preachers of the gospel.[19] *And the hills like new-born lambs*: these are the people to whom the apostle says, *In Christ Jesus through the gospel I have begotten you* (1 Cor 4:15); these are the ones to whom he says, *I do not write so to shame you; I am simply warning you as my most dear children* (1 Cor 4:14); these are they of whom scripture says, *Bring the offspring of rams to the Lord* (Ps 28(29):1). Mark well, all you in every land who have the faculty of wondering at these things, you who know how to rejoice and sing to the Lord your God; mark well how these things which were done with figurative significance so long ago, and prophesied so long ago, are being fulfilled throughout all nations.

9. Put your questions now, and ask, *What ailed you, sea, that you fled away, or you, Jordan, that you turned back? What ailed you, mountains, that you skipped like rams, and you, O hills, like new-born lambs?* What ailed you, O world, that the hindrances you used to put in our way have ceased to trouble us? Why are you turning to your Lord, all you thousands of believers everywhere, who forsake this world? Why are you so happy, each of you to whom the Lord will say at the end, *Well done, good servant; you have been faithful over a few things. I will set you over many* (Mt 25:21)? Why are you so happy, all you who will be invited at the end, *Come, you whom my Father has blessed; take possession of the kingdom prepared for you since the world was made* (Mt 25:34)?

---

15. See Jer 2:27; 32:33.
16. Variant: "merrymaking."
17. See Phil 3:13.
18. See 2 Cor 3:18.
19. On the apostles as rams, compare Exposition of Psalm 64,18.

Verses 7-10(2). Detailed Christological application

10. All these will give you the same answer you are giving to yourselves: *The earth trembled before the face of the Lord, in the presence of the God*[20] *of Jacob*. But what are we to understand by *the face of the Lord*? Surely the presence of him who promised, *Lo, I am with you throughout all days, even to the end of the ages* (Mt 28:20). The earth has certainly been made to tremble, but it was in a slothful state before it was disturbed. It was set trembling to its profit, that it might be more firmly established before the face of the Lord.

11. *He turned the rock into pools of water, and the crag into leaping springs*. God melted himself, so to speak, turning what had seemed to be a hardness in himself into a gift of water for his faithful ones, that it might become in them a spring of water leaping up to eternal life.[21] As long as they knew nothing of him, he seemed hard. The objectors who complained, *This is a hard saying; who could listen to it?* (Jn 6:61) were disconcerted by the hardness and could not wait until the scriptures were opened and Christ caused a stream, a flood, to pour over them. That rock, that hard rock, was changed into pools of water and those crags into leaping springs when Christ rose from the dead and, beginning from Moses, went through all the prophets, explaining to his disciples that the Christ had to suffer.[22] Then he sent upon them his Holy Spirit, of whom he had said, *Let anyone who is thirsty come and drink* (Jn 7:37).

12. *Not to us, Lord, not to us, but to your name give the glory*.[23] The grace of this water that leaps from the rock—*and the rock was Christ* (1 Cor 10:4)—was not given as a reward for any works that preceded it on our part, but only through the mercy of him who justifies the godless.[24] Christ died for the godless,[25] that men and women might seek not their own glory, but the glory of God's name.

13. *On account of your mercy and truth*, the psalm continues. Notice how often these two qualities, mercy and truth, are found together in the holy scriptures. God has called the impious by his mercy, and in his truth he judges those who though called have refused to come. *Lest the pagans ask, Where is their God?* On the last day, when the sign of the Son of Man appears in the sky, his mercy and truth will be revealed, and then all the tribes of the earth will mourn.[26] They will not ask then, *Where is their God?* for then he will not be preached to them as someone in whom they are asked to believe, but shown to them as one they must fear.

20. Variant: "the Lord."
21. See Jn 4:14.
22. See Lk 24:27.26.
23. In the Hebrew numbering Psalm 115 (Ps 113B in the Latin) begins with this verse. The verse numbers of Psalm 113B are given in brackets.
24. See Rom 4:5.
25. See Rom 5:6.
26. See Mt 24:30.

Verse 11(3). The transcendence of God

14. *But our God is in heaven above.* Not in the sky will they see him, where they see the sun and the moon, works of God that they worship, but *in heaven above*, which transcends all heavenly and earthly creatures. Nor is our God in heaven in such a fashion that if heaven were taken away he would need to fear a fall, being robbed of his throne. *In the heavens and on earth he has done all that he willed.* He does not need his creatures, as though they provided him with a place of stability; on the contrary, he abides unchanging in his eternity, and there abiding he has done whatever he willed in heaven and on earth. They did not first support him so that he could make them; if they had not first been made, they could not be his throne. He dwells in them, and contains them as needy, dependent creatures; he is not contained by them as though needy himself.

Another interpretation of the verse, *In the heavens and on earth he has done all that he willed,* would be this: he has assigned his freely given grace to both the noblest and the least of his people, so that no one may boast of his or her own merits. Whether it is a matter of the mountains skipping like rams, or of the hills like new-born lambs, only before the face of the Lord was the earth made to tremble, and that was what saved them from sticking for ever in their terrestrial mud.

Exposition 2 of Psalm 113[1]

Second Sermon

Verses 1-4. Our God is invisible: Augustine begins his polemic against idolatry

1. For those who diligently study them, it may be obvious that all the psalms are so interconnected that there is always continuity between a psalm and the one that follows it. However this may be, we should at least regard this present psalm as forming a unity with its predecessor. Remember how in that psalm we heard, *Not to us, Lord, not to us, but to your name give the glory on account of your mercy and truth, lest the pagans ask, Where is their God?* We worship a God who is invisible. He cannot be seen by any bodily eye but is known only to very clean hearts, and few of us have those. This might seem to give pagans an excuse to ask, *Where is their God?* since, unlike us, they can show us their gods, visible to our eyes. This is why the foregoing psalm warned us in advance that the presence of our God is to be discerned in his works, for being enthroned *in heaven above, he has done all that he willed in the heavens and on earth.* Let the pagans show us their gods, it seems to be saying, for *the idols of the Gentiles are fashioned of silver and gold, the work of human hands.* We cannot display our God before your eyes, you pagans, though you ought to perceive him through his works; you, on the contrary, can point to the deities you worship. But do not let that lead you astray into empty fantasies. It would do you far more credit to admit you have nothing to show than to prove how blind your hearts are by demonstrating your gods to our bodily eyes. What are you showing us? Only gold and silver.

It is true that the pagans also have bronze idols, and wooden ones, and others of earthenware and all sorts of other similar materials, but the Holy Spirit chose to mention the precious metals only, because when someone begins to be ashamed of what is particularly dear to him, he will turn away much more easily from the veneration of cheaper things. In another scriptural passage the devotees of idols are described as *saying to a piece of wood, You are my father, and to a stone, You begot me* (Jer 2:27). But if anyone thinks himself superior because he does not address wood or stone in those terms, but only gold and silver, let him examine the psalm and bend the ear of his heart to its verdict: *The idols of the*

---

1. Psalm 113B. In the Hebrew numbering Psalm 115.

Gentiles are silver and gold. Nothing worthless or tawdry was mentioned. To a mind not earthly itself, gold and silver are of course no better than earth, but a more beautiful and shining earth, more solid and durable. Do not try to make your case by pointing out that human hands have added value to it. From that metal which the true God made, you want to make a false god or, rather, a false man, whom you then venerate instead of the true God! If anyone were to mistake it for a real human being and try to make friends with it, such a person would be accounted mad. A likeness of the human mortal shape, with its members disposed in an orderly fashion that imitates the human body, attracts fickle hearts and sweeps them along into gross passion. But if you can indicate the several organs in this copy that bewitches you, O human vanity, show us also how they all work.

Verses 5-8. The absurdity and dangers of idolatry

2. *They have mouths, but will never speak; they have eyes, but will not see; ears, but will hear nothing; nostrils, but no sense of smell; hands that will never handle anything; and feet that will never walk; nor will they produce any sound from their throats.* The craftsman who fashioned them is better than they are, because he had the power to make them by moving his limbs and plying his trade; yet you would be ashamed to worship the craftsman, wouldn't you? You yourself are better than they, for although you did not make them, you can do things they cannot do. Even an animal is better, for notice the last point added by the psalm: the idols *will not produce any sound from their throats*. At the beginning of the list it had said, *They have mouths, but will never speak*, so what need was there to return to the sounds uttered from the throat, after running through the other members from head to foot? The psalm chose to return to the mouth, I think, because we are used to thinking of all the other faculties listed as common to humans and beasts. The beasts see, and hear, and smell, and walk; some of them, such as apes, hold things with their hands. But the statement about the mouth at the beginning of the list mentioned a faculty proper to human beings, for animals do not speak. In the light of that, a reader might have assumed that all the other items in the list referred exclusively to human faculties and that thus the psalm was attributing to humans alone a higher dignity than to pagan gods. To guard against this misunderstanding, the psalm added at the end, *Nor will they produce any sound from their throats*, for both humans and animals can do that. On the other hand, if the psalmist had put that statement first, beginning his list with the mouth and simply saying that the idols have mouths but never utter any sound, it would still have seemed to suggest that the whole list envisaged human nature only, and then the hearer's mind would not easily have adverted to any kinship between humans and animals. Instead the psalm first mentioned something about the mouth that is proper to human beings, then enumerated parts of

the body, ending with the feet; and that seemed to have concluded the list. But then it added, *Nor will they produce any sound from their throats*, and thereby alerted the reader or hearer, who would wonder about the addition and so discover that we are being told of the superiority not of humans only, but even of beasts, to pagan idols. If pagans find it shameful to worship an animal, which God has endowed with the power to see, hear, smell, handle objects, walk, and produce sounds from its throat, they must see how much more shameful it is to worship an idol which is dumb and lifeless. It has been given fake human organs only so that a soul dominated by sensuality may feel affection for a thing that appears living and animated, since the worshipper is aware of similar organs as living and animated in himself. Mice and snakes and other live creatures are much better judges of pagan idols, we might say, for they take no notice of the human shape of an object in which they detect no human life. They often build their nests in the idols, and unless driven away by human activity they seek no more secure habitat. But along comes a human being, moving to frighten the animal away from his god; then he worships as powerful an object impotent to move itself, from which the worshipper had to scare off an animal that was better than the idol. He has frightened a seeing creature away from a blind thing, a hearing creature from a deaf thing, a walking animal from an immobile image, a sentient creature from something without feeling, and a living animal from a dead object—indeed, from one worse than dead, for although a corpse is obviously not alive, it is equally obvious that it has been alive. A corpse has more dignity, therefore, than a god who is not alive and never has been.

3. Can anything be more glaringly plain, my dearest brothers and sisters? Could anything stand out more clearly? Would any child, on being questioned, not reply that it is quite certain that pagan idols *have mouths, but will never speak; eyes, but will not see*, and so on, as God's word has spelled it out? Why, then, does the Holy Spirit go to so much trouble to make the point and drive it home to us in several passages of the scriptures, as though we were ignorant, as though all this were not plain and well known to everyone? The reason, I think, is this. We have become accustomed to observing limbs and organs naturally present and alive in animals, and to feeling them alive in ourselves. Now when a humanoid form is skillfully wrought to serve as some sign (as the idolaters claim) and placed on a raised platform, and when the crowd begins to worship it and pay it homage, it engenders in each one of them a most foul misapprehension. The worshippers detect no signs of life or movement in the artifact, but they think the god is hiding. They are misled by the idol's appearance and swayed by the pressure of so-called wise teachers and compliant crowds. They cannot believe that an image which looks so much like a human body has no living tenant.

Popular attitudes of this kind are an invitation to evil demons to take possession of pagan idols. With demons in charge, deadly errors are sown and multiplied through all kinds of deception. The divine scriptures are in various passages watchful about this danger also, lest when the idols are derided anyone protest, "I worship not the visible image but the deity that invisibly dwells in it." Scripture counters this by condemning the gods themselves: *All the gods of the heathen are demons*, it says, *but the Lord made the heavens* (Ps 95(96):5). The apostle concurs. *Not that an idol is anything*, he explains, *but the sacrifices offered by pagans are offered to demons, not to God; and I do not want you to have any truck with demons* (1 Cor 10:19-20).

4. There are people who declare, "I worship neither an idol nor a demon, but I regard the image as a physical sign of what I ought to worship." Such people think themselves practitioners of a purer religion. They interpret their idols in various ways. One is said to be an image of the earth, so they speak of the temple of Tellus.[2] Another signifies the sea and is therefore called Neptune;[3] another the air, whence the name Juno;[4] another is a symbol of fire and is called Vulcan.[5] Another idol represents the morning star and is therefore called Venus.[6] Yet another idol signifies the sun, another the moon, and the devotees call their images by the names of the objects signified, as in the case of Tellus. They impose one star's name on this image, another star's on that, or the name of this or that other creature on some other image again. We cannot enumerate them all. When the worshippers begin to be embarrassed by the charge that they are adoring material things like earth, sea, air, and fire—objects that are readily available for our use—they have the temerity to reply that they are not paying cult to the physical objects themselves but to the deities who preside over and rule them. (Less embarrassment is felt in the case of objects in the sky, since we cannot handle these, or even make contact with them, except visually.) The apostle pronounces both condemnation and punishment in a single sentence: *They changed the truth of God into a lie, and they worshipped and served a crea-ture rather than the creator, who is blessed for ever* (Rom 1:25). In the first half of this sentence he condemned idols and in the second half the interpretations imposed on them. By giving to images made by a craftsman the names of things fashioned by God they change God's truth into a lie; by paying divine honors to the things signified they are serving *a creature rather than the creator, who is blessed for ever.*

5. Does anyone worship or pray with his eyes fixed on the image, without being persuaded that the image is hearing his petition and without hoping that it

---

2. A Roman goddess, personifying the productive power of the earth. Augustine speaks of her and her male counterpart Tellumo in *The City of God* 7, 23.
3. The god of waters and of the sea, brother of Jupiter.
4. The wife and sister of Jupiter.
5. Or Volcan, god of fire, son of Jupiter and Juno.
6. The Roman goddess of love, identified with the Greek Aphrodite, associated with various other things including the planet Venus.

will give him what he wants? Probably not. So thoroughly entangled do people become in such superstitions that they often turn their backs on the real sun and pour out their prayers to the statue they call Sun; or again, while the sound of the sea is battering them from behind they batter the statue of Neptune with their sighs as though it were conscious, that statue which they venerate as representative of the actual sea. What causes this error—almost forces the illusion on them, in fact—is the human likeness with all its bodily parts. The minds of the worshippers are accustomed to living with their own bodily senses, and so they judge that a body very similar to their own is more likely to be responsive than the sun's orb, or the wide waves, or any other object clearly not built on the same plane as the living creatures they are used to seeing.

Weak, carnal human beings can all too easily be trapped by this illusion, but God's scriptures sing a different song to warn us against it, nudging and arousing the minds of men and women by restating to them what they already know so well. *The idols of the Gentiles are fashioned of silver and gold*, it tells us. But God made silver and gold, didn't he? Yes, but the idols are *the work of human hands*: people are venerating what they have made themselves out of gold and silver.

6. It may be objected that we ourselves have many vessels and other accessories made of similar metals, which we use in the celebration of the sacraments. They are consecrated to divine service and are called holy in honor of him who is worshipped through their use for our salvation. Such vessels and implements are obviously the work of human hands: what else could they be? But do they have mouths that will never speak, or eyes that will never see? And does the fact that we make use of them to offer our supplications to God mean that we are begging anything from them? Of course not.

The principal cause of insane, blasphemous idolatry is this: a form resembling that of a living person—a form that by its lifelike appearance seems to demand worship—is more powerfully persuasive to the emotions of its wretched suppliants than the plain fact that it is not alive and ought to be scorned by anyone who is. The evidence of mouths, eyes, ears, nostrils, hands, and feet in the idols has more power to lead an unhappy soul astray than the evident inability on their part to speak, see, hear, smell, handle things, or walk has power to bring such a soul back to the truth.

7. The inevitable result is the deterioration the psalm goes on to describe: *May those who fashion them become like them, and all who put their trust in them*. Let people with open and seeing eyes gaze at images that neither see nor live, and let their minds become closed and dead as they worship.

Verses 9-14. God's blessing upon great and small

8. But *the house of Israel has hoped[7] in the Lord*, for *if hope is seen, it is hope no longer, for when someone sees what he hopes for, why should he hope for it? But if we hope for what we do not see, we wait for it in patience.* (Rom 8:24-25) To ensure that such patience holds out to the end, the Lord *is their helper and defender.*

Someone might think, perhaps, that spiritual persons see already—those spiritual ones, I mean, who gently instruct the carnally-minded[8] and like higher beings intercede for their inferiors. Were that the case, what is still an object of hope for the lower ones would be an experienced reality already[9] for spiritual persons. But no, this is not how things are, for *the house of Aaron* also *has hoped[10] in the Lord.* They too need help if they are to persevere in stretching out to what lies ahead and persevere in the race until they grasp him by whom they have been grasped[11] and come to know even as they have been known.[12] For the house of Aaron also, then, the Lord *is their helper and defender.* Both groups *fear the Lord* and *have hoped in the Lord; he is their helper and defender.*

9. None of us takes the initiative in approaching the mercy of God; *the Lord has been mindful of us and blessed us. He has blessed the house of Israel, he has blessed the house of Aaron*, and in blessing both *he has blessed all those who fear the Lord.* If you wonder what "both" means, the psalm replies, *The little along with the great*; that is, the house of Israel along with the house of Aaron. All those who from that race have believed in Jesus as their Savior are included. *God was not pleased with all of them* (1 Cor 10:5), but *if some of them refused to believe, will their unbelief nullify the faithfulness of God? Absolutely not. For not all who spring from Israel are Israelites, nor are all those sprung from Abraham's stock his children*; but, as scripture testifies, *a remnant has been saved.* (Rom 3:3; 9:6-7,27) Scripture speaks in the person of those Jews who have believed when it says, *If the Lord of hosts had not left us seed, we should have become like Sodom, we should have been like Gomorrah* (Is 1:9; Rom 9:29). The believing remnant is called *seed* because when scattered over the earth it multiplied.

---

7. Variant: "hopes."
8. See Gal 6:1.
9. Augustine's frequent contrast between *spes* and *res* is found again here.
10. Variant: "will hope."
11. See Phil 3:12-13.
12. See 1 Cor 13:12.

10. The great ones of the house of Israel prayed, *May the Lord increase bless-ings upon you, upon you and upon your children;*[13] and this happened indeed, for children of Abraham were raised up even from the stones[14] and they came to the Lord. Sheep that were not from that sheepfold came too, that there might be but one flock and one shepherd.[15] All the believing Gentiles came, and the numbers grew and grew, not of wise priests[16] only but also of obedient peoples; for the Lord was increasing his blessings not only upon the fathers, who had come first to him in Christ and set an example to the rest, but upon their children as well, as the children followed their fathers in dedicated faith. We are reminded of the words[17] of a man to some whom he had begotten in Christ through the gospel: *Be imitators of me, as I am of Christ* (1 Cor 4:16). The Lord increased his blessings not only upon the mountains that pranced like rams but also upon the hills that skipped like new-born lambs.

Verses 15-18. "Heaven's heaven" is for God, the earth for humankind

11. To these great and to these insignificant people, to the mountains and the hills alike, to the rams and the lambs, the prophet now says, *Blessed are you by the Lord, who made heaven and earth*. He seems to be telling them, "You are blessed by the Lord who made heaven in the great among you and earth in the lesser ones." By *heaven* he does not mean the visible sky, full of luminaries perceptible to our bodily eyes, for the psalm continues, *Heaven's heaven is for the Lord*. He has raised up the minds of some of his holy ones and endowed them with such dignity that they can be taught by no man or woman but by their God alone. In comparison with that *heaven's heaven* which is *for the Lord*,[18] every-thing we can discern with our bodily eyes deserves to be called "earth." This

---

13. The codices here have "us . . . us . . . our." The substitution of the second-person pronouns is made in accordance with Augustine's translation as found in his Exposition of Psalm 117, 3, which agrees with the Septuagint underlying it.

14. See Mt 3:9.

15. See Jn 10:16.

16. Or leaders.

17. See 1 Cor 4:15.

18. Augustine is not precise here as to what he understands *heaven's heaven* to be, except to say that it is above the material creation. In his *Confessions* he meditates on the phrase at greater length, taking it to be God's spiritual creation, angels in the first place, and beatified human spirits associated with them. It stands above the temporal flux and participates to some degree in God's eternity (see *Confessions* 12,1,1 – 11,21). "Nothing else can I find that I would more readily call *heaven's heaven, which belongs to the Lord*, than this your household, which contemplates your entrancing beauty, never tiring, never turning aside to any other joy. This pure mind builds up your family of holy, spiritual beings . . . it is the mind of all the citizens of your holy city in that heaven above the heaven we see" (12,11,12). The minds of true teachers draw on the wisdom of heaven even in this mortal life, as he remarks here. See also Expositions of Psalms 67,42 and 101,13 with the notes at both places.

earth is for us to observe and meditate upon, whether in its nobler part which sheds light from above (sometimes called "heaven") or in its lowlier part which is more properly called "earth." As we have explained, the whole of it, in all its parts, is simply "earth" in comparison with the reality called *heaven's heaven*, and this whole *earth he has assigned to human beings*, that by contemplating it they may do their best to infer something of its creator, for without the support of such consideration their still feeble hearts cannot discern him.

12. The words, *Heaven's heaven is for the Lord, but the earth he has assigned to human beings*, are capable of a different interpretation. I ought not to gloss over it, on the excuse that it could distract your attention from what we have said prior to this. We said that the verse, *Blessed are you by the Lord, who made heaven and earth*, is directed to the great ones and the little ones previously mentioned. Thus we can take the great to be indicated by the term, *heaven*, and the lesser by the term, *earth*. But those little ones will eventually grow up to be *heaven*; they are fed on milk at present in the hope of becoming so. The great ones are at present *heaven* in relation to *earth*, since they nourish the little ones; and therefore as they ponder on the hope in which the little ones are nurtured, they can recognize themselves to be *heaven's heaven*. They draw the genuine, richly nourishing quality of their wisdom not from any man or woman, nor from any human source, but from God himself. They have taken on the task of forming little ones who will one day become *heaven*, and in that sense the teachers know themselves to be *heaven's heaven*. All the same, those little ones are as yet still *earth*, to whom they must say, *I planted, Apollos watered, but God gave the growth* (1 Cor 3:6). God well knows how to provide for the earth by means of heaven, and he has given to those human beings whom he makes *heaven* the earth as their work-place.

Let heaven and earth abide in their God who made them; let them live on his sustenance, confess to him and praise him, for if they try to live on their own resources they will die. As it is written, *No confession can be made by a dead person: he is as though non-existent* (Sir 17:26). *The dead will not praise you, O Lord, nor will any who go down to the underworld.* In another passage your scripture cries out, *A person devoid of reverence goes deep into sin and is defiant* (Prv 18:3). *But we, who are alive, bless the Lord, from this day forth and for ever.*

Exposition of Psalm 114[1]

A Sermon to the People

Verses 1-2. Certainty of being heard

1. *I have loved the Lord, because he will hear the voice of my pleading.* Let this be the song of a soul on pilgrimage and away from the Lord;[2] let the sheep that had strayed sing it;[3] let the son who had died and come back to life sing it, he who was lost and found again;[4] let our own soul sing this song, my dearest brothers and sisters, my beloved children. Let us learn from it, and stand fast, and sing with the saints, *I have loved the Lord, because he will hear the voice of my pleading.* But surely that cannot be a motive for loving him, that *the Lord will hear the voice of my pleading*? Would it not make more sense to say that we love him because he has heard us, or that we love him so that he may hear us? What can the psalmist mean by saying, *I have loved him because he will hear*? Did he mean that he hoped God would hear him, and knew that hope usually enkindles love?

2. But what grounds had he for hope? *He has bowed down his ear to me, and in my days I have called upon him.* I have loved him because he will hear me, and he will hear me because *he has bowed down his ear to me*. But how do you know, human soul, that God has bowed his ear down to you? How can you know, unless you say, "I have believed it"? These three remain: faith, hope, and charity:[5] because you have believed, you have hoped, and because you have hoped, you have loved him. If I ask how this soul came to believe that its God had bowed his ear down to it, I know how it will answer. "Because *he first loved us, and did not spare even his own Son, but delivered him up for us all* (1 Jn 4:19; Rom 8:32). But *how will they call upon one in whom they have not yet believed?* asks the teacher of the Gentiles. *And how will they believe in him of whom they have not heard? And how will they hear without anyone to preach to them? And how will any preach, if they are not sent?* (Rom 10:14-15) When I saw all he has done for me, all he has wrought on my behalf, how could I not believe that the Lord has bowed his ear down to me? So unmistakably has he proved his love for us that

---

1. In the Hebrew numbering 116:1-9.
2. See 2 Cor 5:6.
3. See Mt 18:12-13.
4. See Lk 15:24.
5. See 1 Cor 13:13.

Christ died for the godless.[6] When the beautiful feet of those who proclaimed peace and announced the good news[7] made these things known to me, assuring me that *whoever calls upon the name of the Lord will be saved* (Joel 2:32; Acts 2:21; Rom 10:13), then I believed that his ear was inclined, ready to listen to me, *and in my days I called upon him.*"

Verses 3-4. Days of distress

3. What are these days of yours, the days you meant when you said, *In my days I called upon him*? Were they perhaps the days in which the fullness of time arrived, when God sent his Son,[8] the days at which he had hinted when he said, *At the acceptable time I have heard you, and on the day of salvation I have helped you* (Is 49:8)? From some preacher who came to you with beautiful feet you heard the news, *See, now is the acceptable time, lo, this is the day of salvation* (2 Cor 6:2); you knew they were your days, and in your days you called upon the Lord: *O Lord, rescue my soul.*

"What you say is true," our psalmist acknowledges, "but it would be nearer the mark to call my days the days of my wretchedness, the days of my mortality, the days bequeathed to me by Adam, days full of toil and sweat, the days of aging and decay. I am lying prone, *stuck fast in the mud of the deep* (Ps 68:3(69:2)). In another psalm I cried to God, *How old you have made my days!* (Ps 38:6(39:5)). These are my days, the days in which *I called upon the Lord*. These days of mine are very different from the days of my Lord, and I call them 'mine' because in my headstrong willfullness I abandoned him. He is Lord everywhere, omnipotent, holding all things in his hands, and I therefore deserved to be imprisoned in the darkness of my ignorance. The shackles of mortality were the punishment I incurred. *In my days I called upon the Lord*, as in another psalm I cry to him, *Lead my soul out of prison* (Ps 141:8(142:7)). But he helped[9] me on that day of salvation which was his gift to me, and so I know that the groans of fettered captives do find their way into his presence.[10] In these days of mine *the pains of death surrounded me, the perils of hell found me*, as they never would have overtaken me had I not strayed from you. They have found me now with a vengeance. I was not looking for them when I was blithely enjoying prosperity in this world; but amid this world's blandishments the perils of hell disguise themselves all the more successfully.

4. "But I too *found anguish and sorrow*, and then *I called on the name of the Lord*. I had known nothing of any profitable anguish and sorrow, the kind in

---

6. See Rom 5:8-9.
7. See Is 52:7.
8. See Gal 4:4.
9. Variant: "helps."
10. See Ps 78(79):11.

which the Lord comes to our aid, he to whom a psalm prays, *Grant us the help that will pluck us out of our troubles, for human aid is useless* (Ps 59:13(60:11)). I had been accustomed to think of human aid as something to be glad about and celebrate. But then I heard from my Lord, *Blessed are those who mourn, for they shall be comforted* (Mt 5:5), and after that I did not wait for the grief I would experience after losing the temporal goods with which I passed my time so agreeably. Instead I looked hard at the wretched state I was in even while I enjoyed those good things, the things I dreaded losing yet could not keep. I looked at it very intently and courageously, and I saw that I was not only tormented by this world's adversity but also tied down by the prosperity it afforded. That was how *I found* the *anguish and sorrow* that were formerly hidden from me, *and I called on the name of the Lord: O Lord, rescue my soul.*"

Who will deliver me from this death-ridden body, wretch that I am? Only the grace of God, through Jesus Christ our Lord. (Rom 7:24-25) Let God's holy people say, then, *I have found anguish and sorrow, and I called on the name of the Lord,* and let its prayer reach the ears of the pagans who still do not call upon the name of the Lord. Let them hear it and seek him, that they too may find anguish and sorrow, and call on the Lord's name, and be saved. We are not telling them to go looking for misery that is not theirs but to recognize the misery that is theirs already though they do not know it. It is not that we want them to go short of the earthly things they need in this mortal life, but we do want them to bemoan their folly in not only losing heavenly satisfaction but even deserving to feel the lack of those earthly resources which, though necessary for support, are not the stable goods that can yield lasting enjoyment. May they come to know this misery and mourn over it. God, who does not want them to be miserable for ever, will bless them in their mourning.

Verses 5-8. Divine compassion, holy rest, and the experience of redemption already real

5. *The Lord is merciful and just, and our God will be compassionate.* He is merciful, he is just, and he will be compassionate. In the first place he is merciful, for he bowed down his ear to me, and I would never have known how close God's ear was to my mouth had I not been aroused by those beautiful feet to call upon him; for who has ever called upon him without first being called by him? To begin with, then, he is merciful. He is also just, since he whips us, but then again compassionate, because he accepts us. He whips every child whom he acknowledges as his,[11] and I ought to find it less bitter that he whips me than delightful that he accepts me. How could he fail to whip us, when he is *the Lord* who *takes care of little ones*, of the children he looks to see growing up to be his

---

11. See Heb 12:6.

heirs?[12] Is there any child who is not disciplined by his father?[13] *I was humbled, and he saved me.* He saved me because I was humbled, for the pain caused by a surgeon's knife is not a punishment but salutary.

6. *Turn round, my soul, to your rest, because the Lord has treated you well.* Not because you deserve it, or because you attain it by your own efforts, but *because the Lord has treated you well.* Indeed, *he has delivered my soul from death.* It is a curious thing, dearest friends, that after the psalmist had urged his soul to turn toward its rest, because the Lord had treated it well, he added, *He has delivered my soul from death.* Was he telling it to seek rest because it had been delivered from death? Do we not usually call death a time of rest? What kind of activity, then, should we look for on the part of someone for whom life itself is rest, and death disquiet? The activity of the soul should be the kind that tends to peace and freedom from care, not that which accumulates restless work, because the soul has been freed from death by him who said, *Come to me, all you who labor, and I will give you relief. Shoulder my yoke, and learn from me, for I am gentle and humble of heart, and you will find rest for your souls; for my yoke is kindly and my burden light.* (Mt 11:28-30) The activity of a soul that aspires to rest should be gentle and humble, as befits one who follows Christ the Way, but not lazy or half-hearted. It should strive to run its course to the end; as it is written, *Do your work thoroughly in a spirit of gentleness* (Sir 3:19). Notice that gentleness should not degenerate into sloth, for scripture emphasizes, *Do your work thoroughly.* This is the opposite of what we are used to: in ordinary life taking rest in sleep invigorates us for action, but good activity leads us toward a peace that is always awake.

7. God gives us all this; he lavishes it all upon us, God of whom it is said here, *The Lord has treated me well; for he has delivered my soul from death, and freed my eyes from tears, my feet from stumbling.* Whoever experiences the restrictions of the flesh sings of the fulfillment of these prophecies in his or her own case, for what the psalm has said is true: *I was humbled, and he saved me.* But the apostle's word is equally true: *In hope we have been saved* (Rom 8:24). The psalm asserts that we have been delivered from death: we can truly say that this has been verified in us, for we understand it to refer to the death of those who do not believe, those of whom it was said, *Leave the dead to bury their dead* (Mt 8:22), and, in the preceding psalm, *The dead will not praise you, O Lord, nor will any who go down to the underworld. But we, who are alive, bless the Lord.* (Ps 113B(115):17-18) Believers rightly understand that their souls have been delivered from that kind of death by their conversion from unbelief to faith, for of this transition our Savior said, *Whoever believes in me passes even now from death to life* (Jn 5:24). The other declarations in our psalm are verified in those who have not yet departed from this life, but they are verified in hope. When we think

12. Variant: "How does he whip us? He is . . . heirs."
13. See Heb 12:7.

about the most dangerous of our stumbles, our eyes cannot restrain their tears, but in the life to come God will free our eyes from tears as he also frees our feet from stumbling. We shall walk without stumbling then, for there will be no slippery places occasioned by weak flesh. At present, however, although our way is firm, because our way is Christ, we have under our feet the flesh we are bidden to subdue. Chastising it is hard work, and to avoid falling through the weakness of the flesh is a great achievement. But is there anyone who does not even stumble?

Verses 8-9. Flesh and spirit

8. We are in the flesh, yet not in the flesh. We are in the flesh with regard to the bond that is not yet loosened, the bond of which the apostle said: *To be loosed from the flesh and be with Christ is much the best* (Phil 1:23). But we are not in the flesh inasmuch as we have given to God the first-fruits of our spirit,[14] inasmuch as we are able to say that *our life is in heaven* (Phil 3:20). We are able to please God with our heads, as it were, although in our feet, the lowest parts of the soul, we still feel ourselves to be on slippery ground.

Since, then, we are in some sense still in the flesh and in another sense not, listen to the psalm singing of what is still the object of hope, but singing as though it were accomplished already. *He has freed my eyes from tears, my feet from stumbling*, it says; but then it continues, not "therefore am I pleasing to the Lord," but *I will be pleasing to the Lord in the land of the living*. This suggests that the speaker is not yet pleasing in the Lord's sight with respect to that part of himself which is still in the land of the dead, in flesh still mortal; for *those who are in the flesh cannot be pleasing to God* (Rom 8:8). But, as the same apostle goes on to say, *you are not in the flesh*. He justifies this statement by explaining, *the body indeed is a dead thing by reason of sin, but the spirit is life through righteousness*. This means that those to whom he spoke were pleasing to God as to their spirits, for in spirit they were no longer "in the flesh." Who could please the living God while in a dead body? But how does the apostle continue? *If the Spirit of him who raised Jesus Christ from the dead lives in you, he who raised Jesus Christ from the dead will bring life to your mortal bodies too, through his Spirit who dwells in you* (Rom 8:8-11).[15] Then we shall be *in the land of the living*, pleasing in the Lord's sight in every dimension of ourselves. At present, *as long as we are in the body, we are on pilgrimage and away from the Lord* (2 Cor 5:6); but then we shall be distant from him no longer. Insofar as we are still pilgrims,

---

14. Through faith.

15. In Paul's thought "flesh" is not synonymous with "body." One who lacks the indwelling Spirit of God is "flesh" even in his or her mental faculties; Paul castigated the Corinthians as "still flesh" for their sins of jealousy and faction-fighting, and the Galatians for wishing to be justified through the works of the law, though these were not the sins commonly called "sins of the flesh" (see 1 Cor 3:1.3; Gal 3:3). On the other hand, believers indwelt by the Holy Spirit have already begun to be "spirit" even as to their bodies.

we are not yet *in the land of the living.* But *we are full of confidence, and esteem it a more desirable thing to take leave of the body and be at home with the Lord; and therefore we strive to please him, whether we are at home or still on our way* (2 Cor 5:8-9).

We strive for this now, because we still await the redemption of our bodies;[16] but when death has been swallowed up in victory, and what is perishable has been clothed with imperishability, and this mortal frame has put on immortality,[17] then there will be no weeping because no stumbling, and no stumbling because no corruption. And therefore we shall no longer strive to please him; we shall be entirely pleasing in the Lord's sight, in the land of the living.

---

16. See Rom 8:23.
17. See 1 Cor 15:53-54.

Exposition of Psalm 115[1]

A Sermon to the People

Faithful preaching requires truth on the lips and in the heart

1. There is a saying of the apostle which I think is very well known to you, holy brethren:[2] *Not everyone has faith* (2 Th 3:2). You are also aware that unbelievers usually outnumber the rest, which is why scripture asks, *Lord, who has believed our report?* (Is 53:1; Rom 10:16). Among the unbelievers are those of whom the same apostle complains, *They all seek their own ends, not those of Jesus Christ* (Phil 2:21). In another passage he says that they preach God's word from the wrong motives, not from a mind moved by pure and sincere charity but with some hidden agenda.[3] What they really believed was apparent in their conduct, but they preached something different in order to ingratiate themselves with their hearers by their use of the holy name.[4] Of such persons the apostle also says, *They serve not God, but their own bellies* (Rom 16:18). Yet he allows them to preach Christ, because although their behavior, which was leading them toward death, was a truer indication of what they believed, they nonetheless preached an authentic message which could lead others to faith and appropriate action and hence to salvation. Such preachers were not propagating any doctrine contrary to the rule of faith.

The people whom the apostle did exclude were those who preached a false message. *If anyone preaches to you a gospel different from the one you have received, let him be accursed* (Gal 1:9), said Paul. Those who proclaim falsehood are not proclaiming Christ, for Christ is truth. But of the other kind he says that they did preach Christ, though not from unadulterated motives, not from a simple, pure intention, not from a sincere faith that works through love.[5] Prompted by greed for things of earth, they announced the kingdom of heaven; falsehood was in their hearts, though truth was on their tongues. The apostle knew that people were set free by believing even when evangelized by Judas, and so he allowed these insincere preachers also to do their work. *Whether in*

---

1. In Hebrew numbering 116:10-19.
2. *Sanctitati vestrae.*
3. See Phil 1:17-18.
4. Of the Lord, it seems. The sentence could also mean "...with their hearers by acquiring a name for holiness."
5. See Gal 5:6.

sincerity or through opportunism, let Christ be preached (Phil 1:18), he says. It was the truth that they were proclaiming, though not truthfully, not from a true intention. Such people speak of what they do not believe, and that is why they were disowned by the Lord, who yet recognized their usefulness to persons instructed by them: *Do what they tell you, but do not imitate what they do, for they talk, but do not act accordingly* (Mt 23:3). How is that? Surely because they do not believe in the value of what they say.

Others there are who do believe but fail to speak in accord with their belief, either from laziness or from fear. The servant who had a talent, but took no trouble to trade with it, was condemned by the divine judge: *You wicked, lazy servant* (Mt 25:26). In another part of the gospel it is said that many of the leaders of the Jews believed in Christ but dared not acknowledge him openly lest they be expelled from the synagogues;[6] they too were denounced as dishonest, for the evangelist continued, *They prized human esteem more than glory from God* (Jn 12:43).

Both groups are rightly rejected: those who speak the truth but do not believe it, and those who do not speak the truth in which they believe. Who, then, will turn out to be the kind of servant who deserves to be praised as faithful? Who will hear from the Lord, *Well done, good servant; you have been faithful over a few things. I will set you over many. Enter into the joy of your Lord* (Mt 25:21.23)? A servant like this neither speaks before he has himself come to believe nor remains silent once he has believed. He fears to hand out to others what he cannot share himself but also fears lest by not sharing what he has he may lose it; for that is the outcome foretold in the gospel: *Anyone who has will be given more, but if anyone has not, even what he does have will be taken away from him* (Mt 13:12).

Verses 10-12 (1-3). Faithful preaching may entail martyrdom

2. What is this good servant to say, this servant who sings, *Alleluia*, immolating to the Lord a sacrifice of praise? What is he or she to say to the Lord, who will in turn say one day, *Enter into the joy of your Lord* (Mt 25:21.23)? Let the servant leap for joy and say, *I believed, therefore I spoke*. That means, "I have believed perfectly." Those who refuse to speak their belief are not perfect believers, for there is another gospel text that relates to faith: *Anyone who confesses me before men and women, I will confess before the angels of God* (Lk 12:8). The faithful servant in the parable merited his accolade not just because he received wealth but because he spent it and made a profit. This is why the psalm does not simply say, "I believed and spoke"; the psalmist points to the fact that

6. See Jn 12:42.

he believed as his reason for speaking, for he likewise believed both in the reward he could expect for speaking and in the punishment he must dread if fear were to keep him silent. *I believed, therefore I spoke*, he said.

But as for me, I was humiliated exceedingly. The psalmist endured many afflictions on account of the word which he faithfully held and faithfully dispensed, and he was humiliated exceedingly, a consequence feared by others who *prized human esteem more than glory from God* (Jn 12:43). Why does he begin, *But as for me*? He could have said more succinctly, "I believed, therefore I spoke, and I was humiliated exceedingly." Why preface the statement with *But as for me*? Probably because a human speaker can be humiliated by those who contradict the truth, but the truth he believes and speaks cannot be. The apostle suggests a similar thought. He spoke of his chain, then reflected, *But God's word is not bound* (2 Tm 2:9). Our psalmist too, in the name of all holy witnesses, all God's martyrs, says, *I believed, therefore I spoke. But as for me, I was humiliated exceedingly.* Not that which I believed in, not the word I proffered, but I myself, I was humiliated.

3. *In ecstasy I said, Every human being is a liar.* He calls fear *ecstasy.* The fear he means is that to which human weakness is prone when persecutors threaten and the agonies of torture and death draw near. We know this because the voice of the martyrs is plainly heard in this psalm, though there is another meaning to ecstasy: namely, that state where the mind is rapt out of itself not by fear but by some revelation inspired by God.

In ecstasy I said, Every human being is a liar. The speaker was full of consternation when he looked at his own weakness and saw that he could not rely on himself, for when left to ourselves every one of us is a liar. Only by the grace of God is each one rendered truthful and preserved from so yielding to ill-treatment by enemies as to deny what he believes instead of speaking it. Peter made the mistake of relying on himself and denied Christ; he had to be taught that no human strength was dependable. And if no human strength is dependable, obviously no one must rely on himself, for each of us is human. The psalmist was quite correct when in his alarm he looked on every man and woman as a liar; for even those whom no terror can break down, who cannot be forced to yield to the persecutors and lie, even they are the brave people they are not through their own courage but through the gifts of God. Hence the psalm's judgment is very true: *Every human being is a liar.* But God is truthful, and he has told us, *This is my sentence: you are gods, sons of the Most High, all of you; yet you shall die like mortals, and fall as any lordly ruler falls* (Ps 81(82):6). He comforts the humble and fills them not only with faith to believe in the truth but also with confidence to preach it, as long as they persevere in submission to God and do not imitate the devil, who was a lordly ruler but did not stand in the truth. That was why he fell. Every human being is a liar, but in the measure that men and women are not merely human but divine, being children of the Most High, they will be liars no more.

4. The dedicated company of faithful witnesses reflects on these things. It recalls how God's mercy does not forsake the weak humanity that cried out in fear, *Every human being is a liar*. It reflects on how God comforts the humble and fills cowards with such a spirit of boldness that after being almost dead at heart they revive, to put their trust not in themselves but in him who raises the dead[7] and makes the tongues of the dumb fluent.[8] It remembers the Lord's injunction, *When they arrest you and deliver you up, do not wonder how to speak, or what you are to say, for what you are to say will be given you at the time. It is not you who are speaking, but the Spirit of your Father who speaks in you.* (Mt 10:19-20) The psalmist had admitted, *In fear[9] I said, Every human being is a liar*; but when he reflected on these things, and saw that he had been rendered truthful by the grace of God, he cried, *What return shall I make to the Lord for all the recompense he has made to me?* Notice that he did not say, "for all he has given me," but *for all the recompense he has made to me*. What sort of human contribution had there been in advance that would justify calling God's gifts not endowment but recompense?[10] What else had men and women contributed but their sins? God has returned good for evil, unlike human beings who repay him with evil for good. That was how the wicked vine-dressers repaid him, the ones who said, *This is the heir; come on, let's kill him* (Mt 21:38).

Verses 13 and 15 (4 and 6).[11] Drinking from the Lord's cup

5. The psalmist looks for something to give to the Lord in return and finds nothing except the recompense the Lord has first made to him. *I will take in my hands the cup of salvation, and call on the name of the Lord.* Listen, mortal, you who by your sins are a liar but by God's gift truthful and therefore more than human: who gave you this cup of salvation? When you take it and call on the Lord's name you will repay the Lord for all the gifts with which he repaid you. But who gave you the cup? Who else but he who asked, *Are you able to drink the cup I am to drink?* (Mt 20:22) Who endowed you with strength to imitate his own sufferings? Who else but he who first suffered for you? This is why the psalm continues, *Precious in the sight of the Lord is the death of his righteous ones.* He bought their death with his own blood, the blood he first shed for the salvation of his servants, that they might not shrink from shedding theirs for the

---

7. See 2 Cor 1:9.
8. See Wis 10:21.
9. Augustine reads *in pavore* here; in verse 2 he read *in ecstasi*.
10. *Non adtributio, sed retributio*.
11. Augustine omits verse 5 (= verse 14 in the Vulgate). It is omitted by the LXX, and by Prosper of Aquitaine in his commentary (see PL 51, 277-426). It is repeated as verse 18 (9) of the psalm.

name of the Lord. Yet it was not the Lord but they themselves who would profit when they did so.

Verses 16-19 (7-10). God's servants, sons and daughters of his handmaid, pay their vows in Jerusalem

6. Now let this slave, bought at so high a price, admit his servile condition: *I am your servant, O Lord, I am your servant and the son of your handmaid.* He is both purchased and a home-born slave. How can he be both? Was he bought along with his mother, perhaps? Or, since he had been born in the house, did he flee, sinner that he was, and then fall captive to enemies and so have to be bought back once more—redeemed, in fact? He is the handmaiden's son in the sense that all creation is subject to its creator and owes its true master the truest possible service. When creation pays its due, it is free, because it receives from the Lord the grace of serving him not under compulsion but of its own free will.

This slave is therefore a child of the heavenly Jerusalem which is above and is free, she who is the mother of us all.[12] Free she is from sin but handmaid to righteousness; for to those of her children who are still wayfarers scripture says, *You have been called to liberty,* yet it immediately makes slaves of them once more: *But serve one another out of charity* (Gal 5:13). They are also reminded, *When you were enslaved to sin, you were free with regard to righteousness; but now you are set free from sin and bound in service to God. Your gains make for sanctification, with eternal life as its end.* (Rom 6:20,22) Let this servant say to God, "Plenty of people call themselves martyrs, and many style themselves your servants, for all sorts of heresies and errors parade under your name. But they are outside your Church, so they cannot be your handmaid's children. As for me, *I am your servant, and the son of your handmaid.*"

7. *You have burst my bonds; to you will I offer a sacrifice of praise.* I found no merits in myself when you burst my bonds, and therefore I owe you a sacrifice of praise. I will indeed boast of being your servant and the child of your handmaiden; yet I will boast not in myself, but in you, my Lord,[13] in you who burst my bonds in order that when I came back after my desertion, I might be bound again to you.

8. *I will render my vows to the Lord.* What vows will you render to him? What victims did you promise? What burnt offerings? What holocausts? Or are you thinking of what you said just now, *I will take in my hands the cup of salvation, and call on the name of the Lord,* and again, *To you will I offer a sacrifice of praise?* Anyone, I tell you, who honestly faces the question of what he or she ought to dedicate to the Lord, and what vows to make, knows that

12. See Gal 4:26.
13. See 1 Cor 1:31.

self-dedication, the giving of oneself to the Lord, is the offering demanded and owed. After examining a coin the Lord commanded, *Render to Caesar what is Caesar's, and to God what is God's* (Mt 22:21). Caesar's own image is handed back to him; let God likewise receive his back.

9. Those who remember that they are not only God's servants but also sons and daughters of God's handmaid see clearly where they must render to God what they have vowed, because they have been conformed to Christ through the cup of salvation. *In the courts of the Lord's house,* says the psalm. God's house is the same as God's handmaid, and what is God's house, if not his entire people? That is why the psalm speaks of vows being rendered *in the presence of his whole people.* And now it names our mother explicitly: *In your midst, O Jerusalem.* Our offering is acceptable if made from peace and in peace; but those who are not children of this handmaiden have espoused warfare.

It is possible that someone might think that the courts of the Lord's house and his entire people refer only to the Jews: such an interpretation could be put on the psalm's closing words, *In your midst, O Jerusalem,* since this is the name in which the carnal Israelites glory. But such a misunderstanding is excluded by the following psalm, which consists only of four short lines. Listen to it.

Exposition of Psalm 116

Continuation of the preceding Sermon

Verses 1-2. The new people; God's mercy and truth

Praise the Lord, all you Gentiles, praise him, all you peoples.[1] These are the courts of the Lord's house, these form his whole people, these are the true Jerusalem.[2] All those who by cutting themselves off from communion with other nations[3] have refused to be sons and daughters of this city would do well to listen. *For his mercy is confirmed upon us, and the truth of the Lord abides for ever.* Here it is again, this coupling of mercy and truth, to which I drew your attention in Psalm113.[4] The Lord's mercy was *confirmed upon us* when at the sound of his name—that name through which our freedom has been won—the savage rantings of hostile nations fell silent. *The truth of the Lord abides for ever*, vindicated both in the awarding to the just of what he promised and in the sentencing of the godless to what he threatened.

---

1. Augustine omits the Alleluia before this verse.
2. Variant: "these are the words of Jerusalem."
3. The Donatists.
4. See his Exposition 1 of Psalm 113, 13.

Exposition of Psalm 117

A Sermon to the People[1]

"Confession" can mean joyful praise

1. My brothers and sisters, we have heard the Holy Spirit admonishing us, exhorting us, to offer a sacrifice of confession to God. Now confession can be either an offering of praise or an acknowledgement of our sins. Confession of sins is something familiar to everyone; indeed we are so used to it that when the holy scriptures mention confession, the majority of less educated people think it always means that. As a result, no sooner has the word been uttered by the reader than a devout din follows: the sound of people striking their breasts. But they should remember what is said in another psalm: *I will walk into the wonderful tent, even to the house of God, amid the shouts of joy and confession and the sound of people celebrating a festival* (Ps 41:5(42:4)). It is quite obvious from that psalm that the songs and sounds of confession are signs not of penitential grief but of a joyful and very crowded festival. If anyone is still unwilling to accept that plain testimony, what can the doubter say to this passage from Ecclesiasticus? *Confess to the Lord, all you his works. Give magnificent glory to his name, confess to his praise in songs and on the harp. And this is how you must confess to him: All the Lord's works are exceedingly good.* (Sir 39:19-21(14-16)) No one, not even the slowest, can hesitate to affirm that the word "confession" here means the praise of God—or, at any rate, only a person of such perverse mind that he would dare to suggest that our Lord Jesus Christ himself confessed his sins to his Father. If some impious objector were to maintain that he did by pointing to Christ's use of the word, such a one could very easily be refuted by the context. The passage runs like this: *I confess to you, Father, Lord of heaven and earth, because you have hidden these things from the wise and clever, and revealed them to little ones. Yes, Father, such was your good pleasure* (Lk 10:21). Surely no one can fail to understand that he said this in praise of his Father? Is it not obvious to all that this confession was not a cry of the heart's anguish but an outburst of joy, since the evangelist prefaced it with the statement, *At that hour Jesus exulted in the Holy Spirit, and said, I confess to you, Father*?

---

1. Apparently preached in paschal time; see section 22.

Verses 1-5. The goodness of God

2. Dearly beloved, there is no room whatever for doubt that the divine writings customarily use the word "confession" to mean not only the avowal of sins but also the praises of God. We have seen so many mutually corroborative testimonies to the fact, and you can find similar instances in the scriptures for yourselves. Now in this present psalm we begin by singing Alleluia, which means "Praise the Lord," so what could be more appropriate than to understand the next words, *Confess to the Lord,* as an injunction to do just that—namely, to praise the Lord? The praise of God could not have been recommended more briefly than it is by the next explanatory words: *Because he is good.* I can think of nothing nobler than this terse statement of the reason for praising him. Goodness is so essentially the character of God that the Son of God himself, when addressed as *Good teacher,* replied, *Why do you ask me about what is good? None is good except one, God alone.* (Mt 19:16-17; Mk 10:18) The questioner was confronting Christ in the flesh, not understanding the fullness of divinity that was in him and supposing him to be no more than a man. But the Lord's reply was a way of saying, "If you want to call me good, realize that I am also God."

The words of the psalm, however, are prophetic of future events and are addressed to a people set free from all its toil, from the captivity it endures during its exile, and from all taint of association with the wicked. All these blessings are conferred on it by the grace of God, who not only refrains from paying back evil with evil but even repays evil with good. This is why the words that come next are supremely apposite: *Because his mercy endures for ever.*

3. *Let the house of Israel say, He is good, his mercy endures for ever. Let the house of Aaron say, He is good, his mercy endures for ever. Let all who fear the Lord now say, His mercy endures for ever.* I am sure you recognize who the house of Israel is, dearly beloved, and who the house of Aaron is, and that both of these fear the Lord.[2] They are *the little along with the great* (Ps 113(115):13) whom you know all about from another psalm. Let us rejoice that all of us have been included in their number, thanks to the grace of him who is good, whose mercy endures for ever. They were heard, you see, those people who prayed of old, *May the Lord increase blessings upon you, upon you and upon your children* (Ps 113(115):14); for to the Israelites who believe in Christ (among whom are our fathers, the apostles) a throng of Gentiles has been added, Gentiles destined both for the high ranks of the perfect and for the obedience of little ones. All of us, made one in Christ, united into one flock under one shepherd,[3] built into one body with Christ as our head, all of us as one new person can therefore say, *I called upon the Lord in my*

---

2. Variant: " . . . and that these certainly fear the Lord."
3. See Jn 10:16.

distress; he heard me in wide freedom. In our distress we are hemmed into a narrow place, but we are on our way to a wide country that has no bounds, for *who will bring any accusation against those whom God has chosen?* (Rom 8:33)

Verses 6-14. The Church under persecution remembers Christ's passion

4. *The Lord is my helper; I will not fear anything human foes can do to me.* But it is not only human foes that beset the Church, is it? What is a human being whose only interest is in flesh and blood? No more than flesh and blood himself! But the apostle warns us, *It is not against flesh and blood that you have to struggle, but against principalities and powers and the rulers of this world of darkness* (Eph 6:12). That means the rulers of the godless, of those who love this world and are therefore darkness themselves. We were once darkness, but now we are light in the Lord.[4] *Against wicked spiritual beings in heavenly realms* (Eph 6:12), Paul continues, the devil and his angels. In another passage he calls the devil *the prince of the power of the air* (Eph 2:2). Listen, then, to the next verse: *The Lord is my helper, and I shall scorn my enemies.* Let the enemies arise from any quarter they choose, whether from the hordes of bad people or the ranks of bad angels; they will be scorned through the help of the Lord, to whom our confession of praise is offered when we sing Alleluia.

5. We have scorned our enemies, then, but let no friend set himself against me in the guise of a good man, persuading me to put my hope in him, for *it is good to trust in the Lord, better than to trust in mortals.* It is possible that someone may in a manner of speaking be called a good angel, but let not such a person be so esteemed by me that I trust in him, for no one is good save God alone.[5] When human beings and angels seem to be helping us and are doing so with genuine love, it is God who made them good in their measure and is helping us through their agency. *It is good to hope in the Lord,* therefore, *better than to hope in princes.*[6] Angels too are called princes; so we read in the Book of Daniel: *Michael, your prince* (Dn 10:21).

6. *All the nations surrounded me, and I took vengeance on them in the name of the Lord. They encircled me, circled me about, and I took vengeance on them in the name of the Lord.* The first phrase, *All the nations surrounded me, and I took vengeance on them in the name of the Lord,* indicates the Church's struggles and victory. But the question might be asked, "Whence did the Church derive the power to overcome such potent evils?" The psalm therefore looked to the Church's exemplar and pointed to what it first suffered in its head: *They encircled me, circled me about.* There is a good reason for the omission of the words, *all the nations,* in this repetition, because the Jews alone were responsible. *And I*

---

4. See Eph 5:8.
5. See Mk 10:18.
6. Variant: ". . . a prince."

took vengeance on them in the name of the Lord. At the hands of that race whence Christ received the flesh that was crucified, the Church, the faithful people that is Christ's body, experienced persecution. For love of them was wrought everything he did by his hidden godhead in its immortal power, through the mediation of his mortal, visible flesh.

7. *They swarmed around me like bees round a honeycomb, they blazed like a fire amid thorns, and I took vengeance on them in the name of the Lord.* The order of words in this verse corresponds to the chronological order of events. We rightly understand that the Lord himself, who is head of the Church, was surrounded by persecutors as a honeycomb is by bees. But in so describing it the Holy Spirit is speaking subtly and using a comparison full of mystical significance, even though he speaks of the actions of men who did not know what they were doing. Bees make honey in their comb; and the Lord's persecutors unknowingly made him sweeter to us by his suffering, so that we may taste and see how delicious is the Lord[7] who died for our offenses and rose again for our justification.[8] The next words, *They blazed like a fire amid thorns*, are more probably to be understood as a reference to Christ's body, to his people spread abroad everywhere. Since they were drawn from all nations, they were necessarily surrounded by all nations. *They blazed like a fire amid thorns* when those nations with the fire of their persecution burnt sinful flesh and the sharp thorns that represent the piercing troubles of this mortal life. *And I took vengeance on them in the name of the Lord*, the psalm continues. This could mean either that the persecutors were eventually united with the Christian people, once the fiery malice in them that used to harass the just had been extinguished; or else that those others among them who scorned God's merciful appeal in this present era will in the end feel the justice and truth of him who judges them.

8. *I was pushed like a heap of sand to make me topple, but the Lord held me up.* The number of believers had greatly increased, and all had been brought into a single fellowship, like sand into a heap. Even so, what are mortals, that you should be mindful of them?[9] The Church has never claimed, "The hordes of pagans could not prevail against me, because of my superior numbers," but only that *the Lord held me up*. Pagan persecution could find no way to push over and topple the multitude of believers dwelling together in unity of faith, as long as they trusted in him who upheld each one of them and all of them together, wherever they were; for he could never have abandoned those who called upon him.

9. *The Lord is my strength and to him I give glory; and he became salvation for me.* When the attack comes, who are the ones who fall? Those, undoubtedly, who want to be their own strength, and who want glory for themselves. This is

---

7. See Ps 33:9(34:8).
8. See Rom 4:25.
9. See Ps 8:5(4).

obvious, because no one falls in the conflict unless his strength fails and his glory has fallen. But one whose strength is the Lord, whose glory is in praising him, is in no more danger of falling than is the Lord himself. That is why the Lord is said to have become salvation for people of this sort: not because he has become anything that he was not before, but because, without change in himself, he has become the salvation of those who turn back to him. He was not their salvation previously, because they were turned away.

Verses 15-18. Victory is the Lord's work

10. *The voice of joy and victory is heard in the tents of the righteous*, where those who savagely ill-treated the bodies of the just had expected to hear sounds of lament and ruin. They had no inkling of the inner happiness of the saints, the joy that sprang from their hope in the future. The apostle speaks of this happiness: *Seeming sorrowful, we always have cause for joy* (2 Cor 6:10), he says; and again: *What is more, we even rejoice in our sufferings* (Rom 5:3).

11. *The Lord's right hand has proved its might*. What might? *The Lord's right hand has raised me up*. Great might is needed to raise up the lowly, to deify a mere mortal, to make the weak perfect, to grant glory through abasement and victory through suffering. Great might was required to give such help to those in trouble that the true salvation of God lay open before the tormented, while for their tormentors human aid was useless.[10] These are mighty feats, but why are you surprised?[11] Listen as the psalm repeats it. No human being has ever raised up himself,[12] no human has made himself perfect, no human has conferred glory on himself, no man or woman has proved victorious, no human being has saved himself. That is why the psalm repeats, *The Lord's right hand has proved its might*.

12. *I shall not die; I shall live and recount the deeds of the Lord*. The persecutors who spread butchery and slaughter all around believed that Christ's Church was dying; but look at it today! It is recounting the deeds of the Lord. In every place Christ is the glory of his blessed martyrs. By enduring blows he conquered his strikers, by patient suffering he conquered those who caused the suffering,[13] and by love he conquered those who raged against him.[14]

---

10. See Ps 59:13(60:11).
11. Variant: ". . .surprised that the psalm repeats something?"
12. Some codices omit "No . . . himself."
13. The codices read *patiendo facientes*; the CCL editors amend this to *patiendo impatientes* which could suggest: "by patience he conquered those incapable of patience."
14. The subject of the verbs in this sentence could equally well be the persecuted Church rather than Christ. It is typical of Augustine to see both in the same perspective. In the following section the subject is the Church.

13. The psalm nonetheless suggests why such cruelties were the lot of Christ's body, holy Church, the people he adopted as his own. *The Lord chastened me, chastened me severely, but did not deliver me to death.* Savage, godless persecutors were not allowed to attribute anything to their own brute force, for they would have had no power at all had it not been given them from above.[15] The father of a family often gives orders that his children be chastised by the most depraved of his servants, yet he is reserving an inheritance for the children and fetters for the slaves. And what inheritance is in reserve for us? Gold, or silver, or jewels, or farms, or pleasant estates? Observe the way into it, and then recognize what your inheritance is.

Verses 19-21. The glorious prospect: entry into the Lord's wonderful tabernacle

14. *Open to me the gates of righteousness,* says the psalm. Now we know what the gates are. What lies within? *Entering there I will confess to the Lord.* This is the wonderful confession of praise that reaches *even to the house of God, amid the shouts of joy and confession and the sound of people celebrating a festival* (Ps 41:5(42:4)). This is the everlasting happiness of the just, the beatitude of those who dwell in the house of God, praising him for ever and ever.[16]

15. Now listen to how one gains entry through the gates of righteousness. *These are the Lord's gates, and the righteous will enter by them.*[17] Let no unrighteous person whatever attempt to enter that Jerusalem where the uncircumcised are not welcome, where it is said, *Outside are dogs* (Rv 22:15).[18] Let it suffice, says the Church, that during my exile in a far country *I have dwelt among the tents of Kedar,* and that *I dealt peaceably with those who hated peace* (Ps 119(120):5,7). To the very end I bore with the wicked who mingled with my righteous children, but now *these are the Lord's gates, and the righteous will enter by them.*

16. *I will confess to you, O Lord, because you have heard my prayer, and have become my salvation.* How frequently it is demonstrated that the confession here referred to is one of praise! This is not a confession that shows its wounds to the physician but one that gives thanks for healing already received. The doctor himself is our salvation.[19]

---

15. See Jn 19:11.
16. See Ps 83:5(84:4).
17. Variant: ". . . the Lord's gate . . . by it."
18. Jews were accustomed to call uncircumcised Gentiles "dogs." In Phil 3:2 Paul ironically uses the derogatory name for non-Christian Jews.
19. Or "our health."

Verses 22-25. Christ the cornerstone; the day of salvation

17. But of whom are we speaking? Of *the stone rejected by the builders*, for this *became the headstone of the corner*, in order *to create from the two of them one new man in himself, so making peace, that he might reconcile them to God in one body* (Eph 2:15-16), the circumcised and the uncircumcised.

18. *He was made so by the Lord for him*;[20] that is to say, Christ was made the headstone of the corner by the Lord. Admittedly he would not have become this principal stone had he not suffered, but he was not made so by those at whose hands he suffered. On the contrary: they were the builders who rejected him; but in that building which was being raised in secret the Lord made the Christ whom they rejected into the headstone of the corner. *And he is wonderful in our eyes*,[21] in the eyes of our inner selves, in the eyes of those who believe, those who hope, and those who love him; not in the carnal eyes of those who despised and rejected him as no more than a man.

19. *This is the day that the Lord has made*. The speaker remembers that he had said in one of the earlier psalms, *He has bowed down his ear to me, and in my days I have called upon him* (Ps 114(116):2); there he was referring to his own old days, but now he can say, *This is the day which the Lord has made*, the day on which he granted me salvation. This is the day of which the Lord said, *At the acceptable time I have heard you, and on the day of salvation I have helped you* (Is 49:8), the day on which our mediator became the principal stone at the corner. *Let us shout for joy and be happy on it.*[22]

20. *O Lord, save me; O Lord, grant a prosperous journey.*[23] Save me, because today is the day of salvation. We are on our way back to you from our exile in a far-off land; we are distancing ourselves from those who hated peace, though we dealt peaceably with them. When we spoke to them, they fought us to a finish, unprovoked.[24] *Grant a prosperous journey* to us as we return to you, for you have become our way.[25]

---

20. *A Domino factus est ei*, so the best codices; but the dative *ei* is absent from the Septuagint and some codices of the *Expositions*.

21. Here and in the preceding half-verse Augustine's Latin has masculine pronouns, referring to Christ; the Vulgate and a variant have neuters.

22. Or "in him."

23. The Latin has *vero* after *iter*, which is meaningless. It seems to derive from an over-literal rendering of the Septuagint's δή, a Greek particle often inserted to give emphasis or suggest urgency. Augustine omits *vero* when he repeats the petition at the end of section 20.

24. See Ps 119(120):7.

25. See Jn 14:6.

Verse 26. Blessings from the noble house of the Lord

21. *Blessed is the one who comes in the name of the Lord.* We could extend this by saying, "And accursed is anyone who comes in his own name." The gospel authorizes such an inference, for there the Lord says, *I came in the name of my Father, and you have not accepted me; if another comes in his own name, him you will accept* (Jn 5:43).

We have blessed you[26] *in the Lord's name.* I think this must be the voice of the eminent persons addressing the little ones: the voice, I mean, of the great believers whose minds commune with the Word who is God-with-God, insofar as this is possible in the present life. Yet they temper their discourse to the capacity of the little ones, so as to be able to say in all honesty with the apostle, *Whether we are beside ourselves, for God, or in our right mind, for you, the charity of Christ constrains us* (2 Cor 5:13-14). These leaders bless the little ones from the inner regions of the Lord's house, where praise never falls silent for all eternity. Mark, then, what they proclaim from there.

Verses 27-29. The eternal sacrifice

22. *The Lord is God, and he shed his light on us.* The *Lord* referred to here is he who *comes in the name of the Lord*, he who was rejected by the builders but became the principal stone at the corner, Christ Jesus, mediator between humanity and God, and himself human;[27] yet he is God, equal to the Father. He shed his light upon us that we might understand what our faith has taught us and then proclaim it to you who do not yet understand but already believe. But to help your understanding, *appoint a festival day for throngs of people, even to the horns of the altar*, that is to say, reaching even to the inner parts of God's house, whence we have blessed you, and where the loftiest parts of the altar are to be found. *Appoint a festival day*, not half-heartedly or lazily, but a day *for throngs of people*. Then shall we hear the sound *of exultation, the sound of people celebrating a festival*, the sound of those who walk in the precincts *of the wonderful tent, even to the house of God* (Ps 41:5(42:4)). If there is a spiritual sacrifice, an eternal sacrifice of praise, there must also be an eternal priest and an eternal altar which is nothing else but the souls of the just, finally at peace. Brothers and sisters, we want to make this still plainer to you. Those who aspire to understand the very Word of God must not be content to remain at the level of his flesh, that flesh which the Word became for their sake, in order to nourish them with milk. Nor must this earthly festival be enough for them, this solemnity on which the

---

26. Variant: "We bless you."
27. See 1 Tm 2:5.

lamb was slain.[28] Let another festival be celebrated for throngs of people, until the Lord so elevates our minds that we reach even to his inner godhead. To this end he graciously granted us his outer humanity, that we might be nourished on milk.

23. And what else shall we sing, when we attain to his godhead, but his praises? What else shall we say there but *You are my God, and I will confess to you; you are my God, and I will exalt you. I will confess to you, O Lord, because you heard my prayer, and became my salvation?* Not with noisy words shall we say this; rather love will cling to him and cry out to him of itself. For this cry is simply love. Just as the psalm began with praise, so does it end: *Confess to the Lord because he is good, because his mercy endures for ever.* The psalm set out from this point, and on reaching this point it finishes, because nothing can give us more intense joy, or more powerfully further our salvation, than praise of God. It was our joy at the outset, which we have left behind, and it is our joy at the goal to which we return.[29] From first to last may God be praised. Let our song be always Alleluia.

---

28. The Passover, fulfilled in the Christian Easter. The sermon was probably preached in paschal time.
29. This could mean the beginning and end of the psalm, or the beginning and end of our journey to God.

Expositions of Psalm 118

Prologue

With the Lord's gracious help I have expounded as best I could all the other psalms contained in the book which, as we all know, is by the Church's custom called the Psalter. I have done so partly in sermons to the people, and partly by dictation. But always I put off the exposition of Psalm 118, not so much because of its formidable length as because of its profundity, which few can fathom. My brethren took it badly that this psalm alone should lack an exposition in our insignificant writings,[1] inasmuch as it too belongs to the collection of psalms; and they pressed me insistently to discharge the debt. But for a long time I did not yield to their requests or even to their commands, because every time I tried to think about it, it always seemed far beyond the powers of my mind. The plainer it seems, the more profound does it appear to me, so much so that I cannot even demonstrate how profound it is. When in other psalms some passage presents difficulty, at least the obscurity itself is obvious, even though the meaning is hidden; but in this psalm not even the obscurity is evident, for on the surface the psalm is so simple that it might be thought to require a reader or listener only, not an expositor.

Now at long last I approach the task of dealing with it, but I have absolutely no idea what I can manage. All the same I trust that God will be with me and will help me, for so he has done on all those occasions when I have sufficiently expounded matters which at first had seemed to me difficult or almost impossible to understand. I have decided to tackle it in public sermons, which the Greeks call homilies. I think this is the fairest way, because then church congregations will not be denied comprehension of this psalm. They are accustomed to enjoy the sound of it when it is sung, as they do with other psalms.

Let this be enough by way of prologue. Now let us begin to speak about the psalm itself, after what seemed necessary as an introduction.

---

1. *Opusculis nostris.*

Exposition 1 of Psalm 118

First Sermon

Verse 1. The universal longing for happiness

1. From its very first verse, dearest friends, this psalm urges us to seek happiness. Yet there is no one who does not long for this. Is there anyone, has there ever been anyone, will there ever be anyone, who does not want to be happy? Surely not. But if that is the case, why should it be necessary to exhort us to seek something that the human spirit spontaneously desires? When someone exhorts another, he or she does so in order to arouse the will of the person addressed to desire whatever it is that the exhortation is recommending. Why, then, do we need to be invited to will something that we are incapable of not willing? Only because, though men and women all long for happiness, many do not know how to reach it.

The speaker in the psalm therefore teaches us: *Happy are the undefiled in the way, who walk in the law of the Lord*. He seems to be saying, "I know what you want. You are seeking happiness. Very well then; if you want to be happy, be undefiled." All desire the good, but few desire the only route to what they all want. But where will anyone keep clear of defilement, if not in the way? And what way is that, if not the law of the Lord? It is thus no superfluous reminder that we are given when the psalm says, *Happy are the undefiled in the way, who walk in the law of the Lord*, for our minds need to be urged on. To walk unstained in the way of the Lord's law is a very good thing, though many are reluctant to attempt it; and the psalm shows how good it is by pointing out that people who do so are happy. For the sake of what everyone wants—happiness—they undertake what many do not want at all.

Happiness is so great a good that both good people and bad people desire it. We can hardly be surprised that good people are good to gain happiness; what should surprise us is that bad people are bad in their attempts to be happy. A person abandoned to his passions is corrupted and dishonored by self-indulgence, yet what such a person is looking for in this evil conduct is nothing else but happiness. He reckons himself unlucky if he does not experience pleasure and enjoyment in pursuing his lust, and he does not hesitate to boast of his happiness when he does manage to get fun out of it. Again, anyone on fire with avarice hoards wealth by any and every means only in order to be happy. One who thirsts to shed the blood of his enemies, one who is ambitious

343

for power, one who sates his cruelty by destroying other people—each of these is looking for happiness in the midst of his foul deeds.

God's voice calls these erring folk back to the right way, if only they can hear it; he calls back all who chase spurious happiness through misery all too real. *Happy are the undefiled in the way, who walk in the law of the Lord*, he says. He seems to be challenging them: "Where are you going? You are heading for perdition without knowing it. The road you are taking is not the way to where you long to be. You desire to be happy, but the paths along which you are running are wretched, and lead to wretchedness deeper still. Do not seek so great a good through bad conduct. If you want to attain it, come this way, travel by this route. You cannot give up your longing for happiness, but you can and must abandon the malice of your twisted ways. You are tiring yourselves out to no purpose by setting your course to a goal that defiles you." They are not happy who are defiled in waywardness, and walk in the winding ways of the world, but *happy are the undefiled in the way, who walk in the law of the Lord*.

Verses 2-3. Wholehearted search for God through his scriptures

2. Furthermore, notice what the psalm says next: *Happy are those who carefully search his testimonies; they seek him with their whole hearts*. It seems to me that the people here declared happy are the same as the ones spoken of already, for to search the Lord's testimonies carefully, seeking him with one's whole heart, is the same thing as to be undefiled in the way and to walk in the law of the Lord. The psalm continues, *For those who break his law have not walked in his ways*. If people who walk in the way—that way which is the law of the Lord—are the ones who carefully search his testimonies and seek him with their whole hearts, it follows that those who break his law do not search his testimonies carefully. It is true that we have known some people who, although they do break his law, also search the Lord's testimonies, but their purpose in doing so is to appear learned, rather than to be just. We have known others again who carefully search the Lord's testimonies, not because they are already living good lives but because they want to find out how they ought to live.

What I mean is this: there are some people who are not yet free from defilement, not yet walking in the law of the Lord, and so, we must suppose, not yet happy. How then are we to understand the words, *Happy are those who carefully search his testimonies*, when we observe such people searching the Lord's testimonies, people who clearly are not happy, because far from undefiled? What about the scribes and Pharisees, of whom the Lord said, *Do what they tell you, but do not imitate what they do, for they talk, but do not act accordingly* (Mt 23:3)? They were certainly accustomed to search the Lord's testimonies for the purpose of extracting good things to say, though their deeds were bad. Let us disregard them, however, because the objection will rightly be made to us that such people do not really search the Lord's testimonies. It is not the testimonies themselves that they are looking for but what they can get out of them, namely, adulation from other people, or riches. To examine God's testimonies without loving what they reveal, without wanting to be led by them to God—that is not true study. Even if those who search God's testimonies hoping to find and gain possession of something else, rather than God himself, are to be recognized as genuinely searching the scriptures, they certainly do not *seek God with their whole hearts*. The psalm goes on to point this out, and with good reason; for the Spirit is speaking here, and he knows that many engage in careful study of the scriptures with some object other than that for which it is recommended. Accordingly the psalm does not confine itself to saying, *Happy are those who carefully search his testimonies*, but adds, *They seek him with their whole hearts*. It obviously wishes to teach us how, and with what intention, we are to search the testimonies of the Lord. Furthermore, in one of the wisdom books Wisdom herself gives this warning: *The wicked seek me but do not find me, because they hate wisdom* (Prv 1:28-29, LXX); and that amounts to saying, "They hate me." Wisdom is warning, "Those who hate me seek me, but do not find me." In what sense can they be said to seek something they hate? Only inasmuch as they are not seeking the reality for itself but merely as a means to some other advantage. They do not aspire to be wise for the glory of God; they only want to appear wise in order to be glorified by other people. Is this not a hatred of wisdom, which commands us and teaches us to despise the human flattery such students love?

Happy are the undefiled in the way, who walk in the law of the Lord. Happy are those who carefully search his testimonies; they seek him with their whole hearts. They walk undefiled in the law of the Lord by carefully searching his testimonies in such a way as to seek him wholeheartedly. But what about the man who asked, *Good teacher, what good thing should I do to gain eternal life?* (Mt 19:16) Surely he was searching the Lord's testimonies and seeking him? I don't think so, for how could he have been seeking the Lord with his whole heart when he preferred his wealth to the Lord's counsel and departed sadly on hearing it? The prophet Isaiah had something to say about this: *Seek the Lord, and when you have found him let the godless abandon his way, and the lawbreaker his thoughts* (Is 55:6-7).

3. The godless and the lawbreaker are understood to seek God so that when they have found him they may be godless and unjust no more. But then how can those who are searching God's testimonies and seeking him be pronounced happy, if even the godless and the lawbreaker can do the same? Who would dare to call the godless and the unjust happy? Only a godless or unjust observer!

The promised happiness is present in hope

No; we must think of a happiness that is hoped for rather than actually present, as in the saying, *Blessed are those who suffer persecution in the cause of right*: these are happy not because of their present circumstances, for what they are suffering is evil, but because of what will be, *for the kingdom of heaven is theirs*. Again, *Blessed are those who hunger and thirst for righteousness*, not because they are hungry and thirsty now, but because of what is to follow, *for they shall be satisfied*. (Mt 5:10,6) Similarly, *Happy are those who weep*, not because they are weeping now but on account of the promise for their future: *because they will laugh* (Lk 6:21). We must take the psalm's beatitude in the same sense: *happy are those who carefully search his testimonies; they seek him with their whole hearts*. Happy they are not because they carefully search his testimonies and seek him but because they are destined to find what they are seeking, for they seek in no negligent spirit but with all their hearts.

We could go further and say that if in hope they are happy, perhaps in hope they are already undefiled. It is all too clear that even though we walk in the law of the Lord, even though we carefully search his testimonies and seek him with our whole hearts, still if in this life *we say that we have no sin, we deceive ourselves, and the truth is not in us* (1 Jn 1:8). But this matter demands more thorough investigation. The psalm continues, *Those who break his law have not walked in his ways*. From these words we may infer that people who walk in the Lord's way, or in his law, carefully searching his testimonies and seeking him with their whole hearts, can even now be undefiled and free from sin. This is the implication of the verse, *Those who break his law have not walked in his ways*. Yet, as blessed John teaches, *Anyone who commits sin is breaking the law*; and he adds, *That is what sin is, breaking God's law* (1 Jn 3:4).

This is so complex a question that we should not hurry over it in a brief treatment, so it is time to conclude the present sermon.

Exposition 2 of Psalm 118

Second Sermon

Verse 3, continued. All the saints are sinners; true humility

1. In this psalm it is written, *Those who break his law have not walked in his ways.* We read these words and know them to be true. But they need further comment, lest what is rightly said be not rightly understood and the reader or listener be worried. To explain this matter we need the assistance of God, *in whose hands rest our words, as do we ourselves* (Wis 7:16). All the saints declare in unison, *If we say that we have no sin, we deceive ourselves, and the truth is not in us* (1 Jn 1:8). But we must take care to avoid two misinterpretations. The first is to assume that this means the saints do not walk in the Lord's ways, for *sin is breaking God's law* (1 Jn 3:4), and those who break God's law have obviously not walked in his ways. The opposite error would be to conclude that, since it cannot be doubted that they do walk in the Lord's ways, they are to be deemed sinless, which is plainly false. When scripture warns, *If we say that we have no sin, we deceive ourselves*, it is not simply admonishing us to avoid arrogance and pride. Were that the case, it would not have continued the thought by saying, *And the truth is not in us*, but rather, "humility is not in us." This is quite obvious from what follows, for the next words clarify the real sense, disposing of all ambiguity. Blessed John continues, *If we confess our sins, he is so faithful and just that he forgives us our sins, and cleanses us from all iniquity* (1 Jn 1:8-9).

Can the detestable self-conceit of the impious gainsay that? What can they find to say in the face of such testimony? If the saints' refusal to declare themselves sinless is no more than a precaution against arrogance rather than an admission of the truth, why do they confess their sins in the hope of deserving forgiveness and cleansing? Surely confession is not made merely in order to avoid pretentiousness? How will a real cleansing from sins be earned by a confession of sins that is hollow? The hauteur of the proud is self-deceiving. In the hearing of other people it feigns humility by calling itself sinful, while in its impious conceit it declares itself sinless in its own heart. But let it fall silent now and wither away like grass. People who claim to be without sin deceive themselves, and the truth is not in them; but when they make their claim in the hearing of others they mislead not only themselves but others too, through the perversity of their unhealthy teaching. Even if they say it only within their own hearts they

347

lead themselves astray there, for then there is no truth within them. Being self-deceived within, they lose the light of truth from their hearts.

Let Christ's holy family raise a different cry, Christ's holy fellowship that is bearing fruit and growing throughout the whole world,[1] humble in its truthfulness and truthful in its humility. Let it shout, *If we say that we have no sin, we deceive ourselves, and the truth is not in us. But if we confess our sins, he is so faithful and just that he forgives us our sins, and cleanses us from all iniquity.* This declaration must be matched by inner conviction, for humility will be genuine if it is not so much flaunted by the tongue as modeled on the apostle's description: *Not haughty, but of one mind with humble folk* (Rom 12:16). He does not say "speaking with the humble" but "of one mind with them." It is a question of the heart's attitude, not the tongue's protestations. If you say you are a sinner, you hypocrite, while believing in your heart that you have no sin, you are affecting humility outwardly but embracing futility within. In consequence you hold to the truth neither in your mouth nor in your heart. What advantage is it to you that your verbal profession seems humble to other people, if God sees your overweening self-esteem?

Suppose the warning trumpeted in your ears by the divine oracles were: "Be not pretentious in speech"; even then you would deserve condemnation if you spoke humble words in human ears but spoke pretentiously in your heart before God. But that is not what you are told. The command you hear is: *Be not high-minded, but stand in awe* (Rom 11:20). *High-minded*, it says, not "boastful in speech." Why, then, are you not humble inwardly as well, where the mind is sensitive to truth? Is your mind so puffed up by arrogance that the tongue lies when it professes humility? You read or hear the warning, *Be not high-minded, but stand in awe.* Are you so high-minded that you think you have no sin? If you refuse to stand in awe you will be overblown with pride; nothing else is left to you.[2]

Paul walked in the Lord's ways, yet he was a sinner

2. "But what does scripture mean," you ask, "when it says, *Those who break his law have not walked in his ways*? Do the Lord's saints not walk in his ways? Yet the psalm indicates that if they do, they do not break his law, and if they do not break his law they must be without sin, for *sin is breaking God's law*" (1 Jn 3:4).

Arise to help me, Lord Jesus, and send me aid against this proud heretic. Send it through your apostle, who does not hesitate in his confession. Where, O where, is that servant of yours, he who emptied himself in order to be filled with you?

---

1. See Col 1:6.
2. An untranslatable pun: *Quia non vis timere, nihil tibi aliud remanet quam tumere.*

Let us listen to him, brothers and sisters. If you will (and I see that this is indeed what you want), let us question him about this puzzling matter.

Tell us, then, most blessed Paul: did you walk in the ways of the Lord while you still lived in the flesh? "Of course I did," he answers. "How else could I have said, *Let us walk consistently with the level we have attained* (Phil 3:16)? How could I have asked, *Did Titus take advantage of you? Have we not both been walking by the same Spirit? Have we not both trodden the same path?* (2 Cor 2:18) Why did I often say, *As long as we are in the body we are on pilgrimage and away from the Lord, for we walk by faith, not by sight* (2 Cor 5:6-7)? Is anything more undeniably the Lord's way than faith, by which a just person lives?[3] Was it by anyone's way other than the Lord's that I was pressing ahead, when I used to say, *One thing only I do: forgetting what lies behind and straining to what lies ahead, I bend my whole effort to follow after the prize of God's heavenly call in Christ Jesus* (Phil 3:13-14)? And as I neared the end, what other way did I suggest I had been pursuing when I claimed, *I have fought the good fight, I have run the whole course* (2 Tm 4:7)?"

These replies must be sufficient to teach us that the apostle Paul certainly did walk in the ways of the Lord; but we need to question him about something else. Tell us, please, apostle: during your life in the flesh, when you were walking in the Lord's ways, did you sin at all, or were you without sin? Let us listen now, and find out whether he is self-deceived or is of the same mind as his fellow apostle John, for the truth is in them.[4]

Paul replies, "Have you not read the passage where I confess, *I fail to do the good I want to do; what I do is the evil I do not want?*" Yes, we have heard that, but we have another query. How could you have been walking in the ways of the Lord if you were doing evil things you did not want to do, and the holy psalm loudly intones, *Those who break his law have not walked in his ways*? Paul's reply comes swiftly: listen to the next sentence. *If what I do is what I do not want to do*, he says, *it cannot be I who am at work, but the sin that dwells in me* (Rom 7:15-17). We can understand from this how people who walk in the Lord's ways do not commit sin, and yet are not free from sin. It is not they themselves who perform the sinful act but the sin that dwells in them.

More explanation is called for

3. At this point someone will object, "How can both be true: that he performed the evil deed he did not want, and that it was not he himself who did it but the sin that dwelt in him?"

---

3. See Rom 1:17.
4. See 1 Jn 1:8.

Well, the question has been settled provisionally, because it is quite evident on the authority of canonical scripture that the possibility is there: people walking in the ways of the Lord are not without sin, though it is not they themselves who commit sin. Yet we know that *sin is breaking God's law* (1 Jn 3:4), and that *those who break his law have not walked in his ways*. Another sermon is needed to demonstrate how the agent both commits sin because of his death-ridden body, in which the law of sin holds sway, and at the same time does not himself commit sin because of the ways of the Lord, in which he is walking. Accordingly we must bring this sermon to an end now.

Exposition 3 of Psalm 118

Third Sermon

Verse 3, continued. Concupiscence is not the same as deliberate sin

1. A difficult question was raised by a verse in this psalm. We read there, *Those who break his law have not walked in his ways*; and the apostle John asserts that *sin is breaking God's law* (1 Jn 3:4). Yet scripture also says, and rightly, as we know, *If we say that we have no sin, we deceive ourselves, and the truth is not in us* (1 Jn 1:8). How is it possible, then, that the saints are not without sin in this life and yet walk in the Lord's ways, when those who break his law do not walk in them? It is puzzling, but the apostle Paul resolves the difficulty. *It is not I who am at work*, he says, *but the sin that dwells in me* (Rom 7:17). How can Paul be without sin, if sin dwells within him? Yet he walks in the Lord's ways, ways untrodden by those who sin, because it is not he himself who does the bad thing but the sin dwelling in him.

One problem has been solved, however, only to give rise to another that is more difficult: how can someone be said to act, when it is not he himself who performs the action? Paul asserted both these things: *What I do is what I do not want to do* (Rom 7:16), and, *It is not I who am at work, but the sin that dwells in me*. From these texts we must conclude that when it is the sin dwelling in us that is at work, we ourselves are not performing the action, for then our will in no way consents to it and even keeps control over our bodily members to restrain them from obeying sin's desires. If we do not will it, what can sin effect, other than illicit desires? If the will does not consent to such desires, there can indeed be emotional upheaval, but sin is given no scope to achieve its purpose.[1] The apostle commanded us to make sure this is the case: *Do not let sin reign in your mortal body, so as to persuade you to yield to its cravings; and do not make your members available to sin as weapons of iniquity* (Rom 6:12-13). Sin entertains its desires, to which we are forbidden to yield. These desires lead to sin.[2] If we yield to them, we ourselves are acting; but if in obedience to the apostle we do not yield to them, it is not we who act but the sin that dwells in us.

---

1. *Movetur quidem nonnullus affectus, sed nullus ei relaxatur effectus.*
2. *Operantur peccatum haec desideria*: so most codices. A probably better reading is found in three codices: *Operatur peccatum haec desideria*: "Sin produces these desires." This variant suits the context and agrees with what Augustine said a few lines earlier.

If we had no unlawful desires, neither we nor sin itself would do anything wrong in us. When the impulse of illicit desire makes itself felt, however, then even though we do not consent to it and it is therefore not we who are at work, we are nonetheless said to be acting because the desire is not some invasion by a nature not our own, but a symptom of our own sickness. We shall be completely healed from this disease only when we become immortal in soul and body.

To sum up: because we walk in the ways of the Lord, we do not yield to sin's promptings; but at the same time, because we are not sinless, we experience the desires inspired by sin. It is not we ourselves who are at work, because we do not consent to them; the sin that dwells in us is acting and stirring them up. But *those who break his law* by yielding to sin's desires *have not walked in* the Lord's *ways*.

Concupiscence remains after baptism

2. We still need to inquire further. For what are we asking forgiveness when we say to God, *Forgive us our debts* (Mt 6:12)? Do we mean the wrong things we ourselves do when we yield to sinful desires; or are we asking to be forgiven for the desires themselves, which are not our own doing but are produced by the sin that dwells in us?

This is how I understand the matter. To the extent that it is guilty, that sickness or infirmity which stirs up illicit desires and which the apostle calls "sin" is entirely washed away in the sacrament of baptism, together with everything we have ever done in obedience to its promptings, whether by deed, word, or thought. If we never yielded in the slightest to any of the unlawful desires arising from our sickness, whether by action, or in speech, or by tacit consent, the sickness itself would give us no trouble, though still lodged within us until it too should be healed and our prayer heard: *Thy kingdom come* (Mt 6:10), and, *Deliver us from evil* (Mt 6:13). But human life on earth is full of trials,[3] and although we may come nowhere near serious transgressions, we do not lack occasions for consenting to sinful desires by deed, or word, or thought. We may be on our guard against greater sins, but small ones sneak up on the unwary; and even though they lack the weight to break us down when they attack singly, they overwhelm us when they band together. This is why even people who are walking in the ways of the Lord pray, *Forgive us our debts*. This prayer, and this implied confession, are entirely appropriate to the Lord's ways, though sins are not.

---

3. See Jb 7:1.

The sin of unbelief estranges us from the Lord's ways

3. No one commits sin in the Lord's ways, therefore, though everyone does confess in those ways. The Lord's ways are all summed up in one single thing: faith. By this faith he who said, *I am the way* (Jn 14:6), justifies the godless.[4] If anyone sins while walking in Christ, the way, such a person has strayed from the way by sinning; for the sin committed by the deviant has no place in the way. But sins are not imputed to those who keep to the way; they are therefore not accounted sinners. The apostle Paul spoke about them when reminding us of the justification that comes through faith and showed us how the same teaching is found in a psalm: *Blessed are those whose iniquities are forgiven, and whose sins are covered. Blessed is the one to whom the Lord has imputed no sin.* (Ps 31(32):1-2; Rom 4:7-8) This is the grace imparted by the Lord's ways. It follows that iniquity, which is a lack of faith, alienates a person from the way of the Lord, for only one who lives by faith is just.[5] But when someone is walking in this way, in loving faith, either he or she does not commit sin or, if there is some straying and sin occurs, such sin is not imputed because of the way; and the one who commits it is accepted by God as though he or she had not committed it.

In the light of this teaching we may well take the psalm-verse, *Those who break his law have not walked in his ways*, to refer to the kind of iniquity or law-breaking that abandons faith or never approaches faith. The Lord said of the Jews, *If I had not come, they would not be in sin* (Jn 15:22). This cannot mean that they were completely sinless before Christ came in the flesh and only began to be guilty of sin at the time of his coming. No: the Lord intended us to think of a particular kind of sin, namely unbelief: they did not believe in him. People who are guilty not of law-breaking in general but of a certain kind of iniquity, the refusal to believe, have not walked in his ways, because *all the Lord's ways are mercy and truth* (Ps 24(25):10). Both of these qualities are found in Christ, and apart from Christ nowhere else. *I maintain that Christ Jesus was a servant of the circumcised, to save the truth of God and confirm the promises made to our fathers*, says the apostle, *but to give the Gentiles cause to glorify God for his mercy* (Rom 15:8-9). In him there is mercy, because he redeemed us, and truth, because he has honored the promises he made, and will honor the promises he makes now. *Those who break his law* by unbelief *have not walked in his ways* because they have not believed in Christ. Let them be converted and believe with love in him who justifies the godless. Let them find mercy in him when their sins are forgiven, and truth as his promises are kept. That is to say, let them discover all the ways of the Lord. Walking in these they will not break his law, for they

---

4. See Rom 4:5.
5. See Rom 1:17.

will cling not to unbelief but to faith which works through love,[6] to which no sin is imputed.

---

6. See Gal 5:6.

Exposition 4 of Psalm 118

Fourth Sermon

Verses 4-6. We keep the commandments only with God's grace

1. Who is it, dearly beloved, who is speaking to the Lord here? *Most earnestly have you ordained that your commandments be kept. O that my ways may be directed toward observing your ways of justice!*[1] *Then I shall not be put to shame, if I look carefully into all your statutes.* Who says this? Surely every member of Christ, or, rather, the whole body of Christ. But what does this mean: *Most earnestly*[2] *have you ordained that your commandments be kept*? Does it mean, "you have ordained most earnestly," or, "that they be kept most earnestly"? Whichever way we take it, this verse seems to conflict with a noble sentiment fixed in people's memories, a sentiment the Greeks applaud in their wise men and the Latins echo and hold in esteem: "Nothing excessive."[3] If it is true that nothing should be done to excess, how can the psalm be right to declare, *Most earnestly have you ordained that your commandments be kept*? If any course of action pushed to excess is to be deprecated, how can God have either most earnestly ordained anything or expected us to keep his commandments most earnestly? We might perhaps say, "Well, after all, we are not bound[4] by the wisdom of the Greeks, because we keep before our eyes the challenge of scripture: *Has not God turned this world's wisdom into folly?* (1 Cor 1:20) Therefore, it might be said, if any teaching is to be regarded as false, it should be the maxim, 'Nothing excessive,' rather than God's word, where we read and sing, *Most earnestly have you ordained that your commandments be kept*."

We could perhaps argue along those lines, were we not checked by true reasoning—yes, true reasoning, not the high-minded attitude of the Greeks. What I mean is this: *nimis* means "more than is proper." The Latin words *parum* and *nimium* are opposites: *parum* indicates a deficiency, something less than

---

1. *Iustificationes*. In his sixth Exposition of this psalm Augustine explains that by *iustificationes* we are to understand the just actions performed with God's help, while his *iudicia* are the just sentences he pronounces.
2. *Nimis*, literally "too much."
3. *Ne quid nimis*. The famous sentence, attributed to Apollo, was inscribed in the temple at Delphi. It was also attributed to Homer and Solon. See also Terence, *Andria* 1,1,34.
4. Variant: "intimidated."

what ought to be present; *nimium* means something in excess of what is appropriate. Midway between these two lies the just mean, of which we can say, "That is sufficient."[5] If, then, it is a useful rule for life and conduct that we should do nothing at all beyond what is fitting, we must admit that the maxim, "Nothing excessive," is true, rather than rejecting it.

But Latin sometimes uses the word *nimis* in the sense of "very much."[6] We find it employed in this way in the sacred scriptures, and we use it in this sense in our own discourse. So too in the psalm: we shall understand the verse correctly if we take it to mean "very much," or "most earnestly." If we say to a dear friend, "I love you very much,"[7] we obviously do not mean "more than is appropriate"; we simply want the friend to understand that we love him or her very dearly.

In any case, the Greek form of the maxim does not contain the word we have here. It says ἄγαν, which means *nimis*, "excessive," whereas the Greek version of the psalm has σφόδρα, which corresponds to *valde*, "very much." But, as we have explained already, we sometimes find *nimis* used in the sense of *valde*, and we use it so ourselves. That is why some Latin codices have *valde* in this verse of the psalm, instead of *nimis*. Very emphatically has God ordered us to observe his commandments, and very earnestly are they to be kept.

2. But humble piety, pious humility, and a faith that has not forgotten about grace have something to add. Listen: *O that my ways may be directed toward observing your ways of justice!* This you have ordained, I know; but O, may what you have ordained be realized in me! When you hear the phrase, "O that. . !"[8] you must recognize the accents of someone who is yearning. And when you hear this voice of longing and hope, lay aside your overbearing presumption, for no one expresses longing if he is so free to choose that he can bring about the desired outcome with no help from anyone else. If a man or woman is longing for something to happen, something which God has commanded, we must infer that it is absolutely necessary to pray to God, that he may grant what he has himself enjoined.[9] From whom should we hope to win such a gift? From him, of course, concerning whom holy scripture testifies, *Every good gift, every perfect endowment, comes down from the Father of lights* (Jas 1:17).

Some people hold, however, that in order to live righteously we need nothing more in the way of divine help than that God's commandments be brought to our notice, so that, once we know them, they can be fulfilled by the powers of our

---

5. Compare Aristotle's teaching on virtue as the mean between two extremes; e.g. courage is the mean between cowardice and rashness (*Nich. Eth.* 2,2).

6. *Valde.*

7. *Nimis.*

8. *Utinam.*

9. Compare Augustine's famous prayer, *Da quod iubes, et iube quod vis* ("Give what you command, and then command whatever you will") in his *Confessions* 10,29,40. It annoyed Pelagius, as Augustine records in *The Gift of Perseverance* 20,53. See also thefollowing note.

will alone, without any further grace from God.[10] To refute this position the psalmist first speaks of receiving the commandments God has given and then expresses the wish, the prayer, that his ways be directed to the keeping of God's justifying statutes. He begins by saying, *Most earnestly have you ordained that your commandments be kept.* He seems to imply: "Yes, I have received the law; I know it perfectly well, for most earnestly have you ordained that your commandments be kept. Your commands are holy, and just, and good, but sin uses this good thing to deal death to me,[11] unless your grace aids me. Therefore I pray, *O that my ways may be directed toward observing your ways of justice!*"

3. *Then I shall not be put to shame, if I look carefully into all your statutes.* Whether we read God's commandments, or turn them over in our memories, they are like a mirror into which we must gaze. The apostle James reminds us of this: *Anyone who is merely a hearer of the word, and not a doer, is like a man studying the face he was born with in a mirror, but then going away and immediately forgetting what he was like. But a person who has looked into the perfect law of liberty and steadfastly remained in it, becoming not a forgetful hearer but an effective doer, will be blessed in his undertakings.* (Jas 1:23-25) The psalmist aspires to be the kind of person who can gaze into God's commandments as into a mirror and not be shamed by what he sees: he wants to be not only a hearer but a doer of the commandments. This is why he prays with longing that his ways be directed to observing the divine demands that make for holiness. How else could he be directed, if not by God's grace? Without grace he will have God's law, but not as a reassurance; if he tries to peer into commandments which he is not keeping, they will shame him.

Verses 7-8. Why the Lord seems to abandon us

4. The psalm continues, *I will confess to you in straightforwardness of heart, O Lord, because I shall have learned your just judgments.* This is a confession not of sins but of praise, like the confession of him in whom there was no sin: *I confess to you, Father, Lord of heaven and earth* (Mt 11:25), and as it is written in the Book of Ecclesiasticus: *This is how you must confess to him: All the Lord's works are exceedingly good* (Sir 39:20-21). Accordingly the psalm prays, *I will confess to you in straightforwardness of heart, O Lord.* If my ways are indeed directed aright I will confess to you, because that will be your doing, and will redound to your praise, not mine. Only if I have a straightforward heart, the consequence of my ways being straight and directed to the keeping of your

---

10. This sounds like an allusion to Pelagius' teaching, which preoccupied Augustine from 412 onward. His sermons on Psalm 118(119) are among the latest of his *Expositions*, as he states in his Prologue, so it is likely that the present sermon belongs to the anti-Pelagian period.
11. See Rom 7:13.

commands that make for holiness—only then shall I *confess to you, because I shall have learned your just judgments.* What use would it be to me to learn them, if my heart were crooked and I wandered into twisting paths? Your commands would not bring me joy but only accuse me.

5. The next words, *I will keep your ways of justice,* are closely connected with the preceding verses. The passage runs like this: *O that my ways may be directed toward observing your ways of justice! Then I shall not be put to shame, if I look carefully into all your statutes. I will confess to you in straightforwardness of heart.* Then follows the declaration, *I will keep your ways of justice.*

But what does the next line mean? *Do not utterly forsake me* (some codices have *usque nimis* here, instead of *usque valde*; the Greek has σφόδρα). It almost looks as though he wants the Lord to abandon him, but not utterly. That cannot be right. Perhaps we should understand it to mean that God had in a sense abandoned the world on account of its sins, but he would have forsaken it utterly only if his wonderful healing remedy had not been provided for it, the grace of God through our Lord Jesus Christ. As it is, this prayer offered by Christ's body has been heard, for *God was in Christ, reconciling the world to himself* (2 Cor 5:19).

An alternative interpretation would run as follows. Someone said in an earlier psalm from his secure position: *I shall be unmoved for ever* (Ps 29:7(30:6)); he was confident then in his own strength. But God wished to prove to him that it was he alone who had added strength to this man's beauty[12] not because of any merit on the part of the recipient but because such was the divine free choice. Therefore God turned his face away, leaving him distraught. This same psalmist seems to recognize himself again here, but no longer does he trust himself. *Do not utterly forsake me,* he cries. Perhaps you have forsaken me, leaving me bereft of your help, so that my weakness may be revealed; but *do not utterly forsake me,* lest I perish. *Most earnestly have you ordained that your commandments be kept;* I can no longer plead ignorance of them, but I am weak. *O that my ways may be directed toward observing your ways of justice! Then I shall not be put to shame, if I look carefully into all your statutes.* Then *I will confess to you in straightforwardness of heart, O Lord, because I shall have learned your just judgments;* then *I will keep your ways of justice.* If the purpose of your forsaking me was to teach me not to boast of myself, *do not utterly forsake me,* for when I have been justified by you, in you I will make my boast.[13]

---

12. See Ps 29:8(30:7).
13. See 1 Cor 1:29.31.

Exposition 5 of Psalm 118

Fifth Sermon

Verse 9. A straight path for the young

1. In the measure that the Lord graciously helps us, dearest friends, let us examine closely the following lines in the psalm we are studying: *By what means does a youth straighten his path? By guarding your words.* The speaker asks himself a question and replies to it. The question is, *By what means does a youth straighten his path?* Then comes the answer: *By guarding your words.* The guarding of the divine words here referred to means acting in accord with the commandments, for it is pointless to retain them in one's memory if they are not kept also in one's life. Some people make it their business to hold onto God's words so as not to forget them but make no effort to live in conformity with those words so as to be straightened out. But the psalmist does not say, "By what means does a youth sharpen his memory?" He says, *By what means does a youth straighten his path?* And it is to that question that the reply is given, *By guarding your words.* A path can certainly not be said to have been straightened if the person's life is still crooked.

2. But why does the psalm speak in particular of a youth? Could it not just as well have asked, "By what means does anyone[1] straighten his path?" or "By what means does a man[2] straighten his path?" Scripture often uses the latter idiom, intending the more highly honored sex to stand for humanity in general; by this mode of speech the whole is signified by a part. So in another psalm we hear, *Blessed is the man[3] who has not gone astray in the council of the ungodly* (Ps 1:1), but of course this does not mean that a woman is not equally blessed if she refrains from doing so.

What we have here, however, is neither "person"[4] nor "man"[5] but *youth.*[6] Does it mean there is no hope for anyone of more mature years? Or that an older person has some other means of straightening his path than the guarding of God's words? Or should we perhaps take the mention of youth as a reminder that

---

1. *Homo.*
2. *Vir.*
3. *Vir.*
4. *Homo.*
5. *Vir.*
6. *Iunior.*

this is the best time to undertake the work of correction? Scripture suggests this elsewhere: *My son, from the days of your youth accept instruction, and even to your gray hair you will find wisdom* (Sir 6:18).

Another way of understanding this verse would be to take it as a reference to the younger son in the gospel, the one who left his father and traveled to a distant country, where he squandered his money by living recklessly with prostitutes. Later, after feeding pigs, he suffered agonies of hunger himself. He came to his senses and said, *I will be off and go to my father* (Lk 15:18). By what means did he straighten out his path? Surely by guarding the words of God, which in his hunger he longed for, as for the bread in his father's house. The elder son felt no need to straighten his path; that is evident from his words to his father: *Look how many years I have been slaving for you! Never have I transgressed your orders.* (Lk 15:29) But the younger son did straighten his. He confessed to his father, *I am no longer worthy to be called your son* (Lk 15:19.21), so perverted and crooked was the path he had been treading.

A third interpretation occurs to me; indeed, to my limited insight it appears better than the other two. The elder could stand for the old self and the younger for the new self.[7] The old humanity bears the image of the earthly man but the new humanity that of the heavenly man,[8] because *it is not the spiritual that comes first; the animal body comes first, and what is spiritual afterwards* (1 Cor 15:46). Anyone, therefore, anyone at all, even though advanced in bodily age and worn out with years, will be youthful before God when converted and made new by grace. Such people straighten their paths by guarding the words of God; that is to say, they accept the word of faith which we preach,[9] a faith that is active through love.[10]

Verse 10. God's initiative of grace

3. This child of grace is the younger people, the new humanity and the new self, the singer of the new song, the heir to the new covenant. This younger son is not Cain but Abel; not Ishmael but Isaac; not Esau but Israel; not Manasseh but Ephraim; not Eli but Samuel; not Saul but David. Hearken to what he says: *I have sought you with all my heart; do not thrust me away from your commandments.* Listen to him praying: he is begging for help in guarding the words of God, which he has recognized to be the means by which a youth straightens his path. That is what his prayer is, a plea for help: *Do not thrust me away from your commandments.* For what else can being thrust away by God mean, if not being

---

7. The "old man" and the "new man" in Pauline teaching.
8. See 1 Cor 15:49.
9. See Rom 10:8.
10. See Gal 5:6.

denied his help? Human weakness cannot adapt itself to God's straight and arduous commandments unless his charity takes the initiative and helps us. If there are any whom he does not help, he is described as thrusting them away; it is as though unworthy persons are debarred by a fiery sword from stretching out their hands to the tree of life.[11]

Yet who is worthy, who ever has been, since sin entered the world through one man, and through sin death, in consequence of which death spread to all men and women, inasmuch as all have sinned?[12] But our well-deserved misery is remedied by the undeserved mercy of God. How could the speaker in the psalm have claimed, *I have sought you with all my heart* unless God had turned back to himself a sinner who had turned away? So another psalm prays to him, *O God, in converting us you will give us life* (Ps 84:7(85:6)). How else could the psalmist make such a claim unless God, who promises, *I will seek out what has perished, and call back the one that has strayed* (Ezk 34:16), sought what was lost and called back the stray?

Verses 11-12. Learning the commandments in theory and in practice

4. The same applies to the straightening of one's paths through guarding the words of God: it is God who straightens and directs us aright, God who does the work. No one could achieve it by himself, as the prophet Jeremiah acknowledges: *I know, O Lord, that a human being's course is not of his own choosing, nor will a man go where he wills to straighten his path* (Jer 10:23). This grace too the psalmist begged from the Lord in an earlier verse, where he prayed, *O that my ways be directed!* His prayer is the same here, for after saying, *I have hidden your declarations in my heart, that I may not sin against you*, he immediately seeks divine help, for it would have been pointless to hide God's declarations in his heart if no good works followed. He adds, therefore, *Blessed are you, O Lord: teach me your ways of justice*. He prays, *Teach me*: let me learn them as people who carry them out learn them, not as those who simply memorize them in order to have something to say. This is in tune with the statement he has just made, *I have hidden your declarations in my heart, that I may not sin against you*.

But why does he now ask to learn what he already keeps hidden in his heart? He could not have hidden them there unless he had previously learned them, could he? Why then does he go on to pray, *Teach me your ways of justice*? It must be because he wants to learn them by putting them into practice, not merely by repeating them and committing them to memory. He recalls the words of another

---

11. See Gn 3:24.
12. See Rom 5:12. For Augustine's understanding of this text, and the translation, "inasmuch as all have sinned," see the note at Exposition of Psalm 50,10.

psalm: *He who gave the law will give a blessing too* (Ps 83:8(84:7)), and so he offers his petition: *Blessed are you, O Lord: teach me your ways of justice.* You have given me the law, for I have hidden your declarations in my heart in order not to sin against you. Give me also the blessing of your grace, that I may learn by practicing what you have commanded in your revelation.

This must be enough for today, if your minds are to be nourished but not wearied. The verses that follow demand a sermon to themselves.

Exposition 6 of Psalm 118

Sixth Sermon

Verse 13. Can anyone articulate all God's judgments?

1. Today's sermon must begin with a discussion of the verse in this psalm which runs, *With my lips I have articulated all the judgments of your mouth.* What is this about, dearly beloved? What can it mean? How can anyone articulate all God's judgments when they are too deep for our scrutiny? Can we hesitate to exclaim with the apostle, *O how deep are God's wisdom and knowledge, how unfathomable his decisions and inscrutable his ways!* (Rom 11:33)? The Lord himself told us, *I have many things to tell you, but at present you are not able to bear them* (Jn 16:12). It is true that he immediately went on to promise his disciples the fullness of truth through the Holy Spirit, but blessed Paul still teaches that *we know only in part* (1 Cor 13:9). He means us to understand that we are indeed being led toward all truth by the Holy Spirit, whom we have received as a pledge, but that this fullness will be ours only when we reach another life[1] beyond the mirror-like, puzzling perceptions proper to our life in the present, and see God face to face.[2]

How, then, can the psalmist claim, *With my lips I have articulated all the judgments of your mouth*? Is this the same person who prayed in an earlier verse—a verse very close to this one—*Teach me your ways of justice*? If he still wants to learn God's ways of justice, how has he been able to articulate all the judgments of God's mouth? Are we to resolve the question by saying, yes, he already knows all God's judgments, but still hopes to learn his ways of justice? Hardly, for it would be stranger still if he already knew the inscrutable secrets of God but was ignorant of the commands God has given to human beings for their observance. Ways of justice are not statements about justice but just deeds, the works performed by just people in obedience to God's commandments. They are said to be God's ways of justice because, although it is we who perform these actions, we can do so only by God's gift. God's judgments, on the other hand, are those pronouncements whereby he judges the world, both now and at the end of time.

---

1. Variant: "face to face vision in another life."
2. See 1 Cor 13:12.

The utterances of God embrace all these realities, however, both his ways of justice and his judgments. How then can the psalmist still pray to learn God's ways of justice, if he declares that he has already hidden God's declarations in his heart? That is what he says: *I have hidden your declarations in my heart, that I may not sin against you*; he follows this with: *Blessed are you, O Lord: teach me your ways of justice*; then he continues: *With my lips I have articulated all the judgments of your mouth*. The first and the third of these statements do not seem to conflict at all; indeed they are harmonious and correlative. Because the speaker has hidden God's declarations in his heart, he proclaims them with his lips, for *the faith that issues in righteousness is in the heart, and the confession that leads to salvation is made with the lips* (Rom 10:10). But in between the two comes the prayer, *Blessed are you, O Lord: teach me your ways of justice*, and this is what raises the difficulty. If a person already holds God's declarations in his heart and has articulated with his lips all the judgments of God, how can he still express the desire to learn God's ways of justice? The only possible answer is that he wants to learn them by putting them into practice, not simply by retaining them in his memory and repeating them. He has demonstrated to us that we must beg this grace from God, because without it we can do nothing.

We dealt with this matter in a previous sermon. The question before us now is this: how can he claim to have articulated with his lips all the judgments of God's mouth, when they have been acknowledged to be inscrutable, and when scripture says elsewhere, *Your judgments are an unfathomable abyss* (Ps 35:7(36:6))? This is the problem we have undertaken to tackle with God's help.

The Church as a whole has articulated God's judgments

2. Well then, apply your minds to the correct understanding of this passage. It cannot be said, can it, that the Church is ignorant of God's judgments? No, obviously the Church does know them. It knows what kind of people will hear the invitation of him who is judge of the living and the dead, *Come, you whom my Father has blessed; take possession of the kingdom*, and to what kind he will say, *Depart from me into eternal fire* (Mt 25:34,41). Let me stress this. The Church knows that neither fornicators nor idol-worshipers nor the various other malefactors whom the apostle Paul enumerates[3] will possess the kingdom of God. It knows what trouble and distress will fall upon the soul of everyone whose deeds are evil: the Jew in the first place, but the Greek also; and that glory, honor, and peace are reserved for everyone who does good: the Jew first of all, but the Greek also.[4] These are judgments of God, plainly expressed; and the Church knows them.

---

3. See Gal 5:19-21; Eph 5:5.
4. See Rom 2:9-10.

But they are not the sum total of his judgments, for there are others which are inscrutable, profound, and secret, like an unfathomable abyss. Should we say, perhaps, that even these are known to certain excellent members of this body which, together with the Savior who is its head, constitutes the whole Christ? Those secret judgments may have been declared inscrutable to human beings because they cannot fathom such mysteries by their own powers; but why should not anyone know them through the gift of the Holy Spirit—anyone, I mean, on whom the Lord confers this gracious gift? After all, scripture asserts that *God dwells in unapproachable light* (1 Tm 6:16), and yet exhorts us, *Draw near to him and receive his light* (Ps 33(34):6). The two texts are easily reconciled when we reflect that God is unapproachable if we are left to our own efforts but can be approached through the gifts he confers.

That sounds like a reasonable argument. Yet to no single one of the saints is it granted to know all the judgments of God, as long as the perishable body weighs down the soul,[5] because this is beyond the capacity of any man or woman. For instance, it is only by a judgment of God that anyone is mentally handicapped or physically crippled: that will give you an idea of how far his judgments exceed the compass of our minds. These things are beyond the understanding of any individual; but the Church, the people God claims as his own,[6] has the right to say in all truth, *With my lips I have articulated all the judgments of your mouth.* This implies, "I have kept silent about nothing in the judgments you choose to reveal to me through your utterances. I have spoken of them forthrightly with my lips." I think this is what the psalm means us to understand, for it does not say simply "all your judgments" but *all the judgments of your mouth*, which suggests, "those of which you have told me." God's mouth means his word, communicated to us through the revelations made to many holy people and enshrined in both Testaments. The Church never ceases to articulate all these judgments with its lips, in every part of the world.

Verse 14. The way of God's testimonies is Christ

3. The psalm proceeds: *I have been delighted with the way of your testimonies, as though with boundless riches.* By the way of God's testimonies we must understand Christ, in whom are hidden all the treasures of wisdom and knowledge.[7] Nothing is more direct, nothing safer, nothing speedier, nothing nobler than this way; that is why the psalmist says he found in it such delight as he might have found in unlimited wealth.

---

5. See Wis 9:15.
6. See 1 Pt 2:9.
7. See Col 2:3.

God's *testimonies* are the means by which he graciously proves to us how much he loves us. The special proof of God's charity toward us consists in this, that when we were still sinners Christ died for us.[8] Speaking of himself, Christ says, *I am the way* (Jn 14:6), evoking the humility of his birth in the flesh and his passion; these are unmistakable testimonies of God's elective love for us, and thus Christ is undoubtedly the way of God's testimonies. Through these testimonies, which we see to have been brought to perfection in him, we look forward to the implementation of the everlasting promises given to us for the future, for *if God did not spare even his own Son, but delivered him up for us all, how can he fail to give us everything else along with that gift?* (Rom 8:32)

Verses 15-16. A fruitful kind of talkativeness

4. The next line is *I will chatter[9] about your commandments, and consider your ways.* The Greek has ἀδολεσχήσω, which some translators render as *I will chatter,* others as *I will be exercised.* These two seem far apart; but if we think of it as the exercise of our natural intelligence, accompanied by a certain delight in argument, the two ideas are united, and out of the blending of the two of them a single notion emerges, so that talkativeness does not seem so far removed from exercise of this kind. Eloquent talkers are sometimes called garrulous; but the Church exercises itself in God's commandments and is talkative[10] in the long-winded disputations of learned men against all the enemies of the Christian and Catholic faith. Such disputations are fruitful if they concentrate on the ways of the Lord which, as scripture says, are *steadfast love and truth* (Ps 24(25):10), the fullness of which two qualities are found in Christ.

From this sweet exercise follows the effect which the psalm now mentions: *I will meditate upon your ways of justice, and I will not forget your words.* My object in meditating on them is to avoid forgetting them. That is the motive of the happy man mentioned in Psalm 1, who meditates on the law of the Lord day and night.

5. We have done our best in this, our own disputation, dearest friends. There is one thing above all that we must remember. The psalmist who has hidden the Lord's declarations in his heart, who articulates with his lips all the judgments of God's mouth, who finds delight in the way of his testimonies as though in boundless riches, who chatters (or exercises himself) over God's commandments, who considers his ways and meditates on his ways of justice in order not to forget his words—this man, so unmistakably revealed as one instructed in the law and the doctrine of God, nonetheless prays to God, saying, *Blessed are you,*

---

8. See Rom 5:8.
9. *Garriam.*
10. *Garrula.*

O Lord: teach me your ways of justice. We can take his prayer in no other sense than this: he is begging for the help of grace, so that he may express in his deeds what he has learned in words.

Exposition 7 of Psalm 118

Seventh Sermon

Verse 17. Four different modes of recompense

1. If you remember the earlier sections of this psalm, dearly beloved, they should help us to understand the verses that follow. They seem to be spoken by a single individual, but in fact it is the members of Christ who speak, the members who belong to one head and form one body.

Now this speaker asked in an earlier verse, *By what means does a youth straighten his path? By guarding your words.* Now he more explicitly begs for help in order to do this. *Pay back your servant,* he prays; *then I shall live, and guard your words.* If by *pay back* he implied a just retribution, the payment of good in return for good, he must have been guarding God's words already. But he did not say, "Pay back your servant, because I have guarded your words," as though demanding a good reward for his good service of obedience; what he said was, *Pay back your servant; then I shall live, and guard your words.* This phrase, *then I shall live,* suggests that the dead are incapable of guarding the Lord's words. The dead in this sense are unbelievers, those of whom the Lord said, *Leave the dead to bury their dead* (Mt 8:22). We can reckon unbelievers to be dead and believers to be alive because it is through faith that a just person lives.[1] But since it is impossible for anyone to guard the Lord's words except through the faith that expresses itself in love,[2] the speaker is begging for this faith when he says, *Pay back your servant; then I shall live, and guard your words.*

Before a person comes to faith, nothing is owed to him or her except evil things in return for evils; yet God has returned good for evil, through undeserved grace. This is the kind of recompense the psalm asks for in praying, *Pay back your servant; then I shall live, and guard your words.* There are four possible modes of recompense. First, evil may be the retribution for evil, as when God will punish the wicked with everlasting fire; second, good things may be the recompense for good, as when he will reward the just with a eternal kingdom; third, evil may be repaid by good, as when Christ justifies the godless through grace;[3] fourth, good may be repaid by evil, as when Judas and the Jews perse-

---

1. See Rom 1:17.
2. See Gal 5:6.
3. See Rom 4:5.

cuted Christ out of malice.[4] Of these four types of retribution the first two are manifestations of justice, in the recompense of evil with evil and of good with good. The third is a manifestation of mercy, when good is rendered for evil. The fourth is alien to God, who has never repaid anyone with evil in return for good. The one I mentioned in third place necessarily has priority, because if God did not repay evil with good there would never be any good people to whom he could render good for good.

How God repaid Paul: first good for evil, then good for good

2. Look at the case of Saul, who became Paul. God saved us, he says, *not in view of any righteous deeds we might have done, but because of his own mercy, through the laver of rebirth* (Tt 3:5); and again, *I was originally a persecutor and a blasphemer, and harmed people, but I received mercy, because I acted in ignorance and unbelief* (1 Tm 1:13). In another passage he says, *I give this as my advice, as one who received mercy from the Lord to enable me to be faithful* (1 Cor 7:25), which is to say, to enable me to live, because it is through faith that a just person is alive.[5] Paul had at first been dead through his own unrighteousness, before he began to live through God's grace. He confesses his dead condition elsewhere: *With the coming of the commandment, sin sprang to life, and I died. The commandment that should have been life-giving spelled death for me* (Rom 7:9-10). But God repaid Paul's evil with good, giving him life in place of death. This is the retribution the psalm begs for: *Pay back your servant; then I shall live, and guard your words.* Paul did live. He guarded the Lord's words, and began to qualify for the other kind of recompense, whereby good is rendered for good. That is why he could say, *I have fought the good fight, I have run the whole course, I have kept the faith; all that remains for me now is the crown of righteousness which the Lord, as a just judge, will award me on that day* (2 Tm 4:7-8). The Lord is called just, and rightly so, in repaying good with good, because he was formerly merciful in rendering good for evil.

All the same, this justice, by which good is repaid with good, is still shot through with mercy; for scripture also says of God, *He crowns you in his pity and mercy* (Ps 102(103):4). How could the man who claimed, *I have fought the good fight*, ever have been victorious except by the grace of God? *Thanks be to God*, he cries, *who gives us the victory through our Lord Jesus Christ* (1 Cor 15:57). He had run his race to the end; but how could he have run at all, much less reached the winning-post, without the help of God? The outcome depends *not on*

---

4. Augustine gave a similar list in his Exposition of Psalm 108,4, though there he counted six possibilities by including the negatives: not to return evil for evil, and not to return good for good.

5. See Rom 1:17.

the one who wills it, nor on the one who runs, but on God who shows mercy (Rom 9:16). He kept the faith, but how could he have done that unless, as he says himself, he had received the mercy that empowered him to remain faithful?

3. There is no place whatever for human pride to rear its head, for when God rewards us with good things he is rewarding his own gifts.[6] But the one who is now praying, *Pay back your servant; then I shall live*, must have begun to live, because if he were entirely dead he would not be praying. He has received from God the glimmerings of good desire and now begs for the true life of obedience. Similarly the disciples who asked, *Lord, increase our faith* (Lk 17:5), had some faith already. Another man, on being asked whether he believed, replied, *I do believe, Lord; help my unbelief* (Mk 9:23); he was confessing his faithlessness yet not disavowing his faith.

The speaker in the psalm is certainly beginning to live when he begs for life, and he already believes as he prays for obedience. He is not asking for a life already safe to be rewarded, but for help, that his life may be saved. One who is renewed from day to day[7] lives every day more fully as life grows.

Verses 18-19. A prayer for understanding

4. The psalmist is aware, however, that God's words cannot be guarded in obedience unless they are grasped with our understanding. He therefore extends his prayer by asking, *Take the veil from my eyes, and I will contemplate the wonders of your law*. Closely connected with this petition is the one that follows: *I am but a lodger*[8] *on the earth; do not hide your commands from me*. Some codices have: *I am but an alien*[9] *on the earth*. In the previous verse he asks, *Take the veil from my eyes*, which corresponds to *Do not hide from me* in this one; and where the preceding verse says *the wonders of your law*, the present verse echoes it in different words with *your commands*. Among God's commands none is more wonderful than *Love your enemies* (Mt 5:44), which amounts to saying, "Render good for evil."

The matter of our status as lodgers or resident aliens on earth demands ample discussion, and we cannot deal with it in our present sermon. You must wait for another, which, with the Lord's help, will be delivered to you.

---

6. See the note at Exposition of Psalm 102,7.
7. See 2 Cor 4:16.
8. *Inquilinus*; see Exposition of Psalm 38,21 and the note there.
9. *Incola*; see Exposition of Psalm 55,9 and the note there.

Exposition 8 of Psalm 118

Eighth Sermon

Verse 19. Who are the true pilgrims on earth?

1. You are expecting a sermon on the next verses of this psalm, dearly beloved,[1] and now you are to get your due. We begin from the verse, *I am but an alien*[2] *on the earth; do not hide your commands from me*; or, as some codices have it, *I am but a lodger*[3] *on the earth.* The Greek word is πάροικος which some of our translators rendered as *lodger,* others as *alien,* and a few as *stranger.*[4] Lodgers are people who have no home of their own, and live in a house belonging to others; resident aliens or strangers are regarded as foreigners.

Now these facts raise an important question about the soul. Obviously it cannot be said of the body, *I am but a resident alien,* or *a stranger,* or *a lodger on the earth,* for the body originates from the earth. But I dare not make any definitive statement in the face of this extremely profound problem. It may be that the complaint *I am but a lodger,* or *an alien,* or *a stranger on the earth,* is quite correctly made on the soul's account, for the soul can by no means be considered to derive from the earth. Or again, it may be that the whole human person makes this lament, because human beings were once denizens of paradise, and the one who speaks in the psalm was certainly not there. Or perhaps (and this interpretation would be less contestable) it is not everyone who utters the complaint but only those to whom an eternal homeland in heaven has been promised. I do not know which is right; but this I do know, that human life on earth is all temptation[5] and lies like a heavy yoke on the children of Adam.[6]

My preference is to discuss the verse in the light of the third interpretation: that we consider ourselves lodgers or aliens on earth because we are aware of a heavenly homeland, that country of which we have received a pledge and from which, once we have gained it, we shall never depart. The person who in another psalm reflected, *I am no more than a lodger in your house and a pilgrim, like all my forebears* (Ps 38:13(39:12)), did not say, "Like everyone else." By speci-

---

1. *Caritatis vestrae.*
2. *Incola.*
3. *Inquilinus.*
4. See Expositions of Psalms 38,21, and 55,9, and the notes in both places.
5. See Jb 7:1.
6. See Sir 40:1.

fying, *like all my forebears*, he undoubtedly meant us to understand the righteous people who preceded him in time, who on this earthly pilgrimage sighed with holy longing for their heavenly country. The Letter to the Hebrews says of them, *All these died in faith. They had not received what was promised, but viewed it from afar and saluted it, acknowledging that they were but pilgrims and exiles on earth. Those who speak so prove that they are seeking a homeland. If they had been thinking of the country they had left behind, they would have had the chance to return there; but now they are longing for a better one, a heavenly country. Therefore God is not ashamed to be called their God, for he has prepared a city for them.* (Heb 11:13-16) Another passage, where we read, *As long as we are in the body we are on pilgrimage and away from the Lord*, must be understood to refer not to all, but only to believers, for *not everyone has faith* (2 Thes 3:2). Moreover we know what the apostle goes on to say after stating that *as long as we are in the body we are on pilgrimage and away from the Lord*: he continues, *For we walk by faith, not by sight* (2 Cor 5:6-7). He means us to understand that this is a pilgrimage only for those who walk by faith. Unbelievers, whom God in his foreknowledge has not predestined to be conformed to the image of his Son,[7] cannot truthfully call themselves pilgrims on earth, for they are in the place where they were born according to the flesh; they have no city anywhere else and hence are not foreigners on earth but earthlings. Scripture says of someone[8] like this, *She has established her house close to death, and to the underworld with the earth-born her paths lead* (Prv 2:18).[9] We should rather say that they are pilgrims and lodgers not on this earth but with respect to the people of God, among whom they are foreigners. To believers on the other hand, to those already beginning to count as their own the holy city that does not originate from this world, the apostle says, *You are pilgrims and lodgers no more; rather are you fellow-citizens with the saints and members of God's household* (Eph 2:19).

To sum up: those who are no more than travelers among the people of God are citizens of the earth; but those who are true citizens among God's people are pilgrims on earth, because this whole people, as long as it is in the body, is on pilgrimage and absent from the Lord. Let it say, then, *I am but an alien on the earth; do not hide your commands from me.*

To love God and neighbor, you must first know yourself

2. But from whom does God hide his commands? Has God not willed them to be preached everywhere? They are clear to many; if only they were dear to as

---

7. See Rom 8:29.
8. *Quodam*, masculine, though the passage quoted refers to a woman.
9. Or ". . .in the underworld with the earth-born the beams of her dwelling."

many![10] What is clearer than the command, *You shall love the Lord your God with all your heart and all your soul*, and *You shall love your neighbor as yourself? On these two commandments depend all the law and the prophets.* (Mt 22:37.39-40) Are these commands hidden from anyone? No, they are familiar to all believers and to many unbelievers as well. How, then, can a believer beg that something be not hidden from him, when he is aware that it is not hidden even from an unbeliever?

Can this be the explanation, that since it is difficult for us to know God, the command, *You shall love the Lord your God,* may also be difficult for us, since we might be in danger of loving the wrong thing? It is obviously much easier to know our neighbor. Every human being is a neighbor to every other human being; no difference of race is important where there is a nature common to both, although the man who asked the Lord, *And who is my neighbor?* (Lk 10:29) did not know even his neighbor, it seems. However, he drew the right conclusion when the Lord told him a story about someone who went down from Jerusalem to Jericho and fell among robbers; he recognized that no one had been a neighbor to the wounded man except the one who showed mercy to him. The story plainly showed that when works of mercy are needed, a person who loves his neighbor must deem no one a stranger.

There are many people, though, who do not even know themselves, for to know oneself in the way a human being should is not given to all. How then can a person who does not even know himself love his neighbor as himself? In the parable about the younger son who set out for a distant region, and there squandered his money in a dissipated lifestyle, we are given a significant detail: he first of all returned to himself. That was what made it possible for him to say, *I will be off and go to my father* (Lk 15:18). He must have traveled so far from home that he had left even himself behind. Yet he could not have returned to himself if he was wholly ignorant of himself, just as he could not have said, *I will be off and go to my Father,* if he was wholly ignorant of God. Hence it is possible for us to know certain things in some degree and at the same time to beg that they be known more and more.

Accordingly we must know God if we are to know how to love God; and if someone is to know how to love his neighbor as himself he must first, by loving God, learn to love himself. But how can he do that, if he does not know God and does not even know himself? He has good reason to say to God, *I am but an alien on the earth; do not hide your commands from me.* They are justly hidden from people who are not aliens on earth, for people of that kind may hear them but do not understand them because they have no taste for any but earthly things. Others, whose citizenship is in heaven,[11] are certainly like pilgrims in their deal-

10. *Utinam quam multis clara sunt, tam multis cara sint.*
11. See Phil 3:20.

ings with earthly affairs. Let them pray to God that his commandments be not hidden from them, for through observance of the commandments comes their chance of being freed from their alien condition here. By keeping the commandments they love God, in whose company they will be for ever, and they love their neighbor, who, as they hope, will be there with them.

Verse 20. Wanting to want God's will

3. But what can be loved by loving if love itself is not loved? This alien on earth prayed to God that the divine commandments be not hidden from him; and since the only—or at least the principal—requirement of the commandments is love, he now proclaims that he wants to love that love. He says, *My soul has passionately wanted to desire your ways of justice*[12] *at all times*. Passionate longing[13] of this sort is praiseworthy, not to be condemned. Not of this longing did the commandment say, *You shall not covet* (Ex 20:17), but of the passionate craving whereby flesh lusts against spirit.[14] But see whether scripture has anything to say about the right kind of passionate wanting by which the spirit longs in opposition to the flesh, and you will find this: *Powerful longing for wisdom leads to a kingdom* (Wis 6:21); and there are many other texts to the same effect. There is an important distinction to be made, however: when good longing is meant, the object of the longing is specified. If no object is mentioned, but wanting or covetousness is named on its own, evil concupiscence is meant. Take, for example, the text I have just quoted, *Powerful longing for wisdom leads to a kingdom*. If the object, wisdom, were not specified, scripture could certainly not have said, "Powerful longing leads to a kingdom." On the other hand, when the apostle laments, *I would not have known what covetousness was, had the law not said, You shall not covet* (Rom 7:7), he makes no mention of the object of covetousness, or of what the law says, *You shall not covet*. Evil concupiscence is certainly to be understood here.

What about the longing expressed in the psalm? What is the speaker hankering after? He has passionately longed, he says, *to desire your ways of justice at all times*. I think he cannot yet have been desiring them when he voiced his passionate longing to have such a desire. But God's ways of justice are just actions, righteous deeds. If, then, a person who already has the desire to act justly does not yet have what he desires, how far from righteous action must he have been who was only at the stage of passionately longing to desire it? And how

---

12. *Iustificationes tuas*.
13. *Concupiscentia*. In the discussion that follows this word is translated as "passionate longing" or "passionate wanting/wishing" to distinguish it from Augustine's other word, *desiderium*.
14. See Gal 5:17.

much further off still are they who do not yet even passionately long for such a desire?

A subtle analysis of how we can want a desire

4. It is a remarkable fact that we can long to have a certain desire yet not have the desire in us, although the wanting of it is in us already. It is not as though we were talking about some beautiful material object, such as gold, or some fair body which a person might desire without possessing it, because it is outside of him, not within him. Everyone knows that passionate wanting is inside a person, and desire is within him too. How is it, then, that desire is passionately wanted, as though it were something that needed to be brought in from outside? Or how is it possible for passionate wanting to exist in the absence of the thing wanted, when that thing is not other than the wanting? For to want something passionately is unquestionably to desire it. What is this strange, inexplicable lassitude?[15]

It is real, as we know. When someone is ill and feels a disgust for food, but wants to recover from his sickly condition, he certainly wants to desire food: this is implied in wanting to be free from his nausea. But in this case the nausea is an indisposition of the body, whereas the vehement wish to desire food—that is, to be rid of the nausea—is not in the body but in the mind. It is not any pleasure in palate or throat that conceives this vehement wish, because any such pleasure is inhibited by the nausea; it is the rational intention to recover one's health and the anticipation that when health returns distaste for food will be banished. There is nothing remarkable if the mind has an appetite for bodily appetite. In this situation there is an appetite in the mind but none in the body.

But when both phenomena are of the mind, and both are forms of wanting, how can I passionately want a desire for God's ways of justice? How can I have in one and the same mind a passionate wish for the desire but not the desire itself? How indeed can these two things be distinct? Are they not the same? Why can I passionately want to desire God's ways of justice yet not passionately want those ways of justice themselves rather than merely a desire for them? How is it possible for me to entertain a passionate wish for a desire for the ways of justice without having a passionate wish for the ways of justice themselves, when the only reason for my passionate wish to conceive the desire is that I passionately want the ways of justice? But if that is the case, I am passionately wanting them already. What, then, is the point of my passionate longing to desire them, when I already have, and feel myself to have, the desire? I could not passionately want a

15. At the time of writing his *Confessions* Augustine had grappled with the puzzling question of how the will can want something and yet not want it; see *Confessions* 8,8,20–9,21. Now, many years later, he analyzes again the condition of the divided will.

desire for righteousness without passionately wanting righteousness itself, could I?

Is this not the same truth that I alluded to earlier: that love itself must be loved? We need to love the very love by which what we are bound to love is loved, just as we must hate the love by which what ought not to be loved is loved. We hate the lusts whereby our flesh lusts against our spirit; and what else is that lust but bad love? We love the passionate longing whereby our spirit yearns in opposition to our flesh; and what is that passionate longing, that yearning, but good love? But when we say, "That is to be loved," what else are we saying, if not, "It is to be passionately wanted"?

The inference must be that if it is right passionately to want God's ways of justice, it is right passionately to want to want God's ways of justice. This could be expressed in other words: if it is right that God's ways of justice be loved, it is right that our love for God's ways of justice should itself be loved.

Should we, perhaps, distinguish between want and desire? I am not saying that desire is not a wanting; but I do say that not all wanting is desire. A person can passionately want both the things he has and things he does not have, for in passionately wanting the things he has, he enjoys those possessions. But when he desires things, he is passionately wanting what is absent. What else is desire but a passionate longing for absent goods?

But then, when can God's ways of justice be described as absent? Only in cases where people do not know them. Or can we also say that they should be considered absent when they are known but not observed? Yes, because those ways of justice are good works, not words. Hence it is possible for them to be undesirable because of our infirmity of soul, while at the same time our rational mind passionately wants to desire them, seeing how useful and wholesome they are. It often happens that we see what ought to be done, but do not do it, because we take no pleasure in doing it; yet we wish we could take pleasure in so acting. The intellect flies ahead, but weak human feelings follow tardily, if at all. This is why the psalmist passionately wanted to desire things he perceived to be good. Seeing the reason for them, he wished also to find pleasure in them.

Conclusion: the psalm has indicated stages

5. The psalm does not say, "My soul passionately wants," but, *My soul has passionately wanted to desire your ways of justice at all times.* Perhaps the person who said this was so truly an alien on earth that he had already attained what he had passionately longed for and already desired those things which he now remembered he had formerly wanted to desire. But if he now desired them, why did he not have them? There is only one thing that hinders us from possessing God's ways of justice, and that is lack of desire for them, as when we have no burning charity in their regard, although their light shines upon us. But

should we perhaps think that the speaker in the psalm did have them and observed them? This seems likely, for a little later he says, *Your servant was busily employed in your ways of justice* (v. 23). He has pointed out to us the steps by which they are reached. The first stage is that we see how profitable and honorable those ways are; then we passionately long to desire them; finally, as light and health increase, we take delight in putting into practice those righteous precepts which earlier appealed only to our reason.

This sermon is already rather long. It will be more convenient to postpone the next verses and discuss them in another sermon, with the Lord's help.

Exposition 9 of Psalm 118

Ninth Sermon

Verse 21. The penalty of pride

1. The next verses of this psalm, the ones we are to discuss now, warn us to keep the cause of our wretched condition before our minds. The psalm has just said, *My soul has passionately wanted to desire your ways of justice at all times*, and these last words are important. *At all times* means when things go well with us, and equally when we meet with trouble, because justice should bring us joy even amid struggle and pain. Our love for justice in peaceful times should not be such that we forsake it when our affairs are in turmoil; justice is to be embraced all the time. The psalmist then immediately continues, *You rebuked the proud; accursed are those who turn away from your commandments*, for it is the proud who turn away from the commands of God. It is one thing to fail through weakness or ignorance in carrying out God's commands, but something quite different to turn away from them out of pride. This is what our first parents did, those who passed on to us a life doomed to death and subject to the evils we experience. The promise, *You will be like gods* (Gn 3:5), intrigued them and so through pride they turned away from God's command, a command they knew he had laid upon them, one which they were capable of obeying with the greatest ease, because they had no weakness that could distract or hinder them or slow them down.

And look at the result! Look at all this hard, unhappy predicament we mortals endure, and observe how the rebuke to the proud has become hereditary. When God said, *Adam, where are you?* (Gn 3:9) he was not ignorant of Adam's whereabouts; he was rebuking that proud man. He was not trying to find out where Adam was—or, in other words, what kind of wretchedness he had sunk into—but by his question rebuking Adam and admonishing him. But notice a further point. After saying, *You rebuked the proud*, the psalm might have continued, "Accursed were those who turned away from your commandments," thus confining our attention to the sin of the first human beings. But it did not: it said, *Accursed are those who turn away*; for all of us need to be deterred by their example from turning away from God's commands, and taught how, by loving justice at all times, we may regain even through this world's hardships what we lost by self-indulgence in paradise.

Verse 22. Christian martyrdoms, once an object of contempt, are now held in honor

2. The proud do not submit, however, even at so powerful a rebuke. They have been thrown down under the punishment of labor and death, yet they exalt themselves in swollen arrogance, imitating the self-exaltation of those doomed to fall and deriding the humility of those who rise. The body of Christ accordingly prays for them, *Take from me the insults and contempt I suffer for having ardently sought your testimonies.* This word "testimonies" is *martyria* in Greek, and the Greek word has passed over into our language.[1] People who were humiliated and subjected to various torments on account of their witness to Christ, and fought for the truth even to death, we call "martyrs," using the Greek word even though we could just as well call them "witnesses" in our own tongue. Since you are more accustomed to the former word, and rather fond of it, let us take the present verse in this sense: *Take from me the insults and contempt I suffer for having ardently sought your martyrdoms.*

But when the body of Christ makes this plea, it surely cannot be regarding the insults and contempt heaped on it by unbelievers as some kind of punishment? Are they not rather the way to its crown? Why, then, does Christ's body pray to be relieved of these things, as though they were a heavy, unbearable burden? The only possible answer, as I have suggested, is that it is praying for its enemies. To fling the name of Christ at Christians as something shameful, to despise Christ's cross, derided by the Jews, and along with it the whole healing process of Christian humility, is harmful to the Church's enemies, for it is only by these means that our tumor can be cured. Through that tumor of pride we fell, and as we lay there we became more swollen still. Yet it is this same persistent and mounting pride that motivates the enemies of Christ's body in their contempt.

But the body of Christ has learned to love its enemies. Let it therefore say to the Lord, its God, *Take from me the insults and contempt I suffer for having ardently sought your martyrdoms.* It is because I have sought your martyrdoms that I hear these insults and am the butt of this contempt, so take them from me. You command me to love my enemies, but those enemies are dying, perishing on every side, as they despise your martyrs' witness and make it a reproach against me. They will certainly come back to life and be found again if they come to see these martyrdoms as my title to honor.

This is indeed what happened; this is what we see today. Martyrdom in Christ's cause is no longer something shameful but something to be revered, even in the estimation of ordinary people and in this world. The death of his holy ones is precious not only in the sight of the Lord[2] but in human eyes as well, and

---

1. He says Latin, of course.
2. See Ps 115(116):15.

his martyrs are now not only free from contempt but even held in high honor. The younger son in the parable used to feed pigs,[3] being accustomed to pay cult to unclean demons. He abandoned his pigs and laid claim to the more excellent portion[4] that was his among the tiny handful of Christians. Consider him now, this younger son: with fervent devotion he is preaching among great and populous nations those martyrs on whom he used to heap shame and commending in the most honorific terms those whom he used to insult. Of him it can truly be said that he once was lost but now is found.[5]

In pursuit of so great a gain through the correction, conversion, and redemption of its enemies, the body of Christ prays, *Take from me the insults and contempt I suffer.* In case there should be any doubt as to the grounds of the insults and contempt, it adds, *For having ardently sought your martyrdoms.*

Verses 23-24. By loving its persecuting enemies, the Church wins them

3. Where are those insults today? Where that contempt? They have faded away and disappeared; they are lost, because the people who were lost are found. Yet at the time when the Church was offering that prayer it was still enduring the insults and contempt. *For indeed rulers took their seats and spoke against me,* it declares. That the leaders, men in lofty positions on their judicial benches, sat down to decree the persecution was a sign of its gravity. Compare this with the experience of the head himself; there you will find that the leaders of the Jews sat in council, devising a plan to do away with Christ.[6] Now compare it with the experience of his body, the Church, and you will find that earthly rulers drew up plans and gave orders that Christians should be eliminated from every place.

Indeed rulers took their seats and spoke against me, but your servant was busily employed in your ways of justice. Anyone who wishes to ascertain the nature of this busy employment should pay attention to the next verse: *For your testimonies are the subject of my meditation, and your ways of justice my project.* Remember how I have already pointed out that those testimonies are acts of martyrdom. Remember also that among the Lord's ways of justice none is more difficult, and none more wonderful, than the command to love one's enemies. This, then, was the employment of Christ's body: meditating on the martyrdoms and loving those who persecuted the Church, the persecutors who all the while insulted and despised it on account of those very martyrdoms. As I

---

3. See Lk 15:15. Augustine identifies the younger son with the Christian Church drawn from the Gentiles, the "younger people."
4. *Particulam*: this could mean either a portion of the inheritance, or a morsel of food, as contrasted with his starving condition.
5. See Lk 15:24.32. This phrase becomes a refrain in the next section.
6. See Mt 26:3-4.

emphasized before, the Church was praying not for itself but for those on whose behalf it begged, *Take from me insults and contempt.*

Well, then, *rulers took their seats and spoke against me, but your servant was busily employed in your ways of justice.* How was it so employed? In that *your testimonies were the subject of my meditation, and your ways of justice my project.* Project against project: the project of the rulers on their judgment-seats to find the martyrs and see them lost; the project of the martyrs in their torments to see that those lost enemies were found. The former were rendering evil for good, the latter good for evil. What wonder, then, if the former were by killing defeated, while the latter by dying conquered? What wonder, I ask, if the martyrs most patiently endured temporal death at the hands of raging pagans, whereas the pagans were enabled to reach eternal life through the praying martyrs? While Christ's body is so employed that it both meditates on the martyrdoms and begs for good things to come to the evil persecutors of the martyrs, this is the result.

Exposition 10 of Psalm 118

Tenth Sermon

Verse 25. My soul is stuck to the hard floor

1. In this very long psalm the next verse we must study, and, as the Lord enables us, thoroughly discuss, is this: *My soul has stuck to the hard floor; give me life according to your word.* What does it mean by saying, *My soul has stuck to the hard floor*? Since the words that immediately follow are: *Give me life according to your word,* we may assume that the preceding phrase supplies the reason why the psalmist is asking to be given life. By saying, *My soul has stuck to the hard floor,* he indicates the background to his request. Now if he gives that as the reason why he asks to be brought to life, we can hardly suppose that the condition of being stuck to the floor signifies anything good. On the contrary: the whole petition is probably equivalent to: "I am dead. Bring me to life."

What then is this hard floor?[1] If we care to represent the whole world as a single enormous house, we can regard the sky as its vaulted roof and the earth as its hard floor. The psalmist is therefore praying to be plucked free from the things of earth, so that he can say with the apostle, *Our way of life is in heaven* (Phil 3:20). To stick fast in earthly things is death to the soul. The remedy for this calamity is life, for which the psalm begs: *Give me life.*

2. The question arises, however, as to how these words can be attributed to the same person whose recent statements seemed to indicate that he was cleaving to God rather than to the floor, so much so that his way of life appeared to be heavenly, rather than immersed in earthly things. How could anyone be stuck fast in things of earth if he was in a position to say, *Your servant was busily employed in your ways of justice, for your testimonies are the subject of my meditation, and your ways of justice my project?* That is what he said earlier, yet now here he is saying, *My soul has stuck to the hard floor; give me life according to your word.*

Perhaps we should understand it this way: however far a person has advanced in the Lord's ways of justice, he is still conscious of the desire of mortal flesh for those earthly things amid which human life on earth is one long temptation.[2] But if he perseveres and continues to make progress, he is brought back to life every day from that deathly condition, for he is constantly given life by God, whose

---

1. *Pavimentum*, a floor composed of stones beaten down hard, or a paved floor.
2. See Jb 7:1.

grace renews our inner self day by day.[3] When the apostle told us that *as long as we are in the body we are on pilgrimage and away from the Lord* (2 Cor 5:6), and that he was longing to be set free so as to be with Christ,[4] his soul was stuck to the floor. It makes good sense to think of the body itself as the floor, since it is made from earth. Because it is still corruptible and weighs down the soul,[5] we cannot but groan wearily in it and say to God, *My soul has stuck to the hard floor; give me life according to your word.* This is not to say that when we are with the Lord for ever[6] we shall be without our bodies; no, but they will not be burdensome to our souls then, because they will no longer be subject to decay. To state the case exactly, we shall not be cleaving to our bodies, but rather they will cleave to us, as we to God. This is why another psalm includes the words, *My good is to hold fast to God* (Ps 72(73):28). This implies that our bodies will live from us, by cleaving to us, but we shall live from God,[7] since to hold fast to him is our good.

The kind of cleaving or sticking fast of which the psalmist says, *My soul has stuck to the hard floor*, is something different, or so it seems to me. It does not mean the conjunction of flesh and soul, although some have understood it in that way; I think it means the carnal impulses by which the flesh lusts against the spirit.[8] If this interpretation is correct, it follows that when the psalmist prays, *My soul has stuck to the hard floor; give me life according to your word*, he is not asking to be released from this death-ridden body[9] by corporeal death itself, for the final day of anyone's life will see to that sooner or later, and, since life is short, it is likely to be sooner. Rather does the prayer beg that the concupiscence with which the flesh lusts against the spirit may be progressively diminished, and the passionate longing of the spirit in opposition to the flesh be progressively intensified, until the lust of the flesh is completely consumed in us and the longing of the spirit reaches its consummation[10] through the Holy Spirit who has been given to us.[11]

Verse 26. He confesses his own ways, and asks to learn those of the Lord

3. The speaker quite rightly asks, *Give me life*, not according to what I deserve, but *according to your word*. What else can that mean but "according to

---

3. See 2 Cor 4:16.
4. See Phil 1:23.
5. See Wis 9:15.
6. See 1 Th 4:17.
7. We could also translate *vivant corpora ex nobis . . . nos autem vivamus ex Deo* as "live on us . . . live on God": as the body now lives on food and air, it will then live on the soul, as the soul already does on God.
8. See Gal 5:17.
9. See Rom 7:24.
10. *Donec ista consumatur in nobis, et illa consummetur.*
11. See Rom 5:5.

your promise"? He aspires to be a child of the promise, not a child of pride, so that under the regime of grace the promise may be effective for the whole progeny of Abraham. This is the word of promise: *It is through Isaac that posterity will be yours*, which is to say, *It is not the children of Abraham's flesh who are children of God; it is the children of the promise who are accounted Abraham's descendants* (Rom 9:7-8).

In the words that follow the psalmist confesses what he was when left to himself: *I declared my ways, and you heard me*. Some codices read *your ways*, but most, particularly the Greek ones, have *my ways*, which means "my bad ways." The sense of the verse is, I think, "I confessed my sins, and you heard me—heard me, that is, by forgiving my sins. *Teach me your ways of justice*. I have confessed my own ways, and you have blotted them out; now teach me yours. But teach them to me in such a way that I may act in accordance with them, and not merely know what I ought to do." It was said of the Lord that he *knew no sin* (2 Cor 5:21), and this is understood to mean that he committed none; conversely it is only a person who acts justly who can truly be said to know justice.

This is the prayer of one who is making progress. If he had not advanced at all in the Lord's ways of justice, he obviously could not have said, as he did in an earlier verse, *Your servant was busily employed in your ways of justice*. He is therefore not hoping to learn from the Lord those ways of justice in which he is already well versed; he wants to move on to others, thus making progress and new growth.

Verses 27-29. Through God's mercy and the "law of faith" the petitioner advances to wonders

4. The psalmist then prays, *Initiate*[12] *me in your ways of justice*; or, as some codices have it, *Instruct me,*[13] which better captures the meaning of the Greek: "Make me understand." *And I will be employed about your wonders*. Those more advanced ways of justice, which he longs to apprehend as he makes progress, he now calls God's wonders. Some of God's ways of justice are so wonderful that in the eyes of people who have never tried them they are thought to be unattainable by human weakness. This is why the speaker in the psalm, struggling and almost worn out by the difficulty, continues, *My soul has fallen asleep through weariness; strengthen me in your words*. What can he mean by *My soul has fallen asleep*, if not that his soul has lost the warmth of that hope which formerly inspired it to believe it would apprehend God's ways of justice? But, it prays, *strengthen me in your words*, lest through sleepiness I fall away

---

12. *Insinua.*
13. *Instrue.*

even from the place I know I have reached. Strengthen me in those of your words to which I hold already, those I already act upon, so that I may advance from them to others.

5. But what prevents any man or woman from so surely walking in God's ways of justice as to reach his wonders with ease? It can be nothing else but the hindrance of which the psalmist speaks next, begging that it be removed from him: *Put far from me the way of iniquity.* But he has more to say, because *the law* of works *entered stealthily that sin might abound* (Rom 5:20); so he continues, *On the basis of your law have mercy on me.* What law can he mean? The law of faith, undoubtedly. Listen to the apostle: *What room is left for your boasting? It is completely ruled out. By what law? The law of works? No; but by the law of faith.* (Rom 3:27) The law of faith is this: that we believe and pray to be empowered through grace to accomplish what we cannot do by ourselves, lest being ignorant of God's justice and attempting to set up our own, we fail to submit to the justice of God.[14] The justice of God who commands us is expressed in the law of works, but the mercy of him who helps us is exercised through the law of faith.

Verses 30-32. Running with hearts enlarged

6. He has begged the Lord, *On the basis of your law, have mercy on me.* Now he lists the benefits he has already received, as though they were an entitlement to further benefits he has not received yet. *I have chosen the way of truth and have not forgotten your judgments. I have clung to your testimonies; do not put me to shame, O Lord.* He says, *I have chosen the way of truth,* in which to run; *I have not forgotten your judgments,* and that is why I had the strength to run. *I have clung to your testimonies* while running. *Do not put me to shame, O Lord,* but let me push on in my course and arrive at the goal; for the outcome depends not on the one who wills nor on the one who runs, but on God who shows mercy (Rom 9:16).

The next verse declares, *I have run the way of your commands, for you enlarged my heart.* There is no doubt that this verse is the key to the statements he made just now: *I have chosen the way of truth and have not forgotten your judgments. I have clung to your testimonies,* for to behave so is to run in the way of God's commandments. But in making these claims he is not flaunting his own merits before the Lord, but acknowledging the good things he has received. It is as though someone now asked him, "How did you manage to run in that way? How were you able to choose that course, and not forget God's judgments, and cling to his testimonies? Were you strong enough to do all that by yourself?" No, he replies. "How did you do it, then?" *I have run the way of your commands, for*

---

14. See Rom 10:3.

you enlarged my heart. Not by my own decision, as though it needed no help from you, but only because *you enlarged my heart.*

Enlargement of heart means delight in righteousness. This is a gift of God. With it we are not cramped by fear in the observance of his commands but led into the broad freedom of love as we delight in justice. He promises us this wide space in his pledge, *I will dwell in them, and walk about in them* (2 Cor 6:16). How spacious must be the place where God walks! In this breadth of heart there is poured out in us that charity which comes from the Holy Spirit who has been given to us.[15] Another text suggests the same truth: *Let your waters run widely in your streets* (Prv 5:16). The word "street"[16] derives from the Greek word πλατύ, which means something wide. The waters here mentioned are those of which the Lord cried out, *Let anyone who is thirsty come to me and drink. If anyone believes in me, as scripture says, rivers of living water shall flow from within that person.* And the evangelist explains the meaning of the Lord's invitation: *He said this of the Spirit which those who believed in him were to receive.* (Jn 7:37-38)

Much more could be said concerning this breadth of heart; but we have already exceeded the due limits of this sermon.

---

15. See Rom 5:5.
16. *Platea.*

Exposition 11 of Psalm 118

Eleventh Sermon

Verse 33. The continuing search for the law of freedom and love

1. The next verse in this great psalm, the one we now have to consider and expound with the Lord's help, runs as follows: *Impose your ways of justice as a law upon me, O Lord, and I will always seek it out.* The apostle says, *Law is not imposed on a righteous person, but upon the unjust and insubordinate . . . and on all other wickedness opposed to the sound teaching that accords with the gospel of the glory of our blessed God, the gospel entrusted to me* (1 Tm 1:9-11). Was it an unrighteous person like this who prayed, *Impose your law upon me, O Lord*? Was he the kind for whom Paul declared the law to be intended? We can hardly think so. If he had been that sort of person, he could not have said earlier, *I have run the way of your commands, for you enlarged my heart.* Why then is he praying that the Lord will impose a law on him, if it is not imposed on a righteous person?

This may be the explanation: the law is not imposed on a righteous person in the same way as it is upon those obstinate people for whom it is written on stone tablets, rather than upon the tablets of human hearts.[1] That was how the Old Covenant was imposed at Mount Sinai, for Sinai is the mountain that brings its children forth into slavery.[2] Very different is the New Covenant, of which the prophet Jeremiah wrote, *Lo, the days are coming, says the Lord, when I will conclude with the house of Israel and the house of Judah a new covenant, not like the covenant that I established with their ancestors when I led them out of the land of Egypt; for they did not abide by my covenant, so I disregarded them, says the Lord. But this is the covenant that I will establish with the house of Israel after those days, says the Lord: I will put my laws into their minds, and write them upon their hearts.* (Jer 31:31-33) This is how the psalmist wants the Lord to impose a law on him: not as it was upon the unjust and insubordinate who belonged to the Old Covenant, and not written upon tablets of stone. He wants the kind of law that is appointed for the holy children of the heavenly Jerusalem,[3] the children of promise, the children for whom an eternal inheritance is kept. This law is imprinted in their minds by the Holy Spirit, as though by the finger of

---

1. See 2 Cor 3:3.
2. See Gal 4:24.
3. See Gal 4:26.

God; it is written in their hearts. It is not a law to be retained in their memory but neglected in their lives. It is a law they will know through their own understanding and observe by loving choice in the wide freedom of love, not in the constriction of fear. Clearly, if anyone performs a work prescribed by law out of fear of punishment rather than love of justice, such a person obeys the law unwillingly. But if he acts unwillingly, that means he would prefer that no such order were laid upon him, if that were possible. Hence he is no friend of the law (since he would wish it not to exist), but its enemy; and the work he performs does not cleanse him, because his own will renders[4] him unclean. A person of this type cannot make his own the words of the psalmist in an earlier verse: *I have run the way of your commands, for you enlarged my heart*, because enlargement of heart symbolizes charity which, according to the apostle, is the perfect implementation of the law.[5]

2. But in that case, why is the psalmist still asking to have this kind of law laid down for him? He could not have been running with wide-open heart along the way of God's commands unless it had been imposed already, could he? The answer must be that the speaker is a person gaining ground. He knows that his progress is a gift from God, and when he asks for a law to be laid upon him, his request means that he sees it as a means of advancing more and more. It is like the request of a very thirsty person: if you hold a full cup in your hand and begin to give it to him, he drains it but still asks for more.

When a law written on stone tablets is imposed on the unjust and insubordinate, however, the effect is to make them guilty of transgression, not to make them children of promise. Similarly guilty is a person who remembers the law but does not love it; the memory of it is for him a tablet which does bear some kind of inscription, but it oppresses rather than ennobles him; it is a ponderous burden, not a title to honor.

But the psalmist calls his law God's way of justice, and this is for him nothing else than the way of God's commands, along which he has been running with heart enlarged. He ran, and he is still running, intent on winning the prize, God's call to life on high.[6] After saying, *Impose your ways of justice as a law upon me, O Lord*, he adds, *and I will always seek it out*. How can he seek out something that is his already? He has it inasmuch as he acts upon it, but he seeks it out that he may make further progress.

3. But why does he say *always*? One possibility is that this means there will be no end to our seeking. In the same sense another psalm says, *His praise shall be in my mouth always* (Ps 33:2(34:1)), for there will never be an end to our praise of God. Even when we reach his eternal kingdom we shall not stop praising him,

---

4. Variant: "his own thought and will render."
5. See Rom 13:10.
6. See Phil 3:14.

for we read, *Blessed are they who dwell in your house; they will praise you for
ever and ever* (Ps 83:5(84:4)).

Alternatively we could take *always* to mean "as long as this life lasts," because
progress is lifelong. But if someone has made good progress here, will he or she not
be made perfect hereafter? Of certain women scripture says that they are *always
avid to learn*; but that must be taken in a bad sense, for the passage continues, *But
they never arrive at knowledge of the truth* (2 Tm 3:7). One who is always
advancing and improving in this world arrives at the goal to which his or her efforts
are tending; after that there is no more progress, because the person stands perfect
and stable without end. But such is not the case with those people of whom scripture said just now that they are *always avid to learn*; these will not persist after
death in their search for useless, unprofitable scraps of knowledge. The sequel to
such pursuits will not be further study but everlasting punishments.

A person seeks out God's law in this world as long as he or she is making
progress in it by knowledge and love; but in the world to come the fulfillment of
that law remains to be enjoyed, and nothing further is to be sought. The same
idea is conveyed in another psalm, where we are bidden, *Seek his face always* (Ps
104(105):4). Where else but in this world can we seek it *always*? We shall not be
seeking God's face in that other world, for there we shall see him face to face.[7]
Perhaps, though, it does make sense to say that we seek something if that thing is
loved without any weariness, and we seek it by taking care never to lose it. In that
sense we shall certainly seek God's law without end, for it is nothing else but
God's truth. This same psalm declares, *Your law is truth* (Ps 118(119):142). We
seek it here in order to hold fast to it; we shall hold fast to it there, so as never to
lose it. There is a certain analogy in what scripture says of the Spirit of God: that
he scrutinizes all things, even the depths of God,[8] certainly not in order to find
out something he does not know but in the sense that nothing whatever remains
outside his knowledge.

Verse 34. The real thrust of the law

4. It is quite clear, then, that when the psalmist asks the Lord that a law be
imposed on him, our attention is being drawn to the grace of God. This must be
so because as far as the letter was concerned the psalmist knew the law already.
But the letter is death-dealing; the Spirit gives life.[9] He prays, therefore, that
through the Spirit he may put into practice what he knew through the letter;

---

7. See 1 Cor 13:12.
8. See 1 Cor 2:10.
9. See 2 Cor 3:6. According to *Confessions* 6,4,6 it was Ambrose's frequent emphasis on this
principle that resolved much of Augustine's difficulty in understanding the anthropomorphic
passages in the scriptures.

otherwise the charge of disobedience might be brought against him for having known the commandment but not observed it.

Only someone to whom the Lord grants understanding can know the law as it ought to be known; that is to say, the true intention of the law, why it was imposed on people who were not going to keep it, and what was the point of it when we are told that *the law entered stealthily that sin might abound* (Rom 5:20). Only if the Lord grants understanding can we comprehend this, and so the psalmist goes on to say, *Give me understanding, and I will study your law, and I will keep it with my whole heart.* When someone has studied the law, and attained to those lofty precepts on which the whole of it depends, he must thence-forth love God with all his heart, all his soul, and all his mind, and his neighbor as himself, for on these two commandments the whole law and the prophets depend.[10] This is what the psalmist seems to have promised in saying, *I will keep it with my whole heart.*

5. All the same, he is quite incapable of doing this by his own strength; he needs help from the author of the commandment to do what is commanded. He prays, therefore, *Lead me in the path of your commandments, because that is what I have willed.* My own will is insufficient; you must yourself lead me in what I have willed. This path to which he refers is the same thing as the way of God's commands, which he said earlier he had been running with heart enlarged. He now calls it a path because the way that leads to life is narrow,[11] and being so narrow it can be run only by someone with a wide heart.[12]

Verse 36. Disinterested service of God

6. The psalmist is still gaining ground, still running. But he knows that the outcome depends not on the one who wills, nor on the one who runs, but on God who exercises mercy,[13] and that even our act of willing is created in us by God,[14] since the will itself is made ready by the Lord. He therefore continues, *Bend my heart to your testimonies, and not to covetousness.* What does it mean to have one's heart bent toward something? Surely, to will that thing. This means that the psalmist has willed it, yet at the same time prays to will it. He has willed it, for he says, *Lead me in the path of your commandments, because that is what I have willed*; but he also prays to will it, by saying, *Bend my heart to your testimonies, and not to covetousness.* He makes this prayer that he may advance in his willed decision.

---

10. See Mt 22:37.39-40.
11. See Mt 7:14.
12. An example of the paradox of which Augustine is fond, though he does not develop it here.
13. See Rom 9:16.
14. See Phil 2:13.

Now what can God's testimonies be, if not those things by which he bears witness to himself? A testimony is the means by which something is proved. Thus God's ways of justice and God's commandments are attested by God. If God wants to persuade us of anything, he persuades us by his own testimonies. The psalmist begs that his heart be bent to these testimonies, and not to covetousness.

By his testimonies God gives us good reason to worship him disinterestedly, but the obstacle to worshiping gratis is covetousness, the root of all evils. The word *covetousness* corresponds to a Greek word with wider connotations, meaning an appetite on anyone's part for more than enough; for πλέον means "more," and ἕξις means "having," from the verb "to have." Thus we get the noun πλεονεξία, which some translators have in this context rendered *gain*,[15] others *advantage*,[16] and the better ones *covetousness*.[17] The apostle teaches that *covetousness is the root of all evils* (1 Tm 6:10); but in the Greek, from which these words were translated into our tongue, this text from the apostle reads not πλεονεξία (the term used in the psalm) but φιλαργυρία, "love of money" or "avarice." We need to recognize, though, that the apostle was using a specific term to indicate a generic vice: he mentioned love of money but meant greed in general, any kind of greed, which is indeed the root of all evils. The progenitors of the human race themselves would not have been deceived and overthrown by the serpent had they not wished to get more than they had been given and to be more than they had been created to be. But this is what the tempter promised them: *You will be like gods* (Gn 3:5). They were ruined by πλεονεξία. By trying to get more than they had received, they lost even what they had received. This truth became part of universal human wisdom, and a trace of it has been captured even in forensic jurisprudence, the principles of which ordain that an overstated case shall collapse. That is to say, if a plaintiff claims more than is owed to him, he loses even what was owed.

But all greed is cut away[18] from us by disinterested worship of God. The enemy himself went so far as to challenge Job on this point amid Job's struggle with temptation: *Job hardly worships God for nothing, does he?* (Jb 1:9). The devil thought that just man's heart was inclined toward greed, as though he worshiped God for what he could get out of it, for the temporal advantages that were his from the goods with which the Lord had enriched him. The devil thought of Job as a mercenary, who served the Lord for the sake of these rewards. But the trials Job underwent revealed the disinterested character of his service. If we, then, have hearts not bent toward covetousness, we worship God for nothing

---

15. *Emolumentum.*
16. *Utilitatem.*
17. *Avaritiam.*
18. *Circumciditur*, literally "is circumcised." There may be an allusion to Col 2:11; Rom 2:28-29.

else but God himself: he is himself the reward for service offered to him. Let us love him in himself, love him in ourselves, and love him in the neighbors whom we love as ourselves, either because they possess him or in order that they may possess him. The possibility of doing so is conferred on us by his gift, which is why the psalm says to him, *Bend my heart to your testimonies, and not to covet-ousness.*

The points that emerge next must be dealt with in another sermon.

Exposition 12 of Psalm 118

Twelfth Sermon

Verse 37. The vanity of earthly things, especially of human approval

1. In the psalm we have undertaken to expound, the next verse makes this prayer: *Turn my eyes away that they may not see vanity; give me life in your way.* Vanity[1] and truth are opposites. To covet this world[2] is vanity; but Christ, who frees us from this world, is truth. He is also the way, in which the psalmist prays to be given life, as he is also both truth and life. This is what he told us: *I am the way, the truth, and the life* (Jn 14:6).

But what can it mean to pray, *Turn my eyes away that they may not see vanity?* Is it possible for us to avoid seeing vanity as long as we are in this life? *All creation has been subjected to vanity* (Rom 8:20), says scripture, for vanity is within human beings. *All things are vanity. How much more wealth does a person gain by all his toil, all his labor under the sun?* (Eccl 1:2-3) Perhaps that text provides a clue, for the psalmist may be praying that his life be passed not under the sun but in Christ the way, in whom he begs to be given life. Christ indeed ascended not merely above the sun but *above all the heavens, to fill all things* (Eph 4:10). People who listen to the apostle, and listen to good effect, live not so much under the sun as in Christ. This is what the apostle urged: *Seek what is above, where Christ is seated at the right hand of God. Have a taste for the things that are above, not the things on earth; for you are dead, and your life is hidden with Christ in God.* (Col 3:1-3) If our life is there, where truth is, then it is not in the home of vanity, under the sun.

But this most excellent state is ours in hope; we do not yet possess it in reality.[3] The apostle's exhortation is couched in the language of hope; for after noting that *all creation has been subjected to vanity,* he goes on to say that this happened *not by creation's own choice, but through him who subjected it in hope* (Rom 8:20). This means that we have been subjected to vanity for the time being, but subjected in the hope of one day cleaving to the truth in contemplation. This whole creation—spiritual, animal, and material—is present in human

---

1. Vanity in the biblical tradition means the condition of being without reality, purpose or usefulness. The word is applied in particular to idols by the prophets: idols are "nothings." Human life is vanity insofar as it is turned away from God; and the entire universe is frustrated (temporarily) by human sin, as Augustine goes on to discuss.
2. Or "what this world covets."
3. Augustine's habitual antithesis: *in spe . . . in re.*

393

beings; indeed a human being comprises all of them. In him all creation sinned by its own choice and became an enemy of the truth. It was justly punished by being subjected to vanity against its will.

A few lines further on the apostle continues, *But not creation only: we ourselves, though we have the first-fruits of the Spirit, groan inwardly as we await our adoption as God's children, the redemption of our bodies. In hope we have been saved. But if hope is seen, it is hope no longer, for when someone sees what he hopes for, why should he hope for it? But if we hope for what we do not see, we wait for it in patience.* (Rom 8:23-25) In saying, *We ourselves, though we have the first-fruits of the Spirit,* he indicates that we are not yet subject to God with the whole of our being but only with the part that makes us superior to the animals, that is, with the *first-fruits of the Spirit.*[4] As long as we live in the flesh here, awaiting with patient hope the full adoption and redemption of our fleshly nature, so long are we living under the sun, subjected to vanity.

How, then, is it possible for us, while this is our condition, not to see vanity? We are subject to it, though we live in hope. What can the psalmist mean when he prays, *Turn my eyes away, that they may not see vanity?* Perhaps this is what he is asking: not that the hope we cherish may find fulfillment in this life but rather that it may become a reality in that blessed state which eventually will be achieved in him too, when he *will be set free from his enslavement to decay* in spirit, soul, and body, *and share in the glorious freedom of the children of God* (Rom 8:21). And there at last he will see no vanity.

2. It is quite legitimate to understand the verse in the aforesaid sense; we do not depart from the rule of faith in doing so. But there is another possible interpretation which, I admit, seems to me preferable. In the gospel the Lord says, *If your eye is clear, your whole body will be filled with light. But if your eye is unhealthy, your whole body will be dark. If then the very light that is in you is dark, how deep will the darkness itself be?* (Mt 6:22-23) From this we learn that when we do something good, what we have in view matters a great deal. Any service we render is to be evaluated not in itself but according to the end on which we have our eye; we must consider not only if what we do is good but also whether we are doing it for a good purpose. The psalmist is asking that the eyes with which we envisage the end of our actions may be averted from vanity or, in other words, that when he does something good, he may not fix his gaze on vanity as the motive of his action.

---

4. In the Pauline text this phrase means the initial gift of the Holy Spirit to the believer, given as the pledge of the full harvest to come. Augustine's understanding is different: for him it means the offering made to God in faith of the highest part of the human spirit, as a pledge of the dedication of the whole person that will follow. Compare his description of the vision at Ostia, when he and Monica, at the climax of the experience, "left the first-fruits of our spirit captive there" (*Confessions* 9,10,24).

Among all vain human objectives, the vainest is winning the praise of others. Many people reputed great in this world have achieved their manifold great deeds with a view to winning praise. They have been highly extolled in pagan civilizations, these heroes who sought glory not with God but in human estimation. For the sake of fame and glory they have lived prudently, bravely, temperately, and justly;[5] they won praise indeed, but in attaining it they received their reward: vain men won a vain prize. The Lord wants to turn the eyes of his followers away from this. *Be careful*, he says, *not to do your righteous works in the sight of other people, to attract their attention. Otherwise you will have no reward from your Father, who is in heaven.* (Mt 6:1) He goes on to detail some elements in this righteous behavior, giving us instructions about almsdeeds, prayer, and fasting; and in each case he warns us that nothing must be done ostentatiously, to win human adulation. He repeatedly stresses that people who act from this motive have had their reward: not the eternal reward kept in store for the saints with their Father, but the fleeting requital pursued by those who act with their eyes on vanity.

This is not to say that human admiration is in itself to be condemned (for what can be more salutary for people than to admire what they ought to imitate?); what is blameworthy is to make the attracting of admiration the motive for one's action, for this is to set one's sights on vanity in all one does. If it happens that a just person does attract human praise in some degree, such praise must not be the object of his or her actions. Praise must be redirected to the glory of God, for whose sake truly good people perform their good actions, because such people become good not by their own powers but by God's gift. Moreover in the same sermon the Lord said, *Let your deeds shine before men and women in such a way that they see the good you do, and glorify your Father who is in heaven* (Mt 5:16). He thus determined the goal we must keep in view when we do some good deed if our eyes are to be averted from vanity; that goal is the glory of God. The praise given by other people must not be the purpose of our good works; let us rather correct such praise and refer everything to the praise of God, since whatever in us rightly deserves praise comes from him.

If it is a vain attitude to do good for the sake of earning human commendation, how much more vain is it to do so in order to win money, or increase it, or hold onto it, or for any other temporal advantage that comes to us from outside ourselves? *All things are vanity. How much more wealth does a person gain by all his toil, all his labor under the sun?* (Eccles 1:2-3) Not even for the sake of temporal health or safety must we do good, but for the eternal salvation which is our hope. In that eternal salvation unchangeable good will be ours to enjoy, the good that will come to us from God, the good which will be God himself. If

---

5. The four cardinal virtues honored in classical antiquity; see the note at Exposition of Psalm 39,9.

God's saints performed their good works with a view to temporal well-being, Christ's martyrs would never have carried through the good work of their confession at the cost of losing temporal well-being. But they received help in tribulation and had no eyes for vanity, because human help is vain.[6] Nor did they seek the sunshine of human approval,[7] for a mere man is like vanity, and his days pass away like a shadow.[8]

Verse 38. Grace and holy fear

3. When prayer is offered to God that he may grant us things which might have seemed to be within our own power, such as the aversion of our eyes from vanity, to what is our attention drawn? Surely to his grace. There have been plenty of people who did not turn their gaze away from vanity; such were those who believed that they could become just and good by their own efforts. They prized human esteem more than glory from God.[9] Though no more than men, they were mightily pleased with themselves and overrated the power of their own wills. But this too is vanity and spiritual presumption.[10]

The psalmist thought otherwise. At first he said, *Turn my eyes away that they may not see vanity*. Then he added, *Give me life in your way*, because that way is not vanity, but truth. Now he continues, *Establish your utterance for your servant, to make me fear you*. What is this about? It must mean, "Grant me to act in conformity with your utterance." God's utterance is not established for people who destabilize it in themselves by contravening it, but it is established in those for whom it is immovable. We can infer, then, that God has established his utterance—an utterance that inspires fear of him—in people to whom he gives the spirit of fear but not the fear of which the apostle says, *You have not received a servile spirit of fear all over again* (Rom 8:15); for this kind of fear is cast out by charity made perfect.[11] The fear for which the psalm asks is that which a prophet called the spirit of the fear of the Lord.[12] This is a chaste fear that abides for ever,[13] the fear that dreads any offense to the beloved. An adulterous wife fears her husband; so does a chaste wife, but differently. The adulteress fears that he may come home; the chaste wife, that he may leave her.

6. See Ps 59:13(60:11).
7. See Jer 17:16.
8. See Ps 143(144):4.
9. See Jn 12:43.
10. See Eccles 6:9.
11. See 1 Jn 4:18.
12. See Is 11:3.
13. See Ps 18:10(19:9).

Verse 39. Do not judge others by yourself

4. *Cut away that shame of mine which I suspected, for sweet are your judgments.* Does anyone suspect his own shame? Surely everyone knows his own shame better than that of anyone else? One may suspect another's shame, but scarcely one's own, because only what is unknown is suspected, whereas in the case of one's own shame there is no room for suspicion; there is knowledge, because there conscience speaks. What is the psalmist talking about when he says, *That shame of mine which I suspected*?

The idea conveyed by this verse is doubtless to be understood from the verse that precedes it, for as long as a person does not turn his eyes away to prevent them from seeing vanity, he will suspect that what goes on in himself goes on in others too. So, for instance, he thinks that his own motives for worshiping God are theirs also, or he thinks that another person does good works for the same reason as he does. This happens because although other people can see our actions, the end we envisage is hidden. Hence the possibility of suspicion arises, and someone may take it upon himself to judge the hidden motives of others. Such conclusions are generally mistaken; and even if they are correct, the self-appointed judge has no right to suspect something of which he is ignorant.

The Lord warns us against a suspicious attitude at the end of the passage where he speaks about the object on which we must keep our eye in acting rightly. He tells us not to perform good deeds for the sake of winning praise from others, for he wishes to turn our eyes away from vanity. Thus he says, *Be careful not to do your righteous works in the sight of other people, to attract their attention*; and again he warns us, *Do not lay up treasures for yourselves on earth*, and, *You cannot serve God and mammon.* (Mt 6:1,19,24) He admonishes us also not to allow even anxiety about necessary food and clothing to dictate our actions: *Do not be anxious about your life and what you can eat, or about your body and how to clothe it* (Mt 6:25). But after giving us all these warnings he says something else, lest we suspect people whom we see to live good lives, but whose purposes we do not see, of being motivated in their well-doing by some such motive as he has mentioned. He immediately goes on to command us, *Do not judge, lest you be judged* (Mt 7:1).

This is why, after praying, *Cut away that shame of mine which I suspected*, the psalmist continues, *for sweet are your judgments.* What he means is, "Your judgments are true," for what is true is saluted by a lover of truth as sweet. The judgments passed by human beings on the motives of others are not sweet but rash. The psalmist therefore acknowledges the suspicions he has entertained about other people as his own shame. He remembers also what the apostle said: *Comparing themselves with one another* (2 Cor 10:12), they do not understand, for a person all too readily suspects in another what he is conscious of in himself. The psalmist prays for the removal of that shame which he has felt in himself and suspected in others, for he does not want to be like the devil, who imputed false motives to holy Job. The devil suspected that Job's worship of God was not disinterested[14] and begged leave to tempt him, hoping to find some charge he could bring against him.

Verse 40. Charity is the remedy for suspicion

5. It may happen that someone takes pleasure in suspecting dishonorable motives in another person; in this case malicious envy is at work. The good deed itself cannot be faulted, because it is open to scrutiny, so the malicious person suspects the hidden facet of it, the motive for which it is undertaken. This facet, being concealed, lends itself to anyone who delights in suspecting evil. He does not see what is secret and is jealous of what shows. To enjoy suspecting evil that one cannot see is a disease, but there is a remedy, and that is charity, which is never jealous.[15] The Lord prescribes this above all: *A new commandment I give you: that you love one another*; and again, *By this all will know that you are my disciples, that you have love for one another.* (Jn 13:34,35) In another passage, speaking about love for God and our neighbor, he says, *On these two commandments depend all the law and the prophets* (Mt 22:40).

With these things in mind the psalmist prays, desiring to see his shameful suspicion cut away, *Lo, I have longed for your commandments; in your justice give me life.* Look at me: I have longed to love you with all my heart, all my soul, and all my mind, and my neighbor as myself. Give me life, but give it not in recognition of any justice of my own; *in your justice give me life.* Fill me with the charity I long for. Help me to do what you ordain, give me what you command. *In your justice give me life*, because what I had in myself is enough to kill me. Only in you do I find my hope of life. Your justice is Christ, *who has been made for us by God wisdom, and justice, and sanctification, and redemption. As it is written, Let anyone who boasts, boast in the Lord.* (1 Cor 1:30-31) In him I find your commandments, for which I have longed, so that in your justice—in your Christ, I mean—you may give me life. He is God, the Word, but the Word was made flesh, that he might also be my neighbor.

---

14. See Jb 1:9.
15. See 1 Cor 13:4.

Exposition 13 of Psalm 118

Thirteenth Sermon

Verse 41. The mercy and salvation prayed for is Christ himself

1. This sermon, which will deal with the verse that comes next, is to be taken in conjunction with the foregoing sermon, the one we preached most recently on this longest of all psalms. The next words are, *And let your mercy come upon me, O Lord*. This clearly belongs with the previous verse, because here the psalm does not say, "Let your mercy come," but, *And let your mercy come*. The psalmist has just said, *Lo, I have longed for your commandments; in your justice give me life*. now he goes on, *And let your mercy come upon me, O Lord*. So what is he asking? That the commandments he has longed for may be obeyed through the mercy of the one who commanded. He gives us a kind of explanation of what he meant by saying, *In your justice give me life*, for now he adds, *And let your mercy come upon me, O Lord, your salvation, according to your word*. This last phrase is equivalent to "according to your promise." The apostle wants us to be recognized as children of the promise by our determination to ascribe nothing of what we are to ourselves and everything to the grace of God, for Christ *has been made for us by God wisdom, and justice, and sanctification, and redemption; as it is written, Let anyone who boasts, boast in the Lord* (1 Cor 1:30-31). When the psalmist asks, *In your justice give me life*, he is longing to be given life in Christ; this is the mercy that he prays will come upon him. Christ himself is the *salvation* of God, and is to be identified with the mercy prayed for in that plea, *and let your mercy come upon me, O Lord*.

If then we ask, "What mercy do you want?" we need only listen to the psalmist's next phrase: *Your salvation, according to your word*. Salvation has been promised to us by him who *calls into being things that do not exist, as though they already were* (Rom 4:17). Those to whom he made that promise did not even exist, so there could be no question of any of them boasting that they deserved it. We can say more: the people to whom the promise was made were themselves the object of promise, so that the whole body of Christ can say, *By God's grace I am what I am* (1 Cor 15:10).

399

Verse 42. The word for the accusers

2. *And I will reply to those who reproach me with a word.*[1] It is uncertain whether we should take this as *those who reproach me with the Word*, or as *I will reply with the Word*; but whichever it is, the verse rings with the name of Christ. Some make the Word himself a matter of accusation against us; these are objectors for whom the crucified one himself is a stumbling-block or foolishness,[2] for they do not know that he is the Word who was made flesh and dwelt among us, the very Word who was with God in the beginning, the Word who was God.

Or it may be that the Word himself is hidden from our accusers, who have no notion of his divinity and spurn the weakness he showed on the cross. In this case they do not precisely cast the Word himself in our teeth as a reproach. But we can still answer them with this Word and need not feel threatened or ashamed at their charges, for if they had known the Word they would never have crucified the Lord of glory.[3] A believer on whom the mercy of God has come will reply with the Word to those who reproach him, for on him the salvation of God has descended, but as a protection, not as a crushing weight. As a crushing weight Christ will indeed come upon certain others, who, by scorning his lowly demeanor now, trip over him at this present time and are dashed against him. So the gospel foretold: *Anyone who trips over this stone will be dashed against it, and anyone on whom it falls will be crushed* (Lk 20:18); and so it happens, for those who accuse us trip over him and fall.

For our part, let us not fear their reproaches, lest we too stumble and fall; but let us reply to them with a word, *the word of faith which we preach. If you believe in your heart that Jesus is Lord, and confess with your lips that God raised him from the dead, you will be saved, for the faith that issues in righteousness is in the heart, and the confession that leads to salvation is made with the lips.* (Rom 10:8-10) It is not enough to have Christ in your heart if you are afraid to confess him when threatened by reproaches; you must respond with this Word to your traducers. The martyrs were promised the power to do this when they were told, *It is not you who are speaking, but the Spirit of your Father who speaks in you* (Mt 10:20). This is why, immediately after saying, *I will reply with a word to those who reproach me*, the psalmist continues, *Because I have hoped in your words*, which plainly means "in your promises."

---

1. Or "I will reply with a word for those who reproach me." Augustine's Latin could mean either; he considers both and in both cases takes the "word" to mean Christ, the divine Word of God.
2. See 1 Cor 1:23.
3. See 1 Cor 2:8.

Verse 43. The Church has never entirely lost the word of truth

3. There have been many people, however, who, although they belonged to the body whose words we are considering, lacked the fortitude to endure the reproaches cast at them when persecution waxed heavy. They weakened and denied Christ. With these in mind, the psalmist continues, *Do not take the word of truth altogether away from my mouth.* Notice that it says, *my mouth*, for this is the unity of the body speaking; even those who have weakened and denied Christ for a time but later repented and come to life again are counted among its members. So too are they who let slip the palm of martyrdom but afterward renewed their confession and seized it. The word of truth was not altogether[4] taken away from Peter's mouth (or *taken away finally*,[5] as some codices have it; but the sense is the same: it means "entirely"); and Peter was a type of the Church in this respect. He was thrown off course by fear and for a time denied Christ, but he was made new again by his tears[6] and later crowned for his confession.

In the present verse of the psalm it is thus the whole body of Christ that is speaking, the universality of holy Church. The word of truth was not taken away from its mouth altogether, for within the whole body some remained brave and fought for the truth even to death, even while many were denying the faith; and even out of those who had denied it, many were rehabilitated.

The expression, *Do not take it away*, must be understood to mean, "Do not allow it to be taken away." We use the same idiom when we pray, *Do not bring us into temptation* (Mt 6:13). The Lord himself told Peter, *I have prayed for you, Peter, that your faith may not fail* (Lk 22:32), which amounts to saying, "I have prayed that the word of truth may not be *altogether* taken away from your mouth."

The psalm continues, *Because I have hoped in your judgments.* Some translators have rendered the Greek verb more exactly with *I have hoped above measure*; that Latin word *supersperavi* is unusual in its composite form, but necessary for complete accuracy. We need to be particularly careful in investigating the sense of this verse, so that, insofar as the Lord helps us, we may understand its bearing on what went before: *I have hoped in your words; I have hoped above measure in your judgments.* The psalmist declared, *I will reply with a word to those who reproach me, because I have hoped in your words*: because, he means, this is what you yourself promised me. So now *do not take the word of truth altogether away from my mouth, because I have hoped above measure in your judgments.* The judgments I mean are your decisions to correct me and whip me. Not only do they not take my hope away; they even increase it, for the

---

4. *Usque valde.*
5. *Usquequaque.*
6. See Lk 22:62.

Lord disciplines those whom he loves and whips every child he acknowledges as his.[7] I have seen how the holy and humble-hearted who put their trust in you did not flinch under persecution. I have seen also how some others who trusted in themselves and failed the test still belonged to the body, for on discovering their weakness they wept and found your grace more steadily because they lost their pride. Therefore do I pray, *Do not take the word of truth altogether away from my mouth, because I have hoped above measure in your judgments.*

Verse 44. The fullness of the law, in time and eternity

4. *And I will always keep your law.* If you do not take the word of truth away from my mouth, *I will always keep your law.* He continues, *To the end of time and for ever,* which makes more precise what he meant by *always.* In some contexts *"always"* means only *"as long as this life lasts,"* but not here, as he indicates by adding, *To the end of time and for ever.*[8] The law he refers to is that of which the apostle says, *The fullness of the law is charity* (Rom 13:10). The saints, from whose mouth the word of truth will not be taken away, will keep this law, which is to say that Christ's Church itself will keep this law not only until the end of the present age but also in the age beyond, as suggested by the phrase, *To the end of time and for ever.* Not that in eternity the precepts of the law will be proposed to us for our observance, as happens here; no, but we shall keep the very fullness of the law, as I have said, and keep it without any fear of sin. This is because when we see God more fully we shall love him and our neighbor too, for God will be all in everyone.[9] There will be no possibility of unjust suspicion arising with regard to our neighbor, because no one there will be hidden from anyone else.[10]

---

7. See Heb 12:6.
8. *In saeculum et in saeculum saeculi.* Augustine's next sentence is omitted from the translation: he says he prefers this Latin rendering to *in aeternum et in saeculum saeculi.*
9. See 1 Cor 15:28.
10. A reference to his preceding sermon; see Exposition 12 of Psalm 118,4.

Exposition 14 of Psalm 118

Fourteenth Sermon

Verses 45-48. The psalm switches from petition to narrative: prayer has been heard

1. The preceding verses of this long psalm were a prayer. The ones that follow now, the ones we have to discuss, are in narrative mode. This man of God has hitherto been begging for the help of God's grace, as he constantly prayed, *In your justice give me life; and let your mercy come upon me, O Lord*. There are similar petitions both before this point and after it. But now he says, *And I walked continually in wide freedom, because I sought your commandments. And I spoke of your testimonies in the presence of kings, and was not put to shame. And all the while I pondered on your commandments, which I loved. And I lifted my hands to your commandments, which I loved; and I was constantly employed about your ways of justice*. These are the words of one who recounts facts, not those of a suppliant: it seems that he must have obtained what he pleaded for, and now praises God as he confesses that the mercy of the Lord, which he begged might come upon him, has made him the kind of person he is.

We are obliged to take the verses in this sense: it is not as though he had linked them to the foregoing passage by saying, "Do not take the word of truth altogether away from my mouth, because I have hoped above measure in your judgments. And I will always keep your law, to the end of time and for ever; and I will walk in wide freedom because I sought your commandments. And I will speak of your testimonies in the presence of kings, and I shall not be put to shame," and so on. That is how he ought to have expressed himself if he had meant these present verses to be simply a continuation of the previous ones. But it is not so: he says, *And I walked continually in wide freedom*. The conjunction *and* looks odd, even illogical, since he does not say, "And I will walk," as he has just said, *And I will always keep your law*. Even if we regard the verb *keep* in the earlier verse as an optative, meaning, "May I keep it," it still does not match the verbs in the present passage, as though both expressed a wish and a request, for he does not say, "May I walk in wide freedom." What he says is, *And I walked continually in wide freedom*.

If the conjunction *and* had been omitted and the sentence, *I walked continually in wide freedom*, had stood alone, disconnected from what went before, there would have been nothing unusual in this mode of speech that could discon-

403

cert the reader or make one think that some hidden meaning needed to be sought here. But the use of the conjunction makes it quite plain that the speaker wishes us to understand something he has not directly said, namely, that his prayer has been heard. Then he goes on to say what kind of person he has become. It is as though he had written, "When I prayed for these graces you heard me, and then *I walked continually in wide freedom*," and so with the rest of the statements he puts together in narrative style.

The gift of the Spirit

2. Now, what does it mean to say, *And I walked continually in wide freedom?* Nothing else than "I walked continually in charity," the charity poured out in our hearts through the Holy Spirit who has been given to us.[1] One man who was walking in this wide freedom was he who said, *Our mouth is open to you, Corinthians, and our heart is thrown wide open* (2 Cor 6:11). But this charity is summed up, whole and entire, in the two great commandments: love of God and love of our neighbor, on which all the law and the prophets depend.[2] After stating, *I walked continually in wide freedom*, the psalmist therefore indicates the reason for it: *because I sought your commandments.* (A few codices have not *commandments* but *testimonies*. However, we have found *commandments* in the majority, especially of the Greek codices; and it is generally agreed that the Greek are more trustworthy as they are in the earlier language, whence our translations derive.)

If we wish to know how he sought these commandments or how we in our turn are to seek them, we must see if our good master, our teacher and giver of good gifts,[3] has anything to say. *Ask, and you will obtain; seek, and you will find; knock, and the door will be opened to you* (Mt 7:7). And a little further on he reinforces this: *If you, then, bad as you are, know how to give good gifts to your children, how much more will your Father, who is in heaven, give good things to those who ask him?* (Mt 7:11) These words show plainly that when he said, *Ask, seek, knock*, he was recommending urgent, persevering petition in prayer. Furthermore, another evangelist has a different version of this saying. He does not say that God *will give good things to those who ask him*, for this could be understood in various senses, of bodily or spiritual blessings. He cuts away all other references and very carefully names the gift which the Lord wanted us to demand so urgently and insistently: *How much more will your heavenly Father give the good Spirit to those who ask him?* (Lk 11:13). This is the Spirit through whom charity is poured out in our hearts, so that by loving God and our neighbor

---

1. See Rom 5:5.
2. See Mt 22:40.
3. Or "giver of the commandments."

we may carry out the divine commands. This is the Spirit in whom we cry, *Abba! Father!* (Rom 8:15) He makes us ask for the one we most desire to receive; he makes us seek the one we long to find; he makes us knock at the door of him into whose presence we strive to come. This is what the apostle is teaching us when he says that we cry out, *Abba! Father!* in the Holy Spirit. Again in another place he says, *God has sent into our hearts the Spirit of his Son, crying, Abba! Father!* (Gal 4:6) How can we be said to cry out if the Spirit himself is crying out in us? Surely because he has been making us cry out, ever since he first began to dwell in us. Once we have received him he works in us, empowering us to go on demanding more, so that by asking, seeking, knocking, we may receive him in ever greater plenitude. All those who are impelled by the Spirit of God are sons and daughters of God,[4] whether their prayer arises from a good life or begs that a good life may be granted to them.

I walked continually in wide freedom, says the psalmist, *because I sought your commandments*. He sought them and found them, because he asked for and received the good Spirit. Made good by the Spirit, he was able to do good things well from the faith that operates through love.[5]

3. *And I spoke of your testimonies in the presence of kings, and was not put to shame*. He asked, and he received, and so he has been enabled to reply with a word to those who reproached him and been assured that the word of truth will not be taken away from his mouth. Strengthened to fight for the truth even to death, he was not ashamed to speak it even in the presence of kings. These testimonies, of which he says he spoke, correspond to μαρτύρια in Greek; we use this word in our tongue also, and from it we derive the name "martyrs." To the martyrs Jesus foretold that they would confess him even before kings.[6]

Love proved by thought and action

4. *And all the while I pondered on your commandments, which I loved*, he continues. *And I lifted my hands to your commandments, which I loved*. Some codices have, in both verses, *I loved ardently*,[7] or *intensely*,[8] or *passionately*,[9] for so the translators chose to represent the Greek σφόδρα. How was he able to love God's commandments? By the same power that enabled him to walk continually in wide freedom: by the Holy Spirit through whom love itself is poured out, that love which enlarges the hearts of the faithful.

---

4. See Rom 8:14.
5. See Gal 5:6.
6. See Mt 10:18.
7. *Valde.*
8. *Nimis.*
9. *Vehementer.*

But he loved the commandments in both thought and deed. With regard to his thoughts, he says, *All the while I pondered on your commandments*; and of his deeds he says, *And I lifted my hands to your commandments*. To both these statements he added, *Which I loved*, for the end of the commandment is charity springing from a pure heart.[10] When an action is performed from that motive—when God's command, I mean, is obeyed by one who has that end in view—the action is truly good. Preparing to speak about charity, the apostle said, *Now I will point out to you a supremely excellent way* (1 Cor 12:31); and, in another place, *May you know the charity of Christ that is more excellent than all knowledge* (Eph 3:19). If anyone carries out God's commands with an eye to being rewarded with earthly happiness, that person's hands are not being lifted up but are drooping, because the action is performed for the sake of earthly gain, which is found not above but below.

The next phrase, *And I was constantly employed about your ways of justice*, envisages both thoughts and actions. Many interpreters prefer this translation, *I was employed,*[11] rather than *I was happy,*[12] or *I chattered,*[13] by which some chose to translate the Greek ἠδολέσχουν. All contain some truth, for a person who loves God's commandments and keeps them delightedly in thought and deed is certainly happy in God's ways of justice and is even inclined to chatter about them.

---

10. See 1 Tm 1:5.
11. *Exercebar*.
12. *Laetabar*.
13. *Garriebam*.

Exposition 15 of Psalm 118

Fifteenth Sermon

Verses 49-50. The word that gives hope

1. With the Lord's help let us turn our attention to the next verses of this great psalm. *Remember your word to your servant, by which you gave me hope. This comforted me in my humiliation, for your word brought me to life.* Surely God is not prone to forgetfulness, like human beings? But if not, why does the psalm urge him to remember? Admittedly this expression is freely used in other passages of holy scripture; we find, for instance, *Why have you forgotten me?* and, *Why do you forget our need?* (Pss 41:10(42:9); 43(44):24) And through a prophet God himself declares, *I will forget all his iniquities* (Ez 18:22). Similar phrases occur everywhere in the scriptures, but they are not to be understood as applying to God in the same way as to men and women. God is sometimes said to repent when he changes a situation in some unlooked-for fashion; but in these cases he has not really changed his plan, for the designs of the Lord abide for ever.[1] Similarly he is said to forget when he seems to delay in coming to our help, or to be slow in fulfilling his promises, or when he does not seem to be punishing sinners as they deserve, or something else of the kind. Then it looks as though an action that human beings hope for, or dread, has slipped his memory, and that is why it does not take place. These statements are accommodated to our understanding, couched in a form that appeals to human sensibility; but in fact God arranges things in accord with his determined purpose, not because his memory has failed, or his intelligence is darkened, or his will has changed. When, therefore, the psalm begs him *to remember*, it is not admonishing God as though something had escaped his memory; this is simply the expression of longing on the part of the one who prays, a longing for what God has promised, a longing that is both articulated and further stretched by this prayer. *Remember your word to your servant,* he says, which is a way of saying, "Fulfill your promise to your servant." *By which you gave me hope,* he continues: you made me hope in your word, because on your side that word was a promise.

2. *This comforted me in my humiliation.*[2] *This* must be the hope given to the humble, according to scripture: *God thwarts the proud, but gives grace to the*

---

1. See Ps 32(33):11.
2. Or "in my humility"; Augustine considers both meanings.

humble (Jas 4:6; 1 Pt 5:5). From the Lord's own lips we hear, *Anyone who exalts himself will be humbled, but the one who humbles himself will be exalted* (Lk 14:11; 18:14).

We may well take this psalm-verse to refer also to a different kind of humility: not that by which a person voluntarily humbles himself by confessing his sins and refusing to claim any righteousness for himself, but the state of someone who is humiliated and cast down by some trouble which he brought on himself by pride or which is sent to train him and test his endurance. In this perspective the psalm says a little further on, *Before I was humiliated, I was found wanting* (verse 67). The same idea occurs in the wisdom literature: *Stand firm in suffering, and in your humiliation be patient, for gold and silver are assayed by fire, and acceptable men and women in the furnace of humiliation* (Sir 2:4-5). That text gives us hope and comforts us in humiliation by introducing the word *acceptable.* The Lord Jesus, even when foretelling the humiliation that persecutors would bring on his disciples, did not leave them without hope. Hope was what he gave them, a hope full of consolation, for he told them, *By enduring you will save your lives* (Lk 21:19). He even reassured them about their bodies, which could be killed and, so it seemed, entirely destroyed by their enemies, for he promised, *Not a hair of your head will perish* (Lk 21:18).

This is the hope given to the body of Christ, the Church, to comfort it in its humiliations. Buoyed by hope the apostle Paul proclaimed, *If we hope for what we do not see, we wait for it in patience* (Rom 8:25). But that is the hope of eternal rewards. There is another kind of hope which is a great source of comfort when we are brought low by distressing circumstances, the kind given to the saints by God's word that promises grace, to save them from falling away. Of this the apostle says, *God is faithful, and he does not allow you to be tempted more fiercely than you can bear, but along with the temptation ordains the outcome, so that you may withstand it* (1 Cor 10:13). The Savior himself offered the same hope: *This very night Satan has asked to sift all of you like wheat; but I have prayed for you, Peter, that your faith may not fail* (Lk 22:31-32). He also inculcated this hope in the prayer he taught us, for he warned that we are to say, *Do not bring us into temptation*, which implied a promise on his part that what he wanted his faithful to pray for, he would give them in their time of peril.

Most clearly of all is this same hope spoken of in our psalm: *This comforted me in my humiliation, for your word brought me to life.* Some translators put here not *word,* but *declaration,* and they are more accurate, for the Greek has λόγιον, which means a "saying" or "declaration,"[3] not λόγος, which means "word."[4]

---

3. *Eloquium.*
4. *Verbum.*

Verses 51-54. Hope for the persecuted and for the human race since its origin

3. The psalm proceeds, *The proud behaved very wickedly indeed, but I did not turn aside from your law.* By *the proud* he means us to understand those who persecute devout believers; this is why he adds, *But I did not turn aside from your law,* for that was what the persecutors tried to make him do. He says that they *behaved very wickedly indeed,* because not only were they impious themselves but they tried to force the pious into impiety as well. Brought low in this distress, Christians found comfort in the word of God that promised them such effective help that the martyrs' faith would not fail. They were consoled by the presence of his Spirit, who imparted strength to struggling souls, that they might escape from the snare of the hunters and proclaim, *If the Lord had not been among us, perhaps they would have swallowed us alive* (Ps 123(124):2-3).

4. Could we perhaps take the words, *This comforted me in my humiliation,* to refer to the humiliation our race suffered when it was flung out of paradise and sunk into death, in consequence of that sin which was so unhappily committed in the happy state of paradise? In this degraded condition men and women are reduced to emptiness, their days pass away like a shadow,[5] and all are children of wrath[6] except those who, predestined for eternal salvation before the world was made,[7] are reconciled to God through the mediator. From ancient times the just put their hope in this mediator, for through the spirit of prophecy they foresaw that he would come in the flesh. A word about him reached them, and if we are prepared to hear their voice in this psalm, we can identify the word they heard with the one spoken of here: *Remember your word to your servant, by which you gave me hope. This comforted me in my humiliation* (that is to say, in my mortal condition), *for your word brought me to life.* Thus I was given hope of life even after being cast down into death. *The proud behaved very wickedly indeed*: not even the humiliation of mortality sufficed to quell their pride. *But I did not turn aside from your law,* as the proud were trying to force me to do.

5. *I have been mindful of the judgments you established from the very beginning, O Lord, and I was comforted*—or, as other codices have it, *I was encouraged,* which implies, "I received encouragement." Both meanings can be derived from the Greek verb, παρεκλήθην. The words, *from the very beginning,* indicate the whole period since the origins of the human race; throughout this time *I have been mindful of the judgments* you have pronounced upon the vessels of wrath prepared for perdition. But *I was comforted* too, because through those same judgments you have revealed the riches of your glory upon the vessels appointed for your mercy.[8]

---

5. See Ps 143(144):4.
6. See Eph 2:3.
7. See Eph 1:4.
8. See Rom 9:22-23.

6. *Disgust possessed me at the sinners who abandon your law, but your ways of justice have been the theme of my song in this place of my sojourning,*[9] or, as other codices translate, *in this place of my pilgrimage.*[10] This is a reference to the lowly condition of wayfaring humanity in this land where it is subject to death, having left paradise and the heavenly Jerusalem. It went down from Jerusalem to Jericho, but on the way it fell among robbers.[11] Yet thanks to the mercy lavished upon it by the Samaritan, God's ways of justice have become the theme of its song in the land of its pilgrimage, although disgust possesses it at the sinners who abandon God's law; for it is forced into temporary association with them while this life lasts, until the time of winnowing arrives.[12]

We may regard these two verses as a reiteration, in different words, of the two parts of the preceding verse. Thus where it was said, *I have been mindful of the judgments you established from the very beginning, O Lord*, the following verse develops the idea with: *Disgust possessed me at the sinners who abandon your law*; and where the earlier verse declared, *And I was comforted*, the later one says, *Your ways of justice have been the theme of my song in this place of my pilgrimage*.

Verses 55-56. Searching for God in the night

7. The speaker continues, *I remembered your name in the night, O Lord, and I kept your law*. Our night is our humiliated estate, where we taste the bitterness of being mortal; our night is the pride of those who behave very wickedly indeed; our night is the disgust that possesses us at the sinners who abandon God's law; finally, our night is the pilgrimage in which we must trudge along *until the Lord comes; for he will light up the dark, hidden places, and reveal the purposes of our hearts, and then there will be praise for everyone from God* (1 Cor 4:5). In this night each one of us must remember the name of God, to ensure that *anyone who boasts may boast in the Lord* (1 Cor 1:31). In the same vein another psalm prays, *Not to us, Lord, not to us, but to your name give the glory* (Ps 113B(115):1). In this way each one will keep the law of God, as the psalmist here claims he did: *I remembered your name in the night, O Lord, and I kept your law*; but we shall not keep it by any righteousness of our own. Each of us will keep it to God's glory, since any righteousness we have is not ours but God's and is conferred on us by God. No one could have kept it by relying on his own strength and forgetting the name of the Lord. That would be impossible, because *our help is in the name of the Lord* (Ps 123(124):8).

---

9. *Incolatus mei.*
10. *Peregrinationis meae.*
11. See Lk 10:30-36.
12. See Mt 3:12.

8. The next phrase continues the thought: *This happened to me*[13] *because I sought your ways of justice.* He explicitly says, *your ways of justice,* those by which you justify the ungodly: not my own, for any self-justification makes me not devout, but proud. The psalmist was not like those who *failed to recognize the righteousness that comes from God, and, by seeking to set up a righteousness of their own, did not submit to God's righteousness* (Rom 10:3). Through God's ways of justice men and women, who of themselves have no power to be just, are freely justified by the grace of God. Some translators render the Greek by *acts of justice*[14] in this verse, but the better ones have *justifying acts,*[15] because the Greek text reads not δικαιοσύνας but δικαιώματα.

But how are we to understand the words, *This happened to me?* What does *this* refer to? Can it mean the law, of which he has just said, *I kept your law?* If this is the right interpretation, the phrase would mean, "This law happened to me." But we need not waste time inquiring how God's law could be said to have "happened to" anyone, because the Greek from which our translation derives makes it quite clear that the law is not alluded to in the phrase, *This happened to me.* "Law" is masculine in Greek, but a feminine pronoun is used for *this.* Our first job, then, is to find out what *this* is, and then how whatever it is happened to him. *This happened to me,* he says, and he certainly does not mean "this law," because, as I have explained, the Greek excludes it.

Possibly, therefore, he means "this night." Taken whole, the previous verse runs, *I remembered your name in the night, O Lord, and I kept your law*; then it continues, *This happened to me.* Plainly, what happened to him was not the law but the night. What does it mean, then, to say, "The night happened to me, *because I sought your justifying acts*"? If he sought God's justifying acts, it would have been light that came upon him, wouldn't it, rather than night? If, however, we rightly understand the statement, *This happened to me,* we shall take it to mean "This happened for me," or "This happened for my benefit." Our humbled state of mortality can reasonably be called a night, for the hearts of men and women are hidden from each other; and from the darkness arise innumerable dangerous temptations. Beasts of the forest prowl through the night, young lions roaring and demanding their food from God.[16] From this night emerges the mighty lion that roars and hunts for people to devour;[17] accordingly the Lord warned us, as I have reminded you already, *This very night Satan has asked to*

---

13. *Haec facta est mihi.* In the following paragraphs Augustine spends some time discussing the reason for the feminine pronoun, "this." i) It could refer to "law"; but this is excluded by the Greek, in which "law" is masculine. ii) It may refer to "night"; he finds this acceptable. iii) It is an idiomatic use of the feminine for an unspecified object which would more naturally be expressed by the neuter, paralleled in another psalm.

14. *Iustitias.*

15. *Iustificationes.*

16. See Ps 103(104):21.

17. See 1 Pt 5:8.

sift all of you like wheat (Lk 22:31). Many a forest predator prowls about in this night, he seems to say; but that most powerful of lions has begged God to hand you over to him as his prey.

Well now, this lowly condition of ours during our pilgrimage, rightly called a night, works to the advantage of those who are disciplined by it on their way to salvation, because it teaches them not to be proud. The wicked sin of pride was the reason for humanity's being plunged into this night in the first place, for *the starting-point of human pride is rebellion against God* (Sir 10:14). But once a person has been freely justified, he can reach a better understanding of how to profit from the manifold temptations and trials that beset him in this lowly state. Then let him say, as the psalmist will in a later verse, *It is good for me that you have humbled me, so that I may learn your ways of justice* (verse 71). What else does that mean—*It is good for me that you have humbled me*—if not "This lowly condition called night *happened to me*, happened *for* me, for my good"? Why? Because it forced me to seek *your justifying acts*, not any justification I could bring about myself.

9. There is another sense in which we may interpret the words, *This happened to me.* The pronoun *this* may be taken neither as the law nor as the night but may be understood in the same way as the pronoun in another psalm, where we read, *One*[18] *have I begged of the Lord, and that*[19] *I will seek after* (Ps 26(27):4). There too the pronoun is feminine. The psalmist does not say what this "one" is, but the feminine gender does duty as a neuter. It is certainly contrary to custom to say "one" in the feminine without indicating what is meant; it would be more usual to say, "One thing[20] have I begged of the Lord, and that[21] I will seek after: to live in the Lord's house." When neuters are used like this it is not always necessary to specify what is being referred to: we do not have to say "one good thing" or "one gift" or anything of the kind. But whatever the object referred to, normal usage employs neuter pronouns, even though the object itself is of the masculine or the feminine gender, when the object is not named but only suggested vaguely. So in our present text *"Haec facta est* to me" is equivalent to *"Hoc factum est* to me."

If we take it this way, the "thing" referred to may be what he mentioned earlier: *I remembered your name in the night, O Lord, and I kept your law.* This thing—namely, my keeping of your law—was not something I did by myself, but rather something that happened to me, and obviously by your doing. It happened because *I sought your justifying acts*, not my own. The apostle tells us, *It is God who is at work in you, inspiring both will and work, for his own good purpose* (Phil 2:13); and God promises through a prophet, *I will make you walk*

---

18. *Unam*, feminine.
19. *Hanc*, feminine.
20. *Unum*, neuter.
21. *Hoc*, neuter.

in my ways of justice, and cause you to observe my decrees, and do them (Ez 36:27). If God can say, *I will cause you to observe my decrees, and do them*, there is every reason for the psalmist to acknowledge, "This thing happened to me." If you ask him, "What thing?" he can only answer with what he has told us already: "That I kept the law of God."

This sermon has gone on too long. The next verses will be more satisfactorily dealt with under a new heading, as the Lord allows us.

Exposition 16 of Psalm 118

Sixteenth Sermon

Verses 57-60. Keeping the commandments through the grace of the Spirit

1. In obedience to God's will we now propose to deal with the verses of this great psalm which begin, *The Lord is the portion allotted to me* or, as other codices understand it, *You are my allotted portion, O Lord*. This means that anyone who clings to the Lord participates in him. As another psalm declares, *It is good for me to cling tightly to God* (Ps 72(73):28). Human beings do not, of course, become gods, but they are divinized by participation in him who alone is the true God. Another interpretation of these opening words suggests itself: in this world men and women choose, or are allotted, their various activities or spheres of ownership. One chooses this, another that, and each lives by his allotted portion. So God himself can be called the allotted share of his faithful followers, because they expect to live through him for ever. Neither of these interpretations is unreasonable. But let us listen to the words that succeed the opening phrase: *I have pledged myself to keep your law*. The matter is clarified now. *You are my allotted portion, O Lord; I have pledged myself to keep your law*. What else can that mean if not that the Lord will be the portion of everyone who has kept his law?

2. But how are we to keep it unless the life-giving Spirit grants us the power and comes to our help? Without him the letter of the law will be death-dealing,[1] and sin will seize its chance through the law to produce in men and women all kinds of disordered desires.[2] We must invoke him, then, for through prayer faith obtains what the law can only command,[3] and everyone who invokes the name of the Lord will be saved.[4] See how the psalm continues: *I entreated your face with all my heart*. Then he tells us the content of this heartfelt prayer: *Have mercy on me, according to your word*.

But it seems that he has already been heard and helped by the one to whom he prayed, for he continues, *Because I considered my ways, and turned away my feet toward your testimonies*. He means that he turned his feet *away* from his own paths, which had become loathsome to him, to direct them toward God's

---

1. See 2 Cor 3:6.
2. See Rom 7:8.
3. For this crucial idea compare Augustine's *The Spirit and the Letter* 13,22; 14,26; 21,36.
4. See Jl 2:32; Acts 2:21; Rom 10:13.

testimonies and there find life. Several codices, however, read not *Because I considered,* but simply *I considered.*[5] In place of the statement, *I turned away my feet,* some codices have *Because I considered, and you turned away my feet,* which more explicitly ascribes the change to God's grace, in line with the apostle's teaching that *it is God who is at work in you* (Phil 2:13). Elsewhere the request is made to God, *Turn my eyes away that they may not see vanity* (Ps 118(119):37). If he turns away our eyes from seeing vanity, why not our feet from following wrong paths? Another text carries the same lesson: *My eyes are on the Lord continually, for he will pluck my feet from the snare* (Ps 24(25):15). But whether we accept as the true reading *You turned away my feet* or *I turned away my feet,* it comes to the same thing, for what we do is God's doing; our action is effected through him whose face the psalmist entreated with all his heart, and to whom he said, *Have mercy on me, according to your word.* Your word is your promise. The children of the promise are reckoned as Abraham's progeny.[6]

3. Fortified by the gift of grace, the psalmist declares, *Undismayed, I am ready to keep your commandments.* The Greek for "to keep" is φυλάξασθαι, which the Latin codices translate variously.[7]

Verses 61-62. Fidelity and courage under persecution

4. His next words demonstrate how ready he is to keep the divine commandments. *The ropes of sinners were entwined around me, but I did not forget your law.* These *ropes of sinners* are the entanglements put in our way by our enemies: both our spiritual enemies—the devil and his angels, I mean—and our enemies of flesh and blood, for in all the children of unbelief the devil is at work.[8] We must understand the verse to mean *the ropes of sinners,* not "the ropes of sin"; the Greek makes this clear.[9] When sinners utter cruel threats to frighten good people and make them think they will suffer for their loyalty to God's law, they are entangling the just in their ropes, as surely as they would with strong, unbreakable twine, for they are dragging out their sins into a long cord.[10] They do their best to bind the saints, and sometimes they are allowed to succeed. But

---

5. Augustine seems to feel that the omission of "because" ties the statement more closely to the idea that the prayer has been heard: the "considering" is the result of grace given and received.
6. See Rom 9:8-9.
7. Augustine read in his text *ut custodiam mandata tua.* He notes some of the variations in a phrase omitted from the English translation. It runs, "Some have rendered this as *ad custodiendum mandata tua,* others as *ut custodirem,* others again as *custodire.*"
8. See Eph 2:2.
9. In Augustine's Latin version *funes peccatorum* could mean either; but the Greek from which it derives is unambiguous, ἁμαρτωλῶν.
10. See Is 5:18.

even if the body is entangled, the psalmist's mind, which has not forgotten God's law, remains free, for God's word is never bound.[11]

5. *At midnight I arose to confess to you over your just judgments*, for even the ropes of sinners that entwine a righteous person are the manifestation of the just judgments of God. The apostle Peter warns that *it is time for judgment to take place, beginning from the house of the Lord; and if it originates with us, what will be the outcome for those who do not believe in the gospel of God? What will become of the wicked and the sinner if the righteous will scarcely be saved?* (1 Pt 4:17-18) He had in mind the persecutions the Church was enduring at the time, when the ropes of sinners were knotted around it.

I think that *midnight* symbolizes the most severe phase of such tribulations. But the psalmist says, *I arose* at that hour, for it did not so daunt him as to cast him down; rather did it challenge him to rise up. He used the distress itself as a spur to confess God more valiantly.

Verses 63-64. Christ speaks in his own person, and in his members

6. Such a victory comes by the grace of God, through Jesus Christ our Lord; and therefore the Savior uses this prophetic psalm to join his own voice to that of his body. I think the words that follow belong to him personally: *I share with all those who fear you and keep your commandments*. This is the teaching of the Letter to the Hebrews: *He who sanctifies and those who are sanctified are all of one stock; that is why he is not ashamed to call them his brothers*; and, a little further on, *Since "children" share in the same flesh and blood, he too just as truly shared in them*. (Heb 2:11,14) This plainly declares that Christ was made a participant in our nature. We could not have become sharers in his godhead if he had not become a sharer in our mortality. The gospel teaches that we have indeed become sharers in his divinity: *He gave them power to become children of God; those, that is, who believe in his name, who are born not of blood, nor by the will of the flesh, nor by the will of man, but of God*. But it goes on to show how this became possible through Christ's coming to share in our mortality: *The Word was made flesh, and dwelt among us*. (Jn 1:12-14) Through his becoming one with us, grace is dispensed to us, so that we may fear God with pure hearts and keep his commandments.

Most surely Jesus himself is speaking in this prophecy. But he says certain things in the person of his members, in the unity of his body, as though in the voice of a single human being diffused throughout the whole world and continually growing as the ages roll on; and other things he says in his own voice, as our head. That is why he says here, *I share with all those who fear you and keep your commandments*. He fully shared in the lot of his brothers and sisters, God with

---

11. See 2 Tm 2:9.

human beings, the immortal with mortals. Thus the grain of wheat fell into the earth, to die and bear a rich yield. Contemplating that abundant harvest, the psalmist cries, *The earth is full of your mercy, O Lord.* How does he fill it with mercy? By justifying sinners. So the psalmist adds a plea that he may grow in knowledge of Christ's grace: *Teach me your ways of justice.*

Exposition 17 of Psalm 118

Seventeenth Sermon

Verses 65-66. Sweetness, discipline, and knowledge

1. The verses of the psalm which, in response to God's will, we are about to discuss begin as follows: *You have provided sweetness for your servant, O Lord, according to your word,*[1] or, better, *according to your declaration.*[2] Where the Greek has χρηστότητα some of our translators have written *sweetness,*[3] others *goodness.*[4] We have to remember that sweetness can be found in evil, for unlawful deeds can be enjoyable, and it can occur even in legitimate carnal pleasure. We must therefore understand the sweetness, the χρηστότητα of the Greek text, to be that afforded by the good things of the spirit. To avoid ambiguity, some of our translators therefore preferred to call it *goodness.* Now when the psalm says, *You have provided sweetness for your servant,* I think it means neither more nor less than "you determined that I should be delighted with what is good"; for to find enjoyment in goodness is a great gift from God. If the opposite is the case, and some good action enjoined by law is performed not out of delight in righteousness but from dread of punishment, because God is feared but not loved, that action is done as a slave would do it, not in a spirit of freedom. *But a slave does not stay in the house permanently, whereas a son stays for ever* (Jn 8:35), because *charity made perfect casts out fear* (1 Jn 4:18). And so, Lord, *you have provided sweetness for your servant* by turning one who was a slave into your son or daughter. This you did *according to your declaration,* which means your promise, so that under the regime of faith the promise may be valid for all Abraham's descendants.[5]

2. *Teach me about sweetness, and instruction, and knowledge, for I have believed in your commands.* He must be asking for these things to be increased and brought to perfection in him; for since he has already acknowledged that *you have provided sweetness for your servant,* how can he now pray, *Teach me about sweetness,* unless he is pleading that God's grace may become more and more

---

1. *Verbum.*
2. *Eloquium.*
3. *Suavitatem.*
4. *Bonitatem.* The Greek word he refers to is related to *kind* in 1 Cor 13:4: *Charity is patient and kind.*
5. See Rom 4:16.

familiar to him through the sweetness of what is good? After all, the disciples who prayed, *Lord, increase our faith* (Lk 17:5), truly had faith. As long as our life in this world lasts, this request must be the song of those who are on their way.

The psalmist continues by asking for instruction,[6] or, as several codices have it, *discipline.*[7] But our scriptures customarily use the word *discipline* as a translation of the Greek παιδεία in contexts where painful instruction is meant. So, for example, we read, *Those whom the Lord loves, he corrects, and he whips every child whom he accepts* (Heb 12:6). This is the sort of discipline usually envisaged in the Church's writings when the Greek speaks of παιδεία. The word occurs a little further on in the Letter to the Hebrews: *All discipline seems at the time a matter for sadness, not joy; but afterward it yields the peace-giving harvest of righteousness in those who have been trained by it* (Heb 12:11). We must infer from this that anyone to whom God has granted sweetness, anyone in whom he graciously inspires a delight in what is good, must pray earnestly that this gift may be increased to such a point that its recipient not only learns to set little store by all other joys in comparison with this but is even prepared to endure any suffering for the sake of it. To speak more plainly, the person I have just described is one to whom God grants charity: love for God, and love of neighbor for God. It is thus very salutary that discipline be added to sweetness. We must pray and hope for discipline to toughen the sweetness we experience, the goodness of holy charity we are granted, for what is to be disciplined is not some feeble, paltry gift; it is a charity that under the weight of discipline cannot be quenched but is kindled the more ardently the more the pressure mounts, like an enormous flame under the onslaught of the wind. This is why it would not have been enough for the psalmist to give thanks because *you have provided sweetness for your servant.* He had to go further and beg the Lord to teach him about a sweetness so intense that it has the power to submit to discipline with the utmost patience.

The third lesson he asks for concerns knowledge. He puts it last because if knowledge outranks charity in importance, it does not build anyone up but only puffs him up.[8] However, when charity in its sweet benevolence has grown so great that it cannot be quenched by the tribulations to which discipline subjects it, then knowledge will be profitable. Through the gift of knowledge a person comes to know himself better. He discerns what he has merited by his own acts, and what gifts have been bestowed on him by God. He realizes that through those endowments he is capable of things he formerly knew to be impossible for him, things he certainly could not have done by himself.

---

6. *Eruditionem.*
7. *Disciplinam.*
8. See 1 Cor 8:1.

3. Now what about the form of the petition? Why does he say, *Teach me*, rather than "give me"? How can sweetness be taught, if it is not given? Many people know things that afford them no delight; they have knowledge of some subject but get no sweetness from it, for sweetness cannot be learned unless delight is present. Of discipline, his second request, something similar can be said. Discipline, in the sense of tribulation that corrects us, is learned through acceptance. Not by listening, or reading, or thinking is it learned, but by experience.

So far, so good; but the third item of which he said, *Teach me*, was knowledge, and knowledge is imparted through teaching. What else is teaching but giving knowledge? These two are so closely connected that one cannot exist without the other. No one is taught unless he learns, and no one learns unless taught. If a student is not able to take in what is said by the teacher, the teacher cannot say, "I taught him, but he did not learn." All he can claim is, "I said to him what had to be said, but he did not learn, because he did not perceive, or comprehend, or understand at all." This is undeniable, because if the teacher had really taught him, the student would have learned.

When God wants to teach anyone he first gives understanding, without which no man or woman can learn truths imparted by divine teaching. Accordingly the psalmist begs, a few verses later, *Give me understanding, that I may learn your commandments* (verse 73). A human being who desires to teach someone is quite capable of saying the same things that the Lord said to his disciples after rising from the dead; but he cannot do what the Lord did, for the gospel tells us, *Then he opened their minds to understand the scriptures, and he said to them . . .* (Lk 24:45). What he said to them can be read there, but they took in what he said only because he had opened their minds and enabled them to do so.

We see, then, that God teaches us sweetness by breathing delight into us, teaches discipline by sending us the right measure of tribulation, and teaches knowledge by empowering us from within to understand. It is to be noted, though, that we learn some things only to know them, but others in order to do them as well. When God teaches us, he teaches us in such a way that we know what we need to know, by opening the truth to us; but he also teaches us so effectively that we do what we ought to do, by inspiring us with sweetness. The prayer in another psalm is full of meaning: *Teach me, that I may do your will* (Ps 142(143):10). That is what it asks: "Teach me that I may do it," not just that I may know it. Deeds rightly done are the harvest we yield to our farmer; but scripture emphasizes, *Truly the Lord will give sweetness, and then our earth will yield its fruit* (Ps 84:13(85:12)). And what earth is this, if not that which cries out to him who bedews it with sweetness, *My soul is like waterless earth before you* (Ps 142(143):6)?

4. After pleading, *Teach me about sweetness, and discipline, and knowledge*, our psalmist adds, *for I have believed in your commands*. We may well wonder why he said not "I have obeyed" but *I have believed*. Commands are one thing,

promises something else. We undertake to carry out the commands so that we may deserve to receive what has been promised. Therefore we believe in promises, but we obey commandments. What can it mean, then, to say, *I have believed in your commands*? Surely it means, "I have believed that it was you who so commanded us, not some mere mortal, even though your commands are passed on through human beings to other human beings." And since I have believed that these are your commandments, let the faith by which I believe it win from you the grace I need to do what you have commanded. If someone who is no more than human were to lay those commands on me from outside, would he also help me from within to do what he ordered? Of course not. Do you, then, teach me sweetness by inspiring charity, teach me discipline by granting me patience, and teach me knowledge by illuminating my intelligence, because *I have believed in your commands.* You are God, and I have believed you to be both the author of the commandments and the giver of grace whereby you cause men and women to do what you command.

Verses 67-72. Penal humiliation, fruitful humility

5. *Before I was humiliated, I was found wanting; therefore have I kept your word,*[9] or, as others translate, *your injunction;*[10] evidently he kept it in order not to be humiliated again. This is best understood of the humiliation suffered by Adam, in whom the entire human creation was corrupted at its root and was subjected to futility[11] because it refused to be subject to the truth. The experience proved advantageous to the vessels destined for mercy,[12] for once pride has been dethroned, obedience can be chosen and loved. Wretchedness can then be banished, never to return.

6. *Sweet are you, O Lord.* Some codices have *Good are you;* we have already discussed these two words. *In your sweetness teach me your ways of justice.* Since he wants to learn God's ways of justice from the one to whom he says, *Sweet are you,* and wants to learn them in that sweetness, clearly his desire is to follow those ways of justice.

7. The psalm proceeds, *The iniquity of the proud lay heavy upon me,* the iniquity of those proud persons who have learned nothing and profited nothing from the humiliation suffered by the human race after its fall. *But as for me, I will study your commandments with my whole heart.* However iniquity may increase, he says, the charity that is in me shall not grow cold.[13] This sounds like the voice of one who is learning God's ways of justice in God's own sweetness.

---

9. *Verbum.*
10. *Eloquium.*
11. See Rom 8:20.
12. See Rom 9:23.
13. See Mt 24:12.

The sweeter one finds the commands of him who helps us, the more lovingly does one study them; then one acts on what is known and comes to know better by acting, because God's commandments are most perfectly known when obeyed.

8. *Their hearts are curdled like milk.* Whose hearts? Surely the hearts of the proud, whose iniquity has been lying heavy upon him, as he has just complained. The word he uses suggests hardness of heart, obduracy, in this context; in other contexts it can have a good meaning, as in the sixty-seventh psalm, where we read of *a mountain full of curds, a rich mountain* (Ps 67:16(68:15)). Some of our translators used the word *curdled* in that psalm, and there it signifies "full of grace." But in the context of our present psalm the sense is different, for look what the psalmist sets over against the hardened hearts of the people who oppress him: *But for my part, I ponder your law.* What law does he mean? The most just and most merciful law, undoubtedly, concerning which he prayed, *On the basis of your law have mercy on me* (verse 29). God thwarts the proud, and they become hardened; but he gives grace to the humble[14] that they may learn to love obedience and deserve true glory. Through meditation on this law we establish in ourselves willing humility, so that we may avoid being punished by humiliation. The psalm goes on to explain this point.

9. *It is good for me that you have humbled me, so that I may learn your ways of justice.* Only a few verses earlier he said, *Before I was humiliated I was found wanting; therefore have I kept your injunction.* He now demonstrates how good it is for him to have been humiliated by pointing to the fruitful results, though in the earlier verse he also indicated that some fault on his part had preceded the humiliation and brought it on. In that verse he said, *Therefore have I kept your injunction,* whereas here he prays, *that I may learn your ways of justice*; I think the comparison of the two verses proves that to know them and to keep them are the same thing. It was said of Christ that *he knew no sin* (2 Cor 5:21); and yet he rebuked sin, and he cannot have rebuked something he did not know. Clearly he did know it with a certain kind of knowledge; but, on the other hand, there was a different sense in which he was ignorant of it. We may compare this with the way in which many people learn God's ways of justice and yet fail to learn them. They know them with a certain kind of knowledge, yet in another sense they know nothing about them, because they do not live in accordance with those ways of justice and hence remain ignorant of them. The psalmist bears this danger in mind when he asks *that I may learn your ways of justice*: with the kind of knowledge, he means, that will make them real as a way of life for me.

10. Such an outcome is possible only through love, and love is born when a person finds God's ways of justice delightful. This is why the psalmist prayed, *In your sweetness teach me your ways of justice.* The next verse reinforces the same

---

14. See Jas 4:6; 1 Pt 5:5.

idea: *The law of your mouth seems good to me, better than thousands of gold and silver coins.* More dearly than greed loves thousands of gold and silver coins does charity love the law of God.

Exposition 18 of Psalm 118

Eighteenth Sermon

Verse 73. The creative hands of God

1. When God created man from dust and breathed life into him,[1] scripture does not say that he used his hands to do it. I cannot understand, therefore, why some people maintain that, while God created all other things by a word, he made the first human, his noblest creation, with his hands. Presumably they base their opinion on the fact that the man's body was formed from dust, and they think such a work could have been done only by hand. They seem to forget that the gospel statement about God's Word, *Everything was made through him* (Jn 1:3), would not be true if it did not include the human body. This does not convince them, however; they appeal to the testimony of our psalm. "Look at that!" they say. "The psalmist was a human being, wasn't he? And he unambiguously cries out to God, *Your hands made me and fashioned me.*" Anyone would think there were no other scriptural passages to refute such a view. What about the following? *I shall see the heavens, the work of your fingers* (Ps 8:4(3); and, just as plain, *The heavens are the work of your hands* (Ps 101:26(102:25)); and, clearer still, *His hands laid down the dry land* (Ps 94(95):5). God's *hands* are obviously God's power. If the use of the plural—*hands* rather than "hand"—upsets them, let them take God's hands to mean his strength and his wisdom. The one Christ is called by both these names,[2] and he is also the arm of the Lord, according to the text, *To whom has the arm of the Lord been revealed?* (Is 53:1). Alternatively they can understand God's *hands* to be the Son and the Holy Spirit, for the Holy Spirit is co-worker with the Father and the Son. That is why the apostle says, *The one same Spirit is at work in all these operations* (1 Cor 12:11). He emphatically says, *the one same Spirit,* to exclude the notion that there might be as many spirits as there are works, not to suggest that the Spirit works alone, without the Father and the Son.

We are free to interpret references to God's hands in whatever way seems best, as long as we do not deny that what he makes with his hands he makes also by his Word, and what he makes by his Word he can also be thought of as making with his hands. However, we may not attribute any bodily shape to God just

---

1. See Gn 2:7.
2. See 1 Cor 1:24.

because his hands are mentioned, nor imagine that he has a right hand and a left. Neither must we believe that statements about his Word imply any vocal sound or passing thought in God as he does his work.

2. Some interpreters have drawn a distinction between the two verbs in the phrase, *Your hands made me and fashioned me*. They think that God made the soul, but fashioned the body, because God says elsewhere of the soul, *Every living breath, I made* (Is 57:16), whereas of the body we read, *God fashioned man from the dust of the earth* (Gn 2:7). Everything that is fashioned is also made, they say, but not everything that is made is fashioned. So they hold that the soul was made but not fashioned, because it is not corporeal but spiritual. But they forget another text in scripture which says of God, *He fashioned the spirit of man within him* (Zech 12:1).

Nonetheless, provided that we do not deny that both human components, soul and body, are created by God, it makes for elegance of expression to distinguish the two verbs in contexts where both are used, and to speak of the soul being made, and the body fashioned, or shaped, or molded. I mention these last three words—fashioned, shaped, molded—because some translators have shied away from saying *fashioned*,[3] a word customarily associated with something fictitious or simulated; they have preferred *molded*,[4] a word closer to the Greek, though less usual in Latin.

3. There are two possible ways of understanding the statement, *Your hands made me and molded me*. First, we can take them as spoken with reference to Adam. Since all human beings were propagated from him, is there anyone who cannot say that he or she was made when Adam was made, in virtue of origin and carnal descent? The second possibility is to take the psalm's statement as a reference to the birth of each individual, because though all of us were made from our parents, we came into existence through the work of God: he creates when our parents produce us. If God's creative power is withdrawn from things, they perish. Nothing is born, whether from the elements of nature, or from parents, or from seeds, except by God's operation. This is why he says to the prophet Jeremiah, *Before I formed you in the womb, I knew you* (Jer 1:5).

The relation between reason and faith

But the verse in the psalm runs like this: *Your hands made me and molded me; give me understanding.* Are we to gather that God ever made any human being without understanding, either Adam, or anyone who comes to birth? Surely not. Is not understanding a quality inherent in human nature, distinguishing us from

---

3. *Finxerunt.* The English word "fashioned" does not of course carry the suggestion of "fiction" associated with the Latin.
4. *Plasmaverunt.*

the beasts? Or is human nature so badly deformed by sin that even its reason needs reformation? Yes, perhaps it does, for the apostle says to all who are reborn, *Be renewed spiritually in your minds* (Eph 4:23), and obviously understanding is exercised through the mind. Again he says, *Allow yourselves to be reformed by the renewal of your minds* (Rom 12:2). But when he speaks of those who have no share in the new birth, he warns, *This I must say, and adjure you in the Lord: Walk no more now as the pagans walk. Their minds are empty; they are darkened in their understanding and estranged from the way of God by the ignorance that is in them, owing to the blindness of their hearts.* (Eph 4:17-18) The blindness of the inner eyes is a lack of understanding, but as hearts are cleansed by faith[5] eyes are opened and become ever clearer. It is true that without some understanding no one can believe in God; but the faith whereby we begin to believe in him has a healing effect, so that we come to understand more. There are some things that we do not believe unless we understand, and others that we do not understand unless we believe. What I mean is this: since faith comes by hearing, and hearing receives the word of Christ,[6] how can anyone believe a preacher of the faith unless he or she at least understands the language that is spoken, not to mention all else? On the other hand, there must be some things that we cannot understand unless we first believe, for the prophet says, *Unless you believe, you will not understand* (Is 7:9, LXX).

We must conclude that our understanding develops to grasp more firmly the truths we have believed and that our faith grows to believe more firmly what we have begun to understand. By its very act of understanding the mind develops and thus penetrates the truths of faith more deeply. This process occurs not through our natural powers but by the help and gracious gift of God; it is a process not of nature but of healing, which imparts to a diseased eye the power to see.

The person who in this psalm begs God, *Give me understanding, that I may learn your commandments*, is not wholly devoid of understanding like an animal; nor is he, though human, to be reckoned one of those who walk *as the pagans walk: their minds are empty; they are darkened in their understanding and estranged from the way of God* (Eph 4:17). If he were, he would not be offering this prayer. On the contrary, it is a mark of no slight understanding to know whom we should ask for understanding. And if the petitioner, who said earlier that he had kept the Lord's decrees, is still begging to be given understanding in order to learn the commandments, it should prompt us to reflect on how much more deeply the commandments need to be understood.

---

5. See Acts 15:9.
6. See Rom 10:17.

God may use a creature to give someone understanding, but always he is its source

4. Our translators wrote, *Give me understanding*, but the Greek is more compact: συνέτισόν με. Greek can compress into one word, συνέτισον, the idea for which we require two: *give understanding*. It is as though we had no verb "to heal," and so we had to say not "heal me" but "give me healing" or "make me healthy," as we might also have said here in the psalm, "Make me intelligent."

Now on occasion an angel seems to have had the power to do this for someone. An angel said to Daniel, *I have come to give you understanding* (Dn 10:14). The Greek expression here is συνετίσαί σε, the same idiom that we find in our psalm. (The Latin translator has to use the longer phrase, *give you under-standing*, where the Greek can do it in one word, just as we noticed above with respect to "heal" and "give healing." The Latin would not have adopted this roundabout phrase, *give you understanding*, if a single verb had been available to express "make you understand," as there was in the case of healing.) But if this service can be rendered by an angel, why does the psalmist ask God to do it for him? Because God had ordered the angel to do it? Yes, indeed; Christ gave his orders to the angel. We know this from another passage in the same prophet: *It came to pass that while I, Daniel, was seeing the vision, and seeking to under-stand, one who looked like a man stood before me; and I heard a human voice[7] calling to him across the Ulai,[8] saying, Make this man understand the vision* (Dn 8:15-16). Here the verb in Greek is the same as that in our psalm, συνέτισον. God is light, and of himself he illuminates faithful souls, imparting to them under-standing of what is divinely revealed or said to them. If he chooses to use an angel as his minister, the angel can produce an effect in the human mind, enabling it to receive God's light and so to understand. In this sense an angel is said to give understanding to a human being—to "intellectualize" him, so to say—as a person could be said to give light to a house—to illuminate it—when he makes a window. Yet the man who makes the window does not flood the house with light from himself; all he does is make an opening through which the house can be lighted up. The sun shines in through the window and irradiates the house, yet not even the sun created the house, or created the man who made the window, or told him to do it, or helped him in his work, or did anything at all to cause an opening to be made through which it might pour in its light. But God made the rational, intelligent mind of human beings, with which they can receive his light; and God made the angel into the kind of being who can bring about some change in the human mind to make it capable of admitting the divine light;

---

7. Human, and therefore suggestive of Christ, whom Augustine has just mentioned as the angel's mentor.
8. The name occurs in this form in the Hebrew and the Septuagint. Augustine's Latin has Ubal, which seems to derive from the Greek of Theodotion. The River Ulai flowed through Susa.

and God works on the human mind to make it responsive to the angel's influence; and, finally, God illumines the mind from himself, so that it not only grasps what is revealed to it by the truth but progresses toward an understanding of the truth itself.

Our discussion has ranged over questions which I consider necessary, but they have resulted in a rather long discourse. Let us therefore defer study of the next verses of the psalm and bring this sermon to a close.

Exposition 19 of Psalm 118

Nineteenth Sermon[1]

Final comments on verse 73

1. The Lord Jesus has just prayed for understanding to be conferred upon his body by God, that it may learn his commandments. He asked this favor through the prophet as though he were asking it on his own behalf, because the life of his body—his people, that is—is hidden with him in God;[2] and so he himself experiences need in his body and begs in the name of his members for all that they lack. *Your hands made me and molded me; give me understanding, that I may learn your commandments.* You formed me, so now reform me, he asks. Only so can there be in Christ's body the renewal which his apostle urges: *Allow yourselves to be reformed by the renewal of your minds* (Rom 12:2).

Verse 74. Fear now, vision and rejoicing hereafter

2. *Those who fear you will see me and be glad,*[3] *because I have hoped in your words.* Some codices read *will rejoice,*[4] in place of *will be glad.* This hope is hope in what you have promised, that those who fear you will be children of the promise, the offspring of Abraham, in whom all nations are blessed.[5]

Now who are these people who fear God, and who is it that they will see, and rejoice at seeing, because he has hoped in the words of God? If the voice we are hearing is that of Christ's body, the Church, uttering its prayer through Christ, then surely the speakers themselves are among *those who fear God*? And the same is true if the voice is that of Christ speaking as of himself but in and from the Church. But if it is the God-fearers themselves speaking, who is it that they see and rejoice to see? Should we say, perhaps, that this people sees itself and rejoices? If this is the right way to understand it, the verse, *Those who fear you will see me and rejoice because I have hoped in your words*, must mean "Those who fear you will see your Church and be glad, because I have hoped above

---

1. The fairly impersonal tone, and the absence of any remarks at the end about deferring the next verses until another day, suggest that this sermon may never have been preached.
2. See Col 3:3.
3. *Iucundabuntur.*
4. *Laetabuntur.*
5. See Gal 3:29; Gn 12:3.

429

measure in your words" (*hoped above measure*,[6] because that is how some trans-lators have more accurately rendered the word). And the people who see the Church and are glad are none other than the Church itself.

Why does it not say, "Those who fear you see me now and are glad now"? It puts the verb in the present tense, but the verbs *will see* and *will be glad* are in the future. Perhaps we should take this distinction as a reminder that fear is proper to the present time, when human life on earth is one long temptation,[7] whereas the gladness to which it looks forward must be awaited until the just shine like the sun in the kingdom of their Father.[8] Another psalm speaks of that future happi-ness in a similar way: *How great, how immense, is your sweetness, Lord, which you have hidden for*[9] *those who fear you!* As long as they are under this present dispensation they fear and do not see what God has hidden, but later *they will see and be glad*, for that other psalm continues, *You have brought it to perfection for those who trust in you* (Ps 30:20(31:19)).

The psalm we are studying now echoes this: *I have hoped in your words*. The composite form, *hoped above measure*, which a more painstaking translator used, reminds us that God *has power to do all things far more abundantly than we ask or understand* (Eph 3:20). Since what God does is more wonderful *than we ask or understand*, it would not be enough to hope for those things; we must hope above measure.

Verses 75-78. Our present life is shadowed by death, but mercy and true life will follow

3. But in this present life the Church is still in a state of holy fear, not yet seeing itself in the kingdom where serene joy will reign. It struggles along in this world amid perilous temptations, heeding the apostle's warning, *Anyone who thinks he stands must take care not to fall* (1 Cor 10:12). It is keenly aware of the wretchedness that besets its mortal condition, in which a heavy yoke lies upon Adam's children from the day they leave their mothers' wombs, and burdens every one of them until the day when they are buried in the earth, mother of us all.[10] Even those born anew are forced to groan still under its weight as they feel the lusting of flesh against spirit.[11] Reflecting on all these woes, the Church prays, *I know, O Lord, that your judgments are passed in justice, and that in your truth you have humbled me. But let your mercy be with me to console me, according to your declaration to your servant*. The divine scriptures insistently

---

6. *Supersperavi.*
7. See Jb 7:1.
8. See Mt 13:43.
9. See the note at Exposition 4 of Psalm 30,6.
10. See Sir 40:1.
11. See Gal 5:17.

draw our attention to mercy and truth, so much so that in one place we read, *All the Lord's ways are mercy and truth* (Ps 24(25):10). Similar texts are found elsewhere, especially in the psalms. In the present case the psalmist mentions truth first, because we have been humbled even to death by the judgment of God, whose decrees are justice itself. Then he mentions mercy, whereby we are renewed and brought to life by the promise of God, whose gift is grace.

The psalm therefore adds the words, *according to your declaration to your servant*, which allude to God's promise. Whether we think of the regeneration which makes us sons and daughters of God even now, or of the threefold endowment of faith, hope, and charity, which are being built up in us (although they come from the mercy of God), these gifts are not the joys of the blessed but the solace of the wretched in this woeful, stormy life. And so the Church prays, *Let your mercy be with me to console me.*

4. Yet after these trials—indeed, through them—the joys of the blessed will come to us; and therefore the psalm continues, *May your manifold mercies come upon me, and I shall live.* Live I shall, most truly, when I need fear no threat of death. The only life that deserves to be called simply "life" without qualification is eternal, happy life. That alone merits the name. In comparison with that, what we have now should be called death more properly than life. True life is envisaged in the gospel, where someone is bidden, *If you wish to enter into life, keep the commandments* (Mt 19:17). Did the Lord specify "eternal life" or "blessed life"? No. Nor did he when he spoke about bodily resurrection. *Those who have done good will rise again to life* (Jn 5:29), he said; and here again he did not add "eternal" or "happy." So too in our psalm. *May your manifold mercies come upon me*, begs the psalmist, *and I shall live.* He does not say, "I shall live for ever," or "I shall live in happiness"; he takes it for granted that the only state really deserving of the name *life* is life without end and without any misery.

How is it won? *Because I meditate on your law*, he says. But no one ever arrives at true life unless such meditation is carried on in the faith that works through love.[12] I think it necessary to stress this point, in case anyone imagines that he will gain life because he has committed the whole law to memory and very frequently sung it by heart, never keeping quiet about its precepts yet not living according to those precepts either. No one must think that by so doing he has followed the psalmist's example. No such person is in a position to claim, *I meditate on your law*, or to expect the outcome for which the psalmist begged as the fruit of his constant meditation: *May your manifold mercies come upon me, and I shall live.* This is not the case. The meditation referred to by the psalm is a lover's meditation, the pondering of one who is so much in love that the charity fostered in his meditation will never grow cold, however thickly the sins of others may swarm about him.

---

12. See Gal 5:6.

5. The psalm proceeds, *Let the proud be put to shame for unjustly injuring me; but I will earnestly observe your commandments.* See the effect of meditation on[13] God's law. It would be truer to say that his meditation is itself the keeping of God's law.

Verse 79. Christ speaks in his own name

6. *Let those who fear you, and recognize your testimonies, turn to me.* (In some codices, both Greek and Latin, I have found *convertantur mihi,* but I think this comes to the same thing as *convertantur ad me.*) Who is it who issues this invitation? No ordinary human being would dare to speak so; or, if he did, he would not deserve a hearing. It can be said only by him whom we heard speaking in his own person a few verses earlier, when he testified, *I share with all those who fear you.* He became a sharer in our mortality that we might become sharers in his divinity; we have become participants in the one Christ unto life, because he partook with many unto death. To him all those who fear God now turn, all who recognize God's testimonies; for God bore witness to Christ long beforehand through the prophets, and their testimonies were verified by his miracles when he was among us not so long ago.

Verse 80. Purity of heart, achieved through grace

7. *Through your justifying actions let my heart be unsullied, that I may not be put to shame.* Here Christ speaks once more in the voice of his body, his holy people, and prays that his heart—the heart of his members, that is—may be free from stain. This can come about only through God's justifying work, not through any efforts of their own, and so cleanness of heart is prayed for, not presumed. The phrase, *that I may not be put to shame,* is reminiscent of words we met in the opening lines of this psalm, *O that my ways may be directed toward observing your ways of justice! Then I shall not be put to shame, if I look carefully into all your statutes.* But there the expression used was *O that . . . !* which indicates a wish; here we have instead the language of prayer, *Let my heart be unsullied.* However, there is no disagreement between them, and neither displays the arrogance of free will trusting to itself in opposition to grace.[14] In the earlier verse the psalmist said, *I shall not be put to shame,* and now he prays *that I may not be put to shame.*

The heart of Christ's members, the heart of his body, is rendered immaculate by the grace of God that flows to it through its head, that is, through Jesus Christ,

---

13. Variant: "See what he means when he spoke of meditation on."
14. Probably an echo of the Pelagian controversy; see the note at Exposition 4 of Psalm 118,2.

our Lord. Grace flows to Christ's members through the laver of rebirth,[15] in which all our past sins have been destroyed. It comes also through the help of the Spirit,[16] thanks to which we foster desires opposed to those of the flesh[17] and so are not defeated in our warfare. It comes too from the efficacy of the Lord's Prayer, in which we ask, *Forgive us our debts* (Mt 6:12). In all these ways, through the new birth given to us, through help afforded to us in our struggle,[18] and through prayer poured out, our heart is purified from its pollution, so that we may not be put to shame. And something else belongs to God's ways of justification. It is this: among his other commands he bade us, *Forgive, and you will be forgiven; give, and gifts will be given to you* (Lk 6:37-38).

15. See Tt 3:5.
16. Or perhaps "through spiritual help."
17. See Gal 5:17.
18. Variant: "through the confession we are helped to make."

Exposition 20 of Psalm 118

Twentieth Sermon

Verse 81. The Church of the ages longs for Christ

1. The section of this great psalm which we have undertaken to study and expound, with the Lord's help, begins, *My soul has fallen away with longing for your salvation, and for your word I have hoped.* Not every sign of weakness is to be regarded as evidence of guilt or deserving of punishment; there is also an exhaustion that is praiseworthy and to be desired. Making progress and falling away through exhaustion are opposites, to be sure, and it is more usual to understand progress as something good and to take falling away in a pejorative sense. This is common usage, as long as nothing is added or implied as to what one is progressing toward or falling away from. But when the object is mentioned, advancing toward it can mean a bad development, and falling away can be good. The apostle says explicitly, *Avoid profane and sensational chatter, for those who engage in it advance toward godless ways* (2 Tm 2:16); and concerning certain people he warns, *They go from bad to worse* (2 Tm 3:13). To fall away from the good toward evil is a bad thing, but to fall away from evil ways is good. It was a holy form of weakness that prompted the cry, *My soul falls away with longing for the courts of the Lord* (Ps 83:3(84:2)). Our present psalm, likewise, does not say, "My soul has fallen away from your salvation through weakness," but *My soul has fallen away with longing for your salvation,* that is, my soul in its faintness is looking toward your salvation. This is a salutary kind of falling away, for it signals a desire for some good not as yet won but longed for with fierce intensity.

Who speaks of such desire? The chosen race, obviously, the royal priesthood, the holy nation, the people God has made his own.[1] From the dawn of humanity until the end of this world, in all who at any time have lived, are alive now, or will live, this people longs for Christ. The holy old man Simeon gave voice to this longing when he took the child into his arms and prayed, *You give your servant his discharge in peace, now, Lord, for my eyes have seen your salvation* (Lk 2:29-30). He had received an assurance from God that he would not taste death until he had seen the Lord's Anointed. We must believe that the intense desire cherished by that old man was shared by all the holy people of ancient times. The

---

1. See 1 Pt 2:9.

Lord himself referred to it when he said to his disciples, *Many a prophet, many a king, has longed to see what you see, but not seen it, and to hear what you hear, but never heard it* (Lk 10:24). It is the voice of all these that rings through the psalm: *My soul has fallen away with longing for your salvation.* The longing of these saints was never appeased; nor is it appeased even now in Christ's body, the Church; nor will it be until the end of the world, until, as God promised through a prophet, *He shall come whom all nations desire* (Hag 2:8). With his eyes on that fulfillment the apostle says, *All that remains for me now is the crown of righteousness which the Lord, as a just judge, will award me on that day, and not to me alone but to all those who look with love for his appearing* (2 Tm 4:8). The yearning voiced in this psalm, the yearning of which we speak, springs from this love for his appearing, of which Paul says elsewhere, *When Christ appears, Christ who is your life, then you too will appear with him in glory* (Col 3:4). The early ages of the Church, before the Virgin's childbearing, had their saints, men and women who longed for his coming in the flesh. These later ages since his ascension into heaven likewise have their saints, who long for his manifestation as judge of the living and the dead. Never has there been any diminishment of this longing from the first, nor will there be until the end of this age, apart from the time when Christ consorted with his disciples in his flesh.

We are therefore fully justified in hearing the voice of Christ's entire body groaning in this life, when the psalm says, *My soul has fallen away with longing for your salvation, and for your word I have hoped.* God's *word* is his promise. This hope strengthens the Church to wait patiently for what it believes but does not see as yet.[2] In this verse the Greek once more has the compound verb which some of our translators have chosen to represent with *hoped above measure,*[3] because we cannot doubt that what is to come is greater than can be expressed.

Verses 82-83. How hard it is to wait!

2. *My eyes have grown weary in longing for your word; they cry, When will you console me?* Here we find again the same praiseworthy, blessed falling away, but this time it is in the eyes—the inner eyes, obviously. It arises not from any mental infirmity but from a powerful desire for what God has promised; that is why the speaker says he longs for God's word. But how can anyone's eyes ask, *When will you console me?* It is not usually the eyes that speak but the tongue; so it must mean that the psalmist is praying and groaning with all his hope and intention focused on this fulfillment. We could say that the voice of the eyes is prayerful desire.

---

2. See Rom 8:25.
3. *Supersperavi.*

The question, *When will you console me?* reveals the psalmist's anguish at the delay he feels he is enduring, and it reminds us of the complaint in another psalm, *And you, O Lord: how long?* (Ps 6:4(3)). Perhaps God delays so that the joy may be all the sweeter for being long awaited. Or perhaps this is simply an impression on the part of those who are yearning, for an interval of time which is brief to one who brings help is long for the lover. But the Lord knows what he wishes to do and when to do it, for he disposes all things by measure, and number, and weight.[4]

3. When spiritual desires burn keenly, the desires of the flesh certainly cool down. This is why the psalmist continues, *Because I have become like a wineskin in the frost, I have not forgotten your ways of justice.* There is no doubt that by the wineskin he intends to suggest our mortal flesh, and by frost the heavenly gift which subdues carnal passions as though they were frozen. The consequence is that God's ways of justice no longer fade from one's memory, because one is not thinking of anything else, and the apostle's injunction is heeded, *Make no provision for the flesh or the gratification of your desires* (Rom 13:14). Thus after saying, *Because I have become like a wineskin in the frost*, he adds, *I have not forgotten your ways of justice*. The reason why I am not forgetful, he implies, is that I am a different person now. The heat of passion has died down, allowing the memory of charity to burn hot.

Verses 84-88. The Church is persecuted for the truth

4. *How many days remain for your servant? When will you judge those who persecute me?* In the Book of Revelation the martyrs ask the same question, and they are told to be patient until the tally of their brethren is complete.[5] Here we have the body of Christ inquiring as to the number of days it must spend in this world. But no one must interpret this as a sign that the Church will not last until the end of the world, leaving a period of earthly time in which the Church will no longer be here. Not at all. The psalmist rules out such a notion by following his question with a further question about judgment; this clearly shows that the Church will continue on earth until the day of judgment brings punishment upon its persecutors.

Someone may be troubled by the psalmist's query, recalling how, when the disciples put a similar question to their teacher, he replied, *It is not for you to know the times which the Father has appointed by his own authority* (Acts 1:7). But why should we not believe that this verse in our psalm was a prophecy that they would ask? The Church's voice, resounding prophetically so many centuries earlier, was proved true when they put this very question.

---

4. See Wis 11:21, a favorite text with Augustine.
5. See Rv 6:10.

5. The next verse runs thus: *The unrighteous have told me titillating tales, but they cannot compare with your law, O Lord.* The Greek has ἀδολεσχίας, for which it is so difficult to find a single word in Latin that some of our translators have put *jokes*,[6] others *titillating tales*.[7] We can take it that some kind of verbal agility is meant, some playfulness that is fun, more or less.[8] Stories of this sort, dealing with various topics and from different walks of life, are found both in secular literature and in the Jewish collection called the Mishnah,[9] which contains thousands of tales in addition to the canon of the divine scriptures. There are examples of the genre also among the vapid, random chatter of the heretics. The psalmist means us to understand that all such iniquitous persons told him ἀδολεσχίας, verbal contrivances to give him pleasure. but no, he says, *They cannot compare with your law, O Lord*, because what gives me pleasure in your law is truth, not games with words.

6. He adds, *All your commandments are truth: they have persecuted me unjustly, so help me.* The sense of this prayer depends on his earlier questions, *How many days remain for your servant? When will you judge those who persecute me?* They told me their clever, amusing stories to catch me, but I preferred your law, which afforded me more delight because *all your commandments are truth*, whereas their words are nothing but nonsense. That was what provoked their unjust persecution, for what they persecuted in me was simply the truth. *Help me* then, that I may fight for the truth even to death, for this too is your commandment and so is part of the truth.

7. When the Church took that line it suffered the fate mentioned next: *They almost made an end of me on earth*; for there was a great slaughter among the martyrs who were confessing and preaching the truth. But the prayer, *Help me!* was not made in vain, and so the Church could say, *But I did not abandon your commandments.*

8. The Church prayed for grace to persevere to the end. *In accordance with your mercy give me life*, it implored, *and I will guard the testimonies of your lips.* For *testimonies* the Greek word is μαρτύρια; this fact should not be passed over in silence, because it evokes for us the precious and beloved name, "martyrs." When the cruelty of the persecutors waxed so fierce that the Church was almost blotted out from the earth, the martyrs could not possibly have guarded the testimonies of God unless the prayer in our psalm had been answered for them: *In accordance with your mercy, give me life.* True life was indeed granted to them, lest by clinging to natural life they should deny the life that matters, and, by

---

6. *Delectationes.*

7. *Fabulationes.*

8. In Expositions 6,4 and 14,4 of this psalm, Augustine reflects on the verb related to the Greek noun used here.

9. Augustine calls it *Deuterosis*, "second" or "repetition." The Mishnah was not an original work, but the authoritative collection of Jewish Oral Law which forms the basis of the Talmud.

denying it, lose it. And so it came about that they refused to let go of the truth to save their lives, and by dying for the truth they found life.

Exposition 21 of Psalm 118

Twenty-first Sermon

Verses 89-91. The stability of God's creation, heaven and earth

1. The speaker in the psalm sounds as though he is weary of the instability of human affairs, which subjects us to a life full of trials. He complained earlier about some of his troubles when, he said, *The unrighteous persecuted me unjustly . . . they almost made an end of me on earth.* But now, afire with longing for the heavenly Jerusalem, he raises his eyes and says, *Your word, O Lord, abides in heaven for eternity,* among the angels who keep their ranks with never a thought of desertion.

2. After that verse about heaven we now have one that looks to the earth. Each verse forms part of a stanza of eight, all beginning with the same letter, and each stanza is headed by the corresponding letter of the Hebrew alphabet, right through to the end of this very lengthy psalm.[1] *Your truth lasts from generation to generation; you have founded the earth, and it stands firm.* He has gazed up to heaven, and now he directs the contemplation of his believing mind to the earth. There he finds something not found in heaven: human generations. *Your truth lasts from generation to generation,* he says. Possibly the repetition of the word indicates that all generations are meant; God's truth has never been absent from any of them, but is found in his saints in every generation, sometimes in few, at other times in many, as circumstances change. Or it may be that by saying, *from generation to generation,* the psalmist means us to think of two generations, one being the age of the law and the prophets, the other that of the gospel.

He points to the reason why truth has never been lost throughout these generations by saying, *You have founded the earth, and it stands firm. Earth* here means earth-dwellers. Scripture tells us that *no one can lay any other foundation than that which is laid, which is Christ Jesus* (1 Cor 3:11). But this is not to say that Christ was not just as truly the foundation of the generation of the law and the prophets, for they, after all, bore witness to Christ.[2] Nor does it imply that Moses and the prophets are to be considered sons of the bondwoman who bears her children for slavery rather than of the free woman who is our mother.[3] To her,

---

1. An acrostic psalm, with 22 stanzas corresponding to the 22 letters of the Hebrew alphabet. We have reached lamed, the twelfth letter.
2. See Rom 3:21.
3. See Gal 4:22-31.

439

the free Zion, *You are my mother, a man will say, he who was made man in her; and the Most High himself founded her* (Ps 86(87):5). Christ is the Most High with the Father, but for our salvation he became most low in his birth from his mother,[4] for though as God he is above her, *he was made man in her.*

On this sound base, Lord, *you have founded the earth, and it stands firm*, for it is stabilized by its foundation and will never be shifted;[5] this earth abides for ever in the persons of those to whom you mean to give eternal life. But the children of the slave-woman belong to the Old Covenant and do not stand firm, because they are interested only in earthly promises, for all that the Old Covenant contained secret hints of the New. *A slave does not stay in the house permanently, whereas a son stays for ever* (Jn 8:35).

3. *By your ordinance the day endures.* All these things we see are *the day*; and they are the day which the Lord has made, so let us exult and be joyful in it[6] and walk honorably as people do in daylight.[7] *For all things serve you*: all these things of which the psalm has been speaking, all that belong to this day: all of them serve you. But the godless do not serve you, and indeed scripture says of them, *I have likened your mother to the night* (Hos 4:5, LXX).

Verses 92-96. A dedicated life

4. Now the psalmist looks about him to see how this earth is set free and made ready to abide on its stable foundation, and he says, *Had your law not been the subject of my meditation, I would perhaps have perished when I was brought low.* The law he means is the law of faith: not an idle faith but the faith that is active through love.[8] In response to such faith believers receive the grace that strengthens them in temporal troubles, so that they do not perish in the humiliations attendant on our mortality.

5. *I will never forget your ways of justice*, he continues, *for in them you have given me life.* This is how it came about that he did not perish when he was brought low. If God does not give life, what is any man or woman? We had the power to kill ourselves, but have no power to bring ourselves to life.

6. The psalmist now declares, *I belong to you, save me, for I have searched earnestly for your ways of justice.* We must not pass hurriedly over this remarkable statement, *I belong to you.* Is there anything that does not belong to God? Is it to be supposed that, because God is acknowledged to be in heaven, there is anything on earth that is not his? How is that possible, when we remember another psalm's cry, *The earth is the Lord's, and all that fills it, the round world*

---

4. Probably Zion, or the Jewish race, here, rather than Mary individually.
5. See Ps 103(104):5.
6. See Ps 117(118):24.
7. See Rom 13:13.
8. See Gal 5:6.

and all who live in it (Ps 23(24):1)? But if this is how things stand, why does the psalmist think it appropriate to commend himself to God in this familiar way, saying, *I belong to you, save me*? I think he means us to understand that to his own harm[9] he had tried to belong to himself; for that is the original evil and the greatest of all, the sin of disobedience. It is as though he were saying, "I tried to own myself, and all I did was lose myself. *I belong to you, save me, for I have searched earnestly for your ways of justice*, not my own willful ways, whereby I tried to be my own property, but *your ways of justice*; because I want to belong to you."

7. *Sinners lay in wait to destroy me, but I understood about your testimonies*, he reflects. What does he imply by saying that they lay in wait to destroy him? Does he mean they set an ambush along his road, intending to kill him as he passed by? But surely he was not afraid of bodily death? No, of course he wasn't. What else, then, can *they lay in wait* mean but that they hoped to make him consent to their evil designs? If they had succeeded, they would indeed have destroyed him.

But he tells us how he escaped destruction: *I understood about your testimonies*—or, better, your μαρτύρια, for this Greek word is more familiar to the ears of the Church: "I understood about your martyrdoms." As long as I did not consent to their wishes I would not have perished even if they had killed me, provided that I was confessing you by martyrdom. But they, bent on destroying me, went on waiting for my consent and tortured me while I confessed to you.

Throughout it all he did not let go of what he had understood. He kept his eyes on what he saw in faith: the end that would have no end, if only he persevered to the end.[10]

8. Now he declares, *I have seen the outcome of unwavering perfection; your commandment is exceedingly wide*. He has entered God's sanctuary, and seen what the final outcome must be.[11] It seems to me that *unwavering perfection* in this context must signify fighting for the truth even to death,[12] and enduring all adversities for the true, supreme good. The outcome of such perfection is a glorious destiny in the kingdom of Christ, which has no end. There the victor enjoys a life that knows neither death nor sorrow, a life of high honor won by death and pain and disgrace endured in the life of this world.

The psalmist adds, *Your commandment is exceedingly wide*. This, I think, must mean the commandment of charity. For what would have been the point of facing any kind of death-threat, or making a martyr's confession amid the most atrocious torments, if the one who made the confession lacked charity? Listen to

---

9. Or "by his own evil conduct"
10. See Mt 24:13.
11. See Ps 72(73):17.
12. See Sir 4:33.

the apostle's words on this point: *If I deliver my body to be burnt, yet have no love, it profits me nothing* (1 Cor 13:3). But *the charity of God has been poured out into our hearts through the Holy Spirit who has been given us* (Rom 5:5); and in the wide outpouring of that charity there is wide freedom for us. Even the narrow way[13] can be walked without constriction in that generous freedom. This is the gift of God, to whom another psalm gives thanks: *You have made room for my steps under me, and my footsteps have not grown faint* (Ps 17:37(18:36)). The commandment of charity is broad indeed, and it is a double commandment, enjoining love of both God and our neighbor. What could be wider than a command on which all the law and the prophets depend?[14]

---

13. See Mt 7:14.
14. See Mt 22:40.

Exposition 22 of Psalm 118

Twenty-second Sermon

Verse 97. Love for God's law

1. We have often pointed out that when we put God's commandments into practice we experience a wonderfully spacious freedom, which is to be identified with charity. In the verse of this great psalm which we examined most recently the psalmist reflected, *Your commandment is exceedingly wide.* In the verse that follows he indicates the source of this wide freedom, exclaiming, *How I love your law, O Lord!* The breadth of the commandment is revealed as love.[1] But is it possible to love the object that God orders us to love without loving the order itself? Probably not; and this order is his law. *All day long I ponder on it,* says the psalmist. You can see how dearly he loves it, if he makes it the subject of his meditation all day long,[2] or rather, as the Greek emphasizes, *throughout the whole day,*[3] which better conveys the prolonged continuity of his meditation. The expression means "continuing uninterruptedly" or "always."

Love like this drives out intemperate desire, which often conflicts with the commands imposed on us by the law, because the flesh lusts against the spirit.[4] The spirit, for its part, pitting its own desires against those of the flesh, must love God's law so dearly that it ponders on the law all day long. Yet the apostle makes an important distinction: *What room is left for your boasting? It is completely ruled out. By what law? The law of works? No; but by the law of faith* (Rom 3:27). This is the faith that works through charity;[5] for by seeking, asking, and knocking it receives the good Spirit,[6] through whom love itself is poured out in our hearts.[7] All those, whoever they may be, who are moved by the Spirit of God are sons and daughters of God,[8] and they are welcomed into the kingdom of heaven to sit down there with Abraham, Isaac, and Jacob.[9] But Israel according to the flesh is no son but a servant, who cannot remain in the house perma-

---

1. *Dilectio*, the love of deliberate choice.
2. *Tota die.*
3. *Totam diem.*
4. See Gal 5:17.
5. See Gal 5:6.
6. See Lk 11:9-13.
7. See Rom 5:5.
8. See Rom 8:14.
9. See Mt 8:11.

nently,[10] and is expelled. To Israel the Lord says, *You will see Abraham, Isaac, Jacob, and all the prophets in God's kingdom, but yourselves cast out. And people will come from east and west, north and south, and sit down in the kingdom of God. And lo, those are last who used to be first, and first who used to be last.* (Lk 13:28-30) As he who was God's chosen instrument[11] testifies, *The Gentiles who were not pursuing righteousness found righteousness, but it was a righteousness based on faith. Israel, pursuing righteousness through the law, did not attain it. Why not? Because what they sought was a righteousness based not on faith but on works; and so they tripped over the stumbling-block.* (Rom 9:30-32) Thus did they become enemies of him who here speaks in prophecy.[12]

Verse 98. Wise understanding with regard to the law

2. The psalm proceeds, *You have given me wisdom to understand your commandment better than my enemies, because it is mine for eternity.* They have zeal for God, certainly, but not a zeal informed by knowledge. Ignorant of the righteousness that comes from God, and attempting to set up their own, they were not submissive to God's righteousness.[13] But the psalmist wisely understands God's commandment better than those enemies of his, and wants to be ranged with the apostle, having no righteousness he can call his own, such as might have derived from the law, but only that which comes from God, through faith in Christ.[14] I do not mean to suggest that the law his enemies study is not from God but only that they have no true sensitivity to it, as he has. He can claim the wisdom to understand it better than his enemies, because he is firmly clasped to the stone over which they stumbled.[15] Christ is the end of the law, bringing justification to everyone who believes,[16] a justification that comes freely through his grace.[17] His enemies are in quite a different situation, for they aspire to observe the law by their own efforts and strive to establish a righteousness which, though apparently conformed to God's law, is in essence their own. The psalmist, by contrast, is like the child of promise who hungers and thirsts for righteousness,[18] and by asking, seeking, and knocking[19] begs it from his Father, knowing that as one adopted through the only-begotten Son he will receive it.[20]

---

10. See Jn 8:35.
11. See Acts 9:15.
12. Probably Christ is meant.
13. See Rom 10:2-3.
14. See Phil 3:9.
15. See Rom 9:32.
16. See Rom 10:4.
17. See Rom 3:24.
18. See Mt 5:6.
19. See Mt 7:7.
20. Or "that as an adopted child he will receive it through the only-begotten Son."

But how could he have acquired such wise insight into God's commandment if God had not made him wise? So he confesses, *You have given me wisdom to understand your commandment better than my enemies.* Those enemies were born into slavery, as children of Hagar,[21] and so what they looked for from the commandment was temporal rewards. This is why they could not regard the commandment as eternal, as the psalmist does. The better translations have *for eternity*[22] rather than *to the end of the age*[23] because the latter could imply that when this world ends there will no longer be any legal commandment. It is true that there will be none if we think of commands written on visible tablets or in books. But on the tablets of the heart[24] the law of love for God and our neighbor will abide for eternity; and on this double commandment the whole law and the prophets depend.[25] God, who issued this commandment, will himself be the reward for keeping it; none other than the Beloved will be love's recompense on that day when God shall be all things in all of us.[26]

Verse 99. Christ speaks in his own person

3. How are we to interpret the next line, *I understood more than all who taught me*? Who is this, whose understanding outstripped that of his teachers? Who is this, who is bold enough to claim superiority in understanding over all the prophets, who in their pre-eminent authority not only taught their own contemporaries by word of mouth but even instructed posterity by their writings? Admittedly Solomon was endowed with such great wisdom that he seemed to surpass all his predecessors;[27] but we can hardly believe that David, his father, was speaking prophetically about Solomon in this text, especially when the words that occur a few lines further on cannot possibly have been spoken by Solomon: *I have held back my steps from every sinful path* (verse 101).

It is much more acceptable to think that the prophet, who is foretelling Christ, distributed his prophetic words in such a way that at one moment they come from the head, who is our Savior, and at another from his body, which is the Church. But the psalmist makes the two speak as one, foreseeing the great sacrament of unity, of which scripture says, *They will be two in one flesh.* I have no difficulty in recognizing him who understood more than all who taught him, for when he was twelve years old the boy Jesus stayed on in Jerusalem and was

---

21. See Gal 4:24.
22. *In aeternum.*
23. *In saeculum.*
24. See 2 Cor 3:3.
25. See Mt 22:40.
26. See 1 Cor 15:28.
27. See 1 Kgs 3:12.

found by his parents[28] three days later in the temple, sitting among the teachers, listening to them and asking them questions. All who heard him were astonished at his discernment and his replies.[29] They had good reason to be, for this was the child who had said in prophecy so long before, *I understood more than all who taught me.*

More than all my human teachers, he means, not more than God the Father, of whom the Son asserts, *As the Father has taught me, so I speak* (Jn 8:28). This claim is very difficult to understand if made by the Word in his own divine person, unless one has the capacity to grasp that for the Son it is one and the same to be taught by the Father and to be begotten by the Father. For the Son, to be and to be taught are not two different realities: for him to be and to be taught are identical. It follows that since he receives his divine nature from the Father, so too he is taught by the Father.

If, however, we take the statement as proceeding from his humanity, in which he accepted the nature of a slave,[30] it is easier to see that he learned what to say from the Father. Older people might well have regarded him in his servile status as someone who needed to be taught, especially while he was a child; but because the Father taught him he understood more than all his would-be teachers.

Because I pondered on your testimonies, he continues. This is why he understood better than all who tried to teach him: God's testimonies were the subject of his meditation, and these he understood of his own accord, far better than they did. He pointed out to his challengers, *You sent messengers to John, and he gave testimony to the truth. I do not need human testimony, but I say these things that you may be saved. John was a burning, shining lamp, and you were prepared to rejoice in his light for a while. But I have a witness greater than that of John.* (Jn 5:33-36) Those were the kind of testimonies on which he was pondering when he understood more than all who taught him.

Verse 100. God's commands versus the tradition of the ancients

4. The psalm immediately adds something about elders, and I think we can identify these with the teachers mentioned in the preceding verse. *I understood better than the elders,* it says. I think the reason for the repetition is that the psalm wants us, the readers, to remember the age of Jesus recorded in the gospel, when in his boyhood days he was sitting among older men—as a youngster amid elders, in fact—and was outstripping his teachers in understanding. A lesser and

---

28. Variant: "by those who were looking for him."
29. See Lk 2:42-47.
30. See Phil 2:7.

a greater person are usually called junior and senior in relation to each other, even though neither has attained old age or even approached it.

There is, however, a more direct reference to seniors or elders in the gospel, if we care to look for it, and for an instance of understanding that surpassed theirs. The scribes and Pharisees challenged Jesus, *Why do your disciples infringe the tradition of the elders? They do not wash their hands before eating bread.* (Mt 15:2) So the charge against him is transgression of the tradition of the elders. But he *understood better than the elders* and had an answer for them. Let us consider it: *And you, why do you transgress God's commandment, preferring your own tradition?* (Mt 15:3) Not long after this encounter Jesus called the crowds to him and said to them, *Listen and understand* (Mt 15:10). His intention was that not only he himself, the head of the body, but also his members should understand better than those elders whose tradition concerning hand-washing had been cited. He seemed to be telling the people, "You too must understand better than those elders. I want it to be perfectly clear that the prophetic words, *I understood better than the elders,* are true of you as well and are applicable to the whole Christ: not to the head only but also to the body." He explained to them, *It is not what enters your mouth that defiles you, but what comes out; that is what defiles a person* (Mt 15:11). This is something not understood by the elders who had passed on their orders about the washing of hands as though they were important commandments.

But although the head had understood better than the elders, his members had not yet grasped what he had told them. Accordingly Peter shortly afterward asked him, *Explain this parable to us.* He still thought it must be a parable, though the Lord had spoken straightforwardly and not in figures. Jesus replied, *Are you still without comprehension? Do you not understand that whatever enters the mouth passes into the stomach, and is discharged into the drain? But the things that come out of the mouth arise from the heart; and these are the things that defile a person.* (Mt 15:15-18)

And what about you? Are you too still without comprehension? Do you not understand better than those elders? Surely now that we have listened to so great a master each of us can say, *I understood better than the elders;* for the next words of the psalm are also applicable to Christ's body: *Because I earnestly sought your commandments.* Your commandments, not human injunctions; your commandments, not the commandments of the elders who, though aspiring to be doctors of the law, understand *neither what they are saying nor the matters on which they pronounce* (1 Tm 1:7). To those who set their own authority above the truth, the question was justly addressed, *And you, why do you transgress God's commandment to establish your own tradition?* The divine commandments are to be earnestly sought, that they may be understood better than those elders understood them.

Verses 101-102. Chaste love in the keeping of the law

5. The next lines do not seem suitable for the head, but are apt for his body: *I have held back my steps from every sinful path, that I may keep your words.* Our head, the Savior of the body, was never swayed by carnal lust toward any sinful path; he had no need to restrain his feet, as though they had been inclined to stray by their own impulses. But this is what we do when we curb our perverse desires and withhold them from sinful paths—perverse desires which Christ did not have. We can keep God's words only if we do not chase after our evil cravings;[31] otherwise they will lead us into the very evils we crave. We need to restrain them by the authority of the spirit whose desires oppose those of the flesh,[32] or they will seize us and sink us by plunging us into sinful ways.

6. *I have not turned away from your judgments,* he continues, *for you have prescribed a law for me.* He has already spoken of the fear that restrained his feet from every sinful path. What is he saying now, when he declares, *I have not turned away from your judgments,* if not what he says in another verse, *I have been in awe of your judgments* (verse 120)? I have steadfastly believed in them, *for you have prescribed a law for me.* You, who are more intimate to me than my inmost self, have set a law within my heart by the action of your Spirit, as though writing it with your finger. You have written it within me so that I may not dread it like a loveless slave but love it with chaste fear like a son or daughter and fear it with chaste love.

Verse 103-104. The sweetness of wisdom

7. The next verse develops this thought: *How sweet in my mouth are your words* (or, following the Greek accurately, *your declarations*), *more delicious than honey and honeycomb to my taste!* This is the sweetness the Lord gives so that our earth may yield its fruit[33] and we may do good in the right way, not out of fear of some material misfortune but from delight in spiritual good. A few codices lack the mention of the honeycomb, but many have it. Wise teaching open to all is like honey; but doctrine concerning more recondite mysteries is like goodness obtained from a honeycomb, because it is squeezed out, as though from waxen cells, by the mouth of the teacher as he chews the mysteries, so to say. Such wisdom is sweet and tasty, but to the mouth of the heart, not that of the body.

8. Now what can the psalmist mean by his next words, *I have found understanding through your commandments?* It is one thing to say, "I have understood

---

31. See Sir 18:30.
32. See Gal 5:17.
33. See Ps 84:13(85:12).

your commandments," but another to say, *I have found understanding through your commandments*. He seems to suggest that on the basis of God's commands he has understood something else. I think he means that by keeping God's commandments he has attained understanding of further matters he had longed to know about. This is why another passage of scripture advises, *You long for wisdom; keep the commandments, and the Lord will grant it to you* (Sir 1:26(33)). Such advice is a warning to anyone who tries to put things back to front, wanting to scale the heights of wisdom before embracing humility and obedience; for no one can comprehend wisdom except by reaching it in due order. If anyone thinks he can, let him listen to further counsel: *Seek not what is above you, and do not scrutinize loftier matters; but let your mind run always on what the Lord has entrusted to you* (Sir 3:22). These texts make it plain that any man or woman attains to the wisdom that penetrates secret things only through obedience to the commandments. Notice that in recommending, *Let your mind run on what the Lord has entrusted to you*, scripture includes the word, *always*; because while we must practise obedience in order to gain wisdom, when we have been granted wisdom we must never abandon obedience.

It is evident, then, that the voice we are listening to here is that of the spiritually-minded members of Christ. *I have found understanding through your commandments*, it says. Christ's body can rightly make this claim in the persons of those who keep the commandments and are granted a richer perception of wisdom. *Therefore I hate every sinful path*, continues the psalm, for any true love of righteousness must of necessity hate all iniquity. Such love is all the more ardent in the measure that it is intensified by the sweetness of a fuller gift of wisdom, imparted to one who obeys God and finds understanding through his commandments.

Exposition 23 of Psalm 118

Twenty-third Sermon

Verse 105. The Word is the true light; humans are illumined

1. As far as our God-given ability permits, we must now examine and explain the next verses of this psalm. The section we approach today opens with the verse, *Your word is a lamp for my feet, and a light for my paths.* Evidently *light* is a repetition of *lamp*, and *paths* corresponds to *feet.* How, then, are we to understand *your word*? Does it mean the Word who was God-with-God in the beginning, the Word through whom all things were made?[1] No, that cannot be right, for the Word is a light, not a lamp. A lamp is something created, not the creator; a lamp is only kindled by participation in the unchangeable divine light. One such was John, of whom the Word, God himself, testified, *He was a burning, shining lamp* (Jn 5:35). In a sense John was both a light and a lamp, but when compared with the Word, of whom the gospel says, *The Word was God* (Jn 1:1), John was not the light but was sent to bear witness concerning the light.[2] The true light is that which does not derive its radiance from elsewhere, as human beings do; the true light is that which enlightens all creatures.[3]

But there is a sense in which a lamp can be called a light, for Christ said to the apostles, *You are the light of the world* (Mt 5:14). He guarded against misunderstanding, though, for he said of himself at another time, *I am the light of the world* (Jn 8:12), for he did not want them to equate themselves with him. He continued, *A city founded upon a mountain cannot be hidden, nor do people light a lamp and then put it under a bushel basket; they place it on a lampstand to give light to everyone in the house. So let your deeds shine before men and women.* (Mt 5:14-16) He was making it plain to them that they were like lamps ignited from the one light that burns unchangeably. No created being, not even a rational, intellectual creature, is the source of its own light; it is kindled by participation in everlasting truth. Sometimes a created element is called "day," but even then it is only the day which the Lord has made,[4] not the day which is the Lord himself, the day of which a psalm says, *Draw near to him and receive his light* (Ps 33:6(34:5)). On account of this participation, and in view of his

---

1. See Jn 1:1-3.
2. See Jn 1:8.
3. See Jn 1:9.
4. See Ps 117(118):24.

humanity, the Mediator himself is called a lamp in the Book of Revelation.[5] But that text is an exception. God never says, nor would it ever be right to say, of any of the saints, *The Word was made flesh* (Jn 1:14). Only of the one Mediator between God and the human race[6] could that be said.

We have seen that the only-begotten Word who is equal to his begetter is called the light and that a human being illumined by the Word can also be called a light, or a lamp, as was the case with John and the apostles. We have seen too that none of these humans is the Word and that the Word by whom they were illumined is not a lamp. Well then, what is the word of which the psalm speaks, a word that can also be called a lamp? That is what the psalm says, *Your word is a lamp for my feet, and a light for my paths.* We must surely understand it to be the word that came to the prophets and was preached by the apostles. It is not the Word who is Christ, but Christ's word, concerning which scripture says, *Faith comes by hearing, and hearing through the word of Christ* (Rom 10:17). The apostle Peter also compares the prophetic word to a lamp: *We have the trusty message of the prophets to rely on, and you will do well to attend to it, for it is like a lamp burning in a dark place* (2 Pt 1:19). Unquestionably, then, the word which the psalm means when it says, *Your word is a lamp for my feet, and a light for my paths,* is the word contained in all the holy scriptures.

Verses 106-107. Faith and martyrdom

2. *I have sworn, and have decided, to keep the judgments of your justice,* says the psalmist, like a person walking steadily toward that lamp and keeping his paths straight. The second verb he uses clarifies the first; for we might have wondered what *I have sworn* signified, so he adds *and have decided.* What he had decided in virtue of a sacred pledge he termed an oath,[7] because the mind ought to be so firmly intent on observing God's just decrees that its decision has the same inviolability as an oath.

3. But faith is needed for the keeping of God's just judgments, faith to believe that under God, the just judge, nothing done rightly will lose its reward and no sin go unpunished. For this faith Christ's body has suffered many grievous wrongs. *I have been humbled exceedingly,* it says. Notice that it does not say, "I

---

5. See Rv 21:23.

6. See 1 Tm 2:5.

7. *Hoc . . . appellavit iuramentum quod statuit per sacramentum.* This last word had in Augustine's day not yet acquired the precise reference to the "seven sacraments" that was attached to it in the thirteenth century but still bore some traces of its original meaning as a sacred oath. Augustine, following the New Testament usage of the word to represent the Greek μυστήριον, generally understands *sacramentum* to mean a sign of a sacred mystery, or some visible sign of grace. In the present context he does not seem to be alluding to the baptismal commitment, which would in any case be inappropriate for an Old Testament psalmist. See further in the notes to Expositions of Psalms 67,16, and 73,2.

humbled myself," which would have obliged us to refer the statement to the kind of humility incumbent on it as a duty. It says rather, *I have been humbled exceedingly*, because it has endured fierce persecution on account of its oath and its decision to observe the judgments of God's justice. In such deep humiliation faith itself could be in danger of failing, and so the psalm continues, *Give me life, O Lord, according to your word*, which means "according to your promise," for the word that enshrines God's promises is a lamp for its feet and a light for its paths. This prayer to be given life amid the humiliating circumstances of persecution recalls earlier verses: *They almost made an end of me on earth, but I did not abandon your commandments. In accordance with your mercy give me life, and I will guard the testimonies of your lips*. By "guarding God's testimonies" the psalm meant the profession that leads to martyrdom, as we have seen. We learn from these passages that if the Lord does not give life to his Church by endowing it with patient endurance, what will be slaughtered in persecution is not the body but the soul, which will fail to keep the judgments of God's justice by accepting martyrdom. With reference to these trials the Lord promised, *By patiently enduring you will save your lives* (Lk 21:19); and of the Lord another psalm declared, *My patience comes from him* (Ps 61:6(62:5)).

Verses 108-110. Abiding in the hands of God

4. *Make the free-will offerings of my mouth acceptable to you, O Lord.* Make them pleasing in your sight, he means; approve them, do not refuse them. Sacrifices offered to praise God, prompted not by fear or compulsion but by an outpouring of charity, are appropriately called *free-will offerings* of the mouth. Another psalm voices the same intent: *Of my own free will I shall offer sacrifice to you* (Ps 53:8(54:6)).

But what is the meaning of the words added next? *And teach me your judgments*, he implores. Did he not say in an earlier verse, *I have not turned away from your judgments*? How could he say that, if he did not know them? But if he did know them, how can he now pray, *Teach me your judgments*? Probably we should understand this apparent inconsistency in the same way that we did when, after acknowledging that *you have provided sweetness for your servant, O Lord*, the psalmist went on to ask, *Teach me about sweetness.*[8] As we explained in that context, we should regard these words as spoken by one who has made some progress but is begging for further gifts to be added to those already received.

5. *My soul is constantly in your hands.* A few codices read *in my hands*, but most have *in yours*. This latter reading makes obvious sense, for the souls of the

---

8. See verses 65-66, Exposition 17 of Psalm 118,1-2.

just are in the hands of God,[9] and in his hand also are we and our words.[10] The psalmist proceeds, *And I have not forgotten your law*, as though the hands of God, in which his soul is held, were also helping his memory not to forget God's law.

I cannot make much sense of the alternative reading, *my soul is in my hands*, for the speaker is a just person, not a transgressor: someone returning to the Father, not deserting him. We could imagine the younger son in the parable wanting to take his soul into his own hands when he said to his father, *Give me the portion of the property that is due to me* (Lk 15:12). But that was what brought about his death; it was the cause of his downfall. Perhaps, though, we could take *my soul is in my hands* to mean that he is offering his soul to God, with a plea that it be given life. This would accord with his prayers elsewhere, *To you have I lifted up my soul* (Ps 24(25):1) and *Give me life* (verse 107).

6. *Sinners have laid a snare for me, but I have not strayed away from your commandments*. How did he avoid straying if not by leaving his soul in God's hands or keeping it in his own to offer to God, that it might be given life?

Verses 111-112. The eternal inheritance of the just

7. *I have acquired your testimonies by inheritance for eternity*. Some translators, wishing to render in one word what the Greek takes only one word to convey, have put not *hereditate adquisivi*, "I have acquired by inheritance," but *hereditavi*, "I have bestowed by inheritance." This could be good Latin, but the word would be more appropriate to the one who gives the inheritance than to the one who receives it; *hereditavi*, "I have bestowed by inheritance," is too much like *ditavi*, "I have enriched." The sense is better conveyed by using an expression such as "I have possessed by inheritance" or "I have acquired by inheritance"; and we should keep the form *by inheritance*, because *inheritance* is not the direct object of the verb.

If we then ask what the speaker acquired by inheritance, the answer is *your testimonies*. What does he mean to suggest? Surely that it was a grace conferred on him by his Father, something given him as the Father's heir, that he became God's witness and confessed God's testimonies; that is to say, it was by God's grace that he became a martyr for God and witnessed to the truth by martyrdom. Many people wanted to do this but were not able to; but among those who did manage it, all wanted it; for without the will to bear witness to God they would never have had the strength. Yet even this will was prepared in them by the

---

9. See Wis 3:1.
10. See Wis 7:16.

Lord.[11] Recognizing this, the psalmist testifies that he obtained the grace by inheritance and that its results would last *for eternity,* because the glory of the martyrs is not like the transient celebrity of people who chase vain things; it is the eternal glory of those who suffer for a short spell but reign everlastingly. The psalmist therefore continues, *For they are the joy of my heart.* In the body they meant pain, but for the heart vibrant joy.

8. Finally he adds, *I have bent my heart toward the observance of your ways of justice for eternity, because of the reward.* The psalmist who here declared, *I have bent my heart,* prayed earlier, *Bend my heart to your testimonies* (verse 36), to show us that this was the work both of divine grace and of his own will. But shall we really be observing God's ways of justice for eternity? The works we perform to meet the needs of our neighbors cannot be eternal, because the needs themselves will not be. If we perform them without love, they will be ineffective for justification. But if we perform them out of love, the love itself is eternal, and for love a reward has been prepared. The psalmist says that he has bent his heart toward the observance of God's ways of justice with a view to that reward, so that, loving eternally, he may deserve to possess eternally what he loves.

---

11. For the idea of God's preparing the will of his faithful, compare Exposition 11 of Psalm 118,6; Prv 8:35 (LXX); Phil 2:13.

Exposition 24 of Psalm 118

Twenty-fourth Sermon

Verses 113-114. Devotion to the law

1. The section of this psalm which by God's will we are to discuss begins with the words, *The iniquitous I have hated, but I have loved your law*. The psalmist does not say, "The iniquitous I have hated, but I have loved the just"; nor does he say, "Iniquity I have hated, but I have loved your law." First he declares, *The iniquitous I have hated*, and then he explains why: because *I have loved your law*. He expresses himself like this to show that what he hates in unjust persons is not their nature, which makes them human, but the iniquity that makes them enemies of the law he loves.

2. He continues, *You are my helper and supporter*. God is his helper in his good works and his supporter in his efforts to avoid evil. When he adds, *I have hoped above measure in your word*, he is speaking as a son of the promise.

Verse 115. How hard it is to study the law when constantly interrupted!

3. But what can the next verse mean? *Go away from me, you spiteful people, and then I will thoroughly explore the commandments of my God*. Observe that the speaker does not say, "And then I will carry out the commandments," but *I will thoroughly explore* them. He wants spiteful people to leave him alone, and he even drives them away by force, so that he may come to know God's commandments perfectly in a spirit of love. Malevolent persons give us plenty of practice in carrying out the commandments but distract us from any deep study of them. This happens not only when the ill-disposed persecute us and try to take us to court but also when they are compliant and flattering yet insistently demand that we engage in furthering their vicious, greedy business and spend our time on them. Or again, they harass weak people and force the victims to bring their cases to us. Yet we dare not say to such plaintiffs, *Tell me, fellow, who appointed me a judge or arbiter between you?* (Lk 12:14) for the apostle appointed ecclesiastical assessors to hear such cases and forbade Christians to litigate in the civil courts.[1] Even when those who appeal to us are not out to get their hands on other people's property but are seeking greedily to recover their

---

1. See 1 Cor 6:1-4.

own, we do not say to them, "Be on your guard against any kind of acquisitive-ness"; we hesitate to remind them of the man to whom the Lord said, *You fool: your life will be taken from you this very night; and then who will own what you have amassed?* (Lk 12:20) Even if we do say something like this, they do not go away and leave us alone; they insist and crowd in on us and plead and rant and pester, so that we are taken up with the things that matter to them rather than with exploring God's commandments, which matters to us.[2]

What weariness with the hordes of importunate people and what intense longing for the divine words wrung this cry from the psalmist, *Go away from me, you spiteful people, and then I will thoroughly explore the commandments of my God!* We are not speaking here about the obedient faithful who rarely trouble us with their secular disputes and willingly acquiesce in our decisions. May all these forgive our remarks, for they do not wear us out with their litigation; rather do they console us by their obedience. But with the other sort in mind, the ones who quarrel among themselves, who when they have plagued innocent people reject our ruling, who oblige us to waste time that ought to be spent on the things of God—with all these in mind, I say, we too must be allowed to cry out in words uttered by Christ's body, *Go away from me, you spiteful people, and then I will thoroughly explore the commandments of my God.*

Verses 116-117. The hope of being led to true life

4. He has swatted these flies away from the eyes of his heart, and now he turns to the Lord. He said a moment ago, *You are my helper and supporter; I have hoped in your word,* and now he extends his prayer: *Support[3] me according to your word, and I shall live; and do not disappoint me of my hope.* He has already addressed the Lord as his supporter,[4] and now he begs to be supported more and more efficaciously, and to be brought safely to that blessedness for the sake of which he endures so many hardships; for he is confident that there he will be more truly alive than he can be in this dream-like human existence. His words look to the future: *I shall live,* he says, implying that there is no real life in this death-ridden body; for the body is dead because of sin.[5] As we await the redemption of our bodies we are saved in hope, and as we hope for what we do not yet see, we wait for it in patience.[6] And our hope is not disappointed if God's charity is poured abroad in our hearts through the Holy Spirit who has been given to us.[7]

---

2. See Augustine's *The Work of Monks* 37 for similar complaints.
3. *Suscipe*; the word has rich overtones and can be variously translated. See the notes at Expositions of Psalms 45,11 and 83,9.
4. *Susceptor.*
5. See Rom 7:24; 8:10.
6. See Rom 8:23-25.
7. See Rom 5:5.

Begging for a yet more generous outpouring of the Spirit the psalmist cries out to the Father, *Do not disappoint me of my hope.*

5. And now he seems to hear the Lord silently answering him: "You do not wish to be disappointed of your hope? Then never give up pondering on my ways of justice." The psalmist knows how often such meditation is hindered by weariness or sickness in the soul, so he prays in reply, *Help me, and I shall be saved, and I will meditate unceasingly on your ways of justice.*

Verses 118-119. The source of sin is in evil thoughts

6. *You have spurned* (or, following the Greek more exactly, *reduced to nothing*) *all those who depart from your ways of justice because their thoughts are unjust.* He had good reason to plead in the preceding verse, *Help me, and I shall be saved, and I will meditate unceasingly on your ways of justice,* for God brings to nothing all those who abandon his ways of justice. Why do sinners abandon them? *Because their thoughts are unjust.* There, in the mind, both loyalty and desertion occur. All our actions, whether bad or good, proceed from our thoughts, and it is in a person's thoughts that he or she is deemed innocent or guilty. This is why scripture teaches, *Holy meditation will keep you safe* (Prv 2:11); and elsewhere it is written, *An inquiry will be instituted into the thoughts of a godless person* (Wis 1:9). The apostle's teaching is the same: *Their thoughts may either accuse or defend them* (Rom 2:15), he says. Where can anyone find happiness if he is unhappy in his thoughts? And how can he not be unhappy if he has been reduced to nothing? Iniquity is the most sterile of conditions. Another psalm spoke truly: *Let them be confounded, the unjust whose actions are worthless* (Ps 24:4(25:3)); their actions are futile because they have been brought to nothing.

7. The next verse of the psalm runs thus: *I have counted*[8] (or *considered*[9] or *reckoned*[10]) *all sinners on earth as violators of the law.* Our translators have had recourse to various words to represent the one Greek verb ἐλογιάμην. But the idea expressed in this verse is profound and must be examined more carefully in another address, if the Lord helps us. What I mean is this: after the words just quoted the psalm immediately adds, *Therefore I have always loved your testimonies,* which makes the matter still more profound,[11] for the apostle says, *The law brings anger,* and explains his statement by adding, *Where there is no law, there is no violation of it* (Rom 4:15). This proves that not everyone is a lawbreaker, because not everyone has the law. This fact he declares more plainly in another

---

8. *Deputavi.*

9. *Putavi.*

10. *Existimavi.*

11. Why it makes it still more profound is not entirely obvious in the present context, but Augustine develops his ideas in the next sermon. See in particular section 5 there.

passage: *Those who have sinned without the law will perish without the law* (Rom 2:12). In view of these texts, what can the psalm mean by saying, *I have counted all sinners on earth as violators of the law?*

It must suffice for the present merely to raise this question; we will discuss it, God willing, in another sermon. Otherwise our present discourse would be unduly prolonged, and then we would have to explain the matter in fewer words than are needed to make it fully intelligible.

Exposition 25 of Psalm 118

Twenty-fifth Sermon

Verse 119. How can Paul's teaching on law be reconciled with the psalm?

1. We must now address a difficult question, and see whether, through God's kindness, we can find the right way to understand a puzzling verse in this great psalm. *I have counted all sinners on earth as violators of the law*, it says, or rather *as violating the law*, for the Greek is παραβαίνοντας, not παραβάτας. So how are we to interpret this verse, in the face of the apostle's teaching that *where there is no law, there is no violation of it* (Rom 4:15)? The apostle said this when drawing a distinction between the law and the promises. The meaning of his statement can be gathered more fully from the lines that precede and follow it: *Not on the basis of law was the promise made to Abraham or his posterity, that he should inherit the world, but through the righteousness that comes from faith. If those who hold to the law are the heirs, faith is null and the promise is void; for law brings retribution, but where there is no law, there is no violation of it either. Therefore the promise was grounded on faith, so that under the dispensation of grace it may stand firm for all his posterity; not for that only which lives under the law, but for that also which shares the faith of Abraham, who is the father of us all.* (Rom 4:13-16) Why did the apostle speak so? Undoubtedly because he wanted to show that, without the grace of the promise, the law was not merely powerless to remove sin but even increased it. That is why he said in another passage, *The law entered stealthily that sin might abound.* But he immediately added, *Where sin abounded, grace abounded all the more* (Rom 5:20), because all sins are forgiven by grace, not only those committed where law is absent but also those committed under the law.

We must therefore recognize that the apostle does not reckon all sinners to be lawbreakers. He calls those who transgress the law violators of it, and those only; for, as he says, *Where there is no law, there is no violation of it.* According to the apostle, then, every violator of the law is a sinner, because he or she sins within the regime of law; but not every sinner is a lawbreaker, because some commit sins outside it, and *where there is no law, there is no violation of it.* Furthermore, if nobody ever sinned outside the scope of the law, the same apostle would not have said, *Those who have sinned without the law will perish without the law* (Rom 2:12).

But our psalm regards all sinners on earth as violators of the law, which means that there is no sin that does not involve lawbreaking; and since there is no violation of law where law is absent, the psalmist must think there cannot be any sin that does not fall within the scope of law. When he says, *I have counted all sinners on earth as violators of the law*, he means us to understand that there are no sinners, none whatever, who are not guilty of a breach of law. Yet in implying this he collides head-on with the apostle, who said, *Those who have sinned without the law will perish without the law*. According to Paul, there are sinners who are not violators of the law, because they have sinned outside the law, and *where there is no law, there is no violation of it*. But according to the psalmist, there is no sinner who cannot be charged with breach of law, for he reckons *all sinners on earth as violators of the law*. We must conclude, then, that in the psalmist's view no one sins outside the law, since *where there is no law, there is no violation of it*.

How can we reconcile the two views? Should we say, perhaps, that it is indeed true that in the absence of law there is no lawbreaking, but that it is untrue to say that anyone has ever sinned outside all regime of law? Or must we say that it is true indeed that some people have sinned outside the law, but untrue that where law is absent, violation of it is impossible? Yet the apostle says that some have sinned outside the law and also that, without law, law-breaking cannot occur; and both these statements must be true, because both were made by the apostle through whom Truth himself spoke. How, then, can we square this with the psalm, seeing that the same Truth undoubtedly spoke there too, saying, *I have counted all sinners on earth as violators of the law*? If we follow the psalm, we shall be challenged: "What has become of the people who, according to the apostle, have sinned outside the law? How can they be reckoned violators of the law if, according to the same apostle, there can be no breach of law where no law exists?"

Paul meant the Mosaic law

2. It is quite clear, however, that when the apostle said, *Those who have sinned without the law will perish without the law*, he was talking about the law which God gave through his servant Moses to his people Israel. The context puts the meaning of his words beyond doubt. He was arguing about the status of Jews and Greeks, these latter being the uncircumcised; and he called them people without the law because they had not received the law which the Jews boasted of having been given. That boasting was what prompted the apostle to say. *You bear the name of Jew, and take your stand on the law, and boast of your God* (Rom 2:17). Now look carefully at how he builds up the argument which leads him to his assertion that *those who have sinned without the law will perish*

without the law. It goes like this: *Anger and wrath, tribulation and distress upon every human soul whose deeds are evil, the Jew first, but also the Greek; but glory and honor and peace upon everyone who does good, the Jew first, but also the Greek; for God has no favorites* (Rom 2:8-11). He then makes the statement that is so difficult to reconcile with what our psalm has said: *Those who have sinned without the law will perish without the law; and those who have sinned under the law will be judged by the law* (Rom 2:12). He obviously means us to understand that the latter group are Jews, the former Greeks. But at the moment he is considering the situation of the Jews, and he demonstrates that they, as much as the Gentiles, are in sin, because he wants to bring both to confess their need of grace. This is why he says, *There is no distinction: all have sinned, and are in need of the glory of God; and they are justified freely by his grace, through the redemption effected in Christ Jesus* (Rom 3:22-24). When he asserts that all are sinners, whom does he mean, if not the Jews and the Greeks, of whom he has just said that there is nothing to choose between them? A few lines before this he said, *We have argued that Jews and Greeks are all under sin* (Rom 3:9). He has demonstrated that *those who have sinned without the law* (outside the law of which the Jews boasted) *will perish without the law, and those who have sinned under the law* (the Jews) *will be judged by the law.* They will be saved from perishing only by believing in him who came to seek what would have perished.[1]

3. There have been some expositors, even Catholic ones, who through insufficient attention have misinterpreted these words of the apostle, taking them to mean that, while those who have sinned outside the law will indeed perish, those who have sinned under the law do not perish, but are judged only. These are to be purified by temporary punishment, according to such expositors, like the hypothetical person of whom the apostle says, *He himself will be saved indeed, though it be through fire* (1 Cor 3:15). But to understand the latter text in the right way we must attribute this person's eventual salvation to the fact that he or she is founded on Christ. Paul has just said, *I laid the foundation like a skilled master-builder, and another imposes the superstructure. But let everyone look to what he builds on the foundation. No one can lay any other foundation than that which is laid, which is Christ Jesus.* (1 Cor 3:10-11) And so he goes on, until he reaches the place where he says that the person who is saved by fire is one who builds on that foundation not in gold, silver, or precious stones but in wood, hay, and straw, yet has not scorned the foundation or abandoned it after accepting it. Such a person is entrapped by all his carnal pleasures and yields to them; but when the critical moment arrives, and he must choose between abandoning them and abandoning Christ, he prefers Christ, the foundation, to all the rest. If at that juncture he does not give preference to Christ, it shows that Christ is not his

---

1. See Lk 19:10.

foundation.[2] Obviously the foundation of a building has priority over all the parts added later.

So, according to some interpreters, the people of whom scripture says that *they will be judged by the law* do not perish. Such interpreters cannot, in my view, have thought of them as having anything other than Christ as their foundation. The trouble with their interpretation is simply that they have not given enough attention to the fact that the apostle was here speaking of Jews who are adrift from Christ, the foundation, as we have pointed out and as scripture plainly indicates. Would any Christian propound the view that a Jew who does not believe in Christ does not perish, but is only judged? Did not Christ himself testify that he had been sent to the Jewish people for the sake of the lost sheep among them?[3] Did he not warn them that on the day of judgment it would go less hard for the Sodomites (who clearly perished outside the law) than for a town in Judea which did not believe in him, though he had worked such mighty miracles there?[4]

But the natural law is available to all human beings, Gentiles and Jews alike

4. When the apostle said that Gentile nations did not have the law, he was referring to the law which God gave through Moses to the people of Israel but not to other peoples. That much is clear. How, then, are we to take the statement in our psalm, *I deemed[5] all sinners on earth violators of the law*, unless we refer it not to the law given through Moses but to some other law, according to which sinners even among other nations are rightly accounted law-breakers? For *where there is no law, there is no violation of it*. What can this other law be? Surely that mentioned by the apostle: *The Gentiles who do not have the law act by nature as the law requires, for though they do not have the law, they are a law to themselves* (Rom 2:14). The phrase, *they do not have the law*, means that they are outside the Mosaic law and will perish outside it; but the phrase, *they are a law to themselves*, means that there is good reason to reckon all sinners on earth violators of law. No one injures another without at the same time hoping the same will not be done to himself, and in this respect he transgresses the law of nature; the very fact that he does not want to suffer the fate he inflicts on someone else means that he cannot plead ignorance of the natural law.

Was this natural law not present in the people of Israel? Certainly it was, for they too were human. They could no more have been without the natural law

---

2. See Exposition 2 of Psalm 29,9 and Exposition of Psalm 37,3 for similar interpretations of this passage in 1 Corinthians.
3. See Mt 15:24.
4. See Mt 10:15.
5. He uses yet another verb this time: *aestimavi*.

than they could have been alien to the human condition itself. But the divine law turned them into still worse lawbreakers, because by the divine law the natural law was established, or amplified, or put on a firmer footing.

Not even babies are exempt from the charge of lawbreaking, but God's testimonies are good news

5. Now it is not unreasonable to include babies also with all sinners on earth, for they too are demonstrably involved in violation of the law through the bonds of original sin, which makes them lawbreakers like Adam. He committed the primordial breach of law, after a law had been imposed on him in paradise. In view of the bonds of original sin, all sinners on earth, all without exception, are to be reckoned violators of the law. *All have sinned, and are in need of the glory of God* (Rom 3:23). The grace of our Savior found all guilty of breaking the law, some more, some less; for the better a person knows the law, the less excuse there is for sin, and the less excuse there is for his sin, the more flagrant is his violation of the law. Nothing therefore was left for humanity except that God's righteousness should come to its rescue: not its own, but God's, the righteousness conferred by God. This is why the apostle says, *Through the law comes consciousness of sin* (Rom 3:20): not the removal of sin, but only consciousness of it. He continues, *But now, independently of law, God's justice has been manifested; the testimony of the law and the prophets support it* (Rom 3:21); and this is the very reason why the psalmist went on to say, *Therefore I have loved your testimonies.* He seems to imply: the law turned all sinners on earth into law-breakers, whether we think of the law imposed in paradise, or the law instilled into human nature, or the law promulgated in writing. But that is why *I have loved your testimonies,* the testimonies enshrined in your law, which tell of your grace, bidding me look in myself for no righteousness of my own but only yours. The function of law is to send us to grace.[6] Not only does law bear witness to the justice of God to be revealed outside the law; it also turns those who know the law into law-breakers, to such a point that the letter is death-dealing.[7] In either case, the fear it arouses forces us to flee to the life-giving Spirit, through whom every kind of sin is blotted out and charity is breathed into us, that we may act aright. *Therefore,* says the psalmist, *I have loved your testimonies.*

Some codices add the word *always,* others do not. But if it is correct to read *always,* we must understand it to mean "as long as this life lasts"; for it is in this life that we need the testimonies of the law and the prophets, which witness to the righteousness of God whereby we are justified; and it is in this life that our testi-

---

6. *Lex . . . ad hoc prodest, ut mittat ad gratiam*: a lapidary formula summing up the teaching of Paul and Augustine himself on the significance of law in God's saving dispensation.
7. See 2 Cor 3:6.

mony too is required, that witness borne by the martyrs who gave up the very life
they lived here.

Verse 120. Crucified with Christ

6. The psalmist has come to know the grace of God, which alone frees us from
the guilt of law-breaking incurred through our knowledge of law. Now he prays,
Pierce my flesh with fear of you. The Greek expressed the idea in a single verb,
καθήλωσον, but some of our translators rendered this accurately by using two
words, *confige clavis,* "pierce with nails." Other translators, endeavoring to
match a single Greek word with a single Latin word, wrote only *confige,*
"pierce," omitting *clavis,* "with nails," but in so doing they did not adequately
capture the meaning. In our Latin word, *confige,* the idea of "nails" is not
present, whereas καθήλωσον is unintelligible without reference to nails. It is
correct, therefore, to translate it with two Latin words, *confige clavis.*

What are we to make of this prayer? We must associate it with the apostle's
aspiration, *Far be it from me to boast, save in the cross of our Lord Jesus Christ,
through whom*[8] *the world has been crucified to me, and I to the world* (Gal 6:14).
Again he says, *With Christ I have been nailed to the cross; and now I live my own
life no longer; it is Christ who lives in me* (Gal 2:19-20). This is another way of
saying, "The righteousness in me is not my own righteousness obtained by the
law, for the law only turned me into a violator of it. What is in me is God's righteousness, that which is from God, not from myself. The 'I' who lives is not
myself but Christ, *who has been made for us by God wisdom, and justice, and
sanctification, and redemption; as it is written, Let anyone who boasts boast in
the Lord*" (1 Cor 1:30-31; 2 Cor 10:17). Elsewhere Paul says, *Those who belong
to Christ have crucified their flesh, with its passions and desires* (Gal 5:24).
Observe that in this saying of the apostle it is Christ's disciples who have themselves *crucified their flesh,* whereas in our psalm God is entreated to do this:
Pierce my flesh with fear of you. This difference teaches us that even our own
right action is to be ascribed to the grace of God, for he is at work in us, inspiring
both will and work, for his own good purpose.[9]

7. But what is the logic of the next phrase? After praying, *Pierce my flesh with
fear of you,* the psalmist added, *for I have been fearful of your judgments.* If he
had been afraid already, and was still afraid, why did he continue to pray that
God would crucify his fleshly self with fear of him? Should we think, perhaps,
that he wanted his fear to increase to the point where it would be strong enough to

---

8. In the original Greek this pronoun could refer either to Christ or to the cross, as both are
masculine: "through whom" or "through which." In Augustine's Latin it can refer only to
Christ.
9. See Phil 2:13.

induce him to crucify his carnal urges and desires? His prayer then would mean, "Bring the fear of you to perfection in me, though I already do fear your judgments."

But there is another, deeper sense which we must tease out by searching the heart of this scriptural passage, insofar as God enables us. *Pierce my flesh with fear of you; for I have been fearful of your judgments*, prays the psalmist. This is what he means: "Let my carnal desires be curbed by that chaste fear of you which abides for ever.[10] I was indeed fearful of your judgments when the law, itself impotent to give me righteousness, threatened me with punishment, but that is not enough." When charity is made perfect it casts out the fear of punishment,[11] for charity sets us free, inspiring us to act not out of fear of punishment but out of delight in goodness. The kind of fear which makes us dread being punished, but instills no love of righteousness, is a servile fear; and because it is carnal, it is useless for crucifying the flesh. The will to sin remains unaffected and breaks out into action wherever one hopes to escape the consequences. If there is reason to believe that punishment will follow, the will to sin lives on, hidden but undiminished. A person controlled by this kind of fear would like to do what the law forbids and is peeved because it is forbidden, because he is not spiritually delighted by the good which the law exists to serve but carnally terrified by the penalty it threatens.

Very different is the chaste fear inspired by charity, which casts out servile fear. Charity dreads committing sin, even if there is no prospect of punishment. Indeed, it cannot think of impunity as even possible, since its love for righteousness is so strong that it regards sin itself as a punishment. The flesh is crucified by this fear, because carnal pleasures, forbidden but hardly kept at bay by the letter of the law, are overpowered by pleasure in spiritual well-being.[12] When spiritual joy grows to perfection, victory over carnal lusts is complete. *Pierce my flesh with fear of you; for I have been fearful of your judgments*, prays the psalmist. Grant me chaste fear, he means, for it was to this that the fear instilled by the law, my pedagogue,[13] led me. Terror-stricken by the law, I was fearful of your judgments.

---

10. See Ps 18:10(19:9).

11. See 1 Jn 4:18.

12. This sentence contains an Augustinian assonance not reproducible in English: carnal pleasures which *vetantur potiusquam vitantur . . . vincuntur.*

13. See Gal 3:24.

Exposition 26 of Psalm 118

Twenty-sixth Sermon

Verse 121. True judgment is just judgment; pray against temptation

1. We now undertake to deal with the verses in this great psalm which begin, *I have wrought judgment and justice; do not hand me over to those who harm me*. It is hardly surprising that he has acted in accordance with judgment and justice, for in the preceding verses he has been begging that his flesh—by which he means carnal lusts—be pierced by the fear of God: chaste fear, obviously. Such carnal lusts distort our judgment.

Now in common parlance judgment may be either right or wrong; it is that faculty in human beings concerning which we are warned in the gospel, *Do not judge by appearances, but form a right judgment* (Jn 7:24). But in the present context the term "judgment" is used in such a way as to imply that only just judgment deserves the name. Were this not the case, it would not have been enough to say, *I have wrought judgment*; the psalmist would have needed to say, "I have wrought honest judgment." The Lord Jesus was using the word in the same way as does the psalm when he said, *You have neglected the weightier matters of the law: judgment, and mercy, and good faith* (Mt 23:23); here too it is assumed that judgment would not be judgment at all if it were perverse. The word is used with this assumption in many passages of the divine scriptures; for example, *I will sing to you of your mercy and judgment, O Lord* (Ps 100(101):1), and again in Isaiah, *I looked to it for the work of judgment, but its work was only iniquity* (Is 5:7). He does not say, "I looked to it for the work of righteous judgment"; he takes it for granted that it can be called judgment only if it is just. If unjust, it is not judgment.

No such ambiguity attends the word "justice." We are not accustomed to speak of good justice or bad justice, as we sometimes do speak of good or bad judgment. If it is justice, it is automatically good. The conventions of speech allow us to talk of good judgment or bad judgment in some instances, as also of a good judge and a bad judge; but we never speak of good justice and bad justice, or of a good just person and a bad just person. If someone is just, it immediately implies that he or she is good.

Justice is an important virtue in the mind, and one specially worthy of commendation, but there is no need to discuss it at length now. Judgment (when the term is used in the strict sense, to denote only good judgment) is this virtue's mode of operation. When a person is imbued with justice he or she judges rightly; or rather, strictly speaking, anyone who is imbued with justice judges. That is enough, because if he does not judge rightly, he is not judging.

However, the word "justice" in this context signifies not the virtue itself but its work; for who creates justice in human beings? He only, who justifies the godless; that is to say, he who by his grace turns the impious into the just. Hence the apostle says, *They are justified freely by his grace* (Rom 3:24). We conclude, therefore, that as the work of grace is to create justice in just persons, so will those just persons act justly, manifesting the work of the justice they have within them.

2. *I have wrought judgment and justice, O Lord, do not hand me over to those who harm me.* Since I have judged justly, he means, do not deliver me to those who persecute me on this account. Some codices make this sense explicit by reading, *Do not hand me over to those who persecute me.* The Greek has τοῖς ἀντιδικοῦσι, and some have translated this as *those who harm me*, others as *those who persecute me*, others again as *those who traduce me*. But I am surprised that none of the codices on which I could easily lay hands had the reading, *my adversaries*; this is strange, because the Greek ἀντίδικος is incontestably represented by the Latin *adversarius*, "adversary." When the psalmist prays not to be delivered by the Lord to his adversaries, what is he asking if not what we ask in prayer when we say, *Lead us not into temptation* (Mt 6:3)? It is this adversary that Paul has in mind when he says, *I was afraid that the tempter might have tempted you* (1 Th 3:5). God hands over to the tempter anyone whom he himself abandons. The tempter cannot deceive a person whom God does not abandon; to human beauty in someone like that, God in his kindly will adds strength.[1] But from one who boasts, *I shall be unmoved for ever* (Ps 29:7(30:6)), God turns his face away, and the creature is dismayed, being shown up to itself.

When, therefore, a person has crucified the flesh through chaste fear of God, is corrupted by no carnal allurement, practices judgment, and deals justly, such a one should pray not to be delivered to his adversaries, lest through fear of suffering a horrible fate he yield to the persecutors and commit horrible deeds instead. Pray he must, because God who grants him the victory over concupiscence, so that he is not dragged away by sensuality, grants him also strong, steadfast endurance, so that he is not broken by pain. Of the Lord it is said, *He will give sweetness* (Ps 84:13(85:12)), but of the Lord also, *My patience comes from him* (Ps 61:6(62:5)).

---

1. See Ps 29:8(30:7).

Verses 122-123. The humility of the cross

3. *Take your servant into good; let not the proud slander me.* They are pushing me to make me fall into evil, but you, for your part, take me into good. Instead of the dative, *non calumnientur mihi*, some Latin translators have used the accusative, *non calumnientur me*, because they followed the Greek literally, though this usage is less familiar in Latin. But possibly *non calumnientur me* implies the idea, "Let them not trap me with their slanders."

4. The slanders of the proud are many, and by all of them Christian humility is disparaged. If we are thinking of proud human beings, the greatest slander is probably that by which we are despised for worshiping a dead man. Christian humility is powerfully brought home to us by the death of Christ and is enjoined on us from heaven. This particular slander is common to both kinds of unbelievers, Jews and pagans. The heretics too have their favorite calumnies, each proper to each heresy. And the schismatics have theirs. It is pride that severs all these people from the organic unity of Christ's members. But how monstrous and flagrant was the devil's slandering of a certain just man! *Job hardly worships the Lord for nothing, does he?* asked the devil (Jb 1:9). The calumnies of all these proud slanderers are like so many varieties of snake's venom, and all are robbed of their power when we gaze with very attentive and very loving devotion on Christ crucified. To foreshadow him, Moses was directed by our merciful God to raise up in the wilderness an image of a snake on a pole,[2] so that the likeness of sinful flesh[3] which was to be crucified in Christ might be displayed in advance. As we contemplate his healing cross we rid ourselves of all the poison injected by the slanders of the proud. Even the psalmist was in some sense gazing at the cross with great intensity when he said, *My eyes grew weary with looking for your salvation, and for the edict of your justice.* Through the likeness of sinful flesh assumed by Christ, God made him into sin for us, that we might become the justice of God in him.[4] The psalmist tells us that his eyes grew faint with longing for this edict of God's justice as he waited for it ardently and thirstily; aware of human weakness in himself he yearns for divine grace in Christ.

Verses 124-125. Pray always for deeper understanding

5. With this in mind the psalmist continues, *Act toward your servant according to your mercy*, not according to any righteousness on my part. *And*

---

2. See Num 21:8-9.
3. See Rom 8:3.
4. See 2 Cor 5:21.

teach me your ways of justice: those ways by which God makes people just, not anything they achieve by themselves.

6. *I am your servant*, for when I tried to be my own free person rather than your servant, it did me no good. *Give me understanding, that I may know your testimonies*. We must never cease to offer this prayer, for it is not enough to have received understanding once and learned God's testimonies once; we need to keep on receiving it all the time and to be drinking continually from the fountain of eternal light. As a person grows in understanding, so do God's testimonies become known more and more.

Verses 126-128. Love for the commandments in the era of grace

7. *It is time for the Lord to act*: this is the reading in most codices, though a few have, "It is time to act, O Lord."[5] What time did he mean, and what sort of action did he want the Lord to take? Surely the kind of action he prayed for two verses back: *Act toward your servant according to your mercy*. This is the action of the Lord for which the time has come. What else could it be but the grace which in its due time was to be revealed in Christ? The apostle speaks of this due time: *When the fullness of time had come, God sent his Son* (Gal 4:4); and elsewhere he adduces prophetic testimony to indicate the time of grace: *At the acceptable time I have heard you, and on the day of salvation I have helped you. See, now is the acceptable time; lo, this is the day of salvation.* (Is 49:8; 2 Cor 6:2)

But the psalmist adds another phrase which seems to suggest why this is the right time for the Lord to act. *They have fragmented your law*, he says, as though the Lord's action is needed against proud persons who have frittered it away, persons ignorant of God's righteousness and minded to set up their own, refusing to be subject to God's righteousness.[6] What else does *they have fragmented your law* mean if not, "By sinfully transgressing, they have failed to keep the law in its integrity"? It was necessary for a law to be given to proud people who put all their reliance on their own free will, so that when they found they had transgressed it they might be stung by remorse and humbled and thereafter cast off dependence on the law and run by faith toward the grace that could help them. The time when the law had been fragmented was therefore the time for the mercy of God to be sent to us through the only-begotten Son. The law sneaked in that sin might abound. By sin the law was broken to pieces, and so at this most opportune time Christ came, so that where sin abounded, grace might abound even more.[7]

---

5. *Tempus faciendi, Domine*, instead of *tempus faciendi Domino*.
6. See Rom 10:3.
7. See Rom 5:20.

8. *Therefore I have loved your commandments more than gold and topaz*, continues the psalmist. The effect of grace is that God's commandments, which could not possibly be implemented by fear, are fulfilled by love; for through grace *the charity of God has been poured out into our hearts through the Holy Spirit who has been given us* (Rom 5:5). This is why the Lord himself declared, *I came not to annul the law, but to bring it to fullness* (Mt 5:17); and the apostle concurred: *The fullness of the law is love* (Rom 13:10). So the commandments are prized *more than gold and topaz*, or, as another psalm puts it, *more than gold and the most precious gem* (Ps 18:11(19:10)), for people certainly call topaz a very precious gem.

The Israelites, however, did not understand the grace that lay hidden in the Old Covenant; it was as though a veil came between it and their minds, just as when they were not strong enough to look at the face of Moses.[8] Accordingly they put their efforts into obeying God's commands with a view to an earthly and material reward; but they did not carry them out because what they were setting their hearts on was not the commandments but something extraneous. The commandments were therefore not patterns for willing service but rather burdens laid on reluctant shoulders.

When the commandments themselves are loved more dearly than gold and very precious stones, any earthly reward appears tawdry, for no human goods can in any respect compare with these good commandments whereby human beings themselves become good.

9. *Therefore I was corrected, in alignment with all your commandments.* Certainly I was corrected, because I loved them and clung in love to those straight and true commands in order to become straight myself. The psalmist's next statement indicates the effect of his correction: *Every crooked way I hate.* How could it be otherwise? How could anyone in love with the straight way not hate the crooked one? If he had set his love on gold and precious stones, he would undoubtedly hate anything that could damage his treasures. So too, because he loves God's commandments, he hates the way of iniquity, hates it as he would hate a huge rock encountered on a voyage at sea, on which he must inevitably see his precious goods shipwrecked. But anyone who sails on the wood of the cross, with the divine commandments as cargo, steers well clear of such a rock and so avoids disaster.

---

8. See Ex 34:30.33-35; 2 Cor 3:13.

Exposition 27 of Psalm 118

Twenty-seventh Sermon

Verse 129. Is it presumptuous to explore God's testimonies?

1. With the Lord's help we must now discuss these words of the psalm, *Your testimonies are wonderful; that is why my soul has explored them carefully.* But who can enumerate, even in a general fashion, the testimonies God has borne to himself? The sky and the earth, his visible and his invisible creations, bear witness in their own way to his goodness and greatness. In every species of creature nature pursues its regular course as rapacious time rolls on; creatures are time-bound and mortal, and we are so used to them that we take little notice, yet the familiar sequence of natural changes, when considered thoughtfully by a devout mind, bears witness to the Creator. Is there any single element in these processes that is not wonderful, if we measure each one not by our habituation to it but by reason? And if we venture to embrace them all in one contemplative intuition, do we not cry out with the prophet, *I have pondered your works, and trembled* (Hb 3:2)? Yet the speaker in the psalm is not afraid; on the contrary, he points to the wonderful character of God's works as the very reason why he had to explore them so carefully. After acknowledging, *Your testimonies are wonderful*, he continues, *that is why my soul has explored them carefully.* He seems to hint that the difficulty of examining them with such care made him all the more curious; for when the causes of something are particularly obscure, it is the more wonderful for that.

2. Well then, suppose we come across someone who tells us that his motive for closely examining God's testimonies is that they are wonderful; and suppose we are aware that all creation, both what we can see and what we cannot see, is full of God's testimonies, should we not put a restraining hand on our inquirer, advising him, *Seek not what is above you, and do not scrutinize loftier matters; but let your mind run constantly on what the Lord has commanded you* (Sir 3:22)? Suppose further that he replies by pointing out, "But the very things the Lord has commanded us, the things you order me to think about, are wonderful testimonies to him. They proclaim him to be the Lord because he issues the commands and proclaim him to be both good and great by the character of what he commands." Surely then we shall not be so officious as to discourage this seeker from careful study of God's testimonies? Shall we not rather urge him to pursue his study assiduously and to spend on so great an enterprise all the effort

he can? Or are we to say that, while God's commandments do indeed bear testimony to his goodness, they are not anything to provoke our wonder? After all, we might say, what is wonderful about a good Lord ordering good conduct?

Such a view is wrong. There is indeed something to marvel at in this, something that demands our scrutiny to find out why it should be so. A good God has issued good commands, yet he gave his good law to people who could not be given life by it. Nor could they gain any righteousness whatever from that good law. *If a law capable of giving life had been granted to us, then of course righteousness would have been obtainable through the law* (Gal 3:21). Why was it given, then—a law impotent to give life, one from which no justification could follow? This is indeed something to wonder at. It is cause for real amazement.

These are the wonders in the testimonies God has borne to himself, and this is why the psalmist's soul explored them carefully, for not on their account could he be admonished, *Do not scrutinize loftier matters; but let your mind run constantly on what the Lord has commanded you* (Sir 3:22). These are the very things that the Lord has commanded us, and we have a corresponding duty to think about them continually. All the more reason, then, why we should see what his soul explored, and what he discovered.

Verses 130-133. The "little ones" keep the law through the Spirit, the Breath of God

3. *The unfolding of your words gives light, and imparts understanding to little ones*. What is meant by *little ones*? Surely people who are humble and weak. Be not proud, then, and do not rely on your own strength, because it amounts to nothing. If you are humble you will come to understand why a good God gave a good law, which yet was powerless to bring anyone to life. This is why it was given: to turn you from a great person into a little one, and to prove you incapable of keeping the law by any strength or virtue of your own, so that in dire need of help you would in your poverty run to grace for refuge, and cry, *Have mercy on me, Lord, because I am weak* (Ps 6:3(2)). The little one who speaks in the psalm understood through his exploration the truth that Paul demonstrated—Paul, the least of the apostles,[1] so indeed a little one himself—that a law powerless to give life was given because *scripture included all things under sin, so that through faith in Jesus Christ the promise might be given to believers* (Gal 3:22).

Yes, Lord, deal with us in this way, O merciful Lord: give commands that cannot be fulfilled, or, rather, that can be fulfilled only through your grace, so that when men and women have failed to implement them by their own powers, *every self-justifying mouth may be shut* (Rom 3:19) and no one think himself great. Let all be little, and let the whole world be held guilty in your presence, for

---

1. See 1 Cor 15:9. A pun on the name Paul, "small."

no mortal shall be justified in your sight, because through the law comes only consciousness of sin. But now, independently of law, God's justice has been manifested, and the testimony of the law and the prophets supports it. (Rom 3:20-21) These are your wonderful testimonies, explored by the soul of the little one in the psalm; and the only reason why he discovered them was that he was humbled and became small. Who keeps your commandments as they should be kept, through faith expressing itself in love,[2] unless that very love is poured abroad in his heart by the Holy Spirit?[3]

4. Our "little one" confesses this directly: *I opened my mouth and drew breath, because I longed for your commands.* What else was he longing for, if not to observe God's commandments? But a weak person has no means of performing mighty feats, nor could a little one achieve great things; so he opened his mouth to confess that he could not do it of himself, and he drew in the Breath that would empower him to do it. He opened his mouth to ask, seek, and knock;[4] he thirsted, and he drank in the good Spirit, through whom he would be able to do what he could not do unaided: observe the command that was holy, and just, and good.[5] If we, evil as we are, know how to give good gifts to our children, how much more will our Father in heaven give his good Spirit to those who ask him?[6] It is not those impelled by their own spirit, but all those moved by the Spirit of God, who are children of God.[7] This does not mean they do nothing but that they are moved by the good Spirit in what they do, for otherwise they might be active indeed but do nothing good. The more generously the good Spirit is bestowed on someone by the Father, the more he or she becomes a good son or daughter of God.

5. Our psalmist is still making his petitions. He has already opened his mouth and drawn in the Breath, but he is still knocking at his Father's door and seeking. He is drinking, but the sweeter the taste as he drinks, the more burning is his thirst. Listen to the words of this thirsty petitioner: *Look upon me, and have mercy on me, according to your wonted judgment on those who love your name.* According to the judgment you have already pronounced on those who love your name, he means, because you loved them first, in order that they might love you. This is the teaching of the apostle John: *We love God,* he says; and then, as though someone had asked what made him love, he adds, *because he first loved us* (1 Jn 4:19).

6. Look what the psalmist asks for, and asks in the plainest terms: *Guide my steps according to your word, and let no iniquity get the better of me.* What else

2. See Gal 5:6.
3. See Rom 5:5.
4. See Mt 7:7.
5. See Rom 7:12.
6. See Lk 11:13.
7. See Rom 8:14.

is he saying, if not, "Make me straight and free, as you have promised"? The more God's charity is sovereign in a person, the less dominion does iniquity have over him. If this is so, what is the psalmist asking in the present verse, if not that by God's gift he may love God? By loving God he also loves himself, so that he may love his neighbor as himself with the love that leads to salvation. And on these two precepts the whole law and the prophets depend.[8] What else does the psalmist's prayer amount to but a petition that the commandments God imposes by his authority he may cause to be fulfilled by his aid?

Verses 134-135. Obedience to the law when falsely accused

7. But what does he mean by his next request? *Rescue me from the slanders of others, and I will keep your commandments*, he prays. If the allegations people make against him are true, they are not slanders; but if they are false, why does he want to be delivered from slanders—that is, false charges—which can do him no harm? A false accusation, a calumny, does not make a person guilty, except perhaps in the view of a human judge. Where God is the judge, no one is hurt by a false allegation, for it is imputed to the one who made it, not to the one against whom it is made.

Should we perhaps interpret the verse as a prefiguration of the Church's prayer and of the prayer of the whole Christian people, delivered as it is now from the accusations by which Christians throughout the world used to be harassed? But that is not the Church's motive for keeping God's commandments, is it? Did not the holy people, when beset by tribulations, keep God's commands all the more gloriously amid those calumnies that used to boil all around it, when it refused to yield to its persecutors and commit acts of blasphemy? Of course it did.

More probably the request, *Rescue me from the slanders of others, and I will keep your commandments*, is to be understood as follows: Pour your Spirit into me, and strengthen me, so that my slandering enemies may not overcome me with their terrors and lead me away from your commandments to their evil practices. If you do this for me, if you endow me with patient endurance so that I am not intimidated by the false accusations they hurl at me, you will have rescued me from their slanders, and then I will indeed keep your commandments, slanders notwithstanding.

8. *Make your face shine upon your servant*, he now prays; that is, manifest your presence by coming to my help and giving support. *And teach me your ways of justice*: clearly he means, "Teach me in such a way that I may put them into practice." Another psalm expresses this more plainly: *Teach me, that I may do your will* (Ps 142(143):10). If people hear but do not act on what they hear, they

---

8. See Mt 22:40.

cannot be deemed to have learned, even if what they hear remains fixed in their memories. The Word himself testified, *Everyone who has heard the Father, and learned, comes to me* (Jn 6:45). One who does not act according to what he hears—does not "come," that is—has not truly learned.

Verse 136. Tears of repentance

9. The psalmist now calls to mind his painful repentance after his transgression. *My eyes ran down freshets of water*, he recalls, *because they did not keep your law*. My eyes did not keep it, he is saying; the reading in some codices makes this explicit: *Because I did not keep your law*. By *freshets of water* he means floods of tears. He says his eyes ran down them, using the idiom we might use in saying, "My feet descended the mountains," without needing to say, "on the mountains" or "by mountain paths." Similarly we can say that someone "came down the ladder," without explaining that he came down by the ladder; or that "he swam the river," without specifying that he swam in the river.[9] Appropriately he says that his eyes *ran down,* suggesting that he descended in humility. Some people had ascended, raising themselves up through obstinate pride and self-satisfaction. Thinking themselves elevated and important, they attempted to set up a righteousness of their own, ignorant of God's righteousness.[10] But they grew weary and embarrassed at their violations of the law, so they came down from their high station in tears to seek and obtain God's righteousness through repentance.

Some codices read *surpassed* instead of *ran down*; this would be a hyperbolic statement by the psalmist that his eyes outdid springs of water (for that is how we would have to take *freshets of water* in this case). He means that he wept more copiously than springs gush with water. Why should anyone weep so bitterly over failure to keep the law? Surely in order to obtain the grace which will efface the penitent's iniquity and strengthen the believer's resolve.

---

9. Literally, "He descended the pool"; the idiom that Augustine uses in Latin has been adjusted to English usage.
10. See Rom 10:3.

Exposition 28 of Psalm 118

Twenty-eighth Sermon

Verses 137-138. God is just when he condemns

1. The singer of this psalm has recalled in the preceding verse, *My eyes ran down freshets of water, because they did not keep your law*; he has testified to the copious tears he shed over his transgression. Now he goes on to explain why he had to weep so bitterly and grievously over his sin. *You are just, O Lord, and you judge with equity. You have imposed just commands as testimonies to yourself, and insisted on your truth.* For everyone who sins this justice of God is to be feared: his upright judgment and his truth are terrible, because all who are condemned by divine decree are condemned by his justice. No condemned person whatever has any grounds for appeal against a just God. There is good reason for a penitent's tears, for if his heart were condemned impenitent, such condemnation would be absolutely just. The psalm is right to call God's testimonies justice, for indeed God proves himself just by commanding us to act justly. And this justice of God is also his truth, for he makes himself known to us by bearing this witness to himself.

Verse 139. Jealousy for God

2. What can the psalmist mean by his next words? *My jealousy made me waste away*, he says; or, as other codices have it, *your jealousy.* Some codices read *jealousy for your house,* and follow this not with *made me waste away* but with *consumed me.* I think this latter reading was thought to be an emendation; it is obviously imported from another psalm, where we find, *Jealousy for your house devoured me* (Ps 68:10(69:9)), a text which, as we know, is quoted in the gospel.[1] But in any case, *made me waste away* is similar in meaning to *consumed me.*

With regard to the difference between *my jealousy* and *your jealousy,* the former, which is the reading of most codices, raises no difficulty. What is remarkable about a person wasting away under the influence of his own jealousy? The alternative reading offered by some, *your jealousy,* suggests the jealousy felt by someone on God's behalf, not on his own; but that can still

---

1. See Jn 2:17.

reasonably be called *my jealousy*. Of what else is the apostle speaking when he warns, *I am jealous about you with the jealousy of God* (2 Cor 11:2)? In saying, *I am jealous about you*, whose jealousy is he manifesting if not his own? But when he speaks of *the jealousy of God*, he shows that it is not on his own behalf that he is jealous but on God's. God inspires this jealousy by his Spirit in his faithful, for it is the jealousy of love, not of spite. What anxiety prompted the apostle to speak as he did?[2] *I have prepared you for presentation to your one husband, Christ, as a chaste virgin*, he says. *But I am afraid that, just as the serpent seduced Eve by his cunning, so too your minds may be led astray, and fall away from that simplicity and chastity which you have in Christ.* (2 Cor 11:2-3) Jealousy for God's house was consuming him, but he was jealous on Christ's behalf, not his own. It is the bridegroom who is jealous on his own account over his bride; the bridegroom's friend has no business to be jealous on his own behalf, but only for the bridegroom.[3]

The psalmist's jealousy is therefore to be commended, for he indicates the motive for it: *Because my enemies have forgotten your words*. We gather from this that his enemies were returning evil for good. While he was so intensely and ardently jealous over them on God's behalf that he could say his jealousy was causing him to waste away, they were showing their hostility for this very reason: that he wanted them to love God. His jealousy sprang from love. He had himself been God's enemy but was now reconciled to him, and he was not ungrateful for the grace of God that had effected his reconciliation. So now he loved even his enemies and was jealous about them on God's account, groaning and wasting away because they had forgotten God's words.

Verses 140-144. The faith of the younger son

3. The mention of God's words reminds him of the source of that fire of love that burned within him: *Your word burns fiercely, and your servant loves it*. He has every reason to be jealous over the impenitent hearts of his enemies, who have forgotten God's words, for he burned with longing to bring them back to that divine word which he himself loved so passionately.

4. *I am younger, and despised; but I have not forgotten your ways of justice*, he says, not like my enemies who have forgotten your words. It looks as though the speaker, a younger person not unmindful of God's ways of justice, is grieving over his enemies who, though senior to him, have forgotten. What else can his declaration mean: *I am younger, but I have not forgotten*? It must mean, "They may be older, but they have forgotten." The word for "younger" in Greek

---

2. Variant: "Why did the apostle speak as he did?"
3. See Jn 3:29.

is νεώτερος, which is used in an earlier verse (9): *By what means does a younger man straighten his path?* It is a comparative adjective, and implies a contrast with someone older. We should recognize here two peoples who wrestled with one another even in Rebecca's womb;[4] for *not on the basis of works, but by the choice of him who calls, was she told, The elder will serve the younger* (Rom 9:12; see Gn 25:23). The younger man in the psalm says he was despised, but this is why he became the greater;[5] for God has chosen the low, contemptible things of this world, things that seem to be nothing, to bring to nought the powers that be.[6] And lo, they who were first are last, and those who were last are first.[7]

5. They who, oblivious of God's righteousness, tried to set up their own[8] could hardly be anything but unmindful of the words of God; but the younger son has not forgotten them, because he wants no righteousness of his own[9] but only God's. Of this he now testifies, *Your justice is an eternal justice, and your law is truth.* How could the law be anything but truth, since through it comes consciousness of sin,[10] and since it bears witness to the righteousness of God? So the apostle tells us, *God's justice has been manifested, and the testimony of the law and the prophets supports it* (Rom 3:21).

6. For his fidelity to it[11] the younger suffered persecution at the hands of the elder, which wrung from him the cry, *Trouble and hardship have befallen me, yet I ponder on your commandments.* Let them rage, let them persecute, provided that God's commandments are not flouted. And in accordance with those commandments let even those who rampage be loved.

7. *Your testimonies are eternal justice; give me understanding and I shall live.* The younger son begs for understanding, yet if he did not have it already he would not have understood more than the elders.[12] But what he asks for now is the kind of understanding that amid his trouble and hardship would make him realize how despicable is anything his enemies can take away from him—those enemies by whom he says he was himself despised. In the light of this understanding he says, *And I shall live.* If the trouble and hardship become so extreme that his present life is terminated at the hands of his persecutors, he will live for ever, because he holds the justice that is eternal dearer than any temporal gains. The righteousness that stands firm through trouble and hardship is martyrdom, witness to God. For such witness were the martyrs crowned.

---

4. See Gn 25:22.
5. *Maior*, the same word that means "older" or "elder" in the preceding lines.
6. See 1 Cor 1:28.
7. See Mt 20:16.
8. See Rom 10:3.
9. See Phil 3:9.
10. See Rom 3:20.
11. Either the law, or God's manifest justice; the latter seems more likely.
12. See verse 100.

Exposition 29 of Psalm 118

Twenty-ninth Sermon[1]

Verses 145-146. Wholehearted prayer for wisdom

1. When people pray, they cry out to the Lord. If their cry is only a sound made by the voice, while the heart is not intent upon God, the cry is futile. If, however, it is made from the heart, then even though the bodily voice is silent, and the prayer inaudible to other people, it is not inaudible to God. When we pray to God, therefore, whether with our voice when that is appropriate, or in silence, we must cry to him from our hearts. The cry of the heart is the mighty concentration of our thought, and when this takes place in prayer it expresses the mighty will of one who is longing and begging for the result he hopes will follow.[2]

Furthermore, crying out with our whole heart means not thinking of anything else. Prayers of this quality come rarely to most people, frequently to few. Whether there is anyone who always prays like this, I cannot say; but the singer in this psalm indicates that his prayer was of this kind when he says, *I have cried out with my whole heart; hear me, O Lord.* Then he articulates the intention that prompted his cry: *Let me seek your ways of justice.* So that is why he cried out with his whole heart, that is what he desires from the Lord who hears him: that he may seek out God's ways of justice.

So this prayer, it seems, asks that we may seek out what we are ordered to do. What a distance there still is between the seeking and the doing! There is no certainty that the seeker will find or that the one who finds will act upon what is found, although no one can act on it unless he has found it first or find it unless he has searched. Yet the Lord Jesus gave us great hope when he bade us, *Seek and you will find* (Mt 7:7). But Wisdom speaks differently—and what else is Wisdom, if not the Lord Jesus? *The wicked will seek me, but not find me* (Prv 1:28, LXX), she warns. So are we perhaps meant to understand that the invitation, *Seek, and you will find,* is addressed only to good people? No, that cannot be right, because only a few verses later the Lord says to his hearers, *If you, bad as*

---

1. Like all the Expositions of Psalm 118, this one is classed as a Sermon (see Augustine's Prologue to this group). But the tone and preoccupations do not suggest that it was ever preached. Like others on this psalm, the present Exposition may have been more a collection of sermon notes prepared by Augustine for his own use or that of other preachers.
2. A dense Augustinian sentence: *Magnum exprimit desiderantis et petentis affectum ut non desperet effectum.*

479

you are, know how to give good gifts to your children . . . (Mt 7:11). How then
can he say to bad people, *Seek and you will find,* when Wisdom says in that other
context, *The wicked will seek me, but not find me*? Can the Lord have intended
them to seek anything other than wisdom, when he promised that they would
find if they sought? Hardly, for in wisdom are to be found all the things that need
to be sought by those who desire happiness; and these, of course, include God's
ways of justice.

There is only one explanation left to us. It is not all bad people who fail to find
Wisdom when they seek her but only those who are so very bad that they hate
her. This is indeed what Wisdom herself says: *The wicked will seek me, but not
find me, because they hate wisdom* (Prv 1:28-29, LXX). Because they hate it,
they do not find it. But then, if they hate it, why do they seek it? Surely because
they are not seeking it for its own sake, but for the sake of something else that
attracts bad people, something they think to gain more easily by means of
wisdom. There are plenty of people who study wise sayings most assiduously
because they want wisdom to show up in their teaching but do not want it in their
lives. Their object is not to conduct themselves as wisdom orders to gain God's
light, which is wisdom itself, but to use words taught by wisdom to win human
praise, which is vainglory. They are therefore not truly seeking wisdom even
when they appear to be doing so, because they are not looking for wisdom in
itself. If they were, they would shape their lives by it. What they want is to puff
themselves up by using wise words; and the more puffed up they become, the
more estranged they are from wisdom.

But the psalmist is begging from the Lord the very thing which the Lord
commands him to do, so that the Lord himself may perform in his servant what
he commands; for it is God who is at work in us, inspiring both will and work, for
his own good purpose.[3] *I have cried out with my whole heart; hear me, O Lord.
Let me seek your ways of justice,* he prays. He wants to seek them in order to
follow them, of course, not merely to know them; for if that were all, he would be
like the obstinate servant who, though he has understood, will not obey.[4]

2. *I have called; make me whole;*[5] or, as some codices have it, both Greek and
Latin, *I have called you; make me whole.* What does he mean by *I have called
you*?[6] Clearly, "I have invoked you with my cries." But after his petition, *Make
me whole,* what does he say next? *And let me keep your testimonies.* He is afraid
he could recant through weakness. Health in the soul causes it to act in the way it
knows to be right and to fight for the truth of God's testimonies even to the point

---

3. See Phil 2:13.
4. See Lk 12:47.
5. *Salvum me fac*: "save me." But *salus* means both salvation and health, and the latter meaning
   seems uppermost in the following lines.
6. *Clamavi te*, an awkward phrase in Latin.

of bodily death, if the ultimate testing demands it. Where health of soul is absent, weakness will succumb and truth will be forsaken.

Verses 147-148. Watching for dawn

3. The next verse introduces some obscurity, which calls for a somewhat longer explanation. *I came before you at dead of night, anticipating the due time, and I cried out.* Several codices have *prematurely,*[7] instead of *at dead of night;*[8] scarcely a single one doubles the preposition, reading *in immaturitate,* "prematurely." The unfit or premature time of night is the portion that is not suitable or not opportune to be awake and doing things, so we commonly speak of an unseasonable hour. The middle of the night or the dead of night[9] is called unseasonable because it is the time for rest; it is not an opportune time for wakeful activity. The ancients spoke of an opportune time as seasonable, and an inopportune time as unseasonable. The word *tempestivus,* "seasonable," is derived from *tempus,* "time," not from *tempestas,* "tempest," in the sense of stormy weather. Indeed, historians freely use the expression *ea tempestate* to signify "at that time." An outstanding poet said,

> *Unde haec tam clara repente*
> *Tempestas?*[10]

He did not mean by *tempestas* a sky stormy with clouds and winds, but a sudden, radiant period of brilliant calm.

The Greek has ἐν ἀωρίᾳ, two words, a preposition and a noun. Some of our translators have represented this with a single word, *intempesta,* or *immaturitate*; others have imitated the Greek by using two, *in immaturitate,* for in Greek ἀωρία is the noun "unfitness," and ἐν ἀωρίᾳ is the noun with the preposition, as with *in immaturitate.* It is as though we not only said *intempesta nocte,* using the other Latin word, but even doubled the preposition: *in intempesta nocte,* with one preposition indicating "at" what time and the other forming part of the compound noun. But as there is no difference in meaning whether someone says he did something "early" or "at cockcrow,"[11] so there is no difference of sense whether the psalmist says that he called on God *intempesta nocte* or that he called upon him *in intempesta nocte.* Either way, it means at an unsuitable time of night.

---

7. *Immaturitate noctis.*
8. *Intempesta nocte.*
9. *Nox intempesta.*
10. Virgil, *Aen.* 9,19-20: "Whence comes suddenly so fair a time?" Iris, messenger of the gods and goddess of the rainbow, has been sent to Turnus by Jove and Juno. Turnus is surprised that a clear, cloudless sky should follow so soon after her visit, as she could ordinarily be seen only against a cloudy background.
11. *Egisse se aliquid galli cantu, an in galli cantu*; the English has been altered a little, as we cannot omit a preposition before "cockcrow."

All the foregoing discussion concerned an obscure expression. Now let us look at the sense.

4. *I came before you at dead of night, anticipating the due time, and I cried out; I hoped in your words.* We could take this literally and refer it to each one of the faithful, for it often happens that at such an unseasonable hour of night our love for God is wakeful, and as a strong desire for prayer urges us[12] we do not wait for the customary time for prayer after cockcrow but anticipate it. Alternatively, we can regard the whole of the present age as a night, in which we certainly cry out to God at an unseasonable hour, anticipating the fit and right time[13] when he will render to us what he has promised. So too we find elsewhere the invitation, *Let us forestall him by coming into his presence confessing* (Ps 94(95):2). Or again, we may wish to understand the premature nocturnal prayer as that offered before the fullness of time had come,[14] before the mature time at which Christ was to be manifested in the flesh. Even then the Church was not silent but anticipated the due time by crying out in prophecy; it was hoping in the words of God, who had power to do what he had promised: that in Abraham's seed all nations would be blessed.[15]

5. This same Church of old speaks in the next verse: *My eyes anticipated the morning, that I might meditate on your sayings.* We can take the morning to be that time when, for those who were sitting in the shadow of death, light arose.[16] In the persons of the saints who were on earth at that early time, the eyes of the Church anticipated the morning, because they foresaw what would come to pass. They watched in anticipation in order to meditate on the sayings of God that were available to them at the time and announced through the law and the prophets the things that were to come.

Verses 149-151. Mercy and judgment

6. *Hearken to my voice, O Lord, according to your mercy, and in accordance with your judgment give me life.* God first relieves sinners of the punishment due to them, acting according to his mercy; and then when they are righteous he gives them life in accordance with his judgment. The order is significant when another psalm prays, *I will sing to you of your mercy and judgment, O Lord* (Ps 100(101):1). Yet even the time of mercy is not exempt from judgment. The apostle says of it, *If we judged ourselves, we should not fall under the Lord's judgment; but when we are judged by the Lord we are corrected by him, to save us from being condemned with the world* (1 Cor 11:31-32). His fellow-apostle

---

12. Variant: "rises up."
13. *Maturitatem temporis.*
14. See Gal 4:4.
15. See Gn 12:3; 22:18.
16. See Is 9:2.

speaks similarly: *It is time for judgment to take place, beginning from the house of the Lord; and if it originates with us,*[17] *what will be the outcome for those who do not believe in the gospel of God?* (1 Pt 4:17) Nor will the final judgment be without mercy, for, as another psalm says of God, *He crowns you in his pity and mercy* (Ps 102(103):4). Judgment without mercy will be reserved for those only who are on the Lord's left hand because they showed no mercy.[18]

7. *Those who persecuted me in their wickedness drew near;* or, as some codices have it, *those who persecuted me wickedly.* Persecutors draw near when they directly attack the flesh of their victims, to torture and destroy it. This is why in the twenty-first psalm, where the Lord's passion was prophesied, he says, *Do not leave me, for anguish is very near* (Ps 21:12(22:11)), although what is being described is what the Lord endured not when his passion was looming, but when it was actually present. However, he spoke of the anguish as very near because it was being inflicted on his flesh, and nothing is nearer to the soul than the flesh it carries. Similarly the persecutors are depicted in our present psalm as having drawn near because they tormented the flesh of those they persecuted.

Notice the next phrase: *But they distanced themselves from your law.* The nearer they drew to the just whom they were bent on persecuting, the farther they withdrew from justice. But how could they harm the people to whom they drew near in their malevolence, when the nearness of the Lord was far more intimate to those sufferers who were in no way abandoned by him?

8. The psalm continues, *You are near, O Lord, and all your ways are truth.* This is the customary confession of the saints, who even in the midst of their distress acknowledge the truth of God's ways, confessing that their sufferings are not undeserved. So it was with Queen Esther,[19] so with holy Daniel,[20] and the three men in the furnace,[21] and so too with others of their peers in holiness: all make this confession.

It may be asked why the present psalm says, *All your ways are truth,* when in another psalm we read, *All the Lord's ways are mercy and truth* (Ps 24(25):10). In fact all the Lord's ways are mercy with regard to his saints, and equally all his ways are truth in their regard, because even in judging them he helps them, and thus there is no lack of mercy, while in showing mercy he is fulfilling his promises, and thus there is no lack of truth. All the Lord's ways are mercy and truth in his dealings both with those he sets free and with those whom he condemns, because in cases where there is no mercy, his truth is plainly vindicated. He sets free many who do not deserve to be freed, but he condemns no one who does not deserve it.

---

17. Variant: "you."
18. See Mt 25:41-6; Jas 2:13.
19. See the supplementary section of Esther inserted into the Greek text and the Old Latin after Est 4:17, but relegated by Jerome in the Vulgate to the end of the book, 14:6-7.
20. See Dn 9:3-19.
21. See the insertion made by the Greek version of Daniel between verses 3:23 and 3:24 of Daniel.

Verse 152. The Church has been holding to God's testimonies from the beginning

9. *I knew about your testimonies from the beginning, knew that you have established them for eternity.* The Greek has κατ᾽ἀρχάς, which some of our translators have represented with *from the beginning,* others with *at the beginning,* others again with *at the beginnings.* Those who chose this last, plural form followed the Greek exactly. In Latin the ordinary idiom is *ab initio* or just *initio.* It is true that the Greek looks like a plural, but this is because the word is used adverbially. We use a similar idiom when we say *alias* : we appear to be using a feminine plural, but it is really an adverb signifying "at some other time."

What, then, is the meaning of *I knew from the beginning*—or, better, to use an adverbial phrase, *I knew about your testimonies originally, knew that you have* established *them for eternity*? He declares that those testimonies were established by the Lord and about the Lord, that they were established to stand for ever, and that he himself has known about them from the beginning. Obviously this knowledge could have come from no other source than the testimonies themselves. What testimonies can they be, if not those in which God testified that he would confer an everlasting kingdom on his children? Because he swore that he would give it in his only-begotten Son, of whom scripture says, *His kingdom will have no end* (Lk 1:33), the testimonies themselves are said to be established eternally, for what God promised through them is eternal. This does not mean that the testimonies will still be needed when we behold the reality itself; the testimonies are necessary now only because we must believe in what they promise.

The testimonies are said to have been *established* because their truth is demonstrated in Christ, and *no one can establish any other foundation than that which is already established, which is Christ Jesus* (1 Cor 3:11). But how could anyone have known about them from the beginning? This is possible because it is the Church that is speaking here. The Church has been present on earth since the dawn of humanity; holy Abel was its first-fruits, Abel, who was slain[22] in witness to the blood that would be shed one day by the Mediator, put to death in his turn by a faithless brother. From the very beginning it was also decreed that *they will be two in one flesh* (Gn 2:24), and the apostle Paul explains that this was a major prophetic sign: *This is a great mystery, but I am referring it to Christ and the Church* (Eph 5:32).

---

22. See Gn 4:8.

Exposition 30 of Psalm 118

Thirtieth Sermon

Verses 153-154. Humility is followed by exaltation

1. No one who has a place in Christ's body should think the next verse has no bearing upon him or her. The section we are to discuss opens with this prayer: *Behold my humiliation and deliver me, because I have not forgotten your law.* The entire body of Christ finds itself in a position to say this, for it is very used to being humiliated. And, given the context, no other law of God can be more appropriately understood here than his immovable decree that everyone who exalts himself must be humbled, and everyone who humbles himself, exalted.[1] While a proud person is associated with evildoers in order to be humbled, a humble person is delivered from evildoers in order to be exalted.

2. *Give judgment in my cause, and redeem me*, the psalm continues. This is almost a repetition of the previous verse, in different words. What was there expressed as *behold my humiliation* is here represented by *give judgment in my cause*; and the earlier plea, *deliver me*, here becomes *redeem me*. Moreover, as the preceding verse supported its plea with an argument: *Because I have not forgotten your law*, so too this verse has a matching argument: *Because of your decree, give me life*. The thought is the same, for God's decree is God's law, which the speaker has not forgotten, the law that inspired him to humble himself so as to be exalted. The prayer, *Give me life*, envisages this exaltation, because the exaltation of the saints is eternal life.

Verses 155-156. If you have sought God's righteous ways, it is by his gift

3. *Salvation is far from sinners, for they have not sought out your ways of justice.* Who marks you out as different,[2] you who say, *Salvation is far from sinners*? Who marks you out as different from sinners, that you can claim that salvation is close to you though far away from them? This is what makes you different, that you have done something they have not done, namely, sought God's ways of justice. But *what have you that you did not receive?* (1 Cor 4:7). Are you not the person who was saying just now, *I have cried out with my whole*

---

1. See Mt 23:12; Lk 14:11; 18:14.
2. See 1 Cor 4:7.

heart; hear me, O Lord. Let me seek your ways of justice (verse 145)? Your prayer was answered, then. From God, to whom you cried out, you received the grace to seek those ways of justice. It is therefore he who marks you out as different from those others, from whom salvation is far off because they have not sought out God's ways of justice.

4. The speaker himself saw that this was true. I could not have seen it myself if I had not seen it through the eyes of Christ,[3] if indeed, I had not been in him; for these words are the words of Christ's body, of which we are members. The psalmist saw this truth, I repeat; and therefore he immediately added, *Manifold are your mercies, O Lord.* The very fact that we seek your ways of justice is a manifestation of your mercies. *Give me life in accordance with your judgment,* for I know that when your judgment falls upon me it will not be without your mercy.

Verses 157-160. The glorious witness of many martyrs

5. *Those who persecute me and harass me are many, but I have not turned away from witnessing to you.*[4] This is a fact; we know it, we remember it, we acknowledge it. The whole earth is reddened with the blood of martyrs; heaven is flowering with martyrs' garlands; our churches are adorned by the memorials of martyrs; our calendars are studded with martyrs' festivals; cures obtained through martyrs' merits grow ever more frequent. How could all of this have happened, had there not come to pass what was foretold and spread throughout the world about that one person: *Those who persecute me and harass me are many, but I have not turned away from witnessing to you?* We recognize this, and we give thanks to the Lord our God. You, the speaker in this psalm, you yourself are the one who said in another psalm, *If the Lord had not been among us, perhaps they would have swallowed us alive* (Ps 123(124):2-3). There you have the reason why you did not turn aside from witnessing to him, and why, at the hands of the many who persecuted and harassed you, you attained the palm of God's heavenly call.[5]

6. *With chagrin I watched the fools,* he admits; or, as other codices have it, *I watched those who did not keep the bargain.* This latter reading is supported by many of them. Who are the people who have not kept the bargain? Who else but those who did turn aside from witnessing to God, unable to bear the harassment inflicted on them by their many persecutors? Now this is the bargain: that

---

3. *In ipso*; we could take this as "in the psalmist," but Augustine believes that the speaker is always in some sense Christ, as the following words show.
4. *A testimoniis tuis*: in earlier verses this has generally meant God's testimonies to himself, but here the thought seems rather to mean the martyrs' testimony to him.
5. See Phil 3:14.

whoever conquers will be crowned.[6] People who could not endure the persecution, who turned aside from witnessing to God and denied him, failed to keep the bargain. The psalmist observed them with chagrin, because he was a lover. Such zeal is good, for it springs from love, not malevolence. He clarifies what he meant about breaking the agreement: *For they did not guard your decrees.* Under duress, they disowned those decrees of God.

7. He now puts his finger on the difference between the apostates and himself: *See how I have loved your commandments.* He does not say, "I did not deny your words or your testimonies." That was what the persecutors tried to force the martyrs to do, and when the martyrs refused, they underwent unbearable torments. No; the psalmist points instead to the fruit borne by all that suffering, for *if I deliver my body to be burnt, yet have no charity, it profits me nothing* (1 Cor 13:3). With this in mind, the psalmist says, *See how I have loved your commandments.* Then he demands his reward: *In your mercy, O Lord, give me life.* They put me to death; do you give me life. He appeals to God's mercy for a reward due to him in justice, and rightly, for how much more generously was mercy lavished in order that the victory might be won, that victory to which the reward was owed?

8. *The origin of your words is truth, and your just judgments abide for eternity.* Your words proceed from truth, he says, and therefore they are truthful. These words, in which life is promised to the just, and punishment for the godless, can deceive no one. These are the righteous judgments of God, and they abide for ever.

---

6. See Rv 2:10.26; 3:12.21.

Exposition 31 of Psalm 118

Thirty-first Sermon

Verse 161. Loyalty to Christ does not exclude civic loyalty

1. We are well aware of the persecutions suffered by Christ's body—holy Church, that is—at the hands of earthly kings. We should therefore have no difficulty in recognizing the Church's words here again,[1] when the psalm says, *Princes persecuted me for no reason, but what my heart feared was your words.* What harm had Christians done to earthly sovereignties, even though their own king had promised Christians the kingdom of heaven? In what way, I ask, had they injured earthly kingdoms? Their king did not forbid his soldiers to render all the devoted service they owed to their earthly rulers, did he? When the Jews endeavored to incriminate him on this score, did he not retort, *Render to Caesar what is Caesar's, and to God what is God's* (Mt 22:21)? Did he not take a coin from a fish's mouth to pay tribute on his own behalf?[2] What about his precursor? What had he to say to soldiers owing allegiance to earthly rulers, when they asked him what they should do to gain eternal salvation? Did John advise them, "Throw your military belt away, throw down your weapons, desert your sovereign, and then you will be free to fight for the Lord"? No; what he said was, *Treat no one with violence, make no false accusations against anyone, and be content with your pay* (Lk 3:14). Then there was one of the Lord's own soldiers, a dearly loved comrade,[3] who told his companions in arms, and indeed Christ's civilians[4] too, *Every soul must be subject to the higher powers* (Rom 13:1). And shortly after this he spelled out the implications: *Pay all your debts: tribute to whom tribute is owed, tax to whom tax is owed, reverence to one to whom you owe reverence, and respect to those you should respect. Be in no one's debt, apart from owing love to each other.* (Rom 13:7-8) Did the apostle not also instruct the Church to pray for kings themselves?[5]

Of what offense, then, did they hold Christians guilty? What duty had Christians failed to perform? In what matter did they not comply with the orders of their earthly rulers? Clearly, the kings of the earth persecuted Christians for no

---

1. Compare sections 5-7 of the preceding Exposition.
2. See Mt 17:24-26.
3. *Comes*, a companion, sometimes used of a follower, or attendant, or member of staff.
4. *Provincialibus.* See Exposition 1 of Psalm 90,10 and the note there.
5. See 1 Tm 2:2.

reason. But notice the second part of the verse: *What my heart feared was your words.* The earthly potentates certainly used threatening words: "I will banish you, proscribe you, and kill you; I will torture you with hooks, roast you over a fire, expose you to wild animals, and tear you limb from limb." Yet, says the psalm, it is not their words, but yours, that terrify me; for you have said, *Do not fear those who kill the body, but after that have nothing else they can do. Fear him rather who has the power to destroy both body and soul in hell.* (Lk 12:5) *What my heart feared was* those words of yours. I scorned my human persecutor and overcame the devil who tried to lead me astray.

Verses 162-163. Delight in and love for God's words

2. The next words of the psalm are: *I will exult over your words like one who finds much booty.* He has come through victorious, thanks to the very words of God which he said he feared. Booty is seized from a vanquished foe, like the strong man mentioned in the gospel who was defeated and despoiled: *No one can get into a strong man's house and carry off his implements, unless he has tied up the strong man first* (Mt 12:29). But abundant booty was gained when the persecutors themselves, amazed at the steadfast bravery of the martyrs, came to believe. Those who had done their best to inflict damage on our king by hurting his soldiers were instead won over to his allegiance. We see the truth of this verse, then: anyone who, fearing to be worsted in the conflict, stands in awe of God's words will exult over those same words as a conqueror.

3. We must not suppose that any hatred for God's words has insinuated itself as a result of such fear. To begin with, the psalmist has just said that he exults over the words of God, and he would not have said that if he hated them. But to make the point more clearly, he goes on to say, *I hate and loathe injustice, but I love your law.* His awe and fear of God's words have certainly not engendered hatred for them but rather kept charity flourishing. There is no question of God's words or utterances being anything other than his law. It is therefore unthinkable that love should perish through fear, where fear is chaste. With such chaste fear fathers are both respected and loved by dutiful children. A chaste wife regards her husband fearfully, lest he desert her, but so loves him as to enjoy his company. If a human father, or a human husband, ought to be both feared and loved, far more true is this of our Father in heaven and of him who as the bridegroom surpasses all humankind in beauty,[6] though it is the beauty of goodness and not of the flesh. Who are the lovers of God's law, if not the lovers of God? What is there in a father's law that could grieve good children? His practice of disciplining those he loves, perhaps, and whipping every child whom he

---

6. See Ps 44:3(45:2).

acknowledges as his?[7] But anyone who refuses God's punishment is excluded also from his promises. Let our Father's judgments be praised even when he whips us, if his promises are loved when he gives us our reward.

Verses 164-165. Sevenfold praise; how not to be scandalized

4. The psalmist obviously shared this attitude, for he now proclaims. *I praised*[8] *you seven times a day over your righteous judgments.* The expression, *"seven times a day,"* signifies "always." The number seven is often used to indicate universality; thus scripture speaks of six days of divine work followed by a day of rest,[9] and so through the constant recurrence of the seven-day week the whole of time rolls on. The same thought underlies another text: *The just person will fall seven times a day, and rise again* (Prv 24:16). It means that though a just person is abased in every way, he or she has not transgressed; this is implied by the adjective *just.* Because such a person is cast down, as others see it, by all sorts of disasters, scripture says that he falls seven times; but because he profits even from his tribulations, it is said that he will rise again. This saying is amply illuminated by the words that follow: *But the godless will be weakened in their evil doings* (Prv 24:16, LXX). This is what is meant by the just person's falling and rising again seven times: he is not weakened by all his troubles.

The Church therefore has good reason to praise God seven times a day over his righteous judgments, for when the time came for judgment to begin from the Lord's house[10] the Church was not weakened but glorified by the crowning of its martyrs.

5. *There is plentiful peace for those who love your law, and they are never scandalized.* This could mean either that the law itself does not scandalize those who love it, or that for those who love it there is no danger of scandal from any other quarter. Either interpretation yields an acceptable sense. If anyone loves God's law, he acquiesces even in those provisions within it that he does not understand. If anything appears meaningless to him, he assumes that his own intelligence is falling short and that something important must be concealed there. Thus God's law does not scandalize him. As to the other interpretation, in order to avoid scandal altogether, a sensible person regards the practitioners of any holy profession in such a way that his faith does not depend on their good conduct. Otherwise, if some of those whom he held in high honor chanced to fall, he would himself be ruined by the scandal he would suffer. Instead he sets his love on the law of God for its own sake, and the result for him is plentiful peace

---

7. See Heb 12:6.
8. Variant: "will praise."
9. See Gn 2:2.
10. See 1 Pt 4:17.

and no scandal at all. He is quite safe in loving God's law, for even if many sin against it, the law itself is incapable of sin.

Verses 166-168. Keeping God's commandments from love; living under his gaze

6. *While awaiting your salvation, O Lord, I loved your commandments.* What use would it have been to the righteous of ancient times to love God's commandments, if Christ, who is God's salvation, had not come to set them free? Indeed, it was only because his Spirit had been communicated to them that they were able to love God's commands. But if those who loved God's commandments were awaiting his salvation, how much more necessary was Jesus, God's salvation, for the saving of people who did not even love the commandments?[11]

This prophecy can also be applied to the saints of the present era, when grace has been promulgated and the gospel is being preached, because those who love God's commandments are still waiting for Christ, so that when he is revealed—Christ who is our life—we too may appear with him in glory.[12]

7. *My soul has guarded your testimonies, and I have loved them dearly*, he says. Some codices read, *My soul has guarded your testimonies and loved them dearly*; it comes to the same thing, whether *I* or *my soul* is the subject. God's testimonies are guarded when they are not disowned. To guard them thus is the job of the martyrs, for *testimonies* are *martyria* in Greek.

But if someone lacks charity, even being burnt up for the sake of God's testimonies is useless,[13] and the psalmist therefore adds, *And I have loved them dearly.* In the preceding verse he said, *I loved your commandments*; now he says, *I have guarded your commandments and loved them*; then in the next verse he says, *I have kept* both *your commandments and your testimonies.* Anyone who loves keeps them truly and wholeheartedly. But it often happens that when God's commandments are loved, enemies arise, and then the commandments have to be kept in the teeth of their opposition. Then too the testimonies of God must be guarded bravely and not denied under the pressure of persecuting enemies.

8. The psalmist claims to have done both these things, and now he ascribes to God the power that enabled him to do so: *Because all my ways are open to your scrutiny, O Lord.* This how I had the strength to *keep your commandments and your testimonies*, he says: it was *because all my ways are open to your scrutiny.* He implies, "If you had turned your face away from me I should have been thrown into distress and incapable of keeping your commandments and your

11. He probably means the Gentiles in particular.
12. See Col 3:4.
13. See 1 Cor 13:3.

testimonies. But I did keep them, *because all my ways are open to your scrutiny.*" Clearly he means us to understand this in the sense that God sees all his ways with a gracious countenance, ready to help. So too another psalm prayed, *Do not turn your face away from me* (Ps 26(27):9). God's gaze also rests on evildoers, certainly, but in their case it is a frown, to blot them out from the earth;[14] clearly the psalmist does not mean that God regarded his ways in that sense. He means that the Lord gazed upon his ways as he knows the ways of the just;[15] in this sense too the Lord told Moses, *I know you better than all others* (Ex 33:17, LXX). The psalmist must have been sure that having his ways under God's eye helped him to make progress; otherwise he would not have given this as the reason why he had kept God's commandments and testimonies. He has heard and understood the injunction, *Serve the Lord in fear, and rejoice before him with trembling. Take hold of discipline, lest the Lord at some time grow angry and you disappear from the righteous path* (Ps 2:11-12), for if his path had not been open to the Lord's scrutiny, it would not have been righteous. The apostle Paul enjoins the same fear and trembling on his faithful disciples: *Work out your own salvation in fear and trembling; for it is God who is at work in you, inspiring both will and work, for his own good purpose* (Phil 2:12-13).

The ways of the righteous are thus open to the Lord's gaze so that he may guide their steps, for theirs are the ways of which the Book of Proverbs says, *The ways on the right are known to the Lord, but those on the left are crooked* (Prv 4:27). We are meant to understand that these perverse ways are unknown to the Lord in the sense that he will say to certain crooked persons, *I never knew you* (Mt 7:23). But Proverbs goes on to show the purpose of the Lord's knowing the ways of the just at his right hand, for immediately it adds, *He will direct your steps, and further your journey in peace* (Prv 4:27). There we have the reason why the psalmist says, *I have kept your commandments and your testimonies.* If we were to ask him how he did it, he would reply, *All my ways are open to your scrutiny, O Lord.*

---

14. See Ps 33:17(34:16).
15. See Ps 1:6.

Exposition 32 of Psalm 118

Thirty-second Sermon

Verses 169-170. The Lord is near as the psalmist prays

1. Let us now listen to the voice of him who prays, for we know who this praying person is, and, unless we are counterfeit, we acknowledge ourselves to be among his members.[1] *May my prayer draw near in your presence, O Lord;* this means, "May this prayer of mine, which I offer in your presence, draw near to you." The Lord is near to those who have bruised their hearts.[2] *According to your word, give me understanding.* He is claiming something already promised; his expression, *according to your word,* is equivalent to "according to your promise." The Lord promised this gift when he said in another psalm, *I will give you understanding* (Ps 31(32):80).

2. *May my pleading come into your presence, O Lord; according to your word, deliver me.* This is almost a repetition of what he has just said, for the first half of the preceding verse, *May my prayer draw near in your presence, O Lord,* is very similar to the first half of this one: *May my pleading come into your presence.* And what he asked before, *According to your word, give me understanding,* fits in with what he asks now: *According to your word, deliver me.* By being given understanding he is delivered, because when he did not understand he was self-deceived.

Verses 171-175. The ministry of the word entails risks

3. *My lips will blurt out a hymn when you have taught me your ways of justice,* he continues. We know how God teaches those prepared to accept his teaching, for all who have heard from the Father and learned from him come to[3] the one who justifies the godless.[4] They come in order to learn God's ways of justice, not simply by retaining them in the memory but by keeping them in practice. So it happens that everyone who boasts is boasting not of self but of the Lord,[5] and the resulting outburst is a hymn.

---

1. A brief and allusive restatement of Augustine's constant teaching that it is always in some sense Christ who prays in the psalms.
2. See Ps 33:19(34:18).
3. See Jn 6:45.
4. See Rom 4:5.
5. See 1 Cor 1:31.

4. He has learned, and he has praised God, his teacher, so now he wants to be a teacher himself: *My lips will declare your words, for all your commandments are justice.* Since he says he will declare them, he is undoubtedly becoming a minister of the word. God teaches from within, but faith comes through hearing.[6] And how will people hear without a preacher?[7] God gives the increase, unquestionably, but that does not mean there is no need for planting and watering.[8]

5. He knows what perils he will face from adversaries and persecutors, however, if he becomes a spokesman for the utterances of God. Accordingly he continues, *Let your hand be there to save me, for I have chosen your commandments.* I have chosen them because I want to be free from fear, and because I hope not only to hold onto your words in my heart[9] but also to proclaim them with my tongue. I have chosen your commandments, and by so doing I have quelled fear with love. Let your hand be there to save me from the hand of others. God did indeed save the martyrs, but in such a way that he did not allow their souls to be killed. As far as the body is concerned, human aid is unimportant.[10]

There is another possible way to understand the prayer, *Let your hand be there.*[11] The hand of God could mean Christ, if we recall Isaiah's question, *To whom has the arm of the Lord been revealed?* (Is 53:1) Considered as the only-begotten Son, he was not "made," for all things were made through him.[12] But he was made from the seed of David[13] so that he who was our creator might become Jesus, our Savior. However, the expression, *The hand of the Lord was there,*[14] is common in scripture,[15] and I do not know whether the explanation I have proposed would be suitable in all its occurrences.

What is less controversial is that when we hear the next line of the psalm, *I have passionately longed for your salvation, O Lord,* we spontaneously refer it to Christ, however little our enemies may like it: Christ, who is God's salvation. The just of ancient times confessed with the utmost sincerity that they longed for him; the Church of those early days longed for him as the one who would come from the womb of his mother; and the Church of today longs for him as the one who will come from the right hand of his Father. The concluding phrase of this verse confirms the thought. *And your law is the subject of my meditation,* it says, for the law bears witness to Christ.

---

6. See Rom 10:17.
7. See Rom 10:14.
8. See 1 Cor 3:6.
9. Variant: "not only to be unafraid in my heart."
10. See Ps 59:13(60:11).
11. *Fiat manus tua,* literally "Let your hand become" or "be made."
12. See Jn 1:3.
13. See Rom 1:3.
14. *Facta est manus Domini.*
15. See, for instance, Ez 1:3 .

6. But now, in the era of faith, when the believing heart finds justification, and confession is made with the lips for salvation,[16] let the Gentiles rage and the peoples devise futile schemes,[17] let my flesh be slain as long as it preaches you, for *my soul will live and praise you,*[18] *and your judgments will be my help.* The judgments mentioned here are those which at the appointed time began from the house of the Lord.[19] But the psalm says that they *will be my help.* Is it not obvious that the blood shed by the Church did indeed help it? What an enormous crop has sprung up all over the world from that sowing![20]

Verse 176. The lost sheep, partly found, still being sought

7. And now, at the very end, he reveals himself openly and shows us who has been speaking throughout the psalm. *I have strayed like a lost sheep*, he prays. *Seek your servant, for I have not forgotten your commandments.* Some codices read *give life to* instead of *seek.* There is only one syllable in Greek to distinguish ζῆσον from ζήτησον, which is why the codices disagree. But whichever is right, let the lost sheep be sought and the lost sheep be given life. For the sake of this one sheep the shepherd left the ninety-nine in the mountains[21] and was torn by Jewish thorns as he looked for it. But it is still being sought; even though partly found, let it be sought still. As to the part which says, *I have not forgotten your commandments*, it is found already. But through the work of those who choose God's commandments, weigh them mentally,[22] and love them, the sheep is still being sought; and through the blood of its shepherd, poured out and spread abroad, the sheep is being found among all nations.

Augustine's conclusion on this long psalm

8. I have carefully treated and expounded this great psalm to the best of my ability and to the extent that the Lord helped me in the task. Wiser and more learned expositors have certainly done it better, or will in the future. But that was no excuse for refusing to offer my service in the matter, especially when my brethren insistently demanded it, and this ministry is one I owe them.[23]

I have said nothing about the Hebrew alphabet, which is used here in such a way that the stanzas of eight verses are headed by successive letters of the

---

16. See Rom 10:10.
17. See Ps 2:1.
18. Variants: "may my soul live"; "my soul lives and has praised."
19. See 1 Pt 4:17.
20. Compare Tertullian, *Apol.* 50: "The blood of Christians is a seed."
21. See Mt 18:12; Lk 15:4.
22. This phrase is omitted by some witnesses.
23. Compare his Prologue to the Expositions of this psalm.

alphabet, so that the whole psalm is bound into a unity. I omitted to mention this because I found nothing in the psalm that seemed to be affected by the letters; after all, this is not the only alphabetical psalm.[24]

But I will just say this for the benefit of those who cannot verify it in the Greek and Latin versions (since the pattern is not preserved there): in the Hebrew text not only is each stanza of eight verses headed by a successive letter of the alphabet, but within each stanza every verse begins with that letter. So we are informed by those who know the language. This means that the psalm was far more carefully structured than the so-called alphabetical psalms our own people have generally composed, whether in Latin or in Punic. In these each stanza begins with a particular letter, but this letter initiates only the opening line; the pattern is not maintained through the whole stanza.

---

24. Others are 9(9-10), 24(25), 33(34), 36(37), 110(111), 111(112), and 144(145).

Exposition of Psalm 119

A Sermon to the People

General introduction to the "Songs of Ascents"

1. The psalm we have just heard, and to which we have sung our response, is a short one, and very profitable for our instruction. Listening to it will not be too long a job for you, and when you put it into practice your labor will not be unfruitful.

As the title that prefaces the psalm informs us, this is a *Song of Ascents.*[1] In Greek the title is ἀναβαθμῶν. Now ascents, or steps, can be used for either going up or going down, but the steps that appear in these psalms represent people going up. We too are to ascend, but we must not try to climb with our bodily feet; rather should we remember what was written in another psalm: *God arranges ascents in his heart, in the valley of weeping, to the place he has appointed* (Ps 83:6-7(84:5-6)).[2] *Ascents,* it said. Where? In the heart. What is the starting point? The valley of weeping. But whither are we mounting? That is hard to say, for human speech falters and the destination cannot be described, perhaps cannot even be conceived in thought. When the lesson from the apostle was read just now, you heard about something that *eye has not seen, nor ear heard, nor has it risen into the human heart* (1 Cor 2:9). So it has not risen into the human heart? Then let the human heart ascend to it instead. But if *eye has not seen, nor ear heard nor has it risen into the human heart,* how can we say anything about that place to which we are called to ascend? Since it is indescribable, the earlier psalm simply says, *To the place he has appointed.* The psalmist, through whom the Holy Spirit was speaking, seems to say, "What else can I tell you about it? That we are going to a place like this . . . or like that . . .? Whatever I say to you, you will think in earthly terms, you who crawl along the ground with your burden of flesh, for *the corruptible body weighs down the soul, and this earthly dwelling oppresses a mind that considers many things* (Wis 9:15). To whom can I speak? Who will hear? Can anyone comprehend where we shall be after the

---

1. Psalms 119-133(120-134) were regarded by Jewish tradition as a distinct group. In his Expositions Augustine also viewed them so, as mutually connected and different from the rest of the psalter. His explanation of the overall title, given here at the beginning of his Exposition of Psalm 119, is an introduction to all of them; the essential themes of his treatment are found here. It appears that his sermons on these *Songs of Ascents* were preached at Hippo between December 406 and April 407, or, less probably, a year later.
2. A key text for Augustine's interpretation of these psalms.

present life, if we have ascended in our hearts? No, no one; and you will do better to hope for a place of happiness beyond all telling, which he who arranged ascents in your heart has appointed for you."

But where did God arrange them? *In the valley of weeping.* This closed-in valley[3] symbolizes humility, as a mountain stands for height. The mountain we have to climb is a height of the spirit. Who is the mountain? Who else but our Lord Jesus? He made himself into a valley of weeping for you in his passion; and he is the mountain of your ascent because he remains where he has always been. What is the valley of weeping? *The Word was made flesh, and dwelt among us* (Jn 1:14). What is the valley of weeping? *He offered his cheek to one who struck him; he was drenched with insults* (Lam 3:30). He was punched, smeared with spittle, crowned with thorns, and crucified. This is the valley of weeping from which your upward climb must begin.

But whither are you to ascend? *In the beginning was the Word, and the Word was with God; he was God* (Jn 1:1). It was this same Word who *was made flesh, and dwelt among us.* He came down to you, but in such wise that he remained in himself; he came down to you so that for you he might become a valley of weeping, but he remained in himself so that he might be for you the mountain of your ascent. *In the last days the mountain of the Lord's house shall be revealed on the summit of all mountains* (Is 2:2), says Isaiah. To that height you are to climb, but do not imagine some earthly expedition. When you hear of the mountain, do not think of elevated ground; when you hear of a rock or a stone,[4] do not let your mind conjure up something flinty; when you hear Christ called a lion,[5] do not suppose that he is fierce; and when you hear of a lamb,[6] do not picture an animal to yourself. In himself he is none of these things, but he became all of them for you. He is the starting point of your ascent and the goal of your ascent; you climb from his example to his divinity. He gave you an example by humbling himself.

When certain of his friends disdained to begin from the valley of weeping, he rebuked them. They were ambitious for an over-hasty ascent; they aspired to high honors but gave no thought to the route of humility. Mark what I am saying, beloved.[7] Two disciples wanted to sit beside the Lord, one at his right, the other at his left. The Lord saw that they were getting things back to front and thinking about honors prematurely, for they should have been learning first of all how to be humbled in order to be exalted.[8] So he said to them, *Are you able to drink the cup I am to drink?* (Mt 20:22). He was destined to drink the cup of suffering in

---

3. *Convallis*, a valley enclosed on all sides.
4. See 1 Cor 10:4.
5. See Rv 5:5.
6. See Jn 1:29; Rv 5:6.
7. *Caritas vestra.*
8. See Mt 23:12; Lk 14:11; 18:14.

the valley of weeping; but they, paying no heed to Christ's humility, wanted to seize the high dignity of Christ. He recalled them to the way like lost travelers, not because he meant to refuse them what they wanted but in order to show them how to reach it.

2. Therefore, my brothers and sisters, since we are to ascend in our hearts, let us sing this psalm about ascending. A certain descent occurred first, a descent right down to our level, without which no ascent would have been possible for us. Jacob saw a vision of ladders, and on those ladders some were shown to him mounting and others coming down; he saw the movement in both directions.[9] We may perhaps think that the climbers he saw were those making progress,[10] and those coming down were backsliders, because this is in fact what we find in the people of God: that some make progress and others fall away. The ladders may possibly suggest these, but perhaps it is better to think that all those on the ladders, whether ascending or descending, are good people; for it was no accident that the text spoke of some as descending, not as falling down. There is a vast difference between descending and falling, for it was because Adam fell that Christ descended. The one fell, the other descended; the one fell through pride, the other descended in mercy. Yet he did not descend alone. Well, yes, he did descend alone from heaven, of course, but there are many holy people who imitate him by descending to us, and have done so in the past. On what a height must the apostle have been accustomed to dwell when he said, *If we are beside ourselves, it is for God* (2 Cor 5:13)! By going forth in his mind he had gone forth to God. Mentally leaving behind all human frailty, all the temporal concerns of this world, all these transient things that dwindle to nothing as they are born and sink into death, his heart dwelt in a contemplation that defied description, insofar as such a state was possible for him. Of that state he said that the one who experienced it *heard things beyond utterance, of which no human tongue may speak* (2 Cor 12:4). Of those realities he could not speak to you, but he himself was able to see them in some degree, though he could not pass them on. If therefore he had chosen to tarry for ever in what he saw but could not express, he would not have lifted you to a height where you too could see them. But what did he do? He came down. In the same letter he says, *If we are beside ourselves, it is for God; if we restrain ourselves, it is for you* (2 Cor 5:13). What does he mean by *restrain ourselves*? "We speak in a fashion you can understand." And this was because Christ also, by being born and suffering, made himself such that people could talk about him; for humans easily talk about another human. Can any mortal talk about God, as God truly is? But men and women readily speak about someone human like themselves. If great people were to come down to little ones and yet speak to them only of him who is great, it was necessary for him who was great to

---

9. See Gn 28:12.
10. *Visos proficientes*. Variant: *viros proficientes*, "men making progress."

become little himself, so that great human teachers could speak of him to little people. And this he did.

What I am telling you now is what you heard about when the lesson from the apostle was read. If your ears were attentive you heard him say, *Not as spiritual persons could I speak to you, but only as carnal* (1 Cor 3:1). On the heights he conversed with spiritual beings, but in order to speak to those who are carnal he comes down. And when he comes down, he speaks of the one who himself descended. If you are not sure of this, listen to what John said of Christ when he was abiding in himself: *In the beginning was the Word, and the Word was with God; he was God. He was with God in the beginning. Everything was made through him; no part of created being was made without him* (Jn 1:1-3). Take that in, if you can. Seize it, for it is solid nourishment. But you will say to me, "Yes, he is solid food, to be sure, but I am an infant. What I need is milk, so that I can grow up and become capable of eating solids." Christ knew this. He is solid food, but you can only take milk; and so he who was solid food was processed through flesh to reach your palate. A mother does this: she eats solid food and processes it through her flesh to pass it on to her baby in the form of milk; similarly the Word, the Lord, the food of angels, was made flesh, and so the apostle could say, *I gave you milk to drink, rather than solid food. You were not capable of it then, nor are you even now* (1 Cor 3:2). He descended to little ones to give them milk, and because he descended, he gave them the one who descended; for he asked them, *Did I ever claim to know anything among you, save Jesus Christ and him crucified?* (1 Cor 2:2) If he had said simply, *save Jesus Christ*, we might have thought he meant Jesus Christ in his divinity, in his reality as the Word with God, Jesus Christ the Son of God. But him the little ones cannot grasp—not when he is spoken of like that. How can they take him in, these little ones who can take only milk? *Jesus Christ, crucified*, says the apostle. Suck what he became for you, and you will grow toward what he is.

There are climbers, and there are some who descend. On those ladders, some mount, some descend. Who are the climbers? Those who are making progress toward an understanding of spiritual things. Who are the ones who descend? People who, though they enjoy as much understanding of spiritual things as human beings can, nonetheless come down to the level of the little ones to tell them all they can take in. Thus these little ones, nourished on milk, may grow fit and strong until they are able to absorb solid spiritual food. Consider, brothers and sisters, how Isaiah too was one of the teachers who came down to us. The very stages of his descent can be discerned. When he spoke of the Holy Spirit he put the Spirit's gifts in a definite order: *The spirit of wisdom and understanding shall rest upon him, the spirit of counsel and strength, the spirit of knowledge and piety, and the spirit of fear of the Lord* (Is 11:2-3). He began with wisdom and brought the list down to the fear of the Lord. As he, your teacher, descended from wisdom to fear, so you, the learner, must ascend from fear to wisdom if you are to make progress; for scripture says, *The fear of the Lord is the beginning of wisdom* (Ps 110(111):10; Prv 1:7; 9:10; Sir 1:16).

Listen now to the psalm. Let us picture to ourselves a man or woman called to make the ascent. Where will it take place? In the heart. What is the starting point? Humility, the valley of weeping. Whither is he to ascend? To a reality that cannot be put into words, of which another psalm says, *To the place* God *has appointed* (Ps 83:6-7(84:5-6).

Verses 1-2. The would-be climber encounters cunning dissuaders

3. When someone thus addresses himself to the ascent—or, rather, to put it more plainly, when a Christian begins to think about making headway—he or she soon suffers from the tongues of people with opposing ideas. Anyone who has not yet had any trouble of this kind has not yet made any progress; and if anyone is not prepared to endure it, that person had better not make any attempt to advance. Does such a one[11] want to understand what we are saying? It is more a matter of our listening together, and reflecting on our own experience. Let anyone begin to move forward, begin to want to make the ascent, begin to scorn earthly, perishable, temporal things and to set little store by the prosperity this world offers; let such a one begin to think of God alone, disdain to gloat over his gains or lament his losses; let him even resolve to sell all he owns, give the proceeds to the poor, and follow Christ. What happens? Let us see how he has to put up with the talk of people who try to pull him back,[12] who raise all kinds of objections, and—what is worse—attempt to turn him away from salvation as though they had his best interests at heart. Anyone who genuinely wants to promote another's interests wants that person's salvation, wants whatever will profit the other; but the false counselor holds the other back from salvation. Cloaked as an adviser, he dispenses a murderer's venom, and so he is reckoned a guileful tongue. The person essaying the climb should therefore pray to God first of all for protection against such tongues. This is what the psalmist did: *I cried to you, Lord, when I was troubled, and you heard me.* How did the Lord hear him? In such a way as to set him on the steps, ready to ascend.

4. As he prepared to ascend, his plea was heard. What does he pray now? *O Lord, rescue my soul from wicked lips and the guileful tongue.* What is a guileful tongue? A sly tongue, one that feigns friendliness but does real mischief. People of guileful speech ask, "Do you mean to attempt what no one else has done? Do you aim to be the only real Christian?" If the aspiring climber points to others who are doing the same, and reads out the gospel passages where the Lord commanded it, or reads the Acts of the Apostles, what is the reply of people with

11. Variant: "Do you . . .?" (plural).
12. Variant: "disparage him."

cunning tongues and iniquitous lips? "But you may not have the strength for that. What you propose is too arduous an undertaking." Some try to deter him by discouragement, others make it even harder for him by their positive commendation; for this is the way of life that has conquered the world, and so great is Christ's authority that not even a pagan dare criticize Christ. So he who is above criticism is read out, and we hear him counseling, *Go and sell all you possess and give the money to the poor. Then come, follow me.* (Mt 19:21) Christ cannot be faulted, then? The gospel cannot be gainsaid? Very well, the guileful tongue resorts to deterrence through praise. If you want to praise him, guileful tongue, you should be encouraging me; why make things difficult for me with your praise? You would do better to insult the Christian enterprise than to praise it deviously. If you were to insult it openly, what would you say? "Have nothing to do with it! That is a foul way of life, a wicked course!" But you know that if you take that line you can be refuted by the authority of the gospel, so you turn to a different tactic to dissuade me: by your insincere praise you try to hold me back from true praise; indeed, by praising Christ you attempt to hold me back from Christ. You say, "But what does it mean? Others have achieved it, have they? Wonderful! But you will probably not be strong enough. Are you setting out to climb? You will fall." The speaker may sound like an adviser, but he is a snake, with a guileful tongue, and venomous. Pray against a tongue like that, if you want to ascend. Say to your God, *O Lord, rescue my soul from wicked lips and the guileful tongue.*

Verses 3-4. The climber is armed with sharp arrows and burning coals: God's words and the examples of the saints

5. The Lord your God says to you, *What is to be given to you, what shall be provided for you, that you may withstand the guileful tongue?* What defense will you have, he asks, against the guileful tongue, with what weapon will you meet the guileful tongue, how are you to arm yourself against the guileful tongue, *what is to be given to you, what shall be provided for you?* He asks to test you, for he is going to answer his own questions. He responds to his own interrogation: *Sharp arrows of the mighty one, with destructive, all-devouring coals.* Whether you say *destructive* or *all-devouring*—for there are variations among the codices—it comes to the same. Look at it like this: coals are called all-devouring because by laying waste and depopulating a region they quickly reduce it to desolation. Now what are these coals? It would be better if you were first to understand what the arrows are, beloved. *Sharp arrows of the mighty one* are the words of God. Watch them as they are launched, and see how they pierce hearts! But when human hearts are transfixed by the arrows of God's word, the effect is not death but the arousal of love. The Lord is a skilled marksman with his eye on

love, and no one shoots more accurately at love than he who shoots with the word. He shoots at his lover's heart for the good of the lover; he shoots to turn you into his lover. We shoot with his arrows when we deal in words.

What about the all-devouring coals? It is not enough to counter the sly tongue and the wicked lips with words. Words alone are insufficient; we need examples too. The destructive coals are examples. You shall have a brief explanation, beloved, as to why they are called destructive; but first consider how we should use examples. A sly tongue can devise nothing more insidious than to say, "Take care, you may not be able to carry your enterprise through. It is too much for you to tackle." Now you have made the gospel precept your own, and so you have an arrow, but as yet you have no coals. There is some danger that an arrow alone may not prevail against the guileful tongue; but there are still coals. Suppose, for instance, you hear God beginning to say to you, "If you are not strong enough to do this, how can that other person do it? Or how was So-and-So able to manage it? You are hardly more delicate than that senator, are you? Are you weaker in health than X or Y?[13] Are you weaker even than women? If women have been strong enough to follow this way of life, is it too much for men? Rich people, delicately nurtured, have been robust enough: is it too rough for the poor?" The person so challenged replies, "But I have committed so many sins; I am a wretched sinner." Then he is reminded of how many people have sinned greatly, and loved all the more because they were forgiven more. As the gospel tells us, *one who is forgiven little loves little* (Lk 7:47).

All these arguments have been rehearsed, and the names have been listed of people who found the necessary strength. The hearer who had already been pierced to the heart by God's word now has destructive coals heaped upon him, and his earthly way of thinking is purged. What does it mean, to be despoiled and depopulated? It means the place is left bare and empty. Plenty of rank plants used to flourish in him: many carnal thoughts, many worldly loves. All these are burnt up by the destructive coals to leave a clean, empty place. In this pure place God can erect his building, for the devil's abode has been dismantled and Christ is now being built up there. As long as the devil makes it his home, Christ cannot be built. But the destructive coals arrive and demolish the evil building. Then on the desolate site the edifice of perpetual happiness is raised.

Consider now why they are called coals. When people are converted to the Lord they pass from death to life. But live coals were once extinct, dead, before they were kindled. Coals that are not on fire can be called dead; burning ones are called live coals. Thus the examples of the many sinful people who have been converted to God are called coals. You may hear others marveling at what has happened, saying, "I knew him once. I knew what a drunkard he was, what a

---

13. Variant: "weaker than this or that invalid?"

scoundrel, what a fan of the circus and the amphitheatre,[14] and how dishonest. But now, look how he serves God, and what a blameless life he leads!" Do not be surprised. He is a piece of coal. You rejoice to see him a live coal, because you deplored his dead state. But while you praise this live coal—if you praise him wisely—you will apply him to another who is dead, and set fire to him or her as well. What I mean is this: if anyone is still reluctant to follow God, put the coal that used to be dead near him. Equip yourself with the arrow of God's word and the destructive coal, and so go out to confront the iniquitous lips and the sly tongue.

Verse 5-6. The miseries of exile, living among the dark tents of Kedar

6. What comes next? The speaker has taken up his burning arrows; let him now take the destructive coals as well. He is already fending off the sly tongue and the wicked lips, already mounting the first step and beginning to make headway; but he is still living among bad people, among the wicked. The winnowing has not taken place yet. Think of it this way: does the mature condition of the grain mean that it is already in the barn? Clearly not. Inevitably it is still pressed down under a load of straw; and so it is with Christians. The more progress they make, the more evident and serious in their eyes are scandals among the people; for if they are not advancing themselves they will not notice prevalent sins, and if they are not true Christians themselves they will not detect impostors. The Lord teaches us this in the parable about the wheat and the tares, brothers and sisters. *When the shoots had grown up and borne fruit, then the weeds became apparent* (Mt 13:26). This suggests that no one notices bad people except an observer who has become good, for only *when the shoots had grown up and borne fruit* did the weeds really show up. The psalmist is one who is beginning to make progress. He therefore notices bad people and many evils of which he was previously unaware; and so he cries out to God, *"Alas, alas, how long-drawn-out is my exile!* I have gone so far away from you. My pilgrimage is so wearisome! I have not yet arrived in that homeland where I shall live untroubled by any evil.[15] Not yet have I attained to the fellowship of the angels, where I shall have no scandals to dread. Why am I not yet there? Because *my exile is so long-drawn-out."* An exile[16] implies a pilgrimage or journey abroad. A person who lives in a foreign land, away from his own country, is called an exile.[17] Thus the psalmist laments, *How long-drawn-out is my exile!* And where is he, in this prolonged exile?

---

14. On Augustine's severe view of these entertainments see Exposition of Psalm 39,8 and the note there.
15. Or "by any bad person."
16. *Incolatus.*
17. See Exposition of Psalm 55,9 and the note there.

It sometimes happens that someone on a journey lives among more congenial people than perhaps he did back at home; but this is not the case with us when we remember that we are travelers, far away from the heavenly Jerusalem. A person may leave his own country and find himself better off during his travels: he comes across trustworthy friends on the journey, unlike any he found at home. Indeed, in his own land he had enemies; that was why he was driven out and forced to journey abroad; and on his way he finds what he never found in his homeland. But Jerusalem, our homeland, is not like that, for there all the citizens are good. Anyone on a journey away from Jerusalem is thrust among bad people and cannot escape from them, except by returning to the society of the angels, to be at home in that place from which he is distanced by his travels. There dwell all the righteous and holy ones who enjoy God's word without reading, without letters, for what is written on the page for us they behold in the face of God. What kind of homeland is it? A very great country, and wretched are they who are so far from home.

7. But what of the psalmist; what has he to say? *How long-drawn-out is my exile!* This is definitely the voice of pilgrims and exiles, the voice of the Church as it struggles along on earth. It is the voice of one who cries out from far-off countries in another psalm: *From the ends of the earth I have called to you* (Ps 60:3(61:2)). Is there any one of us who cries from the ends of the earth? No: not I, nor you, nor he, nor she; but the whole Church[18] cries from the ends of the earth. The whole inheritance of Christ cries out, and of the Church a psalm said in prophecy, *Ask of me, and I will give you the nations as your inheritance, and the ends of the earth for your possession* (Ps 2:8). Christ's domain extends to the furthest bounds of the earth; all the saints are his possession; and all the saints form a single person in Christ because the Church is a holy unity. Therefore it is this single person who laments, *From the ends of the earth I have called to you, as my heart was wrung with pain* (Ps 60:3(61:2)).

Perhaps this one person might be asked, "With whom are you living, then, that you groan like this?" He reiterates, *My pilgrimage is so long-drawn-out.* Yes, but might he not have good neighbors? No, for if he had, he would hardly say *Alas,* would he? *Alas* is a word that indicates misery; it is a sound of calamity and unhappiness, yet it also expresses hope, because the one who uses it has at last learned to grieve. There are many others, just as wretched, who do not grieve; they are exiles too, but have no desire to go home.

The psalmist certainly does want to go home, for he experiences the misery of his exile. Because he recognizes it he is on the way already. He is beginning his ascent, for he is beginning to sing the song of ascents. Where is he groaning, then? Among whom is he living? *I have been dwelling among the tents of Kedar.* That is a Hebrew word, and I am sure you did not understand it. What does the

---

18. Variant: "only the Church."

phrase mean: *I have been dwelling among the tents of Kedar?* As far as I
remember the interpretation of Hebrew names,[19] Kedar signifies "darkness."
We can take Kedar as equivalent to "darkness" in our language.

Now you know that Abraham had two sons.[20] The apostle refers to them and
makes them stand for the two covenants, one being born from the slave-girl, the
other from the free wife.[21] Ishmael was born from the maid-servant; but Isaac,
conceived through faith in what seemed a hopeless situation, was born from the
free Sarah.[22] Both were Abraham's offspring, but they were not both Abraham's
heirs. One of them, though born from Abraham, was not born to an inheritance.
The other was his heir: not only his son, but his heir too. Ishmael personifies all
who worship God from carnal motives. Their province is the Old Covenant, for
the apostle says to them, *You who want to be subject to the law, have you not
heard the law? It is written that Abraham had two sons, one by the slave-girl,
and the other by the free woman; and this story is symbolic. The two allegorically prefigure the two covenants.* (Gal 4:21-22.24) What covenants does he
mean? The old and the new. The Old Covenant was from God, and the New
Covenant is from God, just as both Ishmael and Isaac were sons of Abraham. But
Ishmael was destined for earthly rule, Isaac for a heavenly kingdom. The Old
Covenant embodied earthly promises: an earthly Jerusalem, an earthly Pales-
tine,[23] an earthly kingdom, earthly salvation,[24] the subjugation of enemies,
plenty of children, abundant harvests. All these are earthly promises. But they
can be understood in a spiritual sense, as symbols, for the earthly Jerusalem was
a shadow of the heavenly city and the earthly kingdom a shadow of the kingdom
of heaven. Ishmael was in shadow, Isaac in the light. And if Ishmael was in
shadow, we might as well say he was in darkness, for darkness is nothing but
deeper shadow. If, then, Ishmael's place was in darkness, but Isaac's in light, we
can say that all those who, even in the Church, seek earthly prosperity from God
still belong to Ishmael. These are the same ones who oppose spiritually-minded
persons who are making progress and disparage them. They have iniquitous lips
and sly tongues.

Our psalmist on his upward journey prayed against them, and he was supplied
with destructive coals and the sharp arrows of a mighty warrior, for he still has to
live among such people until the whole threshing-floor is cleared at winnow-
ing-time. This is why he complained, *I have been dwelling among the tents of
Kedar.* Ishmael's tents bear this name, Kedar. Genesis indicates this, for it tells

---

19. See Jerome, *Nom. hebr.* 4,6.
20. See Gn 16:15; 21:2.
21. See Gal 4:22-31.
22. Or perhaps ". . .was born from the free Sarah through faith, once she had given up her
despairing attitude"; see Gn 18:10-15.
23. Augustine seldom uses this name for the Holy Land in his Expositions.
24. Or possibly "good health."

us that Kedar belonged to Ishmael.[25] Isaac and Ishmael are represented as close companions, which signifies that people who belong to Isaac live among those who belong to Ishmael. The former want to ascend, but the latter try to pin them down below. The former long to fly to God, but the latter try to pluck out their wings. The apostle gives hints of this, for he says, *As at that time the son begotten according to the flesh persecuted the one begotten according to the Spirit, so it is today* (Gal 4:29). Spiritual persons suffer persecution from the carnally-minded. But what does scripture say? *Cast out the slave-girl and her son. The son of a slave-girl shall not be heir with my son Isaac.* (Gn 21:10) But when will that command be implemented: *Cast them out?* When winnowing begins on the threshing-floor. But for the present, before they are expelled, *alas, how long-drawn-out is my exile! I have been dwelling among the tents of Kedar.* Thus the psalm indicates to us whom it means by the tents of Kedar.

8. *My soul has been on pilgrimage for a long time.* He says it is his soul that has been on pilgrimage, to make sure you do not think only of bodily journeys. The body travels from place to place; the soul travels by its affections. If you are in love with the earth, your journey is taking you far from God. If you are in love with God, you are climbing toward him. Let us exert ourselves in charity toward God and our neighbor, that we may make our way back to charity. If we fall to earth we wither and become moldy. The psalmist had fallen, but a descent had occurred for his sake, down to his level, so that he might ascend. Reflecting on the time his pilgrimage had lasted, he says he is an exile in the tents of Kedar. Why? Because *my soul has been on pilgrimage for a long time.* His pilgrimage is going on in the place where he is to ascend. Just as his pilgrimage is not a bodily one, so his ascent will not be in the body either. Where does he ascend? *The ascents are in his heart,* we were told in another psalm.[26] If he is to ascend in his heart, there can be no ascent for him unless his soul is on pilgrimage. But until he arrives, he complains, *My soul has been on pilgrimage for a long time.* Where? In the tents of Kedar.

Verse 7. A plea for peace and unity addressed to the Donatists

9. *I dealt peaceably with those who hated peace.* I want you to hear how true these words are, brothers and sisters. You can test the truth of what you are singing only if you are beginning to act in harmony with your song. However much I say about this, in whatever way I explain it, whatever words I use, the truth will not penetrate anyone's heart unless he or she has already begun to practice it. Begin to act on it, and then see for yourselves what we are telling you. Then your tears will flow at every word; then as the psalm is sung your heart will

---

25. See Gn 25:13.
26. See Ps 83:6(84:5).

be engaged in what it sings. How many people there are who make plenty of noise with their voices but are dumb in their hearts! And how many others have no sound on their lips but shout with their love! God's ears are alert to the human heart. Just as a person's ears are open to the speech of another, so are God's ears open to a person's heart. Many are heard without opening their mouths, and many others are not heard even though they shout loudly.

We must pray with our affections, and say, *My soul has been on pilgrimage for a long time; I dealt peaceably with those who hated peace.*[27] "Learn to know peace; love peace," we say to them. "You call yourselves righteous. If you were righteous you would be genuine wheat, yes; but you would be still among the straw, groaning there." There are wheat-grains in the Catholic Church—real grains. They put up with the straw until the time comes for winnowing on the threshing-floor and they keep crying out, *Alas, how long-drawn-out is my exile! I have been dwelling among the tents of Kedar.* "I have lived among the straw," they imply. But as burning straw gives off thick smoke, so does thick darkness emanate from Kedar. *I have been dwelling among the tents of Kedar, and my soul has been on pilgrimage for a long time.* This is the authentic voice of the wheat-grains, groaning amid the chaff.

We point out these things to those who hate peace. We say to them, *I have dealt peaceably with those who hate peace.* Who are the ones who hate peace? Those who tear our unity apart. If they had not hated peace, they would have stayed within that unity. But their motive for seceding was the desire to be righteous, and not be mixed up with the unrighteous.[28] Whose voice is it in this psalm—ours or theirs? You must decide! The Catholic Church says, "Unity must not be sacrificed; God's Church must not be rent apart. God will judge later between the bad and the good. If the bad people cannot be sorted out from the good now, they must be borne with for the time being. Bad people can be with us on the threshing-floor, but cannot be in the barn. In any case, those who appear to be bad today may be good tomorrow, just as those who today are proud of their own goodness may tomorrow turn out to be bad. Anyone who humbly tolerates bad people for a time will attain everlasting rest." This is the Catholic voice.

What tone do they adopt, those who understand *neither what they are saying nor the matters on which they pronounce* (1 Tm 1:7)? *Touch nothing unclean* (Is 52:11; 2 Cor 6:17), they say. "*Anyone who touches what is unclean shall be*

---

27. The following lines make it clear that the Donatists are in Augustine's mind. In 406-407, the probable date of his Expositions of the "Songs of Steps," the conflict with the Donatists was still a burning issue.

28. At the heart of the Donatist crisis were two different conceptions of the Church. For the schismatics, the Church was meant to be the society of the pure; for Augustine it was a mixed crop of good and bad, growing together until judgment day, with the hope that some of the weeds would be revealed as wheat in the end. Meanwhile, the bad serve God's purposes by exercising the good in tolerance and charity. See also the Expositions of Psalms 10,1; 64,2.9; 95,2, and the notes in these places.

defiled (Lv 22:4). Let us take ourselves off; we don't want to get mixed up with bad people."

We plead with them, "Love peace, set your hearts on unity. Don't you realize how many good people you are leaving behind when you stigmatize them all as evil?" But they are ferociously angry when we say this; they even try to kill us. Their open attacks have often been notorious, and so too the traps they have set. Since we have to live among the ambushes they lay for us, and since the very people whom we exhort to love peace range themselves against us, can we not recognize our own voice in the psalm? *I have dealt peaceably with those who hate peace; when I spoke to them, they waged war on me without justification.*

What is the force of those last words, brothers and sisters? *They waged war on me?* That would not amount to much, if the psalm had not added, *without justification.* When we say to them, "Love peace, love Christ," do we say, "And pay honor to us"? Certainly not! We say, "Pay honor to Christ." We want him to be venerated, not ourselves. How unimportant we are by comparison with the apostle Paul! Yet he kept saying to those little ones of his, whom wicked people and evil counselors tried to drag away from unity into schism—what did he keep saying to them? *Was Paul crucified for you, or were you baptized in Paul's name?* (1 Cor 1:13) We are saying the same: "Love peace, love Christ." If they love peace, they will love Christ, for in saying, "Love peace," we are implicitly urging them to love Christ. You ask why? Because the apostle says of Christ, *He is himself our peace, since he united the two* (Eph 2:14).

If Christ is peace because he made two into one, how can you make one into two? In what sense are you promoters of peace, if when Christ makes two into one, you make one into two? When we say these things to them, we deal peaceably with those who hate peace. And whenever we have spoken to these haters of peace, they have waged war on us without justification.

Exposition of Psalm 120

A Sermon to the People[1]

A "Song of Ascents" is appropriate to the festival of a martyr; the need for perpetual vigilance

1. We now approach the second psalm in the collection entitled *Songs of Ascents*. This is a group of psalms which deal with our[2] upward climb, as you have heard already in our exposition of the first one. The ascent is made in our hearts as we mount toward God through the valley of weeping, which symbolizes the humility of our very distressed condition. The ascent can succeed for us only if we are first of all humbled and remember that it is from this valley[3] that our climb must begin. A valley[4] is a sunken region of the earth: just as high areas are called mountains, so is a lowly place called a valley. Were we to forget that this must be our starting-point we would be getting things upside down and seeking exaltation before the proper time; and then we would not ascend but fall headlong. The Lord himself taught us that there can be no ascent except from the valley of weeping. For our sake he graciously willed to be humbled even to death on a cross and to suffer. Let us not neglect his example. The martyrs understood about the valley of weeping. How did they gain understanding? You ask how? By mounting in their turn from the valley of weeping, to receive their crowns.

2. This *Song of Ascents* is apposite today,[5] for of the martyrs scripture says, *They went on their way weeping, as they scattered their seed* (Ps 125(126):6). This is the activity proper to the valley of weeping, where seeds are scattered by people in tears. What are these seeds? Good works performed amid earthly woes. One who is diligent in good works in the valley of weeping is like a farmer who sows in the winter. Is he deterred from his job by the cold? Definitely not. Nor should we be deterred by the hardships of this world from doing good; for notice what comes next in that passage of scripture: *When they come back they will come leaping for joy, carrying their sheaves.*[6]

---

1. Preached on the festival of the martyr Saint Crispina (see section 13), probably on 5 December 406 or 407, a few days after the Exposition of Psalm 119.
2. Variant: "your."
3. Variant: ". . . only if we are first of all mindful that it is from this valley of humility."
4. The word in these lines is *convallis*, literally a valley closed in on all sides.
5. The feast of Saint Crispina.
6. The best reading seems to be *gremia*, perhaps "bunches"; compare Sermon 313D, 3. Variant: "sheaves."

3. These songs have only one thing to teach us, brothers and sisters, and that is how to ascend. But our ascent must be made in the heart, by a good intention, in faith and hope and charity, in a desire for eternity and everlasting life. That is what the ascent is. Now we need to explain[7] how to accomplish it.

You heard plenty of rather terrifying things when the gospel was read, beloved![8] You are well aware that *the Lord's hour will come like a thief in the night* (1 Th 5:2). *If the householder had known at what hour the thief would come, I tell you truly, he would not have allowed his wall to be breached* (Mt 24:43). Now you are saying, "But if the hour will come like a thief, who can know the time of the Lord's coming?" You don't know the time of it? Be vigilant all the time, then, so that even if you don't know when he is coming he will find you prepared when he does. Perhaps the very purpose of your being kept ignorant of the time is to ensure that you are always ready. It is the householder in the story who will be overtaken suddenly by the unexpected timing, and the householder represents proud persons. Take care not to aim at being a householder, and then it will not overtake you unawares. "What am I to be, then?" you ask. Another psalm showed you the kind of person you must be: *I am poor and sorrowful* (Ps 68:30(69:29)); for if you are poor and sorrowful you will not be a householder, to be overtaken suddenly by that hour and suddenly overwhelmed. Householders are the kind who promote their greedy impulses, dissipate their energies on the pleasures of this world, become swollen with pride and overbearing toward humble folk, and insult holy people who recognize the narrow way that leads to life.[9] The hour will come suddenly upon such persons. That was how some were behaving in the days of Noah; you heard their story in the gospel. *The coming of the Son of Man will be as it was in the days of Noah. People were eating and drinking, marrying and taking wives, setting out new plants and building, until Noah entered the ark. Then the flood came, and destroyed them all.* (Mt 24:37-39; Lk 17:26-27)

How are we to understand this passage? Does it mean that all who engage in these activities will perish—all who are given in marriage or take wives, all who set out new plants, all who build? No; but those who put their whole reliance on doing such things, who prefer these things to God, or are ready to offend God for the sake of them: these will perish. Others, who either disengage themselves from such insubstantial occupations or else engage in them without being totally engaged,[10] people who rely more on the giver than the gifts, who even amid the gifts are sensitive to his consolation and his mercy and not so completely taken over by the gifts that they fall away from the giver—these will not be found unprepared when the hour strikes like a thief.

---

7. Variant: "learn."
8. *Caritas vestra.*
9. See Mt 7:14.
10. See 1 Cor 7:31.

To persons so disposed the apostle said, *You are not in darkness, that the day should catch you out like a thief, for you are all children of light and children of the day* (1 Th 5:4-5). When the Lord warned us to be as wary of that hour as of a thief, he likened it to night, as did also the apostle: *The day of the Lord will come like a thief in the night* (1 Th 5:2). Are you hoping that it will not catch you unprepared? Take care not to live in the night. What does that mean? *You are children of light and children of the day; we do not belong to the night or to the darkness* (1 Th 5:5). Who are the children of night and darkness? The wicked, the godless, and unbelievers.

Verses 1-2. The Lord's light reaches us from the mountains

4. But even the careless must hearken before the hour strikes. Let the apostle remind them: *You were darkness once, but now you are light in the Lord* (Eph 5:8). Let them be vigilant, as our psalm urges them.[11] The mountains are already bathed in light; why are these people still asleep? Let them lift their eyes to the mountains, whence comes their help. What does it mean to say that the mountains are illumined already? The sun of righteousness has risen,[12] the gospel has been preached by the apostles, the scriptures have been promulgated, all the sacraments[13] are thrown open, the veil is rent apart,[14] and the secret recess of the temple lies open. Now at last let them lift their eyes to the mountains, whence comes help for them. Thus does the psalm command, this psalm which is the second in the collection called *Songs of Ascents.*

But they must not on that account put their trust in the mountains, because the mountains do not give off light of their own. They transmit light from him of whom scripture says, *He was the true light, which illumines every human person who comes into this world* (Jn 1:9). We can take the mountains to be symbols of great and illustrious people. And is anything greater than John the Baptist? What a mountain he was! Of him the Lord himself testified, *There has never arisen a mother's son greater than he* (Mt 11:11). You can certainly see in him a lofty mountain bathed in light; but listen to his confession: *From his fullness we have all received* (Jn 1:16). Help comes to you not from the mountains themselves but from him whose plenitude endows the mountains. All the same, unless you lift your eyes to the mountains through the scriptures, you will not be brought near[15] to be illuminated by him.

---

11. Some witnesses here insert the first two verses: *I have lifted my eyes to the mountains, from where comes help for me. My help is from the Lord, who made heaven and earth.*
12. See Ml 4:2. This was a favorite image for Christ's resurrection.
13. Or perhaps more generally, "the mysteries of the faith."
14. See Mt 27:57.
15. Variants: "will not draw near"; "will not be instructed."

Verses 3-4. How to keep your footing. Israel's unsleeping guardian

5. Well then, sing the next verses of the psalm. If you want to hear how to set your feet very firmly on the steps, so that you will be in no danger of either growing tired in the climb or slipping and falling, say the next verse: *Do not let my foot be dislodged.* How do feet get dislodged? In the same way as someone's foot was dislodged in paradise. But before thinking about him, reflect how one whose place used to be among the angels was dislodged, and fell, and was transformed from an angel into a devil; for he fell when his foot slipped. Inquire why he fell: he fell through pride. Pride is the only thing that dislodges a foot. Pride alone causes someone to lose his foothold and come crashing down. Charity moves us to walk and make progress; pride pushes us into a fall.

In view of this, what does the speaker say in another psalm? *The children of men will hope in the protection of your wings* (Ps 35:8(36:7)). If they are under his protection they are always humble, ever hopeful of God, and never reliant on themselves. They *will hope in the protection of your wings*, Lord, because they are not sated with happiness deriving from themselves. What comes next? *They will be inebriated by the rich abundance of your house, and you will give them the torrent of your delights to drink* (Ps 35:9(36:8)). They are athirst, and they have been inebriated; they are thirsty, and they drink; but they do not drink from themselves; they are not their own fountain. Whence do they drink? *They will hope in the protection of your wings.* They cannot help being humble if they are under God's wings. Why? *With you is the fountain of life* (Ps 35:10(36:9)), says the psalm. The mountains are not irrigated from their own source, any more than they are illumined with their own light; for see what follows: *In your light we will see light* (Ps 35:10(36:9)).

If then we shall see light in his light, who can fall away from the light? Only the one who tries to be a light to himself and will not have the Lord for his light: this is the one who falls out of the light that enlightens him. The psalmist well knew that no one falls except one who wants to be a light unto himself, whereas of himself he is darkness; and so he immediately added the prayer, *Let not the foot of pride come near me, nor the hand of sinners dislodge me* (Ps 35:12(36:11)). Let not any imitation of the ways of sinners impel me, he means, and cause me to fall away from you. But why were you afraid, psalmist? Why did you pray, *Let not the foot of pride come near me?* He answers, Because *that was how they fell, all who work iniquity* (Ps 35:13(36:12)). The ones you see working iniquity now are already condemned, but they earned their condemnation by falling, there where the foot of pride first approached them.

The would-be climber who does not wish to fall in his ascent has heard this lesson aright. He wants to make progress from his starting-point in the valley of weeping, and not faint or fail through swollen pride. He prays to God, *Do not let my foot be dislodged.* And God replies, *Neither let him grow drowsy, your guardian.* Consider this carefully, beloved. Two voices speak, but they are saying almost the same thing. The human speaker is climbing up and singing his song of ascents: *Do not let my foot be dislodged*; and God seems to be answering him, "You are making your plea to me, *Do not let my foot be dislodged.* But add a further plea: *Neither let him grow drowsy, your guardian,* and then your foot will not be dislodged."

6. Now suppose the climber responds, "But is it in my power to determine whether he who guards me falls asleep? I certainly hope he will not sleep or grow drowsy." If that is what you want, choose a guardian for yourself who will not sleep or grow drowsy, and then your foothold will be assured. God is never sleepy. You want an unsleeping guardian? You are right, perfectly right, to pray, *Do not let my foot be dislodged,* but he says something further to you: *Neither let him grow drowsy, your guardian.* Perhaps you were on the point of turning to human protectors, and asking, "Whom can I find who will not fall asleep? What person can ward off drowsiness? Whom shall I find? Where shall I go? Where am I to turn?" God shows you: *Lo, he will not be drowsy or sleep, the guardian of Israel.* Do you want a guardian who never dozes off or feels drowsy? *Lo, he will not be drowsy or sleep, the guardian of Israel,* for Christ is Israel's guardian.

That means you must be Israel. What is Israel? The name is interpreted as "One who sees God."[16] But who sees God? We see him first by faith, later by vision.[17] If you cannot yet behold him by sight, see him by faith. If you cannot behold his face, because sight would be needed for that, see his back. That was what the Lord told Moses: *You cannot see my face. But you shall see my back when I pass by.* (Ex 33:20,23,22) Are you waiting for him to pass? He has passed already, so you can see his back. When and where did he pass? Listen to John: *When the hour had come, at which Jesus was to pass from this world to the Father . . .* (Jn 13:1). Our Lord Jesus Christ has already accomplished his passover. The word "pasch" means a crossing over. It is a Hebrew word; some people think it is Greek, and associated with "passion," "suffering"; but this is not true. Careful and learned scholars have proved that the word "pasch" is Hebrew, and means not passion but passover. By his passion the Lord passed over from death to life and opened a way for us who believe in his resurrection, that we too may pass over from death to life. It is no great thing to believe that Christ died: pagans and Jews and all bad people believe that. All of them are sure that he died. The faith of Christians is in Christ's resurrection. This is what matters to us, that we believe he rose from the dead.

This is why he wanted to be seen precisely when he "passed by," that is to say, when he had risen. He wanted us to believe in him when he passed by, because *He was delivered to death for our transgressions, and rose for our justification*

---

16. A popular etymology. The aspiration of the true Israel is to see God; compare Jn 1:46-51.
17. See 2 Cor 5:7.

(Rom 4:25). It was faith in Christ's resurrection that the apostle emphasized more than anything else, for *if you believe in your heart that God raised him from the dead, you will be saved* (Rom 10:9). He did not say, "If you believe that Christ died," for pagans and Jews and all his enemies believed that. He said, *If you believe in your heart that God raised him from the dead, you will be saved.* To believe that is to be Israel, one who sees God. Perhaps all you see is his back, but if you have believed in his back, you will attain to the vision of his face.

What does that mean? What is his face, in the beginning? *In the beginning was the Word, and the Word was with God; he was God* (Jn 1:1). And his back, his state afterward, what was that? *The Word was made flesh, and dwelt among us* (Jn 1:14). If you have believed in what Christ afterward[18] became for you, if you have believed in what Christ afterward assumed for you, if you believe in what the Word became for you, if you believe that he rose in the flesh to save you from despairing about your own flesh, you will become Israel.

When you have become Israel, he who guards you will not grow drowsy or fall asleep, because you are Israel now, and you have heard the psalm's assurance, *Lo, he will not be drowsy or sleep, the guardian of Israel.* Christ did sleep indeed, but he arose. What does he say in another psalm? *I slept, and took my rest.* Did he remain asleep? No, for he continues, *I arose, because the Lord upheld me* (Ps 3:6(5)). If he has arisen, then, he has already passed over, and if he has passed over, contemplate his back. What does it mean, to contemplate his back? Believe in his resurrection. Remember how the apostle said, *Though he was crucified in weakness, he is alive by the power of God* (2 Cor 13:4), and again, *Rising from the dead, Christ will never die again, nor will death ever again have the mastery over him* (Rom 6:9). The psalm has good reason therefore to sing to you, *Lo, he will not be drowsy or sleep, the guardian of Israel.*

But you, with your carnal mind, are you perhaps still wondering, "Is there anyone who will not sooner or later be drowsy and sleep?" If you look for one among ordinary human beings you will never find such a one. Do not rely on any of them, for everyone dozes off or grows sleepy. When do ordinary men or women get drowsy? When they are carrying weak flesh. When do they sleep? When they die so you cannot rely on them. A mortal may grow drowsy; and when he dies, he falls asleep. It is no good looking for an unsleeping guardian among your fellow men and women.

---

18. *Posterius*, "later," "afterward." There is a pun, difficult to convey in translation, on the *posteriora*, the "after parts" or "back" of God in Moses' encounter with him (Ex 33), and what Christ became "later" (*posterius*) in the incarnation.

Verse 5. The hand of your right hand; the significance of right and left

7. And who, you ask, will guard me? Who will neither grow drowsy nor sleep? Listen to the next words: *The Lord will guard you.* Not some drowsy, sleepy fellow-human, but the Lord guards you.

How does he guard you? *The Lord will be your defense, better than the hand of your right hand.*[19] Well, brothers and sisters, let us try to understand with the Lord's assistance what is meant by the words: *The Lord will be your defense, Better than the hand of your right hand.* I think there must be some hidden reason why the psalm did not say simply, *The Lord will be your defense,* and leave it at that, but added, *better than the hand of your right hand.* What can it mean? Does the Lord guard our right side but not our left? Did he not make the whole of us? Did not he who made a right hand for us make a left hand too? But in any case, if the psalm wanted to affirm something concerning the right hand only, why did it say, *better than the hand of your right hand,*[20] rather than just "better than your right hand"?[21] Why did it speak so? Surely because some secret meaning is hidden here, which we are to discover by knocking at its door.[22] It could have said either, *The Lord will be your defense,* and added nothing else; or, if it wanted to mention the right side, it could have said, "The Lord will be your defense at your right"; or again, if the hand had to be mentioned, it could have said, "The Lord will be your defense, better than your right hand."[23] There was no need for the awkward phrase, *super manum dexterae tuae,* was there?

I will set before you the ideas that the Lord may himself suggest to me. He dwells in you too and will undoubtedly cause you to recognize the truth of what I say. At the moment you do not know what we are about to tell you, but once we have said it there will be no need for us to prove to you that what we say is true; you will yourselves acknowledge the truth of it. And how will you do that? The Lord who dwells in you will himself demonstrate it, insofar as you belong to the number of those who pray, *Do not let my foot be dislodged,* those to whom it is said, *Let him not grow drowsy, your guardian.* It is important that Christ should not sleep within you; and if he does not, you will understand that what we say is true. Are you going to ask me what I mean by that? If your faith goes to sleep, Christ is asleep in you; for your faith in Christ is the means by which he dwells in your heart. The apostle prays that *Christ may dwell in your hearts through faith*

19. *Super manum dexterae tuae,* an almost meaningless phrase, translated literally from a variant in the Greek of the Septuagint. It is necessary to retain it in this awkward form in English because Augustine, believing that any obscure expression could invite him and his hearers to search for hidden spiritual mystery, meditates on it in the following paragraphs, and further in section 11.
20. *Super manum dexterae tuae.*
21. *Super dexteram tua.*
22. See Mt 7:7.
23. *Super manum dexteram tua.*

(Eph 3:17). In a person whose faith does not go to sleep, Christ is wakeful. And if perhaps your faith was asleep, and you were therefore tossed about by this difficult passage, you were like the boat which was battered in a storm while Christ was aboard and sleeping.[24] Wake him up, and the storms will subside.

8. I want to put a few questions to your faith, then, dearest friends.[25] Because you are children of the Church, and have made progress in the Church, and are making progress in the Church, and will make progress in the Church if you are not doing so already, and, if you have already made progress, need to be helped in the Church to make even more,[26] I am asking you what you customarily understand by the saying in the gospel, *Do not let your left hand know what your right hand is doing* (Mt 6:3). If you have understood that, you will discover what the right hand is, and what the left. You will realize that though God made both, the left has nonetheless no business to know what the right hand is up to.

Our left hand symbolizes all we have in the temporal sphere; the right hand stands for all the eternal, unchangeable goods the Lord promises us. He who will one day give us eternal life also comforts us in our present life with temporal things, and thus it is evident that he made both right hand and left. A psalm of David says of certain people, *Their mouths have spoken empty words, and their right hand is a hand that deals unjustly* (Ps 143(144):11). It appears that he found people he needed to rebuke, because they regarded their right hand as their left, and treated their real left hand as though it were the right. He explains shortly afterward who these people are. If anyone thinks that the only happiness available to human beings cannot exist except amid temporal possessions and a profusion of the wealth this world offers, such a person is foolish and misguided, and has made what should be his left hand into his right. The kind of people rebuked by the psalm were like that. It was not as though even their temporal possessions were anything but God-given; but because they thought that a happy life consisted solely in such goods and sought nothing further, they deserved the rebuke. Listen to how they are characterized in the following lines: *Their mouths have spoken empty words, and their right hand is a hand that deals unjustly*, the psalm has said; then it continues, *Their sons are like well-set saplings, their daughters are adorned and gathered round them like the pillars of the temple, their storerooms are full to overflowing, their ewes fruitful, increasing at every lambing-time, and their oxen are sturdy. Never is their hedge broken down or*

---

24. See Mt 8:24-26; Mk 4:37-39; Lk 8:23-24.

25. *Carissimi.*

26. Conjectural translation: *Et in ecclesia profecistis . . . proficietis qui nondum profecistis, et in ecclesia proficiendi estis.* The last verb is difficult since a gerundive is normally passive, and there seem to be few, if any, examples of the use of the verb *proficere* in the passive with a personal subject. It may be that Augustine's rhetoric was sweeping him along, and the enthusiasm of the people for the build-up in the sentence led him to stretch grammar a little. Some copyists smoothed the difficulty by substituting *perficiendi,* "you need to be made perfect."

their property invaded, nor is there rioting in their streets. (Ps 143(144):11-14)
This is a description of the great good fortune enjoyed by some. A just person
could have had the same good fortune as Job did, but Job regarded it all as his left
hand; he did not mistake it for his right. The only kind of happiness he looked
upon as his right hand was perpetual, unending happiness with God. His left
hand was made vulnerable, but his right hand was enough for him. How was his
left hand injured? By the devil's temptations. The devil suddenly took all his
possessions away, though only by God's permission, in order that a just man
might be proved, and the wicked one punished. Job knew his left hand for a left
hand, and knew his right hand for what it was: his right hand. How did he support
himself with his right hand, how did he exult in the Lord? He was comforted over
his losses, for he suffered no loss of interior riches: he had a heart full of God.
The Lord gave, and the Lord has taken away, he said. *This has happened as the
Lord willed: may the Lord's name be blessed* (Jb 1:21). That was his right hand:
the Lord himself, eternal life, the light that was in him, the fountain of light, the
vision of light in God's light. *They will be inebriated by the rich abundance of
your house* (Ps 35:9(36:8)). All this was his right hand. His left hand had been
there as a help and comfort, but not as the foundation of his happiness; for his
true, genuine happiness was God.

What of the others, the ones of whom David said that *their mouths have
spoken empty words, and their right hand is a hand that deals unjustly*? He did
not rebuke them because they had a profusion of goods, but because *their
mouths spoke empty words.* How do we know this? Because after listing all their
wealth he continued, *They have called blessed people who have these things.*
The empty words they mouthed consisted in this, that they reckoned as blessed
all who have such riches. But what is your judgment, you who know what your
left hand is, and what your right? You will say what the psalm goes on to say:
Blessed rather is the people whose God is the Lord (Ps 143(144):15).

9. Now give me your attention, beloved.[27] We have seen the left hand, and we
have also observed the right. Listen to how our interpretation is confirmed in the
Song of Songs. *His left hand is beneath my head,* we read. The bride is speaking
of the bridegroom; the Church is speaking of embracing Christ in fidelity and
love. What does the bride say? *His left hand is beneath my head, and his right
hand will embrace me* (Sg 2:6). What should we gather from the fact that when
he embraces her the bridegroom places his right hand on top, and his left
beneath? He places his left hand below to comfort her, and his right hand above
for her protection. *His left hand is beneath my head,* she says. The left hand is
God's gift; it is called *his* left hand, for he gives all temporal things. How
empty-headed they are, and how impious, who beg for such things from idols,
from demons! And what a lot of people beg them from demons, and do not get

---

27. *Caritas vestra.*

them! There are others who do not beg them from demons, and yet have them; but these goods are not given by demons. On the other hand, many beg them from God, and do not get them, for he who calls us to the happiness of the right hand well knows how best to dispense the goods of the left.

If you possess this left-hand fortune, let it be your left hand; let it be under your head, and let your head rest upon it. By that I mean let your faith be above it, for in your faith Christ dwells. Do not give temporal things precedence over your faith, and then the left hand will not be on top of your head. Subordinate all temporal things to your faith, and let your faith be supreme over all of them. Then his left hand will be under your head, and his right hand will embrace you.

10. The Book of Proverbs also clarifies what is meant by the right hand and the left. Listen to what it says about Wisdom: *Length of days and years of life are in her right hand, but in her left are riches and fame* (Prv 3:16, LXX). This *length of days* is eternity. Scripture is in the habit of calling what is eternal "long," for anything that comes to an end is short. In another passage God promises, *I will fill him completely with length of days* (Ps 90(91):16). If length of days did not signify eternal life, would God be pledging anything special when he commands, *Honor your father and your mother, that you may have a long life in the land* (Ex 20:12)? To what land does this refer if not the land of which the psalmist says to God, *You are my hope, my portion in the land of the living* (Ps 141:6(142:5))? And what does it mean to enjoy a long life there? What else but to live for ever? After all, what does a long life in this world entail? Arriving at old age! Our span of life here may seem long, but when it is complete[28] we see how short it was, because it has ended. Moreover, there are many who speak ill of their parents and yet grow old on this earth, whereas many others who are dutiful toward their parents go quickly to the Lord. The promise of long life is hardly fulfilled, is it, if it refers to the present life? Scripture must be using long life as a symbol of eternity. This kind of long life is in Wisdom's right hand; but riches and fame, which represent all we need in the present and all that popular opinion reckons good, are the gifts of Wisdom's left hand.

Now suppose someone comes along and wants to wound you in your right hand. He wants to take your faith away from you. You have been slapped on your right hand: offer him your left. Let him take away anything that is temporal, but not your eternal possessions. Listen to how the apostle Paul did this. People were hounding him because he was a Christian: that is, they were hitting his right hand. He retaliated with his left, warning them, "I am a Roman citizen."[29] They despised his right hand, but he scared them with his left. They could not feel threatened by his right hand, because they had not believed in Christ.

---

28. Variant: "when death comes."
29. See Acts 22:25.

Well now, if Christ's right hand embraces you, and his left hand is beneath your head, what is the meaning of the gospel command, *Do not let your left hand know what your right hand is doing* (Mt 6:3)? It means, "When you perform a good work, do it in view of eternal life." If you do some good deed on earth with the object of acquiring a wealth of earthly commodities, your left hand knows what your right is doing, and you have mixed up your right hand with your left. Act only with a view to eternal life. If you do that, you will act with a tranquil mind, for it was for this purpose that God tempted him.[30] If you act in whatever you are doing solely for the sake of gaining some human advantage, with no motive apart from the present life, your left hand is working alone. If you act for the sake of eternal life your right hand is working alone. If, however, your will is directed toward eternal life, but some covetousness associated with temporal life creeps into your motive, so that you keep this also in view as you perform your good work and hope for some reward here, your left hand is interfering with the activities of your right, and this God forbids.

The power of your right hand is God-given, but the Lord himself must defend it

11. Now let us go back to the words of the psalm, *The Lord will be your defense, better than the hand of your right hand.* The psalm calls power a hand. How can we prove this? From the fact that God's own power is referred to as a hand. When the devil tempted Job he said to God, *Just stretch out your hand and touch all his belongings* (Jb 1:11).[31] What else can the challenge, *Stretch out your hand*, mean except, "Put forth your power"? But listen to a still clearer proof, my brother, my sister, for you may still be thinking in carnal terms and supposing that God is distributed among many bodily organs. Listen to a still clearer piece of evidence, then. Scripture says somewhere, *Death and life are in the hands of the tongue* (Prv 18:21). We know what tongues are: small pieces of flesh that by moving in our mouths and striking against the palate and the teeth produce the distinct sounds with which we speak. So now let someone show me the hands of the tongue. Surely the tongue does not have hands? Yet it does, in a way. What are its hands? The power of the tongue; for what is meant by the warning, *Death and life are in the hands of the tongue*? The gospel tells us: *Out of your mouth you will be justified, and out of your mouth you will be condemned* (Mt 12:37).

If the hand represents power, what is the hand of the right hand? I can think of no better way of understanding it than to assume that the power of the right hand

---

30. *Ad hoc enim tentavit Deus eum*, so the codices. If this is correct, the reference may be to Job, who was mentioned in section 8. Variant: *hoc enim mandavit Deus* ("for this is what God commanded").

31. Some witnesses continue the quotation: *and see if he does not curse you to your face.*

is the power God has given you to be at Christ's right hand, if you choose. All the impious will be at his left, and all God's good sons and daughters at his right. To these he will say, *Come, you who are blessed by my Father, take possession of the kingdom prepared for you since the creation of the world* (Mt 25:34). But you have received power to be at his right, power to become a child of God. What power is that? The power of which John speaks: *He gave them power to become children of God.* And how did that power come to you? Through faith, for John specifies, *To those, that is, who believe in his name* (Jn 1:12). If you are a believer, this power has been given to you, the power to be among the children of God. But to be among the children of God is to be entitled to a place at Christ's right hand. This means that your faith is *the hand of your right hand.* The power conferred on you to find a place among God's children is therefore *the hand of your right hand.*

But what is the use of even this power given to us, if the Lord does not protect it? A Christian is someone who has come to believe and is already walking in faith. But he or she is weak, and is harassed by temptations, by all sorts of distress, by the allurements of sensuality, by stirrings of avarice, by the crafty tricks and traps of the enemy. Can the power a believer has received hold out against all these? Is it enough that he has believed in Christ, so as to be numbered among God's children? Woe betide him if the Lord does not also protect the faith he has. Your chances are poor unless the Lord ensures that you are not tried beyond your strength, as the apostle guarantees that he will: *God is faithful, and he will not allow you to be tempted more fiercely than you can bear* (1 Cor 10:13). God it is who does not allow us to be tried beyond our strength, even though we are already believers, even though the hand of our right hand is already within us; and God it is who covers us with a defense better than the hand of our right hand. It is not enough for us to have the hand of our right hand, unless he protects this very gift, the hand of our right hand.

Verse 6. The danger of being burnt by scandals related to either the sun or the moon

12. I said all that with reference to trials and temptations; now observe what follows. The Lord protects you *better than the hand of your right hand,* I told you, and I think you recognized the truth of that. If you had not recognized it—and, moreover, recognized it as taught by the scriptures—you would not be raising your voices to demonstrate to me that you have understood. Well then, brothers and sisters, since you have understood, consider the next verse. Think why the Lord needs to protect you, even better than the hand of your right hand. He is a better guardian for us even than faith itself, through which we have received power to become children of God and claim a place at Christ's right hand.

Why is it necessary for the Lord to protect us? Because of scandals. But where do scandals come from? We must beware of scandals from two sources, which correspond to the two commandments on which the law and the prophets depend: namely, love for God and love for our neighbor.[32] The Church is loved for our neighbor's sake, but God for his own sake. The psalm speaks figuratively of God as the sun and figuratively of the Church as the moon. A person may go wrong by holding mistaken beliefs about God: for instance, by not believing that the Father and the Son and the Holy Spirit are of one and the same substance. If such a person, deceived by the cunning of the heretics, especially the Arians,[33] believes that either the Son or the Holy Spirit is in any sense less than the Father, he or she has stumbled over a scandal concerning God. But again, anyone may be scandalized concerning the Church, thinking that it exists in one region only[34] and failing to see that it is spread throughout the whole wide world; or he may put his faith in those who say, *Look, here is Christ!* or, *There he is!* (Mk 13:21) as you heard just now when the gospel was read. Persons so deceived do not realize that Christ, by paying such an enormous price, purchased the whole world; and thus they could be said to have stumbled over a scandal concerning their neighbors. They are burnt by the moon.

We conclude, then, that anyone who wanders into error touching the very substance of the truth is burnt by the sun, and burnt in daylight, for he or she has strayed from the wisdom of which scripture says, *Day speaks the word to succeeding day* (Ps 18:3(19:2)). This is why the apostle speaks of *interpreting spiritual truths to people possessed of the Spirit* (1 Cor 2:13). *Day speaks the word to succeeding day: interpreting spiritual truths to people possessed of the Spirit. Day speaks the word to succeeding day: we speak wisdom among the perfect.* (1 Cor 2:6) But what does the rest of that psalm-verse suggest: *And night imparts knowledge to night* (Ps 18:3(19:2))? To little ones the humility of Christ is preached, and the flesh of Christ and the crucifixion of Christ, because this is the milk suited to little ones. These little ones are not abandoned in the night, because the moon shines then; this symbolizes the Church which is preached through the reality of Christ's flesh; for the very flesh of Christ is the head of the Church. Those who are not scandalized over this, not made to stumble over the Church or over the flesh of Christ, are not burnt by the moon. Those who are not made to stumble over the truth that exists unchangeably and beyond the reach of defilement are not burnt by the sun. In this context the sun does not mean the sun in the sky, which flies and cattle see along with us, but that sun of which the impious will say at the end, *What good has our pride done us, or what benefit has*

---

32. See Mt 22:40.
33. Augustine's language is reminiscent of the Council of Nicea (325). On the Arians, see the note at Exposition of Psalm 54, 22.
34. The Donatists' contention.

come to us from our vaunted wealth? All these things have passed away like a shadow. And they will continue, *No doubt of it, we strayed from the path of truth. On us the light of righteousness did not shine, nor did the sun rise for us.* (Wis 5:8-9.6) We cannot think, can we, that the sun we see in the sky does not rise for wicked people? God has arranged that it shall; of him it is said, *He causes his sun to rise over the good and the wicked* (Mt 5:45). There is a sun which God has made, which he causes to rise over good and bad people alike, the sun which both good and bad can see; but there is another sun which is not made but begotten, he through whom all things were made, and in whom is the understanding of unchangeable truth. Of this sun the wicked lament, *The sun did not rise for us* (Wis 5:6). Those who do not go astray from wisdom itself are not burnt by the sun. Those who do not go astray concerning the Church, or the flesh of the Lord,[35] or all those things done for our sake in his temporal dispensation, are not burnt by the moon. But all of us, even though already believers in Christ, will fall into error concerning the one or the other, unless the promise made in the psalm is fulfilled in us: *The Lord will be your defense, better than the hand of your right hand.* This is why, after the psalm has made that promise, the believer seems to be inquiring further, "But look: I have the hand of my right hand, for I have already chosen to believe in Christ. I have received the power to be numbered among the children of God. Why do I still need God to defend me even more effectively, better than does the hand of my right hand?" The psalm explains: *The sun will not burn you by day, nor the moon at night.* The Lord gives you extra protection, even better than that afforded by the hand of your right hand, so that neither the sun in the daytime nor the moon at night may scorch you.

This assurance is enough to make you understand, brothers and sisters, that the language is figurative. If we think literally of the visible sun, we know that it certainly can burn us during the day; but does the moon burn us at night? No, of course it doesn't. But what does burning suggest? Scandal. Listen to what the apostle says on that subject: *Is anyone weak, and I am not weak too? Is anyone tripped up, without my being afire with indignation?* (2 Cor 11:29)

Verses 6-8. The example of Saint Crispina

13. *The sun will not burn you by day, nor the moon at night.* Why not? Because *the Lord will guard* [36] *you from every evil.* May he guard you[37] from scandals relating to the sun, scandals relating to the moon, and every kind of disaster, for he is *your defense, better than the hand of your right hand,* and *he*

---

35. Variant: "the resurrection of the Lord."
36. Variant: "guards."
37. Variant: "he will guard you."

does not sleep or grow drowsy. Why do we need such protection? Because we are beset by temptations. *The Lord will guard*[38] *you from every evil.*

May the Lord guard your soul. Yes, your very soul. *May the Lord guard*[39] *your going in, and your coming out henceforth and for ever.* It does not say he will guard your body, for the martyrs were slain as to their bodies; rather *may the Lord guard*[40] *your soul,* because as far as their souls were concerned the martyrs did not yield. The persecutors turned their rage against Crispina,[41] whose birthday[42] we celebrate today. They unleashed their savagery against a rich woman, delicately nurtured; but she was strong, because the Lord was for her a better defense than the hand of her right hand, and he was guarding her. Is there anyone in Africa who does not know about these events, brothers and sisters? Scarcely, for she was extremely famous, of noble stock and very wealthy. But all these advantages belonged to the left hand and were under her head. The enemy attacked, intent on striking her head, but all that was presented to him was the left hand, which was beneath her head. The head was on top, and Christ's right hand was embracing her from above. Had the persecutor power to do anything, even against so delicate a woman? She was of the weaker sex, perhaps enfeebled by riches and quite frail in body in consequence of the life to which she had been accustomed. But what did all this signify, compared with the bridegroom whose left hand was beneath her head, whose right hand was embracing her? Was the enemy ever likely to overthrow one so fortified? He struck her, certainly, but only in the body. What does the psalm say? *May the Lord guard your soul.* The soul did not yield, though the body was struck down. And even the body was slain only for a time, for it is destined to rise again at the end. He who graciously willed to be the Church's head surrendered his own body to be killed, but only for a time. He raised his flesh to life again on the third day, and he will raise ours at the end. The head was raised that the body might wait expectantly and not faint.

May the Lord guard your soul. May it not yield; may your soul not be shattered against stumbling-blocks when persecutions arise and tribulations surround you. May it not faint or give way,[43] for the Lord bids us, *Do not be afraid of those who kill the body, but cannot kill the soul. Fear him rather who has the power to kill both soul and body in hell.* (Mt 10:28) May the Lord guard

---

38. Variant: "guards."
39. Variant: "the Lord will guard."
40. Variant: "the Lord will guard."
41. Born at Thagara in the Province of Africa, Crispina was a noble Roman matron and the mother of children. During the persecution of Diocletian she was brought before the tribunal and ordered to worship the gods. She steadfastly refused, despite the tearful pleas of her children. She was executed on 5 December 304, and her festival was celebrated on that day in Augustine's time.
42. *Natalicia*; see the note at Exposition of Psalm 63, 15.
43. Variant: "fall."

this soul of yours, so that you never yield to an evil persuader, never yield to one who makes false promises, and never yield to anyone who threatens you with temporal disaster. *May the Lord guard*[44] *your soul.*

We "go in" when tempted and "come out" from temptation; the Lord guards us in both cases

14. Finally, *may the Lord guard your going in, and your coming out henceforth and for ever.* Notice how it says, *Your coming out henceforth and for ever,* whereas your *going in* is only for a time. Focus your attention on this: *may the Lord guard your going in, and your coming out henceforth and for ever.* May he *guard your coming out.* What is our *going in*? What is our *coming out*? When we are tempted, we go in; when we conquer the temptation, we come out. Listen to what scripture has to say about going in and coming out: *Pots are proved in the kiln, and righteous persons in temptation and trouble* (Sir 27:6). If good people are like a potter's vessels, it is necessary for them to be put into the fire like pots. Not when they go in is the potter free from anxiety, but only when they have come out. The Lord, by contrast, is free from anxiety all the time, because he *knows his own* (2 Tm 2:19) and knows which ones will not crack. The ones who do not crack are those in whom are trapped no bubbles of pride.

Thus humility is your guardian in all temptation, for we are climbing up from the valley of weeping, singing our song of ascents; and the Lord is guarding our entrance that we may go into it and be safe. When temptation comes upon us let us keep our faith whole and strong. Then he will guard our *coming out henceforth and for ever,* for when we have finally come through all temptation there will be no further temptation to daunt us for all eternity, no concupiscence ever again to make its insolent demands. Listen to the apostle reminding you, as I reminded you myself not long since, that *God is faithful, and he does not*[45] *allow you to be tempted more fiercely than you can bear.* So you see, your going in is guarded. When God does not allow any temptation to befall you that you cannot bear, he is guarding your going in; now see whether he also guards your coming out. The apostle continues, *But along with the temptation he ordains*[46] *the outcome, so that you may withstand it* (1 Cor 10:13). Can we offer any other interpretation of the psalm than the one taught us by the apostle's words, brothers and sisters? Guard yourselves, but not by any strength of your own, for the Lord is your defense and your guardian, the Lord who neither grows drowsy nor sleeps. Once only did he sleep for us; but he rose again, and now he will never sleep any more.

---

44. Variant: "the Lord guards."
45. Variant: "will not."
46. Variant: "will ordain."

None of us must rely on ourselves. We are ascending from the valley of weeping; let us not linger on the way. There are steps ahead of us, and we must neither linger nor fall through pride. Let us pray to God, "Do not let our feet slip." Let him not sleep, your guardian. It is up to us[47] to make him our guardian, the Lord who neither sleeps nor gets drowsy, the Lord who guards Israel. What "Israel" is this? The one who sees God. Thus will your help come from the Lord; thus will he be *your defense, better than the hand of your right hand*; thus will your going in be guarded, and your coming out *henceforth and for ever*. If you rely on yourself, your foot has slipped already; and if your foot has slipped, you will be deceived into thinking you have already mounted to some particular step. You will fall off it, if you are proud. The humble person in the valley of weeping prays, *Do not let my foot be dislodged*.

Conclusion: this has been a rich feast of the word

15. Although this is a short psalm, our examination of it has taken a long time, and this sermon has been a long one. Put it to yourselves this way, brothers and sisters: I invited you to blessed Crispina's birthday party, and I have prolonged the banquet somewhat beyond what was expected. But could this not happen to you if some officer[48] invited you to his table, and compelled you to drink more than you meant to? Well then, we ought to be allowed to do the same with God's word, leaving you inebriated and filled with it. Just so has the Lord in his gracious mercy drenched the earth with his seasonal rain.[49] This has prevented us from going with greater joy to the shrine of the martyrs,[50] as we promised yesterday. Beyond all suffering and toil, the martyrs are here with us.

---

47. Some witnesses insert "by God's grace."
48. *Militaris*.
49. Or perhaps "his temporal, material rain," in contrast to the spiritual potations of which Augustine has spoken.
50. *Dominus pluvia sua temporali terram dignatus est irrigare, ut cum maiore gaudio nos non sineret ire ad locum martyrum*. The translation offered above follows the CSEL text. But weighty witnesses, followed by the CCL edition, omit the *non*; if this is correct, the sentence could be differently understood, as follows: "Just so has the Lord drenched the earth with his seasonal rain, sending us with all the more joy to the shrine of the martyrs. . . ."

Index of Scripture

(prepared by Michael Dolan)

(The numbers after the scriptural reference refer to the section of the work)

Old Testament

Genesis

1:1	III, 103, 4
1:6	I, 103, 7
1:6.26	II, 101, 12
1:14	109, 16
1:31	102, 8
2:7	I, 103, 13; XVIII, 118, 2
2:24	XXIX, 118, 9
3:5	II, 103, 11; IX, 118, 1; XI, 118, 6
3:9	IX, 118, 1
3:14	IV, 103, 11
3:15	IV, 103, 6
3:19	IV, 103, 11
3:19.18	102, 17
12:3	100, 3
15:10	III, 103, 5
17:4	I, 113, 2
21:10	119, 7
22:16-18	109, 17
22:18	I, 113, 2
25:23	I, 113, 2; XXVIII, 118, 4
45:7	II, 101, 15

Exodus

3:13-14	II, 101, 10
3:14	I, 103, 3; 104, 4
3:14.15	II, 101, 14
3:15	104, 4
15:1	105, 12
20:5	108, 15
20:12	120, 10
20:17	VIII, 118, 3
32:31-32	105, 21
33:17, LXX	XXXI, 118, 8
33:20.23.22	120, 6

Leviticus

22:4-6	119, 9

Deuteronomy

19:21	108, 4
25:4	102, 12; III, 103, 9
32:35	102, 14
32:39	I, 101, 8
32:49	I, 103, 8

Job

1:8, LXX	100, 12; IV, 103, 8
1:9	104, 40; XI, 118, 6; XXVI, 118, 4
1:11	120, 11
1:21	IV, 103, 7; 120, 7
7:1	111, 2
9:33, LXX	IV, 103, 8
14:4-5, LXX	IV, 103, 6
41:24-25, LXX	IV, 103, 9
42:7	IV, 103, 8

Psalms

1:1	109, 20; V, 118, 2
1:4	I, 101, 15
2:1-4	109, 9
2:2	109, 18
2:7	109, 9
2:8	109, 9; 119, 7
2:9	109, 10
2:11	IV, 103, 16
2:11-12	XXXI, 118, 8
3:4(3)	105, 19

527

Proverbs

Ecclesiastes

Song of Songs

22:37.39-40	VIII, 118, 2	6:30	102, 12; III, 103, 10
22:40	102, 25; I, 103, 10;	6:37-38	111, 4; XIX, 118, 7
	XII, 118, 5	7:39-44	100, 8
22:42	109, 6	7:47	119, 5
22:43-45	109, 3	10:6	III, 103, 5
23:3	100, 10; 115, 1; I, 118, 2	10:8.7	III, 103, 9
23:23	XXVI, 118, 1	10:21	117, 1
23:31.35	108, 18	10:24	XX, 118, 1
23:37	I, 101, 8; 108, 6	10:29	VIII, 118, 2
23:38.37	II, 101, 6	11:7	102, 10
24:14	II, 101, 9; II, 101, 12	11:13	XIV, 118, 2
24:17	I, 101, 7	11:15	108, 4
24:35	I, 103, 17	12:5	XXXI, 118, 1
24:37-39	120, 3	12:8	115, 2
24:40-41	99, 13	12:14	XXIV, 118, 3
24:43	120, 3	12:20	I, 101, 10; XXIV, 118, 3
25:21	I, 113, 9	12:49	I, 103, 16
25:21.23	115, 1; 115, 2	13:26-27	100, 7
25:21.30	108, 9	13:28-30	XXII, 118, 1
25:26	99, 10; 115, 1	13:32	105, 36
25:26.27	I, 101, 7	14:11	XV, 118, 2
25:34	109, 15; 111, 5; I, 113, 9;	14:13-14	III, 103, 10
	120, 11	15:12	XXIII, 118, 5
25:34.41	VI, 118, 2	15:18	V, 118, 2; VIII, 118, 2
25:41	111, 5	15:19.21	V, 118, 2
25:45	108, 19	15:29	V, 118, 2
25:46	109, 15	16:9	III, 103, 10
26:38	100, 6	16:28	108, 17
26:38.39	III, 103, 11	17:5	VII, 118, 3; XVII, 118, 2
26:39	100, 6	17:26-27	120, 3
27:25	108, 20	17:34	99, 13
27:40	I, 103, 5	18:13	105, 2
27:40.42	100, 9	18:14	110, 3; XV, 118, 2
28:19	III, 103, 2	18:14.13	110, 3
28:20	99, 17; II, 101, 8;	20:18	109, 18; XIII, 118, 2
	I, 113, 10	20:21-22	I, 101, 9
		21:18	XV, 118, 2
		21:19	XV, 118, 2; XXIII, 118, 3
Mark		21:24	109, 11
		22:31	XV, 118, 8
2:11	100, 4	22:31-32	100, 12; III, 103, 22;
9:23	VII, 118, 3		XV, 118, 2
10:14-15	112, 1	22:32	XIII, 118, 3
10:18	102, 8; 117, 2	22:33	III, 103, 9
10:21	III, 103, 16	23:34	100, 9; I, 101, 8;
10:28	III, 103, 16		I, 101, 15; 108, 4; 108, 5
13:21	120, 12	24:45	XVII, 118, 3
14:34	100, 6; 108, 24	24:46	109, 10
14:69	III, 103, 9	24:47	109, 10
Luke			
		John	
1:33	XXIX, 118, 9		
2:14	111, 2	1:1	I, 103, 8; III, 103, 20;
2:29-30	XX, 118, 1		XXIII, 118, 1; 119, 1;
2:30	105, 5		120, 6
2:34-35	104, 13	1:1-3	I, 101, 1; 119, 2
3:14	XXXI, 118, 1	1:1.10	III, 103, 3
6:21	I, 118, 3		

1 Corinthians

3:29	100, 3; 104, 5; I, 113, 2
4:4	XXVI, 118, 7
4:5	I, 101, 14
4:6	XIV, 118, 2
4:19	I, 101, 8
4:21-22.24	119, 7
4:24	I, 103, 13
4:25	110, 8
4:26	110, 8
4:27	II, 101, 6; II, 101, 7
5:2	III, 103, 7
5:13	99, 7; III, 103, 9; 115, 6
5:15	100, 9
5:17	106, 6
5:24	XXV, 118, 6
6:3	106, 14
6:9	111, 3
6:14	XXV, 118, 6

Ephesians

2:2	III, 103, 23; 105, 36; 117, 4
2:3	I, 101, 11; 102, 17; I, 103, 6; 112, 6
2:8-10	112, 6
2:9-10	110, 3
2:10	IV, 103, 14
2:14	119, 9
2:15-16	117, 17
2:19	VIII, 118, 1
2:19-22	111, 1
3:14-19	I, 103, 14
3:17	120, 7
3:19	XIV, 118, 4
3:20	XIX, 118, 2
4:2-3	99, 9
4:10	XII, 118, 1
4:13	I, 101, 2
4:17	XVIII, 118, 3
4:17-18	XVIII, 118, 3
4:23	XVIII, 118, 3
4:26	III, 103, 19
5:8	I, 103, 6; II, 103, 2; 112, 6; 120, 4
5:25.24	III, 103, 4
5:27	I, 103, 7
5:32	XXIX, 118, 9
6:12	117, 4

Philippians

1:18	115, 1
1:23	100, 6; 114, 8
1:23-24	112, 4
2:6	I, 103, 5
2:7	IV, 103, 8
2:7-8	I, 103, 5
2:8-11	109, 20

2:9-10	109, 7
2:12-13	102, 29; IV, 103, 16; XXXI, 118, 8
2:13	105, 3; XV, 118, 9; XVI, 118, 2
2:21	115, 1
3:13-14	II, 118, 2
3:16	II, 118, 2
3:20	112, 4; 114, 8; X, 118, 1
4:17	102, 12; 106, 13

Colossians

1:13	105, 36
3:1-2	IV, 103, 11
3:1-3	XII, 118, 1
3:4	XX, 118, 1

1 Thessalonians

3:5	XXVI, 118, 2
4:16-17	I, 103, 11
5:2	120, 3
5:4-5	120, 3
5:5	120, 3

2 Thessalonians

2:3-4.8-12	105, 37
3:2	115, 1; VIII, 118, 1
3:14.15	100, 8

1 Timothy

1:5	102, 25
1:7	XXII, 118, 4; 119, 9
1:9-11	XI, 118, 1
1:13	I, 103, 6; 112, 6; VII, 118, 2
1:13.16	100, 2
1:17	109, 10
2:5	IV, 103, 8; 104, 10
5:18	102, 12; III, 103, 9
6:10	110, 8; XI, 118, 6
6:16	VI, 118, 2

2 Timothy

2:8.9	109, 4
2:9	115, 2
2:16	XX, 118, 1
2:19	104, 34; 106, 13; 106, 14; 120, 14
2:26	105, 36
3:1-2	106, 14
3:7	XI, 118, 3

Index

(prepared by Joseph Sprug)

The first number in the Index is the Psalm number.
More than one Exposition is cited by the number in parentheses, for example (2)
The number after the colon is a paragraph number.
Different expositions in the same heading are separated by a semi-colon.
Biblical texts/words are in italics.

539

creation of, 118(18):1,2
flesh vs. spirit, 114:8
soul as alien, 118(8):1
See also flesh; soul
bones, 101(1):4
booty, 118(31):2
boredom, 106:6
bosom, 109:16
brazier, 103(3)5
bread, 101(1):5; 103(3)12,14
breath, 103(4)13,14
bulls, 106:14

Caesar, 115:8
camel, 110:6
Canaan, 104:6,7,8,9
Catholic Church, 99:12; 119:9
cattle, 103(3)9
cedars of Lebanon, 103(1):18; 103(3)15,17
charity, 99:6,7,10; 101(1):4; 102:3,25;
    103(1):10,16,19; 103(3)9; 118(14):5;
    118(17):2; 118(25):7; 119:8; 120:5
    enduring faults of bad people, 99:12
    enlarged heart, 118(11):1
    exceedingly wide, 118(21):8
    higher regions of the scriptures, 103(1):9;
        103(2):3
    lover's meditation, 118(19):4
    spacious freedom, 118(22):1
    walked continually in..., 118(14):2
    works as assets, 102:12
cheerfulness, 99:7,8,14
childlikeness, 112:1-2
children, 101(2):15; 108:14
    sins of their fathers and, 108:15
children of God, 118(27):4; 120:11,12
children's children, 102:25
Christ, *See* Jesus Christ
    Christian life: build on rock; not on sand,
        102:28
    duty to imitate the Father, 100:1
    early church, 101(1):15
    flesh crucified, 118(25):6
    meet to form one perfect man, 105:36
    new creation, 101(1):19; 103(3)26; 103(4)3
    serving Christ, 100:10
    taste for things that are above, 103(4)11
    See also commandments; spiritual life
Christianity, 119:4
Christians, 109:10
    bad mixed with the good, 99:12
    called together from whole world, 106:9
    false accusations against, 118(27):7
    name "Israel" not alien to, 113(1):2,5
    seed of Abraham, 100:3
    your servant, son of your handmaid,
        115:6,7,9
Church, 100:3; 101(1):8; 101(2):7; 103(3)25;

104:5; 106:8,13,14; 108:32; 110:1;
118(13):3; 118(19):2,7; 118(20):1,7;
118(27):7; 118(31):1; 118(32):5,6;
119:7; 120:8,12
    arrayed in light as in a garment,
        103(1):7; 103(2):2
beauty, 103(1):6
Christ and the body of, 100:3; 111:1
Christ as foundation of, 103(1):17;
    103(2):5
earth as figure of, 103(1):17
end of the world, 101(2):9
figure: Noah's ark (animals as nations),
    103(3):2
gifts conferred on, 103(1):9
hidden with Christ in God, 118(19):1
holy fear in, 118(19):3
humiliations, 118(15):2
judgments of God, 118(6):2
left hand; right hand, 120:9
made white, 103(1):6
moon and, 103(3)19; 120:12
one person: Christ and Church, 101(1):2;
    118(29):9
one soul, one heart, 103(1):4
persecutions in the future, 103(2):7
power to overcome evils, 117:6
present from the beginning, 118(29):9
prophecy: head or body, 118(22):3
ships as churches, 103(4)5
unity, 101(1):18; 101(2):8; 106:14
vineyard, 103(1):11
watch-tower, 101(2):4
will continue until judgment day,
    118(20):4
Zion, 101(2):4
See also Mystical Body of Christ;
    persecution
circumcision, 103(3)7; 113(1):2
clergy, 99:12,13
clouds, 103(1):11,19
coals, 119:5
commandments, 102:25; 110:1; 111:2;
    118(5):3; 118(11):6; 118(13):1;
    118(14):1; 118(17):7; 118(18):3;
    118(19):1,5; 118(26):9; 118(27):7;
    118(28):6; 118(32):4,5,7
    believing in, 118(17):4
    chatter about, 118(6):4
    grace and fulfillment of, 118(27):3,4
    guarded, 118(31):7
    guarding your words..., 118(5):1,4;
        118(7):1
    hearer and doer, 118(4):3
    I understood better than elders,
        118(22):4
    love God by keeping, 118(8):2,3;
        118(16):3,4,6